(Continued on back endsheets)

American Short-Story Writers, 1910-1945
First Series

Dictionary of Literary Biography • Volume Eighty-six

American Short-Story Writers, 1910-1945 First Series

Edited by
Bobby Ellen Kimbel
Pennsylvania State University, Ogontz Campus

A Bruccoli Clark Layman Book
Gale Research Inc.
Detroit, London

Advisory Board for
DICTIONARY OF LITERARY BIOGRAPHY

Louis S. Auchincloss
John Baker
William Cagle
Jane Christensen
Patrick O'Connor
Peter S. Prescott

Matthew J. Bruccoli and Richard Layman, *Editorial Directors*
C. E. Frazer Clark, Jr., *Managing Editor*

Printed in the United States of America.

Published simultaneously in the United Kingdom
by Gale Research International Limited
(An affiliated company of Gale Research Inc.)

The paper used in this publication meets the minimum requirements
of American National Standard for Information Sciences—Permanence
Paper for Printed Library Materials, ANSI Z39.48-1984. ∞™

Copyright © 1989
Gale Research Inc.
835 Penobscot Bldg.
Detroit, MI 48226-4094

ISBN 0-8103-4564-1
89-34227 CIP

for my children
William, Andrew, and Kate

Contents

Plan of the Series

. . . Almost the most prodigious asset of a country, and perhaps its most precious possession, is its native literary product—when that product is fine and noble and enduring.

Mark Twain*

The advisory board, the editors, and the publisher of the *Dictionary of Literary Biography* are joined in endorsing Mark Twain's declaration. The literature of a nation provides an inexhaustible resource of permanent worth. We intend to make literature and its creators better understood and more accessible to students and the reading public, while satisfying the standards of teachers and scholars.

To meet these requirements, *literary biography* has been construed in terms of the author's achievement. The most important thing about a writer is his writing. Accordingly, the entries in *DLB* are career biographies, tracing the development of the author's canon and the evolution of his reputation.

The purpose of *DLB* is not only to provide reliable information in a convenient format but also to place the figures in the larger perspective of literary history and to offer appraisals of their accomplishments by qualified scholars.

The publication plan for *DLB* resulted from two years of preparation. The project was proposed to Bruccoli Clark by Frederick G. Ruffner, president of the Gale Research Company, in November 1975. After specimen entries were prepared and typeset, an advisory board was formed to refine the entry format and develop the series rationale. In meetings held during 1976, the publisher, series editors, and advisory board approved the scheme for a comprehensive biographical dictionary of persons who contributed to North American literature. Editorial work on the first volume began in January 1977, and it was published in 1978. In order to make *DLB* more than a reference tool and to compile volumes that individually have claim to status as literary history, it was decided to organize volumes by topic, period, or genre. Each of these freestanding volumes provides a biographical-bibliographical guide and overview for a particular area of literature. We are convinced that this organization—as opposed to a single alphabet method—constitutes a valuable innovation in the presentation of reference material. The volume plan necessarily requires many decisions for the placement and treatment of authors who might properly be included in two or three volumes. In some instances a major figure will be included in separate volumes, but with different entries emphasizing the aspect of his career appropriate to each volume. Ernest Hemingway, for example, is represented in *American Writers in Paris, 1920-1939* by an entry focusing on his expatriate apprenticeship; he is also in *American Novelists, 1910-1945* with an entry surveying his entire career. Each volume includes a cumulative index of subject authors and articles. Comprehensive indexes to the entire series are planned.

With volume ten in 1982 it was decided to enlarge the scope of *DLB*. By the end of 1986 twenty-one volumes treating British literature had been published, and volumes for Commonwealth and Modern European literature were in progress. The series has been further augmented by the *DLB Yearbooks* (since 1981) which update published entries and add new entries to keep the *DLB* current with contemporary activity. There have also been *DLB Documentary Series* volumes which provide biographical and critical source materials for figures whose work is judged to have particular interest for students. One of these companion volumes is entirely devoted to Tennessee Williams.

We define literature as the *intellectual commerce of a nation:* not merely as belles lettres but as that ample and complex process by which ideas are generated, shaped, and transmitted. *DLB* entries are not limited to "creative writers" but extend to other figures who in their time and in their way influenced the mind of a people. Thus the series encompasses historians, journalists, publishers, and screenwriters. By this means readers of *DLB* may be aided to perceive litera-

*From an unpublished section of Mark Twain's autobiography, copyright © by the Mark Twain Company.

ture not as cult scripture in the keeping of intellectual high priests but firmly positioned at the center of a nation's life.

DLB includes the major writers appropriate to each volume and those standing in the ranks immediately behind them. Scholarly and critical counsel has been sought in deciding which minor figures to include and how full their entries should be. Wherever possible, useful references are made to figures who do not warrant separate entries.

Each *DLB* volume has a volume editor responsible for planning the volume, selecting the figures for inclusion, and assigning the entries. Volume editors are also responsible for preparing, where appropriate, appendices surveying the major periodicals and literary and intellectual movements for their volumes, as well as lists of further readings. Work on the series as a whole is coordinated at the Bruccoli Clark Layman editorial center in Columbia, South Carolina, where the editorial staff is responsible for accuracy of the published volumes.

One feature that distinguishes *DLB* is the illustration policy—its concern with the iconography of literature. Just as an author is influenced by his surroundings, so is the reader's understanding of the author enhanced by a knowledge of his environment. Therefore *DLB* volumes include not only drawings, paintings, and photographs of authors, often depicting them at various stages in their careers, but also illustrations of their families and places where they lived. Title pages are regularly reproduced in facsimile along with dust jackets for modern authors. The dust jackets are a special feature of *DLB* because they often document better than anything else the way in which an author's work was perceived in its own time. Specimens of the writers' manuscripts are included when feasible.

Samuel Johnson rightly decreed that "The chief glory of every people arises from its authors." The purpose of the *Dictionary of Literary Biography* is to compile literary history in the surest way available to us—by accurate and comprehensive treatment of the lives and work of those who contributed to it.

The *DLB* Advisory Board

Foreword

The bleak and cheerless vision that we have come to associate with American literature in the first half of the twentieth century was not invented by the men and women who lived and wrote during the period. We find no greater affirmation in the poetry of Alfred Tennyson, A. E. Housman, and Edwin Arlington Robinson than in that of T. S. Eliot, Ezra Pound, and Robinson Jeffers and no greater claim for meaning or purpose in the world of human beings in the fiction of Thomas Hardy, Joseph Conrad, Hamlin Garland, and Henry James than in that of Theodore Dreiser, Ernest Hemingway, F. Scott Fitzgerald, and William Faulkner. Nineteenth-century science had abruptly and conclusively provided us with a world with nothingness at its center, a world in which the activities of men and women were, in Bertrand Russell's phrase, only "secular hurryings through space." And literary artists, reflecting as they invariably do the currents that define their own time and place, created poetry and fiction of despair: events, characters, and the natural world were depicted as clearly God-abandoned. But late-nineteenth-century writers had retained at least the externals of order; one finds in their works a continuity with established traditions of metrics and rhyme, of carefully structured plots, of trustworthy narrators, of consecutive chronologies. As the twentieth century advances, this adherence to rhetorical strategies of the past disappears, giving way to a new compression of material, a fragmentation of narrative, a break in rhythmic patterns, a dislocation of time, a freshness of language, a convolutedness and open-endedness of plot. The break with traditional forms becomes the hallmark of twentieth-century writing—compare even the look of a page of Tennyson's poetry with one of Eliot's—and nowhere is this shift more evident than in the American short story.

Gertrude Stein's *Three Lives* (1909) and Sherwood Anderson's *Winesburg, Ohio* (1919) are among the earliest examples of stories (both of these are written as collections) which exhibit marked departures from what had earlier been established as acceptable structure for the short-

story form. Stein's accomplishment was in recording the process of consciousness itself: the effect is primitive, the technique extraordinarily sophisticated. The method she employed—careful limitation of vocabulary, absence of traditional punctuation, consistent use of present participles, repetition of simple words and phrases, distortion of syntax—allowed her to establish the unique personality of each of her characters and to suggest as well a mirroring of the mind as it perceives the world and experiences events. In the *Winesburg, Ohio* stories Anderson broke with those still obedient to the rhetorical strictures of the past. While many of his contemporaries were engaged in creating short fictions defined by Aristotelian plot structure, linear chronology, verisimilitude of character and event, and the assumption of available (if not often utilized) moral codes, Anderson created brief, intense moments in which his nearly always desperate characters are revealed in a sudden flash of illumination. The effect is epiphanic: often only a single gesture or bit of dialogue catches the complexity, the allusiveness of character or moment, and it remains uninterpreted, merely suggestive. His treatment of sexual longing as a defining characteristic of American loneliness in the industrial age is as much as anything else in Anderson shockingly new, and this, coupled with his use of those unusual linguistic cadences rooted in the American oral tradition, created possibilities for fiction writers not earlier available to them.

Anderson often acknowledged his debt to Stein; Hemingway acknowledged his to both of them (if only grudgingly to Anderson); all three are the stylistic children of Mark Twain whose *Adventures of Huckleberry Finn* (1884) first brought to American literature a native idiom. The reaction against the "literary" (which is to say inflated, sentimentalized, rhetorically grand) style of the nineteenth century can be seen in the stories of George Ade, Ring Lardner, Stephen Crane, Gertrude Stein, Sherwood Anderson, and Ernest Hemingway, all of whom infused their works with the language of everyday speech—direct, colloquial, and in its effect, spontaneous.

The most famous exemplar of this increasingly characteristic prose idiom is Ernest Hemingway, whose 1924 collection of prose fiction, *In Our Time*, reveals his indebtedness to both Twain and Stein: "The kid came out and had to kill five bulls because you can't have more than three matadors, and the last bull he was so tired he couldn't get the sword in. He couldn't hardly lift his arm." The passage, like many in the collection, is in the American vernacular–deliberately loose, slangy, and ungrammatical. This flat, direct observation of experience, unmediated by any reflection upon its meaning, defines the Hemingway style. Critics are in general agreement that this distancing of event from response to it is a defense against feeling (articulated most convincingly in Philip Young's "wound theory"). But it reveals as well Hemingway's background as a working journalist on the *Kansas City Star* and the *Toronto Star*.

It is a fact often remarked upon that many of the finest practitioners of the short-story form in the first half of the twentieth century began their writing careers as newspaper reporters. Jack London, Stephen Crane, Dreiser, Lardner, Damon Runyon, Anderson, Katherine Anne Porter, Hemingway, all served their apprenticeships in that intense, deadline-driven environment of the newsroom. Their awareness of the editor's blue-penciling developed an ear for transcribing the vitality of spoken language, an eye for recording the telling detail, and the ability to restructure the flabby and inchoate human scene into tightly organized and vivid tales. We know from the essays and memoirs of many of these men and women that a number of their best-known short-fiction works had first lives as reported news events.

At the same time that newspapers provided a training ground for the sharpening of storytelling skills, American magazines, proliferating everywhere, became a source of income for struggling young writers and a forum which exposed their works to the public. Although by 1910, *Century*, *Harper's*, the *Atlantic*, and the *North American Review* were languishing (due in part to a misguided clinging to outworn editorial and advertising principles and in part to an increasingly literate but less discriminating populace), mass-circulation magazines flourished and under wise editorship continued to publish the works of America's literary artists. Throughout the next two decades stories by Edith Wharton, Ernest Hemingway, and Thomas Wolfe appeared with regularity in *Scribner's* magazine. In the 1930s the

Saturday Evening Post featured the illustrations of Norman Rockwell on its cover, his stolid figures gazing benignly and reassuringly at the reader, while inside were printed many of the radically new, often unsettling fictions of F. Scott Fitzgerald and William Faulkner. (Fitzgerald received as much as four thousand dollars per story from the *Post* and in the combined years of 1928 and 1929 had an income of nearly fifty thousand dollars for the pieces the magazine published.) H. L. Mencken's *American Mercury*, although not, strictly speaking, a mass-circulation magazine, was influential, and writers as important as Sinclair Lewis, Dreiser, and Fitzgerald knew they had an appreciative audience when Mencken published their works. When Harold Ross's the *New Yorker* first appeared in 1925 with Ross's celebrated admonition that its published works must make no concessions to "the little old lady from Dubuque," the most sophisticated, urbane of American magazines had arrived. The importance of this periodical for short-story writers of real talent cannot be overstated. In its nearly sixty-five years of publication, it has functioned, informally, but incontrovertibly as a *New Yorker* school of short-story writing, shaping its audience to expect and applaud the cool, allusive, frequently satiric, and usually brilliant works of such authors as Kay Boyle, John O'Hara, Irwin Shaw, Dorothy Parker, E. B. White, James Thurber, John Cheever, and John Updike.

For many serious readers and writers of short fiction, the little magazines provided the ideal medium for the publication of short fictions considered avant-garde at the time, but now regarded as indisputable classics of the canon. According to Frederick Hoffman, Charles Allen, and Carolyn Ulrich in their *The Little Magazines: A History and A Bibliography* (1947), since 1912 eighty percent of our most important writers (this includes critics as well as poets and fiction writers) and every significant literary movement found sponsorship in the little magazines. The function of these literary periodicals is described in this way:

A little magazine is a magazine designed to print artistic work which for reasons of commercial expediency is not acceptable to the money-minded periodicals or presses. Acceptance or refusal by commercial publishers at times has nothing to do with the quality of the work. If the magazine can obtain artistic work from unknown or relatively unknown writers, the little magazine purpose is further accomplished. Little magazines are willing to lose money, to court ridicule, to ignore public taste, willing to do almost anything–steal, beg, or undress in public–rather than sacrifice their right to print good material.

In general, then, the founding of the little magazine was an expression of revolt against the conservativism of both the general public and the editorial policies of commercial periodicals; indeed, the titles of several–*Blast*, the *Anvil*, the *Left*, and *Masses*–reveal a political as well as a literary bias. But the risk of economic failure was great, and although there were as many as fifty new little magazines in the mid 1930s, relatively few of them survived the war years.

Beginning in 1912 and for several years following, these literary journals acted as a forum for some of the country's most remarkable young writers. There were those publications designed exclusively for poetry: *Poetry: A Magazine of Verse; The Poetry Journal; Contemporary Verse; The Fugitive;* and *Others* are among the best known, and it is no exaggeration to say that for nearly every poet of note these small presses provided the first and often the only outlet for their work. For short-story writers whose fictions seemed unsuitable for and were therefore rejected by the mass-circulation magazines, publication in the little magazines frequently functioned to establish their careers. Hemingway's first six stories were printed in the little magazines; and the early work of Jean Toomer, Conrad Aiken, James Stephens, Sherwood Anderson, Kay Boyle, William Faulkner, Erskine Caldwell, and Katherine Anne Porter found a sophisticated and responsive readership in subscribers to such periodicals as *The Double Dealer, Hound and Horn, Broom, transition,* and *Story*.

Although two world wars and an economic boom and catastrophe have allowed literary and other historians of the twentieth century neatly to categorize the 1920s, 1930s, and 1940s, the forces at work in the first two decades were not as felicitously deployed. Until the beginning of the Great War in 1914 and most perceptibly in the disillusionment which followed it, American culture seemed of a piece with that of the late nineteenth century. To observe that throughout that complacent period of expansion and industrialization the very rich continued to become very much richer without the threat of taxation or of labor legislation; to note that at the same time, the number of immigrants arriving in the United States formed a huge underclass, the effect of

which was to keep millions unemployed or working for low wages in incredibly poor conditions; to remember that there coexisted, sometimes within only a few miles of each other, the squalor and misery of slums and the grandeur of palatial estates is but to recount the most obvious social data. The frontier and the midwestern plains, once glowing alternatives to life in the metropolitan East, no longer promised either the riches of gold or the welcoming smiles of farmers who were now experiencing drought and foreclosures. The growth of industrial communities brought a gray unvarying pattern to the cityscape, and people of clashing nationalities, languages, and customs were daily thrown into uneasy alliances with each other. And America, which at least in the eyes of the privileged and the governing had seemed superior and inviolable, was slowly drifting toward involvement with other nations, and finally into the Great War.

Neither the dislocations undergirding the culture nor the rumblings of approaching disaster were reflected in the popular magazine stories of the time. Their subjects tended toward the sentimental and were treated in a cheerful, allusive way, and plots nearly always had a happy ending. They were, quite simply, false to experience, and the language in which they were written was, predictably, banal and lifeless. Philip Stevick, in his introduction to *The American Short Story, 1900-1945* (1984), observes that the magazine fiction of this period had an "obsessive adverbial quality," while works from that time that endured reveal a greater reliance on nouns and verbs to carry the burden of meaning. His examples, taken from one contemporary magazine story, make the point: "he said, indolently"; "nodding his head, sagaciously"; "he answered, gravely"; "replied Braithwaite, snappishly"; "he continued, ecstatically"; "he said, wearily." There is a tendency for such rhetoric to draw attention to itself as arch and knowing; at the same time, focus is shifted away from character and action, and the reader feels removed from the narrated events. The authors of such works were bound, or at least felt that they were, by the taboos of subject matter and language inherited from the past. And yet, those transitional figures–Willa Cather, Theodore Dreiser, Henry James, and Edith Wharton–remained resistant to the complacency around them and unfazed by the meretricious stories with which they had to compete for inclusion in many of the magazines of the day. They went on doing what they had to do, that is, writing with originality and conviction. Their short stories of this period (among them, James's "The Beast in the Jungle," Wharton's "Souls Belated," Dreiser's "Free," and Cather's "Paul's Case") reveal textures more tough and sinewy and truths much darker than the typical contemporary short fictions, but they are still read, taught, analyzed, anthologized, and emulated today, while the more esteemed writers of the period, courting popularity by maintaining the tradition of the genteel and precious, have long since been forgotten.

The social upheavals of the postwar decade and the extraordinary fiction, poetry, and drama to which they gave birth have made the 1920s the most consistently scrutinized of any period in American literary history. Despite the bitterness of the young men and women returning from service overseas to a country untouched by the war and insensitive to its brutality, and the consequent expatriation of great numbers of artists to France and England, and despite the growing power of the Ku Klux Klan, gangsterism, prohibition, the increasing alienation and suspicion between the generations, and a tenacious Main Street repressiveness, the period evokes an unmistakable glamour. Women won the vote; the automobile, now available through mass production to enormous numbers of people (a Ford car sold for $290 in 1924), functioned as a means of escape from boredom and sexual restraint; jazz, formerly a subversive musical idiom played primarily by black performers, now defined the era; movies (attended by one hundred million people weekly by 1926) suggested a sensuous reality further reinforced by the popularization of Sigmund Freud's theories of the libido; new fashions in dancing and dress dictated social status and were taken up and cast off with equal impetuousness. It was, in Fitzgerald's words, "the greatest, gaudiest spree in history."

The American fiction writers of the 1920s who fled to Paris after the war in revolt against the nation of "philistines" remained curiously apolitical. Of those who either made Paris their home or traveled there often enough to be labeled "expatriates"–Gertrude Stein, Sherwood Anderson, F. Scott Fitzgerald, Ernest Hemingway, John Dos Passos, Kay Boyle–only Dos Passos and Boyle espoused specifically political views. Those authors most closely identified, then as now, with the modernist spirit in fiction works of the 1920s and the decade which followed– Hemingway, Fitzgerald, and Faulkner (who

served in the Canadian Royal Air Force during the war and then returned to his home in Oxford, Mississippi)–discovered methods of protest more rooted in the literary imagination. While the reputations of these three writers grow primarily out of their work in novelistic fiction, their steady output in the short-story form (even when dictated more by economic need than aesthetic impulse) reshaped and redefined its contours. Fitzgerald traced the psychic as well as the social history of the times (he is much more than the chronicler of that period, a debasing of his extraordinary talent still exercised today in some quarters), and his stories catch with superb irony the hysterical abandonment to youth, riches, glamour, and amusement that became both his subject and his personal fate. Hemingway, in his conviction that the past provides no source of value, the future no hope, focuses on the moral choices made from moment to moment as the only meaning available in human experience, and this theme and its variation throughout his stories are a powerful expression of American existentialism. And Faulkner's intricate weaving of southern myth with archetypal ritual, his stretching of American vocabulary and cadences to reveal complexities of chronology and consciousness, establish thematic and linguistic patterns undreamed of before his work appeared.

The years between 1910 and the end of World War II–the period covered by this volume (the third on American short-story writers in the *Dictionary of Literary Biography* series)–are dominated by fiction writing. Eugene O'Neill is the only genius writing for the American stage during this period; and although the poetry of such figures as Edwin Arlington Robinson, Ezra Pound, T. S. Eliot, Robert Frost, Hart Crane, and Wallace Stevens is extraordinary in its range of subjects and techniques and inevitably in its influence, the number of novels and stories published and avidly read by intellectuals and general readers alike make the first half of the twentieth century the era of American fiction. The increasing prominence of the short-story form is particularly apparent. In part, this is due to a new "packaging." In the 1920s two short-story annuals began publication, *The Best Short Stories* and *O. Henry Memorial Award: Prize Stories.* Thus, it was not unusual for stories of real artistic merit to find two forums–the first in a commercial magazine, the second in one of the two annuals whose inclusion in their titles of the lustrous and beckoning words, "best" and "prize," worked to insure a large readership. At the same time, a new format emerged for individual writers of the short story. Following the publication of Sherwood Anderson's *Winesburg, Ohio* in 1919, there appeared several collections, among them Willa Cather's *Youth and the Bright Medusa* (1920); F. Scott Fitzgerald's *Flappers and Philosophers* (1922); Jean Toomer's *Cane* (1923); Ernest Hemingway's *In Our Time* (1925); Ring Lardner's *The Love Nest* (1926); Thomas Wolfe's *From Death to Morning* (1935); Richard Wright's *Uncle Tom's Children: Five Long Stories* (1938); and Eudora Welty's *A Curtain of Green* (1941).

But it was content even more than availability that created a continued demand for the short story. While the received ideas of Sigmund Freud, Carl Jung, Karl Marx, and G. S. Fraser (whose studies in cultural anthropology brought an awareness to the Western world of the cross-cultural pervasiveness and centrality of myths) are everywhere in evidence in the evolution of the form, the sources of its power are in native American material. Whether in the melancholy atmosphere of small towns (in the works, for example of Anderson, Cather, Welty), the glamour and danger of the big city (as in O. Henry, Fitzgerald, James T. Farrell), or the capacity for violence, both potential and actual, lurking in the natural world (particularly in Hemingway, Faulkner, Katherine Anne Porter), our finest writers in the genre have found the means to make the regional universal. It is interesting to note how many of these authors lived on the fringes of the world about which they wrote so that they are themselves the "marginal figures," the members of a "submerged population group," about which Frank O'Connor (in his *The Lonely Voice*, 1963) speaks when he describes the solitary beings that populate the modern American short story. It may well be that the lonely wanderers who dominate these works are compelling precisely because they are the projected lives of their creators; in them the thoughtful readers of the nation and the world have been able to recognize themselves.

—Bobby Ellen Kimbel

Acknowledgments

This book was produced by Bruccoli Clark Layman, Inc. Karen L. Rood is senior editor for the *Dictionary of Literary Biography* series. J. M. Brook was the in-house editor.

Production coordinator is James W. Hipp. Systems manager is Charles D. Brower. Art supervisor is Susan Todd. Penney L. Haughton is responsible for layout and graphics. Copyediting supervisor is Joan M. Prince. Typesetting supervisor is Kathleen M. Flanagan. William Adams, Laura Ingram, and Michael D. Senecal are editorial associates. The production staff includes Rowena Betts, Nancy Brevard-Bracey, Joseph M. Bruccoli, Teresa Chaney, Patricia Coate, Marie Creed, Allison Deal, Holly Deal, Sarah A. Estes, Brian A. Glassman, Cynthia Hallman, Susan C. Heath, Mary Long, Kathy S. Merlette, Laura Garren Moore, and Sheri Beckett Neal. Jean W. Ross is permissions editor.

Walter W. Ross and Jennifer Toth did the library research with the assistance of the reference staff at the Thomas Cooper Library of the University of South Carolina: Lisa Antley, Daniel Boice, Faye Chadwell, Cathy Eckman, Gary Geer, Cathie Gottlieb, David L. Haggard, Jens Holley, Jackie Kinder, Marcia Martin, Jean Rhyne, Beverly Steele, Ellen Tillett, Carol Tobin, and Virginia Weathers. William E. Grant, Bowling Green State University, assigned some of the entries in this volume.

American Short-Story Writers, 1910-1945
First Series

Dictionary of Literary Biography

Sherwood Anderson
(13 September 1876-8 March 1941)

David D. Anderson
Michigan State University

See also the Anderson entries in *DLB 4: American Writers in Paris, 1920-1939; DLB 9: American Novelists, 1910-1945;* and *DLB Documentary Series: 1.*

BOOKS: *Windy McPherson's Son* (New York: Lane / London: Lane, Bodley Head, 1916; revised edition, New York: Huebsch, 1922; London: Cape, 1923);

Marching Men (New York: Lane / London: Lane, Bodley Head, 1917 / Toronto: Gundy, 1917);

Mid-American Chants (New York: Lane / London: Lane, Bodley Head, 1918);

Winesburg, Ohio: A Group of Tales of Ohio Small Town Life (New York: Huebsch, 1919); republished as *Winesburg, Ohio: Intimate Histories of Every-day People* (London: Cape, 1922);

Poor White (New York: Huebsch, 1920; London: Cape, 1921);

The Triumph of the Egg: A Book of Impressions from American Life in Tales and Poems (New York: Huebsch, 1921); republished as *The Triumph of the Egg, and other stories* (London: Cape, 1922);

Horses and Men: Tales, long and short, from our American life (New York: Huebsch, 1923; London: Cape, 1924);

Many Marriages (New York: Huebsch, 1923);

A Story Teller's Story: The tale of an American writer's journey through his own imaginative world and through the world of facts, with many of his experiences and impressions among other writers—told in many notes—in four books—and an Epilogue (New York: Huebsch, 1924; London: Cape, 1925);

Culver Pictures

Dark Laughter (New York: Boni & Liveright, 1925; London: Jarrolds, 1926);

3

The Modern Writer (San Francisco: Lantern Press, 1925);

Sherwood Anderson's Notebook: Containing Articles Written During the Author's Life as a Story Teller and Notes of his Impressions from Life scattered through the Book (New York: Boni & Liveright, 1926);

Tar: A Midwest Childhood (New York: Boni & Liveright, 1926; London: Secker, 1927);

A New Testament (New York: Boni & Liveright, 1927);

Alice and The Lost Novel (London: Matthews & Marrot, 1929);

Hello Towns! (New York: Liveright, 1929);

Nearer the Grass Roots (San Francisco: Westgate Press, 1929);

The American County Fair (New York: Random House, 1930);

Perhaps Women (New York: Liveright, 1931);

Beyond Desire (New York: Liveright, 1932);

Death in the Woods and Other Stories (New York: Liveright, 1933);

No Swank (Philadelphia: Centaur, 1934);

Puzzled America (New York & London: Scribners, 1935);

Kit Brandon: A Portrait (New York & London: Scribners, 1936; London: Hutchinson, 1937);

Plays, Winesburg and Others (New York & London: Scribners, 1937);

A Writer's Conception of Realism (Olivet, Mich.: Olivet College, 1939);

Home Town (New York: Alliance, 1940);

Sherwood Anderson's Memoirs (New York: Harcourt, Brace, 1942);

Selected Short Stories of Sherwood Anderson (New York: Editions for the Armed Services, 1944);

The Sherwood Anderson Reader, edited by Paul Rosenfeld (Boston: Houghton Mifflin, 1947);

The Portable Sherwood Anderson, edited by Horace Gregory (New York: Viking, 1949; revised, 1972);

Sherwood Anderson: Short Stories, edited by Maxwell Geismar (New York: Hill & Wang, 1962);

Return to Winesburg: Selections From Four Years of Writing for a Country Newspaper, edited by Ray Lewis White (Chapel Hill: University of North Carolina Press, 1967);

The Buck Fever Papers, edited by Welford Dunaway Taylor (Charlottesville: University Press of Virginia, 1971);

The "Writer's Book," edited by Martha Mulroy Curry (Metuchen, N.J.: Scarecrow Press, 1975);

France and Sherwood Anderson: Paris Notebook, 1921, edited by Michael Fanning (Baton Rouge: Louisiana State University Press, 1976);

Sherwood Anderson: The Writer at His Craft, edited by Jack Salzman, David D. Anderson, and Kichinosuke Ohashi (Mamaroneck, N.Y.: Appel, 1979).

Sherwood Anderson, now regarded as one of the most important American writers in the short-story form, was born to Irwin McLain Anderson and Emma Smith in Camden, Ohio, on 13 September 1876 and raised in Clyde, Ohio. After a variety of jobs in Clyde (his education was interrupted often by the necessity of having to help support the family), he was successively a laborer in Chicago and a private and corporal in an Ohio volunteer infantry company in the Spanish-American War. After the war he returned to school for one year before embarking on a business career as an advertising copywriter and salesman in Chicago. On 16 May 1904 he married Cornelia Lane, the daughter of the head of a wholesale firm. In 1906 he became president of a mail-order company in Cleveland, and in 1907 he founded his own mail-order paint company in Elyria, Ohio. In Elyria he had apparently begun to write, well before his abrupt break with the business world in 1913. After leaving Elyria following a mild breakdown, he returned to Chicago and copywriting, and soon after separated from his wife (they were divorced in 1916, at which time Anderson married Tennessee Mitchell, an aspiring Chicago artist). He turned, too, to serious writing, establishing himself as a member of the modernist literary movement known as the Chicago Renaissance. With a trunkful of manuscripts brought with him from Elyria, where he had been working in isolation, he began thinking about his new identity as a writer, at the same time rewriting old material and seeking out new subject matter and new approaches to it.

Anderson's first literary publication was in the first issue of the *Little Review,* which appeared in March 1914. Edited by Margaret Anderson, the journal was to become the voice of the Chicago Renaissance. Anderson's contribution was an essay called "The New Note," essentially an attempt to define what he had learned about writing in the nine months since he had returned to

Chicago. The essay was neither a definition of modernism nor a plea for artistic liberation, however; it was an affirmation of the work he had begun and a statement of the sense of craft that was to dominate his work to the end of his life and career twenty-seven years later.

He also pointed out in the essay the direction in which his work was to go in the future: he would write in a literary language drawn out of the living language of the American heartland, as had Mark Twain more than a generation earlier; he would employ a new literary technique that would penetrate appearance to lay bare psychological reality; he would use as his subject matter the commonplace lives of commonplace people.

Nevertheless, when Anderson published his first short story, "The Rabbit-Pen," in *Harper's* (July 1914), there was little evidence of what he had called "the new note" in this work. The manuscript of the story may or may not have been among those Anderson brought with him from Elyria, as apparently were early drafts of *Windy McPherson's Son* (1916) and *Marching Men* (1917), his first two novels to be published. In concept and execution "The Rabbit-Pen" seems closer to the two novels than to the stories that started to appear in 1916 and that were incorporated into *Winesburg, Ohio* in 1919.

Certainly not the realistic story that Anderson saw it to be at the time, "The Rabbit-Pen" is reminiscent of the unreal portions of *Windy McPherson's Son.* In it Anderson attempts to fuse a realistic element, the struggle of a mother rabbit to save her newborn litter from a rampaging male, with the fantasies of a successful writer concerning marriage and with the competition between a wealthy suburban mother and a German housemaid for the love of the woman's children. Set in a wealthy Chicago suburb and in a downtown office, it has overtones of the exotic, and it depends on a twisted ending for the limited effect that it has: the writer is shocked to learn that the German housemaid, whose confidence, strength, and control he had admired and to whom he had fantasized marriage, has married the gardener and returned to Germany. With her departure, the woman's children become unmanageable.

Not only is the story dependent on the ending for its effect, but Anderson's handling of dialogue is as yet undeveloped and the writer, the central character, is too naive to be credible. Only the rabbit-pen episode resembles

Anderson, circa 1900 (courtesy of The Newberry Library)

Anderson's later use of vivid, harsh incidents in his short stories, but this scene is of marginal importance to the structure of the story, although it apparently is meant to be symbolic. The portrayal of the maid has overtones of Anderson's later idealized portraits of his mother, and there is some indication of Anderson's future concern with love and the ironies of appearance, but the story is essentially apprentice work.

Anderson's second published story was "Sister" (*Little Review*, December 1915). A two-page sketch, impressionistic rather than realistic in technique, it marks Anderson's first published attempt to use the subject matter and techniques that he was to fuse in the stories that became *Winesburg, Ohio.* The prose is straightforward and natural, in the first-person manner of an oral storyteller. The story contains no dialogue, perhaps because none was necessary, but more likely

Anderson (third from left) with his siblings: Karl, Ray, Stella, Irwin, and Earl (courtesy of The Newberry Library)

because Anderson realized, as "The Rabbit-Pen" demonstrates, that he had not yet learned to construct conversations in the easy rhythms and idiom of the Midwest.

In technique and execution the story is a substantial advance over "The Rabbit-Pen." There is no plot; the story consists of a description, told by an omniscient narrator, of the relationship between a brother and sister, both of them exiled from their father's house, who meet occasionally in the brother's room. The sister, we are told, has always been "strange," that is, a tomboy and a loner, who at fifteen had suffered a severe beating from the father when she announced to him that she was about to take a lover.

In the telling, two incidents point to the future development of Anderson's subject matter. The father becomes ill after the beating, suggesting a sensitive dimension of the father completely lacking in the vicious portrayal of the father in *Windy McPherson's Son* and not to appear again in Anderson's work until his refurbished father-image in "The Triumph of the Egg" in 1920 and *A Story Teller's Story* in 1924, when he portrays his father characters sympathetically. Furthermore, the narrator departs from surface real-

ism to penetrate into the deeper dimensions of human relationships when he declares that he had no idea how he learned of the beating, that he had neither witnessed it nor been told of it although he knew it had occurred.

In the final paragraphs Anderson moves beyond the incident to define its meaning, not, however, in the individual, personalized manner of most of the stories in *Winesburg, Ohio,* but in universal terms:

> I am the world and my sister is the young artist of the world. I am afraid the world will destroy her. So furious is my love for her that the touch of her hand makes me tremble. . . .
>
> In the evening after my sister is gone I do not try to work any more. I pull my couch to the opening by the window and lie down. It is then that I begin to understand my sister. She is the artist's right to adventure in the world, to be destroyed by the adventure, if that be necessary, and I, on the couch, am the worker in the world, blinking up at the stars that can be seen from my window when my couch is properly arranged.

Although Anderson was apparently unaware of it, "Sister" was his first published attempt to use, in the portrait of the sister, what he was later in *Winesburg, Ohio* to call the "grotesque," a human being twisted by circumstance and the lack of love and understanding into a person psychologically if not physically deformed, yet oddly lovable and uniquely worthy of compassion. The grotesque is, however, in Anderson's terms, doomed to misunderstanding by those who see only the surface of life. "Sister" foreshadows Elizabeth Willard, Kate Swift, and the other memorable women in *Winesburg, Ohio.*

In February 1916 Anderson published the first of what were to become the *Winesburg, Ohio* stories in *Masses.* "The Book of the Grotesque" was to become the prefatory sketch of the collection, and, as Anderson originally conceived it, the title story of the volume. The following month, March 1916, he published "Vibrant Life" in the *Little Review* and "Hands," the second of the *Winesburg, Ohio* stories, in *Masses.*

During the last months of 1915 and the early months of 1916 Anderson discovered that in the short-story form he could best apply the principles that he had defined in "The New Note." In those months Anderson passed from modest to substantial achievement in his work, from the tentative sketch "Sister" to the work of art that is "Hands." So sudden was this accomplish-

Anderson at the time he ran a mail-order paint company in Elyria, Ohio

ment that he tried on several occasions, most notably in two different accounts in his twice-edited *Memoirs* (1942), to describe both in mythical and metaphorical terms what had happened.

In the first, he wrote,

> What dreams, hopes, ambitions. Sometimes it had seemed to me, when, as a young man I sat at the window of that room, that each person who passed along the street below, under the light, shouted his secret up to me.
>
> I was myself and still I fled out of myself. It seemed to me that I went into the others.
>
> What dreams. What egotism. I thought then, on such evenings, that I could tell all of the stories of all the people of America. . . .
>
> And then came the night that it happened. . . .
>
> I had been working so long, so long. Oh, how many thousands, hundreds of thousands of words put down.
>
> Trying for something.

> To escape out of old minds, old thoughts put into my mind by others, into my own thoughts, my own feelings. . . .
>
> To at last go out of myself, truly into others, the others I met constantly in the streets of the city, in the office where I then worked, and still others remembered out of my childhood in an American small town.
>
> To be myself, and yet at the same time the others.
>
> And then, on a day, late in the afternoon of a day, I had come home to that room. I sat at a table in a corner of the room. I wrote.
>
> There was a story of another human being, quite outside myself, truly told.
>
> The story was one called "Hands." It was about a poor little man, beaten, pounded, frightened by the world in which he lived into something oddly beautiful.
>
> The story was written that night in one sitting. . . .
>
> "It is solid," I said to myself. "It is like a rock. It is put down."

The second account, which may apply to "The Book of the Grotesque," apparently the first of the stories to be written, rather than to "Hands," differs substantially in detail but not in spirit:

> it was a late fall night and raining and I had not bothered to put on my pajamas.
>
> I was there naked in bed and I sprang up. I went to my typewriter and began to write. It was there, under those circumstances, myself sitting near an open window, the rain occasionally blowing in and wetting my bare back, that I did my first writing.
>
> I wrote the first of the stories, afterwards to be known as the Winesburg stories. I wrote it, as I wrote them all, complete in one sitting. I do not think I afterwards changed a word of it. . . .
>
> The rest of the stories in the book came out of me on succeeding evenings, and sometimes during the day when I worked in the advertising office. . . .

It is irrelevant whether these accounts are factual or have been transmuted into myth in order to explain the inexplicable. At this point Anderson had discovered the means by which he could transform his theory of "the new note" into literature. He had found, for the subject matter of his best work, those people who are deformed psychologically, people he was to call grotesques. He had found, too, his language, the easy rhythms of the American heartland, and his

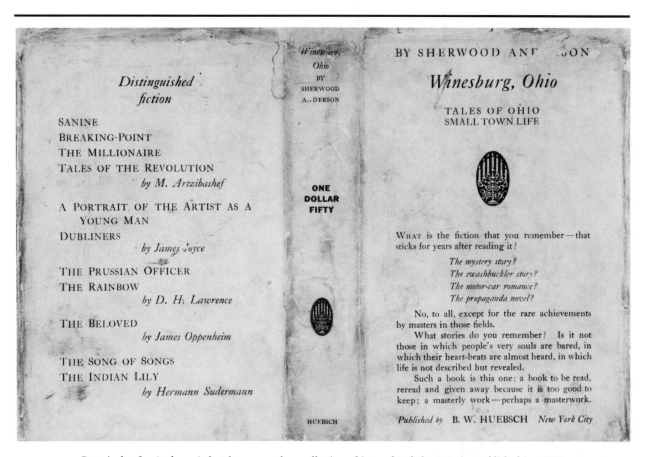

Dust jacket for Anderson's best-known work, a collection of interrelated short stories published in 1919

form, the seemingly artless but carefully controlled meandering of an ancient oral tradition.

Again, whether or not these accounts are factually correct, certain elements in "Vibrant Life" suggest that this two-page sketch is, like "Sister," a transition to *Winesburg, Ohio.* It is not a fully developed story, its emphasis is upon a grotesque incident rather than a human being become a grotesque, and its shocking ending is related to that of "The Rabbit-Pen" rather than the introspective understanding at the end of "Sister." Nevertheless, its action reflects the confusion exhibited by many of the characters of *Winesburg, Ohio,* those who mistake lust for love, who see only the surface of life rather than its substance.

In "Vibrant Life" two people are sitting up with the corpse of a man shot by a jealous husband: the dead man's older brother, who, after a scandalous youth, has become a successful lawyer, and a nurse who had been in love with the dead man. The two drink wine; they look at each other, and then the man notices a magazine lying on a nearby table. It is open to a picture of a magnificent stallion. He remembers such a stallion from his youth, and he tells the nurse, "It was a

wonderful sight.... The great animal was all life, vibrant, magnificent life...." Then, leaning over the woman, he tells her "We are like that.... The men in our family have that vibrant, conquering life in us." He seizes her, she resists, and the two bump the coffin. The dead body of brother and lover rolls onto the floor.

Anderson makes clear in the story that neither the woman who had loved the dead man nor the rounder turned lawyer have any more understanding of life or love than the young George Willard, who in "Nobody Knows" (first published in *Winesburg, Ohio*) mistakes a lonely plea for an invitation to a sexual encounter. The two people in "Vibrant Life," particularly the lawyer, are as grotesque as any of the people of *Winesburg, Ohio.* The relationship of "Vibrant Life" and "Sister" to "Hands" is a major step in the evolution of Anderson's literary ability. The difference between the two simultaneous publications is so startling that perhaps it can best be explained in Anderson's terms.

"Hands" is superb, a perfectly executed story that is almost immeasurably superior to anything Anderson had written earlier. It is the

Anderson, circa 1922 (Chicago Historical Society, DN #9914)

story of Wing Biddlebaum, a fat, bent, frightened old man who lives in a dilapidated house on the edge of Winesburg, and of George Willard, a reporter on the *Winesburg Democrat* (renamed the *Winesburg Eagle* in *Winesburg, Ohio*).

Wing is a semirecluse, the target of much abuse and teasing by the young people of the town, yet, curiously, the town is proud of his remarkable hands, so adept that he can pick berries faster than anyone else. But Wing is ashamed of his hands, and he tries to conceal or control them when he is talking to his young friend, George Willard. The two, the old recluse and the young reporter, seek each other out to walk and talk in the evenings. The old man knows that there is much he can teach George about life and the ability to dream, but he is afraid to speak. George senses this fear, and he knows intuitively that Wing's hands, so potentially expressive, are the source of his isolation in the town, but he is afraid to ask about them. In an encounter between the two Wing becomes excited while warning George not to accept the values of the town, and his hands begin to move

wildly. Suddenly aware of them, Wing becomes frightened and sends the boy away; George, frightened at Wing's behavior, no longer wants to know his secret.

Anderson as narrator reveals the man's secret: twenty years before, as Adolph Meyers, a young schoolmaster in a Pennsylvania town, Wing often became excited when he talked to his students in an all-male class. As he told them of his dream, he touched them or tousled their hair. Men of the town misunderstood his actions, and one night he was beaten and driven out of the town, with the warning, "Keep your hands to yourself" echoing in his ears.

The story concludes with Wing, still nervous from his encounter with George, alone in his house. His hands quickly and involuntarily pick bits of bread off the floor and carry them to his mouth. Anderson concludes, "The nervous expressive fingers, flashing in and out of the light, might well have been mistaken for the fingers of the devotee going swiftly through decade after decade of his rosary."

Wing's hands and his dream fuse in the story. His dream is of human love and fulfillment, and his hands, like the hands of a craftsman, a surgeon, or a lover, are the means by which he can communicate that dream, like all dreams, difficult to articulate. But the language of hands, like that of any other medium of communication, is easily misunderstood. For Wing, misunderstanding had occurred, and the dream had become a nightmare, driving him into himself and forever precluding love or fulfillment for him.

The story, like "The Rabbit-Pen," "Sister," and "Vibrant Life," employs a moment of horror as a crucial element in its structure, but here it is low-keyed, not exploited but integral to the plot structure and intensely real. It provides a momentary insight into what had made Wing a grotesque, turned in upon himself, afraid to speak in his most eloquent language, instead permitting his hands to be instruments of pointless activity and the subject of idle curiosity.

With the publication of "Hands" Anderson reached his artistic maturity in the mastery of the language, form, and character type that were to be his major and most lasting contributions to American literature. While Anderson continued to write advertising copy in Chicago, his stories began to appear as regularly and rapidly in the literary journals as Anderson later said they had been written: "The Philosopher," *Little Review* (June-July 1916); "The Strength of God," *Masses*

Manuscript page for "Godliness," one of the stories in Winesburg, Ohio *(courtesy of The Newberry Library)*

Caricature by William H. Cotton of Anderson "conceiving a love lyric"

(August 1916); "Queer," *Seven Arts* (December 1916); "The Untold Lie," *Seven Arts* (January 1917); "Mother," *Seven Arts* (March 1917); "The Thinker," *Seven Arts* (September 1917); "Seeds," *Little Review* (July 1918); and "An Awakening," *Little Review* (December 1918).

All of these, as well as "The Book of Grotesques" and "Hands," were to appear in *Winesburg, Ohio* in 1919, following his third book, the collection of verse *Mid-American Chants,* in 1918. When Anderson had begun to conceive of the internal relationships of the stories it is impossible to tell, but each of the stories appeared in the book essentially as it had first appeared. In form *Winesburg, Ohio* is perhaps most accurately called a short-story sequence, a form developed by Anderson in this and later collections, but Anderson later referred to the collection as a novel in a form invented by himself, although he called each of the individual sections a short story. In the *Memoirs* he commented that the novel is not an appropriate form for American writers, that "What is wanted is a new looseness; and in *Winesburg* I have made my own form. There

were individual tales but all about lives in some-way connected. . . . Life is a loose flowing thing. . . ."

That Anderson did, almost from the beginning, perhaps from the writing of "The Book of the Grotesque" and "Hands," conceive of the stories as an integrated whole is clear from the manuscript of *Winesburg, Ohio* in the Newberry Library. Because most of the stories were written on the backs of earlier fragments of an unpublished novel, it is clear that Anderson wrote them not as isolated stories and sketches but as a unified series or sequence in which the geographical reality of a town takes form, the psychological reality of its people is made clear, and the spiritual maturity of a young man becomes possible.

Although the originality of the form and substance of *Winesburg, Ohio* and its individual stories and sketches is indisputable, its relationship to the ferment of the Chicago Renaissance is clear: Edgar Lee Masters had published *Spoon River Anthology,* an obvious comparison, in April 1915; the Chicago Little Theatre had presented Cloyd Head's one-act play, "Grotesques, a Decoration in Black and White," on 16 November 1915; and Arthur Davison Ficke had published "Ten Grotesques" in the *Little Review* in March 1915. However significant the artistic cross-fertilization of those years in Chicago may have been, Anderson's achievement in *Winesburg, Ohio* is the most important and influential work of a time, a place, and a movement that gave him the stimulation that made the book possible, if not inevitable.

Critics have debated whether the three concluding stories, "Death," "Sophistication," and "Departure," all previously unpublished, were written because Anderson saw that they were necessary or his publisher, B. W. Huebsch, suggested that they be written; whether John Lane had turned down the collection because *Mid-American Chants* had sold so poorly or Anderson had given Lane the collection of verse to fulfill his contract for three books so that he might publish *Winesburg, Ohio* with Huebsch; whether Anderson, Huebsch, or Floyd Dell suggested the final title rather than Anderson's original "The Book of the Grotesque." These questions are as yet unresolved but unimportant in light of the accomplishment.

Equally unresolved by too many scholars and anthologizers in spite of its obviousness is the unity of *Winesburg, Ohio* as well as that of Anderson's three later collections of stories, *The*

Advertising Men

Harry knew he shouldn't have done it. He said so. He said that
Mildred,his wife,was a damn good little woman. "She belongs to
Church",he said. "I tell you her people are O k. They got good
blood in them too. She tries to do right by the kids. She wants
them to be eduaated,go to the best colleges-Yale or Priceton or
University of Virginia,eh,what.

"I'm faithful to her,after my fashin,"he said.George said
he stle that line. He said-"I've been with other women,when I was
spiffed or something,but I never kissed a damn one of them on the
lips,"he said.

Alfred T said-"lets have another drink. How we going to stand up
to this racket,write the stuff we do write,year after year,without
hooch?
"Hooch and women,"he said,"our wives shouldn't blame us.
"Damn wives anyway,"he said.

Carl told one-how he came home,one night,less than a week before. He hadn't got himself squared yet. He said he crept in,
shoes in his hand. He made it O K.
The,"like a fool",he said,"I left my shorts,hanging on a chair.
"They were all red",he said.

"Well,you know...advertising",Alfred T said.

Will always wanted to hurt one of them. He said that,over at
his agency they were always having conferences. here was a long
room,with a mahogany conference tale. There were heavy glass ink
wells on the table.

Corrected typescript page for an unpublished sketch by Anderson (courtesy of The Newberry Library)

Triumph of the Egg (1921), *Horses and Men* (1923), and *Death in the Woods* (1933). Although each of the stories in each collection is complete in itself and many have been frequently anthologized, each diminishes perceptibly in its effect when taken out of the context in which Anderson conceived, wrote, and published it.

Winesburg, Ohio is unified in time, place, character, theme, style, and form to a greater extent than any of the later collections. The time of the stories is that which Anderson later defined in *Poor White* (1920) as a time of waiting, in which America and the Midwest, having fought and won the Civil War, paused for a moment before rushing headlong into industrial development and the acceptance of material values. The stories in *Winesburg, Ohio* are set in the late nineteenth century, but they are not of that time. The trains that travel through Winesburg connect the town to the greater world of American destiny beyond the flat northwestern Ohio horizons. Echoes of change are heard in the town, promising a fulfillment that many of the town's people have yet to find, that perhaps they can never find.

The town itself, its geography gradually defined as the stories develop (a geography close to that of Clyde, Ohio, Anderson's boyhood home), becomes a living thing to its people. Winesburg is refuge, it is nurturer, it is prison, it is point of departure; it provides, sometimes simultaneously, psychological support and spiritual torment as it plays its active part in the lives of its people, providing at once the walls that isolate them, the values that alienate them, and the ideals that liberate them.

But the stories are not about a time or a place; they are about the people who give life and identity to the town, those who, as Anderson later commented, came from "everywhere about me, in towns in which I had lived, in the army, in factories and offices." Each of them becomes the focal point and the substance of a story, as the nature of each is laid bare in a moment of Anderson's insight into what makes his people grotesques.

In "The Book of the Grotesque" Anderson defines the nature of his people, the substance of the stories, the technique of each, and the theme of the book. In it, in the portrayal of an old writer who had written an unpublished book called "The Book of the Grotesque," Anderson describes, in symbolic terms, the origins of human grotesquerie, and, in metaphorical terms, his own

experience in writing the stories of *Winesburg, Ohio*. The old writer had a dream in which all the people he had ever known passed by him, and he recognized that all were grotesques, some of them horrible, some beautiful. He awoke and began to write his book. In it he declared that in the beginning of the world there were many thoughts but no such thing as truth. People combined these thoughts into what were called truths, a great many of them and all beautiful. Then people seized upon the truths, made them their own, and tried to live by them. In so doing the people became grotesques and the truths became falsehoods.

In the following twenty-one stories and sketches, Anderson uses the concept of the grotesque–some attractive, some repulsive, some strange, some apparently conventional–as the controlling concept in each. Thus, each story is character-plotted (Anderson remarked on several occasions that there are no plots in human life); each examines the place of the central character in the life of the community; and in a revealing moment Anderson penetrates suddenly and sometimes shockingly to the character's psychological reality, to whatever it was that made the character a public or private grotesque.

Perhaps most important in this delineation of psychological reality is Anderson's attitude toward each of his people. Unlike William Faulkner, Carson McCullers, Flannery O'Connor, and others who later used Anderson's concept of the grotesque as the basis of many of their characters, Anderson insisted that all of his people, whether public or private grotesques, were worthy of love and compassion, not in spite of but because of their very grotesqueness. They were, he wrote, like the apples left behind by the pickers in the orchards around Winesburg because they were imperfect. Small boys and the poor sought these apples eagerly because they knew that they were the sweetest in the orchards, perhaps because of the imperfections that made them unsalable.

The first three stories, "Hands," "Paper Pills," and "Mother," define at once both the origins and the nature of the grotesque, and the three major sources of grotesquerie. At the same time, Anderson makes clear that the fact that the principal characteristic of the grotesque is his or her alienation from the community through an isolation that often terrifies the grotesque into overt as well as covert grotesque behavior.

Three Anderson Brothers, *painting by Karl Anderson of Earl, Sherwood, and Irwin Anderson (courtesy of Yale University Art Gallery)*

In each of the three stories the grotesque is isolated from the community because he or she is unable to communicate an inner vision to those for whom he or she cares. Thus, in "Hands" Anderson demonstrates the inability of a male school teacher in a small Pennsylvania town to communicate his vision of fulfillment to his boy students, the misunderstanding of the townspeople, and the teacher's ensuing fearful exile in Winesburg; in "Paper Pills," the story of Doctor Reefy, Anderson writes of an old physician who writes his thoughts on bits of paper, crumples them in his pockets, and when they become hard balls dumps them on the floor, or throws them at his friend John Spaniard, the nurseryman, laughing; only once, the narrator reveals, did Reefy read those thoughts to another: a beautiful young woman who had been his patient and then his wife and then had died. In "Mother," the story of Elizabeth Willard, Anderson writes of a woman who, married to an unsympathetic man, dreams of an escape into fulfillment for her son, a dream the town's mores had denied her. But, like Reefy and Biddlebaum, she is unable to com-

municate that dream to her son, who sees her as the conventional Winesburg wife and mother. Again, Anderson reveals what made her what she was: the girlish dreams, impossible to fulfill, that led her to scandalous behavior in the town.

In each of these three stories the central character has an inner vision, but in attempting to communicate it to others, he or she is misunderstood, and what is beautiful becomes, instead, a perversion. In two of the stories Anderson employs George Willard, young reporter on the *Winesburg Eagle,* son of Elizabeth, and promising young man of the town, in the role in which he appears in most of the following tales. George not only provides unity in the stories as he appears in various roles but he grows from intuitive sensitivity in "Hands" to empathetic understanding in "Sophistication" and archetypal young American man seeking opportunity in "Departure."

In the development of the book George slowly learns to understand and appreciate the intrinsic worth of others, but to each of the grotesques he is what that person wants him to be: a pupil, a lover, an extension of self, one who lis-

Anderson at Ripshin Farm, near Troutdale, Virginia. He purchased the property in 1925 with proceeds from his novel Dark Laughter.

tens and understands, one who becomes what the grotesque is not and cannot be. Thus, Wing Biddlebaum wants him to share a vision that Wing cannot articulate in words and is afraid to express with his hands; to his mother George can escape into the freedom that she was unable to seek; to Louise Trunnion in "Nobody Knows" he is a romantic lover who knows and values what she is; to others he is seen as a friend and a channel of entry into the life of the town.

But understanding is rare; not only does George not understand but understanding can only be sought or found in the intense moments of empathetic insight when both seeker and recipient can transcend the conventional means of communication, most frequently words and hands, both of which are subject to misunderstanding, and the barriers of appearance, especially of sex, that define the individual to the town, isolate him or her from the townspeople, and prevent both understanding and fulfillment. Thus, when Louise sends George a lonely plea for love, he mistakenly accepts it as an invitation to a surreptitious sexual adventure, just as when Wing attempts to

define his vision to George and instead frightens him.

But understanding can come, gradually, when one transcends the barriers, as George learns. When Kate Willard in "The Teacher" embraces him in her search for language, George misunderstands at first but later realizes that he had missed what Kate was trying to tell him. Finally, in "Sophistication" he and Helen White walk quietly through the deserted fairgrounds at night, finding, in a moment of mutual love, understanding, and acceptance, whatever it is that, Anderson says, makes adult human life possible. George is, in "Departure," finally wise enough to go into the larger world, West in the traditional American path of destiny and fulfillment, and to the city, Chicago, the symbol of a new age, a new fulfillment, and a new century.

Many of the people of Winesburg contribute to George's understanding and his determination to escape not from the town but from whatever it is that made the others grotesques. To Doctor Parcival, in "The Philosopher," George is a listener to whom he can tell the stories out of his past, the things that taught him to hate, and finally, after refusing to accept the futility of attending a child killed by a runaway team, he reveals the secret of a compassion beyond measure: his conviction that each of us is Christ, crucified for our very humanity.

In "A Man of Ideas," the story of Joe Welling's twin pursuits of the order beyond physical fact and of the tall, pale Sarah King, George functions as friend and reporter, but his attempts to write are frustrated by fear. "Respectability" is the story of Wash Williams, a physical as well as a psychological grotesque. Wash is the dirtiest and ugliest man in town but a skilled telegrapher; George, who notes Wash's well-kept hands, functions as listener. To him Wash pours out the cause of his grotesquerie and the destruction of his love, as his insensitive mother-in-law conspired to effect his reconciliation with his unfaithful wife by having him see her naked. But his love becomes hatred of all women, makes him ugly and violent, and George is chilled by the power of Wash's hatred of life.

In "The Thinker" the young, quiet Seth Richmond, known in the town as "a deep one" like his father, attempts to tell Helen White, the banker's daughter, of dreams and ideas he cannot articulate. But he mistakes her young sentiment for indifference, and he goes off into the night, convinced that she loves George Willard, whom he insists is a fool who talks a lot.

"The Strength of God," the story of the Reverend Curtis Hartman, and "The Teacher" are two of the most tightly interwoven stories in the sequence, not only because of George's presence as observer in the first and catalyst in the latter but because in both cases he is misled by appearance while keeping his lonely vigil in the *Winesburg Eagle* office as he tries to write. In the first story Hartman, spying on the unclothed Kate Willard in her bedroom from a cracked stained-glass window in his study in the bell tower of the Presbyterian church, is convinced of his sin but unable to stop. Finally, one stormy winter night, he sees her praying in anguish. Convinced that God had visited him in Kate's form, he smashes the window and then dashes into the winter night and to the *Eagle* office, where he announces to a startled George that he had seen God in Kate. His need for something more than routine faith had been distorted first into a neurotic sense of sin and then into an equally neurotic renewal of faith.

In "The Teacher" the source of Kate's anguish is revealed. Torn by her loneliness, her plainness, and, at thirty, her sense that she can never find fulfillment, she attempts to communicate her hope for George to him. The previous evening, Kate had attempted unsuccessfully to talk to him. George, misunderstanding her passion but sensing that somehow he had misunderstood, is sitting in bewilderment after her return, her embrace, and her sudden flight. When the minister bursts in upon him a short while later, it seems to George that the town has suddenly gone insane. But he lies awake that night, knowing that there is much that he has to learn.

In "Loneliness," the story of Enoch Robinson, George learns about the solitariness of human beings, the futility of flight, and the peculiarly intense isolation of one who aspires to become an artist. Enoch tells George his story: fifteen years before, he had gone to New York to become an artist among artists; his new marriage then failed because there was neither communication nor love nor understanding between him and his wife. Then, after becoming an advertising artist, he was driven into a lonely room. Finally, as a failed artist, he returns to Winesburg and a lonely old age in a lonely room.

In "An Awakening" and "Queer" George is taken further along the path to understanding, but in each he is assaulted by those who see him as something other than he is. The former is the story of Belle Carpenter, the daughter of the bullying cashier in the Winesburg bank. She is George's friend, with whom he occasionally walks in the evening and to whom he tries to talk of his dreams and ideas. But the story is that, too, of Ed Hanby, the bartender in Ed Griffith's saloon, crude, uncouth, and unable to express his love for Belle, just as she is unable to express hers for him. One evening George and Belle walk out of town to the Winesburg Fair Grounds, unaware that Ed Hanby is following. George, in his excitement, takes Belle in his arms; Belle, silent, stands waiting. Ed, cursing, springs out of the bushes, knocks George down, and takes Belle away, bullying her, while George, in sudden, unfamiliar humiliation, runs home through streets suddenly become squalid.

In "Queer" Elmer Cowley is the younger member in the firm of Cowley and Son, unsuccessful and eccentric merchants, both of whom are considered "queer" in the town. But Elmer, determined to destroy the reputation and break out of his isolation, attempts without success to talk to a half-witted man of the town. Then he seeks out George Willard but is unable to talk to him. Later, he plans to leave the town. As he leaps on a train, he strikes out, knocking George down. As he runs across the tops of the moving cars he shouts out his victory over George and over his reputation in the town.

"Drink" is the story of quiet, gentle, maladjusted, dreamy Tom Foster, secretly in love with Helen White, his intoxication with a spring night, his experimental drunkenness as a result, and his encounter with George Willard. As the boy begins to talk of walking with and making love to Helen, George becomes upset. But Tom talks of his dreams, his suffering, his recognition that everyone suffers, and his attempt to find experience, and George is drawn to the strange, sobering boy.

With the three concluding stories, "Death," concerning the long, secret, fulfilling relationship between Doctor Reefy and Elizabeth Willard, "Sophistication," concerning the mutual understanding and maturity of Helen White and George Willard, and "Departure," George's transition into the larger world and into manhood, the story of Winesburg as nurturer and teacher is complete. But George is not escaping from the village, as Anderson makes clear; he is entering into the American mainstream, taking Winesburg, its values, and the memory of its people with him.

Anderson with Katherine Anne Porter at Olivet College, 1940 (Trustees of the Sherwood Anderson Literary Estate)

But others, those whose lives have not touched George's, the grotesques who must live and die alone in Winesburg, remain behind, unfulfilled: Doctor Reefy, alone after Elizabeth's death; Jesse Bentley, of "Godliness," the old farmer turned Old Testament patriarch, hurt and confused, lying on the ground as his grandson David Hardy runs off into the night; Alice Hindman of "Adventure," whose lost love for Ned Currie sends her running naked into a rainy night, and then, humiliated, back to her lonely bed; the seven-year-old daughter of Tom Hard in "Tandy," who understands the vision of a drunken stranger, displaced in time; Ray Pearson of "The Untold Lie," who learns that there are two dimensions of truth and falsehood; Butch Wheeler, the lamplighter, Turk Smollet, the half-witted Mook, Tom Willard alone in the fading glory of the New Willard House, all of them the substance of the dreams George will paint as he finds himself in the city.

Winesburg, Ohio, as Anderson conceived and executed it, is both myth and poetry, an affirmative work, but misconceptions and misinterpreta-

tions began at its publication and continue to obscure the greatness of Anderson's achievement. Anderson was not "revolting from the village" as Carl Van Doren insisted in the *Nation* in 1921, a misconception that unfortunately continues to mislead readers and critics alike. Nor was he constructing a myth of the village as some more recent critics continue to insist. Neither is the book a Freudian exposé of sexual mores, a naturalistic study of biological and social determinism, a realistic portrayal of village life, or a primitivistic study of primitive people, all critical comments that have been applied to it.

Nor, in the final analysis, is it the story of George Willard's adolescent initiation into adult life, although George grows in understanding and compassion in the year's cycle of the book. Rather, it celebrates people as it explores the American promise that implies happiness at the end of the search. Each of the stories is the life of a person encapsulated in a moment that reveals the nature of that search and its end. Neither the prototype of the American Midwestern village at the end of the nineteenth century nor

Photograph of Anderson by Carl Van Vechten (by permission of Joseph Solomon, Trustee for the Estate of Carl Van Vechten)

an America in microcosm, *Winesburg, Ohio* is rather a microcosm of the human spirit as it yearns for understanding and love within the confused context of the values it has been taught.

Widely used as a textbook of the short story, its individual stories frequently anthologized, *Winesburg, Ohio* is the keystone of Anderson's literary reputation, and it is an impressive achievement. It is a work in which Anderson not only defines the problem of human isolation but asserts that it can be overcome, if only in moments, if we learn to transcend the walls that society and biology have erected among us.

Although Anderson began almost immediately to work on *Poor White*, the novel that was to bring the people of Winesburg into the modern age, he also began to write and publish many of the stories that were to be included in *The Triumph of the Egg*. Although there is no suggestion in his correspondence or memoirs that he had planned and written the stories as a short-story sequence—the stories in *The Triumph of the Egg* are not unified in character, setting, or time—the collection is unified by a consistent thematic state-

ment and by the inclusion of two free-verse poems, "The Dumb Man" at the beginning and "The Man With the Trumpet" at the end.

In the first, actually the nucleus of what might have been a story, Anderson describes an incident in a house in which are three men—a dandified youth, an old man, and a man "who has wicked eyes"—and a woman who waits upstairs, craving love. A fourth man comes to the house to see the woman. He, Anderson says, may have been Death, and the woman may have been Life. While the couple is upstairs, the wicked man runs back and forth, the old man dies, and the dandy laughs constantly. Anderson concludes "I have a wonderful story to tell but know no way to tell it," bemoaning his lack of understanding as well as his lack of words.

The incident is reported, but the narrator is unable to penetrate it to the reality beyond. Each of the characters is isolated from the observer and the others, and even if the barriers are penetrated or transcended, the underlying reality cannot be explained or defined. This feeling of inadequacy, frustration, despair, the inability to understand or penetrate the barrier, marks the lives of each of the grotesque characters in the following stories. Anderson, as in *Winesburg, Ohio*, however, intuitively grasps the essence of each character as he defines their tragic inadequacy.

The opening story, "I Want to Know Why," first published in *Smart Set* (November 1919), is set in the late nineteenth century, as are the Winesburg tales, at a racetrack. Ostensibly a boy's story of a lad who loves horses but cannot understand why men pursue shoddy substitutes for beauty and love with prostitutes, it is not, however, the story of a boy's initiation into adulthood; it is, instead, an expression of the most adult of human tragedies: the inability to understand or accept the contradictory values and emotions inherent not only in society but in each human being.

The first of these contradictions is simple: a black man will not tell on a boy; a white man will. But they become increasingly complex: a good, generous man is condemned because he is a gambler; other men refuse to see the beauty of running horses but regard them as instruments for gambling. But the ultimate contradiction is that which provides the lament of the narrator: the trainer of a beautiful, coordinated horse, a man who perceives real beauty, is seen through the window of a brothel consorting with a wom-

Anderson at his writing table, 1941 (courtesy of Walt Sanders of Black Star)

an who, superficially attractive, "is not clean" and who has "a hard, ugly mouth."

While the boy protests the incident, Anderson protests the confusion of values that prevents the trainer from distinguishing between the beautiful and the tawdry, the reality and the appearance, love and its superficial substitute. At times Anderson's persona slips; the boy is confused at the dichotomy of values; the adult despairs that he can do nothing about it.

The second story, "Seeds" (*Little Review*, July 1918), is closely related to the theme defined in "The Book of the Grotesque." In it Anderson begins with a dialogue between the narrator and a psychiatrist, and he concludes with a sketch of a relationship between a woman from Iowa and a young male artist in a Chicago boardinghouse. In the first, the psychiatrist, exhausted spiritually, attempts to find peace, but the narrator protests that what he has been trying to cure is the universal illness, that "It is given to no man to venture far along the road of lives." In the latter sketch, the young man refuses to become the woman's lover because, he realizes, the woman needs more than he can offer: "All the people in the

world are grotesques," he tells the narrator; "We all need to be loved," but he cannot love her because "I am paying old debts. Old thoughts and beliefs–seeds planted by old men–spring up in my soul and choke me," and the two part forever, his and the woman's isolation complete. Only for a moment the two had come together, holding hands on a park bench as had George Willard and Helen White in "Departure"; then the woman, loveless, returns to Iowa while the young man seeks a cleanness, perhaps in death, that eludes him.

In "The Other Woman" (*Little Review*, May-June 1920; republished in *The Best American Short Stories of 1920*), Anderson as narrator retells a story told by another man: the man is in love with his new wife, a wise woman who insists that they are human beings before they are a man and a woman, but the man is obsessed with his brief affair with another man's wife just before the wedding. He knows, however, that the obsession will pass because he had talked of it. Anderson, as narrator, withholds comment, and the implication is clear: that the man perhaps protests too much. Like Wash Williams in "Respectability" he can tell his story, but he does not understand either the other woman or himself, and the relationship will haunt him.

"The Egg" (first published as "The Triumph of the Egg," *Dial*, March 1920) is the most complex of the stories and as nearly humorous as any of Anderson's fictions. It has been widely anthologized and translated, and it was dramatized in one act by Raymond O'Neil for the Provincetown Players and presented as a curtain raiser for Eugene O'Neill's two-act *Diff'rent* in New York on 10 February 1925. It had a run of twenty-two performances. The story explores the frustrations of one of Anderson's displaced persons, a chicken farmer turned restaurant owner, a grotesque for whom life is a sequence of failures and frustrations as he attempts to become a success as defined by the values of society.

Again Anderson uses an adolescent narrator, the son of the grotesque, who sympathizes with his father, but who can only speculate on the cause of his father's failures and ultimate despair. As the father displays his collection of preserved deformed chickens to customers of his restaurant, the parallel is clear to the reader but not to the narrator, as Anderson probes beneath the seemingly humorous and ridiculous to define the man as a grotesque. In nature, Anderson makes clear, physical deformity is resolved by death, as the preserved deformed chickens illustrate, but Anderson's frustration parallels that of the father and clarifies that which is expressed in the opening verse of the collection and in "Seeds." The human psychological grotesque is doomed to live out his grotesque life, and we–the son, the author, the reader–can only observe with the compassion the grotesque's nature demands and needs.

This note of frustration and hopelessness continues through the rest of the collection as each of the characters finds it impossible to transcend his isolation. In "Unlighted Lamps" (*Smart Set*, July 1921) a young girl seeks love and understanding, first from her father and then from a young man, but she is misunderstood and repulsed, and at the end she is alone and unfulfilled. "Senility" (*Little Review*, September 1918) portrays a man who can cure "coughs, colds, consumption, and the sickness that bleeds," but not the sickness in his own heart. In "The Man in the Brown Coat" (*Little Review*, January-March 1921), a college professor can understand the secrets of ancient civilizations but he cannot find the secret to a meaningful marriage, and in his resulting despair he is "as alone as ever any man God made."

In two of the stories, "Brothers" (*Bookman*, April 1921; republished in *The Best American Short Stories of 1921*) and "The Door of the Trap" (*Dial*, May 1920), the protagonists attempt unsuccessfully to break down the barriers that isolate them from others, and their isolation is consequently intensified. In the former, an old man who proclaims his kinship with others is called insane; in the latter, a college professor realizes that he is misunderstood, and he withdraws to become a grotesque.

In "The New Englander" (*Dial*, February 1921), an unmarried woman seeks vainly to find fulfillment in the new, fertile Midwest, but she finds instead that she is imprisoned by the old, dead ideas she brought with her from the East, and, knowing that she is condemned to infertility, she also knows that she will never find the understanding she needs. The two following sketches, "War" (first published as "The Struggle," *Little Review*, May 1916) and "Motherhood," reinforce and extend the pervasive despair that emanates from the lives of the grotesques and the frustrated vision of the narrator.

In the last story, "Out of Nowhere Into Nothing" (*Dial*, July-September 1921), a romantic young woman leaves her small-town home to seek personal freedom and fulfillment in the city, but failing to find either in the city's impersonal atmosphere she returns home, hoping that somewhere in that more intimate atmosphere she can find what she seeks. But her momentary hope is destroyed, and she runs off into the night, into the emptiness that she has found to be the universal human reality.

As Anderson concludes the collection with his free-verse poem "The Man With the Trumpet," he proclaims "that life was life," that "life was sweet, that men might live"; that they must reject their "fleeing married minds," that they must "build temples to themselves." But none of the characters perceive that their only fulfillment can be momentary, that each of them can best be seen in Dr. Parcival's terms in *Winesburg, Ohio*, as he declared that "Everyone in the world is Christ and they are all crucified." In the collection, Anderson's theme is clear: that his people cannot break through the barriers of isolation, and that each is on the point of a mindless, irrational rebellion, a rebellion that he portrayed in his next novel, *Many Marriages* (1923).

The Triumph of the Egg is, like *Winesburg, Ohio*, a significant achievement as a unified collection and equally successful in the quality of the individual stories. Two of the stories, "I Want to Know Why" and "The Egg," are among Anderson's best; "Seeds," "The New Englander," and "Out of Nowhere Into Nothing" are more complex but less well executed. Anderson's style is that of the oral storyteller in its midwestern rhythms and idioms. None of the stories is a failure, and the opening and closing verses serve as useful commentary by the omniscient narrator who makes clear the fragile humanity of his people.

Like *Winesburg, Ohio*, *The Triumph of the Egg* is about people, each of whom contains within his or her shell a human essence, but like the egg in the title story, each retains its secret inviolate. In effect, Anderson's people in this collection are the people of Winesburg without a George Willard to listen to them, and they are without hope. Just as "I Want to Know Why" voices a desperate, youthful plea for insight into human nature, "Out of Nowhere Into Nothing" concludes with the hopeless confusion of the adult who knows that she can never find that insight. The continued accumulation of human despair links the two stories and unifies the collection.

In the winter of 1921-1922 Anderson took up residence in New Orleans to work on *Many*

Marriages, first serialized in the *Dial* (October 1922-March 1923), and then expanded for novel publication later in 1923. At this time, Anderson, now separated from Tennessee Mitchell and living in Greenwich Village, began collecting recent stories for *Horses and Men,* also to be published in 1923 to a generally enthusiastic critical reception. Although *Many Marriages,* an ultimately unsatisfactory and much misunderstood novel, describes the rebellion of John Webster and ends with a note of momentary optimism–as Anderson always ended his novels–*Horses and Men* emphasizes the collective despair that characterizes *The Triumph of the Egg,* in some cases to the extent of near insanity as well as psychological torment, until gradually a muted, tentative optimism and affirmation emerge from the stories.

As in the earlier collection, Anderson unifies this volume in theme, and he sets that thematic note in a foreword. His purpose, he says, is to continue to probe beneath the dark surface of life and to define its essence. But almost immediately in the preface, the inability to do so that had earlier been proclaimed in "The Dumb Man" is heard. "I had pushed myself off into a world where nothing has any existence," he writes. "It may be that my eyes are blind. . . . It may be that I am deaf. . . . Now, alas, I am absorbed in looking at my own hands. With these nervous and uncertain hands may I really feel for the form of things concealed in the darkness?" The stories are the result of such fumbling, directed only by compassion and love for his people.

Like *The Triumph of the Egg, Horses and Men* opens with the story of a youth who follows and likes horses and who finds ultimately that the larger world is much more complex than that of the stables. In this story, "I'm a Fool" (*Dial,* February 1922; republished in *The Best American Short Stories of 1922*), as in the opening story in the earlier volume, Anderson uses the young narrator's bewilderment to point to the adult despair that marks the following stories. If here, as in "I Want to Know Why," Anderson points out the confusion inherent in mistaking appearance for reality, he also suggests that if the problem baffles his adolescent protagonist, causing his disgust with himself and others, it is equally evident that few adults–and none of the grotesques in the following stories–can make the distinction. Unlike the earlier collection, however, the note of despair is not sustained through the volume, as Anderson begins gradually to mitigate despair with

a ray of hope until he concludes the last story with a note of unabashed optimism.

"I'm a Fool" is the story of a youth growing into manhood as he follows the Ohio racetrack circuit. His life as a stable swipe is, while often crude and sometimes brutal, nevertheless innocent, honest, and uncomplicated. On his day off, he dresses up to go to the races as a spectator; stopping in a hotel bar, he sees a well-dressed young man whom he automatically resents. To show his contempt he pushes the man aside and has two drinks of whiskey. Then at the track he meets a well-bred young lady, and he lies about his background to impress her. Although she accepts him, he knows that because of his lies he can never see her again. In the end he concludes that he's a fool and that the dude is one, too, for making him resent his own background. He is ready to kick himself or to strike out at the dude, but he knows that either is futile as he goes back to a life no longer simple.

In this, as in all his racetrack stories, Anderson points out the dichotomy of appearance and reality, and in emphasizing appearance in the youth's relationship with the young woman, the youth makes impossible the achievement of a real relationship with her. Although he had lied and drunk whiskey before, often to impress country rustics, he found that the combination made him unacceptable in her world, and his punishment, self-inflicted, is not only physical, but psychological exile.

As in the other stories, the adult narrator is evident. This story is set in the days "before prohibition and all that foolishness," as the mask deliberately slips, but the narrator is as bewildered as the boy he had once been; there is a difference between appearance and intrinsic worth, he knows, but he is not yet able to resolve the dichotomy in his own mind. The boy is appealingly pathetic in his naiveté; the narrator is bewildered by an event he has never understood, and the boy's bewilderment has become adult frustration. But the frustration is not as deep as that of "I Want to Know Why," just as the baffling incident is less significant if more personal, and frustration remains more baffling than despairing.

"The Triumph of a Modern" (*New Republic,* 31 January 1923) examines the same confusion of values in terms of the modernist Chicago Renaissance, which by 1920 had run its course. In this story a "liberated" young man who prides himself on his rejection of puritan values writes a letter to a maiden aunt whom he has never seen. De-

Eleanor and Sherwood Anderson boarding the Santa Lucia
*on 28 February 1941 for a goodwill tour of South America
(by Acme, courtesy of The Newberry Library)*

liberately using the word *breasts* rather than the more conventional *bosom* in attempting to convey a love for her that he does not feel, he so appeals to her frustrated emotions that she wills him her fortune.

The young man's triumph is real, but it is dishonest, Anderson makes clear. Rebellion against dead principles has become, for the young man, a tool of selfishness and greed rather than a statement of the principles of personal freedom. Reflecting Anderson's own disenchantment with what he saw as an increasingly dishonest movement—a disenchantment that was to provide the impetus for his novel *Dark Laughter* (1925)—the story suggests that the liberation movement had become a material end in itself rather than a means that would bring about human fulfillment. The modern has, he suggests, won a minor battle but has given up the war.

These first two stories demonstrate the structural and thematic patterns that unify the collection. Anderson alternates between rural late-nineteenth-century and urban twentieth-century settings, and, with the exception of the last story, which combines both settings, each story of each

pair is designed to complement the other as he shows that the problems inherent in human society—alienation, isolation, the dichotomy of appearance and reality—are individual rather than social problems, that human fulfillment is beyond our grasp, that truth, the basis of understanding and love, cannot transcend the barriers of isolation when it is denied by the naiveté of the country rustic or the urbanity of the city sophisticate.

The next pair of stories, "Unused" and "A Chicago Hamlet" (first published as "Broken," *Century*, March 1923), are concerned with an attempt to carry through an honest rebellion which culminates in tragedy. The first, set in Bidwell, Ohio, is the story of a young woman from a disreputable family whose attempts to rise above her origins are misunderstood. In her despair she runs into the lake and is drowned. As the narrator views the girl's body after it has been recovered, he is filled with compassion, and the bedraggled ostrich feather on her hat remains with him as a symbol of her failed attempt to find beauty. He shares her despair as he remembers her fleeting escape and her tragedy.

"A Chicago Hamlet" tells the story of a man who has failed in his rebellion and "had gone the road of surrender to ugliness and to dreary meaningless living." As the man drinks, he reflects that "It is horrible stuff, this whiskey, eh, but after all this is a horrible town." And the narrator reflects on the millions on Chicago's West Side, where "the streets are equally ugly," where they "go on forever and ever," who can find their only escape in cheap prohibition whiskey.

In the next pair of stories, "The Man Who Became a Woman" and "Milk Bottles" (first published as "Why There Must Be a Midwestern Literature," *Vanity Fair*, March 1921), Anderson writes of a young man forced by social pressure to deny his individuality. In each story the penalties of nonconformity are exacted in moments of horror, in the first story among the discarded bones behind an abandoned small-town slaughter house; in the second among the rubbish heaps in the shadow of a city tenement.

"The Man Who Became a Woman" is one of Anderson's best stories, but unfortunately, perhaps because of confused interpretations of Anderson's theme and symbolic structure, it is rarely anthologized. Another story of the racetrack life and a youthful lover of horses, it goes beyond the adolescent's initiation into adulthood, and it denies the suggestion of homosexuality implied in the title as it deals with the two sides of human nature, masculine brutality and feminine compassion, each seeking ascendancy or at least a stormy balance in the boy's character.

This story, too, is told by an adult narrator looking back on and attempting unsuccessfully to explain to himself an incident that had taken place in his youth. In the incident, the boy, alone at the track, decides to go to town. Stopping in a rough bar, he remembers past dreams in which he thought he was a girl. Looking into the mirror behind the bar, he sees a girl's face instead of his own. Frightened, he flees as a fight starts in the bar, and he goes back to the stables to sleep. Later, awakened by two drunken swipes who mistake him for a girl, he runs off into the night, where he falls into the broken bones behind the slaughterhouse. There he hides for the night, recalling that his fear was so great that "It burned all that silly nonsense about being a girl right out of me." The next morning he leaves the racetrack life forever.

Nevertheless, the narrator puzzles over the incident, knowing that somewhere in it he had surrendered a significant part of his identity to convention. Important, too, to the narrator is the recognition, in tones reminiscent of Wing Biddlebaum in "Hands," that appearance denies reality, that "a man don't dare own up that he loves another man, I've found out, and they are afraid to admit such feelings to themselves, even. I guess they're afraid it may be taken to mean something it don't need to at all."

Perhaps Anderson did not publish this story in a periodical because he was still smarting under the charges of "sex-obsessed" that had been leveled at *Winesburg, Ohio* and more recently at *Many Marriages*, but his careful control of complex structure and execution clarifies his concern with the duality of human nature and its suppression by puritan and masculine social values. Human beings will never be free because they permit brutality and compassion to clash, with each side defined by sexual identity, instead of being allowed to merge into the oneness that makes up a complete person, compounded of the brutality and the innocence that nature had defined and men had destroyed.

In "Milk Bottles" Anderson develops the same theme in an urban, modern setting. A young advertising writer is determined to write truth, but the lies by which he earns his living and the grimness of the city make it impossible to write honestly, and eventually the lies become truth for him. In the background, the lost people of the city serve, like a Greek chorus, to lament the lives that they lead and the city in which they live. Behind the sign advertising milk as "The health and freshness of a whole countryside," bottles of milk stand sour on window sills. The reality is not merely denied by city lies; it is smothered by them, and the tortured people, unable to perceive reality, are unable to save themselves.

The last pair of stories, "The Sad Horn Blowers" (*Harper's,* February 1923) and "The Man's Story" (*Dial,* September 1923; republished in *The Best American Short Stories of 1923*), return to the futility of attempts to find permanent fulfillment. But optimism emerges, as in *Winesburg, Ohio,* as Anderson points out that fulfillment can be found in moments if the seeker accepts the moments in which it is possible. In the first story a young man flees the small town, which he sees as dehumanizing, to find himself condemned to drilling meaningless holes in meaningless pieces of iron. He can only blow an old man's cornet in muted, tuneless protest, recognizing that he and the old man are still children seeking adulthood.

In "A Man's Story" a married man runs off with another woman, as did John Webster in *Many Marriages.* But Anderson's suggestion of hope at the conclusion of that novel is here carried through to its violent conclusion. In the city to which they flee, the woman is murdered, and the man is arrested but freed after another confesses. He knows that neither love nor hope is possible, and Anderson emphasizes the momentary nature of what he once had: "The man had come up out of the sea of doubt, had grasped for a moment the hand of the woman, and with her hand in his had floated for a time upon the surface of life–but now he felt himself again sinking into the sea."

In "An Ohio Pagan," previously unpublished and apparently a fragment of an uncompleted novel, Anderson returns to the rural scene, and he concludes the story with a note of solid affirmation: a young man who loves horses and is something of a poet resents the social pressures of the town. He runs off to the city, but its impersonality frightens him, and he returns to the countryside where he finds, through a simple stableman, that there is meaning in both the countryside and in the city, that, like George Willard in "Departure," he had but to seek it in the moments in which it would be revealed to him.

In this final story Anderson has returned to the youthful optimism with which he had concluded *Winesburg, Ohio,* perhaps reflecting his own decision to take a third wife, Elizabeth Prall, to make his home permanently in rural western Virginia, and to return to the cities–New York, Chicago, New Orleans–only when it pleased him to do so. In Virginia he found the simple society that had been eliminated in the Midwestern towns with the inroads of industrialism in the late nineteenth century. He purchased, and for two years edited, the *Smyth County News* and the *Marion Democrat,* two weekly newspapers in Marion, Virginia, and he continued to write, publishing occasional stories and frequent essays that reflected his experiences in the southern towns and countryside. He published, too, a book of optimistic verse, *A New Testament* (1927); a volume of newspaper pieces, *Hello Towns!* (1929); and two essays under the title *Nearer the Grass Roots* (1929). That year, he also published, in a limited edition, *Alice and the Lost Novel,* comprising two stories, both of which reflect his new experiences as a writer in the rural South.

"Alice" (first published as "Beauty," *Harper's Bazaar,* January 1929; republished in *The Best American Short Stories of 1929*) is a portrait, an attempt to define the inner beauty of an east Tennessee mountain girl, her intuitive wisdom, and her willingness to give of herself to others. "The Lost Novel" (first published in *Scribner's,* September 1928; republished in *The Best American Short Stories of 1929*) is an attempt to define or explain the mystic qualities of the creative experience in which that act is itself more important to the artist than the completed work.

In 1930 Anderson published his brief, affirmative essay *The American County Fair* in a limited edition and in 1931 the essays in *Perhaps Women,* an assertion that men had surrendered to the machine age and that consequently perhaps the only hope for a humanized future lay in women. In 1932, flirting with communism as a solution to the depression, he published *Beyond Desire,* his first novel using the southern experience and a tentative proletarian novel in which a woman like Alice is prominent. In 1933 he published his last collection of stories, *Death in the Woods.*

Anderson's most consistent collection, *Death in the Woods* is, unfortunately, also his least known, in part because his publisher, Horace Liveright, went bankrupt before it was distributed. In it Anderson dispensed with preface, introduction, or thematic statement; instead, he wrote the last story, "Brother Death," as a capstone for the collection. Determined that the collection

would be his best, he rewrote and reordered the stories extensively in the proofs and eliminated several that he felt were unsatisfactory or out of context.

The result is impressive, containing two of his best stories, "Death in the Woods" and "Brother Death," and demonstrating clearly Anderson's continued mastery of the form. To give unity to the collection he uses these two stories as companion pieces in mood and theme, as in the first, a boy contemplates the unknowable, and in the last a girl comes to understand it.

Not only did Anderson consider "Death in the Woods" one of his best short stories, explaining his continued concern with the story itself by commenting that he "wrote, threw away, and rewrote many times," but three earlier versions unpublished in Anderson's lifetime and three published versions exist. The previously unpublished versions, now in print, are in *France and Sherwood Anderson: Paris Notebook, 1921* (1976), "Father Abraham: A Lincoln Fragment" in *The Sherwood Anderson Reader* (1947), and "The Death in the Forest" in the critical edition of *Tar: A Midwest Childhood* (1969). The versions published in Anderson's lifetime are as a part of *Tar: A Midwest Childhood* (1926), as a short story in *American Mercury* (September 1926), and as the lead story in *Death in the Woods,* which also appeared in *O. Henry Memorial Award Prize Stories 1926* (1927) and in the anniversary volume of that series, *Fifty Years of the American Short Story* (1970), as well as in dozens of other short-story anthologies and textbooks.

The reasons for such attention to the story by Anderson and others are immediately evident. The old woman who dies in the woods is one of Anderson's grotesques, one who in life had been exploited by her husband and sons. Told by an adult narrator who cannot forget seeing in his youth the old woman dead in the woods, in the three versions Anderson published, the old woman's death and her life are unforgettable, and the meaning of what he had observed without understanding as a boy becomes clear to the man in the telling.

In the story, Anderson concludes, the woman had been beaten into perpetual silence by the men; her main function had been to provide them with food. One night, as she returned from the town with meat given her by a kindly butcher, she had sat down in a clearing in the woods to rest in the snow; a few days later she is found naked and dead. Dogs had taken the meat, torn off her clothes, but left her untouched, the tracks in the snow indicating that the dogs, reverting to their natural instincts, had circled silently like wolves around her.

The narrator tells how he and his brother had, when the word spread, gone into the woods to view the body, and at this point for the boy the experience seems to initiate him into the mysteries of sex: "One of the men turned her over in the snow," he recalls, "and I saw everything. My body trembled. . . . None of us had ever seen a woman's body before. It may have been the snow, clinging to the frozen flesh that made it look so white and lovely. . . ."

But as an adult the narrator realizes that the experience, however revealing or profound, was more than sexual initiation. The woman's death, he realizes, had so completed and complemented her life that it had a beauty of its own; she had been a feeder of animal life–cows, pigs, chickens, horses, men, and dogs–and she had died carrying food for animal life, and in death she had continued to feed it. Death, he realized, is not terrible or frightening but somehow appropriate, and the old woman's death was not a tragedy nor was it pathetic; it was, in essence, a silent celebration of her life and of the silent, welcome deaths among his people.

"The Return" (*Century*, May 1925; republished in *The Best American Short Stories of 1925*), placed in a contemporary setting, portrays a futile attempt by a city man to return to his home town after an eighteen-year absence. The protagonist realizes that the automobile that had taken him home had not only made a return in spirit impossible but had provided him with the means to flee from the town and the corruption that modern values and transportation had brought there. "There She Is–She is Taking Her Bath" is another contemporary story, of a seemingly humorous incident in which Anderson defines the inarticulateness of partners in a modern marriage, the minor spiritual crises of unproductive work and modern marriage, and the sudden fear of the narrator when he knows that his hands will shake and that he will spill his dessert as his doubts continue unresolved.

Anderson includes in this group "The Lost Novel," followed by "The Fight" (*Vanity Fair*, October 1927), a contemporary story of two men, cousins, who in the small midwestern town from which they came, had, as boys, been rivals who had always wanted to fight but never did. In adulthood, as each makes a modest success, their ri-

valry continues until finally they exchange futile blows. Their rivalry, Anderson makes clear, is pointless; the adult fight had failed to resolve what had begun long before.

Anderson also includes "Alice," retitled "Like a Queen," followed by "That Sophistication," republished from the 23 May 1929 *Smyth County News*, in which he carries the theme of pseudo-intellectual mindlessness into the American expatriate Bohemian revolt of the 1920s in Paris and of the dilettantes who proclaim their sophistication and their talents. Only one woman, deliberately naive, points out that the life they lead could just as well have been led in Chicago.

"In a Strange Town" (*Scribner's*, January 1930) further explores the futile attempt to intellectualize human relations and to control human experience through rational action. The narrator, a wanderer, reflects on the patternless reality of the surface of the lives and incidents he observes in bits and pieces. An observer rather than a participant, he feels refreshed as he watches without attempting to analyze what cannot be analyzed or to understand what cannot be understood.

"These Mountaineers" (*Vanity Fair*, January 1930), "A Sentimental Journey" (*Vanity Fair*, January 1928), and "A Jury Case" (*American Mercury*, December 1927) are all drawn from Anderson's experience in the Virginia hill country. In many ways the lives of the mountain people parallel those of the people of small-town Ohio whom he knew as a boy but who had disappeared in the industrialization of the Midwest and the disintegration or growth of the towns. "These Mountaineers" depicts the fierce primitive pride of an old man, a young man, and a young woman who live in isolated independence in a hill cabin; "A Sentimental Journey" describes an encounter between a mountaineer moonshiner and a writer, in which the mountaineer tells of his brief experience in the larger world of a mining town. "A Jury Case" describes a mountain rivalry that erupts into violence, murder, and legal action, contrasting mountain justice with legality as it describes the peculiar means by which mountain juries make the law work.

These three stories contrast sharply with the stories of twentieth-century urban life as they compare the urban trivial with the mountain profound, primitive with modern values, and human beings who act upon inner strength with those who attempt to live by social appearance. To Anderson it is evident that these people are as yet uncorrupted by materialism or by the acceptance of appearance as reality. These people, not only primitive and sometimes violent but also innocent, reflect Anderson's earlier grotesques, especially those craftsmen who, in *Poor White*, fight unsuccessfully against the factories that destroy their independence, their skills, and their values, and ultimately destroy them. Anderson's mountaineers are America's last free and uncorrupted human beings.

"Another Wife" (*Scribner's*, December 1926; republished in *The Best American Short Stories of 1927*) is the story of the romance of two moderns, a sophisticated woman of thirty-seven and a forty-seven-year-old physician. It takes place in a primitive mountain setting and is told from the physician's point of view. "A Meeting South" (*Dial*, April 1925) is a fictionalized treatment of Anderson's meeting with William Faulkner in New Orleans. Faulkner is presented as David, an aspiring young poet. Like "Another Wife," it is a story of intuitive spiritual recognition among the poet, a southerner; the sixty-five-year-old former madam, Aunt Sally, a midwesterner who had lived in New Orleans for thirty years; and the narrator, a midwestern writer, the three of whom belong in some strange, strong way to the romantic and sub-tropical city.

"The Flood" describes a scholar who is unable to write a book on values because he learns that they cannot be defined; he knows intuitively that they can neither be intellectualized nor communicated to another. "Why They Got Married" (*Vanity Fair*, March 1929) is a modern story in which two young people find each other in spite of the ambiguous values, material and social, of the world in which they live.

Throughout the collection Anderson weaves an intricate thematic thread that leads directly to "Brother Death," the story he wrote to conclude the collection and, as he commented, "one of the finest stories I've ever done." The collection begins with an apparent tragedy that is not tragedy at all, and it examines the human attempt to search for the reality beneath the surface of life, sometimes protesting the inability or unwillingness to do so, sometimes celebrating the ability to see the underlying reality. As the stories proceed, it is evident that Anderson sees modern urban industrial society and its values, whether material or intellectual, as detrimental to the search for meaning, while the primitive values of a simple society, those that come from within, permit an understanding that is intuitive and emotional rather

than rational or social. Yet, Anderson focuses not upon social structures but upon the people who live in them, the grotesques who have been distorted emotionally or psychologically by values they do not understand and who remain isolated and frustrated or upon those who have learned to seek out the moments of understanding that make their lives tolerable.

In "Brother Death" Anderson combines the competing value systems that either permit fulfillment or deny it in a remarkable story set in the rural South. The first conflict in the story describes the relationship between a young girl and her younger brother, who has a heart condition so serious that he may die at any moment. In the effort to prolong his life the family prevents him from playing normally. The girl protests, and finally the boy is allowed to play as other children do. After a year or two he dies peacefully in his sleep.

The second plot describes the struggle between the father of the family and the older son, who disagree about running the farm. The conflict erupts over two huge oak trees, beautiful but functionless, which stand in the pasture. The father wants to cut them down, but the son protests. Eventually the father has his way, and the son must either accept the decision, protecting his position as heir, or leave the farm. He remains, thus surrendering his individuality to the father. The young girl realizes that the physical death of her younger brother was both human and natural, but that her older brother had suffered a horrible spiritual death. To die physically, Anderson shows, is to celebrate one's life; spiritual death is, conversely, the surrender of one's values to another.

"Brother Death" encapsulates Anderson's conviction that whatever meaning lies in human life can be found only in distinguishing between appearance and reality, between substance and dross, and in refusing to accept the shoddy substitutes for reality that a materialistic society offers. All too often, he reiterates, Americans are willing to accept material values at the price of their own individuality, and the nature and quality of their lives are diminished as a result.

On 6 July 1933 Anderson married Eleanor Copenhauer, twenty years his junior and the daughter of a prominent Marion attorney. During the last eight years of his life, he traveled extensively, always returning to Ripshin, his home in the Virginia hills, and he wrote another novel, *Kit Brandon* (1936), based on his Virginia experience, two volumes of essays, including *Puzzled America* (1935), an examination of America in the depression, and *Home Town* (1940), a celebration of life in the towns. He also continued to publish essays and short stories in journals. On 8 March 1941 he died of peritonitis in Colón, Panama Canal Zone, while on a goodwill tour of South America. The illness was precipitated by Anderson's swallowing part of a toothpick at a farewell party.

Much of the short fiction of those last eight years was collected and published posthumously in *The Sherwood Anderson Reader*, a collection of both published and unpublished works, edited by Paul Rosenfeld, and in *Sherwood Anderson: Short Stories* (1962), edited by Maxwell Geismar, which draws from Anderson's collections as well as those included in *The Sherwood Anderson Reader*.

Neither of these collections is as Anderson would have organized it. Some stories are included that Anderson published in journals but rejected in collections; others, Anderson chose not to publish in any form. Of these stories, unpublished or uncollected at Anderson's death, the ten best appear, together with selections from *Winesburg, Ohio*, *The Triumph of the Egg*, *Horses and Men*, and *Death in the Woods*, in *Sherwood Anderson: Short Stories*. (All of the stories Anderson chose not to publish and those left uncollected also appear in *The Sherwood Anderson Reader*.)

"The Corn Planting" (*American Magazine*, November 1934) is the story of a seventy-year-old man and his sixty-year-old wife. Both setting and mood are reminiscent of *Winesburg, Ohio* as the narrator describes the couple's closeness to the land and to their only son, an art student in Chicago. When the son is killed in an accident, the narrator and a friend of the son's go out to the farm after midnight to tell them. The two old people listen silently, and then, in their nightclothes, go out to the field and plant corn all night by hand. The next morning they are calm, and the narrator and the friend know that they have gotten strength from the land.

"Nobody Laughed" (written in 1939) is set in a small Tennessee town. It is the story of Pinhead Perry, a member of the town's leading family, but a good natured, slow-minded grotesque, who marries quiet, crippled Hallie Albright of the rough Albright clan. Town jokesters tell Pinhead that Hallie has lovers, devise a method for him to prove her infidelity, and hide in the bushes to watch as Pinhead ties Hallie to a chair, scatters flour on the floor and porch, and hides,

crying, in the bushes. When the jokesters tell the story in town, no one laughs; "It was as though they had all suddenly begun disliking each other," Anderson concludes.

"A Part of the Earth" (written in 1936) is a first-person narrative set in Chicago and built around a conversation between a well-known writer who must write advertisements of dubious taste in order to live and a banker who wants the writer to work for him as a racehorse trainer. The writer rejects the offer, telling the banker about his life, suggesting that the banker give him money to free him from his advertising career. But the banker refuses to give him money without working, and the two part amicably. Included in the story is one of the several versions Anderson told at various times of the experience of writing "Hands."

"Morning Roll Call" (written in 1940) returns to Smoky Pete, the small-town Jeremiah of Bidwell, Ohio, in *Poor White*, who calls down judgment each morning on Main Street on the town's businessmen seen going into the local brothel the night before. "The Yellow Gown" (published posthumously in *Mademoiselle*, September 1942), set in Chicago early in the twentieth century, describes the course of love and artistic success as well as artistic fraud among Harold, an artist, Mildred, his lover, and the narrator, who finds himself alone on a park bench as the others reject him.

"Daughters" (written in 1935) is set in a small southern town. It is the story of John Shepard, who works as a section hand and tries desperately but futilely to understand his two adolescent daughters, Kate, studious and hardworking, and Wave, a flirt. The longest story in the group, it also explores the generation gap between the older men who accept and like their low-status, hardworking lot, and the younger people, male and female, who seek to become something more than their fathers.

"White Spot" (written in 1939) is more an autobiographical sketch than a short story, as Anderson, by name, writes nostalgically in the first person of women, passion, beauty, and the reflected white spot on the ceiling of a cheap hotel room at night. The following story, "A Walk in the Moonlight" (first published as "A Moonlight Walk," *Redbook*, December 1937), set in a small town, is also in first person, the narrator retelling a story told him on fishing trips by a small-town doctor of the women who tempted him and of his closeness to his wife and crippled daughter, a relationship almost interrupted by an unfortunate woman with whom he had once walked in the moonlight.

The last two stories, "His Chest of Drawers" (*Household Magazine*, August 1939) and "Not Sixteen" (published posthumously in *Tomorrow*, March 1946), are brief pieces. The first, set in an advertising agency, is the story told the narrator by a man who, with a wife, four daughters, and mother-in-law, finds his clothes storage space reduced from a closet to a chest of drawers, and finally to a part of the bottom drawer, whereupon he goes to town to get drunk in order that he might have the illusion of importance. The latter describes the brief, touching romance of a young racing enthusiast and a farmer's daughter, their restraint, and his sudden departure in the night because she is too young for marriage.

None of the stories in this group from Anderson's last years is a major work, but none is a failure, and four are impressive achievements. The best of the ten, "Nobody Laughed," could take its place in any of Anderson's earlier collections, including *Winesburg, Ohio*, both in setting and theme, as it explores the loss of innocence as a town creates its own grotesque; "Daughters" and "A Walk in the Moonlight" are substantial stories that deal with the themes of alienation and the complexities of human relations that Anderson had explored in much of his best work; "The Corn Planting," too, could take its place in *Winesburg, Ohio* as the two old people, simple rural grotesques, pursue the only reality they know.

Although Anderson was in critical disfavor when he died (the common critical consensus insisting that he had written little of value since *Winesburg, Ohio*), and his accomplishments during the previous twenty years were consequently almost entirely overlooked, critics and scholars during those twenty years and after have given his earlier works much more attention than those of writers often considered more important. In the past decade critical disfavor has been replaced by increasing reconsideration of many of his works, and his strengths and accomplishments are being reassessed for contemporary readers.

This reassessment has particularly focused on his short stories, especially those included in *Winesburg, Ohio*, but also on Anderson's ability to construct sequential collections in which each story is an intrinsic part. Being reassessed also is the durability of the literary qualities that he contributed to American literature in his century. Particularly important are his contributions to the form of the short story, the style of American writing as we know it, and our understanding of the American grotesque. The spirit of his works is the spirit of human life and his compassion for it, often expressed with lyric beauty, even in despair. Not considered a major author in his own time, he has come to be seen as a pioneer in the short-story form. His work has endured, continuing to provide interest in its own right as well as for the influence it exerted on such later masters as Ernest Hemingway, William Faulkner, and Saul Bellow.

Letters:

Letters of Sherwood Anderson, edited by Howard Mumford Jones in association with Walter B. Rideout (Boston: Little, Brown, 1953);

Sherwood Anderson / Gertrude Stein: Correspondence and Personal Essays, edited by Ray Lewis White (Chapel Hill: University of North Carolina Press, 1972).

Bibliographies:

Eugene P. Sheehy and Kenneth A. Lohf, *Sherwood Anderson: A Bibliography* (Los Gatos, Cal.: Talisman Press, 1960);

G. Thomas Tanselle, "Additional Reviews of Sherwood Anderson's Work," *Papers of the Bibliographical Society of America,* 56 (Third Quarter 1962): 358-365;

Ray Lewis White, *The Merrill Checklist of Sherwood Anderson* (Columbus, Ohio: Merrill, 1969);

Walter B. Rideout, "Sherwood Anderson," in *Sixteen Modern American Authors: A Survey of Research and Criticism,* edited by Jackson R. Bryer (Durham, N.C.: Duke University Press, 1974), pp. 3-28;

Douglas G. Rogers, *Sherwood Anderson: A Selective, Annotated Bibliography* (Metuchen, N.J.: Scarecrow Press, 1976);

Tanselle, "Addenda to Sheehy and Lohf's *Sherwood Anderson:* Copyright Information and Later Printings," in *Sherwood Anderson: Centennial Studies,* edited by Hilbert H. Campbell and Charles E. Modlin (Troy, N.Y.: Whitston, 1976), pp. 145-150;

White, *Sherwood Anderson: A Reference Guide* (Boston: G. K. Hall, 1977).

Biographies:

James Schevill, *Sherwood Anderson: His Life and Work* (Denver: University of Denver Press, 1951);

Irving Howe, *Sherwood Anderson* (New York: Sloane, 1951);

Elizabeth Anderson and Gerald R. Kelly, *Miss Elizabeth: A Memoir* (Boston: Little, Brown, 1969);

William A. Sutton, *The Road to Winesburg: A Mosaic of the Imaginative Life of Sherwood Anderson* (Metuchen, N.J.: Scarecrow Press, 1972);

Kim Townsend, *Sherwood Anderson* (Boston: Houghton Mifflin, 1987).

References:

Richard Abcarian, "Innocence and Experience in *Winesburg, Ohio*," *University Review*, 35 (Winter 1968): 95-105;

David D. Anderson, *Critical Essays in American Literature* (Karachi, Pakistan: The University of Karachi, 1964);

Anderson, *Sherwood Anderson: An Introduction and Interpretation* (New York: Holt, Rinehart & Winston, 1967);

Anderson, ed., *Critical Essays on Sherwood Anderson* (Boston: G. K. Hall, 1981);

Anderson, ed., *Sherwood Anderson: Dimensions of His Literary Art: A Collection of Critical Essays* (East Lansing: Michigan State University Press, 1976);

Karl James Anderson, "My Brother, Sherwood Anderson," *Saturday Review of Literature*, 31 (4 September 1948): 6-7, 26-27;

Howard S. Babb, "A Reading of Sherwood Anderson's 'The Man Who Became a Woman,'" *PMLA*, 80 (September 1965): 432-435;

Joseph Warren Beach, *The Outlook for American Prose* (Chicago: University of Chicago Press, 1926), pp. 247-280;

Percy H. Boynton, "Sherwood Anderson," *North American Review*, 224 (March-April-May 1927): 140-150;

Richard Bridgman, *The Colloquial Style in America* (New York: Oxford University Press, 1966), pp. 152-164;

Louis J. Budd, "The Grotesques of Anderson and Wolfe," *Modern Fiction Studies*, 5 (Winter 1959-1960): 304-310;

Rex Burbank, *Sherwood Anderson* (New York: Twayne, 1964);

Hilbert H. Campbell and Charles E. Modlin, eds., *Sherwood Anderson: Centennial Studies* (Troy, N.Y.: Whitston, 1976);

Ralph Ciancio, "'The Sweetness of the Twisted Apples': Unity of Vision in *Winesburg, Ohio*," *PMLA*, 87 (October 1972): 994-1006;

Malcolm Cowley, Introduction to *Winesburg, Ohio* (New York: Viking, 1960), pp. 1-15;

Hart Crane, "Sherwood Anderson," *Double Dealer*, 2 (July 1921): 42-45;

Edward Dahlberg, *Alms for Oblivion: Essays by Edward Dahlberg* (Minneapolis: University of Minnesota Press, 1964), pp. 3-19;

Bernard Duffey, *The Chicago Renaissance in American Letters: A Critical History* (East Lansing: Michigan State College Press, 1954), pp. 194-209;

James T. Farrell, "A Memoir on Sherwood Anderson," *Perspective*, 7 (Summer 1954): 83-88;

William Faulkner, "Sherwood Anderson: An Appreciation," *Atlantic Monthly*, 191 (June 1953): 27-29;

John H. Ferres, ed., *Sherwood Anderson, Winesburg, Ohio: Text and Criticism* (New York: Viking, 1966);

John T. Flanagan, "Hemingway's Debt to Sherwood Anderson," *Journal of English and Germanic Philology*, 54 (October 1955): 507-520;

Edwin Fussell, "*Winesburg, Ohio*: Art and Isolation," *Modern Fiction Studies*, 6 (Summer 1960): 106-114;

Maxwell Geismar, *The Last of the Provincials: The American Novel, 1915-1925* (Boston: Houghton Mifflin, 1947), pp. 223-284;

Harry Hansen, *Midwest Portraits: A Book of Memories and Friendships* (New York: Harcourt, Brace, 1923), pp. 109-179;

Anthony Channell Hilfer, *The Revolt from the Village, 1915-1930* (Chapel Hill: University of North Carolina Press, 1969), pp. 147-157, 235-243;

Frederick J. Hoffman, *Freudianism and the Literary Mind* (Baton Rouge: Louisiana State University Press, 1957), pp. 229-250;

Forrest L. Ingram, *Representative Short Story Cycles of the Twentieth Century: Studies in a Literary Genre* (The Hague: Mouton, 1971), pp. 143-199;

Dale Kramer, *Chicago Renaissance: The Literary Life in the Midwest, 1900-1930* (New York: Appleton-Century, 1966), pp. 37-51, 167-184, 232-243, 288-305;

John S. Lawry, "'Death in the Woods' and the Artist's Self in Sherwood Anderson," *PMLA*, 74 (June 1959): 306-311;

Thomas M. Lorch, "The Choreographic Structure of *Winesburg, Ohio*," *CLA Journal*, 12 (September 1968): 56-65;

Rosemary M. Loughlin, "Godliness and the American Dream in *Winesburg, Ohio*," *Twentieth Century Literature*, 13 (July 1967): 97-103;

Glen A. Love, "*Winesburg, Ohio* and the Rhetoric of Silence," *American Literature*, 40 (March 1968): 38-57;

Luther S. Luedtke, "Sherwood Anderson, Thomas Hardy, and 'Tandy,' " *Modern Fiction Studies*, 20 (Winter 1974-1975): 531-540;

John J. McAleer, "Christ Symbolism in *Winesburg, Ohio*," *Discourse*, 4 (Summer 1961): 168-181;

James M. Mellard, "Narrative Forms in *Winesburg, Ohio*," *PMLA*, 83 (October 1968): 1304-1312;

William V. Miller, "Earth-Mothers, Succubi, and Other Ectoplasmic Spirits: The Women in Sherwood Anderson's Short Stories," *Midamerica I* (1974): 64-81;

Newberry Library Bulletin, Sherwood Anderson Memorial Number, second series, no. 2 (December 1948); Special Sherwood Anderson Number, 6 (July 1971);

William L. Phillips, "How Sherwood Anderson Wrote *Winesburg, Ohio*," *American Literature*, 23 (March 1951): 7-30;

Phillips, "Sherwood Anderson's Two Prize Pupils," *University of Chicago Magazine*, 47 (January 1955): 9-12;

Walter B. Rideout, ed., *Sherwood Anderson: A Collection of Critical Essays* (Englewood Cliffs, N.J.: Prentice-Hall, 1974);

Paul Rosenfeld, *Port of New York: Essays on Fourteen American Moderns* (New York: Harcourt, Brace, 1924), pp. 175-198;

Epifanio San Juan, Jr., "Vision and Reality: A Reconsideration of Sherwood Anderson's *Winesburg, Ohio*," *American Literature*, 35 (May 1963): 137-155;

Shenandoah, Sherwood Anderson Number, 13 (Spring 1962);

Benjamin T. Spencer, "Sherwood Anderson: American Mythopoeist," *American Literature*, 41 (March 1969): 1-18;

Maaja A. Stewart, "Scepticism and Belief in Chekhov and Anderson," *Studies in Short Fiction*, 9 (Winter 1972): 29-40;

Story, Homage to Sherwood Anderson Issue, 19 (September-October 1941); reprinted in *Homage to Sherwood Anderson: 1876-1941*, edited by Paul P. Appel (Mamaroneck, N.Y.: Appel, 1970);

David Stouck, "*Winesburg, Ohio* and the Failure of Art," *Twentieth Century Literature*, 15 (October 1969): 145-151;

Stouck, "*Winesburg, Ohio* as a Dance of Death," *American Literature*, 48 (January 1977): 525-542;

Tony Tanner, *The Reign of Wonder: Naivety and Reality in American Literature* (Cambridge: Cambridge University Press, 1965), pp. 205-227;

Welford Dunaway Taylor, *Sherwood Anderson* (New York: Praeger, 1977);

Jarvis Thurston, "Anderson and 'Winesburg': Mysticism and Craft," *Accent*, 16 (Spring 1956): 107-128;

Lionel Trilling, *The Liberal Imagination: Essays on Literature and Society* (New York: Viking, 1950), pp. 24-33;

Twentieth Century Literature, Sherwood Anderson Issue, 23 (February 1977);

Charles Child Walcutt, *American Literary Naturalism, A Divided Stream* (Minneapolis: University of Minnesota Press, 1964), pp. 222-239;

Brom Weber, "Anderson and 'The Essence of Things,' " *Sewanee Review*, 59 (Autumn 1951): 678-692;

Weber, *Sherwood Anderson* (Minneapolis: University of Minnesota Press, 1964);

Michael D. West, "Sherwood Anderson's Triumph: 'The Egg,' " *American Quarterly*, 20 (Winter 1968): 675-693;

T. K. Whipple, *Spokesmen: Modern Writers and American Life* (New York: Appleton, 1928), pp. 115-137;

Ray Lewis White, *The Merrill Studies in Winesburg, Ohio* (Columbus, Ohio: Merrill, 1971);

White, ed., *The Achievement of Sherwood Anderson: Essays in Criticism* (Chapel Hill: University of North Carolina Press, 1966);

The Winesburg Eagle, Official Publication of The Sherwood Anderson Society, 1975- .

Papers:

The major collection of Anderson's papers is in the Newberry Library in Chicago.

Kay Boyle

(19 February 1902-   )

Elizabeth S. Bell
University of South Carolina, Aiken

See also the Boyle entries in *DLB 4: American Writers in Paris, 1920-1939; DLB 9: American Novelists, 1910-1945*; and *DLB 48: American Poets, 1880-1945*.

BOOKS: *Short Stories* (Paris: Black Sun Press, 1929);

Wedding Day and Other Stories (New York: Cape & Smith, 1930; London: Pharos Editions, 1932);

Plagued by the Nightingale (New York: Cape & Smith, 1931; London & Toronto: Cape, 1931);

Landscape for Wyn Henderson (London: Curwen Press, 1931);

A Statement (New York: Modern Editions Press, 1932);

Year Before Last (London: Faber & Faber, 1932; New York: Harrison Smith, 1932);

The First Lover and Other Stories (New York: Smith & Haas, 1933; London: Faber & Faber, 1937);

Gentlemen, I Address You Privately (New York: Smith & Haas, 1933; London: Faber & Faber, 1934);

My Next Bride (New York: Harcourt, Brace, 1934; London: Faber & Faber, 1935);

The White Horses of Vienna and Other Stories (New York: Harcourt, Brace, 1936; London: Faber & Faber, 1937);

Death of a Man (London: Faber & Faber, 1936; New York: Harcourt, Brace, 1936);

Monday Night (New York: Harcourt, Brace, 1938; London: Faber & Faber, 1938);

A Glad Day (Norfolk, Conn.: New Directions, 1938);

The Youngest Camel (Boston: Little, Brown, 1939; London: Faber & Faber, 1939);

The Crazy Hunter and Other Stories (London: Faber & Faber, 1940); republished as *The Crazy Hunter: Three Short Novels* (New York: Harcourt, Brace, 1940);

Primer For Combat (New York: Simon & Schuster, 1942; London: Faber & Faber, 1943);

Kay Boyle

Avalanche (New York: Simon & Schuster, 1944; London: Faber & Faber, 1944);

American Citizen Naturalized in Leadville, Colorado (New York: Simon & Schuster, 1944);

A Frenchman Must Die (New York: Simon & Schuster, 1946; London: Faber & Faber, 1946);

Thirty Stories (New York: Simon & Schuster, 1946; London: Faber & Faber, 1948);

1939 (New York: Simon & Schuster, 1948; London: Faber & Faber, 1948);

His Human Majesty (New York, London & Toronto: Whittlesey House / McGraw-Hill, 1949; London: Faber & Faber, 1950);

The Smoking Mountain: Stories of Postwar Germany (New York, London & Toronto: McGraw-Hill, 1951; London: Faber & Faber, 1952);

The Seagull on the Step (New York: Knopf, 1955; London: Faber & Faber, 1955);

Three Short Novels (Boston: Beacon, 1958);

The Youngest Camel Reconsidered and Rewritten (New York: Harper, 1959; London: Faber & Faber, 1960);

Generation Without Farewell (New York: Knopf, 1960; London: Faber & Faber, 1960);

Collected Poems (New York: Knopf, 1962);

Breaking the Silence: Why a Mother Tells Her Son About the Nazi Era (New York: Institute of Human Relations Press, American Jewish Committee, 1962);

Nothing Ever Breaks Except the Heart (Garden City, N.Y.: Doubleday, 1966);

Pinky, the Cat Who Liked to Sleep (New York: Crowell-Collier/London: Collier-Macmillan, 1966);

Pinky in Persia (New York: Crowell-Collier, 1968);

Being Geniuses Together, 1920-1930, by Robert McAlmon, revised, with supplementary chapters, by Boyle (Garden City, N.Y.: Doubleday, 1968; London: Joseph, 1970);

Testament For My Students and Other Poems (Garden City, N.Y.: Doubleday, 1970);

The Long Walk at San Francisco State and Other Essays (New York: Grove, 1970);

The Underground Woman (Garden City, N.Y.: Doubleday, 1975);

Fifty Stories (Garden City, N.Y.: Doubleday, 1980);

Words That Must Somehow Be Said: The Selected Essays of Kay Boyle, 1927-1983 (Berkeley: North Point Press, 1985);

This Is Not a Letter and Other Poems (Los Angeles: Sun and Moon Press, 1985).

TRANSLATIONS: Joseph Delteil, *Don Juan* (New York: Cape & Smith, 1931);

René Crevel, *Mr. Knife, Miss Fork* (Paris: Black Sun Press, 1931);

Raymond Radiguet, *The Devil in the Flesh* (Paris: Crosby Continental Editions / New York: Harrison Smith, 1932; London: Grey Walls Press, 1949).

OTHER: Gladys Palmer Brooke, *Relations & Complications, Being the Recollections of H. H. The Dayang Muda of Sarawak*, ghostwritten by Boyle (London: John Lane / Bodley Head, 1929);

Boyle, photographed by her mother in Beach Haven, New Jersey, circa 1912 (collection of Sandra Spanier)

Ernest Walsh, *Poems and Sonnets*, anonymously edited by Boyle (New York: Harcourt, Brace, 1934);

365 Days, edited by Boyle, Laurence Vail, and Nina Conarain (London: Cape, 1936; New York: Harcourt, Brace, 1936);

Bettina Bedwell, *Yellow Dusk*, ghostwritten by Boyle (London: Hurst & Blackett, 1937);

Fourteen of Them, includes a memorial chapter on Anthony John Rizzi by Boyle (New York & Toronto: Farrar & Rinehart, 1944);

The Autobiography of Emanuel Carnevali, compiled, with a preface, by Boyle (New York: Horizon Press, 1967);

Enough of Dying! Voices for Peace, edited by Boyle and Justine Van Gundy, with an introduction and three selections by Boyle (New York: Laurel, 1972);

"Report from Lock-Up," in *Four Visions of America*, by Boyle, Erica Jong, Thomas Sanchez, and Henry Miller (Santa Barbara: Capra Press, 1977).

PERIODICAL PUBLICATIONS: "Passeres' Paris," *This Quarter*, no. 1 (1925): 140-143;

"Flight," *This Quarter*, no. 2 (1925): 161-171;

"Collation," *Calender of Modern Letters*, 3 (October 1926): 171-174;

"Plagued by the Nightingale," *This Quarter*, no. 3 (1927): 165-203;

"Written for Royalty," *transition*, no. 13 (Summer 1928): 60-64;

"War in Paris," *New Yorker*, 14 (26 November 1938): 18-20;

"Poor Monsieur Panalitus," *New Yorker*, 15 (20 January 1940): 19-22;

"St. Steven's Green," *Atlantic Monthly*, 245 (June 1980): 41-44.

As a member of the expatriate literary community in Paris in the late 1920s and 1930s, Kay Boyle was well known for her novels, poetry, and short fiction, but it is as a short-story writer that she excelled. During the entire decade of the 1930s her work appeared consistently on lists of the year's best short stories and won two major short-fiction awards. Noted as a stylist and as an architect of words, she received the accolades of peers and readers alike.

Boyle was born to Howard P. and Katherine Evans Boyle in St. Paul, Minnesota, on 19 February 1902. In her own biographical sketches Boyle places her date of birth as 19 February 1903, but the fact that she was actually born one year earlier has come to light in recent years. Named Katherine for her mother, the child grew up in affluence. She traveled extensively in Europe during her early childhood years; in fact, in the autobiographical chapters she added to the 1968 edition of Robert McAlmon's 1938 memoir, *Being Geniuses Together*, she mentions several trips to England and Europe prior to World War I.

She was influenced intellectually by her maternal grandmother, Eva Evans, and by her mother, two rather extraordinary women who introduced the child to radical ideas. For example, they took her to the controversial Armory Show in 1913 and exposed her to the avant-garde writing of James Joyce and Gertrude Stein, among others. These active and dedicated women endowed

Cover for a 1925 issue of the Paris little magazine that included Boyle's experimental poem "Flight"

Boyle with a love of art and an excitement for progressivism, whether political or artistic, which helped to shape her later responses to life.

During and after the war the Boyle family suffered financial reverses that led them to Cincinnati, Ohio, where Boyle was able to attend briefly the Conservatory of Music and, from 1917 to 1919, the Ohio Mechanics Institute. She financed her way through secretarial school by working as a cashier in her father's business, but as soon as she graduated, she left for New York to join her sister Joan, who was then on the staff of *Vogue* magazine. Boyle worked at the magazine briefly for fashion writer Margery Welles.

Richard Brault, a French exchange student whom Boyle had met in Cincinnati and who had just graduated from the University of Cincinnati with a degree in electrical engineering, joined Boyle in New York. They were married on 24 June 1922 at the New York City Hall and, in deference to Richard's very traditional Catholic family,

Boyle with Laurence Vail, 1929 (Special Collections, Morris Library, Southern Illinois University, Carbondale)

Boyle (third from left) in 1929 with the Countess of Polignac, Laurence Vail, Hart Crane, and Caresse Crosby

they were remarried two weeks later by a priest. Their life in New York, headquartered in a one-room apartment on East Fifteenth Street, was one of extreme poverty. By this time Boyle was working for Lola Ridge in the New York office of *Broom* magazine. Through her experiences at *Broom* she met such writers as John Dos Passos, Elinor Wylie, Waldo Frank, Gorham Munson, Edwin Arlington Robinson, Monroe Wheeler, Glenway Wescott, Marianne Moore, and William Carlos Williams. By this time Boyle's first poems were being published: "Morning" in *Broom* (January 1923) and "Shore" in *Contact* (June 1923).

In June 1923 Boyle and Brault decided to vacation with Brault's family in France. Boyle's rather unpleasant experiences with the Braults are recorded in her fictionalized but autobiographical first novel, *Plagued by the Nightingale* (1931). As soon as possible Boyle and Brault left for Paris. Not long after her arrival Boyle met Robert McAlmon, who had founded *Contact* magazine with William Carlos Williams in 1920. It was to be a fortunate friendship, for McAlmon was deeply involved with the active young American and European writers of the emerging decade and was to prove valuable to Boyle's career.

Brault soon found a job in LeHavre, and the couple was forced to relocate. For the next two years Boyle's fledgling literary career suffered a setback for she did not publish again until two of her poems appeared in *Poetry* in early 1925. Shortly thereafter Boyle received a letter from Ernest Walsh, coeditor with Ethel Moorhead of *This Quarter*, soliciting manuscripts for the magazine's first issue. He had read the poems she had published in *Broom* and *Poetry* and was impressed with her work. Two of her poems, "Summer" and "Passeres' Paris," appeared in the spring of 1925 in the maiden issue of *This Quarter;* thereafter her works appeared regularly in the pages of the journal.

A steady correspondence grew between Walsh and Boyle, with her sending him excerpts from her novels and poems. The relationship became much more serious, as Boyle describes in *Being Geniuses Together*. In the early winter of 1926 she contracted bronchitis, which was mistakenly diagnosed as tuberculosis. She wrote of this to Walsh, who was suffering from tuberculosis, and received a telegram from him asking her to join him in the warmer climate of southern France. Brault's family provided her with the money to travel to Grasse, where Walsh and Moorhead had rented a villa for the winter. Boyle's con-

dition improved rapidly, and as she was finishing her first novel in a pension, Walsh came to tell her he loved her and wanted her to live with him. Boyle became Walsh's lover and companion for the last months of his life as they traveled from village to village in southern France and Italy trying to find a hotel that would allow the terminally ill Walsh to stay for longer than a few days. During this time Boyle also helped Walsh with the editorial duties involved with *This Quarter*.

Brault wrote to Boyle saying that he had found a good job and wanted to reestablish their marriage if possible. He had refrained from telling his conventional family about Kay's new life, and he felt that a divorce was impossible. Meanwhile, Boyle discovered that she was pregnant with Walsh's child, and she chose to remain with him even though she was fully aware of the precariousness of their future. Within weeks Walsh's illness became worse, and on 16 October 1926 he died.

Brault again sought a reunion with Boyle and was willing to accept her infant daughter. Her reminiscences of the next year, as recorded in *Being Geniuses Together*, are laced with humiliation, for she returned to Brault simply because she had nowhere else to go. This was a period of spiritual drifting, for by her own admission, she was living a life that denied everything honest and affirmative in which she believed. Perhaps as an antidote, Boyle resumed her writing during this year, 1927, publishing almost exclusively in *transition*, edited by Eugene Jolas. She was at this time beginning to write short stories.

In the spring of 1928 English poet Archibald Craig and his cousin the Dayang Muda of Sarawak (the former Gladys Palmer of the United States) requested that Boyle come to Paris in order to ghostwrite the Dayang Muda's memoirs. With very little deliberation Boyle accepted the job, severing forever her life with Brault. During her stay in Paris Boyle met Raymond Duncan, brother of the famed Isadora Duncan and the leader of a communal artists' colony. He offered Boyle the opportunity to work with other artists and at the same time provided care for her daughter, Sharon, who would become a ward of the colony. By the time she had become disillusioned with the colony and decided to leave, Boyle had already signed Sharon into the group's custody. As a result of this rather bizarre circumstance, she was forced to kidnap her own daughter. She was aided in this venture by

PROCLAMATION

TIRED OF THE SPECTACLE OF SHORT STORIES, NOVELS, POEMS AND PLAYS STILL UNDER THE HEGEMONY OF THE BANAL WORD, MONOTONOUS SYNTAX, STATIC PSYCHOLOGY, DESCRIPTIVE NATURALISM, AND DESIROUS OF CRYSTALLIZING A VIEWPOINT...

WE HEREBY DECLARE THAT :

1. THE REVOLUTION IN THE ENGLISH LANGUAGE IS AN ACCOMPLISHED FACT.

2. THE IMAGINATION IN SEARCH OF A FABULOUS WORLD IS AUTONOMOUS AND UNCONFINED.
(*Prudence is a rich, ugly old maid courted by Incapacity*... Blake)

3. PURE POETRY IS A LYRICAL ABSOLUTE THAT SEEKS AN A PRIORI REALITY WITHIN OURSELVES ALONE.
(*Bring out number, weight and measure in a year of dearth*... Blake)

4. NARRATIVE IS NOT MERE ANECDOTE, BUT THE PROJECTION OF A METAMORPHOSIS OF REALITY.
(*Enough ! Or Too Much !*... Blake)

5. THE EXPRESSION OF THESE CONCEPTS CAN BE ACHIEVED ONLY THROUGH THE RHYTHMIC " HALLUCINATION OF THE WORD ". (Rimbaud).

6. THE LITERARY CREATOR HAS THE RIGHT TO DISINTEGRATE THE PRIMAL MATTER OF WORDS IMPOSED ON HIM BY TEXT-BOOKS AND DICTIONARIES.
(*The road of excess leads to the palace of Wisdom*... Blake)

7. HE HAS THE RIGHT TO USE WORDS OF HIS OWN FASHIONING AND TO DISREGARD EXISTING GRAMMATICAL AND SYNTACTICAL LAWS.
(*The tigers of wrath are wiser than the horses of instruction*... Blake)

8. THE " LITANY OF WORDS " IS ADMITTED AS AN INDEPENDENT UNIT.

9. WE ARE NOT CONCERNED WITH THE PROPAGATION OF SOCIOLOGICAL IDEAS, EXCEPT TO EMANCIPATE THE CREATIVE ELEMENTS FROM THE PRESENT IDEOLOGY.

10. TIME IS A TYRANNY TO BE ABOLISHED.

11. THE WRITER EXPRESSES. HE DOES NOT COMMUNICATE

12. THE PLAIN READER BE DAMNED.
(*Damn braces ! Bless relaxes !*... Blake)

— *Signed* : KAY BOYLE, WHIT BURNETT, HART CRANE, CARESSE CROSBY, HARRY CROSBY, MARTHA FOLEY, STUART GILBERT, A. L. GILLESPIE, LEIGH HOFFMAN, EUGENE JOLAS, ELLIOT PAUL, DOUGLAS RIGBY, THEO RUTRA, ROBERT SAGE, HAROLD J. SALEMSON, LAURENCE VAIL.

Manifesto for "The Revolution of the Word," published in the June 1929 issue of transition

Caresse and Harry Crosby, whom she had met through Jolas. They not only participated in the actual kidnapping but they provided a place for Boyle and Sharon to stay until future plans could be made.

In addition to their personal friendship, the Crosbys also offered professional aid to Boyle. Their publishing house, the Black Sun Press, published her first book, *Short Stories*, in 1929. This collection contained seven stories, four of which had originally appeared in *transition* in 1927 and 1928.

At this time Boyle met Laurence Vail, an expatriate artist who was in the midst of his divorce from Peggy Guggenheim, and their relationship began to erase some of the pain and grief she had felt since Walsh's death. In 1929 the first of their three daughters, Apple-Joan, was born, and Vail's two children by his previous marriage joined them at their home in the south of France. Boyle and Vail were married on 2 April 1932, following Boyle's divorce from Brault. They and their children moved to Austria in 1933, then to England in 1936, where Vail's son was attending school. Then they returned to France and bought a chalet in the Alps where they lived until 1941 when the pressures of wartime Europe forced them to return to the United States.

Boyle photographed by Laurence Vail in the south of France, 1930

During the 1930s Boyle entered a period of immense literary activity, publishing her six most important novels as well as several novellas and collections of short stories. In 1930 her second collection of short stories, *Wedding Day and Other Stories*, was published in New York by Jonathan Cape and Harrison Smith and was dedicated to Laurence Vail. It contained the seven pieces which had previously appeared in *Short Stories* plus six others, including the title story and "Episode in the Life of an Ancestor" (*Hound and Horn*, October-December 1930), the first of her stories to gain significant attention from literary critics and scholars.

Set in nineteenth-century Kansas, "Episode in the Life of an Ancestor" is Boyle's tribute to her grandmother. It examines the generation gap between a young woman (called "the grandmother" in the story) and her widowed father. Although the grandmother is the central character of this story, her actions are recorded only as they appear to her father who long since has failed to understand her and to the horse who car-

ries her joyously across the prairie on a nocturnal gallop. She fears neither the vastness nor the dangers that may surround her. In contrast, the father's concerns about her move rapidly during the course of the evening through three stages: from disappointment that she does not care for traditionally "feminine" duties such as sewing or cooking, to a fear that the local schoolmaster may have seduced her on the prairie, and finally to a recognition that she is too vital to be attracted by the "poor squat little periwinkle with his long nose always thrust away in a book." In this story Boyle introduced technical innovations that she would develop more completely in later works. For example, the grandmother appears only briefly as actor during the events of the story. The main focus is on impressions of her the reader receives from other characters in the story. Furthermore, Boyle ends this chronicle at the traditional beginning of the narrative: at the point at which the conflict is defined. Thus, this particular story ends as the grandmother and her father confront each other, before any words are exchanged or actions taken. Yet, as innovative as "Episode in the Life of an Ancestor" appears to be, it is not the most impressive of Boyle's early stories.

"Kroy Wen" (*Front*, December 1930; collected in *The First Lover and Other Stories*, 1933) is a deceptively simple, technically innovative venture. Essentially plotless in the traditional sense, its power derives from its acute observations of human behavior and its reliance on nuance to establish the character relationships that provide its movement. Set on board a tramp steamer, the *New York*, its action deals with a movie director's compulsive attempts to manipulate–as if they were actors in one of his movies–the actions and reactions of an Italian acrobat and his pregnant wife, en route to their homeland in a desperate effort to reach Italy before the child's birth. "Kroy Wen" is a study based on contrasts, between art and nature, image and reality, crassness and dignity, exploitation and human concern. At its center the artificiality and shallowness of the movie director, who is trying to recover from a nervous breakdown, contrasts dramatically with the natural poetry and dignity of the Italian woman, battling steerage, nausea, and incipient labor pains to reach her goal. Wurthenberger, the director, sees in her desperation a subject for his camera, and he begins to film her agony and her husband's concern, congratulating himself in the process for his touching, emotional rendition of the human condition. Oblivious to the real suffering the pair are enduring, however, he demands that they conform to the artistic conception of suffering that his imagination creates. Finally, frustrated by their "obstinance," he tells the woman to scream aloud in her agony of childbirth, but the woman quietly refuses to be exploited in such a way by him. Her refusal, final and nonnegotiable, ends the story. The title "Kroy Wen" refers to the predominant symptom of Wurthenberger's illness: at the height of his nervous disorder he reads words backwards. Thus this title illustrates in short form two of the real strengths of Boyle's style: her acute awareness of the potentials for manipulating words for special effects and her biting irony, symbolized in this case by Wurthenberger's distorted vision of reality and his inability to recognize the meaning of the situations he observes. These two elements of her style, noticeable in effective patterns in this early work, became trademarks of Boyle's fiction.

Yet, her most remarkable early story, "Rest Cure" (*Front*, April-May 1931; collected in *The First Lover and Other Stories*), received even more favorable attention and was republished in the Edgar J. O'Brien anthology *Best Short Stories of 1931*. Again Boyle deals with three characters in tandem. This time her protagonist is a terminally ill writer who, in the presence of his wife and his publisher on a terrace bordering the Mediterranean one late afternoon, must learn to deal with the inescapable reality that he is dying. Unable to admit his fear, even to himself, he lashes out in irritation at both wife and publisher. As representatives of the healthy, they will live after his death, and he hates them for it. Yet, these two people pale in importance to him as the story progresses. In a striking movement that in less-skillful hands would have become ludicrous, Boyle takes the reader deep into her protagonist's psyche to describe the mystic bond he intuitively feels with the live langouste his wife brings for his lunch. Holding it with its pinchers bound, he looks into its face and sees his long-dead father waiting to embrace him. Strangely the langouste serves as a kind of talisman for him, and as the story ends he calls out to his father to help him face his own death.

Boyle uses physical surroundings and inner landscapes to provide the dramatic contrasts in this story: the writer associates the afternoon sunlight, his wife's geraniums, and a glass of sparkling golden champagne with life, while his visions and memories of the dark, sunless coal

Boyle in 1932 (Special Collections, Morris Library, Southern Illinois University, Carbondale)

mines in which his father once worked serve to remind him of the death that awaits him. As the story progresses, this imaginary inner landscape becomes increasingly more real to the writer than his physical surroundings. His father communicates with him more personally and profoundly than either wife or publisher can. In essence, during the course of these events, Boyle redefines reality until at the story's end the symbolic is more valid than the literal, and the imagination conveys more knowledge than the senses.

Thus "Rest Cure" serves as a showcase for Boyle's skill as a stylist. She creates a setting and uses details within it to contribute to the thematic unity within the story by prefiguring death in its many guises. For example, the writer's hands appear to him as "emaciated strangers" and as skeletons. The geraniums, which he destroys, have been personified as "weary washer-women" with "their meager bundles of dirty linen on their heads." When he attacks them, he "finger[s] them at the waist a moment, and then snap[s] off each stem." The sun beginning to set will soon leave him with the dark of night, the golden champagne he drinks will soon be finished, and his living talisman soon will be dead. This story illustrates the dramatic tension and condensation that mark Boyle's style, a style of prose writing that grew out of her work as poet.

Boyle's work appeared regularly during the 1930s and 1940s in such prestigious magazines as *Harper's*, *Scribner's*, and the *New Yorker*. Her story "The First Lover" (*Harper's Monthly*, June 1931; collected in *The First Lover and Other Stories*) appeared in the *O. Henry Memorial Award Prize Stories of 1932*. The award committee praised Boyle for her unusual turns of phrase, and they ranked this story as second among the four stories represented in this volume.

"The First Lover" focuses on the reactions of three young German sisters to a chance encounter with a handsome young Englishman. The sisters, sent by their father, Professor Albatross, on a vacation from the poverty and hardship of post-World War I Germany, associate the Englishman with the affluence to which they aspire but cannot attain. His mannerisms and bearings supply grist for their impression. For example, the reader learns that he takes his food for granted and that he has no idea "that people sometimes had less or did without." He seems aloof and untouched by human problems. The oldest of the sisters fantasizes about him, planning to interest him in herself by fabricating a story of her prosperous life and the power and influence of her father, whom she decides should be the *Baron* Albatross. The Englishman destroys her daydream by asking if the three of them are the daughters of the Professor Albatross with whom he had once studied. The sisters, unable to indulge their fantasy, are thrown back abruptly into their reality and can barely answer as the Englishman walks away and out of their lives. They prefer the fiction to the real, and they cannot deal with their realization that the fiction has been denied to them. In this story Boyle displays the fragility of the human ego and its powers of self-delusion. Her women lose—because they long so intensely for a dream life—any chance of achieving it.

Furthermore, Boyle also hints at the beginning of a sociopolitical involvement she would develop more forcefully in later fiction. She touches briefly and subtly on the political reality

of Europe in the late 1920s and 1930s by contrasting the poverty of the sisters' Germany with their "new country of greed and plenty," and she lets the sisters choose the latter, deciding to "forget . . . everything that had made their hearts like winter apples." The action of this story is understated, with very little dialogue to maintain it. It is, in fact, a chronicle of interior action with the human mind as its arena. The story sustains its interest by tracing the changing nuances of mood, personality, and ego among the characters.

During the next few years Boyle continued to write short fiction in addition to her other work. She saw her first four novels published, to mixed reviews, and she worked as translator of various works from French, including Raymond Radiguet's *The Devil in the Flesh* (1932). In 1933 she collected fourteen short stories in *The First Lover and Other Stories*. By 1934 she was well enough established as a writer to receive a Guggenheim Fellowship for research dealing with a long poem on aviation. Segments of this poem later appeared in *transition* and in Eugene Jolas's *Vertical* (1941).

In April 1935 Boyle published "The White Horses of Vienna" in *Harper's Monthly*. This story won the O. Henry Memorial Award first prize of three hundred dollars for the best short story of the year. The next year she used this story as the title piece for a collection of eighteen stories—*The White Horses of Vienna and Other Stories* (1936)—and it has since become one of her most widely anthologized works.

"The White Horses of Vienna" delves more deeply into the political setting of Europe during the 1930s than any of Boyle's previous fiction, but as always her concern is with the relationships among her characters, this time played out against the backdrop of intensely explosive social and political movements. Divided into three parts, the story pits an anti-Semitic Tyrolian doctor and his wife against a young Jewish student-doctor sent to help them during the doctor's recovery from an accident. Part 1 introduces the undercurrents of the story. It describes the doctor's family as loving and closely knit and explains in passing that the doctor's injury was the result of a fall he had sustained while coming home from lighting fires on the mountain." Only when the student-doctor, Heine, appears does tension begin to build in the story. The doctor's wife turns pale at the sight of Heine's "long, dark, alien face," the "arch of his nose and the quality of skin." At this point she appears to be the anti-

Semite because her husband seems not at all concerned that his helper is Jewish. Part 2, however, establishes the ironies that pervade the story. First of all the reader learns that the mountain fires the doctor frequently starts are, in fact, swastika fires. His kindly behavior toward Heine disguises the truth of his pro-Nazi feelings, clearly revealed in a puppet show that he conducts. In it he ridicules a clown named "Chancellor" and glorifies a magnificent grasshopper called "Leader" in a thinly veiled allusion to Engelbert Dollfuss and Adolf Hitler. Thus, even the doctor's entertainment is laced with political tensions. In addition his wife projects her stereotypical hatred of Jews onto Heine, assuming he has no sense of homeland and is motivated solely by greed. Because of this she completely misinterprets a story he tells the family.

This story, about the famous Lippizaner horses of Vienna, provides the central metaphor for the events that follow. In it one of the famous horses is bought for an exorbitant sum by an Indian maharaja who wishes to take it home with him, but the groom who has trained the horse since its birth cannot bear to let the horse leave him. Although it may destroy the horse's ability to perform, he cuts one of the horse's hooves in an effort to keep it in Vienna. When that hoof heals, he cuts another, but this time the horse develops blood poisoning and must be killed. In grief, but not remorse, the groom commits suicide on the day the horse dies. The doctor's wife assumes Heine is impressed with the shrewdness of the people who sold the horse for an excessive price and held the maharaja to that amount even after they had learned that the animal was injured, but instead Heine is impressed with the strength of the groom's devotion, even though it leads to his and the horse's ruin. Because Heine is not political, he cannot use political criteria to interfere with the relationships and bonds that develop between people. In this way he differs from the doctor and his wife.

Part 3 concludes the story with the doctor's arrest. Dollfuss has been assassinated and the authorities recognize the doctor's pro-Nazi activism. Heine, not realizing the anti-Semitic implications of the doctor's political activities, follows them from the house asking what he can do to help the doctor. Like the groom in his story, he acts from personal devotion to a man he considers a friend. This irony, much more poignant and biting from a post-World War II perspective, was in 1935 a subtle examination of the varieties of artificial boundaries which divide individuals from each other.

To a large extent the story's power depends on the reader's knowledge of the sociopolitical situation in Europe during the 1930s. Boyle alludes to events and attitudes one must understand in order to recognize the tension among the characters. Thus, the fact that she merely suggests the larger context provides both the story's most serious potential weakness and its most striking and important strength. She explores her world through the emotions of individual characters, each of whom is seen at various turns to be sympathetic. Placed together, however, they live out the conflicts that led eventually to World War II.

From the mid 1930s Boyle's literary output became more diverse. She produced not only short fiction and novels but also reviews and articles. In 1936 she, Laurence Vail, and Nina Conarain edited a collection of short stories entitled *365 Days*, and in 1937 she ghosted a book–*Yellow Dusk*–for Bettina Bedwell. In addition she reestablished herself as a poet by publishing a group of twenty-four poems as *A Glad Day* (1938). While her short stories continued to appear in prominent periodicals, they did not receive the attention granted "The White Horses of Vienna." Finally she published "Anschluss" (*Harper's Monthly*, April 1939; collected in *Nothing Ever Breaks Except the Heart*, 1966), which was republished in both *Best Short Stories of 1940* and *O. Henry Memorial Award Prize Stories of 1939*.

Although it was well received critically, "Anschluss" did not gain the popular attention some of Boyle's earlier works had. This story also deals with the effect of political barriers on the relationships among people, this time a Paris fashion writer in Austria and her two Tyrolian friends, Fanni and her brother Toni. In Fanni she finds a friend, and in Toni she discovers a lover who cherishes her because she is different from the local people. His political leanings, however, disturb her: he lights swastika fires and spends time in jail. Then the *anschluss* (the annexation of Austria to Nazi Germany) he has helped to bring about becomes reality, and all is changed; Toni and Fanni are changed, for they become absorbed by the new militarism of the Nazis. No longer welcomed, seen as a stranger with inappropriate mannerisms and customs, the fashion writer leaves the country. In effect she has been driven from her beloved retreat by the regimented stifling atmosphere of the new political order. Again, in this story, Boyle portrays the destructive power of political dogmas which create barriers between people and inhibit communication at a human level. Metaphorically the story describes in individual terms the divisions evident on a national and international level in Europe at the time.

In 1941 Boyle again won the O. Henry Memorial Prize Award for the year's best short story, "Defeat" (*New Yorker*, 17 May 1941; collected in *Thirty Stories*, 1946). A chronicle of the fall of France in 1940 presented from the perspective of a "quiet-mouthed little bus driver" who tells his story only once and then only to strangers, "Defeat" focuses on the discrepancy between the man's expectations of compatriots' behavior and their subsequent actions. As an escaped prisoner of war, the bus driver travels through France during the days immediately following Germany's victory over the French army. He is surprised at the hostility he encounters from some of his fellow Frenchmen, but he maintains his morale by reassuring himself and his *copain* that their country would not be defeated "as long as its women aren't." Arriving in a village on the evening of the fourteenth of July (Bastille Day), he sees German soldiers decorating for a dance, which he is certain will be ignored by the villagers. Perhaps, he tries to convince himself, it was the magnificent food or maybe the festive occasion that made the difference, but later, as he looked out of the window of the hayloft where he was hiding, he watched the women join the dance.

The story is starkly told, concentrating on the soldier's reactions to the events around him. Nevertheless, it contains more of a traditional plot than most of Boyle's stories, for it narrates the journey through the French countryside of the escaped soldier, and it reaches a climax as he realizes at the dance scene that France is, indeed, defeated. His journey, however, is metaphorical as well; it covers the distance from naiveté to painful knowledge, from hope to despair. "Defeat" captures the mood of France during the early years of World War II and portrays through the disillusionment of one ordinary man the grief of a nation.

Boyle's fiction of the early 1940s consistently explored war-torn Europe with the insights of an insider and the skill of an artist. She published these stories in magazines such as *Harper's*, the *New Yorker*, and *Saturday Evening Post*. Yet, although Boyle concerned herself with Europe and its ordeal, as the war became more involved she

and her family had to be evacuated from France; even so, it was at the latest possible moment. They traveled to America by way of Spain to Lisbon, Portugal, where they waited for six weeks before being able to arrange passage for the entire family. They arrived in New York on 14 July 1941.

After returning to the United States Boyle and her four daughters lived in Nyack, New York, and later in Mt. Vernon. At this time her marriage to Vail was deteriorating rapidly over what Boyle characterized as major political differences. In November of 1942 their divorce became final. Meanwhile Boyle had met Joseph Franckenstein, an Austrian nobleman who was then serving in the American armed services, and they were married in 1943. Earlier in the 1930s Boyle had worked to arrange U.S. visas for European Jews and other political exiles, and she had done so for Franckenstein, a Roman Catholic who opposed the Nazi regime.

In the early 1940s three of Boyle's stories, "Poor Monsieur Panalitus" (*New Yorker*, 20 January 1940), "Their Name is Macaroni" (*New Yorker*, 3 January 1942; collected in *Thirty Stories*), and "The Canals of Mars" (*Harper's Bazaar*, February 1943; collected in *Thirty Stories*), appeared in the O. Henry Memorial Award prize-story collections. All these stories deal with facets of the war experience, but the last moves its action from Europe to New York. In "The Canals of Mars" Boyle describes the last few shared hours of husband and wife as they prepare for his departure with other military inductees for a life in the armed services. This departure differs from previous ones, however, such as the time he "went to concentration camp." Boyle offers no real explanation for these experiences beyond saying, "This isn't like the other times. . . . This time you're not just one man bearing the burden alone of what you've decided to do. There's a national sanction to it." She leaves the reader to infer that as an Austrian with pro-Allied sympathies, his past experiences in Europe demanded real courage and forced him into the isolation of official condemnation. This time, however, he is one of many, and as she stands with other families gesturing to other inductees, she watches him disappear in formation and in uniform, "the other trappings for the thing in which we had believed." Less tightly written than "The White Horses of Vienna," this story, too, relies on the reader's knowledge of political events to sustain the drama of the story. However, because this outside knowledge is, in this case, more selective and private, the story loses some of its power and is less convincing than Boyle's earlier work.

After the war Boyle and Franckenstein returned to Europe where Franckenstein worked with the U.S. State Department and Boyle wrote for the *Nation*. In 1948 Boyle was hired as a foreign correspondent for the *New Yorker*, and she used her considerable knowledge of Europe to add dimension to the articles and short stories she produced during these years. Some of these postwar stories were collected in *The Smoking Mountain: Stories of Postwar Germany* (1951). Boyle and her family settled in Germany and, in addition to her writing assignments, Boyle taught for four years in a German women's prison.

In the 1950s both Boyle and Franckenstein fell victim to McCarthyism. She was dismissed from the *New Yorker*, as was he from the State Department. Against the advice of European friends, the two returned to the United States in 1953 and tried to clear themselves. They taught in private schools while they waited and worked for exoneration. During these years Boyle wrote regularly and eloquently for the *Nation*, which was not only an effective forum for those writers blacklisted elsewhere but also one of the few magazines that would publish her work. Her nonfiction, drawn from her experiences in postwar Europe coupled with her own commitment as creative artist in a less-than-perfect world, displays the same style and tension of the best of her short stories, demonstrating her mastery of yet another genre. Finally, when the hysteria of McCarthyism was laid to rest, Boyle and her husband succeeded in clearing their names, and Franckenstein was reinstated in the Diplomatic Corps. In 1961 Boyle was granted her second Guggenheim Fellowship, and in 1962 she published *Breaking the Silence: Why a Mother Tells Her Son About the Nazi Era*, a monograph designed to explain to adolescents the Jewish experience in Europe during the Nazi years.

Franckenstein died of lung cancer in 1963, a few months after Boyle accepted a position teaching creative writing at San Francisco State University. She became extremely active in the civil rights movement and in protesting the U.S. involvement in Vietnam. During the late 1960s she was arrested twice for her participation in nonviolent sit-ins at the Army Induction Center in Oakland, California. Her experiences became the basis for several articles, stories, and a novel, *The Underground Woman* (1975).

Boyle continues to write and to teach, serving as visiting professor at Eastern Washington State University in 1982. She continues also to be a vocal supporter of human rights and human dignity, as she has consistently in her long and productive literary career. Her concern has always been with people, evident in her fiction in her emphasis on character and the drama taking place within the human psyche. Her canon—the short stories, novels, articles, and poems—constitutes an impressive document of the dignity and resilience of the human being.

References:
Elizabeth S. Bell, "Henry Miller and Kay Boyle: The Divided Stream in American Expatriate Literature, 1930-1940," Ph.D. dissertation, University of Louisville, 1979;

Richard C. Carpenter, "Kay Boyle: The Figure in the Carpet," *Critique*, 7 (Winter 1964-1965): 65-78;

Frank Gado, "Kay Boyle: From the Aesthetics of Exile to the Polemics of Return," Ph.D. dissertation, Duke University, 1969;

Patricia Holt, "Kay Boyle," *Publishers Weekly*, 218 (17 October 1980): 8-9;

Byron K. Jackson, "The Achievement of Kay Boyle," Ph.D. dissertation, University of Florida, 1968;

"Kay Boyle," in *Talks with Authors*, edited by Charles F. Madden (Carbondale & Edwardsville: Southern Illinois University Press, 1968), pp. 215-236;

Harry T. Moore, "Kay Boyle's Fiction," in *The Age of the Modern and Other Essays* (Carbondale & Edwardsville: Southern Illinois University Press, 1971), pp. 32-36;

Sandra Whipple Spanier, *Kay Boyle: Artist and Activist* (Carbondale & Edwardsville: Southern Illinois University Press, 1986);

Dan Tooker and Roger Hofheins, "Kay Boyle," in *Fiction! Interviews with Northern California Novelists* (New York & Los Altos, Cal.: Harcourt Brace Jovanovich / William Kaufman, 1976).

Papers:
The primary collection of Boyle's papers is held at the Morris Library, Southern Illinois University, Carbondale.

Roark Bradford
(21 August 1896-13 November 1948)

Wade Hall
Bellarmine College

BOOKS: *Ol' Man Adam an' His Chillun: Being the Tales They Tell about the Time When the Lord Walked the Earth Like a Natural Man* (New York & London: Harper, 1928);

This Side of Jordan (New York & London: Harper, 1929);

Ol' King David an' the Philistine Boys (New York & London: Harper, 1930);

John Henry (New York & London: Harper, 1931);

Kingdom Coming (New York & London: Harper, 1933);

Let the Band Play Dixie and Other Stories (New York & London: Harper, 1934);

How Come Christmas: A Modern Morality (New York & London: Harper, 1934);

The Three-Headed Angel (New York & London: Harper, 1937);

John Henry [play] (New York & London: Harper, 1939);

The Green Roller (New York: Harper, 1949).

PLAY PRODUCTION: *John Henry*, book by Bradford, music by Jacques Wolfe, New York, 44th Street Theatre, 10 January 1940.

Roark Whitney Wickliffe Bradford had an ideal background for writing the plantation stories and sketches of southern black people that made him a celebrity in the 1920s and 1930s. He was born to Richard C. and Patricia Adelaide Tillman Bradford on 21 August 1896 on his family's cotton plantation in Lauderdale County, Tennessee, near the Mississippi River. That plantation, and the black sharecroppers who worked it, provided the primary influence for the settings and characters of much of his fiction. Although he was descended from William Bradford, Puritan governor of Massachusetts, his ancestors had moved to Virginia in the early eighteenth century, and both of his grandfathers had fought for the Confederacy.

After study at home and in the public schools, Bradford attended the University of California. During World War I he was a first lieuten-

Roark Bradford

ant in the U.S. Army Artillery Reserve and was stationed in the Canal Zone. He remained in the army until March 1920. After his discharge he worked as a newspaper reporter for the *Atlanta Georgian* and the *Macon Telegraph*, then moved to Louisiana, where he worked first for the *Lafayette Advertiser* and then for the *New Orleans Times-Picayune* until 1926, when he resigned to spend his entire time writing. He was married twice, first to Lydia Sehorn of Columbia, Mississippi, and then, several years after Sehorn's death, to Mary Rose Sciarra Himler, with whom he had one son. He made the French Quarter in New Orleans his home and helped bring about the city's artistic renaissance.

Bradford made his decision to become a professional writer at the age of fifteen. Even then he was attracted to the character and stories of the poor black people who worked on the plantations of the lower South. Indeed, much of the material of his fiction was based on black men and women he knew as a boy. From them he developed his own style of storytelling and his interpretation of black dialect.

For over twenty years his stories of black plantation life appeared in such popular magazines as *Collier's*, the *Saturday Evening Post*, the *Delineator*, *Harper's*, the *Golden Book*, *Forum*, and the *Dial*. One of his first stories, "Child of God" (*Harper's*, April 1927), won the O. Henry Award in 1927. The main source of Bradford's popularity was his comic interpretation of the southern Negro—considered stereotypical today but the only portrait of the Negro accepted at that time by most readers. In such stories blacks were portrayed as simpleminded menials who could survive in white civilization only if they were supervised and protected by white people. In most of Bradford's stories black people are happy and content, religious, superstitious, sometimes lazy and shiftless but usually hardworking; they never presume equality with their white overlords.

Bradford's best-known stories are his depictions (they are actually distortions) of black religious life. His first collection of Bible tales in Negro dialect, *Ol' Man Adam an' His Chillun* (1928), was an immediate best-seller. The thirty-two stories are based on familiar characters and incidents from the Bible, all but two from the Old Testament. These "Tales They Tell about the Time When the Lord Walked the Earth Like a Natural Man" are written in the language of a backwoods black preacher who is presumably instructing a class of Sunday-school children. Here are dialect renderings of the familiar stories of Eve and the snake, Cain and Abel, Noah and the flood, Abraham and Sarah, Abraham and Isaac, Lot and his wife, Moses, Joshua, David, Job, Samson and Solomon—plus two characters from the New Testament, that "mean jege" named Pilate and "Nigger Deemus," who reluctantly gives up his fishing pole to follow "de Lawd."

The stories are based on gross distortions, confusions, and literal readings of Bible characters and incidents. They abound in anachronisms, including frequent references to people, objects, and events familiar to plantation blacks. "Populating the Earth," for example, is Bradford's version of the story of Cain and Abel. In

Dust jacket for a later edition of Bradford's first collection of short stories

the "preacher's" words: "Well, Adam and Eve had two chilluns name Cain and Abel. So when Adam got to gittin' along in de years so's he couldn't do no heavy work, he called his boys and say: 'Well, you boys better settle down and git to work. I and de old lady been s'portin' y'all up to now and hit's about time y'all was s'portin' me and yo' maw.'" The boys get into a fight when Abel announces that he will herd sheep and Cain comments: "You smells like a sheep, anyhow." The antagonism between the brothers is climaxed one day when Abel, sitting in the shade to watch Cain plow, calls out: "Me, I'd be skeered to git out in dat hot sun. Hit might cook my brains. . . . Cou'se hit ain't gonter cook yo' brains 'cause you ain't got no brains to git cooked." Cain loses patience, throws a large rock at his brother, and kills him. The Lord discovers the murder and warns Cain that since the new district judge is very strict he ought to leave the country. Therefore Cain "rid for fawty days and fawty nights" and arrives in a place called Nod, where he meets "a big gorilla gal," settles down, raises a family, and "peopled de yearth."

In 1930 *The Green Pastures*, Marc Connelly's dramatization of the tales from *Ol' Man Adam an' His Chillun*, was awarded a Pulitzer Prize, which enhanced Bradford's reputation and popularity. That same year Bradford published a new collection of Bible tales, *Ol' King David an' the Philistine Boys*, which includes comic portraits of such Old Testament personages as Esther, Jonah, Elijah, Jezebel, and Ruth. As in the earlier collection, divine beings and earthly sinners mingle in familiar fellowship, and the voice of the backwoods preacher remains: "Efn de Lawd has ever yit made a mistake, well ain't nobody ever kotched him." Why? "'Cause de Lawd is a man which is got a haid on him as long as a mule and he knows what he's up to, all de time." "De Lawd" himself speaks a language of contemporary allusion, similar to the preacher's, full of warning and promise: "I lets my people grind dey own cawn.... And sometimes dey wanders away f'm de mill whilst I ain't watchin'. But I kin always git 'em straightened out in time to git de meal home for de supper hoecakes."

One of Bradford's most popular stories, "How Come Christmas" (*Harper's*, December 1930; published in book form in 1934), also uses the preacher-narrator. It is a retelling of the Christmas story to six black children in Sunday school, but in this version the Christ Child is in company with Moses, Methuselah, George Washington, and Santa Claus.

When it was published in 1929, *This Side of Jordan* was called a novel. It is actually a collection of nineteen loosely connected sketches of black life centered on characters living on the Whitehall Plantation, located in the Bayou Rouge community of Louisiana near the Mississippi River. Here more than three hundred black men, women, and children live in small cabins behind the plantation mansion. Their lives are filled with the routines of work and play: "Day after day they journeyed into the fields and plowed or hoed or picked, and when night came they retired to their village for rest and amusement." The book presents a picturesque gallery of vivid portraits, including Aunt Crippled Lou, a mistress of cures, charms, and signs; Daddy Jack, the black foreman; and Preacher Wes, who has his hands full caring for the souls of his people.

The legendary hero of the lower Mississippi is the subject for Bradford's next book, *John Henry* (1931). Narrated in standard English, it is a collection of tales about the adventures of one of the most virile of American folk heroes. At his birth John Henry weighed forty-four pounds. He named himself and prophesied his future fame: "I might preach some ... but I ain't gonter be no preacher. I might roll cotton on de boats, but I ain't gonter be no cotton-rollin' rousterbout. I might got blue gums like a conjure man, but I ain't gonter git familiar wid de sperits. 'Cause my name is John Henry, and when fo'ks call me by my name, dey'll know I'm a natchal man." The book was dramatized by the author in 1940.

The Green Roller (1949) is a "legend" made up by Bradford about a preacher who preached up and down the swamplands of Louisiana for a hundred years and then died, leaving twelve men to continue his work. The book includes twelve sermons in poetry by his fiery followers. Three of his faithful disciples are Sin Splitting Samuel, Elder Johnson, and Butt-Cut Bostick, who figure prominently in several stories published in *Collier's*.

In "Money in the Sack" (*Collier's*, 24 May 1941) Sin Splitting Samuel rids a community of a runaway from the Georgia chain gang, gets his mule Baalam a free bushel of corn and a bale of pea-vine hay, and obtains a sack of money for himself. When the good people do not provide food enough, he "borrows" it. Surely, he reasons, "Takin' cawn for a hongry old mule ain't no sin." After all, the old itinerant preacher is doing the Lord's work: "Were the odor of sin detected, the Sin Splitter would fall upon a community and do battle with Satan." He fights evil with passion. Before one of his encounters he prays: "Lawd, you knows how things is, good as me. I and ole Satan fixin' to tangle up for who-laid-de-rail. I ain't axin' for no he'p. I just want to let you know dat a mighty big battle is fixin' to take place betwixt yo' prophet and de devil and efn you got any special need for Satan in yo' plans, you better git set to pull him out f'm under me. Amen." Indeed, so successful is Sam in fighting evil that he becomes legendary: "The word among the cotton croppers and wage makers was that when the pair, the gaunt preacher and the bony mule, appeared, Old Satan picked up his marbles and went home."

Bradford's first story to appear in *Collier's* was "Tricker," published in the 31 December 1927 issue. During the next twenty-one years *Collier's* published more than one hundred of his stories. Although the stories include Cajun sketches

People not only quit speaking to him—they quit speaking about him; for the first time in his life, Zeno was lonely

"I put de curse on you!" she snapped. "Moles gonna on-bury yo' money and tote it off!"

Illustrations for Bradford's story "Rich Man, Rich Man," published in the 13 November 1948 issue of Collier's

Bradford (third from left) in New Orleans, circa 1934. The woman on the left is Sheila K. Smith; the first man on the right is Lyle Saxon (courtesy of The Historic New Orleans Collection).

("The Pirate-in-Law," 19 December 1942) and other unconnected stories, many of them take place at a fictional place called Little Bee Bend Plantation, a Louisiana farm on which more than sixty black families work for their seldom-seen white overlords. These uncollected stories present a profile of teeming plantation life in the black quarters.

Many of the Little Bee Bend stories deal with religion. "Red Pants Ain't No Sin" (*Collier's*, 29 March 1941) is a character sketch of "Br'r Charlie," the plantation's religious but slow-witted "one-legged preaching blacksmith." Every time he has an idea, it gets him into trouble. One time he decides to rid the village of the danger of a large tree. He chops it down, but unfortunately it falls across his house and wrecks it. Another time he chides a young woman convert for wearing red overalls. He tells her to go home and put on a decent dress. But he begins to think too much about her "hot-lookin' strut" and concludes–by

some curious twist of logic–that too much hard work leads to sin. Also, he gets himself into trouble with the foreman when he takes a vacation from his blacksmith work.

Another not-too-bright citizen of Little Bee Bend Plantation is Po-Chile Albright, a strapping young black man who is mature in body but not in mind ("Poor-Chile No More," *Collier's*, 5 July 1941). He has been a problem for Giles, the black overseer, from the moment he arrived on the plantation. Now he wants to marry Little Livvy, but she says no–that is, till he goes into Shreveport, plays a slot machine at the Elite Club, hits the jackpot, and becomes "wealthy."

One of the busiest characters on Little Bee Bend Plantation is the Widow Duck, a prominent member of "Ole Ship er Zion Church." In addition to her church work, she also helps out Cupid. In "Cupid up the Bayou" (*Collier's*, 28 February 1948) she is engaged in her favorite pastime when she gets herself into trouble as she stops by the Hi-Way Club and consumes too much wine.

All the black croppers on the plantation have to work–or have someone work for them. Eutaw Graves is a lazy man ("The High Hip Rider," *Collier's,* 31 July 1948) whose wife Beena does his field work, despite the plantation rule that women are not allowed to plow. But one day Beena's neighbor, Cissie Lee, tells her that "de mens got to plow in de field and de ladies kin go fishin'," and Beena refuses to do any more plowing. Suddenly Eutaw changes, and Beena does not like her new husband. When the foreman is out of sight, therefore, they go back to their old routine: Beena in the field plowing and Eutaw in the shade picking his guitar and singing.

Bradford's last story to appear in *Collier's* was "Low-Down Cotton" (26 February 1949), published some three months after his death. It is a story that in its way is a prophecy of the end of the plantation system. Unaware of what it means to their way of life, the plantation workers are excited about the arrival of the first cotton-picking machine they have ever seen. But it means trouble for Bee Bee Dorcas. His proposal of marriage is refused by Shully T, the daughter of the best cotton picker on the place, because he cannot drive a tractor. "You ain't nothing but a field hand," she accuses him.

Bradford's stories present an idealized picture of plantation life. The black workers are pleased with their existence despite their second-class status. They seldom come into meaningful contact with their white bosses. When they do, it is usually an old black / young white relationship reminiscent of the Uncle Remus stories of Joel Chandler Harris. "The Butter Paddle" (*Collier's,* 6 July 1946), for example, is the story of how a little white boy, Robert E. Lee Hughes III, learns to accept his relationship with his family's black cook. Although he has been told by a lower-class white boy that "ain't no nigger got the right to paddle a white boy," Robert's father tells him that when he needs to be punished, it is the cook's rightful job to paddle him.

The stories are usually loosely constructed sketches and seldom follow the traditional short-story format of rising action, climax, and denouement. Nevertheless, even a generation after they were written they hold the reader's attention by the force of their vivid characterizations and the uniqueness of the world they reveal. Indeed, Bradford created a vivid fantasy world that never existed outside the pages of his books. Despite the fact that he lived among blacks most of his life and observed them closely, he was still an outsider who was seldom able–or willing–to penetrate black consciousness. Bradford admitted his limitations. In the preface to *The Green Roller* he stated: "The entire contents of this book is the product of my own imagination; it has no foundation in fact, legend, or folklore." Even the stories based on observation are largely caricatures of black people and their culture. Perhaps, as critic Lewis P. Simpson has concluded, Bradford was "the last of a line of Southern storytellers who more or less invented a Negro folk culture."

Roark Bradford died 13 November 1948 from an amoebic infection he contracted while serving in the U.S. Navy during World War II. In its 26 February 1949 issue *Collier's* editorialized: "No living writer has equaled him in his chosen field. None is likely to replace him." A short obituary in the *Saturday Review of Literature* (27 November 1948) concluded: "He lived a full and busy life; he was a skilled fisherman and horseman, a student, a talented writer, and a fascinated listener who could catch the colorful and sad nuances in song and storied legend of the deep South." After his death the world of Bradford's fiction ceased to exist, in fact and fiction. Perhaps that is why, except for a handful of graduate-school theses, so little critical attention has been paid to his work.

Reference:

Lewis P. Simpson, "Roark Bradford," in *A Bibliographical Guide to the Study of Southern Literature,* edited by Louis D. Rubin, Jr. (Baton Rouge: Louisiana State University Press, 1969), pp. 159-160.

Louis Bromfield

(27 December 1896-18 March 1956)

David D. Anderson
Michigan State University

See also the Bromfield entries in *DLB 4: American Writers in Paris, 1920-1939* and *DLB 9: American Novelists, 1910-1945*.

SELECTED BOOKS: *The Green Bay Tree* (New York: Stokes, 1924; London: Unwin, 1924);

Possession (New York: Stokes, 1925); republished as *Lilli Barr* (London: Unwin, 1926);

Early Autumn (New York: Stokes, 1926; London: Cape, 1926);

A Good Woman (New York: Stokes, 1927; London: Cape, 1927);

The Strange Case of Miss Annie Spragg (New York: Stokes, 1928; London: Cape, 1928);

Awake and Rehearse (New York: Stokes, 1929; London: Cape, 1929);

Twenty-Four Hours (New York: Stokes, 1930; London: Cassell, 1930);

Tabloid News (New York: Random House, 1930);

A Modern Hero (New York: Stokes, 1932; London: Cassell, 1933);

The Farm (New York & London: Harper, 1933; London: Cassell, 1933);

Here Today and Gone Tomorrow (New York & London: Harper, 1934; London: Cassell, 1934);

The Man Who Had Everything (New York & London: Harper, 1935; London: Cassell, 1935);

The Rains Came (New York & London: Harper, 1937; London: Cassell, 1937);

England: A Dying Oligarchy (New York & London: Harper, 1939);

It Takes All Kinds (New York & London: Harper, 1939; London: Cassell, 1939); abridged as *You Get What You Give* (London: Cassell, 1951);

Night in Bombay (New York & London: Harper, 1940; London: Cassell, 1940);

Wild Is The River (New York & London: Harper, 1941; London: Cassell, 1942);

Until the Day Break (New York & London: Harper, 1942; London: Cassell, 1943);

Mrs. Parkington (New York & London: Harper, 1943; London: Cassell, 1944);

Louis Bromfield (Walter M. Laufer)

What Became of Anna Bolton (New York & London: Harper, 1944; London: Cassell, 1945);

The World We Live In (New York: Harper, 1944; London: Cassell, 1946);

Pleasant Valley (New York & London: Harper, 1945; London: Cassell, 1946);

A Few Brass Tacks (New York & London: Harper, 1946);

Kenny (New York & London: Harper, 1947; London: Cassell, 1949);

Colorado (New York & London: Harper, 1947; London: Cassell, 1949);

Malabar Farm (New York & London: Harper, 1948; London: Cassell, 1949);

The Wild Country (New York: Harper, 1948; London: Cassell, 1950);

Out of the Earth (New York: Harper, 1950; London: Cassell, 1951);

Mr. Smith (New York: Harper, 1951; London: Cassell, 1952);

A New Pattern for a Tired World (New York: Harper, 1954; London: Cassell, 1954);

From My Experience (New York: Harper, 1955; London: Cassell, 1956);

Animals and Other People (New York: Harper, 1955; London: Cassell, 1956).

OTHER: "Expatriate–Vintage 1927," in *Mirrors of the Year 1926-27*, edited by Grant Overton (New York: Stokes, 1927);

"A Critique of Criticism," in *Mirrors of the Year 1927-28*, edited by Horace Winston Stokes (New York: Stokes, 1928);

"The Novel in Transition," in *Revolt in the Arts*, edited by Oliver Martin Sayler (New York: Brentano's, 1930).

Louis Bromfield, novelist, short-story writer, columnist, and experimental farmer, was born on 27 December 1896 in Mansfield, Ohio, to a farming family that had settled Richland County in the early nineteenth century and had moved to town in the late nineteenth century as the result of agricultural reverses as Ohio became increasingly industrial. This transition was not only to color most of Bromfield's best fiction but it was to provide the impetus for his decision in 1938 to return to Richland County, after fourteen years' residence in France, to establish Malabar Farm, which he hoped would become fully self-sufficient. From this point onward Bromfield increasingly devoted his creative talents to nature and agricultural writing.

After education in the Mansfield public schools, a period as police reporter on the *Mansfield News*, and an unsuccessful attempt, together with his father, Charles Bromfield, and grandfather, Robert Coulter, to revitalize the family farm, Bromfield went first to Cornell to study agriculture and then to Columbia to study journalism. From Columbia, without graduating, he enlisted in the U.S. Army Ambulance Service in 1917. He served in seven major battles, received the Croix de Guerre, and took his discharge in France. However, he returned to New York, determined on a career as a writer. He married Mary Appleton Wood on 16 October 1921, and while working as a journalist in various capacities, he wrote and destroyed three novels. The fourth, *The Green Bay Tree*, published in 1924, was an immediate financial and critical success.

That novel not only drew on his Ohio and family background, as most of his successful novels and short stories were to do, but it also made clear the strong Jeffersonian idealism that was to dominate his fiction and his personal life to the end. After publishing *Possession*, his second novel, in 1925, he took his family to France, where they were to remain until war threats in 1938 precipitated their return to Ohio. In 1927 *Early Autumn* (1926) received the Pulitzer Prize. It was followed by *A Good Woman* (1927) and *The Strange Case of Miss Annie Spragg* (1928). The next year Bromfield published his first volume of short stories, *Awake and Rehearse*. Although criticism of his earlier works was almost uniformly favorable, this volume marked the beginning of a serious critical decline, resulting initially from charges of commercialism, from which his reputation has never recovered.

Although Bromfield published his first short story, "The Wedding Dress," in *Collier's* for 31 October 1925 and remained for the rest of his life a prolific contributor to *Cosmopolitan*, *Harper's Bazaar*, and other popular journals, he continued to be best known as a novelist (many of his novels appeared in serial or abridged forms in magazines) until his return to Ohio, when he became almost as noted as an experimental farmer and nature writer. Between 1925 and 1955 he published at least fifty stories in periodicals in addition to eighteen novels, as well as four volumes of short stories and one of novellas, three volumes of farm and nature lore, a number of sections of which are actually short stories, and two of economic theory, numerous articles and essays, and a regular newspaper column in the *Cleveland Plain Dealer* that was widely syndicated during the last decade of his life. He also wrote the screen story for *Brigham Young* (1940).

The sheer weight of his productivity, combined with charges of commercialism and, in the 1930s, led by the Marxist critics of the *New Republic*, charges that he had succumbed to reaction and later to Hollywood, has continued to obscure his accomplishments in the short-story form. Yet acknowledgment of his success in the form began early. "The Scarlet Woman," originally published in *McClure's* in January 1927, appeared in *The O. Henry Memorial Prize Stories of 1927* and was collected as "The Life of Vergie Winters" in *Awake and Rehearse*. It later became a successful motion picture. "The Cat That Lived at the Ritz," first published in *Harper's Bazaar* (October 1927), ap-

Bromfield in his U.S. Army Ambulance Service uniform, France, 1918

peared in *The Best Short Stories of 1928* and was collected in *Awake and Rehearse;* "The Apothecary," first published in *Cosmopolitan* (October 1928) as "The Skeleton at the Feast," appeared in *The O. Henry Memorial Prize Stories of 1928* and was collected in *Awake and Rehearse;* "Let's Go to Hinky-Dink's" was published in *McCall's* (September 1927) and appeared in *The World's Best Short Stories of 1928* and *Awake and Rehearse;* "Tabloid News," published in book form by Random House in 1930, was republished in *Cosmopolitan* (February 1931) and appeared in *The Best Short Stories of 1931;* "Crime Passionel," published in the *New Yorker* (25 March 1944), appeared in *The Best American Short Stories of 1945.*

Such a publication record suggests a great deal more distinction and accomplishment in the short-story form than most of Bromfield's critics, then and now, have been willing to concede. His short stories are closely related to his novels in setting, in character, and in theme. His stories are set in "the town," a thinly disguised Mansfield, Ohio; in New York; in Europe, among the interna-

tional smart set and expatriate Americans; or, increasingly in his last decades, in rural Ohio. In character, he often focuses upon the natural aristocrats to whom Thomas Jefferson had ascribed the nation's leadership in the eighteenth century. His themes are often drawn out of the conviction that industrialism, its origins in a curious combination of Puritanism and Hamiltonian economics, has distorted American values and driven the natural aristocrats into geographic, emotional, or psychological exile until they can ultimately restore sanity and meaning to human affairs.

In almost all of his stories, as in his novels, Bromfield focuses upon a central character, often a woman, and upon the interrelationships between that character and the social structure and values of the environment in which the character lives. Such a form, eminently suited to his novels, particularly *The Green Bay Tree, Early Autumn, The Strange Case of Miss Annie Spragg,* and *The Farm* (1933), the works upon which his reputation rests, is less suited to the short-story form, and in most of them one senses a larger story yet un-

Bromfield at work, 1925

told. Perhaps this is why one story, "The Three Faces in the Mirror," which appeared in *Cosmopolitan* (February 1935), was expanded into the novel *The Man Who Had Everything*, published later that year, and several, notably "The Skeleton at the Feast," "The Wedding Dress," "The Scarlet Woman," and "De luxe" (*Cosmopolitan*, December 1932), were extensively rewritten and retitled for later publication in collections.

However successful Bromfield's stories were when published in magazines, *Awake and Rehearse* marked the beginning of the decline of Bromfield's critical reputation because it permitted those who doubted his literary integrity to raise the charges of commercialism that are still directed at his work. The thirteen stories, nine of which appeared in magazines, are uneven at best, marked only by four distinctive stories, "The Life of Vergie Winters" (originally "The Scarlet Woman"), "The Life of Zenobia White" (originally "The Wedding Dress"), "The Apothecary" (originally "The Skeleton at the Feast"), and "Justice," essentially unrevised from its original publication in *Forum* (December 1925).

The best story in the collection is "The Life of Vergie Winters," combining a small-town setting, in which Bromfield was always most confident, and a strong female character as protagonist. With compassion and irony, Bromfield describes the lifetime affair of Vergie, a milliner in the town, and John Shadwell, a politician who becomes a political power. In spite of their discretion, rumors proliferate, and under the double standard of the town's values, Vergie is ostracized, while Shadwell's career advances. Although Vergie is forced to give up her daughter to adoption and indoctrination in the town's values, she is secure in her love. Eventually Shadwell dies, and Vergie lives on in her memories, until finally even the scandal is lost in the town's myth-ridden past, and only a monument to Shadwell remains in the square to stir old memories.

Not only is the portrait of Vergie sharp and sympathetic but Bromfield's depiction of the values and mores of the late-nineteenth-century midwestern town is accurate. Equally clear is his attitude, a curious mixture of revulsion at the impact of those values on human lives and regret at the passage of the closeness that they represent. Vergie is one of the best of Bromfield's long gallery of strong women; Shadwell, spiritually weak, is one of his typical men.

"The Life of Zenobia White" deals, less successfully and with less conviction, with a similar theme, while "The Apothecary," a sound story, deals with the subject matter with which Bromfield was becoming increasingly familiar and which he used with confidence in his novels begin-

Bromfield leading a tour of Malabar Farm, which he purchased in 1938 (Ferguson)

ning with *The Strange Case of Miss Annie Spragg*. It portrays the postwar international set of displaced, impoverished nobility, the new rich who had emerged from the war eager to trade money for position, and the attempts to exploit the innocence of a young American woman by an older American woman of dubious background who serves as the agent of the curious combination of people who are at once haves and have-nots.

"Justice" is an effective story written while Bromfield was reading John Galsworthy in 1925. Like Vergie Winters, the central character in this story is convicted by society and by the weakness of the narrator rather than the evidence. Its structure, however, prevents the intensity of "The Apothecary" and the compassionate depth of "The Life of Vergie Winters," and the closeness of the theme to Galsworthy's *Justice: A Tragedy in Four Acts* (1910) makes clear its origin.

The other stories in the collection, either previously unpublished–"Bavarian Idyll," "Aunt Milly Crosses the Bar," "Mr. Rosie and Max," and "Nigel"–or unrevised after periodical publication–"Let's Go to Hinky-Dink's," "The Letter of a Romantic" (first published as "A Romantic Letter," *Harper's Bazaar*, March 1929), "The Life of Louise Milbrook" (*Century*, February 1926), and "The Urn," (*Harper's Bazaar*, January 1928)– share the common faults of lack of depth and obvi-

ousness, suggesting Bromfield's attitude toward the short-story form. He regarded each as a tentative statement or an experiment rather than a final work, and subject matter, theme, or characters are often reworked in revised stories or novels. The collection, on the whole, was premature, the few first-rate stories insufficient to redeem it.

Bromfield's second collection of short fiction marks the beginning of his long, profitable association with *Cosmopolitan. Here Today and Gone Tomorrow*, published in 1934, contains four novellas, each of which had appeared in somewhat revised form and under different titles: "No. 55" ("Single Night," June 1932), "The Listener" (March 1934), "Fourteen Years After" ("De luxe," December 1932), and "Miss Mehaffy" ("Living In a Big Way," September 1933). The title of the collection suggests Bromfield's sense of irony at the subject matter of the four stories: each is determinedly contemporary in setting, tone, and plot, but the bootleggers, gamblers, and aimless expatriates of the early 1930s, portrayed as character types, were irrelevant at the time of book publication, as the Depression had intensified, and thus the collection provided more ammunition for Bromfield's critical enemies at the *Nation* and the *New Republic*. Nevertheless, each is a portrait, sharply if shallowly etched with irony, of the emptiness of post-World War I society and of the people caught up in it. "No. 55" is set in a Midtown Manhattan town house turned speakeasy, and the story has undertones of permanence perverted by puritan laws.

"The Listener" is the story of an elderly minister's daughter suddenly become wealthy who eavesdrops upon fashionable conversations, and, because of a slight, uses overheard information to destroy a boorish financier at the cost of her own fortune. "Fourteen Years After" takes place among fashionable people aboard a transatlantic liner. In "Miss Mehaffy," the best of the collection, the protagonist, a tearoom operator, visits her young woman friend in New York, outgambles a professional, hospitalizes a gangster by hitting him on the head with a bottle, and returns her protégé safely home.

The stories are ephemeral, and they share a common tediousness; the characters are caricatures, even Miss Mehaffy, who might have been one of Bromfield's strong women. Each of the stories might have provided the substance for a novel, but the stories as published in this collection, in spite of revisions, do not penetrate the surface of a superficial society. Ironically, this collection followed one of Bromfield's best and most enduring novels, *The Farm*, published the year before.

It Takes All Kinds (1939) was Bromfield's first book publication after his return to Ohio. It followed the strong novel *The Rains Came* (1937), set in India, and his *England: A Dying Oligarchy* (1939) and preceded the weaker *Night in Bombay* (1940). Like *Here Today and Gone Tomorrow*, it consists entirely of stories and novellas previously published in *Cosmopolitan*, and it is equally weak. The three novellas, "McLeod's Folly" ("You Get What You Give," July-November 1938), "Bitter Lotus" (January-May 1937), and "Better Than Life" ("And It All Came True," January 1936), are tedious stories that depend largely on trivial incidents and melodrama, although each has the potential of a serious story with depth and dramatic impact. The first, the story of a small-town newspaper's war with the local political machine, is violent, but it is easily resolved; "Bitter Lotus," according to Bromfield a technical experiment, takes characters from *The Rains Came*, places them in a different set of circumstances in an Indian setting, and allows them "to work out their destinies." "Better Than Life" describes the futile attempt of a New York gangster to turn an old boarding house into a nightclub.

The short stories–"New York Legend" (September 1935), "The Girl Who Knew Everybody" (September 1932), "Good Time Bessie" (March 1936), "That Which Returns" (September 1931), "Aunt Flora" (June 1933), and "The Hand of God" (September 1934)–are essentially untouched since magazine publication. In each, Bromfield attempts to capture a character in a moment of conflict with shallow contemporary values. Those who succumb become equally shallow; those who resist find love and human understanding. Only in "The Hand of God" do genuine mood and character emerge, but the motivating incident is not believable.

Perhaps Bromfield selected and published these stories at the time because in almost all of them, particularly in "The Hand of God," a house plays an important part: as focal point, as a reflection of personality, as a symbol of permanence in a changing world. At the time Bromfield was planning and building "The Big House" at Malabar Farm.

With the single exception of *Mrs. Parkington* (1943), all of Bromfield's novels between 1939 and 1944, the date of his next collection of short stories, are inferior to his earlier major works. Most had been serialized in *Cosmopolitan*, where he continued to publish short fiction. *The World We Live In* (1944) collects the shorter fiction written during those years, including, curiously, two of the best constructed, most believable novellas that Bromfield was to write. These works reflect Bromfield's concern with the war and the fate of people caught up in it, but in the background of several is the sense of purpose and fulfillment he found at Malabar Farm.

Of the nine stories in the collection, "The Old House" (first published as "The Wild Swan," *Cosmopolitan*, February 1943) and "Daughters of Mars" are superb. The former, set in an old house built upon Roman foundations on the southeast coast of England, is the story of a lonely woman who defies government bureaucracy and social forces that threaten her but eventually sacrifices the house and herself in an incident of war. The latter is the story of four old ladies, daughters of an expatriate former Confederate officer, forced to live under the German occupation of France as they attempt to maintain a dead tradition in the face of living horror.

"The Pond" (*Cosmopolitan*, August 1944), set on an Iowa farm and in the South Pacific, attempts a mysticism not unlike that in *The Strange Case of Miss Annie Spragg*, but it does not succeed;

Bromfield with his dogs at Malabar Farm (Joe Munroe)

"True Love" (*Cosmopolitan*, June 1944), a romance between a stage electrician and an unsuccessful actress, is not only pointless but unreal. "The Man Who Was in Love With Death" (first published as "These Two Alone . . . ," *Cosmopolitan*, June 1941) and "Thou Shalt Not Covet," the former a cloak-and-dagger story and the latter an indictment of Nazism, are simply weak and improbable.

Two other stories are stronger. "Death in Monte Carlo" (first published as "Twilight in Monte Carlo," *Cosmopolitan*, May 1941) is a study in contrasts between Mrs. Pulsifer, a strong American woman, and the Princess d'Orobelli, both caught up in the German occupation. While Mrs. Pulsifer exhausts herself—and dies—trying to save refugees, the Princess saves her jewels. In "The Great Facade" (*Cosmopolitan*, March 1944) a weak but appealing politician and his friend, a cripple, are destroyed by the foolishness behind the facade.

"Up Ferguson Way" (*Cosmopolitan*, December 1943) is perhaps the most interesting story in the collection. Bromfield is nearly successful in his attempt at constructing an Ohio myth, but his usual technical control is marred by meandering in his struggle to define the sense of identity with nature that marked his increasing concern with the land.

This collection of stories, combined with the weak longer work of the period, makes clear Bromfield's decreasing concern with writing fiction and his increasing interest in the land, a shift so obvious that it led him to say that he continued to write out of habit rather than involvement. When *Kenny*, containing three novellas, "Kenny" (*Cosmopolitan*, October 1946), "Retread" (*Cosmopolitan*, January-February 1945), and "The End of the Road" (*Cosmopolitan*, October 1944), appeared in 1947, followed by his last three novels, *Colorado* (1947), a Western spoof, *The Wild Country* (1948), the story of a twelve-year-old boy on the farm, and *Mr. Smith* (1951), essentially a tract, it was evident that habit was no longer enough. Bromfield's real interest and talent went into the deeply felt nature writing and folklore of *Pleasant Valley* (1945), *Malabar Farm* (1948), *Out of the Earth* (1950), and *Animals and Other People* (1955), while his indignation was spent in *A Few Brass Tacks* (1946) and *A New Pattern for a Tired World* (1954).

To assess Bromfield's short fiction without acknowledging his strengths in the Jeffersonian novels of his early years and the fine nature writing of his last is unfair, because his short fiction suffers inevitably as a result. One of the most prolific writers of this century, he was also one of the most highly regarded critically during his early years and one of the most widely criticized during the 1930s and 1940s, culminating in Edmund Wilson's 1 April 1944 *New Yorker* review of *What Became of Anna Bolton* (1944), entitled by Wilson "What Became of Louis Bromfield." While much of that criticism was philosophical in origin, much of it, too, had its origins in Bromfield's increasingly successful commercial fiction. Nevertheless, in most of his fiction, he wrote well, if too easily, and he told a story convincingly. If his short fiction often lacks profundity and conviction, if the characters are often facile and superficial, it is because Bromfield's talents were best suited to the broad character-based fiction that ranged across competing ideologies, resulting in effective and intelligent interpretations of American life in transition. In the short forms Bromfield often suggests a much larger story than that which he tells, and the resulting understatement is incomplete. Nevertheless, his literary canon, ranging from novels to plays to short stories and novellas, and culminating in the nature writing of his last years, is a substantial contribution to American literature in this century.

References:

David D. Anderson, *Louis Bromfield* (New York: Twayne, 1964);

Ellen Bromfield Geld, *The Heritage: A Daughter's Memories of Louis Bromfield* (New York: Harper, 1962).

Maxwell Struthers Burt

(18 October 1882-29 August 1954)

William P. Toth, Jr.
Bowling Green State University

BOOKS: *In the High Hills* (Boston & New York: Houghton Mifflin, 1914);

John O'May, and Other Stories (New York: Scribners, 1918);

Songs and Portraits (New York: Scribners, 1920);

Chance Encounters (New York: Scribners, 1921);

The Diary of a Dude Wrangler (New York & London: Scribners, 1924);

The Interpreter's House (New York: Scribners, 1924; London: Hodder & Stoughton, 1924);

When I Grow Up to Middle Age (New York: Scribners, 1925);

The Delectable Mountains (New York: Scribners, 1927; London: Hodder & Stoughton, 1927);

They Could Not Sleep (New York: Scribners, 1928);

The Other Side (New York & London: Scribners, 1928);

Festival (New York: Scribners, 1931; London: Peter Davies, 1931);

Entertaining the Islanders (New York: Scribners, 1933; London: Lovat Dickson, 1934);

Malice in Blunderland, With Apologies to Lewis Carroll, Whose Name Has So Often Been Taken in Vain (New York: Scribners, 1935);

Escape from America (New York & London: Scribners, 1936);

Powder River; Let'er Buck, Rivers of America Series (New York & Toronto: Farrar & Rinehart, 1938; London & New York: Rich & Gowan, 1947);

Along These Streets (New York: Scribners, 1942; London: Rich & Gowan, 1943);

War Songs (New York: Scribners, 1942);

Philadelphia, Holy Experiment (Garden City, N.Y.: Doubleday, Doran, 1945; London: Rich & Gowan, 1947).

Maxwell Struthers Burt (photograph by Doris Ulmann)

A frequent contributor to such high-quality magazines as *Scribner's, Harper's,* and the *Saturday Evening Post,* Maxwell Struthers Burt (who usually signed his works Struthers Burt) was a popular short-story writer, novelist, and occasional poet. A Princeton graduate, he deals invariably with the affluent and the genteel, yet he is a writer who is often equally concerned with the beauty and the romantic virtues of the American West. As a result, the reader finds in his works an interesting union of romantic individualism and the refined, orderly world of eastern society and tradition.

Burt was born in Baltimore on 18 October 1882, the son of Horace Brooke Burt, a lawyer, and Hester Ann Jones, but he stressed the fact that he was, in fact, a Philadelphian (he was taken to Philadelphia when he was six months old). Though there were six generations of American-Welsh Baptist ministers on his mother's side, one of his fondest boasts was of his paternal great-grandfather, Nathaniel, who, according to

Burt, "had been born an Irishman and somewhere in the late seventeen-hundreds, indulged in revolution and ruction of sorts, as Irishmen will, had been forced, to use a western expression, to leave Ireland 'between sundown and sunup.' " And though this great-grandfather eventually became a "hawk-eyed and successful merchant" in the bustling commercial cities of the eastern seaboard, Burt relished stories of this ancestor's fur-trading days, tales of his escapades into America's then-wild heartlands and of his encounters with such frontier heroes as Jim Bridger and "Old Tippecanoe" Harrison.

Burt once wrote that "Like a great many other Americans I have always had the West in my blood." Besides his great-grandfather, he was influenced early by an uncle who owned a ranch in California. During his visits east this uncle would regale young Maxwell with cowboy songs and stories of desperadoes and even taught him how to throw a rope.

Burt's precollegiate education was received in private schools in Philadelphia. He graduated in 1898, at age sixteen, and promptly landed a reporter's job on the *Philadelphia Times*. Col. Alexander McClure, a Civil War newspaperman and a former private secretary to Abraham Lincoln, was his editor. His first encouragement to write creatively came from his city editor, Philip Keats Speed, a great-grandnephew of poet John Keats. Thus his "finishing" school became the streets of Philadelphia where he wrote, in the then-fashionable mode of yellow journalism, about fires, suicides, and murders.

In 1900 he entered Princeton University, whose "honor-system and benign traditions" contrasted sharply with his raucous two years as a journalist. He somewhat facetiously claimed this venerable institution to be the "salvation" of his soul. At Princeton he was editor in chief of the *Tiger*, on the editorial board of two other undergraduate papers, and wrote two libretti for the *Triangle*.

After graduating in 1904 Burt spent a year in Germany at the University of Munich and eighteen months at Merton College, Oxford, where he met his future wife, Katherine Newlin, who would later also become a popular writer of western novels. This cosmopolitan experience very likely had an influence on the creation of the characters in his short stories, many of whom are either German or British. Burt once wrote revealingly about the national character traits of the students he had met: "English education devel-

ops a man as an individual; German education develops him as a unit of a multitude. That is why the English are thinkers and the German students are soldiers." Strongly patriotic, he often attacked German militarism, as in "Shining Armor" (*Harper's*, July 1919).

Burt's poetry began to appear in 1912 and his short stories in 1914, when he was thirty-two. He ascribed his comparatively late start to a belief that a creative writer needs experience and must earn a living before he can successfully begin a writing career. He met these personal prerequisites by spending two years as an English instructor at Princeton (1906-1908) and by then moving west to Jackson Hole, Wyoming, in 1908, where he obtained an option on a ranch. In 1912 he and a partner homesteaded the Bar BC ranch.

Burt's first important short story, "Water-Hole," appeared in the 15 July 1915 issue of *Scribner's* and was subsequently republished in *The Best Short Stories of 1915*. As in many of his tales, the protagonist, Hardy, is an intelligent adventurer, a wanderer just returned to civilization from the West. He is educated, refined, and yet willing to live and work in a hostile environment. He is a man who often gives his East Coast friends "a shock of color, as do the deserts and mountains he inhabited." The story, a frame tale, is recounted in a posh New York restaurant and revolves around both an ill-fated love affair and a doomed search for lost gold. The central symbol for the story, the water hole, takes on an ironic dimension: if Hardy saves the life of Jim Whitney, the antagonist, he then kills his chances for the success of his love affair. Critic Blanche Colton Williams wrote of "Water-Hole" that while its "surprise ending discloses apprenticeship" it is nevertheless a "sure product of the craftsman" and a "forerunner of other stories, nearly all of which combine the mountains and the plains of the West with the club life of the East."

The years between "Water-Hole" and Burt's first collection of short stories saw the birth of his two children, Nathaniel and Julia (both born on the Bar BC ranch), as well as a very brief stint by Burt in the Army Air Corps at the end of World War I. During this period much of Burt's time was still taken up with his ranching (which now included a dude ranch and a boy's ranch). Generally his seasonal business activities allowed him only four months of the year to concentrate on writing. Still, he managed to write enough short stories to have Scribners publish his first col-

CHANCE ENCOUNTERS

BY

MAXWELL STRUTHERS BURT
Author of "John O'May and Other Stories"

WITH A FRONTISPIECE BY
N. C. WYETH

NEW YORK
CHARLES SCRIBNER'S SONS
1921

Title page for the collection that includes Burt's 1920 O. Henry Memorial Award story "Each in His Generation"

lection, *John O'May, and Other Stories,* in 1918. In addition to "Water-Hole," it included another *Best Short Stories* entry: "A Cup of Tea" (*Scribner's,* July 1917).

Similar in construction to "Water-Hole," this story is made up of two interrelated frame tales. The first tale is related by Burnaby, another wanderer / adventurer who has just returned to the East from the West. While attending a dinner party, Burnaby relates an encounter with an Englishman, Geoffrey Boisselier Bewsher, who is living in squalor with the Indians. Another member of the dinner party, Sir John Masters, also an Englishman, knows Bewsher intimately and relates to the party how Bewsher came to fall (with his help) to the level that he now occupies. It is, like "Water-Hole," the story of an unfulfilled love affair and, in addition, a study in the effects of the clash between an older, more romantic, yet more gentlemanly world and the highly competitive modern industrial society.

Critical reaction to *John O'May* was generally enthusiastic. Burt's romantic characterization was singled out by most reviewers for special attention, with many seeing this as a positive aspect of the book, though the *New York Times* reviewer saw it otherwise: "Mr. Burt has chosen the wrong hero for his stories. Rather he has chosen the wrong time." Other reviewers noted his cleverness and his "fine competence of phrase," though he was mildly chided for not "staying clear of the current tricks of short story writers." His style was compared in the *Dial* to Katharine Gerould and Edith Wharton with their "air of keen and lucid detachment from . . . characters." And the *Nation* (although the review was generally positive) noted that Burt was "addicted . . . to the quasi-philosophical introductory dictum popularized by Kipling and O. Henry." Yet if he was seen to have affinities with the "tricks" and trends of popular magazine short-story writers, his stories were nevertheless regarded as above av-

Drawn by F. Walter Taylor

THE WAY LAY ALONG A TRAIL CUT INTO THE FACE OF A PRECIPICE

Illustrations for Burt's story "Buchanan Hears the Wind," published in the August 1921 issue of Harper's Magazine

Drawn by F. Walter Taylor

"SO MANY PEOPLE FIND LIFE ALWAYS A DILEMMA"

erage in the quality of their execution.

A closer look at the comparison of Burt to Wharton will perhaps help to clarify Burt's place in the American short-story tradition. It is much more than an "air of keen and lucid detachment" from characters that the two writers have in common. Both, of course, have eastern roots and often set their stories in an eastern milieu. But even more important, they are both concerned with social limitations. In dealing with these limitations, Wharton, unlike Burt, is often aligned with the school of social realism and with the literary techniques of psychological realism developed and articulated by Henry James. Burt also admired James (and Joseph Conrad as well) and, like so many other writers of this period, was involved in what Irving Howe describes as the "anxious and persistent search for values." But in most of his short stories Burt's ultimate solution to this problem aligns him with a much older tradition—that of romance—and gives him more of a kinship with a writer such as James Fenimore Cooper than with Wharton or James. There is, in his short stories, a glorification of the raw, essential qualities of the American spirit that, for Burt, arise out of the land itself: the freedom of the frontier, the grandeur of the mountains, the simplicity of the desert. This glorification leads to that sense of "something more"–be it Ultimate Beauty or Ultimate Love–that his characters often experience. The problem with this focus, however, is that it often approaches, or becomes, mere sentiment.

"Each in His Generation" (*Scribner's,* July 1920), the most notable story in Burt's second collection, *Chance Encounters* (1921), is an exception to this generality. The 1920 O. Henry Memorial Prize-winner, it is one of Burt's best stories, and the clearest example of how he could, on occasion, examine social limitations more in the manner of Wharton. The world of the 1920s, when most of Burt's finest short stories appeared, was a world far different from the world of 1900– when Burt was eighteen and entering Princeton. The conventions of decorum were under attack, there was a trend toward candor, and World War I had had an unsettling effect upon a whole generation. This clash of values is the theme of the story.

The setting is entirely East Coast; there is no wanderer from the West returning to the East. It is a story of contrasts between generations and between attitudes toward conventions. The primary contrast is between Henry Mc-

Cain–a member of the pre-1900 generation, affluent and highly proper–and his nephew, Adrian McCain, a journalist and a writer of political reviews and propaganda. Questions of divorce, extramarital affairs, and even attitudes toward war are blended skillfully in the narrative line. At the heart of the contrasts presented are the ideas of the openness of the new generation (the "roaring twenties") and the decorum and restraint of the older generation (pre-1900 Victorian). While it is too melodramatic to be considered a genuine tragedy of manners, "Each in His Generation" is an excellent story, one that never becomes maudlin.

In 1925 Burt managed to organize his business affairs so that he might spend all his time writing. Though he had already written a best-selling novel, *The Interpreter's House* (1924), which was later made into a movie entitled *I Want My Man,* and though he would continue to write novels, essays, poetry, and history until the mid 1940s, his last collection of short stories, *They Could Not Sleep,* appeared in 1928.

The *New York Times,* in its review of *They Could Not Sleep,* noted the narrative skill exhibited in the collection and rated the stories as above the ordinary run of magazine fare. The book has, in fact, a little bit of everything that Burt did well: fine passages of landscape description; well-crafted romance stories, such as "Buchanan Hears the Wind" (*Harper's,* August 1921), a tale which is also representative of Burt's oftenexpressed theme of the transcendental, almost mystical ideals of love and beauty; and topical stories, such as "The Man Who Grew a Beard" (*Hearst's International,* July 1923), which deals with America's reactions to the Communist revolution in Russia, and "C'est La Guerre" (*Saturday Evening Post,* 5 February 1927), a story concerned with reactions to the war.

During the 1930s Burt published two novels (*Festival,* 1931, and *Entertaining the Islanders,* 1933), a book of political satire (*Malice in Blunderland,* 1935), a collection of essays (*Escape from America,* 1936), and a book for the Rivers of America Series that might be best described as subjective history (*Powder River; Let'er Buck,* 1938)–a genre in which he excelled. His short stories continued to appear in popular magazines, though less frequently (only fourteen during the 1930s as compared to the thirty-seven published in the 1920s). In 1938, at the age of fifty-six, Burt sold his interest in the Bar BC and bought a smaller ranch. The following year there appeared in *Atlan-*

tic Monthly a short story written by Burt entitled "The Fawn" (April 1939). The narrator, who is fifty-six, is riding about his ranch, surveying the countryside and, in turn, the accomplishments of his life. The dramatic tension of the story is supplied by the narrator's sense of something following him–"nothing definitely frightening ... rather a wistfulness, a haunting." He is in love with the beauty surrounding him: the natural beauty of the country, the beauty of his wife and two children, the beauty of the life that he has created. In the end he realizes that the haunting presence, the presence which had been wistfully yet surely stalking him, is time itself.

During the 1940s Burt published only three stories. His last, "The Stuffed Shirt and the Lady," appeared in the 31 January 1948 issue of *Collier's*. In addition he published just one novel, *Along These Streets* (1942), a book of poetry, *War Songs* (1942), and another highly acclaimed subjective history, *Philadelphia, Holy Experiment* (1945). But as fiction and poetry publications dwindled, essays and reviews proliferated. Burt became a frequent contributor to several magazines, including the *Saturday Review of Literature,* in whose pages he became embroiled in two of the literary controversies of the period: one involving the awarding in 1949 of the Bollingen Prize in Poetry to Ezra Pound, and the other, in 1951, centering on the true working relationship between Scribners editor Maxwell Perkins and writer Thomas Wolfe. Burt was also a judge for the 1945 O. Henry Award as well as a contributor to the *World Book Encyclopedia* (he wrote the entry for the city of Philadelphia).

His health began to deteriorate during the 1950s, though he did write a few essays and reviews. In June of 1954, after returning from a fiftieth-anniversary class reunion at Princeton, Burt became ill and entered a hospital at Jackson Hole, Wyoming, where he died on 29 August 1954. His son, Nathaniel, wrote what is perhaps the best of all epitaphs for him: "He is buried in the graveyard above Jackson, a tangled place of aspens, weeds, and wildflowers, with a glimpse of the Tetons, the 'Delectable Mountains' that remained, after his family and friends, among all his various loves his first and last ones. It must certainly be of all burial places, the one he would have preferred."

Bibliography:

Alexander D. Wainwright, "A Check List of the Writings of Struthers Burt '04," *Princeton University Library Chronicle,* 19 (Spring 1958): 123.

References:

Charles C. Baldwin, *The Men Who Make Our Novels* (New York: Dodd, Mead, 1925);

Nathaniel Burt, "Struthers Burt '04: The Literary Career of a Princetonian," *Princeton University Library Chronicle,* 19 (Summer 1958): 109;

Blanche Colton Williams, *Our Short Story Writers* (New York: Moffatt, Yard, 1922).

Papers:

The majority of Burt's papers and manuscripts are in the Princeton University Library.

Erskine Caldwell

(17 December 1903-11 April 1987)

Rodney Simard
California State University, San Bernardino

See also the Caldwell entry in *DLB 9: American Novelists, 1910-1945.*

SELECTED BOOKS: *The Bastard* (New York: Heron Press, 1929);

Poor Fool (New York: Rariora Press, 1930);

American Earth (New York: Scribners, 1931; London: Secker, 1935; revised edition, New York: Duell, Sloan & Pearce, 1950); republished as *A Swell-Looking Girl* (New York: New American Library, 1950);

Tobacco Road (New York: Scribners, 1932; London: Cresset Press, 1933);

God's Little Acre (New York: Viking, 1933; London: Secker, 1933);

We Are the Living (New York: Viking, 1933; London: Secker, 1934);

Kneel to the Rising Sun and Other Stories (New York: Viking, 1935; London: Secker, 1935);

Journeyman (New York: Viking, 1935; revised, 1938; London: Secker & Warburg, 1938);

Some American People (New York: McBride, 1935);

Tenant Farmer (New York: Phalanx Press, 1935);

The Sacrilege of Alan Kent (Portland, Maine: Falmouth Book House, 1936);

You Have Seen Their Faces, text by Caldwell, photographs by Margaret Bourke-White (New York: Viking, 1937);

Southways (New York: Viking, 1938; London: Falcon Press, 1953);

North of the Danube, text by Caldwell, photographs by Bourke-White (New York: Viking, 1939);

Jackpot (New York: Duell, Sloan & Pearce, 1940; London: Falcon Press, 1950);

Trouble in July (New York: Duell, Sloan & Pearce, 1940; London: Cape, 1940);

Say, Is This the U.S.A., text by Caldwell, photographs by Bourke-White (New York: Duell, Sloan & Pearce, 1941);

All Night Long (New York: Duell, Sloan & Pearce, 1942; London, Toronto, Melbourne & Sydney: Cassell, 1943);

Erskine Caldwell, portrait by Margaret Bourke-White inscribed by the author (courtesy of Roger B. White)

All-Out on the Road to Smolensk (New York: Duell, Sloan & Pearce, 1942);

Moscow Under Fire (London, New York & Melbourne: Hutchinson, 1942);

Russia at War, text by Caldwell, photographs and introduction by Bourke-White (London, New York & Melbourne: Hutchinson, 1942);

Georgia Boy (New York: Duell, Sloan & Pearce, 1943; London: Falcon Press, 1947); enlarged as *Georgia Boy, and Other Stories* (New York: Avon, 1946);

Tragic Ground (New York: Duell, Sloan & Pearce, 1944; London: Falcon Press, 1947);

The Stories of Erskine Caldwell, edited by Henry Seidel Canby (New York: Duell, Sloan & Pearce, 1944);

A House in the Uplands (New York: Duell, Sloan & Pearce, 1946; London: Falcon Press, 1947);

The Caldwell Caravan (Cleveland & New York: World, 1946);

The Sure Hand of God (New York: Duell, Sloan & Pearce, 1947; London: Falcon Press, 1948);

The Pocket Book of Erskine Caldwell Stories, edited by Canby (New York: Pocket Books, 1947);

This Very Earth (New York: Duell, Sloan & Pearce, 1948; London: Falcon Press, 1949);

Midsummer Passion, and Other Stories (New York: Avon, 1948);

Where the Girls Were Different, and Other Stories (New York: Avon, 1948);

A Woman in the House (New York: New American Library, 1949);

Place Called Estherville (New York: Duell, Sloan & Pearce, 1949; London: Falcon Press, 1950);

Episode in Palmetto (New York: Duell, Sloan & Pearce, 1950; London: Falcon Press, 1951);

Call It Experience (New York: Duell, Sloan & Pearce, 1951; London: Hutchinson, 1952);

The Humorous Side of Erskine Caldwell, edited by Robert Cantwell (New York: Duell, Sloan & Pearce, 1951);

A Lamp for Nightfall (New York: Duell, Sloan & Pearce / Boston: Little, Brown, 1952; London: Falcon Press, 1952);

The Courting of Susie Brown (New York: Duell, Sloan & Pearce / Boston: Little, Brown, 1952; London: Falcon Press, 1952);

The Complete Stories of Erskine Caldwell (New York: Duell, Sloan & Pearce / Boston: Little, Brown, 1953);

Love and Money (New York: Duell, Sloan & Pearce / Boston & Toronto: Little, Brown, 1954; Melbourne, London & Toronto: Heinemann, 1955);

Gretta (Boston & Toronto: Little, Brown, 1955; Melbourne, London & Toronto: Heinemann, 1956);

Gulf Coast Stories (Boston & Toronto: Little, Brown, 1956; Melbourne, London & Toronto: Heinemann, 1957);

Certain Women (Boston & Toronto: Little, Brown, 1957; London, Melbourne & Toronto: Heinemann, 1958);

Claudelle Inglish (Boston & Toronto: Little, Brown, 1958); republished as *Claudelle* (London, Melbourne & Toronto: Heinemann, 1959);

Caldwell and his mother in Prosperity, South Carolina, in 1908 (by permission of Virginia Caldwell)

Molly Cottontail (Boston & Toronto: Little, Brown, 1958; London, Melbourne & Toronto: Heinemann, 1959);

When You Think of Me (Boston & Toronto: Little, Brown, 1959; London, Melbourne & Toronto: Heinemann, 1960);

Jenny By Nature (New York: Farrar, Straus & Cudahy, 1961; London, Melbourne & Toronto: Heinemann, 1961);

Erskine Caldwell's Men and Women, edited by Carvel Collins (Boston & Toronto: Little, Brown, 1961);

Close to Home (New York: Farrar, Straus & Cudahy, 1962; London, Melbourne & Toronto: Heinemann, 1962);

The Bastard and Poor Fool (London: Bodley Head, 1963);

The Last Night of Summer (New York: Farrar, Straus, 1963; London: Heinemann, 1963);

Around About America (New York: Farrar, Straus, 1964; London: Heinemann, 1964);

In Search of Bisco (New York: Farrar, Straus & Giroux, 1965; London: Heinemann, 1965);

The Deer at Our House (New York: Collier / London: Collier-Macmillan, 1966);

In the Shadow of the Steeple (London: Heinemann, 1967);

Miss Mamma Aimee (New York: New American Library, 1967; London: Joseph, 1968);

Writing in America (New York: Phaedra, 1967);

Deep South (New York: Weybright & Talley, 1968);

Summertime Island (New York & Cleveland: World, 1968; London: Joseph, 1969);

The Weather Shelter (New York & Cleveland: World, 1969; London: Joseph, 1970);

The Earnshaw Neighborhood (New York: World, 1971; London: Joseph, 1972);

Annette (New York: New American Library, 1973; London: Joseph, 1974);

Afternoons in Mid-America (New York: Dodd, Mead, 1976);

Stories of Life, North & South (New York: Dodd, Mead, 1983);

The Black & White Stories of Erskine Caldwell, edited by Ray McIver (Atlanta: Peachtree, 1984);

With All My Might (Atlanta: Peachtree, 1987).

RECORDING: "Naturalism in the American Novel," McGraw-Hill Sound Seminars, Tucson, 1950.

The son of Ira S. Caldwell, a Presbyterian minister, and Caroline Preston Bell, a schoolteacher, Erskine Caldwell was born in White Oak, Georgia, and because of the expediencies of his father's profession, the family moved often, living in various places in the Deep South. Tutored at home by his mother in his childhood, he attended high school in Wrens, Georgia, before going on to Erskine College in Due West, South Carolina, the University of Pennsylvania, and the University of Virginia. He left the last institution, however, without a degree in 1925 to become a newspaper reporter for the *Atlanta Journal*. That same year he married Helen Lannegan, by whom he had three children. In 1926 the family moved to Maine in order for Caldwell to devote himself to a writing career. In 1932 he achieved his first real literary success with his third novel, *Tobacco Road*, but the book did not become a best-seller until after its highly successful dramatization by James Kirkland. With his next novel, *God's Little Acre* (1933), Caldwell became firmly established as a promising young writer. In 1935 he began his collaborations with photographer Margaret Bourke-White, whom he married in 1939, one year after his divorce from Lannegan (Caldwell and Bourke-White were divorced in 1942). After teaching at the New School for Social Research in 1938, he began a four-year period as a traveling newspaper correspondent, visiting and reporting on such diverse places as Mexico, Spain, Czechoslovakia, China, Mongolia, Turkestan, and Russia. From 1941 to 1955 Caldwell edited the American Folkways series of regional books. He married June Johnson in 1942 (divorced 1956), had one son, and in 1957 married Virginia Fletcher. He died in 1987 of lung cancer.

After his sale of "Midsummer Passion" to *The New American Caravan* in 1929 (the story also appeared as "July" in *transition*), Caldwell produced well over a hundred short stories by the early 1940s and was chiefly known as a short-fiction writer. And although his story production dropped off sharply after that decade in favor of the novel, he remarked as late as 1958 that "I don't think there is anything to compare with the short story. I think it's the best form of writing there is." A prolific novelist, Caldwell is perhaps best known for *Tobacco Road* and *God's Little Acre*, which are actually long stories or novellas; he can be most profitably assessed as the author of numerous volumes of short stories, of which James Korges has noted, "one could make a collection of twenty-five of Caldwell's stories which would reveal his talent and which would be a minor classic of American literature, standing in relation to the giant works of our literature much as a selection of de Maupassant's stands in relation to French fiction." Caldwell's stories are ambitiously experimental in both concerns and techniques. His primary technical device is repetition, employed for a wide range of effects, and through this technique he shows an acute awareness of both the American literary tradition and the experiments of his contemporaries.

"Midsummer Passion" (collected in *American Earth*, 1931) is representative of Caldwell's earlier character sketches. Reminiscent of D. H. Lawrence, the brief story describes middle-aged Ben Hackett's attempt to rape Fred Williams's wife symbolically by forcing a pair of found "drawers" on her. The characters are people of the land, and their earthiness is reinforced by the eroticism that suffuses their lives in repressed and ex-

Wood engravings by Ralph Frizzell for Caldwell's 1936 book The Sacrilege of Alan Kent. *This volume has been variously described as a novel or as a collection of short stories.*

Caldwell and his second wife, Margaret Bourke-White, on board a British convoy ship, 1941 (by permission of Virginia Caldwell)

plosive passion, an aspect of Caldwell's writing that helped make his novels controversial best-sellers, and which contributed much to his best fiction, notably the stories and *God's Little Acre*. The story also introduces a motif that runs throughout the Caldwell canon: those associated with the land possess a primal vitality that, by virtue of direction, can be either bestial or transcendent, depending on the basic character of the individual.

In "Saturday Afternoon" (collected in *Midsummer Passion, and Other Stories*, 1948) Caldwell presents the lynching of Will Maxie, a black man hated by the white community because of his intelligence, industry, and prosperity. Narrated from the point of view of the butcher, Tom Denny, the brutal murder becomes only an interlude in the ordinary pattern of this small southern town. Caldwell underscores the inhumanity of both the act and the community by the complacence with which the killing is received by the townsfolk, a device he returns to many times. The selling of Coca-Colas in this story, a prosaic and economic note in the horror of the narrative, demonstrates one of his major uses of repetition. By making Denny fixated on the economic rather than the moral, Caldwell makes the story essentially dramatic, for the butcher's absorption represents and demonstrates his self-serving single-mindedness, his limited range of understanding and perception, and his immovability. The triviality of his insistence

on the cold drinks rather than the outrage he complacently participates in heightens the importance of an essential yet unspoken subtext.

This type of repetition, which can represent fixation, limited awareness, and mounting hysteria or passion, complements the scant dialogue in Caldwell's works. Such a work as *Tobacco Road* has been described as a novel of silence, for several of the main characters do not speak. This silence, which is evident in many of the stories as well, functions to underscore the essential isolation of the characters and the interior, disjointed nature of their lives. Similarly, silence suggests inarticulation, and it represents the importance of what is left unsaid, for silence frequently glosses over pain and suffering, confusion, the threat of physical violence, or a refusal to deal with moral or intellectual complexities. The stories are often largely interior monologues related from a single perspective, and repetition in them, particularly the repetition of a seemingly irrelevant or absurd detail, highlights what is left unspoken or unthought. By emphasizing the trivial, Caldwell heightens the important issues implicit in the stories while remaining essentially objective to his material. His unadorned prose reflects the intellectual and cultural conditions of his characters, at the same time forcing the reader to become an active participant in the world of the story. Caldwell refuses to draw conclusions about the events he narrates, requiring the reader to provide moral and ethical judgments. His method of writing has been described as composition-as-discovery, for he seemed to begin a story with no knowledge of its conclusion. In this regard, his method paralleled the effect of any story, for he created the experience for the reader, upon whom the burden of responsibility must fall for assigning value and meaning. In this regard Caldwell anticipates the experimentation that came to dominate post-World War II fiction.

The sensitivity inherent in his objective presentation is clearly evident in "The Mating of Marjorie" (*Scribner's Magazine*, June 1930; collected in *American Earth*), a story with scant dialogue told from a woman's perspective. Despite the sensational eroticism traditionally associated with Caldwell's work, his portrayal of women is both sympathetic and intelligent; while his female characters often have primal, Lawrentian overtones, as in *God's Little Acre*, they are always formidable human beings in their own right, equals to their men by force of character if not by prevailing social standards. In this story Caldwell presents a sympathetic and sensitive picture of a woman rejected by a prospective husband, and while the author remains objective to his material, his indictment of the social forces that have compromised Marjorie is clear to the reader. Another characteristic aspect of this sensitivity is evident in "Where the Girls Were Different" (collected in *American Earth*), one of Caldwell's stories of adolescence. His account of his young hero Fred as he comes of age is marked by the repetition of the title phrase, representing erotic fixation. As in his treatment of women, Caldwell is psychologically acute in his portrayal of youth, accurately chronicling the indecision and inadequacies of a young man searching for himself.

"Dorothy" (*Scribner's Magazine*, April 1931; collected in *Georgia Boy, and Other Stories*, 1946), which was included in *The Best Short Stories of 1931*, combines many of these elements in its description of a young man's attempt to deal with his guilt over sending the title character to work in a bordello. The narrator meets the strange girl on an Atlanta street and acts as the deciding factor for what they both know is inevitable, and the story is the man's attempt to deal with the guilt he feels while vainly trying to escape his role in Dorothy's fate. Similarly, "After-Image" (collected in *We Are the Living*, 1933) is a complex psychological account of another unnamed narrator's attempt to make sense of the suicide of an

Caldwell as a war correspondent, Moscow, 1941 (by permission of Virginia Caldwell)

abandoned woman with whom he has had a brief but intense relationship, and, as in the earlier story, both the male and female perspectives are sensitively, yet inconclusively, presented. In yet another story representative of this approach Caldwell is less impressionistic; "Warm River" (collected in *We Are the Living*) presents a pair of old friends, Richard and Gretchen, who anguish through their own self-doubts to a realization of their mutual love. Significantly, the man in this story is the one who undergoes the more radical change as he comes to understand that men can love as women do, and that marriage represents fundamental equality.

In "Country Full of Swedes" (*Yale Review*, December 1932; collected in *The Stories of Erskine Caldwell*, 1944), which was included in *O. Henry Memorial Award Prize Stories of 1933*, one can see another, no less characteristic aspect of Caldwell's short fiction, his humor. Set in Maine rather than the South, this story deals with the prejudice the Frosts feel for their neighbors, a family of Swedes, as viewed by their more enlightened farmhand, Stan. Repetition is clearly evident in this story as the hysteria of prejudice mounts, only to be undercut by the benign and virtually slapstick actions of the feared foreigners, who want nothing more than to corral their wayward cats and children. The boisterous, situational humor of this story can be seen as a counterpoint to the humor inherent in a character study such as "Horse Thief" (collected in *Kneel to the Rising Sun and Other Stories*, 1935). A more gentle humor is at work in this account of a young man who is accused of horse theft for having mistaken the horse of his girlfriend's father for his own, after stealing away from a forbidden visit to her in the dark of the night. Heroically he refuses to explain the farcical events in this comedy of mistaken identity in order to preserve the girl's reputation. The reader is both amused and in sympathy with the young man's plight, which has none of the malignant overtones so often evident in Caldwell's treatment of similar situations. "Horse Thief" was included in *The Best Short Stories of 1934*.

A young wife's fears, self-doubts, and socially induced sense of racial division are explored in "Yellow Girl" (collected in *The Pocket Book of Erskine Caldwell Stories*, 1947), another character sketch, significant for its perceptive psychological treatment of one woman's first encounter with the possibility of miscegenation. And in "Maud Island" (collected in *Kneel to the Rising Sun and Other Stories*), included in *O. Henry Memorial Award Prize Stories of 1934*, young Milt comes one step closer to adulthood as he witnesses his religious uncle's lust for a pair of city women who intrude on the men's fishing trip. This sort of account of a boy's coming of age on the Mississippi River clearly points to some of the qualities that have led several critics to suggest that Caldwell is a spiritual heir of Mark Twain.

Another group of Caldwell's stories reveals a no less perceptive and sensitive but far more cynical and accusatory vision of life. His "Kneel to the Rising Sun" (*Scribner's Magazine*, February 1935; collected in *Kneel to the Rising Sun and Other Stories*) is Caldwell's indictment of human brutality. This often-praised story is the account of the evil and malignant Arch Gunnard and his inhuman treatment of his black sharecroppers, as narrated from the perspective of always-hungry Lonnie, who helplessly watches as Gunnard cuts off his dog's tail and who finds his father eaten by Gunnard's hogs. The reader shares in Lonnie's frustration and moral confusion as he becomes a party to the murder of the courageous

Clem Henry, whose only crime is his virtue. The reader's sense of indignation that arises from this story is also generated by "Candy-Man Beechum" (collected in *Kneel to the Rising Sun and Other Stories*). The heroically proportioned title character's unwarranted detention by the unjustifiably suspicious white sheriff is mitigated morally only by the final impression that the black man will avenge the indignity of his treatment before he dies. A similar cynicism about human nature is central to "Man and Woman" (collected in *The Stories of Erskine Caldwell*). This story, which was included in *O. Henry Memorial Award Prize Stories of 1939*, portrays the mistreatment of an ill and grief-stricken couple traveling to the grave of their dead child by a self-righteous and unfeeling woman at whose house they stop for food. And the pathos of the plight of the characters in "The People v. Abe Latham, Colored" (collected in *Jackpot*, 1940) is also representative of this aspect of Caldwell's vision. The reader develops a sympathy for Uncle Abe due to the mistreatment and frustration he and his family suffer as they vainly try to meet their eviction from Luther Bolick's farm.

Like the earlier work *The Sacrilege of Alan Kent* (1936), Caldwell's *Georgia Boy* (1943) is seen by some critics as a novel and by others as a collection of short stories. Nonetheless, the work can be profitably approached as a group of interrelated stories concerning the fortunes of the Stroup family and their servant, Handsome Brown. Representative of the collection is "My Old Man's Baling Machine," a domestic comedy about Martha Stroup's exasperation with her husband Morris, and his purchase of a paper baling machine, into which he tosses her hymnals and love letters in his enthusiasm for quick profits. Narrated by young Williams, the story is a humorous treatment of adults' foibles as perceived by an adolescent, and as a collection the stories have often been praised and admired. One of Caldwell's later stories, "Soquots" (collected in *Gulf Coast Stories*, 1956), is in a similar vein; a domestic farce, the work recounts Pete Ellrod's successful maneuvers to drive away his wife's freeloading cousin, Oscar Strude.

Any brief survey of Caldwell's work cannot give an accurate impression of the texture and wide range of his variations on essentially simple themes. Many topics and techniques are found in multiple treatments, as in the technical accomplishment of "A Swell-Looking Girl" (collected in *American Earth*), wherein repetition is used simultane-

Caldwell at his home in Dunedin, Florida, 1971 (by permission of Virginia Caldwell)

ously to suggest limited self-perception and mounting eroticism. Both "Joe Craddock's Old Woman" (1929; collected in *American Earth*) and "Handy" (*New Republic*, 23 September 1940; collected in *Jackpot*), which was included in *The Best Short Stories of 1941*, are poignant and masterful character studies. Such works as "The First Autumn" (collected in *We Are the Living*), a story about a father's death as witnessed by two small children that was included in *The Best Short Stories of 1933*, and "The Fly in the Coffin" (collected in *Southways*, 1938), an account of a dead man's rising from his coffin to swat a fly, provide examples of Caldwell's ability to construct parables and other folkloric tales. Although relatively limited in thematic scope, Caldwell's stories are all interesting in their individual diversity.

Through the course of his productive literary career Caldwell remained true to the same concerns and issues, cloaking his fiction in issues that were perhaps topically germane to the early decades of this century but always dealing in the timeless qualities of individuals and the society they have created. In all his work he displays a sense of compassionate humanity, unbridled by sexual, economic, and racial barriers. As a novelist Caldwell may be accurately regarded as second to the masters of the genre; however, as a short-story writer, his accomplishments rival those of any American literary figure. Technically innovative and psychologically acute, the stories are now be-

ginning to be recognized for their rightful value and are guaranteed a significant position in the development of the American short story.

Interviews:

Carvel Collins, "Erskine Caldwell at Work," *Atlantic*, 202 (July 1958): 21-27;

Morris Renek, "Sex Was Their Way of Life: A Frank Interview with Erskine Caldwell," *Cavalier*, 14 (March 1964): 13-16, 40-42;

Alan Lelchuk and Robin White, "An Interview with Erskine Caldwell," *Per / Se*, 2 (Spring 1967): 11-20;

Richard B. Sale, "An Interview in Florida with Erskine Caldwell," *Studies in the Novel*, 3 (Fall 1971): 316-331;

Jac Lyndon Tharpe, *Interview with Mr. Erskine Caldwell, Eminent American Author*, Mississippi Oral History Program, 13 (Hattiesburg: University of Southern Mississippi, 1973).

References:

Kenneth Burke, "Caldwell: Maker of Grotesques," in *The Philosophy of Literary Form*, third edition (Berkeley: University of California Press, 1973), pp. 350-360;

Henry Seidel Canby, Introduction to *The Pocket Book of Erskine Caldwell Stories* (New York: Pocket Books, 1947), pp. vii-xvi;

Caldwell and his third wife, Virginia Fletcher Caldwell, in Paris, 1979 (by permission of Virginia Caldwell)

Robert Cantwell, Introduction to *The Humorous Side of Erskine Caldwell* (New York: Duell, Sloan & Pearce, 1951);

Malcolm Cowley, "Georgia Boy: A Retrospect of Erskine Caldwell," in *Pages*, edited by Matthew J. Bruccoli and C. E. Frazer Clark, Jr. (Detroit: Gale, 1976), pp. 62-78;

Louise Y. Gossett, *Violence in Recent Southern Fiction* (Durham: Duke University Press, 1965);

R. J. Gray, "Southwestern Humor, Erskine Caldwell, and the Comedy of Frustration," *Southern Literary Journal*, 8 (Fall 1975): 3-26;

James Korges, *Erskine Caldwell* (Minneapolis: University of Minnesota Press, 1969);

Scott MacDonald, "An Evaluative Check-List of Erskine Caldwell's Short Fiction," *Studies in Short Fiction*, 15 (Winter 1978): 81-97;

MacDonald, "Repetition as Technique in the Short Stories of Erskine Caldwell," *Studies in American Fiction*, 5 (Autumn 1978): 213-225;

John MacLachlan, "Folk and Culture in the Novels of Erskine Caldwell," *Southern Folklore Quarterly*, 9 (January 1945): 93-101.

Papers:

Dartmouth College, the University of Virginia, and the University of Georgia all have holdings of Caldwell materials.

Irvin S. Cobb

(23 June 1876-10 March 1944)

Wade Hall
Bellarmine College

See also the Cobb entries in *DLB 11: American Humorists, 1880-1950* and *DLB 25: American Newspaper Journalists, 1901-1925.*

BOOKS: *Cobb's Anatomy: A Guide to Humor* (New York: Doran, 1912; London: Hodder & Stoughton, 1915);

Back Home; Being the Narrative of Judge Priest and His People (New York: Doran, 1912; London: Heinemann, 1912);

Cobb's Bill-of-Fare (New York: Doran, 1913; London: Hodder & Stoughton, 1915);

The Escape of Mr. Trimm: His Plight and Other Plights (New York: Doran, 1913; London: Hodder & Stoughton, 1914);

Europe Revised (New York: Doran, 1914);

Roughing It De Luxe (New York: Doran, 1914);

"Speaking of Operations—" (Garden City, N.Y.: Doubleday, 1915; London: Hodder & Stoughton, 1916);

Paths of Glory: Impressions of War Written At and Near the Front (New York: Doran, 1915); expanded and republished as *The Red Glutton: Impressions of War Written at and near the Front* (London & New York: Hodder & Stoughton, 1915);

Fibble, D. D. (New York: Doran, 1916);

Local Color (New York: Doran, 1916);

Old Judge Priest (New York: Doran, 1916; London: Hodder & Stoughton, 1916);

Those Times and These (New York: Doran, 1917; London: Brentano, 1927);

"Speaking of Prussians—" (New York: Doran, 1917);

Lost Tribes of the Irish in the South (New York: American Irish Historical Society, 1917);

The Thunders of Silence (New York: Doran, 1918);

The Glory of the Coming: What Mine Eyes Have Seen of Americans in Action in this Year of Grace and Allied Endeavor (New York: Doran, 1918; London: Hodder & Stoughton, 1919);

Life of the Party (New York: Doran, 1919);

Eating in Two or Three Languages (New York: Do-

Irvin S. Cobb

ran, 1919; London: Hodder & Stoughton, 1919);

"Oh Well, You Know How Women Are!" (New York: Doran, 1919);

The Abandoned Farmers (New York: Doran, 1920);

From Place to Place (New York: Doran, 1920);

A Plea for Old Cap Collier (New York: Doran, 1921);

One Third Off (New York: Doran, 1921);

J. Poindexter, Colored (New York: Doran, 1922);

Sundry Accounts (New York: Doran, 1922);

Stickfuls; Compositions of a Newspaper Minion (New York: Doran, 1923);

A Laugh a Day Keeps the Doctor Away (New York: Doran, 1923; London: Hodder & Stoughton, 1924);

Snake Doctor, and Other Stories (New York: Doran, 1923);

Irvin Cobb at His Best (Garden City, N.Y.: Sun Dial Press, 1923);

Goin' on Fourteen: Being Cross-sections out of a Year in the Life of an Average Boy (New York: Doran, 1924);

Indiana: Cobb's America Guyed Books (New York: Doran, 1924);

Kansas: Cobb's America Guyed Books (New York: Doran, 1924);

Kentucky: Cobb's America Guyed Books (New York: Doran, 1924);

Maine: Cobb's America Guyed Books (New York: Doran, 1924);

New York: Cobb's America Guyed Books (New York: Doran, 1924);

North Carolina: Cobb's America Guyed Books (New York: Doran, 1924);

Alias Ben Alibi (New York: Doran, 1925);

"Here Comes the Bride—" and So Forth (New York: Doran, 1925);

Many Laughs for Many Days (New York: Doran, 1925; London: Hodder & Stoughton, 1925);

On an Island That Cost $24.00 (New York: Doran, 1926);

Prose and Cons (New York: Doran, 1926);

Some United States: A Series of Stops in Various Parts of this Nation with One Excursion across the Line (New York: Doran, 1926);

Chivalry Peak (New York: Cosmopolitan, 1927; London: Hodder & Stoughton, 1928);

Ladies and Gentlemen (New York: Cosmopolitan, 1927; London: Hodder & Stoughton, 1927);

All Aboard: Saga of the Romantic River (New York: Cosmopolitan, 1928);

Red Likker (New York: Cosmopolitan, 1929; London: Jarrolds, 1930);

This Man's World (New York: Cosmopolitan, 1929; London: Brentano, 1929);

To Be Taken before Sailing (New York: Cosmopolitan, 1930);

Both Sides of the Street (New York: Cosmopolitan, 1930);

Incredible Truth (New York: Cosmopolitan, 1931);

Down Yonder with Judge Priest and Irvin S. Cobb (New York: Long & Smith, 1932);

Murder Day by Day (Indianapolis: Bobbs-Merrill, 1933);

One Way to Stop a Panic (New York: McBride, 1933);

Faith, Hope and Charity (Indianapolis & New York: Bobbs-Merrill, 1934);

Judge Priest Turns Detective (Indianapolis & New York: Bobbs-Merrill, 1937);

Azam, the Story of an Arabian Colt and His Friends (New York: Rand, 1937);

Favorite Humorous Stories of Irvin Cobb (New York: Triangle Books, 1940);

Glory, Glory Hallelujah (Indianapolis: Bobbs-Merrill, 1941);

Exit Laughing (Indianapolis & New York: Bobbs-Merrill, 1941);

Roll Call (Indianapolis & New York: Bobbs-Merrill, 1942);

Cobb's Cavalcade (New York: World, 1945).

Irvin S. Cobb was a literary man of all trades: short-story writer, novelist, journalist, war correspondent, playwright, essayist, raconteur, and actor. Born to Joshua Clark Cobb and Manie Saunders Cobb in Paducah, Kentucky, on 23 June 1876, he was a prolific and successful author whose more than three hundred short stories and sixty books made him one of the highest paid writers of his time. In 1925 magazines were paying up to four thousand dollars for each of his short stories. He was frequently represented in the annual *O. Henry Memorial Award Prize Stories* volumes. In 1929 his stories were reprinted in nine anthologies of short-story classics. Like his friend humorist Will Rogers, he was a famous public figure. His portly build, bushy eyebrows, multiple chins, and ever-present cigar made him a favorite subject for cartoonists.

Because of family financial troubles, Cobb was forced to leave school at sixteen. He worked briefly on an ice wagon, then started as a cub reporter without pay on the *Paducah Evening News*, where at nineteen he was made managing editor. After working for the *Louisville Evening Post* for a year and a half, he returned to his hometown to edit the *Paducah Democrat*. In 1900 he married Laura Spencer Baker of Savannah, Georgia, who urged him to try his fortune in New York. In August 1904 he took his wife and infant daughter to Mrs. Cobb's parents, borrowed two hundred dollars from his father-in-law, and headed for fame and fortune in the big city. It was not long in coming, but it took some plotting on his part. After spending two weeks in fruitless search for a job and seeing his borrowed finances shrink to three dollars, he devised a stratagem that Benja-

Cobb, circa 1915, as a war correspondent for the Saturday Evening Post

opportunity to present his qualifications in person. He concluded: "A modest appreciation of my worth forbids me doing business with your office boy any longer."

From the five offers of work he received, he accepted a job with the *Evening Sun*. His first important assignment was reporting the Russo-Japanese peace conference in 1905. He later moved to the *Evening World*, where he enhanced his reputation as a reporter with his coverage of the sensational trial of Harry K. Thaw, accused of murdering architect Stanford White. After twenty years of newspaper work, he became a staff contributor to the *Saturday Evening Post*. In 1913 his first visit to Europe resulted in eleven articles in the *Post* under the title "An American Vandal," and in 1914 he made the first of two trips abroad as a war correspondent.

Cobb's work appeared chiefly in the *Post* until the fall of 1922, when he began publishing in *Cosmopolitan Magazine*, to which he contributed regularly for over a decade. He supplemented his writing income on the lecture circuit and with cameo appearances in silent movies.

In 1934 filmmaker Hal Roach invited Cobb to Hollywood. There he made a number of short comedies and several full-length films, including *Steamboat Round the Bend* (1935), in which he starred with Will Rogers. He died in New York on 10 March 1944.

Cobb wrote about a broad range of subjects, and though many of his stories have urban settings, his most popular and significant work was based on anecdotes and incidents from his early life in Kentucky. Many of the characters in his stories are based on people he knew as a boy: doctors, lawyers, merchants, ministers, and black servants. His most popular creation, Judge William Pitman Priest, is a portrait of Judge William Pitman Bishop (1839-1902), a prominent west Kentucky circuit judge. Cobb's first short-story collection, *Back Home; Being the Narrative of Judge Priest and His People* (1912), comprises Kentucky local-color tales originally published in the *Saturday Evening Post*. In the preface Cobb states that the book consists of "a series of pictures, out of the life of a town in the western part of Kentucky." He wrote the "pictures," he asserts, to correct the errors of others who portray southerners as either "venerable and fiery colonels" living "in a feudal state of shabby grandeur and proud poverty on a plantation gone to seed" or as "snuff-dipping" white trash. In this book he intended "to describe what I believe to be an average south-

min Franklin would surely have approved. In the factual but flippant style that was to become his hallmark, Cobb sent identical letters to the editors of thirteen leading New York papers, informing them that he was tired "of studying the wallpaper designs" in their outer offices and wanted an

Cobb, circa 1926, with his mother, Manie Saunders Cobb, and his sister, Reubie Cobb (by permission of Paducah Public Library)

ern community so that others might see it as I had seen it."

The "accuracy" of Cobb's home-based fiction has often been questioned, but its popularity is a matter of sales statistics. In 1911 and 1912, when the first series of Judge Priest stories appeared in the *Post,* circulation soared. From the beginning the American reading public took the garrulous old unreconstructed Kentuckian to its heart. In the first Judge Priest story ("Words and Music," *Saturday Evening Post,* 28 October 1911) John Breckenridge Tandy is on trial in west Tennessee for murdering a popular local man. Judge Priest is called in as a character witness for his fellow Kentuckian and wins acquittal with his reminiscences of the war and the role Tandy played in trying to rid western Tennessee of Yankee soldiers. It takes the jury just six minutes to find the defendant not guilty.

Many readers were quite certain that Judge Priest would be added to the gallery of classic characters in American fiction—a gallery that included James Fenimore Cooper's Leatherstocking, Herman Melville's Captain Ahab, Nathaniel Hawthorne's Hester Prynne, and Mark Twain's Huck Finn. Here was a plain, good-natured Amer-

ican, at home with himself and with the world. "His Mother's Apron Strings" (*Good Housekeeping,* March 1923; collected in *Snake Doctor, and Other Stories,* 1923) shows the judge sitting on a warm spring day in his chamber at an old courthouse: "his mussed, but clean, white linen shirt, with its broad pleats and its big, flat gold studs; his black string tie, threatening now, as it always did, to come undone any minute; his little, white paintbrush of a chin beard, his corncob pipe, his broadtoed shoes; the United Confederate Veteran's button in the lapel of his loose, black alpaca coat. . . ." So popular had the old judge become that the public would not let Cobb abandon the character, and in 1930 and 1931 a new series of Judge Priest stories appeared in *Cosmopolitan Magazine.* The twelve new stories were published in 1932 as *Down Yonder with Judge Priest and Irvin S. Cobb.* In the August 1936 *American Magazine* the judge made his first appearance as an amateur detective in "The Widow Arrives."

In his day Cobb was considered almost the equal of Edgar Allan Poe in creating stories of terror, most of them set in his native South. "The Belled Buzzard" (*Saturday Evening Post,* 28 September 1912; collected in *The Escape of Mr. Trimm,*

Caricature of Cobb by Conrado Massaguer

1913) is set in a swamp where a local squire lures a young peddler to his death, then leaves him "lying where he might lie undiscovered for months or for years, or forever." A bell attached to a buzzard leads to the discovery of the body and the eventual revelation of the murderer. The story probes beneath the macabre surface action to reveal the psychology of guilt. George Horace Lorimer, editor of the *Post,* considered "Fishhead," another of the horror tales collected in *The Escape of Mr. Trimm,* too strong for his readers; it appeared in the 11 January 1913 issue of the *Cavalier.*

The most honored of Cobb's horror stories was "Snake Doctor" (*Cosmopolitan Magazine,* November 1922; collected in *Snake Doctor, and Other Stories*), which was selected by the O. Henry Memorial Award Committee as the best short story published in 1922. It is the story of a hermit who lives in a swamp and is believed to be in unholy communion with snakes. His nearest neighbor, Japhet Morner, is a swamp rat who imagines that his wife, Kizzie, and Snake Doctor are having an affair and plans to kill him in an ambush. Morner believes that he will rid himself of a rival and obtain for himself a fortune he thinks is hidden in Snake Doctor's cabin. However, his plans go awry

when he mistakenly kills his wife and then dies of fright when he enters the darkened cabin and pricks his hand on a piece of barbed wire, which he believes to be a water moccasin guarding the hermit's treasure.

Cobb made his reputation and fortune as a short-story writer, but his works include longer fiction. In 1922 he published his first novel, *J. Poindexter, Colored,* which had appeared in a shorter version in the *Saturday Evening Post.* It is a comic novel of a happy and faithful black valet who accompanies his white boss to New York, where he lectures other blacks on their racial presumptions and assures his boss that when they return "below the Line, I'll know my place an' station an' I'll respec' 'em both."

Cobb doubtless considered himself an enlightened southerner. Yet, despite his intentions to dispel "certain notions about Southern people and Southern ways," in most of his fiction he confirms southern stereotypes. His white characters are benevolently condescending to their black servants, who do not mind serving as choice butts of humor. Most of his stories, in fact, read as quaint, unreconstructed fragments of a South that, even as late as Cobb's death in 1944, still had not brought itself into the twentieth century.

But Cobb's limited racial vision is not his only weakness. In general, his view of human nature was mischievous, superficial, and unsupported by any coherent philosophical underpinning. His stories are, therefore, easy and fun to read–once. They do not invite sustained thought or attention. They abound in pathos and farce, but too seldom take the reader beneath these surface emotions to show the wellsprings of comedy and tragedy that make for fiction of permanent significance. A contemporary critic, Robert H. Davis, intending to praise him, perhaps unwittingly showed Cobb's weakness for cheap grandstand effects when he boasted that Cobb "writes in octaves, striking instinctively all the chords of humor, tragedy, pathos and romance with either hand."

Perhaps Cobb wrote too much and found it too easy to satisfy his editors and his public. In commenting on his enormous productivity, he once admitted that some of his works "never should have been published in the first place." Much of his short fiction seems facile and hastily written. Cobb insisted, however, that he worked long and hard at his craft and never "dashed off" anything. "You should see me some morning when I'm in the mood for dashing off the

Cobb in April 1936

on flaunting colors. The busy sweet gum, which reared almost against the north wall of the old courthouse, was shaking a cosmetic bough, all purple and scarlet and weathered green, in at the nearmost raised window...." ("The Widow Arrives," *American Magazine,* August 1936). Small wonder that in 1923 Kentucky critic John Wilson Townsend called him "the Confederacy's biggest voice in current literature."

Like most extremely popular writers, he exactly suited and reflected the tastes of his time. Major writers struggle against popular taste and rise above it. Irvin Cobb seemed to revel in it. Such acquiescence made him rich, but it left him a literary reputation that hardly survived his death. Nevertheless, Cobb deserves more than cursory mention. His short stories, in particular, have at least the charm and surface realism of a Norman Rockwell magazine cover illustration.

References:

Wayne Chatterton, *Irvin S. Cobb* (Boston: Twayne, 1986);

Elisabeth Cobb, *My Wayward Parent, Irvin S. Cobb* (Indianapolis: Bobbs-Merrill, 1945);

Robert H. Davis, *Irvin S. Cobb, Storyteller* (New York: Doran, 1924);

Anita Lawson, *Irvin S. Cobb* (Bowling Green, Ohio: Bowling Green University Popular Press, 1984);

Fred G. Neuman, *Irvin S. Cobb: His Life and Letters* (Emaus, Pa.: Rodale Press, 1938);

Bess A. Ray, ed., *Biographical and Critical Materials Pertaining to Kentucky Authors,* Kentucky Work Projects Administration, Library Project (Louisville, Ky.: Louisville Free Public Library, 1941);

John Wilson Townsend, "Irvin S. Cobb," in *Library of Southern Literature,* 27, supplement 1, edited by Edwin Anderson Alderman and others (Atlanta: Martin & Hoyt, 1923), pp. 159-180.

stuff," he once wrote. "There I sit, dashing it off at the rate of about an inch and a half an hour, and using sweat for punctuation. I'm the sort of impetuous dasher that the Muir Glacier is.... Every smooth, easy, graceful line means another furrow in the head of its maker. Nearly every recorded statement which deals with verities means study, research, and patient inquiry." Nevertheless, there is a certain flippancy even in his writing about writing.

Other defects include his loosely constructed plots and his seemingly undisciplined writing style–a kind of latter-day version of "Confederate rhetoric." Witness this description: "It was one of those flawless cool-warm days of early October when the Southern summer is putting

Papers:

Irvin S. Cobb's papers are held at the Margaret I. King Library, University of Kentucky, Lexington.

James T. Farrell

(27 February 1904-22 August 1979)

Paul Schlueter

See also the Farrell entries in *DLB 4: American Writers in Paris, 1920-1939; DLB 9: American Novelists, 1910-1945;* and *DLB Documentary Series: 2.*

SELECTED BOOKS: *Young Lonigan* (New York: Vanguard, 1932; London: Panther, 1959);
Gas-House McGinty (New York: Vanguard, 1933);
The Young Manhood of Studs Lonigan (New York: Vanguard, 1934; London: Panther, 1959);
Calico Shoes and Other Stories (New York: Vanguard, 1934);
Judgment Day (New York: Vanguard, 1935; London: Panther, 1959);
Studs Lonigan: A Trilogy (New York: Vanguard, 1935; London: Constable, 1936);
Guillotine Party and Other Stories (New York: Vanguard, 1935);
A Note on Literary Criticism (New York: Vanguard, 1936; London: Constable, 1936);
A World I Never Made (New York: Vanguard, 1936; London: Constable, 1938);
Can All This Grandeur Perish? and Other Stories (New York: Vanguard, 1937);
Fellow Countrymen: Collected Stories (London: Constable, 1937);
The Short Stories of James T. Farrell (New York: Vanguard, 1937);
No Star Is Lost (New York: Vanguard, 1938; London: Constable, 1939);
Tommy Gallagher's Crusade (New York: Vanguard, 1939);
Father and Son (New York: Vanguard, 1940; London: Routledge, 1943);
Ellen Rogers (New York: Vanguard, 1941; London: Routledge, 1942);
$1,000 a Week and Other Stories (New York: Vanguard, 1942);
My Days of Anger (New York: Vanguard, 1943; London: Routledge, 1945);
To Whom It May Concern and Other Stories (New York: Vanguard, 1944);
The League of Frightened Philistines and Other Papers (New York: Vanguard, 1945; London: Routledge, 1948);

James T. Farrell (courtesy of the University of Pennsylvania Library)

Bernard Clare (New York: Vanguard, 1946); republished as *Bernard Clayre* (London: Routledge, 1948);
When Boyhood Dreams Come True (New York: Vanguard, 1946);
Literature and Morality (New York: Vanguard, 1947);
The Life Adventurous and Other Stories (New York: Vanguard, 1947);
The Road Between (New York: Vanguard, 1949; London: Routledge & Kegan Paul, 1949);
A Misunderstanding (New York: House of Books, 1949);
The Name Is Fogarty: Private Papers on Public Matters (New York: Vanguard, 1950);

An American Dream Girl (New York: Vanguard, 1950);

This Man and This Woman (New York: Vanguard, 1952; London: Panther, 1961);

Yet Other Waters (New York: Vanguard, 1952; London: Panther, 1960);

The Face of Time (New York: Vanguard, 1953; London: Spearman & Calder, 1954);

Reflections at Fifty and Other Essays (New York: Vanguard, 1954; London: Spearman, 1956);

French Girls Are Vicious and Other Stories (New York: Vanguard, 1955; London: Panther, 1958);

An Omnibus of Short Stories (New York: Vanguard, 1956);

A Dangerous Woman and Other Stories (New York: Vanguard, 1957; London: Panther, 1959);

My Baseball Diary (New York: A. S. Barnes, 1957);

It Has Come to Pass (New York: Theodore Herzl, 1958);

Boarding House Blues (New York: Paperback Library, 1961; London: Panther, 1962);

Side Street and Other Stories (New York: Paperback Library, 1961);

Sound of a City (New York: Paperback Library, 1962);

The Silence of History (Garden City, N.Y.: Doubleday, 1963; London: Allen, 1964);

Selected Essays, edited by Luna Wolf (New York, Toronto & London: McGraw-Hill, 1964);

What Time Collects (Garden City, N.Y.: Doubleday, 1964; London: Allen, 1965);

The Collected Poems of James T. Farrell (New York: Fleet, 1965);

Lonely for the Future (Garden City, N.Y.: Doubleday, 1966; London: Allen, 1966);

When Time Was Born (New York: The Smith / Horizon Press, 1966);

New Year's Eve / 1929 (New York: The Smith / Horizon Press, 1967);

A Brand New Life (Garden City, N.Y.: Doubleday, 1968);

Judith (Athens, Ohio: Duane Schneider Press, 1969);

Childhood Is Not Forever (Garden City, N.Y.: Doubleday, 1969);

Invisible Swords (Garden City, N.Y.: Doubleday, 1971);

Judith and Other Stories (Garden City, N.Y.: Doubleday, 1973);

Literary Essays 1954-1974, edited by Jack Alan Robbins (Port Washington, N.Y. & London: Kennikat Press, 1976);

Farrell at the Yaddo writers' colony, circa 1934 (courtesy of Cleo Paturis)

The Dunne Family (Garden City, N.Y.: Doubleday, 1976);

Olive and Mary Anne (New York: Stonehill, 1977);

The Death of Nora Ryan (Garden City, N.Y.: Doubleday, 1978);

Eight Short Short Stories & Sketches (Newton, Mass.: Arts End Books, 1981);

On Irish Themes, edited by Dennis Flynn (Philadelphia: University of Pennsylvania Press, 1982);

Sam Holman (Buffalo, N.Y.: Prometheus Books, 1983);

Hearing Out James T. Farrell: Selected Letters, edited by Donald Phelps (New York: The Smith, 1985).

James T. Farrell's reputation rests primarily on his novels of the 1930s, in particular the interrelated series about Studs Lonigan and Danny O'Neill. Farrell repeatedly claimed that, in the tradition of Theodore Dreiser, John Dos Passos, and Sherwood Anderson, he wrote out of his own life, feelings, and experiences–sources, he be-

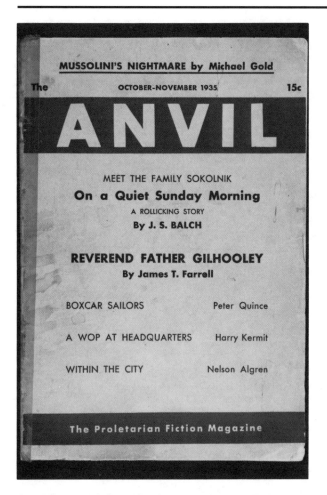

Cover for one of the proletarian magazines in which Farrell published short stories during the 1930s (courtesy of Jack Conroy)

lieved, to which writers had to remain devoted. Hence most of his fifty-odd books focus on his Irish-American origins on Chicago's South Side. Farrell has often been dismissed as of limited importance because of his alleged dedication to the literary-philosophic theory labeled "naturalism"; however, Edgar M. Branch has more accurately described Farrell as a critical realist, "representing characters in a definite time and place and in complex relationship to other individuals. He has shown their destinies being shaped by the milieu and the period, by their particular roles in society, and by their qualities of character." Farrell consequently avoids allegorical or heavily symbolic portrayals, subtle narrative techniques, poetic language, or reliance on the supernatural or mythical; his world, again quoting Branch, is "one of relationship, process, tendency, change, emergence, and time leading onward to death. Most of his fiction, sometimes thought of as a formless overflow of memory, may reasonably be regarded as a selection of experience that imaginatively embodies the world at process." Although Farrell's novels have received a fair amount of criticism, with recent commentary balancing the negative attention he commonly received earlier in his career, his stories have yet to receive much notice, though they focus on the same subjects.

Farrell was born on 27 February 1904, the second oldest of six surviving children (out of fifteen) born to James Francis Farrell (a teamster) and Mary Daly Farrell (a domestic servant). Never well-off financially, crowded into a small wooden house, and with a rapidly growing family, the Farrells were forced to send James to live with his maternal grandparents elsewhere on Chicago's southwest side; the grandparents, living with three of their other children, were relatively prosperous residents of a better neighborhood than Farrell had known. Though he had greater advantages than his siblings, he was also cut off from normal family relationships and was thrown into family squabbles he barely understood. At age seven he started attending the first of several Roman Catholic elementary schools, continuing in the parochial system through the end of high school.

Farrell, like many Catholic adolescents, seriously considered entering the priesthood but instead found his classical education, active social life and dating, sports, and early efforts at writing essays and fiction for a high school publication leading him in a different direction. For two summers while in high school he worked for an express company and after graduation worked full-time while taking pre-law classes at night. He gave up both the express company and night school to work full-time as a gas-station attendant, then after one semester at De Paul University (1924) attended the University of Chicago (1925-1927).

Farrell dropped out of the university during the fall of 1927, determined to become a writer, and traveled to New York to work as a salesman while he continued writing. When he returned to Chicago early in 1928, he reentered the university and wrote frequent articles for university publications, book reviews for New York and Chicago newspapers, and fiction. He soon began writing stories and essays for various magazines and started putting together the characters and incidents for the Studs Lonigan trilogy and other first books. One of his first stories, "The Sheik," was first published in the January 1975 issue of

Chicago and describes the fanaticism created by Rudolph Valentino's visit to a dance hall.

In 1928 Farrell met Dorothy Butler, a fellow student at the university; they married three years later and moved to New York. In April 1931 Farrell and his wife sailed to France for a year's residence. Through the intervention of Samuel Putnam he was able to place "Studs," a story about Studs Lonigan, in *This Quarter* (July-September 1930), and though Vanguard Press had optioned both *Young Lonigan* (1932) and *Gas-House McGinty* (1933) and given Farrell several cash advances, the Farrells were desperate financially. To add to their difficulty, their first child died soon after birth. Alienated from other American expatriates in Paris, Farrell found Ezra Pound's faith in his work encouraging and began a collection of stories on a common theme, eventually published as *Calico Shoes and Other Stories* (1934).

Still impoverished, the Farrells returned to the United States in 1932, during the depths of the Depression, but despite these hardships Farrell rejected an offer to write in Hollywood. However, with the publication of *Young Lonigan* in 1932 and with H. L. Mencken's acceptance of "Helen, I Love You!" for the *American Mercury* (July 1932), he began to achieve recognition, though he never approached financial security. He subsequently spent time in a writers' colony and traveled throughout his life to Europe and elsewhere but henceforth considered New York his home and was an active part of the city's literary circles. In 1935 he and Dorothy separated; they were divorced in 1940. In 1941 he married Hortense Alden; they separated in 1951 and were divorced in 1955, the same year he remarried Dorothy. They separated permanently in 1958; Farrell never remarried.

He contributed stories, essays, and reviews to many journals throughout the 1930s and published several Danny O'Neill and Studs Lonigan novels, a volume of literary criticism, and numerous stories and essays. In 1936 he received a Guggenheim Fellowship. The following year he and Vanguard successfully defended themselves in a censorship case against his novel *A World I Never Made* (1936). During these years he developed a reputation as an articulate non-Marxist leftist; always a vigorous individualist, he had early on rejected the communism that had appealed to many other writers, but he never relinquished his strong sense of political justice, his progressive convictions, and his civil-libertarian opposition to

Farrell, circa 1944 (courtesy of Vanguard Press)

censorship. He remained active in labor, civil-libertarian, and writers' organizations throughout his life, supported liberal political candidates, and wrote incessantly, publishing more than fifty books before his death in New York on 22 August 1979.

Farrell wrote hundreds of stories, many of which concern the same characters and situations as his novels. Indeed, it is this unity and consistency in Farrell's fiction that distinguish it from the work of many other writers of his era, for, like William Faulkner, Farrell repeatedly went back to his own small "postage-stamp" of land as the source for his fiction. Hence the same characters appear in work after work, in some cases with the protagonist of a novel becoming little more than a bit character in a story. Indeed, there are several similarities among most of Farrell's characters, whether from early or late in his career: they typically suffer from an overwhelming, uncontrollable sense of loneliness; they desperately seek love as a respite from loneliness, with sexual love most often being the specific form of escape; they sense a conflict in their lives between the strict Catholicism they grew up with and the escape they crave; they are (with some notable exceptions) relatively weak, often unable to control their lives or their feelings, and they rely excessively on alcohol and sex as ways of dulling reality; many feel themselves doomed to failure, despair, financial ruin, lovelessness, world-weariness, and oblivion but in spite of this fatalistic attitude constantly seek new experiences, new ways of dulling reality, and often dream of what might have been; and as one form of escape, whether from reality or unpleasant surroundings, many of his characters, most notably Danny O'Neill, turn to writing.

During the years Farrell worked on his Studs Lonigan trilogy, comprising *Young Lonigan*, *The Young Manhood of Studs Lonigan* (1934), and *Judgment Day* (1935), he also published *Gas-House McGinty* and two collections of stories, *Calico Shoes* and *Guillotine Party and Other Stories* (1935), as well as many uncollected tales. Many of these early stories, as Robert Morss Lovett said in the introduction to *The Short Stories of James T. Farrell* (1937), comprising the first two collections and *Can All This Grandeur Perish? and Other Stories* (1937), are versions of the early novels themselves. The best stories in *Calico Shoes*, however, are only tangentially connected to the novels. "Scarecrow" (first published in *New Masses*, 29 May 1934), a story about a pathetic young woman who turns to prostitution as a means of counteracting the beatings she receives at home, is a parody of the Cinderella tale, in this case with the young woman dreaming of love and money she can never have except through prostitution. In "A Front-Page Story" the death of a student prompts a reporter to track down her full life story. "Mary O'Reilly" (*Midland*, May 1931), about an old, empty woman who suddenly dies, is sensitive without being maudlin.

Several of the sixteen stories in the book offer a sufficiently hopeless, hard-boiled picture of society that is partially responsible for Farrell's being categorized too simplistically as a naturalist: "Just Boys," for example, offers as desolate a world as that portrayed by Richard Wright, a world in which a white homosexual with venereal disease picks up a financially desperate black youth who then kills the homosexual at a party once he realizes he, too, has been infected. "Honey, We'll Be Brave" also deals with venereal disease, in this more Ibsenesque case with a young married couple; the wife, desperate for money, decides to have an abortion and discovers that she is infected, possibly, it is hinted, by her own father. "Calico Shoes" tells of the social disease of greed and inhumanity in its picture of a

slumlord, and "Meet the Girls" offers a pathetic picture of three drunken, older women, too fat and undesirable to be able to find sexual partners any longer. This first collection illustrates most of Farrell's major concerns, particularly the plight of the dispossessed, hopeless, trapped inner-city people he himself knew so well.

While all the stories in *Calico Shoes* are set in Chicago (it was originally to be called "These Chicagoans"), the nineteen tales in *Guillotine Party* reflect a gradually broadened worldview for Farrell, including both Paris and New York City, locales for many of Farrell's later stories. One finds the same degree of hopelessness in this group, as in "Soap" (first published in 1932 in *Americans Abroad*, edited by Peter Neagoe), again about a poor young couple, and "Studs," set immediately after Studs's death. The most successful of the tales include "All Things Are Nothing To Me," in which a know-it-all family clashes with a University of Chicago student who is gradually aware that there is a larger, more interesting world than he had known previously. "The Benefits of American Life" (*Partisan Review*, January-February 1935) is a parody of the American Dream, inverting the familiar pattern of rags-to-riches in telling of a Greek immigrant, alone and poor at age twenty-five, who enters and wins a dance marathon, developing tuberculosis along the way and returning to Greece with his health broken. "The Merry Clouters" (*This Quarter*, October-December 1932) suggests the degree to which urban youths are unassimilated socially; a gang of youths, drunk and eager for sexual conquest, gang up on and beat a black man, then themselves are involved in a gang fight.

Farrell's great productivity and similarity of subject and approach necessarily led to repetition; for example, "A Casual Incident" (*Story*, September-October 1931) in *Calico Shoes* tells of a young man at a religious rally, during which a homosexual tries to pick him up; "Footnote" in *Guillotine Party* tells of a Columbia University student to whom the same thing happens. Even when plot similarities are not so obvious, the same perspective is sometimes offered, as in the many stories that show the human—and rather unlikable or hypocritical—sides of the Roman Catholic clergy. In "The Little Blond Fellow" in *Guillotine Party* a young priest, incognito, goes with others his age to a whorehouse, later asking the inevitable questions about faith and his church. "Reverend Father Gilhooley" (*Anvil*, October-November 1935), more typical of Farrell's portrayals of priests because of the title character's pride and rigidity, tries to force a Catholic girl and Protestant boy to separate more because of his own ambition and arrogance than anything resembling sincere interest and conviction.

The seventeen stories in Farrell's third collection, *Can All This Grandeur Perish? and Other Stories*, derive mostly from the experiences of his Chicago days but with a greater awareness of the social and political overtones of the Depression. The title story, for example, presents a rich, older couple holding court for their relatives, wholly oblivious to the relatives' poverty and, indeed, to the Depression itself. "The Scoop" (*Daily Worker*, 30 January 1934) grew out of the notorious newspaper circulation wars in Chicago during the 1930s; it offers a particularly vicious, cynical story of a delivery man for one paper killing a newsboy hawking the competition's papers, then using his own paper's headline story the next day about the death of the innocent boy to sell more papers. Several of the stories in this collection suggest the utter hopelessness of the times, as in "A Noble Guy," in which a tenant's child dies and the landlord evicts the family for nonpayment of rent. "Thanksgiving Spirit," like the title story, contrasts an overfed, gluttonous family celebrating the holiday with the poor and hungry outside. A young man and woman in "Seventeen" get involved sexually; when the young woman discovers she is pregnant, she has an abortion and rejects the man. The boy in "The Oratory Contest" is ashamed of his parents not only because of their appearance but even more because his middle-aged mother, with four children to care for, is pregnant once again.

Farrell's perspective in most of these early stories is so earnest that only rarely does a touch of humor intrude. One exception, however, is "Mendel and His Wife," set in a Paris suburb. The protagonists are two disorganized, expatriate Communists, and their comments to each other and with visitors are filled with barbed observations about Communist jargon, intellectual pretensions, art criticism, and bourgeois ambition. Some of this sardonic, underkeyed humor is also evident in "The Professor," about an insecure University of Chicago creative-writing teacher who humors his students, fears the end of life and his reputation, writes reviews for a Hearst paper, and lyrically compares a society woman's novel with Dreiser's *An American Tragedy*, with which it has nothing in common, as a way of maintaining good relations with those in power: "In each of

Farrell in Cap d'Antibes, France, during the twenty-fourth P.E.N. Congress, 1950 (photograph by E. Sottsass, Jr., courtesy of the University of Pennsylvania Library)

her gemlike tales the meaning has transcended the local and the immediate, swooping up, like a glorious bird on the wing, into the empyrean realm of the universal, and thereby becoming fine art." Farrell's forays into humor are rarely subtle: he seems to prefer obvious targets which he can satirize through jargon or through the ironic treatment of recognizable positions or professions.

With the publication of *$1,000 a Week and Other Stories* (1942), a collection of seventeen pieces, Farrell's gradually broadened worldview enabled him to write knowledgeably about Hollywood actors, writers, and producers as well as intellectuals from both the United States and Europe. The title story, for example, concerns a writer hired to rewrite a script for a Cinderella story who discovers that money cannot replace the need for satisfying work and companionship. In "Whoopee for the New Deal!" two partying couples talk wildly against socialism and the Jews and for Roosevelt and Hitler. The central character in "Monday Is Another Day" is a fervent Communist who in seeking a revolution alienates his family. A similar true believer from the opposite end of the political spectrum is found in "Sorel," about a French writer, a Fascist who hates Germans, tourists, and the modern world and who sees the end of civilization rapidly approaching. Yet Farrell also continued to write of the world he knew best, and while some of the Chicago stories in this collection are slight, "The Fate of a Hero" (*North American Review*, Spring 1938) is striking in its depiction of an Iowa farm boy who works hard at his gas-station job, too hard, in fact, since the other workers' morale is so affected by his efforts that he is fired, only to become a hired strikebreaker elsewhere. "The Bride of Christ" vividly shows the lifelong effects of a wasted life of strictness and fanaticism. And "The Only Son" (*Partisan Review*, Spring 1939) is a sensitive account of a man celebrating his twenty-first birthday; his parents do not understand his studies at the University of Chicago, so he is forced to lie to satisfy them regarding the books he reads, his religious faith, and his girlfriend.

Only a few of the thirteen stories in *To Whom It May Concern and Other Stories* (1944) are worthy of individual discussion. The title story is about a writer recently returned from Hollywood, where he has willingly "sold out" his literary goals and ideals; a victim of writer's block, he can think of his wives and lovers but cannot believe in anything any longer. A silent-film star in "Patsy Gilbride" rationalizes his rejection by "the talkies" through drink and anti-Semitism. And "Tommy Gallagher's Crusade" (separately published in 1939) is a powerful novella about a Fascist youth selling Nazi newspapers who is beaten up in a riot with Communist sympathizers; his faith, however, remains unshaken. Gallagher bases much of his belief on the radio preaching of a Father Moylan, a thinly disguised parallel to Father Charles Coughlin, a Fascist priest of the 1930s who used radio to stir up racial prejudice and political unrest.

When Boyhood Dreams Come True (1946) is also a weaker collection than those of the prewar period, though here, too, a few stories are memorable. Farrell's postwar world continues to expand, both geographically and ideologically, but political naiveté still leads some of his characters to a facile acceptance of communism. "John Hitchcock," for example, tells of a poor writer who talks bravely about communism while a woman asserts her interest in individuality; de-

spite her greater dependence on reason, he joins the Party. In "Fritz" an American soldier during World War II reminisces about a conversation he had had with a German in Paris in 1931. The story contrasts Fritz's greater awareness of history in talking about the consequences of World War I on Germany and France with the American's relative innocence and portrays these roles as reversed when Fritz, a Communist, is taken back to an uncertain fate in Germany and the American survives the Depression only to fight another war. They are both lost in history, but Fritz's survival is far less probable.

The best stories in the group, however, are those that do not strive to present a particular political viewpoint, as in the title story. A soldier in New York City, awaiting shipping orders during World War II, meets a rich woman who takes him home with her; much later he recalls the war, especially the fighting and heroism, and starts to fantasize about death, his boyhood friends in Chicago such as Studs Lonigan, and Adam and Eve–all in a surrealistic dream, a futile effort to recapture the past. A similar attempt to avoid reality appears in "Two Brothers," which, as indicated by the explicit Cain / Abel comparison, contrasts two brothers: one studious, one indifferent to discipline; the first a masturbator, the second involved in an affair with a married woman. The first brother, incapable of sinning overtly, eventually finds security in a seminary, and the story shows how the life-denying seminarian is the more pitiable of the two because of his inability to match his brother's involvement in life. Two other stories in this collection of eleven are also worthy of brief comment. "The Power of Literature" is a sardonic but all too revealing account of a writer, author of a successful book about alcoholism, attending a book party given by his publisher at which everyone is drunk. And "The Virginians Are Coming," set on the University of Chicago campus in 1930, tells of a man who, though a graduate of the university, cannot secure any sort of job. When he goes back on campus to work, he sees that everyone is more successful than he is. The title of the story, taken from Vachel Lindsay, suggests that people like the protagonist are similar to those in Lindsay's poem, doomed to hopelessness and futility.

Many of the twenty stories in *The Life Adventurous and Other Stories* (1947) are slight pieces at best, though the collection does include a few memorable tales. "Joe Eliot" is about a widower who longs touchingly and believably for the past. The central character in "The Philosopher," a sixty-nine-year-old professor at the University of Chicago, is also displaced in the modern world; forced to resign by the university's "boy president" (clearly modeled on Robert Maynard Hutchins), the professor can only poignantly recall his past and then die. Indeed, the chaos of the present takes a terrible toll in some of these stories. In "Saturday Night," for instance, a youth criticized by his family for lack of industry goes out drinking, driving, and fighting, with a consequent accident causing several deaths. "A Love Story of Our Time" tells of a would-be writer in love with a Communist woman who persuades him to fight on the Republican side in the Spanish civil war; when he returns, he is rejected as a "false hero" and is jilted by the woman. In all of these stories there is the implicit question asked by the protagonist in "A Love Story of Our Time": "Why did this happen to me?" For the complications of economics, politics, internationalism, and change preclude many of Farrell's characters from sensing any way of handling the present.

An American Dream Girl (1950), a collection of twenty-one stories, ties together Farrell's earlier themes and settings with distinctly postwar ones. "The Fastest Runner on Sixty-First Street" (*Commentary*, June 1950), for example, focuses on two boys, one a runner, the other slower both physically and mentally, who chase a black youth out of their neighborhood. The "fastest runner" catches up with the intruder and, as a result, gets his throat slashed. The heavily ironic title story, which first appeared in the Spring 1950 issue of *General Magazine and Historical Chronicle*, is about a woman's implicit brother-sister incest and an abortion; though superficially a "dream girl," she is in reality promiscuous, decadent, and doomed to deteriorate even further, thus understanding Farrell's rather too obvious contrast between the superficial attractiveness of the woman and the true nature of her character. "A Misunderstanding" (published separately in 1949) is an ironic, bitter account of decayed affection: as a man who has killed his wife reflects on what his marriage was like, it becomes apparent that his obsessive wife simply could never communicate, for whatever he said to her, she replied with a completely irrelevant change of subject. In "I Want to Go Home" an ex-GI, a would-be artist, goes to Paris with a Chicago woman who favors black musicians as lovers, but they never become even slightly adjusted, speaking only English, for in-

stance, and showing an almost complete lack of sensitivity to any larger world. "Digging Our Own Graves" (*New Leader*, 24 June 1948) is a successful fantasy in which the narrator tells how he and other Democrats are either shot or forced into concentration-camp drudgery, a new Five-Year Plan to dig the world's biggest ditch, one even large enough for the Republicans gradually coming into the camp. The story is clever, especially in its suggestion that a Soviet takeover will result in the same circumstances in the United States that anti-Stalinists such as Farrell were increasingly aware had occurred in the Soviet Union. The relatively despairing tone of most of the stories in this collection–including accounts of rejected lovers, a mediocre playwright, a teamster's sense of death upon his retirement, and children in a bombed-out European town after the war who dream of toys and candy–is only partially relieved by a sardonic touch of black humor, as in "Have I Got Sun in My Eyes?," in which a New York woman refuses to make love with the narrator because she, like all New York women, reads Freud and so of course will not be a part of a sexual relationship.

Two of the nine stories in *French Girls Are Vicious and Other Stories* (1955) are as excellent as anything Farrell wrote in the 1930s, particularly "Kilroy Was Here" (*Commentary*, December 1954). An older Danny O'Neill returns to his old neighborhood, which has completely changed from white to black in the twenty-odd years since he had lived there, to visit Bryan, a young black friend who wishes to be a poet, and the conversation necessarily turns to the changes in the neighborhood as well as to black / white relations and writing. Bryan does not want to think about being black but rather about being "another person, a poet, with [his] own feelings" as a way of transcending the hopelessness and squalor of the area and as a way of not being like those around him. Danny had left the neighborhood by defeating the fears within himself, and Bryan knows he has to do the same. In "A Baptism in Italy" Giovanni, an Italian workingman who was a prisoner of war in the Soviet Union during World War II and who wrote a vanity-press book after the war about his experience, is honored by a visit from an American writer and French woman. Giovanni goes to excess to be hospitable, even though he cannot afford to do so, and proudly shows off one humble possession after another, without the guests being especially im-

Farrell with Chicago White Sox second baseman Nelson Fox, July 1957 (courtesy of the University of Pennsylvania Library)

pressed; they seem completely unaware of the contrasts between themselves and Giovanni.

The fourteen stories in *A Dangerous Woman and Other Stories* (1957) range widely in setting–Stockholm, Paris, Switzerland, London, New York, Chicago–but less so in mood. Psychic pain dominates "Norman Allen," about a black man with a Ph.D. in philosophy who has a breakdown, is institutionalized, and dies, all presumably because he was rejected sexually by a white woman at the university. "Little Johnny: A Fable" is effective in showing how a "misunderstood" boy ends up killing people, and "Success Story" is about an apathetic man who writes one successful novel after the war but, unable to write any more, can only kill himself. Apathy and indifference also reign in the life of a teamster in "Memento

Mori" (first published as "The Nothingness of Milt Cogswell," *Swank*, February 1956), who ages, marries, raises a family, develops stomach trouble, and is killed by a car. "Edna's Husband" tells of a freeloading southern couple in Paris who experience tragedy when a "glass contrivance" is broken inside the woman, evidently as part of a botched abortion.

Given the familiar plots, characters, and locales that inform the stories in *Side Street and Other Stories* (1961), these sixteen tales seem little more than rewritings of earlier stories. "Side Street" (*Manhunt*, September 1955), for example, contrasts love as portrayed in movies and popular songs with the harsh realism of a back-street abortion parlor. In "An Old Sweetheart" a middle-aged editor, happily married, is visited by an old love from his university days, a self-centered intellectual who is bored with life and whose dreams are gone. "Shanley" is about an overweight, middle-aged man who feels "melancholy for what used to be, for what was gone, ... for what ... should have been." Similar layers of memory are experienced by the protagonist in "The Stuff That Dreams are Made Of" (*Audience*, Winter 1959), in which he is "lost in an inner chaos of the past" as he reminisces about a series of young loves and his consequent wounded vanity. Such insecurity, indeed, is found in several of these stories, as in "The Old Flame" (*Manhunt*, May 1954), in which a newscaster makes love to his exwife's sister before self-consciously having dinner with his current lover; "Tickle 'Em in the Ribs" (*Bluebook*, June 1961), in which a professor, a Dreiser scholar, returns from a speaking trip, picks up a hitchhiker, and enviously listens to tales of sexual conquest; and "War Widow" and "Not Funny, No, Not Funny," in both of which women wait for their lovers—a wife for her husband, a would-be writer in the army, and a French girl for her American lover. The most effective story is "Aunt Louise," in which a twenty-year-old woman lies dying of tuberculosis in 1911; a boy (presumably based on Farrell himself) is angry at her for dying, although the story is told from a more mature perspective and with profound memories of love and loss.

Sound of a City (1962) is a group of twenty-four stories, most of them merely anecdotes, sketches, or "fables." The tales in this collection cover by-now-familiar territory, as in "Casey" and "William McNally," in which seminarians wrestle with thoughts of sex and other suppressed desires, or "Shorty Leach," in which Danny O'Neill contrasts a 1925 conversation with a boy who defends his lack of success on "the breaks" with a 1950 conversation with the same man, who has not changed and who has wasted his life making excuses for himself. Expatriates again come in for some notice, as in "A Story About Money," in which the dissipated son of a dead businessman finds Europe empty and eventually joins the Communist party, or "Scene at the Coupole (*Bachelor*, September 1961), in which an American woman teases and shocks a British woman in a café by her talk about sex and Puritanism, or "Arrival in England," in which an obnoxious American writer offends his British hosts by his excessive drinking and talk about politics. But there are also some effective though slight tales in which foreigners visit the United States or wish to do so, as

in "I Want to Go to America," set on a plane from Amsterdam to Copenhagen and concerned with Europeans fearing a Russian attack and in particular with a one-armed woman, injured in a bombing, who wants to emigrate but cannot. "Anna" (*Views*, Winter 1955) tells of a Danish woman who is changed because of her one visit to the United States and who wishes to return. Especially effective is "French Post Cards," in which French couples who have spent several years in the United States leave during the McCarthy era and are asked by an American businessman to get obscene postcards, cards they have never seen in Paris and do not know how to obtain. The contrast between the relatively sophisticated Europeans and relatively naive, meretricious Americans is clear; there is a sharp distinction between the Puritanic American businessman's delight at forbidden eroticism and the more blasé French inability to isolate sex from the rest of human experience.

Childhood Is Not Forever (1969) is a group of sixteen stories with much of the same emphasis as in the previous two collections. "Reunion Abroad" (*Meanjin Quarterly*, December 1964), for instance, contrasts an American labor leader visiting Indonesia with an old friend, a foundation executive, with the two of them becoming aware of the increased distance between them as they talk about world power changes. "An American Student in Paris" (*Southern Review*, October 1967) contrasts a lonely, virginal youth with the abundance of life and love in Paris, and "Arlette" contrasts a sad, lonely Frenchwoman, Danny O'Neill's translator, a woman who cannot love and who is afraid of both life and people, with the vitality around her. The title story is about a racist Republican who hates Roosevelt, Truman, all of Europe, and "radicals" such as Danny O'Neill, whom he meets at a restaurant. The title character in "Dumbrovic" (*University of Kansas City Review*, Spring 1956) is an old Yugoslavian leftist living in Italy, a Trotskyite, unable to understand the changes in the Soviet Union since Lenin and whose wife, a Jew, had died in a concentration camp. "Ray Taite," by contrast, is about a tennis prodigy, an ascetic incapable of keeping friendships, meeting Eddie Ryan at the University of Chicago and finding here, too, that an old friend cannot be his to keep since they "were traveling separate roads toward a future that controlled them." "Native's Return" is also about Ryan; now a successful author, he is invited to Chicago to attend an authors' luncheon, a television interview, and an

Farrell in his study, New York, circa 1979 (courtesy of Cleo Paturis)

Adlai Stevenson rally. As with many of Farrell's characters, and especially so in his later works, Ryan has "never lost his anxiety about time," about what Farrell calls elsewhere in the story "the Tyranny of Time." Aware that Stevenson has no chance of winning the presidential election, Ryan recalls A. E. Housman's lines about being "a stranger and afraid, / In a world I never made," also used by Farrell in 1936 as the title of the first Danny O'Neill novel.

Farrell comments in his introduction to *Judith and Other Stories* (1973) that the eleven tales in the book are a "continuation of [his] lifework" in their concern with the "panorama of time." But none of the stories is an advancement upon earlier work, and in some cases they are merely variations on overly familiar topics. When Eddie Ryan returns to Chicago as a celebrity to give a speech in "Episodes of a Return," one immediately recalls "Native's Return" in the previous collection. "Mr. Austin" (*Works in Progress Number Two*, 1971), about a Republican stockbroker talking with Eddie Ryan, recalls "Childhood Is Not Forever" in the same earlier collection. "The Old Timer" and "Only Tomorrow and Tomorrow" are both about trucking-company veterans, the

former about a man who lives in the past and who overrates his ability and importance, the latter about a lonely, autocratic supervisor who suddenly packs up and leaves without notice. "Sister" contrasts two nuns in a 1918 parochial school, a cruel one and a younger replacement who tries to instill both fear and loyalty but without the slightest tinge of joy in religion. The title story, which was separately published in 1969, is about a concert pianist who has an affair with Ryan and finds that although she has success she does not have happiness.

Olive and Mary Anne (1977) groups four stories and one novella, the title piece. Olive in "Olive Armstrong" is a rich, psychotic woman in a bad marriage; she drinks heavily, she is promiscuous, she paints a surreal picture of horror, and after gradually deteriorating she dies. As an unrelieved portrait of physical decline, the novella is an impressive achievement, but it represents no development from the earlier work. "Benjamin Mandlebaum" tells of a youth mistreated in a southern orphanage who escapes after seducing a clergyman's wife and who becomes first a tramp and then a writer; the story is also about the minister himself, who prefers masturbation

On 18 April 1979 Farrell received the American Academy of Arts and Sciences Emerson-Thoreau medal. Victor Weisskopf, president of the academy, is at left; Daniel Aaron, chairman of the award committee, is at right (courtesy of the University of Pennsylvania Library).

to an encounter with his promiscuous wife. "Mary Anne Reade" is also about a southerner, in this case a successful writer in the 1920s who has a prolonged affair with her editor and who dies after traveling to Paris; her reputation is a firm though minor one thirty-five years later when Eddie Ryan reads of her death. "Morris" focuses on a former professor who leads a group to the U.S.S.R. and who feels disgust at himself and irritation at the world; he wonders if anything will ever occur to change his life. And "Joshua" is about an actor, guilt-ridden over his wife's death (misdiagnosed as neurosis) and lost, so dependent has he been on her as a surrogate mother.

Farrell's stories do not show much sense of progression. This is not to say, however, that Farrell lacked talent as a short-story writer; he based the bulk of his output on his own formative experiences in Chicago, and at their best his stories focusing on this period are vivid, compelling, and memorable. But one can note that Farrell simply wrote too much. Even though each of his collections of stories contains two or three works that can stand up with the best of their kind, his ca-

reer as a short-story writer takes second place to that of novelist, perhaps because each successive collection lacked the originality that would have secured his reputation as an artist of the first rank in the form.

Bibliographies:

Edgar M. Branch, *A Bibliography of James T. Farrell's Writings, 1921-1957* (Philadelphia: University of Pennsylvania Press, 1959); see also the supplements by Branch in *American Book Collector*, 11 (Summer 1961): 42-48; 17 (May 1967): 9-19; 21 (March-April 1971): 13-18; 26 (January-February 1976): 17-22; *Bulletin of Bibliography*, 39 (1982): 201-206;

Jack Salzman, "James T. Farrell: An Essay in Bibliography," *Resources for American Literary Study*, 6 (Autumn 1976): 131-163;

Daniel J. Casey and Robert E. Rhodes, eds., *Irish-American Fiction: Essays in Criticism* (New York: AMS Press, 1979), pp. 201-214.

References:

Edgar M. Branch, "Freedom and Determinism in James T. Farrell's Fiction," in *Essays on Deter-*

minism in American Literature, edited by Sydney J. Krause, Kent Studies in English I (Kent, Ohio: Kent State University Press, 1964), pp. 79-96;

Branch, *James T. Farrell* (New York: Twayne, 1971);

Branch, *James T. Farrell*, University of Minnesota Pamphlets on American Writers (Minneapolis: University of Minnesota Press, 1963);

Branch, "James T. Farrell: Four Decades After *Studs Lonigan*," *Twentieth Century Literature*, 22 (February 1976): 28-35;

Branch, "The 1930's in James T. Farrell's Fiction," *American Book Collector*, 21 (March-April 1971): 9-12;

Robert James Butler, "The Christian Roots of Farrell's O'Neill and Carr Novels," *Renascence*, 34 (Winter 1982): 81-98;

Morley Callaghan, "James T. Farrell: A Tribute," *Twentieth Century Literature*, 22 (February 1976): 26-27;

Don Richard Cox, "A World He Never Made: The Decline of James T. Farrell," *College Language Association Journal*, 23 (September 1979): 32-48;

Ann Douglas, "*Studs Lonigan* and the Failure of History in Mass Society: A Study in Claustrophobia," *American Quarterly*, 29 (Winter 1977): 487-505;

Dennis Flynn and Jack Salzman, "An Interview with James T. Farrell," *Twentieth Century Literature*, 22 (February 1976): 1-10;

Lewis Fried, "James T. Farrell: Shadow and Act," *Jahrbuch für Amerikastudien*, 17 (1972): 140-155;

William J. Lynch, "James T. Farrell and the Irish-American Urban Experience," *Proceedings of the Comparative Literature Symposium*, 9 (1980): 243-254;

Barry O'Connell, "The Lost World of James T. Farrell's Short Stories," *Twentieth Century Literature*, 22 (February 1976): 36-51; revised and expanded in *Irish-American Fiction: Essays in Criticism*, edited by Daniel J. Casey and Robert E. Rhodes (New York: AMS Press, 1979), pp. 53-71;

Donald Phelps, "Exegesis: James T. Farrell's 'Mary O'Reilly,' " *For Now*, no. 15 (1976);

Donald Pizer, "James T. Farrell and the 1930s," in *Literature at the Barricades: The American Writer in the 1930s*, edited by Ralph F. Bogardus and Fred Hobson (University: University of Alabama Press, 1982), pp. 69-81;

Irene Morris Reiter, "A Study of James T. Farrell's Short Stories and Their Relation to His Longer Fiction," Ph.D. dissertation, University of Pennsylvania, 1964;

Joseph W. Slade, " 'Bare-Assed and Alone': Time and Banality in Farrell's *A Universe of Time*," *Twentieth Century Literature*, 22 (February 1976): 68-79;

Twentieth Century Literature, 22 (February 1976), special Farrell issue;

Alan Wald, "Farrell and Trotskyism," *Twentieth Century Literature*, 22 (February 1976): 90-104;

Wald, *James T. Farrell: The Revolutionary Socialist Years* (New York: New York University Press, 1978);

Wald, "A Socially-Committed Writer to the End," *Michigan Quarterly Review*, 17 (1978): 263-269;

Barry Wallenstein, "James T. Farrell: Critic of Naturalism," in *American Literary Naturalism: A Reassessment*, edited by Yoshinobu Hakutani and Lewis Fried (Heidelberg, West Germany: Carl Winter Universitätsverlag, 1975), pp. 154-175.

Papers:

The Farrell Archives at the Charles Patterson Van Pelt Library of the University of Pennsylvania contain manuscripts, letters, publications, and other materials. Other, smaller collections are found at the University of Kentucky, the Clifton Waller Barrett Library at the University of Virginia, Columbia University, and the New York Public Library.

Edna Ferber

(15 August 1885-17 April 1968)

Ellen Serlen Uffen
Michigan State University

See also the Ferber entries in *DLB 9: American Novelists, 1910-1945* and *DLB 28: Twentieth-Century American-Jewish Fiction Writers.*

BOOKS: *Dawn O'Hara: The Girl Who Laughed* (New York: Stokes, 1911; London: Methuen, 1925);

Buttered Side Down (New York: Stokes, 1912; London: Methuen, 1926);

Roast Beef, Medium: The Business Adventures of Emma McChesney (New York: Stokes, 1913; London: Methuen, 1920);

Personality Plus: Some Experiences of Emma McChesney and Her Son, Jock (New York: Stokes, 1914);

Emma McChesney & Co. (New York: Stokes, 1915);

Fanny Herself (New York: Stokes, 1917; London: Methuen, 1923);

Cheerful, By Request (Garden City, N.Y.: Doubleday, Page, 1918; London: Methuen, 1919);

Half Portions (Garden City, N.Y.: Doubleday, Page, 1920);

$1200 a Year, by Ferber and Newman Levy (Garden City, N.Y.: Doubleday, Page, 1920);

The Girls (Garden City, N.Y., & Toronto: Doubleday, Page, 1921; London: Heinemann, 1922);

Gigolo (Garden City, N.Y.: Doubleday, Page, 1922; London: Heinemann, 1923);

"Old Man Minick" and Minick, by Ferber and George S. Kaufman (Garden City, N.Y.: Doubleday, Page, 1924; London: Heinemann, 1924);

So Big (Garden City, N.Y.: Doubleday, Page, 1924; London: Heinemann, 1924);

Show Boat (Garden City, N.Y.: Doubleday, Page, 1926; London: Heinemann, 1926);

Mother Knows Best: A Fiction Book (Garden City, N.Y.: Doubleday, Page, 1927; London: Heinemann, 1927);

The Royal Family, by Ferber and Kaufman (Garden City, N.Y.: Doubleday, Doran, 1928; London: French, 1929);

Edna Ferber

Cimarron (Garden City, N.Y.: Doubleday, Doran, 1930; London: Heinemann, 1930);

American Beauty (Garden City, N.Y.: Doubleday, Doran, 1931; London: Heinemann, 1931);

Dinner at Eight, by Ferber and Kaufman (Garden City, N.Y.: Doubleday, Doran, 1932; London: Heinemann, 1933);

They Brought Their Women (Garden City, N.Y.: Doubleday, Doran, 1933; London: Heinemann, 1933);

Come and Get It (Garden City, N.Y.: Doubleday, Doran, 1935; London: Heinemann, 1935);

Stage Door, by Ferber and Kaufman (Garden City, N.Y.: Doubleday, Doran, 1936; London: Heinemann, 1937);

Nobody's In Town (Garden City, N.Y.: Doubleday, Doran, 1938; London: Heinemann, 1938);

A Peculiar Treasure (New York: Doubleday, Doran, 1939; London: Heinemann, 1939);

The Land is Bright, by Ferber and Kaufman (Garden City, N.Y.: Doubleday, Doran, 1941);

No Room at the Inn (Garden City, N.Y.: Doubleday, Doran, 1941);

Saratoga Trunk (Garden City, N.Y.: Doubleday, Doran, 1941; London: Heinemann, 1942);

Great Son (Garden City, N.Y.: Doubleday, Doran, 1945; London: Heinemann, 1945);

One Basket: Thirty-One Short Stories (New York: Simon & Schuster, 1947);

Your Town (Cleveland: World, 1948);

Bravo!, by Ferber and Kaufman (New York: Dramatists Play Service, 1949);

Giant (Garden City, N.Y.: Doubleday, 1952; London: Gollancz, 1952);

Ice Palace (Garden City, N.Y.: Doubleday, 1958; London: Gollancz, 1958);

A Kind of Magic (Garden City, N.Y.: Doubleday, 1963; London: Gollancz, 1963).

SELECTED PLAYS: *Our Mrs. McChesney*, by Ferber and George V. Hobart, New York, Lyceum Theatre, 19 October 1915;

Minick, by Ferber and George S. Kaufman, New York, Booth Theatre, 24 September 1924;

The Royal Family, by Ferber and Kaufman, New York, Selwyn Theatre, 28 December 1927;

Dinner at Eight, by Ferber and Kaufman, New York, Music Box Theatre, 22 October 1932;

Stage Door, by Ferber and Kaufman, New York, Music Box Theatre, 22 October 1936;

This Land is Bright, by Ferber and Kaufman, New York, Music Box Theatre, 28 October 1941;

Bravo!, by Ferber and Kaufman, New York, Lyceum Theatre, 11 November 1948.

Edna Ferber, best known today for her novels, was a short-story writer well before she was an acclaimed novelist. It was not until the appearance of *So Big* in 1924, after the publication of four novels, one play, and seven collections of stories, that her reputation as a novelist became firmly established. The novel earned its creator a Pulitzer Prize as well as a new audience eager for her longer fiction. Ferber, however, continued to produce short-story collections until 1947. Along with thirteen novels, nine plays, and two autobiog-

Ferber, age seven

raphies, she produced twelve collections of stories. Like her work in other genres, these collections are of varying literary merit, but at least three–the memorable Emma McChesney books–have achieved lasting recognition.

McChesney, along with many of the other sharply drawn denizens of Ferber's short stories, is a survivor in a tough world. And so was Ferber. She was born in 1885 of Jewish parents in Kalamazoo, Michigan. Her family–mother, Julia; father, Jacob; and sister, Fanny–moved in 1890 to Ottumwa, Iowa, where her father ran a general store and where they remained until 1897. There Ferber experienced the brutal anti-Semitism which affected her deeply throughout her life. The forced isolation it caused allowed Ferber to read avidly and to begin developing her creative gift. Moreover, the loneliness that resulted from being thought "inferior," or, at best, "different," would stand her in good stead later in her fictional characterizations.

From Ottumwa, the peripatetic Ferbers moved to the prosperous, liberal community of

Appleton, Wisconsin, where Ferber completed high school, the end of her formal education. At seventeen, because she could not afford to study acting, her first professional love, Ferber became a reporter on the *Appleton Daily Crescent*. It was in her journalistic work in Appleton and, slightly later, on the *Milwaukee Journal* that, as she put it, she "learned how to sketch in human beings with a few rapid words." When poor health forced Ferber to return to her family, she began her fiction writing in earnest. Her initial success as a writer occurred in 1909 when she sold her first story, "The Homely Heroine," to *Everybody's Magazine* (November 1910) for the modest sum of $50.60. During this period in her life her father, who had been an invalid for several years, died, and her mother, a domineering woman who would control a great part of Ferber's life for years to come, sold the family business, which she had been running alone for years, and moved herself and her daughters to Chicago. Ferber then began to travel extensively (mostly with her mother, with whom she later lived as well) and to maintain a residence in New York. She remained there, an established and accepted member of the New York literary set, until her death in 1968.

Ferber was, by all accounts, a difficult woman—stubborn, vain, cantankerous, impatient, "a surprisingly well adjusted megalomaniac," as her great-niece and biographer Julie Goldsmith Gilbert puts it. Her relationship with her family was strained throughout her life, yet Ferber was always proud of her middle-class, midwestern, American-Jewish roots. These attributes, she felt, enabled her to imagine vividly the America and Americans about whom she wrote. She wore her Jewishness loudly, arguing often and eloquently against the evils of anti-Semitism. She never married, although she was romantically linked with Moss Hart, George S. Kaufman, Jed Harris, William Allen White, Bert Boyden, and several other prominent men. It is unclear, however, whether Ferber had any sexual life at all. Gilbert speculates that what in most people would be defined as sexual energy, was released by Ferber in her writing. She herself equated not working well with impotence.

Ferber believed that fiction was an escape for both reader and writer, an escape into a universe peopled with products of pure imagination, not, as she said, "copied from life, like a bad painting." In practice, however, the stories are a great deal more real than Ferber perhaps intended.

Her first collection of short fiction, *Buttered Side Down* (1912), is made up of twelve stories previously published in *Everybody's Magazine* or the *American Magazine*, including "The Homely Heroine." The stories are inhabited by such characters as Birdie Callahan, who "had a face that looked like a huge mistake"; the "triumphantly pretty" Sophy Epstein; Rudy Schlachweiler, the "bush league hero"; Effie Bauer; Gussie Fink; and the "homely heroine" herself, Pearlie Schultz. They come from New York, Chicago, or small midwestern towns, but they are typically working people whose stories take place in hotel kitchens, shoe stores, and rooming houses. The people from the cities tend to be more streetwise than the others, but their values and their basic goodness are the same. They are invariably troubled in some way, lonely, hungry, or lovelorn.

Their stories are presented simply. In "The Frog and the Puddle" (*American Magazine*, March 1911), for instance, a "story of Chicago," Gertie, a shop clerk from Beloit, weeps in her boardinghouse room and is heard by the "Kid next Door." They discuss their mutual loneliness, and at the end Gertie decides to return home. In "What She Wore" (*American Magazine*, June 1911) the lovely Sophy, a shoe clerk in a low-cut dress, meets and is attracted to Louie, from Oskaloosa, Iowa, who begins working in the same store. He can never get adjusted to Sophy's taste in attire. When Louie finds another job, promising a better future for both of them, Sophy puts a yoke in her dress.

The stories often begin with a paragraph or two of homey philosophy, authorial intent, or just a brief explanation of what the reader might expect. This creates an easy tone and sets up the relationship between author, reader, and characters. The author often addresses the audience directly in first person while discussing the characters and actions of the story, as if she actually witnessed what she is relating. In fact, in "That Home Town Feeling" (*American Magazine*, January 1912) Ferber herself, or her persona, plays a direct role in the story and, in the doing, describes her literary technique. The narrator explains how she frequents newsstands in Chicago and listens and watches as people buy their hometown papers. Her observations become her fiction. The implication, despite Ferber's earlier protestations to the contrary, is that the resulting stories are closely based on fact. If they are meant, then, as she insisted, to be "escapes," they enable the reader to escape only from immediate reality

A James Montgomery Flagg illustration depicting Ferber's popular salesperson Emma McChesney and her boss, T. A. Buck
(A Peculiar Treasure, *1939*)

(unlike her novels, incidentally, which are indeed escapist in the sense that she suggested). In the stories Ferber's social conscience, of which she was justly proud, reigns supreme over her literary theory.

Ferber's next collection of stories brought a new character to the American literary scene and the American consciousness–the female "salesman"–and solidified her reputation as a writer of short fiction. The popular Emma McChesney stories began appearing in 1911 in the *American Magazine* and continued there and in *Cosmopolitan* until 1915. They were collected in three volumes– *Roast Beef, Medium: The Business Adventures of Emma McChesney* (1913); *Personality Plus: Some Experiences of Emma McChesney and Her Son, Jock* (1914); and *Emma McChesney & Co.* (1915)–and dramatized in 1915 as *Our Mrs. McChesney* by Ferber and George V. Hobart, with Ethel Barrymore cast, or, as Ferber thought, miscast, in the title role. These immensely popular stories form a continuing, loosely chronological, thematically connected saga of the life and times of the heroine, her son, her employer, and her colleagues.

Emma is thirty-six years old when she is introduced in *Roast Beef, Medium* and for the past ten years has been a successful "drummer," representing "T. A. Buck's Featherloom Petticoats." She had been married at eighteen, divorced at twentysix, and has a seventeen-year-old son, Jock. Emma will grow older in the course of the three volumes; the facts of her life will change and, accordingly, so will her reactions to people and events. She will grow both personally and professionally, and the reader follows the growth as it is revealed in Emma's various relationships.

The first two volumes establish Emma's world and set up relationships which will mature in the last collection of stories. Emma's skill at her job, her loneliness on the road, her longing for a settled life, and her fear that her son will turn out to be as much a cad as his father are developed early. In order to teach Jock a lesson in life, she takes him on the road with her for two highly educational weeks. Volume 1 nears an end with Jock leaving for college–and Emma feeling his loss–and with the death of shrewd T. A. Buck, her employer, father-figure, and the man

Photograph, circa 1938, signed by Ferber and Louis Bromfield

who knew her best. The provisions of Buck's will specify that Emma be made secretary of the firm. This enables her to settle, at last, in an apartment in New York. Meanwhile, it has become clear that T. A. Buck, Jr.–described as having "remarkably fine eyes"–who now runs the business and who has gotten over his initial mistrust of his female partner, has fallen in love with her. His proposal of marriage to the now thirty-nine-year-old Emma and her refusal end *Roast Beef, Medium*.

The relationship between Emma and T. A. Buck, Jr., takes second place in *Personality Plus* to the one between Emma and her son, now twenty-one, a brash college graduate, and a novice adman. The stories follow Jock from his first job interview through various failures and successes in his new profession. Emma comforts him, en-

courages him, and, when necessary, admonishes her son for a rare ethical lapse. Emma's attitude toward Jock is, by turns, exasperated, loving, and faintly and affectionately mocking. Under his mother's tutelage Jock matures: he gradually learns to temper his rashness, his vanity, even, at times, his charm. By the last story of the volume, "The Self Starter" (*American Magazine*, September 1914), Jock is well aware that his success–he will be the manager of the new Chicago branch of his agency–is largely due to Emma. As for Emma herself, when Jock leaves she is afraid of her own impending loneliness, but she is also proud: "This was her handiwork. . . . She looked at it, and found that it was good." Emma, the creator, can now relax, assured that her son's successful future is inevitable. There is also a strong suggestion at the end that she will indeed marry T. A. Buck, Jr.

In *Emma McChesney & Co.*, the third and final book of the series, plots and themes introduced in the earlier books coalesce. Emma is briefly working on the road again in "Broadway to Buenos Aires," this time, as the title indicates, in South America, where she successfully creates new skirt markets; in "Thanks to Miss Morrissey" (the title refers to a midwestern buyer and friend of Emma's) Ferber focuses on Buck's new business ability and Emma's ambivalence about his position as the head of the firm; in "Blue Serge" Emma, now married to Buck, tries to adjust to staying at home doing wifely and, to her mind, deadly boring chores and decides, finally, that she must return to work; in the last story, "An Etude for Emma," her reactions are revealed to yet other new roles for her, those of mother-in-law, and grandmother to a new Emma McChesney.

The effect of the McChesney stories is cumulative: Ferber's technique is to present different aspects of Emma and her world until she has presented the whole woman, her milieu, her beliefs and feelings, her friends, and her family. The stories, however, are not strictly connected. Since they were originally published separately, they were meant to be read independently of each other; yet, collected, they form the continuing saga of a woman of her time.

Emma McChesney, as a working woman, is also, by necessity, a feminist, albeit not to the degree the term indicates in contemporary society. Nor did Ferber–or Emma–have much use for organized feminism. Neither was a member of "The Movement," although both sympathized with its causes. Ferber's own brand of feminism derived not so much from any theoretical belief in the equality of women as from a belief that women have a right to share in the American Dream. This means, in practice, that her sympathies lie primarily with working women, the Emma McChesneys of America. It means, too, that Emma's attitudes are, in great part, defensive, based on her knowledge that the world believes women are *not* equal to men. And she is right: even old T. A. Buck, whom she adored and respected, once "complimented" her by saying she "ought to have been a man. With that head on a man's shoulders, you could put us out of business." Emma demands of her world–as represented by a hotel clerk who insists he does not have a room for her–that, since she is doing a

man's job and earning a man's salary, she "be treated with as much consideration as you'd show a man."

She, of course, is well aware of her own worth. Where her confidence falters or her vulnerability exhibits itself too strongly, they do so only temporarily and because they must if she is to be perceived as human. But still, Emma's–Ferber's–feminism is revealed as ambivalent, especially in the *Emma McChesney & Co.* stories. It is fitting that the ambivalence be revealed most strongly in this book since it is here that Emma is married. The ambivalence, in fact, is clearest precisely in the context of Emma's relationship with Buck: when Emma, distressed by Buck's new success as a businessman (or, more to the point, by her own loss of control), confides her feelings to Ethel Morrissey, Ethel tells her that the Lord is simply showing Emma her place. When woman begins to feel herself superior to man, the Lord makes her stumble and fall back a bit on the path to success. "He does this," says Ethel, "just as a gentle reminder to her that she's only a woman after all. Oh, I know all about this feminist talk. But the thing's been proven. Look at what happened to–to Joan of Arc, and Becky Sharpe, and Mary Queen of Scots. . . ." This bit of only mildly disguised advice is not lost on Emma nor, tellingly, is it countered by anyone else. On the contrary, she learns from it: when, on their honeymoon, Buck makes a mistake with their baggage and Emma says nothing, the reader is told that "her conduct that moment shaped the happiness of their future life together."

But Emma finds herself a failure as a housewife and, with Buck's approval, returns to work. At this point, however, it is clear that Buck is as competent as she to run the business, and this fact is doubly important in the fictional world of Edna Ferber: not only must the reader believe that Emma will not overshadow her man, but it must be evident that Buck is himself capable. Work to Ferber is sacred. It is a way to achieve the American Dream and, more, a way to gain humanity. The workers in Ferber's stories, at all levels, are portrayed as sympathetic, and some of the warmest moments in the stories occur in interactions between Emma and her working "sisters." Buck's weeks on the road, then, constitute a baptism of sorts and the final proof that he is deserving of Emma McChesney.

After the McChesney stories, Ferber's energies began to be devoted more and more to the writing of novels, although she continued to produce short fiction over the next three decades.

Ferber in Kotzebue, Alaska, 1956

The volume *Mother Knows Best: A Fiction Book* (1927) is a noteworthy example of the short stories she produced after her Pulitzer Prize for *So Big* and her wide recognition as a writer of extended fiction, since, stylistically and thematically, the stories resemble the novels. In the title story Sally Quail, a former child star, is dead at forty. The story looks at Sally's relationship with her tyrannical mother, who denied her daughter love and freedom in favor of a career; in "Every Other Thursday" Helmi, a Finnish maid, changes her clothes and her identity, has a steam bath, and dances with her lover, Vaino, once every two weeks; in "Holiday" the "devoted Cowans" are off to Atlantic City where, momentarily, Pa has an afternoon of freedom, Mother defies convention and spends extravagantly on underwear, and the unmarried daughter, Carrie, sneaks out of the hotel alone at night and is kissed by a stranger; in "Consider The Lilies" Poli Zbado, married at seventeen, finds freedom years later when her husband's plant goes on strike and, at last, they can travel west; in "Our Very Best People" Rutger G. Tune dies suddenly with his spats on and leaves nothing to his twin girls, so his beautiful, pretentious daughter Hilda lives off her rich eastern friends and plain Hannah finds work as a waitress. The latter marries a destitute brakeman who becomes general manager of the "Santa

Fe road," and after a silence of twenty years Hannah, now well-to-do, accidentally meets her sister, a saleswoman.

All of these stories are about the momentary fulfillment of personal fantasies. Ferber reveals the discrepancy between the public and the internal lives of people, their dreams and desires, and their longing for excitement. Their reality is humdrum but comfortable and safe (the suggestion also of the title of Ferber's earlier collection *Roast Beef, Medium* and a recurrent theme in much of her work). Ferber portrays these people with accurate detail and, when, as it often does, her point of view becomes that of the characters', with a great deal of charm and psychological astuteness. Their innocence creates the narrative tone, allowing Ferber to use only the gentlest of irony.

There is one exception to this, however: "Mother Knows Best," in which the character of the mother falls under Ferber's sharply honed narrative knife. Responsible for her daughter's unhappiness throughout her life, at her funeral the mother is "swathed in expensive mourning which transformed her into a sable pillar of woe through whose transparencies you somehow got the impression that she was automatically counting the house." It has been suggested by Gilbert that the story is a version of Ferber's relationship with her own mother and is "the closest to psychological home that Ferber ever reached on paper." What makes the autobiographical element interesting is that it is worked out in the same terms of wish-fulfillment as the other stories, but with the twist that the heroine, unlike her creator, dies in the prime of life.

At the time of her death on 17 April 1968 Edna Ferber was better known as a novelist than a writer of short fiction. It should be noted, however, that many of the important themes and techniques evident in the novels and transferred to the screen were introduced first in the short stories. Rarely in those stories is there a true villain and rarely are people undeserving of their desserts: wayward lovers return to their good women after realizing their mistakes, and falsely accused people are finally exonerated by the truth. Ferber's language, particularly the breezy dialogue of the earlier stories, may be of its time, but the subject matter of the stories is not dated.

These short fictions deal with recognizable human feelings and reactions unattached to history and so are alive still.

Bibliography:

V. J. Brenni and B. L. Spencer, "Edna Ferber: A Selected Bibliography," *Bulletin of Bibliography*, 22 (1958): 152-156.

Biography:

Julie Goldsmith Gilbert, *Ferber: A Biography* (New York: Doubleday, 1978).

Reference:

Mary Rose Shaughnessy, *Women and Success in American Society in the Works of Edna Ferber* (New York: Gordon Press, 1977).

Papers:

The State Historical Society of Wisconsin holds the principal collection of Ferber's papers.

F. Scott Fitzgerald

(24 September 1896-21 December 1940)

Ruth Prigozy
Hofstra University

See also the Fitzgerald entries in *DLB 4: American Writers in Paris 1920-1939; DLB 9: American Novelists, 1910-1945; DLB Yearbook: 1981;* and *DLB Documentary Series: 1.*

BOOKS: *This Side of Paradise* (New York: Scribners, 1920; London: Collins, 1921);

Flappers and Philosophers (New York: Scribners, 1920; London: Collins, 1922);

The Beautiful and Damned (New York: Scribners, 1922; London: Collins, 1922);

Tales of the Jazz Age (New York: Scribners, 1922; London: Collins, 1923);

The Vegetable (New York: Scribners, 1923);

The Great Gatsby (New York: Scribners, 1925; London: Chatto & Windus, 1926);

All the Sad Young Men (New York: Scribners, 1926);

Tender Is the Night (New York: Scribners, 1934; London: Chatto & Windus, 1934);

Taps at Reveille (New York: Scribners, 1935);

The Last Tycoon, edited by Edmund Wilson (New York: Scribners, 1941; London: Grey Walls, 1949);

The Crack-Up, edited by Wilson (New York: New Directions, 1945; Harmondsworth, U.K.: Penguin, 1965);

The Stories of F. Scott Fitzgerald, edited by Malcolm Cowley (New York: Scribners, 1951);

Afternoon of an Author, edited by Arthur Mizener (Princeton: Princeton University Library, 1957; London: Bodley Head, 1958);

The Pat Hobby Stories, edited by Arnold Gingrich (New York: Scribners, 1962; Harmondsworth, U.K.: Penguin, 1967);

The Apprentice Fiction of F. Scott Fitzgerald, 1909-1917, edited by John Kuehl (New Brunswick, N.J.: Rutgers University Press, 1965);

F. Scott Fitzgerald In His Own Time: A Miscellany, edited by Matthew J. Bruccoli and Jackson R. Bryer (Kent, Ohio: Kent State University Press, 1971);

F. Scott Fitzgerald

The Basil and Josephine Stories, edited by Bryer and Kuehl (New York: Scribners, 1973);

Bits of Paradise: 21 Uncollected Stories by F. Scott and Zelda Fitzgerald, edited by Scottie Fitzgerald Smith and Bruccoli (New York: Scribners, 1973);

F. Scott Fitzgerald's Ledger, edited by Bruccoli (Washington, D.C.: Bruccoli Clark / NCR Microcard Books, 1973);

The Great Gatsby: A Facsimile of the Manuscript, edited by Bruccoli (Washington, D.C.: Bruccoli Clark / NCR Microcard Books, 1973);

F. Scott Fitzgerald's Screenplay for Three Comrades by Erich Maria Remarque, edited by Bruccoli

(Carbondale & Edwardsville: Southern Illinois University Press, 1978);

The Notebooks of F. Scott Fitzgerald, edited by Bruccoli (New York: Harcourt Brace Jovanovich / Bruccoli Clark, 1978);

F. Scott Fitzgerald's St. Paul Plays: 1911-1914, edited by Alan Margolies (Princeton: Princeton University Library, 1978);

The Price Was High: The Last Uncollected Stories of F. Scott Fitzgerald, edited by Bruccoli (New York: Harcourt Brace Jovanovich / Bruccoli Clark, 1979);

Poems 1911-1940, edited by Bruccoli (Bloomfield Hills, Mich. & Columbia, S.C.: Bruccoli Clark, 1981);

The Stories of F. Scott Fitzgerald, edited by Bruccoli (New York: Scribners, 1989).

Although for the general reader F. Scott Fitzgerald's fame rests primarily on one novel, *The Great Gatsby* (1925), his creative life, from youth to early death, found full expression in some 160 short stories. These works not only provided the income that sustained Fitzgerald when writing his novels, but they also enhanced the legend that grew up around Scott and Zelda Fitzgerald after his first novel, *This Side of Paradise* (1920), appeared at the beginning of the Jazz Age. For ten years thereafter the pages of the *Saturday Evening Post, Redbook, Woman's Home Companion*, and other mass-circulation magazines were filled with romantic tales of young lovers, of dreamers and doers, of madcap heroines and sad young men, many of whom seemed to reflect aspects of the lives of their creator and his wife.

Fitzgerald is one of the most widely recognized names in American literature, yet the legend he so carefully cultivated has, paradoxically, tended to obscure the writer as well as his work. Fitzgerald was a major novelist, but at least a dozen of his stories rank among the very best short fiction written in the twentieth century. Fitzgerald's whole life was bound up with his short stories; indeed, the story of his life cannot be told without them. Only through an acquaintance with his career as a short-fiction writer can the complex man who now occupies a major position in the literary and mythic life of the nation be understood.

Perhaps no other American writer has felt himself as inextricably tied to the history of his country as F. Scott Fitzgerald. Born in 1896, at the end of an era of unprecedented national growth, he lived to see the traditions that had guided his parents' generation and his own childhood cast aside; indeed, he was said by his contemporaries to have precipitated the upheaval in manners and morals that accompanied the end of World War I. Never as "lost" as the members of his generation described in Paris by Gertrude Stein, Fitzgerald nevertheless experienced and even personified the "boom" of the 1920s and the "bust" of the 1930s. America had sloughed off its past and headed for, as Fitzgerald said, the "greatest, gaudiest spree in history"; when it was over, he realized that the nation had been living on borrowed time, "a short and precious time— for when the mist rises . . . one finds that the very best is over."

The elegiac note that characterizes his reminiscences of the 1920s is typical of Fitzgerald's writing; its origins were in his early childhood and struggling adolescence. He felt himself always to be an outsider—from the elite society of the St. Paul, Minnesota, of his boyhood, from the spectacular achievements of the athletes of his school days, from the glittering social world of his young manhood, from the wealth and power of the American aristocracy, and even, at the end, from the literary life of his nation.

Fitzgerald's sense of estrangement was rooted in his family background. He never forgot that he was related, however distantly, to Francis Scott Key, a name that conjured up images of America's heroic past. He listened attentively to the tales his father, Edward Fitzgerald, told of the family's Confederate past. He noted the connection between his father's family and, through marriage, Mary Surratt, hanged as a conspirator in Lincoln's assassination. And on the side of his mother, Molly McQuillan, although the ancestry was not as patrician as his father's, he could point to the vitality of his grandfather, an Irishman who epitomized the self-made American merchants in the decades immediately following the Civil War. Fitzgerald admitted in 1933 in a letter to John O'Hara, "I am half black Irish and half old American stock with the usual exaggerated ancestral pretensions. The black Irish half of the family had the money and looked down upon the Maryland side of the family who had, and really had, that . . . series of reticences and obligations that go under the poor old shattered word 'breeding.'" When his own father experienced serious business failures during Fitzgerald's childhood, the boy was distraught. He experienced such severe anxieties that he expected the family to be taken to the poorhouse, and his later finan-

Dust jacket for Fitzgerald's first short-story collection, published in 1920. The illustration refers to "Bernice Bobs Her Hair"; the book also includes "The Offshore Pirate" and "The Ice Palace."

cial insecurity reinforced these childhood traumas. His life suggests that perhaps unconsciously he *had* to live on a financial brink.

The Fitzgerald family became increasingly dependent on the mother's relatives in St. Paul after moves to Buffalo, Syracuse, and back to Buffalo, with several different residences in each city. They moved several times in St. Paul, too, but always lived in rented houses or apartments in the Summit Avenue neighborhood where railroad tycoon James J. Hill kept his residence. The years of Fitzgerald's childhood and early youth were marked in his memory indelibly: he was the outsider, the poor relation, dependent on his grandmother and his aunt, admitted to but never really part of the social center of St. Paul life. That sense of estrangement so characteristic of his formative years marks much of his fiction, from the first short stories, written when he was about thirteen, to his last efforts in Hollywood. Similarly, despite his father's weaknesses and fail-

ures Fitzgerald was never to relinquish his loyalty to him and to the traditions he represented.

Fitzgerald was admitted to the St. Paul Academy, a private high school, in 1908, where he remained for three years. It was there, from 1909 to 1911, that he published his first short stories, in the school literary magazine *Now and Then*. In the late 1920s he re-created these years in the Basil Duke Lee stories, which depict the painful rejections Fitzgerald experienced at St. Paul Academy where he was disliked and socially unsuccessful. He attempted to use sports as a path to acceptance, but he did not have the physique for football stardom. His most cherished memories of the St. Paul experience were those connected with the stage. Fitzgerald always loved drama, and his earliest writing efforts were either in the form of short plays or stories with strong theatrical elements. When his poor grades at St. Paul Academy necessitated his changing schools, he was enrolled at the Newman School in Hackensack, New Jersey, where he could indulge his taste for the theater with a few thrilling trips to New York City, less than an hour away. Here he felt the glamour and excitement he had dreamed about in St. Paul. For the rest of his life New York City would hold a special magic for Fitzgerald: success, vitality, and enchantment.

His popularity improved slowly at Newman, but his opportunities to escape from an unpleasant reality were greater than they had ever been. And it was perhaps the color and excitement of the Broadway theater, particularly the musicals, that so captured Fitzgerald's imagination that he aspired throughout his life to achieve fame as a playwright or librettist. He continued to write short stories at Newman, where the school magazine, the *Newman News*, published three of his efforts. His Newman career was not the failure that the St. Paul Academy had been. At the beginning of his second year he met the person who would become the most influential figure in his early life, both creatively and personally, Father Sigourney Fay, who would become director of the school. Father Fay was a sophisticated, lively esthete, a friend of many well-known figures in arts and letters, including writer Shane Leslie. Fay revealed to Fitzgerald a far more attractive Catholicism than he had ever known and opened a world to him that suggested the beauty and richness of experience he would always try to capture in his writing.

Fitzgerald entered Princeton University in 1913, and although he never graduated, his years there were the most important to his development as a writer. He never lost his interest in sports, but knowing that he could not succeed as a participant, he sought other roads to success and the popularity he would always crave. His major activities at Princeton were in the Triangle Club, the *Tiger*, and the *Nassau Literary Magazine*.

In the first of the two periods he spent at Princeton (he left in his junior year as a result of poor grades and illness, returning the following year only to enlist in the army after the United States entered World War I) he contributed the plot and lyrics to a Triangle show and the lyrics to another, and he wrote a one-act play and a short story, "The Ordeal" (*Nassau Literary Magazine*, June 1915). In 1917, when he returned to Princeton, he wrote five stories and one short play as well as one Triangle show. The stories from this period reveal a growing maturity in the author. Three were later revised for publication in H. L. Mencken's *Smart Set*, two were incorporated into Fitzgerald's first novel, *This Side of Paradise*, and one, "Tarquin of Cheapside" (*Nassau Literary Magazine*, April 1917), later appeared in his second collection of stories, *Tales of the Jazz Age* (1922). Clearly these years were of major importance to his development as a writer.

At Princeton he expanded his literary horizons considerably, largely through his friendships with John Peale Bishop, who introduced him to poetry, particularly that of John Keats, and with Edmund Wilson, who would become the "intellectual conscience" of his life. He admired Christian Gauss, the teacher who recognized the unique quality of Fitzgerald's prose. In the richest intellectual environment he had ever experienced he read Oscar Wilde, Ernest Dowson, Algernon Charles Swinburne, and Compton Mackenzie, whose *Sinister Street* (1913-1914) made a marked impression on him. Later at Princeton he read Bernard Shaw, Rupert Brooke, and H. G. Wells and dabbled in socialist theory. His social life broadened, too. He was elected to the Cottage, one of the most elite Princeton clubs, largely because his standing among his classmates was enhanced by his successes with the Triangle productions.

And it was while at Princeton that Fitzgerald met the girl who would become the prototype for so many of the beautiful but elusive women who appear in his stories and novels, Ginevra King. His meeting with Ginevra was so important that he used it, and his memories of her, in the Basil and Josephine stories over a decade later.

Fitzgerald in the early 1920s

After receiving his army commission, Fitzgerald was stationed in Montgomery, Alabama, where he met the girl who was to become the single most important person in his life, Zelda Sayre. Like Ginevra, Zelda appears throughout Fitzgerald's fictional world. She is Sally Carrol in "The Ice Palace" (*Saturday Evening Post*, 22 May 1920; collected in *Flappers and Philosophers*, 1920), the heroine of "The Last of the Belles" (*Saturday Evening Post*, 2 March 1929; collected in *Taps at Reveille*, 1935), and Jonquil in " 'The Sensible Thing' " (*Liberty*, 5 July 1924; collected in *All the Sad Young Men*, 1926); she is the model for most of the women in his stories and novels until the late 1930s. Zelda was the most popular, daring, and vital girl in Montgomery. For Fitzgerald she represented the glamour of the unattainable, and he fell deeply in love with her. In the ledger that he kept until 1937 (published as *F. Scott Fitzgerald's Ledger*, 1973) Fitzgerald reported that his twenty-second year was "The most important year of life. Every emotion and my life work decided. Miserable and ecstatic but a great success." In the entry for September of that year he notes, "Fell in love on the 7th." Fitzgerald also wrote the first version of *This Side of Paradise* while in the army.

Much has been written about the relationship between Scott and Zelda Fitzgerald. It was stormy, passionate, fierce, often ugly. Despite their quarrels and mutual self-destructiveness, the bond between them was so strong that long after her mental illness had kept them apart he could not divorce her, even when he fell in love with Sheilah Graham during his last years in Hollywood. Zelda lacked any principle of order; she threw herself into the heady celebrations that marked her husband's early success. She competed with him; she goaded him; she joined him in showing the world how an attractive and successful young American couple could defy convention and live for the thrill of the moment.

Zelda wrote many poignant letters after her illness, and, indeed, she has emerged as a pitiable figure, particularly in recent years when she has come to be regarded as a casualty of the American system of marriage–a woman who needed artistic fulfillment of her own, struggling against the domination of a male-oriented society. That kind of conclusion is simplistic; the truth of the relationship cannot really be known. Zelda Fitzgerald, whatever anguish she experienced and caused in those around her, is inseparable from her husband's career. His initial struggle for literary success in 1920 was caused by Zelda's refusal to marry him because he did not have enough money to support them. Subsequently, he kept on writing the short stories that would provide the money for them to maintain the style of life they desired, to maintain her throughout years of medical care and hospitalization, and to pay for their daughter, Scottie's, care and education.

Fitzgerald wrote nineteen short stories in the spring of 1919, all of them rejected by magazines. In June *Smart Set* bought "Babes in the Woods," first published in the *Nassau Literary Magazine* in May 1917, for thirty dollars. (It appeared in the September 1919 *Smart Set* and was later incorporated into *This Side of Paradise*.) Fitzgerald was living in New York, working in advertising, and struggling to finish his novel.

In the summer of 1919 Fitzgerald left New York City for St. Paul, where he finished *This Side of Paradise* and resubmitted it to Scribners, who had previously rejected it but now accepted it for publication in the spring of 1920. While waiting, he sold six stories to the *Smart Set* for $215 in October and two more in November for $300. His big break came when his new agent, Harold

Ober, sold "Head and Shoulders" to the *Saturday Evening Post*, where it appeared in the 21 February 1920 issue, for $400. Ober later sold the film rights to the story for $2,500. In the early months of 1920, soon after the publication of *This Side of Paradise*, Fitzgerald wrote one of his best stories, "May Day," which was rejected by the *Post* but admired by Mencken, who included it in the July 1920 *Smart Set*. On 3 April 1920 Scott and Zelda were married in New York.

Scribners followed publication of the novel with Fitzgerald's first collection of short stories, *Flappers and Philosophers*. Although only three of the stories may be considered among his best ("The Ice Palace," "The Offshore Pirate" [*Saturday Evening Post*, 29 May 1920], and "Bernice Bobs Her Hair" [*Saturday Evening Post*, 1 May 1920]), the volume appealed to the audience that had embraced his novel. The collection sold 15,325 copies by 1922, with six printings. The reviews were not as enthusiastic as those for *This Side of Paradise;* indeed, Mencken made note of the two-sidedness of Fitzgerald's creative life–the serious writer and the popular entertainer. This view of Fitzgerald was to characterize critical judgments of his fiction, particularly in relation to the short stories, from the 1920s to the present day. From this point in his life short stories would provide Fitzgerald's major income. He never made much money from his novels, including *This Side of Paradise* which, despite its success, never achieved the sales of a best-seller. During the next twelve years the *Saturday Evening Post* was Fitzgerald's main outlet for short stories, his fees increasing to $4,000 per story for the years 1929 through 1932.

There is a popular conception about Fitzgerald's work for the *Post*–that his stories were written to slick-magazine specifications, and therefore they represent the commercial side of his talent. It is a common belief that Fitzgerald bartered his gifts by writing short stories acceptable to the *Post*, which was edited from 1899 to 1936 by George H. Lorimer. Lorimer demanded an unusually high standard from his *Post* writers, allowing them wide latitude in choice of subject and form. There were certainly standards of commercial acceptability to which he subscribed, but they depended on professional smoothness, readability, and verve. The *Post* encouraged, but did not demand, strong plots, leisurely narrative, a good mixture of dialogue and action, and vivid characters. These requirements, while not stimulating radical departures from convention, also did not

 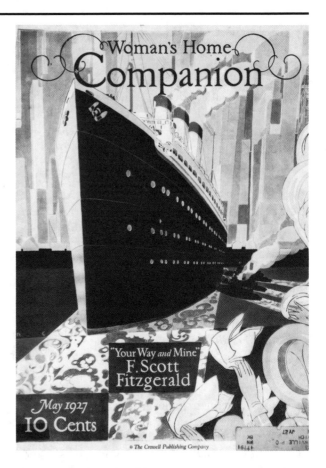

Covers for two magazines featuring short stories by Fitzgerald

necessarily constrict or hamper creative instincts. And they were characteristics of Fitzgerald's fiction long before the *Post* ever accepted one of his stories. Happy endings were not prescribed, as proved by the publication in the *Post* of "Babylon Revisited" (21 February 1931; collected in *Taps at Reveille*), "The Rough Crossing" (8 June 1929), "Two Wrongs" (18 January 1930; collected in *Taps at Reveille*), and "One Trip Abroad" (11 October 1930).

Fitzgerald's letters underscore his independence as well as his dedication to his work. Although commercial writing is, he admitted in a 1940 letter to Zelda, a "definite trick," he felt he brought to it the "intelligence and good writing" to which a sensitive editor like Lorimer might respond. In Wesley W. Stout, Lorimer's successor, "an up and coming young Republican who gives not a damn about literature," he placed the blame for the plethora of "escape stories about the brave frontiersmen . . . or fishing, or football captains, nothing that would even faintly shock or disturb the reactionary bourgeois." He con-

ceded that he had tried but could not write such stories. "As soon as I feel I am writing to a cheap specification my pen freezes and my talent vanishes over the hill. . . ." To Harold Ober he confessed that he was unable to "rush things. Even in years like '24, '28, '29, '30, all devoted to short stories, I could not turn out more than 8-9 top-price stories a year. It simply is impossible–all my stories are conceived like novels, require a special emotion, a special experience–so that my readers . . . know that each time it'll be something new, not in form but in substance."

After their marriage the Fitzgeralds rarely remained in one place more than six months to a year. After a whirlwind descent on New York City, they retreated to Westport, Connecticut, and then to Europe. Back in America, they lived briefly in St. Paul where Fitzgerald revised his novel *The Beautiful and Damned* (1922) and put together *Tales of the Jazz Age*, in which only two pieces, "The Diamond as Big as the Ritz" (*Smart Set*, June 1922) and "Two for a Cent" (*Metropolitan Magazine*, April 1922), had been written after 1920.

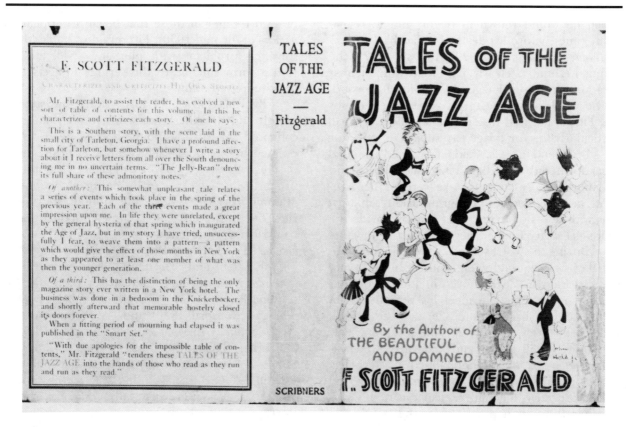

Dust jacket for Fitzgerald's second short-story collection, published in 1922 and including "May Day" and "The Diamond as Big as the Ritz"

The collection contained eleven stories, divided into three sections: "My Last Flappers," "Fantasies," and "Unclassified Masterpieces." The John Held cartoon cover and Fitzgerald's annotated table of contents made it an attractive volume. Sales were good: eight thousand copies sold in the first printing, followed by two more printings in the same year. Readers liked the collection more than the critics did; most of them regarded the stories as diversions and failed to recognize the merit of "May Day" or "The Diamond as Big as the Ritz."

During the next few years the Fitzgeralds moved frequently: from Great Neck to France, to Italy, to Delaware, and even to Hollywood, where Fitzgerald was invited to try his hand at screenwriting. He was, at the same time, writing the major novels for which he received critical acclaim, *The Great Gatsby* and *Tender Is the Night* (1934). During these years Fitzgerald was at the top of his form as a short-story writer not only in the quantity but also in the quality of the fiction he produced. Because he needed money to finance the writing of *The Great Gatsby*, he produced eleven short stories in just four months.

He was able to put together another collection in 1926, and this one, *All the Sad Young Men*, contained some of his finest work: "The Rich Boy" (*Redbook*, January, February 1926), "Winter Dreams" (*Metropolitan Magazine*, December 1922), "Absolution" (*American Mercury*, June 1924), and " 'The Sensible Thing.' " As was his practice, he meticulously edited the magazine versions, careful to remove passages that he had "stripped" from them for use in *The Great Gatsby*. (It was characteristic of Fitzgerald to mine his stories for particularly felicitous passages which could be used in the novels.) This volume, too, was relatively successful, considering that short-story collections rarely sold well. It went into three printings, totaling 16,170 copies in 1926. The critics were decidedly more impressed with this collection than either of the two that had appeared earlier, yet in retrospect it is clear that few recognized its level of artistry.

Just as his months in Europe had provided Fitzgerald with new friendships and influences–Ernest Hemingway, Gertrude Stein, Gerald and Sara Murphy–his two-month sojourn in Hollywood in early 1927 introduced him to a world to which he would return in fiction and in reality many times before his death. In "Jacob's Ladder" (*Saturday Evening Post*, 20 August 1927) the young heroine is clearly patterned after actress Lois Moran, whom Fitzgerald met in Hollywood. As he would continue to do for the rest of his life, Fitzgerald used his own personal experience, particularly his marriage, as subject matter for his stories and novels. Zelda Fitzgerald's mental breakdown did not allow Fitzgerald to suspend his short-story writing to take care of her. Instead, he combined visits to her in various sanatoriums with bouts of writing that would provide the funds necessary for her care and treatment.

During the worst years of economic and emotional crisis Fitzgerald wrote some of his most eloquent stories. As Zelda moved in and out of clinics and he struggled to meet his responsibilities to her and to his daughter, he wrote the Basil Duke Lee stories (1928-1929), the Josephine Perry stories (1930-1931), and the story which is today regarded as an unqualified masterpiece, "Babylon Revisited." The stories from this period are retrospective, meditative, elegiac, certainly sadder than those he had written for the *Post* during the previous ten years, and the *Post* editors did not like them.

By the early 1930s Fitzgerald had lost his taste for writing the stories of young love which had brought him to the top of the magazine pay scale by 1929. Of the forty-two stories written in the six years from 1929 to 1935, eight (the Basil and Josephine stories) draw on autobiographical events and cultural attitudes that reflect the years from World War I through the 1920s. Five of the remaining stories are so trivial as to demand only wonder that they managed to find their way into print. ("The Passionate Eskimo" [*Liberty*, 8 June 1935] and "Zone of Accident," [*Saturday Evening Post*, 13 July 1935] are among them.) But the other twenty-nine provide important insight into Fitzgerald's artistic crisis, when his subjects were as serious as his and the nation's trials demanded, but his plots were outworn, stale, mechanical–unintentional parodies of the exuberant accounts of young love and romantic longing that so captivated audiences during the boom years. These stories show Fitzgerald groping with painful subjects and achieving only intermittent success but on at least two occasions, with "Babylon Revisited" and "Crazy Sunday" (*American Mercury*, October 1932), producing masterpieces that incorporate the matter, if not the manner, of his more commercial contemporary work. In these two stories and in those that began to appear in *Esquire* in the mid 1930s, Fitzgerald was able to resolve his problems with plot and style, and to find a form suitable to the serious subjects that now interested him.

By 1934 Fitzgerald was writing one story a month and drinking excessively, until finally he collapsed. At this low point (he had been disappointed by the poor sales, despite critical praise, of *Tender Is the Night*, which had been published in April) he suggested to his editor at Scribners, Maxwell Perkins, a new collection of short stories, *Taps at Reveille*. The volume contained eighteen stories, including such Basil Duke Lee stories as "The Freshest Boy" (*Saturday Evening Post*, 28 July 1928) and "He Thinks He's Wonderful" (*Saturday Evening Post*, 29 September 1928), the Josephine Perry stories "First Blood" (*Saturday Evening Post*, 5 April 1930) and "A Woman with a Past" (*Saturday Evening Post*, 6 September 1930), and other first-rate examples of his art: "Crazy Sunday," "The Last of the Belles," and "Babylon Revisited." The first printing was 5,100 copies, and the reviews were generally good, but short-story collections at any time were luxuries, and in the Depression, with a $2.50 cover price, the volume did not attract a wide readership. Fitzgerald's *Post* price had dropped to $3,000 per story, and of the nine he wrote in 1935, the magazine accepted only three. His primary outlet in the late 1930s was *Esquire*, whose editor, Arnold Gingrich, encouraged Fitzgerald, agreeing to accept anything he wrote. The stringent space limitations of the magazine coincided with Fitzgerald's search for a new form and a new style, but its low fees ($250 per story) were insufficient to support him. In 1936 he wrote nine stories, semifictional sketches, and articles for *Esquire*, including "Afternoon of an Author" (August 1936) and "Author's House" (July 1936), but they brought him only $2,250. These were Fitzgerald's most anguished years: Zelda was hopelessly ill; his own health had deteriorated badly; his income had shrunk to $10,000 by 1937; and he suffered a serious breakdown, physically and emotionally.

In 1937 Ober secured a contract for Fitzgerald as a screenwriter for M-G-M studios. Although he worked on many films and screenplays, only *Three Comrades* (1937) gives him screen credit (as cowriter). Nevertheless, these last years were among Fitzgerald's most artistically creative and personally satisfying. Despite his family problems and his poor health, he found personal happiness in his relationship with

Hollywood gossip columnist Sheilah Graham. In addition to the uncompleted novel *The Last Tycoon* (1941), Fitzgerald wrote a series of stories for *Esquire* about a Hollywood hack writer, Pat Hobby. Fitzgerald had a heart attack in November 1940 and died on 21 December after suffering a second attack. In his hand was the *Princeton Alumni Weekly*. At his death he was almost forgotten as a writer; his royalty statement for the summer of 1940 was $13.13. Since the 1950s his reputation has grown steadily, and today he is ranked among the most important writers of the century. And the short stories, long neglected or undervalued, are at last receiving the kind of serious attention they have always deserved. But Fitzgerald always knew their value: "I have asked a lot of my emotions–one hundred and twenty stories. The price was high, right up with Kipling, because there was one little drop of something–not blood, not a tear, not my seed, but me more intimately than these, in every story, it was the extra I had."

Fitzgerald did not have a notably idiosyncratic linguistic style, as did Hemingway or William Faulkner, but a Fitzgerald story is recognizable by its romantic rhetoric, characters, settings, and social concerns. Fitzgerald experimented frequently with plots, subjects, and characters. The late stories are markedly different from the early group; both in style and substance they are innovative and experimental. For example, from Hollywood and his experience as a scriptwriter, Fitzgerald borrowed techniques, such as fade-outs and the camera angle as point of view.

The stories reveal a pattern of development and fall into three groups: the early tales about golden flappers and idealistic philosophers; the middle, embarrassingly sentimental, often mawkish stories; and finally, the late works, marked by new techniques–ellipsis, compression, suggestion–curiously enervated, yet deeply moving. Similar to these, yet distinctly separate, stand the Pat Hobby stories, where the old vitality had become corrosive bitterness in a literature of humiliation.

Most of his stories employ standard fictional techniques used in the novels: central complication, descriptive passages, dramatic climaxes and confrontations, reversals of fortune. And like the novels, the stories rarely turn on one action; more often, even in the shortest, slightest story, there are several actions of equal weight. His major problem is with plot; Fitzgerald will often begin with a good idea, create dramatic scenes, and then let the story limply peter out, or resolve

the complications mechanically. An ending technique he used often was to blanket the resolution in lyrical prose, thus concealing the weakness of the story's resolution. Another weakness in the stories is related to point of view and distance, particularly in relation to the protagonists. Fitzgerald is most successful when his central character is both a participant and an observer of the action, weakest when the protagonist is simply a member of the upper class or an outsider.

Fitzgerald's gifts as a writer were primarily lyric and poetic; lapses in plot and characterization did not concern him nearly as much as using the wrong word. His revisions show that he edited primarily for phrase or rhythm in a sentence. Thus, his stories, whatever their plots, are almost always notable for the grace and lyricism of his rhetoric. His descriptive gifts are strikingly apparent; with a few selected details, usually in atmosphere or decor, he creates a mood against which the dramatic situation stands out in relief. In "News of Paris," a late sketch (probably written in 1940, published posthumously in *Furioso* in 1947), merely two lines, "It was quiet in the room. The peacocks in the draperies stirred in the April wind," provide the background for a brief but haunting retrospective account of dissolution, apathy, and tired sexuality in the pre-Depression boom.

Through language Fitzgerald created another world in his stories, a fairy-tale world replete with its own conventions and milieus, free of the tensions in his own all-too-depressingly familiar environment; he projected his imagination through the rhetoric of nostalgia into the past, creating a never-never land of beauty, stupefying luxury, and fulfillment. Fitzgerald's other world is a refuge from fear and anxiety, satiety and void; it is his answer to death and deterioration. Through a profusion of words, images–especially the sights, sounds, smells of luxury–perhaps existence itself might take on new meaning and possibility. The words themselves, for Fitzgerald, may have provided refuge from the storms of his own life. His infusions of charged rhetoric throughout the stories offer unshakable evidence of his belief in and commitment to that other world beyond his own, a world of possibility, hope, and beauty. Through imagery, through sensory appeals, through the evocative re-creation of an idealized past and a fabulous future, Fitzgerald's stories as a whole have the effect of lifting and transporting the reader past the restrictions of his own world. Fitzgerald was not simply playing

Pages from Fitzgerald's Ledger *recording published fiction at the beginning of his professional career*

Produced by	Date	Movie Made by	Sources	Remarks	Disposition 3
Dramatic Club Univ. Ala. Feb 1921		See T.S.of P.	Play in Nassau Litt Mag January 1917		Included in This Side of Paradise
		See T.S.P.	Published in Nassau Litt.		Included in This Side of Paradise
Players League april 16th, 1923 Δ March, 1924				2nd Serial "College Stories"	In Tales of the Jazz Age
					In Flappers and Philosophers
			Story in Nassau Litt Mag. June 1915		In Flappers and Philosophers
Bayard Veiller offer turn down		Metro (Dana) "The Chorus Girl's Romance"			In Flappers and Philosophers
			The Usual Thing Nassau Litt. Dec. 1916.		In Tales of the Jazz Age
		"Fot (Percy) "The Husband Hunter"	Lilah Meets his family april 1917	Stripped and —	Permanently Buried
See Debutante		Famous Players	The Romantic Egotist Nov 1917 – Mar 1918 And destroyed stories 1917	Cheap editions, Burt + Collins. Popular Lions 2nd serial Daily News act	This Side of Paradise
		Still D man R us "Conductor 1492"			In Tales of the Jazz Age
				O'brien, two stars	In Flappers and Philosophers
					In Flappers and Philosophers
				Anthology "Trumps"	In Flappers and Philosophers
		Metro (Dana)			In Flappers and Philosophers
				O'brien, two stars	In Flappers and Philosophers
			Smile, Smile, Smile June 1917	Stripped and ——	Permanently Buried
					In Tales of the Jazz Age

Dust jacket for Fitzgerald's third short-story collection, published in 1926 and including "The Rich Boy" and "Winter Dreams"

on the facile sensibilities of his readers. The stories testify to his abiding faith in the possibility, somewhere, of living a graceful life. That this life might be made up of questionable values–of riches, of Hollywood-like romance, of tinselly fairgrounds and gilded mansions–is less important than that Fitzgerald asks his readers to share, perhaps ingenuously, his dedication to a dream.

His prose is filled with imagery, sensory in the Keatsian manner. He describes bridges, "like dancers holding hands in a row, with heads as tall as cities, and skirts of cable strand" (" 'The Sensible Thing' "); trees, "like tall languid ladies with feather fans coquetting airily with the ugly roof of the monastery . . . delicate lace on the hems of many yellow fields" ("Benediction," *Smart Set*, February 1920; collected in *Flappers and Philosophers*); and moonlight, "That stream of silver that waved like a wide strand of curly hair toward the moon" ("Love in the Night," *Saturday Evening Post*, 14 March 1925). And his stories are filled with colors, bright blue and gold, white and silver, occasionally coalescing in a symbol that evokes a range of meanings beyond the purely decorative. In "May Day" the "great plate-glass front had turned to a deep creamy blue, the color of a Maxfield Parrish moonlight–a blue that seemed to press close upon the pane as if to crowd its way into the restaurant. Dawn had come up in Co-

lumbus Circle, magical, breathless dawn, silhouetting the great statue of the immortal Christopher, and mingling in a curious and uncanny manner with the fading yellow electric light inside."

The world of Fitzgerald's stories is most frequently the world of the very rich. The milieus and manners constitute the backdrop against which a rags-to-riches story may unfold, a struggling young man is rescued by a benevolent tycoon, or a beautiful Cinderella meets her handsome, wealthy prince. Even in the more somber stories, manners and milieu are as important as the plot or the characters.

Although most of the stories can be classified as stories of manners, there are several that fall into the category of fantasy, using supernatural devices, suspense and mystery, and fabulous, fabricated milieus as critical elements of plot. In "The Adjuster" (*Redbook*, September 1925; collected in *All the Sad Young Men*) Fitzgerald combines a realistic surface, homiletic intention, and supernatural agent in a unique, yet not entirely successful, mixture. Dr. Moon, the supernatural figure, is introduced purely as a deus ex machina in a story which is concerned with the growth of maturity and responsibility in a selfish young married woman. Dr. Moon is a strange amalgam, half-psychiatrist, half fortune-teller. He appears at regular intervals when the plot begins to falter, re-

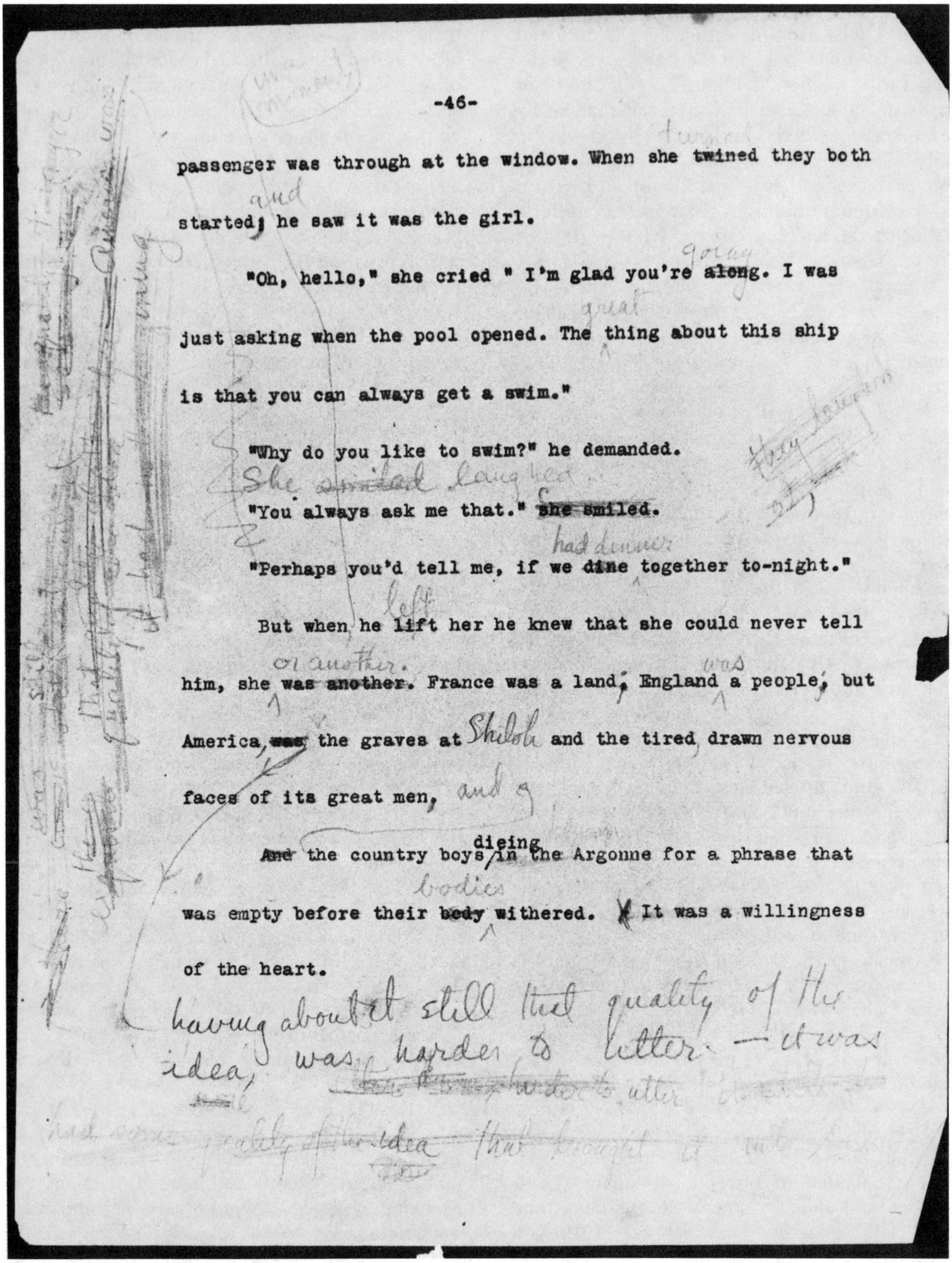

-46-

passenger was through at the window. When she twined they both started; he saw it was the girl.

"Oh, hello," she cried " I'm glad you're along. I was just asking when the pool opened. The thing about this ship is that you can always get a swim."

"Why do you like to swim?" he demanded.

"You always ask me that." she smiled.

"Perhaps you'd tell me, if we dine together to-night."

But when he lift her he knew that she could never tell him, she was another. France was a land England a people but America, was the graves at Shiloh and the tired drawn nervous faces of its great men,

And the country boys dieing in the Argonne for a phrase that was empty before their body withered. It was a willingness of the heart.

having about it still that quality of the idea, was harder to utter — it was

Revised typescript page for the conclusion of "The Swimmers," first published in the 19 October 1929 issue of the Saturday Evening Post *(Bruccoli Collection)*

ordering the events. Thus he prevents the woman, Luella, from deserting her sick husband; he compels her to take up the irksome, neglected role of wife, mother, and housekeeper; and he rewards her at the end by confessing that he has never really existed: she has merely grown up, and he symbolizes her growth. He is on hand, also, to deliver to her a final homily on performing one's duties unselfishly. In a portentous declamation at the end he reveals, "Who am I? I am five years."

Similarly, in another morality tale, "One Trip Abroad," the supernatural element again enters the plot, but here it is worked more closely into the fabric of the story. In this Dorian Gray–like situation a young couple, Nicole and Nelson Kelly, on the path of dissolution and degeneration, see themselves at crucial moments in the process of their decay in the guise of another young couple. The dissipation of which they are unaware in themselves they notice in their doubles. The most vivid scene occurs at the end, where in one horrifying moment the Kellys recognize themselves in the other couple. What adds to the impressiveness of this story is the suggestion of supernatural elements functioning in the background. All nature seems to reflect the tumult and disorder of the Kellys' lives, suggests, in fact, a primordial force surrounding and eventually engulfing them. It follows them through the pleasure haunts of Europe, where nature is majestic and threatening; and in a powerful storm the two supernatural elements, the other couple and the malign forces which seem to have been released into the universe, meet–and in their meeting, the Kellys realize at last that they have lost not only "peace and love and health" but their souls as well.

Whatever the form of the story, Fitzgerald's range of subjects is wide and varied. Within the larger themes of life, love, death, and the American myth of success there are incalculable shades and variations. Many of his later subjects are adumbrated in his juvenilia, collected as *The Apprentice Fiction of F. Scott Fitzgerald, 1909-1917* (1965). "A Debt of Honor" (*Now and Then*, March 1910) is a young boy's exploration of the meaning of heroism as embodied in conventional notions of self-sacrifice and military glory. "Reade, Substitute Right-Half" (*Now and Then*, February 1910) is a classic wish-fulfillment sketch of an underdog who makes good on the football field, whose speed and dexterity outclass his teammates' greater brawn. "Sentiment–and the Use of Rouge" (*Nassau Literary Magazine*, June 1917) contrasts the new, relaxed wartime morality with older, tested values. It touches on the breakdown of sexual codes, on personal morality, on religion and belief, and on the boredom and ritualistic emptiness of upper-class life. In "Shadow Laurels" (*Nassau Literary Magazine*, April 1915) Fitzgerald mourns the unlived life and celebrates the power of the romantic imagination; in "The Spire and the Gargoyle" (*Nassau Literary Magazine*, February 1917) he regrets wasted opportunity and unfulfilled potential. "The Ordeal" (later revised and published as "Benediction") presents a spiritual conflict in the soul of a novitiate between the call of "the world . . . gloriously apparent" and "the monastery vaguely impotent." "The Debutante" (*Nassau Literary Magazine*, January 1917) and "Babes in the Woods" treat class distinctions, young love, manners, morals, and the generation gap. In "The Pierian Springs and the Last Straw" (*Nassau Literary Magazine*, October 1917) the themes are the artist's source of inspiration and the cruelty and hatred that can accompany love.

Most of the stories are brief; the themes are suggested or superficially explored. In "Sentiment–and the Use of Rouge," however, Fitzgerald develops his theme with fictional sophistication. "Sentiment" is about Clay Harrington Syneforth, a soldier in World War I who returns to his home in England for a two-day leave. What he encounters on his visit forms the core of the story. The central theme is change: between the England Clay knew, was raised in, and loved and the new world to which he returns, its looser morals, neglect of conventions, and disillusion with the old ideals of heroism and love, a world totally committed to the present moment and dedicated to pleasure and momentary satisfactions. The war has created a new sexual license; the women who cannot be the wives of the soldiers must discard conventional morality and be as much as they can to the soldiers in the little time they have.

But Clay does not understand. In the last section of the story, on the battlefield, Flaherty, an Irish-Catholic soldier, brings up the question of faith. Flaherty excoriates the English talent for prettying up reality. "Blood on an Englishman always calls rouge to me mind." The English, he says, see death as a game, but "the Irish take death damn serious." Fitzgerald is saying at the end that Clay's devotion to outward forms and conventions prevents him from perceiving what is re-

Advertisement for the 24 June 1933 issue of the magazine with which Fitzgerald was identified

ally important in life. Because he lives and worships the surface symbols of a bygone era, he is incapable of recognizing that underneath the rouge, people have been genuinely and profoundly moved by the events behind the big, important words. Thus he dies uncomprehending, bewildered, frightened—of sex and sexual license, of the new morality, of the unexpected depths of feeling in his contemporaries—more afraid of life than of the death which awaits him on the battlefield.

There are many flaws in the story, particularly its schoolboy seriousness and its consciously "arty" narrative. But it is a very early example of Fitzgerald's concern with a major theme—social change and the accompanying dislocation of values—which he treats memorably years later in "Babylon Revisited."

The major subjects of Fitzgerald's short stories are the sadness of the unfulfilled life and the unrecapturable moment of bliss, the romantic imagination and its power to transform reality, love, courtship and marriage, problems in marriage, the plight of the poor outsider seeking to enter the world of the very rich, the cruelty of beautiful and rich young women, the generation

gap, the moral life, manners and mores of class society, heroism in ordinary life, emotional bankruptcy and the drift to death, the South and its legendary past, and the meaning of America in the lives of individuals and in modern history. To these subjects which intrigued him from adolescence, he added Hollywood, where the American dream seemed to so many of his generation to have reached its apotheosis.

Many of Fitzgerald's finest stories date from the early 1920s. "Bernice Bobs Her Hair" is an early story, slight in intent but animated by an authentic and minute representation of manners and social milieu in which newly emancipated young American women live. It was the kind of story that Fitzgerald came to be associated with, for it typified the changes overtaking the new postwar generation. The central action is the transformation of a socially inept, unpopular girl, Bernice, into a much-sought-after, socially sophisticated "flapper." In the course of Bernice's education, Fitzgerald reveals the intricate system of manners on which social success depends. The plot hinges on Bernice's daring threat to bob her hair and invite her whole crowd to witness the momentous event. In the relationship between Bernice and her cousin Marjorie, Fitzgerald exposes the cruelty underlying the social conventions of young people, the competition for popularity which impels Marjorie to jibe at and cruelly taunt Bernice until she must carry out the threat Marjorie knows she had initially made as a joke. But Marjorie herself is an example of the newly emancipated woman who desires only to shake free from the limitations imposed upon her by society and to face life courageously, unhampered and unfettered. In a short, fervent speech she confesses to Bernice her abhorrence of society's hypocritical expectations of women and exhorts her cousin to relinquish the morals of a defunct generation. In this spirited story Fitzgerald sums up more accurately than any sociological analysis the rebelliousness and determination of the new generation and, particularly, of the new heroine.

Ardita Farnham, the heroine of "The Offshore Pirate," is the prize wealthy young Toby Moreland seeks because she possesses courage and independence, the most valuable attributes of Fitzgerald's flappers and philosophers. The story traces Toby's disguise as a jazz bandleader, Curtis Carlyle, who pirates the Farnham yacht with Ardita on board. A bored, spoiled debutante, she longs for someone with "imagination and the courage of his convictions." She refuses to meet anyone her family proposes and intends to run off with an older playboy. Toby's ruse works; he and Ardita fall in love on the ship, moored in a cavernous alcove, while "Curtis's" band plays music that enchances the romantic possibilities of the tropical paradise. The story seems bathed in the blue, silver, and gold of the sky and sun, and hero and heroine's paeans to courage, conviction, and the possibilities of the romantic imagination seem appropriate to the mood and milieu established by the opening lines:

> This unlikely story begins on a sea that was a blue dream, as colorful as blue-silk stockings, and beneath a sky as blue as the irises of children's eyes. From the western half of the sky the sun was shying little golden disks at the sea—if you gazed intently enough you could see them skip from wave tip to wave tip until they joined a broad collar of golden coin that was collecting half a mile out and would eventually be a dazzling sunset.

Fitzgerald sustains both rhetoric and idea—the power of the romantic imagination—throughout in a story that is among the best of his early works. Curtis Carlyle's tale of lost illusions parallels Fitzgerald's exploration of the meaning of natural aristocracy. The conflict within Fitzgerald between rival claims—aristocracy of the spirit versus aristocracy of wealth—is omnipresent throughout the stories. In his disillusionment he seeks to replace the values common to his society with a completely personal ethical standard; he ultimately exchanges moribund social values for a personal brand of heroism—in itself an aristocracy of the spirit.

Among the early stories, "The Diamond as Big as the Ritz" is notable not only because of the fine writing and historical resonances but because Fitzgerald's gift for fantasy is at its best. John Ungar, a middle-class boy, is invited by his classmate, Percy Washington, to spend his vacation at the latter's home "in the West." En route, Percy reveals that his father has a diamond "bigger than the Ritz-Carlton Hotel." John falls in love with Percy's sister, discovers the secret of the Washington wealth, and is almost killed before he can escape from a lavish and terrifying world. In this story Fitzgerald does not contain his subject and theme within a realistic setting. Here is an American West bigger and more extravagant than in the wildest Western tall story it subtly parodies. As the reader willingly suspends disbelief, the world of Fitzgerald's imagination takes on the col-

orations of the Oriental kingdom belonging to "some Tartar Khan." The Washington chateau is very like the pleasure dome of Kubla Khan, and the sights, smells, and sounds of luxury assault and ultimately deaden the senses until the lavish phantasmagoria moves as in a waking dream.

Remarkably, Fitzgerald sustains this geographic flight from the opening in Hades, "a small town on the Mississippi River," to St. Midas School near Boston, to the twelve wizened old men in the wasteland town of Fish, Montana, to the diamond mountain retreat of Braddock Washington. Yet the action, which departs wildly from probability, is so rooted in the familiar, recognizable patterns of human behavior that after the initial shock has receded and the reader has accepted the fanciful premise, he is forced to make invidious comparisons between the rise of American big business in the nineteenth and twentieth centuries and the growth of Braddock Washington's fortune.

Just as Fitzgerald used the American West in "The Diamond as Big as the Ritz" to explore American values in the context of American history, Fitzgerald used the American South to express the need for tradition, as embodied in his own father's values and manners. "The Ice Palace" is about the differences between the South—which stands for warmth, carelessness and generosity, feeling, tradition, and life—and the North—cold, hard materialism, selfishness, and death. The action involves heroine Sally Carrol Happer's desire for something more than the swimming, dancing, and playing that fill up her languid, somnolent, lazy summer days.

The opening of the story establishes the mood of the South, and at the end of part two, as Sally Carrol walks with her northern suitor, Harry Bellamy, through a Confederate graveyard, she defines the tradition she treasures:

> I've tried in a way to live up to those past standards of noblesse oblige—there's just the last remnants of it, you know, like the roses of an old garden dying all round us—streaks of strange courtliness and chivalry in some of these boys an'stories I used to hear from a Confederate soldier who lived next door.... Oh, Harry, there was something, there was something!

The tempo of the story quickens with the introduction of the northern element, Harry Bellamy, "tall, broad, and brisk." The warm summer is over; it is November and time for the serious business of life. Sally Carrol becomes engaged to

-ꮓ-   -63-

cry.

     She flung herself against ~~her~~ Nelson; even in the

darkness, she saw that his face was as white and strained as her own.

     "Did you see?," she cried in a whisper, "Did

you see them?"

     "God, yes!"

     "They're us! They're us! Don't you see?"

     Trembling ~~Shivering~~, they clung together. The clouds ~~melted~~ merged into the dark mass of ~~into a~~ mountains ~~somewhere merging with its dark mass, and~~

;looking around after a moment, the Nelson and Nicole saw that they were alone, ~~alone~~

together in the ~~quiet~~ tranquil moonlight.

Revised typescript page for the conclusion of "One Trip Abroad," first published in the 11 October 1930 issue of the Saturday Evening Post *(Princeton University Library)*

Harry, and they plan to go North to meet his family. From the first line in part three—"All night in the Pullman it was very cold"—and for all the scenes laid in the North, it is penetratingly cold. There is no relief for Sally Carrol who cannot, for as long as she remains in the alien environment of Harry's home, get warm. The icy weather symbolizes a way of life: no sense of play, no social badinage, no graciousness, no heritage of manners and style, only a chilling obedience to the forms of life. Even the people are gray and desiccated. Harry's "cold lips" kissing her reinforce the pervasive, unrelenting chill.

In the next part the relationship between Sally Carrol and Harry hardens after a quarrel at dinner when Harry refers to southerners as "lazy and shiftless," and later when the vaudeville orchestra plays "Dixie," she is painfully reminded of what she has left behind. Part five again takes up the motif of iciness, and the action builds to an apocalyptic climax as Sally Carrol loses her way in the glittering cavernous maze of the "ice palace, like a damp vault connecting empty tombs." Here, ice, snow, and palace are symbolically linked as death. As she falls down in the palace, she dreams of rejoining the dead Margery Lee, at whose grave she had sat and pondered the southern past back in Tarleton, her home town. The ice palace itself functions brilliantly as a symbol of the imminent death of the spirit, the inevitable accompaniment to life in a new, raw, mercantile northern city.

The last section returns to the original scene; it is April in Sally Carrol's southern town, and "the wealth of golden sunlight poured a quite enervating yet oddly comforting heat over the house where day long it faced the dusty stretch of road." Sally Carrol has experienced a purgatory in ice; chastened, contented, even indolent, she takes up her old life. There is much in the texture of the story that adds to its effectiveness: the decor, like the new but charmless library in Harry's house; dialogue, at the dinner-party where Sally Carrol first experiences disappointment and disillusionment with Harry; characters, the men—hard, brisk, athletic, and the women—faded, dull, apathetic; social position, shades and nuances of class distinction and throughout, wealth of goods going hand in hand with poverty of spirit, death and snow versus life and lilacs.

One of Fitzgerald's most effective and popular stories in which the primary emphasis is on social criticism is "May Day," yet he never wrote another story quite like it. Although the main character's story is characteristically Fitzgerald, the social / political criticism, developed in a sub-plot, is more overt than in most of his stories. He did salvage several structural and technical devices from the story—contrasting and parallel episodes, kaleidoscopic impressions, shifting rhetorical patterns— for use in other short stories but turned to the more expansive novel form to develop the multi-level plot.

Fitzgerald often opens a story with a philosophical passage that sets the tone and adumbrates the theme. In "May Day" the opening lines are heavily ironic, measured, musical, and solemn, with unmistakably biblical overtones.

> There had been a war fought and won and the great city of the conquering people was crossed with triumphal arches. . . . Never had there been such splendor in the great city, for the victorious war had brought plenty in its pain, and the merchants had flocked thither from the South and West with their households to taste of all the luscious feasts and witness the lavish entertainments prepared—and to buy for their women furs against the next winter and bags of golden mesh and varicolored slippers of silk and silver and rose satins and cloth of gold.

The passage serves to unify under a common subject the diverse episodes which follow. And, by offering moral commentary which is supported by the ensuing action, it raises that action to a level beyond its immediate significance.

The opening scenes of this story establish the setting and introduce the characters and major action—Gordon Sterrett's drift to death. The action is constructed around a series of contrasts between Gordon and a former Yale classmate, Philip Dean. Dean's social world, to which Gordon tries frantically to cling, is epitomized in expensive clothes and bodily well-being, the "trinkets and slippers," the "splendor" and "wine of excitement" of the invocation. Gordon asks Dean for a three-hundred-dollar loan that will enable him to extricate himself from the demands of a lower-class young woman with whom he has become involved. Dean, paying careful attention to his body and his wardrobe, listens to Gordon and refuses the loan. Gordon, like so many other poor young men whose dreams have been betrayed by a fiercely competitive system, is unprepared for the cold New York City which tosses people like him to their deaths.

His plight, made more poignant by beautiful Edith Braden's initial interest and subsequent rejection, is contrasted with that of two war veterans, unintentionally caught up in a socialist protest rally in the crowded streets. One of the soldiers, Carrol Key, whose name suggests that "in his veins, however thinly diluted by generations of degeneration, ran blood of some potentiality," is accidentally killed when he is swept up in the embattled crowd determined to put the Bolsheviks to rout. The last part of the story turns into a kind of social parable. The action moves from the Biltmore Hotel to Child's 59th Street restaurant, and to the Biltmore elevator, where the ascent of Mr. In and Mr. Out serves as an ironic counterpoint to the descent of Gordon Sterrett and Carrol Key–and possibly to the struggle upward for success in America.

"Winter Dreams" was written three years before *The Great Gatsby*, "The Rich Boy" immediately after. Both stories are among Fitzgerald's best, and both plots turn on conflicts between the very rich and a representative of the middle class–a contrast explored in the minutiae of social gestures, moods, conventions, and customs. In the former, Dexter Green is the protagonist of the story. In the latter, Anson Hunter is "the rich boy," the subject of the story, which is narrated by an observer-participant in the action, a friend of Anson's who all his life has lived among the rich.

In "Winter Dreams" Dexter Green is a golf caddy at the luxurious club patronized by the wealthy inhabitants of Sherry Island. He meets Judy Jones, from one of the club's leading families, and she and her summer world become the focus of his winter dreams. Judy Jones epitomizes the very rich. She is beautiful, cold, imperious, and maddening. Dexter pursues her, but she eludes him; the struggle to attain Judy Jones becomes for him the struggle to realize his dream of entering the glittering world of those enchanted summers. But the world of Judy Jones–who comes to symbolize both the beauty and the meretriciousness of Dexter's dreams–is clearly revealed as cruelly, coldly destructive. Dexter, listening to the music wafting over the lake at Sherry Island, felt "magnificently attuned to life." His winter dream, simply, was to recapture the ecstasy of that golden moment: the sensation that "everything about him was radiating a brightness and a glamour he might never know again."

The story is richly evocative, containing some of Fitzgerald's best writing. The change of seasons throughout the story reflects and coincides with Dexter's moods; like other Fitzgerald characters, he is extraordinarily sensitive to the natural world, and it is in terms of its effects upon people's lives that nature fascinates Fitzgerald. Dexter's spirits soar with the "gorgeous" Minnesota autumn; October "filled him with hope which November raised to a sort of ecstatic triumph." That ecstasy, linked with the image of Judy Jones, is finally Dexter's vision of immortality, just as Daisy Buchanan was Gatsby's. If he could have had Judy he could have preserved his youth and the beauty of a world that seemed to "withstand all time." When the beauty of Judy Jones fades, his hopes fade with it, and that sense of wonder he cherished over the years is lost "in the country of illusion . . . where his winter dreams had flourished."

"The Rich Boy" is the story of Anson Hunter, who lives in a world of "high finance, high extravagance, divorce and dissipation, of snobbery and privilege." The narrator immediately establishes his relationship to Anson. Brought together by chance as officers in the war, their backgrounds are totally dissimilar. Anson is the easterner, raised without "idealism or illusion," who accepts without reservation the world into which he was born. The narrator is from the West and thoroughly middle class, but he has lived among the "brothers" of the rich. He is thus capable of observing the nuances of upper-class manners and morals. His famous introduction, "Let me tell you about the very rich," clearly distinguishes the narrator from Anson and from the reader, thus effecting the necessary separation between subject and point of view which characterizes Fitzgerald's best stories. As though determined to prove for once that "the country of the rich" need not be "as unreal as fairyland," the narrator traces with clinical care the events and implications of Anson's life to their inevitable end.

Following a series of incidents chronicling Anson's courtship with Paula Legendre, the narrator returns to fill in the events and analyze the changes the last years have wrought in his friend. He is with Anson after the latter had learned of Paula's death in childbirth, and Anson, "for the first time in their friendship," says nothing of how he feels, shows no sign of emotion. The narrator wonders why Anson is never happy unless someone is in love with him, promising him something, perhaps "that there would always be women in the world who would spend their bright-

67

Stories	Record for 1931	$ 4000.	Com 10%	3600 00
	Indecision	4000.	"	3600 00
	A New Leaf	4000.	"	3600 00
	Flight and Pursuit	4000.	"	3600 00
	Emotional Bankrupcy	4000.	"	3600 00
	Between Three and Four	4000.	"	3600 00
	A Change of Class	4000.	"	3600 00
	Half a Dozen of the Other	3000.	"	2700 00
	A Freeze Out	4000.	"	3600 00
	Diagnosis	4000.	"	3600 00
	Total			31,500 00
Other Items	Treatment Metro Goldwyn Mayer	6000.	"	5400 00
	Echoes of the Jazz Age	500.		500 00
	Vegetable Performance	25.00	"	22 50
	New Leaf (English)	£17	"	59 00
	Flight & Pursuit (English)	Guinies 35	"	126 00
	John Jackson's Arcady	2.21	"	2 00
	Total			6,109 50
Books	This Side of Paradise			12 90
	Flappers & Philosophers			4 30
	The Beautiful & Damned			4 40
	Tales of the Jazz Age			3 90
	The Vegetable			1 13
	The Great Gatsby			17 70
	All the Sad Young Men			7 90
	Advance against Bk.			100 00
	Total			
	Less: Not paid in 1931 by Metro	173.72	"	– 155 35
	Grand Total			37,554 00
	New Yorker sketch	50.00		45 00
				37,599 00

Page from Fitzgerald's Ledger *documenting his most remunerative year as a writer before moving to Hollywood in 1937*

est, freshest, rarest hours to nurse and protect that superiority he cherished in his heart."

"Absolution" is one of the very few Fitzgerald stories that focuses directly on religion. Eleven-year-old Rudolph Miller is forced by his parents to go to confession, where the "half-crazed priest," Father Schwarz, listens to the boy's story. It is a tale of a young boy's fears and passions in an environment of rugged austerity and grim religiosity, ending with a lie in the confessional booth. When the confession is over, the priest's complete breakdown reinforces the significance of the boy's story. The pressure of Rudolph's environment has driven him onto the "lonely secret road of adolescence." Father Schwarz had once followed that lonely road to the end years ago, suppressing along the way the natural passions aroused by the rustle of Swedish girls along the path by his window and in Romberg's Drug Store "when . . . he had found the scent of cheap toilet soap desperately sweet upon the air."

Flashback adds dramatic intensity to the encounter by supplying the details leading up to Rudolph's spiritual crisis and connecting Rudolph's background with Father Schwarz's. It also points up the resemblances among apparently dissimilar characters by tying the quality in which Rudolph's father is deficient, the romantic imagination, to Rudolph's conviction that "there was something ineffably gorgeous somewhere that had nothing to do with God," and to Father Schwarz's dream of an amusement park where "things go glimmering." But Rudolph's life is just beginning, and his imagination restores him by providing an outlet for his buried life. He becomes Blatchford Sarnemington, a figure who exists outside of Father Schwarz's world, far from the confessional. Fitzgerald suggests that in Rudolph's perception of Father Schwarz's insanity and in Rudolph's commitment to his own dreams lie freedom and the possibility of romantic fulfillment.

In 1934 Fitzgerald told a critic that "Absolution" "was intended to be a picture of [Gatsby's] early life, but that I cut it because I preferred to preserve the sense of mystery." Fitzgerald told Maxwell Perkins that the story was salvaged from an earlier, discarded version of *Gatsby;* the 1923 start of the novel included a section on Gatsby's childhood, so it is likely that Rudolph is a preliminary version of a character who would become Jay Gatsby.

One of the most moving stories of the early 1920s, " 'The Sensible Thing' " draws upon Fitz-gerald's courtship of Zelda Sayre, as he describes George O'Kelly's rejection by Jonquil Cary because of his poverty and her subsequent acceptance after a year during which he has achieved the success that will now make their marriage possible. Again for Fitzgerald, the glow that first love imparts cannot be recaptured. In her acceptance of conventional advice by her parents, and, indeed, following her own convictions, Jonquil turned away George because he was not financially ready for her at the moment when they realized how much they were in love. Two months later, she tells him, "now I can't because it doesn't seem to be the sensible thing."

Although George does win her after a year in which a series of lucky breaks reward him with the success he had found so elusive previously, he learns that something rare and precious has been lost. "The sensible thing–they had done the sensible thing. He had traded his first youth for strength and carved success out of despair. But with his youth, life had carried away the freshness of his love." Thus, his lament at the end for that loss, "never again an intangible whisper in the dusk, or on the breeze of night. . . . ," conveys Fitzgerald's deepest conviction that the golden moment in one's life comes only once, and that subsequent fulfillment in love or in work can only be second best. Thus he ends the story on a note of both regret and acceptance: "Well, let it pass. . . . April is over, April is over. There are all kinds of love in the world, but never the same love twice."

From 1928 through 1931 Fitzgerald wrote fourteen stories in two series, the first, about Basil Duke Lee (1928-1929), comprising nine stories, one posthumously published, and the second featuring Josephine Perry (1930-1931). The Basil stories, for which Fitzgerald plumbed his own adolescence, take the character from his early school days, age eleven, through his entrance into college. From the beginning, Basil is never wholly accepted by the other youngsters. Because of his sensitivity, intensity, and competitiveness, he differs from them; they know it and resent it. He is frequently the butt of their jokes and recipient of their insults. Fitzgerald handles Basil's anguish and humiliation by bringing to bear the perspective of the adult on the loneliness and misery of an adolescent. Basil not only endures but even learns from each of his painful experiences: upstaging by Hubert Blair, that paragon of youthful charm and virtuosity; rejection by Imogene Bissel, a juvenile femme fatale; and,

TAPS AT REVEILLE
by
F. Scott Fitzgerald

Author of «Tender Is the Night,» «The Great Gatsby,» etc.

In these eighteen stories, chosen by Mr. Fitzgerald as his best short-story writing in the past decade, the author not only brings together in one volume the exploits and adventures of two of his most vividly delineated characters, but adds ten tales which, with one exception, portray various phases of American life from the beginning of the aureate twenties to the bitter end of the age of gold. That one exception is a story, here printed for the first time, that tells what happened to a pair of light ladies who followed the Federal armies to the Civil War battle-field of Chancellorsville and back. It is among the most remarkable stories that have come from the pen of an acknowledged master in the field.

The book begins with five stories about Basil Duke Lee, the freshest, most disturbingly real adolescent who was ever young in the days when "The Quaker Girl" played on Broadway and folks were singing "Everybody's Doing It." These tragically amusing and uncannily perceptive tales of the pre-war 'teen age are followed by three stories of Josephine, not much older than Basil in years, but as old as Lilith in feminine wiles. She is the complete picture of the eternal feminine, in years when the deadliness of the female was perhaps more celebrated than it is today.

The ten stories which make up the rest of the book include such brilliant pieces as "The Last of the Belles," "Family in the Wind," "A Short Trip Home," and one of the best of all Fitzgerald stories "Babylon Revisited."

Scott Fitzgerald's fame as a writer rests quite as securely on his short stories as on his novels. This collection contains much of his finest work and something for every reader of American fiction.

Published by **CHARLES SCRIBNER'S SONS**, New York

Dust jacket for Fitzgerald's fourth short-story collection, published in 1935 and including "Babylon Revisited" and "Crazy Sunday"

more seriously, ostracism and debasement by his prep-school classmates.

Basil's fatal flaw is his loquacity; he cannot resist pointing out his own superiority and his fellows' deficiencies. It is a hard lesson, but he finally learns, after years of misery, the value of discretion. He is, however, destined to remain the outsider, "one of the poorest boys in a rich boys' school." By adopting Basil's hyperbolic evaluation of the situation, the narrative forms an ironic but not unkind commentary on the young hero's driving ambition. Because Fitzgerald understands and takes seriously the problems of adolescence and because he remembers the pain of his own youth, he remains always the detached but totally sympathetic observer.

The central situation in each Basil story is a two-fold struggle, within Basil for mastery over himself and between Basil and society for social acceptance. In each situation, although rebuffed and humiliated by his own fatal penchant for self-advertising and an unwillingness to temper his romantic illusions about others, Basil grows in awareness and perceptivity, particularly of his own character and motives. In "The Freshest Boy" he concludes that "he had erred at the outset–he had boasted, he had been considered yellow at

football, he had pointed out people's mistakes to them, he had shown off his rather extraordinary fund of general information in class." The Basil Duke Lee stories treat the pain of adolescence without the sentimentality so characteristic of the popular Booth Tarkington stories.

Josephine Perry is an embodiment of the alluring yet cruel flapper, and Fitzgerald manages to convey the tragedy inherent in a totally self-absorbed life. Women like Josephine are doomed, he implies; momentary perception of their tragic destinies impels them to strike out at their world, and particularly at the young men who idolize them.

In "First Blood" Josephine is introduced during an argument with her family. Supremely self-confident in her budding beauty, Josephine sets her sights beyond the limits suggested by age and inexperience. She pursues and captures the most eligible "older" man in her set, only to reject his slavish devotion when it is finally proffered. The object of her desires, once attained, loses its fascination. Josephine must go on to ever more thrilling and elusive conquests.

In the first stories Fitzgerald's tone is unvaryingly indulgent toward the young woman and her romantic forays. But as the stories continue,

Josephine's successes invariably prove empty. Perpetually seeking new thrills, she longs for the ideal man who she thinks might satisfy once and for all her craving for romance and novelty. In each story, however, the young man disappoints her. She gradually grows numb with satiety (in Fitzgerald's day promiscuity usually meant only kissing), until a kiss fails to arouse her.

The youthful flirtations of "A Nice Quiet Place" (*Saturday Evening Post*, 31 May 1930; collected in *Taps at Reveille*) deepen in "A Woman with a Past" into a frantic search for fulfillment in love, but each conquest brings Josephine only boredom and ennui. In "Emotional Bankruptcy" (*Saturday Evening Post*, 15 August 1931), the saddest and most serious story of the group, by the time Josephine finally meets the perfect man, a war hero, it is too late for her. She no longer has the capacity to feel anything for anyone. She is emotionally bankrupt, no longer appealingly flirtatious and amusing either to the author or the reader, but empty, frozen, slightly repellent. Fitzgerald drops his ironic detachment at the end and moralizes on the human waste which might be tragic were it associated with someone less trivial and self-centered than Josephine Perry.

From the time Fitzgerald made his first trip to Hollywood in the late 1920s, he was fascinated by what he described as "a tragic city of beautiful girls." By 1940 he reported that there is "no group, however small, interesting. . . . Everywhere there is . . . either corruption or indifference." Hollywood was to provide Fitzgerald with the subject of some of his important fiction, notably the short story "Crazy Sunday," based upon his own experience at actress Norma Shearer's party, and partly inspired by her husband, M-G-M chief Irving Thalberg.

"Crazy Sunday" is a story about Hollywood and about one extraordinary man, Miles Calman, as observed by Joel Coles, a young writer. From the outset Hollywood, a "damn wilderness," vies with Jole and Miles for center stage. Hollywood transcends, compels, structures the plot. The rhythm of the story is the rhythm of Hollywood life, from crazy Sunday, "not a day, but rather a gap between two other days," to the other six days of frantic irrelevancy in a plastic wasteland.

The action begins and ends in Miles Calman's house where the ambience promotes the wildly exhibitionist performance which wins Joel instant notoriety. When Joel regards the assemblage, he is driven in a moment of semi-drunken, lavish goodwill to entertain them, and the ten-

The Fitzgeralds in Paris, 1925: F. Scott, Zelda, and Frances Scott (Scottie)

sions within him, suggested earlier, become insistent and are released in his outrageous performance. The focus of the story, however, is the intricate relationship between Miles and Stella Calman which ensnares Joel. The Calmans fight with one another but remain, to the end, self-sufficient, tightly insulated by mutual desire and mutual dependency. Joel can never really matter to them.

The story culminates, after Miles's death, in the circuslike parade Joel observes at the theater as he waits for Stella. Everything seems tinsely, tawdry, as artificial as a Hollywood B-picture. At the end Joel leaves the Calman house and bitterly takes up his life made empty and futile after the death of "the only American-born director with both an interesting temperament and an artistic conscience." "Crazy Sunday" is a haunting vignette of Hollywood, and it is measure of Fitzgerald's artistry that he succeeds despite the flaw of conflicting centers of interest, Miles and Joel. Joel is able both to evaluate and at the same time participate in events, and Fitzgerald's narration is often indistinct from Joel's observations. Yet the fascination lies, for Joel and for the reader, in Miles Calman, an early version of Monroe Stohr, the subject of Fitzgerald's last, incomplete novel, *The Last Tycoon*.

Many critics and scholars regard "Babylon Revisited" as the best of Fitzgerald's short stories. Written in 1930, at a particularly low point in his own life, it reflects the meditative sadness of a man looking back, in the Depression, on the waste and dissipation of the boom. More than perhaps any of his stories, it blends personal and historical elements to form a commentary on an era. It is about Charlie Wales, who, through indiscretions resulting in the death of his wife, made himself an outsider to the "good" people, represented by his sister-in-law and her husband, Marion and Lincoln Peters. In order to win back his child, Honoria, from the Peterses, who have been caring for her, he must establish for them his new stability and adherence to their values. The difficulty of his task is compounded by Marion Peters's dislike and distrust of him. Fitzgerald constructs the plot around a series of contrasts: between Charlie and the Peterses, past and present, illusion and reality, dissipation and steadiness, gaiety and grimness, Paris and America, adults and children. The author's tone, detached, critical, and ironic, merges with Charlie's self-critical but not self-pitying awareness, heightening the contrasts and adding meaning to even the briefest observation. "I spoiled this city for myself. I didn't realize it, but the days come along one after another, and then two years were gone, and everything was gone, and I was gone."

Charlie Wales of the Depression is no longer the same young man who coasted along on the joyride of the boom years. The story is about his exploration of the problems of character and responsibility, particularly the power of one's past to shape and determine his future. Against a background of change and dislocation wrought by social upheaval, the story of Charlie Wales is a search for latent values residing within the individual, values that provide the courage and resiliency to remake a squandered life. And it is all based on character, the "eternally valuable element." Charlie is left to examine the ruin of the past, to discover what, if anything, is worth the survival. He admits, "I lost everything I wanted in the boom," and his one hope for the future is continuity of character, as if by passing on to his daughter some lesson from his past, he will thus preserve part of himself in her.

"Babylon Revisited" is not a simple morality tale. Charlie is acutely sensitive to himself and to the Peterses, and he is eager to assume responsibility for Honoria's life and for his own. But "character" does not insure happiness for Charlie Wales. In this story, perhaps his most moving statement on the subject, Fitzgerald indicates that it is strictly a mode of individual survival, that not only may character not bring Charlie happiness along with his newly discovered values, but it may even intensify his despair and corrode his hopes.

In his late works, dating from 1936 to his death in 1940, Fitzgerald's style was markedly different from the early lyrical prose. The tone becomes flat, almost essayistic; narrative is unemotional and economical, yet strangely haunting in its dry precision. These are brief, autobiographical sketches, semifictional attempts to reinterpret his life and his art. In "Afternoon of an Author" the protagonist prepares to go outside for a walk, the first one in many days. His thoughts are of mental and physical fatigue–his own and others. On the bus ride, in the barber shop, he ruminates over what he is now, what he once was, what he might have become, his struggles and especially his weariness and inertia. There are no highs and lows, only a quiet drift toward death. The faint note of self-pity stems from physical debility rather than emotional outrage.

The author in "Author's House" surveys his youth, his illness, his mistakes and failures, and waits for death. All he has left is despair, knowing he can never dwell again in the turret of his symbolic house, knowing that success has ultimately eluded him.

In "An Author's Mother" (*Esquire*, October 1936) the title character, with her "high-crowned hat," incipient cataracts, and air of hopeless bewilderment, is a touching relic of another era. The modern world is obviously too much for her. She is proud of but cannot understand her son's success, for she associates "authors" only with Mrs. Humphry Ward, Henry Wadsworth Longfellow, Edna Ferber, and especially the sentimental poetesses Alice and Phoebe Cary. Uncomplaining and uncomprehending, she, too, retreats from life through the back door of her memories. For her there is nothing left but death.

Fitzgerald's vitality did burst forth again in his last years with a series of stories about Pat Hobby, a has-been screenwriter. Pat Hobby is among Fitzgerald's most intriguing characters, perhaps because the author was exorcizing the dark, defeated side of his own nature. Pat is an incompetent, an alcoholic, a petty blackmailer, a dreamer, a would-be lecher, a leech, a whiner, a conniver, a thief, a scab, a coward, an informer, an eternal outsider. He is lazy, ubiquitous, and dishonest. Although he is rigidly excluded from the Hollywood power center, his perverted sense of justice leads him to identify with the producers rather than their hireling writers like himself and the exploited or discarded actors and directors. He aspires to every flashy Hollywood-American success symbol–Filipino servants, swimming pools, liquor, girls, and meals at the Brown Derby. Pat is a firm ally of the status quo, or more properly, the past, into which he seeks to escape the sordid present.

Fitzgerald's technique in the Pat Hobby stories is to devise situations in which Pat, faced with alternatives, consistently selects the action most likely to degrade him further. In one story after another, Pat sinks to lower and lower levels of activity; trickery and connivance are his tools. But for all his duplicity, Pat is pathetically unsuccessful in his attempts to "put one over on them." Each situation ends in debacle, humiliation, and further degradation. And yet, for all his faults, he is a strangely moving figure in these stories of the absurd: the eternal fall guy who admits honestly in a moment of painful clarity, "I've been cracked down on plenty." The language of these stories is racy and colloquial, and the tone consistently ironic and detached. The stories were published in *Esquire* during the last year of Fitzgerald's life and in 1941, after his death. He worked on them as carefully as he could, often sending Arnold Gingrich telegrams requesting minor revisions even after a story had been set in print. At the same time Fitzgerald was working on his other Hollywood story, *The Last Tycoon*. It is probable that the Pat Hobby stories served as a release for his black vision of Hollywood and of his own career, allowing a final blossoming of his artistry.

F. Scott Fitzgerald's reputation as a short-story writer has risen considerably since his death, and at least a dozen of his stories rank with the most notable in American literature. And though his reputation as a major American writer rests primarily on his novels, especially *The*

Great Gatsby, in variety, in range, and in stylistic excellence, his short stories are an intrinsic part of his fictional world.

Bibliographies:

Jackson R. Bryer, *The Critical Reputation of F. Scott Fitzgerald: A Bibliographical Study* (Hamden, Conn.: Archon Books, 1967; supplement, 1984);

Matthew J. Bruccoli, *F. Scott Fitzgerald: A Descriptive Bibliography*, revised edition (Pittsburgh: University of Pittsburgh Press, 1987).

Biographies:

Arthur Mizener, *The Far Side of Paradise* (Boston: Houghton Mifflin, 1951);

Andrew Turnbull, *Scott Fitzgerald* (New York: Scribners, 1962);

Matthew J. Bruccoli, *Some Sort of Epic Grandeur: The Life of F. Scott Fitzgerald* (San Diego, New York & London: Harcourt Brace Jovanovich, 1981);

Andrew LeVot, *F. Scott Fitzgerald: A Biography*, translated from the French by William Byron (Garden City, N.Y.: Doubleday, 1983);

James R. Mellow, *Invented Lives: F. Scott and Zelda Fitzgerald* (Boston: Houghton Mifflin, 1984).

References:

Jackson R. Bryer, ed., *The Short Stories of F. Scott Fitzgerald: New Approaches in Criticism* (Madison: University of Wisconsin Press, 1983);

John A. Higgins, *F. Scott Fitzgerald: A Study of the Stories* (Jamaica, N.Y.: St. John's University Press, 1971);

Richard D. Lehan, *F. Scott Fitzgerald and the Craft of Fiction* (Carbondale: Southern Illinois University Press, 1966);

Henry Dan Piper, *F. Scott Fitzgerald: A Critical Portrait* (New York: Holt, Rinehart & Winston, 1965);

Robert Sklar, *F. Scott Fitzgerald: The Last Laocoön* (New York: Oxford University Press, 1967).

Papers:

The F. Scott Fitzgerald papers are in the Manuscript Department, Princeton University Library.

Nancy Hale

(6 May 1908-24 September 1988)

Laurie Buchanan
Bowling Green State University

See also the Hale entries in *DLB Yearbook: 1980* and *DLB Yearbook: 1988.*

BOOKS: *The Young Die Good* (New York: Scribners, 1932);

Never Any More (New York: Scribners, 1934);

The Earliest Dreams (New York: Scribners, 1936; London: Dickson & Davies, 1937);

The Prodigal Women (New York: Scribners, 1942);

Between the Dark and the Daylight (New York: Scribners, 1943);

The Sign of Jonah (New York: Scribners, 1950; London: Heinemann, 1951);

The Empress's Ring (New York: Scribners, 1955);

Heaven and Hardpan Farm (New York: Scribners, 1957);

A New England Girlhood (Boston & Toronto: Little, Brown, 1958; London: Gollancz, 1958);

Dear Beast (Boston & Toronto: Little, Brown, 1959; London: Macmillan, 1960);

The Pattern of Perfection (Boston & Toronto: Little, Brown, 1960; London: Macmillan, 1961);

The Realities of Fiction (Boston & Toronto: Little, Brown, 1962; London: Macmillan, 1963);

Black Summer (Boston & Toronto: Little, Brown, 1963; London: Gollancz, 1964);

The Life in the Studio (Boston & Toronto: Little, Brown, 1969);

Secrets (New York: Coward, McCann & Geoghegan, 1971);

Mary Cassatt (Garden City, N.Y.: Doubleday, 1975);

The Night of the Hurricane (New York: Coward, McCann & Geoghegan, 1978);

Birds in the House (Charlottesville, Va.: Learning Center, 1985);

Wags (Charlottesville, Va.: Learning Center, 1985);

Those Raccoons (Charlottesville, Va.: Learning Center, 1985).

PLAY PRODUCTIONS: *The Best of Everything,* Charlottesville, Virginia, 7 May 1952;

Somewhere She Dances, Charlottesville, Virginia, 13 May 1953.

Nancy Hale (photograph by Rollie McKenna, N.Y.)

OTHER: *New England Discovery: A Personal View,* edited by Hale (New York: Coward-McCann, 1963);

New England, edited by Joe McCarthy, introduction by Hale (New York: Time-Life Library of America, 1967);

"Who Needs No Introduction," in *A Book for Boston,* edited by Llewellyn Howland and Isabelle Story (Boston: Godine, 1980);

"Miss Dugan," in *An Apple for My Teacher,* edited by Louis D. Rubin, Jr. (Chapel Hill, N.C.: Algonquin Books, 1987).

PERIODICAL PUBLICATIONS: "Child Training at Harvard," *New Yorker*, 33 (15 February 1958): 28-30;

"The Poor Man's War Between the States," *New Yorker*, 37 (25 March 1961): 34-37;

"Handful of R's," *Vogue*, 138 (1 November 1961): 111;

"A Gift from the Shops," *New Yorker*, 37 (11 November 1961): 48-51;

"Handsome, Alert, a Real Young Blade," *Vogue*, 139 (May 1962): 152-153;

"The Feel of Writing," *Saturday Review*, 45 (8 September 1962): 16-18;

"In a Word," *New Yorker*, 39 (27 July 1963): 80;

"Colonel Sartoris and Mr. Snopes," *Vogue*, 142 (1 August 1963): 112-113+ ;

"Girl with the Goat-Cart," *New Yorker*, 39 (30 November 1963): 53-56;

"An Age for Action," *Ladies' Home Journal*, 82 (March 1965): 92-93;

"The Signorina," *Transatlantic Review*, no. 19 (Autumn 1965): 44-51;

"Animals in the House," *Harper's*, 223 (September 1966): 94-100;

"The Most Elegant Drawing Room in Europe," *New Yorker*, 42 (17 September 1966): 55-64;

"Waiting," *Virginia Quarterly Review*, 42 (Autumn 1966): 574-586;

"The Innocent," *Virginia Quarterly Review*, 43 (Spring 1967): 281-296;

"Mr. Hamilton," *Michigan Quarterly Review*, 9 (April 1970): 105-113;

"Dreams of Rich People," *McCall's*, 94 (August 1972): 86-87, 123-126;

"A Ceremony of Innocence," *Virginia Quarterly Review*, 52 (Summer 1976): 389-399;

"The Real Thing," *Virginia Quarterly Review*, 55 (Spring 1979): 275-283;

"The Interior," *Virginia Quarterly Review*, 56 (Spring 1980): 297-306;

"Tastes," *Virginia Quarterly Review*, 58 (Autumn 1982): 594-599;

"A Part," *Virginia Quarterly Review*, 61 (Winter 1985): 76-78.

Nancy Hale is most often recognized as a keen observer of people who is at her best when dealing with fundamental human qualities. Hale, who grew up in Dedham, Massachusetts, worked in New York City, and lived in Charlottesville, Virginia, from the 1940s until her death in 1988, used her own background for the settings and plots of her stories. Her skill as a writer, though, extends beyond the regionalist's acute and percep-

tive drawing of the local coloring of Boston's traditionalism, New York's idle rich, and Virginia's idiosyncrasies. With intensity and objectivity, she portrays the deeper reverberations that result when an individual, particularly a woman, moves from one culture to another where she must develop her own identity amid what often becomes a stifling and antagonistic environment.

Nancy Hale was born on 6 May 1908 in Boston, Massachusetts, the only child of Philip L. and Lilian Westcott Hale. Both her parents were painters, but her mother was the more successful of the two, having more portrait commissions than she could fill. Although Philip Hale continued to paint, he became respected for his art criticism, and he supported his wife and daughter on his teacher's salary from the Boston Museum of Fine Arts. However, Hale, the granddaughter of Edward Everett Hale, had more of the writer in her blood than the painter. Indeed, her first story was published in the *Boston Herald* when she was eleven. While attending Winsor School in Boston she edited the *Winsor Lamp* and, she says, wrote a poem a day.

Hale felt that her early writing fulfilled a need for expression during her lonely years at school. Because her parents were painters instead of wealthy business people, she was largely ignored by the girls at the exclusive Winsor School. Her writing (poetry at this time) became not only a release but a source of recognition, finally, at the school. Asked by a teacher to paraphrase Milton's sonnet "On His Blindness," she chose, instead of following the assignment exactly, to summarize Milton in a sonnet of her own. Finding this neglect of instruction impertinent, the teacher threw the sonnet away. However, the sonnet was found in the wastebasket by the assistant principal, who recognized Hale's talent and gave her special English instructions.

Although aware of her talent for writing at the time, Hale decided to study art after her graduation in 1926. She attended the School of Boston Museum of Fine Arts from 1927 to 1928 and studied with her father in his Fenway Studio. In 1928 she married Taylor Hardin and moved with him to New York City, where her first son, Mark Hardin, was born on 10 March 1930. In New York she was on the staff of *Vogue* from 1928 to 1932, where she worked first in the art department and on the fashion staff and then as assistant editor. In 1933-1934 she was employed on the staff of *Vanity Fair*, and she became the first woman reporter on the *New York Times* in 1935.

Charcoal sketches of Hale by her mother, Lilian Westcott Hale

In addition to these jobs, she was an adviser to an advertising agency from 1930 to 1935. During this time she began publishing short stories in the *New Yorker*, with which her reputation became permanently linked, and also *Harper's*, *Scribner's*, and *American Mercury*, besides publishing two novels, *The Young Die Good* (1932) and *Never Any More* (1934). Some of her short stories from this period are collected in *The Earliest Dreams* (1936), which concentrates on childhood, adolescence, and young adulthood.

The stories that make up *The Earliest Dreams* focus on women, either in adolescence or in the early years of marriage, with some early hints of the command of detail which gives Hale's fiction its immediacy, and the keen awareness of plot and character which distinguishes her as a short-story writer. The adolescent girl in the title story, first published in the April 1934 issue of *American Mercury*, waits eagerly for life to begin for her, in her loneliness finding everything that hints of adulthood mysterious and exciting. Alone in her room at bedtime, the child listens to the sounds of the night which come to her as loudly as the sound of laughter from her parents' gathering downstairs. To this girl, who has ex-

perienced life only in her imagination, the sounds evoke both the mystery and the glamour she is sure will come to her, suggesting a sense of the future that is both sophisticated and stimulating as well as frightful and unknowable.

"No One My Grief Can Tell" (*American Mercury*, October 1932) sets part of a pattern that emerges more fully in Hale's novels and later collections of short stories. The protagonist in this story, although in love with her husband, finds the emptiness of her life overwhelming. When her son is born she feels that she has found some meaning and purpose in life, but as she watches him grow, she realizes that he is making a life for himself independent of her. Like many women, Amanda is faced with a life of love and devotion to family juxtaposed with the frustration of being unable to define and strive for her individual needs.

Also collected in *The Earliest Dreams*, "To the Invader" originates the theme of women trying to maintain their individuality and self-respect among unsympathetic people. This story also distinguishes Hale as a regionalist, for setting is as important in the work as character. The protagonist's emptiness is prompted by her move with

Hale with her son, Mark Hardin, circa 1933

her husband from her home in New England to Virginia, where she finds that any deviation from the southern traditional understanding of what a pregnant woman feels is considered irrational. The story is, in a sense, a continuation of "No One My Grief Can Tell," for the protagonist is married to a loving husband but is lonely because there is no place in his life for her needs. But this character is more psychologically developed, and unlike Amanda, she can define her needs, though she is still frustrated by her inability to fulfill them. Because of the codes of behavior imposed upon her by her southern in-laws, her frustration at being constantly misunderstood or disapproved of overcomes any joy or satisfaction she might find in breaking from these narrow and suffocating codes.

Hale's contemporaries found these stories to be filled with penetrating beauty, formed out of strong emotion and vivid color. Her intensity in portraying character and immediacy in her situations, however, seems to have discomfited some of her critics. "The emotion is tense, the tragedies so many and so poignant that one feels either depressed or strained to too high a pitch. But a writer who can produce that impression

has artistry and skill above many others," said a reviewer in the 19 April 1936 *Springfield Republican*. However, these first stories show an acute perception of character and are rendered evenly and passionately.

Having divorced Taylor Hardin, Hale married writer Charles Wertenbaker in 1937 and moved with him from New York City to his home in Virginia. Her second son, William, was born on 23 February 1938. Although she published a best-selling novel, *The Prodigal Women*, in 1942, she was not a prolific writer during this period in her life. The marriage to Wertenbaker terminated in divorce and led to a period of Jungian analysis in 1943. Soon after her second divorce, she met Fredson Bowers, a professor at the University of Virginia, and married him on 16 March 1942. In 1943 her second collection of short stories, *Between the Dark and the Daylight*, was published.

In an interview with Robert Van Gelder entitled "Nancy Hale . . . An Analyzer of the Feminine," Hale states: "I specialize in women because they are so mysterious to me. . . . My interest in analyzing women is in their relations with men." And indeed, as in her first collection,

Hale with her great-granddaughter Rosalie Morton (courtesy of Janelle Morton)

In "Who Lived and Died Believing" women are again the focus. The depth of Hale's concern for the plight of women is revealed in the parallel circumstances of the two main characters. In a sanatorium, Mrs. Myles is receiving shock treatments so that she can overcome her fears. Her one joy is seeing her nurse in love, but the nurse has doubts about the relationship with her fiancé. Both women are imprisoned: Mrs. Myles by her obsession and the nurse by her relationship. Similarly, both are freed. Mrs. Myles responds to her treatments and the nurse breaks off her engagement. The parallel is set up in the protagonists' situations, and their subsequent release results in the same feelings of peace and freedom.

Hale's deep perception and objective portrayal of characters in crisis have been appreciated by critics. In the *Yale Review* (Summer 1943) Mark Schorer states: "Nancy Hale has command of the kind of detail which gives fiction immediacy," and an unsigned review in the 12 July 1943 *New Republic* summarizes her work thus: "The subject matter is one of intense conflict and the treatment is purely neutral." With few characters and a simple plot, Hale reveals the depths of the human mind in the style of an acute and objective observer.

Hale published another novel, *The Sign of Jonah*, in 1950 and another collection of short works, *The Empress's Ring*, in 1955. Many of these stories are based on her own reminiscences and were again collected in her memoirs. *The Empress's Ring* also includes stories that concentrate less on women and more on concerns of the individual in general. The feeling of despair prevails, however, and one might assume that the intertwining of her childhood stories among the more worldly ones suggests that one finds peace and meaning in the past and in a slower, more simple way of life. Although the stories vary in plot and setting, "A Full Life" best summarizes the general tenor of the collection. In this story an active but bored socialite realizes that her life has been empty and superficial when she meets an old friend who has spent fifteen years in a sanatorium finding fulfillment in herself and in nature. The suggestion, one that prevails in Hale's earliest novels, is reminiscent of the works of F. Scott Fitzgerald: the idle rich live lives of chaos and wastefulness, while the real satisfaction lies in appreciating simplicity.

With the publication of *The Empress's Ring* reviewers again praised Hale's gift for characterization, her perceptive and sensitive understanding

the most penetrating stories in *Between the Dark and the Daylight* focus on women in relationships with men trying to maintain a degree of recognition of their own individuality. Regionalism, again, is used as a backdrop, but the focus is on plot and character. In "Book Review," for example, Hale portrays a woman trying to engage other members of a dinner party in a conversation about fascism and communism, stimulated by a guest's comment on the publication of a "filthy" and radical book by Ernest Hemingway. Defending the author and trying to explain the guest's misunderstanding of Hemingway's point, the speaker is teased and ignored, and it is suggested that she is making the other guests uncomfortable by her insistence on discussing literature and politics with a man at a dinner party. The point of the story is a feminist one: because she is a woman, her views are silly and not worth listening to. Being humored rather than taken seriously even by her husband, her position is one of frustration.

of humanity, and her ability to sketch a story in swift strokes. Some see the work as lacking depth, but taken as a whole, the book has the penetrating quality of the observer forcing one to look at himself and his way of life.

In 1957 Hale published *Heaven and Hardpan Farm*, a collection of short stories drawn together in novel form. *A New England Girlhood*, her memoirs and her own adaptation of her vision of New England life and a companion to her grandfather's book *A New England Boyhood* (1893), was published in 1958, and another novel, *Dear Beast*, which takes up again the themes of antagonism between northern and southern manners, was published in 1959. Hale is again the regionalist, using her settings as the force which causes conflicts for the individual. Another short-story collection, *The Pattern of Perfection* (1960), illuminates the frustrations of women as they move to different areas, facing their own insecurities amid what to them is a contrary environment. Hale has been praised for her "warm, delicate presentation of superb portraits of civilized discontent" on the basis of these stories. With acute perception, she "examines some serious human predicaments thoughtfully and gracefully ... with no gushing or sensationalism." Her concerns are as intense and her presentation as deft here as anywhere in her works, and her vision and skill reveal a deep understanding of the daily conflicts that her characters face.

Midway through her career Hale published *The Realities of Fiction* (1962), a collection of essays on fiction that were given as lectures at various institutions including the Bread Loaf Writers' Conference (1957-1965). In 1963 the novel *Black Summer* and an anthology edited by Hale, *New England Discovery*, were published. *The Life in the Studio*, a book about her parents, was published in 1969, the year in which she won the Henry H. Bellaman Award for literature. Although this book is not an autobiography, Hale reveals something of her relationship with her parents in telling about them. She was very attached to her father, who died when she was twenty-three, but, until her mother was very old, Hale had a somewhat ambivalent relationship with her. Her sensitivity to each of her parents is reflected in the themes of some of her short stories. *Secrets*, a novel which portrays a woman's conflict in integrating her own world from within, was published in 1971. She received the Sarah Josepha Hale award in 1974, and in 1975 she published *Mary Cassatt*, a biography. She also published a

children's book, *The Night of the Hurricane*, in 1978 and three stories for children with learning disabilities in 1985, *Birds in the House*, *Wags*, and *Those Racoons*. For the Virginia Players, the theater department at the University of Virginia, she wrote two plays: *The Best of Everything* and *Somewhere She Dances*, both of which were produced at the university.

Throughout her work Hale portrayed characters in conflict with themselves amid pressures from the outside world. Her individual works compress a universal plot into a moment of vision, and the character, who is Everyman, is forced to make a choice. Summarizing her theory of the short story, Hales states: "The short story, while it can involve a number of personal destinies, or a number of events, does tie them all into a crisis. Now, a crisis in fiction means a decision. . . . One may equate crisis, or decision, with the life of the individual in relation to himself alone, since one's entire autonomous activity can be boiled down to the making of choices." Her stories describe situations and decisions that one faces at various points in life, dramatized through very real characters and told by an acute and compassionate observer of people. Using regionalism as a backdrop, Hale gave meaning to her stories with the subtle force of a skilled and imaginative writer. In effect, her stories work exactly as she intended them to. Hale defined meaning in the short story as "The reverberation of significance beyond matters immediately under observation." Her stories communicate this truth to the readers through careful rendering of character, plot, and setting.

Interview:

Robert Van Gelder, "Nancy Hale ... An Analyzer of the Feminine," in his *Writers and Writing* (New York: Scribners, 1946), pp. 330-333.

References:

James Gray, "Dream of Unfair Women," in *On Second Thought*, edited by Gray (Minneapolis: University of Minnesota Press, 1946);

Eudora Welty, "Women and Children," review of *Between the Dark and the Daylight*, *New York Times Book Review*, 2 May 1943, p. 8.

Papers:

The Smith College Library, Northampton, Massachusetts, holds the largest collection of Hale's papers.

Ben Hecht

(28 February 1894-18 April 1964)

Robert Schmuhl
University of Notre Dame

See also the Hecht entries in *DLB 7: Twentieth-Century American Dramatists; DLB 9: American Novelists, 1910-1945; DLB 25: American Newspaper Journalists, 1901-1925; DLB 26: American Screenwriters;* and *DLB 28: Twentieth-Century American-Jewish Fiction Writers.*

SELECTED BOOKS: *The Wonder Hat*, by Hecht and Kenneth S. Goodman (New York: Shay, 1920);

The Hero of Santa Maria, by Hecht and Goodman (New York: Shay, 1920);

Erik Dorn (New York & London: Putnam's, 1921);

1001 Afternoons in Chicago (Chicago: Covici-McGee, 1922; London: Grant Richards, 1923);

Gargoyles (New York: Boni & Liveright, 1922);

Fantazius Mallare: A Mysterious Oath (Chicago: Covici-McGee, 1922);

The Florentine Dagger: A Novel for Amateur Detectives (New York: Boni & Liveright, 1923; London: Heinemann, 1924);

Cutie, A Warm Mamma, by Hecht and Maxwell Bodenheim (Chicago: Hechtshaw, 1924);

Humpty Dumpty (New York: Boni & Liveright, 1924);

The Kingdom of Evil: A Continuation of the Journal of Fantazius Mallare (Chicago: Covici, 1924);

The Wonder Hat and Other One-Act Plays, by Hecht and Goodman (New York & London: Appleton, 1925);

Broken Necks (Chicago: Covici, 1926);

Count Bruga (New York: Boni & Liveright, 1926);

Christmas Eve (New York: Covici-Friede, 1928);

The Front Page, by Hecht and Charles MacArthur (New York: Covici-Friede, 1928; London: Richards & Toulmin, 1929);

The Champion from Far Away (New York: Covici-Friede, 1931);

A Jew in Love (New York: Covici-Friede, 1931; London: Fortune, 1934);

The Great Magoo, by Hecht and Gene Fowler (New York: Covici-Friede, 1933);

Ben Hecht (Billy Rose Theatre Collection, the New York Public Library at Lincoln Center, Astor, Lenox and Tilden Foundations)

Actor's Blood (New York: Covici-Friede, 1936);

To Quito and Back (New York: Covici-Friede, 1937);

A Book of Miracles (New York: Viking, 1939; London: Nicolson & Watson, 1940);

Ladies & Gentlemen, by Hecht and MacArthur (New York, Los Angeles & London: French, 1941);

Fun To Be Free, Patriotic Pageant, by Hecht and MacArthur (New York: Dramatists Play Service, 1941);

1001 Afternoons in New York (New York: Viking, 1941);

130

Concerning a Woman of Sin (New York: Armed Services Edition, 1943);

Miracle in the Rain (New York: Knopf, 1943);

A Guide for the Bedevilled (New York: Scribners, 1944);

I Hate Actors! (New York: Crown, 1944);

The Collected Stories of Ben Hecht (New York: Crown, 1945);

A Flag Is Born (New York: American League for a Free Palestine, 1946);

The Cat That Jumped Out of the Story (Philadelphia: Winston, 1947);

A Child of the Century (New York: Simon & Schuster, 1954);

Charlie: The Improbable Life and Times of Charles MacArthur (New York: Harper, 1957);

The Sensualists (New York: Messner, 1959; London: Blond, 1960);

A Treasury of Ben Hecht: Collected Stories and Other Writings (New York: Crown, 1959);

Perfidy (New York: Messner, 1961);

Gaily, Gaily (Garden City, N.Y.: Doubleday, 1963; London: Elek, 1964);

Letters from Bohemia (Garden City, N.Y.: Doubleday, 1964; London: Hammond, Hammond, 1965);

In the Midst of Death (London: Mayflower, 1964).

PLAY PRODUCTIONS: *The Wonder Hat*, by Hecht and Kenneth S. Goodman, Detroit, Arts and Crafts Theatre, 1916;

The Hero of Santa Maria, by Hecht and Goodman, New York, Comedy Theatre, 12 February 1917;

The Egotist, New York, Thirty-ninth Street Theatre, 25 December 1922;

The Front Page, by Hecht and Charles MacArthur, New York, Times Square Theatre, 14 August 1928;

The Great Magoo, by Hecht and Gene Fowler, New York, Selwyn Theatre, 2 December 1932;

Twentieth Century, by Hecht and MacArthur, New York, Broadhurst Theatre, 29 December 1932;

Jumbo, by Hecht and MacArthur, New York, Hippodrome, 16 November 1935;

To Quito and Back, New York, Guild Theatre, 6 October 1937;

Ladies and Gentlemen, by Hecht and MacArthur, New York, Martin Beck Theatre, 17 October 1939;

Christmas Eve, New York, Henry Miller Theatre, 27 December 1939;

Hecht, circa 1910

Fun To Be Free, Patriotic Pageant, by Hecht and MacArthur, New York, Madison Square Garden, 1941;

Lily of the Valley, New York, Windsor Theatre, 26 February 1942;

We Will Never Die, New York, Madison Square Garden, 9 March 1943;

Swan Song, by Hecht and MacArthur, adapted from Ramon Romero and Harriett Hinsdale's *Crescendo*, New York, Booth Theatre, 15 May 1946;

A Flag Is Born, New York, Alvin Theatre, 5 September 1946;

Hazel Flagg, New York, Mark Hellinger Theatre, 11 February 1953;

Winkelberg, New York, Renata Theatre, 14 January 1958.

MOTION PICTURES: *Underworld*, screen story by Hecht, Paramount, 1927;

The Front Page, screenplay by Hecht, Charles MacArthur, and Charles Lederer, United Artists, 1931;

Scarface, screen story by Hecht, United Artists, 1932;

Design for Living, screenplay by Hecht, Paramount, 1933;

Twentieth Century, screenplay by Hecht and MacArthur, Columbia, 1934;

Crime Without Passion, screenplay by Hecht and MacArthur, Paramount, 1934;

Viva Villa!, screenplay by Hecht, M-G-M, 1934;

The Scoundrel, screenplay by Hecht and Mac-Arthur, Paramount, 1935;

Barbary Coast, screenplay by Hecht and Mac-Arthur, Goldwyn, 1935;

Once in a Blue Moon, screenplay by Hecht and Mac-Arthur, Paramount, 1936;

Soak the Rich, screenplay by Hecht and Mac-Arthur, Paramount, 1936;

Nothing Sacred, screenplay by Hecht, United Artists, 1937;

The Goldwyn Follies, screenplay by Hecht, United Artists, 1938;

Let Freedom Ring, screenplay by Hecht, M-G-M, 1939;

It's a Wonderful World, screenplay by Hecht, M-G-M, 1939;

Lady of the Tropics, screenplay by Hecht, M-G-M, 1939;

Gunga Din, screen story by Hecht, MacArthur, Joel Sayre, and Fred Guiol, RKO, 1939;

Wuthering Heights, screenplay by Hecht and MacArthur, United Artists, 1939;

Angels Over Broadway, screenplay by Hecht, Columbia, 1940;

Comrade X, screenplay by Hecht and Lederer, M-G-M, 1940;

Lydia, screenplay by Hecht and Samuel Hoffenstein, United Artists, 1941;

China Girl, screenplay by Hecht, 20th Century-Fox, 1942;

Spellbound, screenplay by Hecht and Alfred Hitchcock, United Artists, 1945;

Specter of the Rose, screenplay by Hecht, Republic, 1946;

Notorious, screenplay by Hecht, RKO, 1946;

Her Husband's Affairs, screenplay by Hecht, Lederer, and I. A. L. Diamond, Columbia, 1947;

Kiss of Death, screenplay by Hecht, Lederer, and Diamond, 20th Century-Fox, 1947;

Ride the Pink Horse, screenplay by Hecht and Lederer, Universal, 1947;

The Miracle of the Bells, screenplay by Hecht and Quentin Reynolds, RKO, 1948;

Whirlpool, screenplay by Hecht and Andrew Solt, 20th Century-Fox, 1950;

Where the Sidewalk Ends, screenplay by Hecht, 20th Century-Fox, 1950;

Actors and Sin, screenplay by Hecht, United Artists, 1952;

Hecht with Sherwood Anderson, 1916

Monkey Business, screenplay by Hecht, Lederer, and Diamond, 20th Century-Fox, 1952;

The Indian Fighter, screenplay by Hecht and Frank Davis, United Artists, 1955;

Miracle in the Rain, screenplay by Hecht, Warner Bros., 1956;

The Iron Petticoat, screenplay by Hecht, M-G-M, 1956;

Legend of the Lost, screenplay by Hecht and Robert Presnell, Jr., United Artists, 1957;

A Farewell to Arms, screenplay by Hecht, 20th Century-Fox, 1957;

Circus World, screenplay by Hecht, Julian Halevy, and James Edward Grant, Paramount, 1964.

Ben Hecht began his career as a writer in 1910, at the age of sixteen, when he became a reporter for the *Chicago Journal*. His four years at the *Journal* and the nine years he spent with the *Chicago Daily News* (1914-1923) served as more than an apprenticeship for the novels, short stories, plays, movie scripts, memoirs, and political polemics he completed before his death on 18 April 1964. His work in journalism shaped and to an extraordinary degree defined almost everything he wrote, especially the approximately 250 short stories that he produced. As a result much of this short fiction seems more journalistic–engaging yet ephemeral–than literary. The stories are eminently readable and strikingly inventive, the efforts of a skilled craftsman with an understanding of popular taste. In general, however, they lack artistic depth.

Hecht came to Chicago from Racine, Wisconsin, where he lived most of his youth after being born in New York City on 28 February 1894 to Joseph Hecht and Sarah Swernofsky Hecht, both Russian immigrants. He was married twice–to Marie Armstrong from 1915 until 1925 and to Rose Caylor from 1925 until his death. From the beginning of his newspaper days until their end, Hecht reveled in the kaleidoscopic swirl of urban life that his reporting job let him experience. He was particularly attracted to people and occurrences that were unusual, idiosyncratic, or abnormal. He specialized in writing about criminals (and their victims) and social misfits or outcasts. He mastered the form of the "human interest" article and from 1920 to 1923 wrote a daily column of such stories. A collection of these sketches, *1001 Afternoons in Chicago* (1922), became, according to one commentator, "something of a Bible" for newspaper writers across the country.

While Hecht was gaining his reputation in journalism, he was also trying to become a serious writer of fiction. He read omnivorously and associated with the group of writers–Sherwood Anderson, Carl Sandburg, Maxwell Bodenheim–that came to be known as the Chicago Literary Renaissance. Though imaginatively executed, Hecht's early short fiction is derivative of his newspaper work. His characters and incidents seem, in most cases, to come from the world of the human interest article. He deliberately introduces fictive elements, but the journalist's judgment of what should be "covered" and emphasized guides the rendering of many of the stories.

Hecht's initial efforts appeared in Margaret Anderson's *Little Review* and H. L. Mencken's *Smart Set*, two respected outlets for short fiction. His first story for the *Little Review*, "Life," was published in the November 1915 issue, and it was selected by Edward J. O'Brien for *The Best Short Stories of 1915*. (Hecht included "Life" in his first collection of stories, *Broken Necks*, 1926.) "Life" is an urban vignette that focuses on a sensitive young dramatist, Maisse, and his reactions to what he sees while walking down Halsted Street in Chicago. At the beginning Maisse has an attitude of contempt: "I am the only one in the street whose soul is awake." Later, however, his

view changes when he contemplates an old beggar sleeping along the sidewalk. The beggar's hair teems with lice, triggering Maisse's realization that the life of the lice is similar to the human scene around him. The repulsiveness of Maisse's outlook–his abject cynicism–is undercut at the end when he acknowledges his own involvement in the situation:

> "Life," he murmured again; and
> "I am the old man," he added, "I . . . I . . .[.]"

This story is typical of the work Hecht did for the *Little Review*. It is a poignant sketch of city life by someone awakening to experiences that seem unusual and worth explaining. Hecht creates the young dramatist as his mouthpiece for reporting the incident and its effects.

In "Broken Necks" (*Little Review*, July 1918; collected in *Broken Necks*) Hecht uses a first-person narrator to describe the hanging of two criminals. The prose is vivid in relating what occurs at the executions, but the narrator's reaction is falsely poetic and labored. The speaker tries to use the experience for "adjusting certain important adjectives" in his life, but his response is untempered cynicism devoid of insight. All people, in jail and outside, are seen as "the little greedy half-dead," a phrase that recurs three times. Its weaknesses notwithstanding, "Broken Necks" shows Hecht attempting to experiment with language and technique. He seeks to transmute his experience as a reporter, to elevate his journalism to literature. This story and many of the others written for the *Little Review* and collected in *Broken Necks*–for example, "The Yellow Goat" (December 1918), "Decay" (September 1918), "Dog Eat Dog" (April 1919), "The Bomb Thrower" (September 1920)–are interesting juvenilia, but little more. In preparing five of these early stories for *A Treasury of Ben Hecht: Collected Stories and Other Writings* (1959) Hecht "re-edited" each one, remarking in the preface, "They were written when I was young and full of complex reflections which seem to my present taste a bit silly."

Hecht's contributions to the *Smart Set* demonstrate greater concern for plot and characterization than his impressionistic sketches for the *Little Review*. The narratives are straightforward, completely accessible examples of popular fiction. In most cases the stories revolve around problems between men and women. Although writing with a mass audience in mind, Hecht does not shy away

Hecht (right) in Berlin, 1919, as a foreign correspondent for the Chicago Daily News. *Richard Little of the* Chicago Tribune *is on the left.*

from realism in the resolution of some of the difficulties. For instance, in "The Movie Maniac" (*Smart Set*, November 1917; collected in *Broken Necks*) Wilbur Omar Brown, a copy reader on a Chicago newspaper known for "his general witlessness," is named the paper's movie reviewer. The change in jobs results in a "metamorphosis" in Brown. As his wife observes: "He's got so he can't do anything but strut and mimic the terrible movie actors." Mrs. Brown endures her husband's "preposterous pantomime" for a few months but then obtains a divorce. Hecht cleverly ridicules Brown's affectations, yet he does not allow his humor to lead to a contrived, happy ending. Besides being representative of Hecht's work for the *Smart Set*, "The Movie Maniac" is significant because it foreshadows how Hecht would treat movies and Hollywood in all of his fiction. Despite his later success as a screenwriter, he was critical to the point of contempt of film people and what they did.

The short stories Hecht wrote from 1915 to 1920–along with his daily journalism–enabled him to learn the writer's craft. The five years are a prelude to Hecht's most intensive and productive period as a writer of fiction. From 1921 through 1926 he published eight books of fiction: seven novels–*Erik Dorn* (1921), *Gargoyles* (1922), *Fantazius Mallare: A Mysterious Oath* (1922), *The Florentine Dagger: A Novel for Amateur Detectives* (1923), *Humpty Dumpty* (1924), *The Kingdom of Evil: A Continuation of the Journal of Fantazius Mallare* (1924), and *Count Bruga*

(1926)–and one collection of short stories–*Broken Necks*. Although some of the works were frivolous–*The Florentine Dagger*, for example, was completed in thirty-six hours to win a bet–others were serious efforts of fiction. *Erik Dorn*, a novel about a love triangle that allowed Hecht to draw on his experience as a journalist in revolutionary Germany in 1919, received favorable appraisals. The reviewer for the *New York Times* (9 October 1921) commented that "when Ben Hecht gets himself well in hand, America will have another great realistic writer of novels." In one case Hecht's realism created problems. *Fantazius Mallare* was suppressed by the federal government as obscene.

Beginning in 1927 Hecht devoted less of his attention to fiction so that he could write movie scripts and plays. He won an Academy Award for *Underworld* in 1927. (He won a second Oscar in 1935 for *The Scoundrel*.) *The Front Page*, coauthored with Charles MacArthur, was highly successful on Broadway in 1928; moreover, it established a new tradition in theatrical comedy with its irreverent attitude toward established values. Significantly, *Underworld*, *The Scoundrel*, and *The Front Page* were deeply influenced by Hecht's work in Chicago journalism.

Although Hecht's output of published short fiction declined as he wrote more films and plays, he continued to write a few short stories each year. The short fiction that appeared from 1928 through 1936 was similar to his earlier work in that it featured unusual characters involved in out-of-the-ordinary–frequently criminal–activities. The journalist's interest in abnormal behavior remained constant. In these stories, however, Hecht is more self-consciously inventive. Many of the characters are grotesque freaks, and what they do is often bizarre. For example, in "The Rival Dummy" (*Liberty*, 18 August 1928; collected in *The Champion from Far Away*, 1931) the main character is Gabbo the Great, a ventriloquist, who constantly bickers with his dummy, Jimmy. When Gabbo becomes infatuated with Mlle Rubina, a woman who joins his act, he senses that the dummy is trying to steal Rubina away from him. Gabbo flies into a rage and "murders" Jimmy with an ax. The ventriloquist flees from justice for his "great crime," returning years later with a new identity. The act, however, haunts Gabbo. He is always alone, and he draws a sketch of the dummy on the tablecloth of the restaurant where he dines each evening. Many of Hecht's stories of this period describe psychological disturbances in offbeat characters. Given the weird, incongruous circumstances, there is humor in these narratives. But Hecht seems primarily serious, intent on exploring darker motives of human conduct. In "The Ax" and "The Lost Soul" (both collected in *The Champion from Far Away*) ax murders occur–and the victims are *not* dummies.

"The Champion from Far Away" (*Saturday Evening Post*, 9 August 1930; collected in *The Champion from Far Away*) illustrates another dominant concern of Hecht's short fiction at this time. In this story a Russian immigrant, Vanya Kovelenko, comes to America and gets involved in professional wrestling. A disreputable promoter, Gaspodin Charash, makes the gullible Kovelenko a championship contender and a celebrity by arranging several easy matches for him. Charash bets heavily against Kovelenko for the championship and reaps the benefits when the Russian is brutally beaten. After recovering from his numerous injuries, Kovelenko leaves the limelight to become a restaurant doorman. In this story and others like it–for example, "Lindro the Great" (*Liberty*, 11 July 1925) and "The Bull That Won" (both collected in *The Champion from Far Away*)– Hecht focuses on the downfall of the characters he creates. He satirizes the machinery of publicity that manufactures ephemeral celebrity, and he describes how unscrupulous agents and managers orchestrate the rise and fall of performers and athletes. Hecht attempts to show one-dimensional celebrities in a more rounded way by

explaining how they developed and what became of them. He is successful–to a point. The problem is the unrealistic strangeness of the people he writes about. As one reviewer of this collection noted in the *Saturday Review of Literature* (19 September 1931): "Hecht writes with gusto about all his queer characters.... He does not create many real characters or teach us about human beings, but he carries us along with him into strange byways and shows us grotesque sights and makes us listen to unearthly sounds. In other words, he is an eccentric but a forceful writer."

Hecht's fascination with elaborately plotted mystery stories involving idiosyncratic characters is most pronounced in his collection *Actor's Blood* (1936). The complex twists and turns leading to surprise endings make these stories mildly interesting; however, they are too overtly contrived to merit more than a first reading. The characters, though typically unusual, seem incidental to the action. *Actor's Blood* received the most negative reviews of Hecht's five collections of short fiction. James T. Farrell's dismissal of it is representative of the critical reaction: "The characterizations are established by tricks, by stereotypings, by fitting people to the needs of plots. The older manner of Hecht has gone with mellowness, and the observations are surface and obvious; the humor creaks and is rusty; there is no life, no people here.... It is all entertainment writing, and even in this field Mr. Hecht could do better."

After the publication of *Actor's Blood* and during breaks in his writing of screenplays, Hecht began to work on a series of novella-length stories. From the outset he wanted these narratives to be substantively different from his earlier fiction. Distinctive characters and ingenious plots would remain; however, he wanted all of these stories to explore relationships between God and modern man. The seven novellas were published as *A Book of Miracles* (1939). Some of the "miracles"–such as "A Lost Soul" and "The Missing Idol"–are whimsically religious and profanely sacred; others–such as "The Little Candle" and "Death of Eleazer"–are richly allegorical and devoutly spiritual.

Summarizing the plots of these stories makes them sound too contrived and too bizarre to be successful. In "The Adventures of Professor Emmett," for example, a misanthropic professor of entomology commits suicide. His soul transmigrates into an ant, who heroically warns the president of the United States of the imminent invasion of killer termites. The professor ant hates

A BOOK OF Miracles

BEN HECHT

NEW YORK · THE VIKING PRESS · MCMXXXIX

Title page for Hecht's 1939 collection of allegorical novellas

life until he has a chance to save it, and he dies with hope for the future. The president sees the "miraculous ant" as one of "God's emissaries." As farfetched as this sounds, Hecht's imaginative and careful execution makes this fantastic tale and the others seem oddly plausible. He writes with a seriousness and depth of conviction not to be found in his previous short fiction. He retains control of material that could easily spin off into absurdity or become falsely pious.

Reviewers were unanimous in their praise of the literary merit of *A Book of Miracles*. F. T. Marsh in the *New York Times* (18 June 1939) wrote, "Something of a miracle itself, this book is probably the most amazing work of fiction of the year.... It's not only an amazing book; it's an amazingly good book." Harry Hansen in the *New York World Telegram* went so far as to say: "Ben Hecht has the most fantastic imagination in America. Of all the thousands of story writers in the republic Ben is one of the dozen or so who has the gift of invention." *A Book of Miracles* is Hecht's most artistic and accomplished work of short fiction, and he had a personal fondness for the collection. Assessing his many books in his autobiography, *A Child of the Century* (1954), he remarked that he "was proudest of the Miracle book. The critics praised it greatly. But hardly anyone read it. Even in London, where it was identified as one of the most important books of our time, it remained unread."

Hecht in Nyack, New York, circa 1946

Hecht's last sustained work in short fiction involved the publication of *The Collected Stories of Ben Hecht* in 1945. He selected fifteen of the twenty-one stories from earlier collections–seven from *The Champion from Far Away* and four each from *Actor's Blood* and *A Book of Miracles*. Six other stories pursue themes and approaches Hecht established in the late 1920s and 1930s. In "Concerning a Woman of Sin" (*Collier's*, 27 March 1943) an agent discovers to his dismay that the author of "the most sophisticated sex drama ever filmed" is a nine-year-old girl. Hecht's unmitigated cynicism about the movie industry, his source of wealth, pervades this story and the others. Three of the narratives–"Miracle of the Fifteen Murderers" (*Collier's*, 16 January 1943), "Cafe Sinister" (*Collier's*, 21 August 1943), and "Specter of the Rose" (which Hecht developed as a screenplay for a 1946 film)–are melodramatic mystery stories similar to Hecht's other ventures into psychological abnormality and macabre behavior. "The Pink Hussar" (*Collier's*, 25 Septem-

ber 1943) and "God is Good to a Jew" (*Collier's*, 31 July 1943) probe Hecht's concern for Jews forced to flee Nazism. These poignant stories echo two of the novellas in *A Book of Miracles*, "The Little Candle" and "Death of Eleazer." None of these new stories matched the accomplishment of the narratives in *A Book of Miracles*, and the collection met with tepid reviews.

Hecht dabbled in prose fiction during the last twenty years of his life, producing a children's story, *The Cat That Jumped Out of the Story*, in 1947 and a novel, *The Sensualists*, in 1959. Most of his energy, however, was devoted to his screen writing (approximately thirty scripts from 1944 to 1964), his memoirs (*A Child of the Century; Charlie: The Improbable Life and Times of Charles MacArthur*, 1957; *Gaily, Gaily*, 1963; and *Letters from Bohemia*, 1964), and his polemical works to combat anti-Semitism and to establish an appropriate homeland for Jews (*A Guide for the Bedevilled*, 1944; *A Flag Is Born*, 1946; and *Perfidy*, 1961). Hecht's ability to compose rapidly–a trait he learned as a reporter–and his knowledge of the techniques of several different forms enabled him to be prolific throughout his career.

Hecht's prodigious output and the variety of his work made him one of America's most prominent writers for four decades. Although as a young man he was called "the most promising writer of the whole Chicago group," his reputation as a serious author was tarnished when he became known as the highest-paid scriptwriter in Hollywood. (Gossip columnists enjoyed reporting that he received as much as thirty-five hundred dollars a day churning out screenplays.) Hecht wanted to be taken seriously as a writer of fiction, but he realized that his other work made such an appraisal impossible. At the beginning of *A Child of the Century* he candidly comments: "I can understand the literary critics' shyness toward me. It is difficult to praise a novelist or a thinker who keeps popping up as the author of innumerable movie melodramas. It is like writing about the virtues of a preacher who keeps carelessly getting himself arrested in bordellos."

Hecht's modest standing as a creator of short fiction is not only attributable to the prejudice of critics to his Hollywood ventures. Except for *A Book of Miracles*, he limited himself to the telling of stories that seem primarily journalistic rather than genuinely literary. In one of the few academic assessments of Hecht, Marvin Felheim notes: "Always the reporter, with the mind set and the emotional make-up of the clever journalist out for a scoop or a good newspaper yarn, he never moved away from those preoccupations." Hecht's promise as a fiction writer to be more than momentarily popular and diverting was never fulfilled. His fictional legacy will forever be overshadowed by the achievement of the play *The Front Page* and such films as *Underworld, The Scoundrel, Spellbound* (1945), and *Notorious* (1946).

References:

James T. Farrell, "The Mind of Ben Hecht," in *Literary Essays, 1954-1974*, edited by Jack Alan Robbins (Port Washington, N.Y.: Kennikat Press, 1976), pp. 70-76;

Marvin Felheim, "Tom Sawyer Grows Up: Ben Hecht as a Writer," *Journal of Popular Culture*, 9 (Spring 1976): 908-915;

Doug Fetherling, *The Five Lives of Ben Hecht* (Toronto: Lester & Orpen, 1977);

Gary Fincke, "Polarity in Ben Hecht's Winkelbergs," *Critique: Studies in Modern Fiction*, 15 (Winter 1973): 103-109;

Harry Hansen, "Ben Hecht, Pagliacci of the Fire Escape," in *Midwest Portraits: A Book of Memories and Friendships* (New York: Harcourt, Brace, 1923), pp. 303-357;

David Karsner, "Ben Hecht," in *Sixteen Authors to One* (New York: Copeland, 1928), pp. 235-245;

Roy Newquist, "Ben Hecht," in *Counterpoint* (Chicago: Rand, McNally, 1964), pp. 345-353;

Abe C. Ravitz, "Ballyhoo, Gargoyles, and Firecrackers: Ben Hecht's Aesthetic Calliope," *Journal of Popular Culture*, 1 (Summer 1967): 37-51;

Stuart Sherman, "Ben Hecht and the Superman," in *Critical Woodcuts* (New York: Scribners, 1927), pp. 63-72;

John Wain, "Ben Hecht," in *The Critic as Artist: Essays on Books, 1920-1970*, edited by Gilbert A. Harrison (New York: Liveright, 1972), pp. 343-350.

Papers:

The Newberry Library in Chicago, Illinois, houses the major collection of Hecht's papers, including manuscripts, outlines, notebooks, letters, and clippings.

Langston Hughes

(1 February 1902-22 May 1967)

Winifred Farrant Bevilacqua

Universita Degli Studi di Torino

See also the Hughes entries in *DLB 4: American Writers in Paris, 1920-1939; DLB 7: Twentieth-Century American Dramatists; DLB 48: American Poets, 1880-1945;* and *DLB 51: Afro-American Writers from the Harlem Renaissance to 1940.*

BOOKS: *The Weary Blues* (New York: Knopf, 1926; London: Knopf, 1926);

Fine Clothes to the Jew (New York: Knopf, 1927; London: Knopf, 1927);

Not Without Laughter (New York & London: Knopf, 1930; London: Allen & Unwin, 1930);

Dear Lovely Death (Amenia, N.Y.: Privately printed at Troutbect Press, 1931);

The Negro Mother and Other Dramatic Recitations (New York: Golden Stair Press, 1931);

The Dream Keeper and Other Poems (New York: Knopf, 1932);

Scottsboro Limited: Four Poems and a Play in Verse (New York: Golden Stair Press, 1932);

Popo and Fifina: Children of Haiti, by Hughes and Arna Bontemps (New York: Macmillan, 1932);

A Negro Looks at Soviet Central Asia (Moscow & Leningrad: Co-operative Publishing Society of Foreign Workers in the U.S.S.R., 1934);

The Ways of White Folks (New York: Knopf, 1934; London: Allen & Unwin, 1934);

A New Song (New York: International Workers Order, 1938);

The Big Sea: An Autobiography (New York & London: Knopf, 1940; London: Hutchinson, 1940);

Shakespeare in Harlem (New York: Knopf, 1942);

Freedom's Plow (New York: Musette Publishers, 1943);

Jim Crow's Last Stand (Atlanta: Negro Publication Society of America, 1943);

Lament for Dark Peoples and Other Poems (N.p., 1944);

Fields of Wonder (New York: Knopf, 1947);

One-Way Ticket (New York: Knopf, 1949);

Troubled Island, libretto by Hughes, music by William Grant Still (New York: Leeds Music, 1949);

Simple Speaks His Mind (New York: Simon & Schuster, 1950; London: Gollancz, 1951);

Montage of a Dream Deferred (New York: Holt, 1951);

Laughing to Keep from Crying (New York: Holt, 1952);

The First Book of Negroes (New York: Franklin Watts, 1952; London: Bailey & Swinfen, 1956);

Simple Takes a Wife (New York: Simon & Schuster, 1953; London: Gollancz, 1954);

The Glory Round His Head, libretto by Hughes, music by Jan Meyerowitz (New York: Broude Brothers, 1953);

Famous American Negroes (New York: Dodd, Mead, 1954);

The First Book of Rhythms (New York: Franklin Watts, 1954; London: Bailey & Swinfen, 1956);

The First Book of Jazz (New York: Franklin Watts, 1955; London: Bailey & Swinfen, 1957);

Famous Negro Music Makers (New York: Dodd, Mead, 1955);

The Sweet Flypaper of Life, text by Hughes and photographs by Roy DeCarava (New York: Simon & Schuster, 1955);

The First Book of the West Indies (New York: Franklin Watts, 1956; London: Bailey & Swinfen, 1956); republished as *The First Book of the Caribbean* (London: Edmund Ward, 1965);

I Wonder As I Wander: An Autobiographical Journey (New York & Toronto: Rinehart, 1956);

A Pictorial History of the Negro in America, by Hughes and Milton Meltzer (New York: Crown, 1956; revised, 1963; revised again, 1968); revised again as *A Pictorial History of Black Americans,* by Hughes, Meltzer, and C. Eric Lincoln (New York: Crown, 1973);

Simple Stakes a Claim (New York & Toronto: Rinehart, 1957; London: Gollancz, 1958);

Langston Hughes (Lincoln University Library)

The Langston Hughes Reader (New York: Braziller, 1958);

Famous Negro Heroes of America (New York: Dodd, Mead, 1958);

Tambourines to Glory (New York: John Day, 1958; London: Gollancz, 1959);

Selected Poems of Langston Hughes (New York: Knopf, 1959);

Simply Heavenly, book and lyrics by Hughes, music by David Martin (New York: Dramatists Play Service, 1959);

The First Book of Africa (New York: Franklin Watts, 1960; London: Mayflower, 1961, revised edition, New York: Franklin Watts, 1964);

The Best of Simple (New York: Hill & Wang, 1961);

Ask Your Mama: 12 Moods for Jazz (New York: Knopf, 1961);

The Ballad of the Brown King, libretto by Hughes, music by Margaret Bonds (New York: Sam Fox, 1961);

Fight for Freedom: The Story of the NAACP (New York: Norton, 1962);

Something in Common and Other Stories (New York: Hill & Wang, 1963);

Five Plays by Langston Hughes, edited by Webster Smalley (Bloomington: Indiana University Press, 1963);

Simple's Uncle Sam (New York: Hill & Wang, 1965);

The Panther and the Lash (New York: Knopf, 1967);

Black Magic: A Pictorial History of the Negro in American Entertainment, by Hughes and Meltzer (Englewood Cliffs, N.J.: Prentice-Hall, 1967);

Black Misery (New York: Knopf, 1969);

Good Morning Revolution: Uncollected Social Protest Writings by Langston Hughes, edited by Faith Berry (New York & Westport: Lawrence Hill, 1973).

PLAY PRODUCTIONS: *Mulatto*, New York, Vanderbilt Theatre, 24 October 1935;

Little Ham, Cleveland, Karamu House, March 1936;

When the Jack Hollers, by Hughes and Arna Bontemps, Cleveland, Karamu House, April 1936;

Troubled Island, Cleveland, Karamu House, December 1936; opera version, libretto by Hughes, music by William Grant Still, New York, New York City Center, 31 March 1949;

Joy to My Soul, Cleveland, Karamu House, March 1937;

Soul Gone Home, Cleveland, Cleveland Federal Theatre, 1937;

Don't You Want to Be Free?, New York, Harlem Suitcase Theatre, 21 April 1938;

Front Porch, Cleveland, Karamu House, November 1938;

The Organizer, libretto by Hughes, music by James P. Johnson, New York, Harlem Suitcase Theatre, March 1939;

The Sun Do Move, Chicago, Good Shepherd Community House, Spring 1942;

Street Scene, by Elmer Rice, music by Kurt Weill, lyrics by Hughes, New York, Adelphi Theatre, 9 January 1947;

The Barrier, libretto by Hughes, music by Jan Meyerowitz, New York, Columbia University, January 1950; New York, Broadhurst Theatre, 2 November 1950;

Just Around the Corner, by Amy Mann and Bernard Drew, lyrics by Hughes, Ogunguit, Maine, Ogunguit Playhouse, Summer 1951;

Esther, libretto by Hughes, music by Meyerowitz, Urbana, University of Illinois, March 1957;

Simply Heavenly, New York, Eighty-fifth Street Playhouse, 20 October 1957;

The Ballad of the Brown King, libretto by Hughes, music by Margaret Bonds, New York, Clark Auditorium, New York City YMCA, 11 December 1960;

Black Nativity, New York, Forty-first Street Theatre, 11 December 1961;

Gospel Glow, Brooklyn, New York, Washington Temple, October 1962;

Tambourines to Glory, New York, Little Theatre, 2 November 1963;

Let Us Remember Him, libretto by Hughes, music by David Amram, San Francisco, War Memorial Opera House, 15 November 1963;

Jerico-Jim Crow, New York, Village Presbyterian Church and Brotherhood Synagogue, 28 December 1964;

The Prodigal Son, New York, Greenwich Mews Theatre, 20 May 1965.

Hughes with friends (clockwise: Isidore Kaplow, "Wendel" Gomez, and Irwin Braverman) at Central High School, Cleveland, circa 1919 (courtesy of the Beinecke Rare Book and Manuscript Library, Yale University)

OTHER: Alain Locke, ed., *The New Negro*, includes nine poems by Hughes (New York: A. & C. Boni, 1925);

Four Negro Poets, includes twenty-one poems by Hughes (New York: Simon & Schuster, 1927);

Four Lincoln University Poets, includes six poems by Hughes (Lincoln University, Pa.: Lincoln University Herald, 1930);

Elmer Rice and Kurt Weill, *Street Scene*, lyrics by Hughes (New York: Chappell, 1948);

The Poetry of the Negro, 1746-1949, edited by Hughes and Arna Bontemps (Garden City, N.Y.: Doubleday, 1949);

Lincoln University Poets, edited by Hughes, Waring Cuney, and Bruce McM. Wright (New York: Fine Editions Press, 1954);

The Book of Negro Folklore, edited by Hughes and Bontemps (New York: Dodd, Mead, 1958);

An African Treasury: Articles/Essays/Stories/Poems by Black Americans, selected, with an introduction, by Hughes (New York: Crown, 1960; London: Gollancz, 1961);

Poems from Black Africa, edited by Hughes (Bloomington: Indiana University Press, 1963);

New Negro Poets: U.S.A., edited by Hughes (Bloomington: Indiana University Press, 1964);

The Book of Negro Humor, edited by Hughes (New York: Dodd, Mead, 1966);

The Best Short Stories by Negro Writers, edited, with an introduction, by Hughes (Boston & Toronto: Little, Brown, 1967).

TRANSLATIONS: Federico García Lorca, *San Gabriel* (N.p., 1938);

Jacques Roumain, "When the Tom-Tom Beats" and "Guinea"; Refino Pedroso, "Opinions of the New Chinese Student," in *Anthology of Contemporary Latin-American Poetry*, edited by Dudley Fitts (Norfolk, Conn.: New Directions, 1942), pp. 191-193, 247-249;

Roumain, *Masters of the Dew*, translated by Hughes and Mercer Cook (New York: Reynal & Hitchcock, 1947);

Nicolas Guillén, *Cuba Libre*, translated by Hughes and Ben Frederic Carruthers (Los Angeles: Ward Richie Press, 1948);

Leon Damas, "Really I Know," "Trite Without Doubt," and "She Left Herself One Evening," in *The Poetry of the Negro, 1746-1949*, edited by Hughes and Arna Bontemps (Garden City, N.Y.: Doubleday, 1949), pp. 371-372;

García Lorca, *Gypsy Ballads*, Beloit Poetry Chapbook, no. 1 (Beloit, Wis.: Beloit Poetry Journal, 1951);

Gabriela Mistral (Lucila Godoy Alcayaga), *Selected Poems* (Bloomington: Indiana University Press, 1957);

Jean-Joseph Rabearivelo, "Flute Players"; David Diop, "Those Who Lost Everything" and "Suffer, Poor Negro," in *Poems from Black Africa*, edited by Hughes (Bloomington: Indiana University Press, 1963), pp. 131-132, 143-145.

One of the most eminent black American writers and a literary figure of international renown, Langston Hughes was a serious and innovative artist who helped bring into the mainstream of American literature the experiences, culture, and language of the black population through poetry, fiction, and drama. By way of these literary forms he investigated with a particular combina-

Hughes at Lincoln University, 1928 (courtesy of the Schomburg Center for Research in Black Culture, New York Public Library, Astor, Lenox and Tilden Foundations)

tion of celebration and protest the joys and sorrows, triumphs and defeats of ordinary blacks. Fundamentally an optimist, he clung to his belief that the barriers excluding his people from the American Dream might one day be abolished.

James Langston Hughes was born on 1 February 1902 in Joplin, Missouri, to James Nathaniel and Carrie Langston Hughes. His parents separated soon after his birth, and he was raised in various Midwestern cities by his mother and his maternal grandmother. After graduating from Central High School in Cleveland in 1920, he spent thirteen months living with his father in Mexico. On the trip south he wrote his well-known poem "The Negro Speaks of Rivers," a free-verse exploration of black heritage that was published in the June 1921 issue of *Crisis*. During 1921 and 1922, although enrolled at Columbia University, he devoted himself to getting acquainted with the streets and people of Harlem, then becoming a center of Afro-American artistic development, and to making a real commitment to his literary career by writing several more poems for the *Crisis*. Yet, restless and in need of money, in June 1923 he signed on as cook's helper on the *West Hesseltine*, a freighter bound for West Africa. On completing that journey, he signed on the *McKeesport* for two voyages to Europe, terminating the second by jumping ship in Holland. From there he made his way to Paris, where he worked in nightclubs featuring black musicians playing blues and jazz. Hughes also traveled at this time through southern France and Italy.

Hughes returned to America in November 1924. He enrolled in Lincoln University in 1926 (he was to graduate in 1929) and soon emerged as one of the major voices in the Harlem Renaissance with his essay "The Negro Artist and the Racial Mountain" (*Nation*, 23 June 1926), in which he proclaimed the new cultural independence of the black writer: "to my mind, it is the duty of the younger Negro artist, if he accepts any duties at all from outsiders, to change through the force of his art that old whispering 'I want to be white,' hidden in the aspirations of his people, to 'why should I want to be white? I am a Negro—and beautiful.' " In keeping with the tenets of this literary manifesto, the poems in his first two collections, *The Weary Blues* (1926) and *Fine Clothes to the Jew* (1927), besides projecting an intense pride in blackness and African heritage and conveying a sense of protest against prejudice and discrimination, demonstrate that the colloquial black idiom and the rhythms of blues, jazz, and spirituals could be made a part of the art of poetry. The vigor, simplicity, and sure sense of human relationships characteristic of the best of these early poems also pervade his first novel, *Not Without Laughter* (1930), which in spite of its structural defects and undramatic action offers a moving and authentic picture of the life of a typical black family in the Midwest.

In the spring and summer of 1931 Hughes toured the southern United States as well as Cuba and Haiti, and in June 1932 he joined a group of black Americans who traveled to the Soviet Union for an ill-fated attempt to make a film about the exploitation of blacks in the United States. During the 1930s, except for a brief pamphlet of somber lyrics entitled *Dear Lovely Death* (1931), Hughes's limited poetic production grew out of the social, economic, and political urgencies of the times. *Scottsboro Limited: Four Poems and a Play in Verse* (1932) contains impassioned verse about the hasty judgment passed on a group of black youths accused of raping two southern white girls, while *A New Song* (1938) speaks critically of hunger, eviction, unemployment, a wors-

ening racial situation, and the rise of fascism in Europe. Though frequently marred by ideological rhetoric and sometimes lacking lyric intensity, these poems are important for their revelation of Hughes's militant response to the events of the 1930s and of his sincere yearning for more humane treatment of blacks and other oppressed peoples. Of greater artistic value is the short fiction about the absurdities and dishonesty that so often characterize relations between blacks and whites in the United States that he published in leading literary magazines between 1933 and 1935 and collected in part in *The Ways of White Folks* (1934).

Following the successful Broadway production in 1935 of his play *Mulatto*, an explosive treatment of interracial violence that was hailed as the first major achievement by a black dramatist, he turned his attention to the theater, writing light comedies about urban blacks such as *Little Ham* (1936), a somewhat confused but amusing slice-of-life in Harlem during the 1920s, and dramatizations of black history such as *Don't You Want to Be Free?* (1938), an emotionally charged pageant about the development and aspirations of American blacks from their original enslavement through the Depression, effectively set to the melodies of spirituals, work chants, jazz, and the blues. To further help promote a black national theater he founded the Suitcase Theatre in Harlem (1938), the Negro Art Theater in Los Angeles (1939), and the Skyloft Players in Chicago (1941).

After the publication of *The Big Sea* (1940), the first volume of his autobiography, Hughes proceeded to accomplish his mature work in prose, drama, and poetry. In 1942 he began producing a regular column for the *Chicago Defender*, and in January 1943 he introduced in that column his most popular fictional character, Jesse B. Semple of Harlem or "Simple," as he came to be called. Over the next twenty-three years Hughes displayed his considerable talents as a humorist by presenting Simple's comically astute views on race and the human condition in countless newspaper sketches periodically collected in book form. His other fiction included a second collection of short stories primarily about the black experience, entitled *Laughing to Keep from Crying* (1952), the previously uncollected tales which appeared in his volume of selected short fiction, *Something in Common and Other Stories* (1963), and a second novel, *Tambourines to Glory* (1958). The most memorable of his later works for the theater were *The*

Kolya Shagurin, Langston Hughes, Shaarieh Kikilov, and Arthur Koestler, Central Asia, 1932 (courtesy of the Beinecke Rare Book and Manuscript Library, Yale University)

Barrier (1950), an operatic version of *Mulatto;* the musical comedy *Simply Heavenly* (1957); and *Black Nativity* (1961), a dramatization of the Christmas story in dialogue, narration, pantomime, and gospel songs.

Aside from the delicate lyrics about nature in *Fields of Wonder* (1947), in his mature poetry he continued to offer fresh and insightful portraits of the black community and to utilize the rhythms of black music. Centering mainly on the universal conflict between man and woman, *Shakespeare in Harlem* (1942) is a collection of light verse "in the Blues mood," while *One-Way Ticket* (1949), along with blues songs, angry verses about southern racial brutality, and scenes from black life in various geographical areas, contains the superb series of "Madam" poems, dramatic monologues revealing the humor, shrewdness, resilience, and earthy philosophy of Alberta K. Johnson, the female counterpart of Jesse B. Semple. Subsequently, in both *Montage of a Dream Deferred* (1951), intended as one interrelated poetic jam session full of jazz, ragtime, bebop, and boogie-

woogie rhythms, and in *Ask Your Mama* (1961), twelve verse "moods" to be read aloud to musical accompaniment, he stressed the frustration and disappointment of blacks at the perennial thwarting of their hopes for a better future. Equally foreboding in tone were the new pieces in *The Panther and the Lash*, a thematic collection of his social poetry published posthumously in 1967.

In addition to these varied accomplishments, during his later years Hughes wrote another book of autobiography, *I Wonder As I Wander* (1956), participated in annual lecture tours, and undertook a series of challenging editorial activities, projects which conformed to the chief aim of his life's work in their explication and interpretation of the social, cultural, spiritual, and emotional experiences of black America. Hughes died on 22 May 1967, less than a year after he had attended the First World Festival of Negro Arts in Dakar where he received homage from an international gathering of black writers and artists for whom he had been a major source of inspiration and pride.

The product of an ironic intelligence and a keen honesty applied to an ingenious craftsmanship, Langston Hughes's most accomplished short stories, though lacking the depth and the resonance of those by James Baldwin and Ralph Ellison, still retain their power to engage, provoke, amuse, and educate as they explore the struggles of American blacks against prejudice, poverty, and injustice and as they reveal the values, sensibilities, and cultural forms of the black community. In them, Hughes reaches his most intense imaginative identification with those characters who despite their defeats and humiliations manage to survive and sometimes even discover humor in their absurd or unfortunate external circumstances. Presenting plots that are never complicated and are cast primarily in the mode of social realism, these stories are told in a language which, whether emanating from a cultured narrative persona or reproducing the idioms and cadences of black English, is always lucid, compact, and conversational. All of these qualities make them easily accessible to a general reading audience, able to appreciate their apparently effortless style and deceptively simple surface meanings, as well as to catch their undercurrents of sly humor, quiet bitterness, and social consciousness.

Hughes's career as a short-story writer began rather inauspiciously in the late 1920s with a group of slight tales based on his experiences as a seaman and admittedly written more in the hope of earning quick money than out of a serious commitment to experimenting with this literary form. Set on a freighter making stops along the coast of Africa, "Bodies in the Moonlight," (*Messenger*, April 1927), "The Young Glory of Him" (*Messenger*, June 1927), and "The Little Virgin" (*Messenger*, November 1927) offer glimpses into the daily life of ordinary sailors and have as their common theme initiation into manhood and adult sexuality, while "Luani of the Jungles" (*Harlem*, November 1928) traces in retrospect the happy alliance of a sensuous Nigerian woman and her tragically weak white husband.

It was only in 1933, while in the Soviet Union, that Hughes discovered the full aesthetic potential of the short story through his reading of D. H. Lawrence and decided to attempt a series of provocative stories about American blacks, several of which were published in the *American Mercury*, *Scribner's Magazine*, and *Esquire*. These and other tales written the next year while he lived in Carmel, California, in a house provided by the wealthy businessman Noel Sullivan, appeared in *The Ways of White Folks* (1934), generally greeted with favorable reviews and highly praised for its style and themes by Sherwood Anderson. The stories in this volume focus mainly on blacks whose lives are controlled by white-dominated conventions and standards, and through satire, irony, or subtle protest, expose the misunderstandings and hypocrisy that so often lead to white denial of black humanity. These stories represent a link between the literature of the Harlem Renaissance with its impulse to dissipate prejudice and win sympathy for the black community and the fiction of a later generation of black writers who, headed by Richard Wright, angrily lashed out at the social, political, and economic causes and consequences of discrimination.

Hughes's satiric impulse is most evident in those tales which offer a critical backward glance at the "cult of the Negro" in the Harlem Renaissance, especially as it manifested itself in a glorification of the primitive, a Freudian-inspired curiosity about the habits and pleasures of "uninhibited" blacks, and the often manipulative interest of white patrons in fostering Afro-American artistic growth. Shrewdly connecting the fashionable conception of blacks as exotic primitives to the earlier stereotype of the "contented slave" in "Slave on the Block" (*Scribner's Magazine*, September 1933), the author dissects the curious attitudes of a Greenwich Village couple toward a young black man they hire as part-time butler and part-time muse for their artistic endeavors, and in "Rejuvenation through Joy" he pokes fun at rich white women who seek spiritual uplift at a resort offering them pseudo-African music, dance, and religion. With a more subtle form of satire, in the excellent "The Blues I'm Playing" (*Scribner's Magazine*, May 1934), he chronicles the difficult relationship between a gifted pianist from Harlem whose talents embrace both classical music and the blues and a possessive, unconsciously bigoted white philanthropist who agrees to finance her further education in a classical repertoire if she rejects her black cultural heritage and sublimates her emotional needs. Along with providing a complex dramatization of the sociocultural influence some white patrons tried to exert on black artists in the 1920s, in this work Hughes contrasts two opposing views of how music relates to life, one positing that music transcends ordinary human experience, the other, presented as the essence of the Afro-American approach, affirming that it expresses and reconciles the joys

Hughes in Atlanta during Negro History Week, 1947 (photograph by Griffith J. Davis)

and pains, hopes and bitterness of the human condition.

A second trio of tales blends the kind of socioeconomic observation and critique typical of proletarian literature of the 1930s with investigation of the theme of alienation. This dual concern finds its most powerful expression in "Cora Unashamed" (*American Mercury*, September 1933), which was included in *Best Short Stories of 1934*, where the protagonist, a black housekeeper, not only endures the social and economic evils of racial prejudice but also experiences suffocation of her belief in the sacredness of life and love at the hands of a white community wholly devoted to form and profit. The biting irony pervading the story derives from the fact that Cora, so admirable in the eyes of author and reader for her wise simplicity and humble strength, is considered to be just another invisible or, at best, insignificant black by white characters, whose indifference deprives her of the dignity of defeat and nullifies her very existence. Similar in tone and theme, but less intensely dramatic, are "One Christmas Eve" (*Opportunity*, 1933) and "Berry" (*Abbott's Weekly*, 24 February 1934), each of which portrays the deprivations and isolation suffered by black servants whose individual humanity is far superior to that of their white employers.

Elsewhere in this collection Hughes probes into the psychodynamics of racial intolerance and demonstrates how easily it can lead to psychological and physical violence. The most memorable of these tales are "Father and Son" and "Home" (*Esquire*, May 1934). Derived from the play *Mulatto*, "Father and Son" is the tragedy of Bert Norwood, son of a southern plantation owner, and of his black mistress and servant. Norwood finds that the color of his skin bars him from receiving his father's affection and from enjoying the social status he believes should be his. The tension created by his unfulfilled desires and enforced social inferiority explodes in the last scene when in a fit of anger he strangles his father and then commits suicide, causing his mother to descend into insanity and his brother to become the innocent victim of a lynching mob. Despite its sensational conclusion, the situation described here is firmly grounded in the human social reality of the segregated South as it emerges from the carefully constructed flashbacks revealing how the mother, the father, and Bert are all trapped in the rigid codes governing the caste system, especially as they refer to miscegenation. Shifting from melodrama to tragic lyricism, in "Home" Hughes lays open the irrationality and violence underlying the white man's fear of black sexuality. In this story a sensitive and ailing musician who is the complete opposite of the stereotype of the "Negro brute" returns to his hometown in Missouri and meets a white music teacher who is willing to transcend the racial barrier in order to express her admiration for his immense talent. While out walking one evening, he extends her a gentlemanly greeting and for this gesture, interpreted by onlookers as a threat of rape, is beaten, stripped, and "strung from a tree at the edge of town . . . like a violin for the wind to play."

A strikingly different dimension of Hughes's talent is evident in "Little Dog," which focuses on an unmarried, middle-aged white woman who, to fill the emotional void in her well-regulated and highly circumscribed existence, buys a small dog and through him comes into contact with and is unexpectedly attracted to the gentle black man who works as a janitor in her apartment building. Their meetings each evening when he brings food for her pet become the center of her life until, fearful of her own feelings, she moves away. Linked to the other stories in this book through its implied insistence on the social, psychological, and sexual complications of interracial relations, this work, with its careful balancing of compassion and irony, also delicately treats the theme of lost potential in those individuals who withhold themselves from life.

Largely composed of works written in the mid 1930s and the early 1940s, *Laughing to Keep from Crying* (1952), save for a few stories on nonracial themes, likewise emphasizes the difficult situation of blacks in a white society. The best stories in this volume fall into two categories. The tales in one group, reflective of the radical ideas which the author held during the Depression, either critique the servile behavior of blacks or celebrate their defiance of the white establishment. Hughes's profound disillusionment with those black leaders whose conservatism was helping prolong prejudice and inequality is clearly revealed in "Professor" (*Anvil*, May-June 1935), a bitterly satiric portrait of an accommodationist educator who diminishes himself and his race by "dancing to the tune of Jim Crow education" in order to obtain the funds that will allow his segregated college to survive and to help further his own career. "Trouble with the Angels" (*New Theatre*, July 1935), on segregated theaters in the United

Hughes with Gwendolyn Brooks at a Chicago public library, 1949 (courtesy of the Beinecke Rare Book and Manuscript Library, Yale University)

States, and "Little Old Spy" (*Esquire*, September 1934), set in Cuba during the political unrest of the early 1930s, similarly comment harshly on blacks whose self-seeking, timidness, or insensitivity make them betray the sociopolitical aspirations of oppressed peoples. "On the Road" (*Esquire*, January 1935) instead has a rebellious and visionary protagonist, a cold and hungry black vagrant who after being denied refuge by a minister and being physically abused by policemen for trying to break into the church next to the parsonage, dreams that he converses with a deity who espouses social activism. Skillfully moving from realism to fantasy, this tale both records an emergent revolutionary consciousness among the black population and attacks the institutionalized Church for distorting the original tenets of Christianity.

The other group of superior stories from this collection dramatizes the conflict and suffering experienced by adolescent blacks as they are initiated into the social and psychological complexities of their racial heritage. Discovery of the paradoxical condition of being a mulatto is explored with restrained sentimentality in "African Morning" (*Pacific Weekly*, 31 August 1936), where the mixed-blood Nigerian son of an English banker contemplates suicide when he realizes the full extent of his estrangement from the natives and understands that his father will someday abandon him. In "Big Meeting" (*Scribner's Magazine*, July 1935), depicting the successive phases of a southern revival meeting observed at close range by a black teenager and from a distance by white adults, the author traces the transformation which takes place in the boy as he moves from an initial sharing of the condescending attitudes of the whites toward a more sympathetic understanding of his ethnic traditions. His sensitive delineation of the dilemma of Afro-American youth caught between two identity sources, one deriving from the dominant white culture and the other pertaining to their minority background, is complemented by an eloquent and moving disclosure of the historical and emotional significance of black religion. Finally, the deliberately didactic "One Friday Morning" (*Crisis*, July 1941) brings a high school girl to a confrontation in which her complacently optimistic social outlook is revealed to be inadequate to the conditions of black life when she learns that the scholarship she has won to an art institute is to be withdrawn because of her race. By having her attend the awards ceremony and join the other students in reciting the pledge of allegiance with the thought, "this is the land we must make," Hughes, along with stressing the incongruity between racial discrimination and America's avowed ideals, invites the younger generation to rise above its skepticism and fight for a world in which freedom, economic and social equality, and brotherhood exist.

Hughes's third collection, *Something in Common and Other Stories* (1963), contains twenty prose pieces selected from his previous volumes as well as nine sketches and eight tales assembled for the first time. Of this latter group only three are especially noteworthy: "Gumption" (first published as "Oyster's Sons," *New Yorker*, 12 January 1935), which tells of the unsuccessful battles waged by a black family against racial discrimination in the WPA; "Fine Accommodations," a companion piece to "Professor" in its brutal exposure of the negative attitudes of a black educator toward members of his own race; and "Blessed Assurance," which presents in the form of an interior monologue the anguished thoughts of a father as he comes to realize that his son is homosexual.

The waning of Hughes's interest in the short-story form, evident in the other "new" work in

Something in Common, may find its most plausible explanation in the fact that as his career advanced he channeled his talent in short fiction mainly into his sketches about Jesse B. Semple, which began appearing in 1943 in the *Chicago Defender*, a popular black weekly, and were later collected in five volumes. Short and fast-paced, these sketches are presented as conversations that took place between Simple, an honest and hard-working peasant from the South who has found a freer life in the North, and an educated Harlem acquaintance named Boyd, who represents the views of the cultured black liberal. The clash and interplay of Simple's crude realism and instinctive race consciousness with Boyd's broadminded sophistication and tolerance furnish much of the humor and also serve to accentuate two contending approaches to black life in the United States, one militantly stressing the disparity between being "black" and being "American," the other idealistically seeking points of contact between these dual identities. Typically, Boyd meets Simple in a bar, at a street corner, or on the stoop of his boardinghouse and briefly converses with him until Simple, having warmed into a serious or humorous topic, takes over the dialogue in order to confide in or talk back to his friend. Boyd then asks a question or makes a remark that evokes a seriocomic reply, reinforcing the validity of Simple's views and values and concluding the sketch in a flash of wit.

In most of the sketches Simple denounces with deceptively light humor such inherently unfunny social, political, and economic realities as poll taxes, segregation, job discrimination, hunger, ignorance, unemployment, ghetto living conditions, and the Ku Klux Klan, all of which persistently thwart the ambitions and dreams of average black citizens. The indignation underlying even the most playfully expressed of his laments is regularly set against the conciliatory views held by Boyd who, although he too sees evidence of racial intolerance all around him, keeps trying to believe that a just society in fact exists. The distinction between American ideals and reality as blacks define it is usually made sharp in their closing repartee, as when, for instance, Boyd asserts "Negroes today are . . . advancing advancing!," and Simple replies "I have not advanced one step. Still the same old job, same old salary, same old kitchenette, same old Harlem and the same old color" ("Radioactive Red Caps," collected in *Simple Stakes a Claim*, 1957). When not critiquing racism in all its forms, degrees, and absurdities,

Hughes in Chicago, 1960 (photograph by Roy DeCarava)

Simple, generally to Boyd's amusement but sometimes to his dismay, turns his wit on the foibles of blacks, on life in Harlem, and on his relationships with women. At other times, with great perception and insight that are acknowledged and seconded by Boyd, he comments on such universal human dilemmas as love and hate, war and peace, loneliness and companionship, sympathy, kindness, and death.

Just as Simple's ideas reveal his grounding in the experiences and attitudes of urban blacks in the 1940s and the 1950s, so too his language reflects their characteristic mode of speech. Unlike the stereotyped and condescending black dialect established by some nineteenth-century local-color writers, with its gratuitous misspellings and mispronunciations, the language Hughes creates for Simple is an authentic blend of southern idiom and Harlem jive, sprinkled with mistakes in diction and malapropisms that are clearly the product of the character's lack of education rather than his inferior intelligence. Moreover, as a believably natural orator, Simple is able to deploy a wide range of effective rhetorical devices,

engaging in word play, coining phrases, making puns, offering similies, confusing metaphors, compiling outrageous lists, and employing alliteration and rhyme.

During the more than twenty years of his prominence, Simple reached Hughes's widest and most appreciative audience. Black readers relished Simple's mixture of urban humor and cynicism with down-home simplicity and mother wit, recognizing him as an embodiment of accumulated black experience, and white readers, though often the butt of his satire, nonetheless enjoyed his sardonic levity, valued his perceptiveness, and admired his ability to endure and rise above the forces arrayed against him. The racial turbulence of the early 1960s inevitably made the comic tone of these sketches seem somewhat anachronistic, and in 1965 Hughes wrote in "Hail and Farewell" that Simple was leaving Harlem and would not be heard from again. But like all great literary characters Simple has outlived the circumstances of his creation, and still today his basic humanity, masterful presentation of the little ironic social comedies of life, and wise analyses of the ludicrous paradoxes of America's racial double standard retain much of their power and freshness.

Letters:

Arna Bontemps-Langston Hughes Letters, 1925-1967, edited by Charles H. Nichols (New York: Dodd, Mead, 1980).

Bibliographies:

Donald C. Dickinson, *A Bio-Bibliography of Langston Hughes, 1902-1967* (Hamden, Conn.: Shoe String Press, 1967);

R. Baxter Miller, *Langston Hughes and Gwendolyn Brooks: A Reference Guide* (Boston: G. K. Hall, 1978).

Biographies:

Faith Berry, *Langston Hughes: Before and Beyond Harlem* (Westport, Conn.: Lawrence Hill, 1983);

Arnold Rampersad, *The Life of Langston Hughes*, 2 volumes (New York & Oxford: Oxford University Press, 1986-1988).

References:

Richard K. Bardsdale, "Langston Hughes: His Times and His Humanistic Techniques," in *Black American Literature and Humanism*, edited by R. Baxter Miller (Lexington: University Press of Kentucky, 1981), pp. 11-26;

Black American Literature Forum, special Hughes issue, edited by Miller, 15 (Fall 1981);

Robert Bone, *Down Home: A History of Afro-American Short Fiction from Its Beginnings to the End of the Harlem Renaissance* (New York: Putnam's, 1975);

James Emanuel, *Langston Hughes* (New York: Twayne, 1967);

Emanuel, "The Literary Experiments of Langston Hughes," *CLA Journal*, 11 (June 1967): 335-344;

Nathan Huggins, *Harlem Renaissance* (New York: Oxford University Press, 1971);

Blyden Jackson, "A Word About Simple," *CLA Journal*, 11 (June 1968): 310-318;

David Levering Lewis, *When Harlem Was in Vogue* (New York: Knopf, 1981);

Peter Mandelik and Stanley Schatt, *Concordance to Langston Hughes* (Detroit: Gale Research, 1975).

Papers:

The largest collection of Hughes's letters and papers is deposited in the James Weldon Johnson Memorial Collection at Yale University. Additional materials are in the Schomburg Collection of the New York Public Library, the Lincoln University Library (Pennsylvania), and the Fisk University Library.

Fannie Hurst

(19 October 1889-23 February 1968)

Susan Currier
California State Polytechnic University

BOOKS: *Just Around the Corner* (New York & London: Harper, 1914);

Every Soul Hath Its Song (New York & London: Harper, 1916);

Gaslight Sonatas (New York & London: Harper, 1918);

Humoresque (New York & London: Harper, 1919);

Star-dust: The Story of an American Girl (New York & London: Harper, 1921);

The Vertical City (New York & London: Harper, 1922);

Lummox (New York: Harper, 1923; London: Howard Balker, 1970);

Appassionata (New York: Knopf, 1926);

Song of Life (New York: Knopf, 1927; London: Cape, 1927);

A President is Born (New York & London: Harper, 1928);

Five and Ten (New York & London: Harper, 1929; London: Cape, 1929);

Procession (New York & London: Harper, 1929);

Back Street (New York: Cosmopolitan Book Corporation, 1931; London: Cape, 1934);

Imitation of Life (New York & London: Harper, 1933);

Anitra's Dance (New York & London: Harper, 1934);

No Food with My Meals (New York & London: Harper, 1935);

Great Laughter (New York & London: Harper, 1936);

We Are Ten (New York & London: Harper, 1937);

Four Daughters (New York & Toronto: Longmans, Green, 1941);

Lonely Parade (New York & London: Harper, 1942);

White Christmas (Garden City, N.Y.: Doubleday, Doran, 1942);

Hallelujah (New York & London: Harper, 1944);

The Hands of Veronica (New York & London: Harper, 1947);

Anywoman (New York: Harper, 1950);

The Man with One Head (London: Cape, 1953);

Fannie Hurst (Lotte Neustein)

Anatomy of Me: A Wonderer in Search of Herself (Garden City, N.Y.: Doubleday, 1958; London: Cape, 1959);

Family! (Garden City, N.Y.: Doubleday, 1960);

God Must Be Sad (Garden City, N.Y.: Doubleday, 1961);

Fool, Be Still (Garden City, N.Y.: Doubleday, 1964).

Although rarely read today, Fannie Hurst was one of America's most popular, prolific, and well-paid fiction writers of the 1920s and 1930s. The author of eighteen novels in addition to hundreds of short stories, Hurst wrote sentimental but vivid accounts of America's downtrodden. Her works have been translated into eighteen languages and adapted for the screen, television, and theater.

Hurst was born on 19 October 1889 in Hamilton, Ohio, into a family of German-Jewish back-

151

ground. She was raised in St. Louis, the only child of Samuel and Rose Koppel Hurst, old-fashioned parents who were chagrined by their daughter's peculiar vocation. A thick-set, over-dressed girl, she found herself ill-suited to St. Louis's private and public schools. Nevertheless, she continued her education at Washington University, where she persevered in her writing with much endurance and some success. She graduated in 1909.

Hurst began submitting stories to the *Saturday Evening Post* when she was fourteen. During college she continued at such a rate that the manuscripts bottlenecked at the *Post*, and the rejection slips were returned in batches. Hurst was to receive thirty-five rejections from the *Post* before its editors accepted "Power and Horse Power" (6 July 1912). But, meanwhile, she launched a simultaneous attack on *Reedy's Mirror*, a prestigious midwestern literary journal with offices in St. Louis. Marion Reedy was the first to publish Edgar Lee Masters, Sara Teasdale, Zoë Akins, and Orrick Johns. In due course he also became the first to publish Fannie Hurst. He accepted "Ain't Life Wonderful," which had begun as a successful weekly theme in one of Hurst's college English classes. Then after a few more rejections, he also agreed to publish "Home." Following the story's appearance in *Reedy's Mirror*, Hurst adapted it for a week-long run at Keith's Vaudeville Theatre in St. Louis. Hurst acted in one of the play's principal roles; however, she and her parents were humiliated by her performance. Nonetheless, the production was sufficient to secure her encouragement and recommendations for acting instruction in New York.

The story of "Home" is that of "a young married woman grown restive with her necktie-salesman husband and the disillusionments of domesticity." Although Hurst was not married, she was certainly restive in St. Louis domesticity, and within two years of her college graduation she prevailed upon her parents to send her to New York. There she worked as a waitress, as an elevator operator, and at other odd jobs to gather material for her books. She studied literature and acting with William Dean at Columbia University. A bit part in David Belasco's Broadway hit *The Music Master* (1910) helped her to support herself. Hurst's role was to close an overstuffed suitcase by sitting on it.

Throughout that early period in New York Hurst continued to write even without friends or prospects. Her thirty-fourth submission to the

Post earned a "good try." Her thirty-sixth won an acceptance, three hundred dollars, and a bid for first chance at her future work. *Century Magazine* also requested first option on stories to come. And Theodore Dreiser, editorial staff member of the *Delineator*, mailed her a rejection embedded in impressive if telegraphic praise: "Someday you may be a helluva writer. At present you are not. I have the same complaint that bedevils you. Too many words on hand and I say them all. Two of our readers were for your story. Three of us were not. One of whom I beg to remain. Keep at it." By 1917, however, Hurst's career was secure. Editors began bidding against one another for her stories, and her price quadrupled and then climbed to five thousand dollars.

On 6 May 1914 Hurst married Jacques S. Danielson. A classically trained pianist and a Russian Jew, Danielson was unacceptable to Hurst's parents. Her father never acknowledged his son-in-law, and no public announcement was made of the marriage until 1920. During the interim, husband and wife maintained separate residences and a three-night-a-week arrangement which provoked some scandal when it was made public but which permitted Hurst to pursue the writing career she desired.

Hurst's first volume of short stories, *Just Around the Corner*, appeared in 1914. Like her subsequent collections, it is composed largely of material previously published in magazines. Reviewers found Hurst's stylistic control in this collection "uneven" but the stories promising, nevertheless. In these stories Hurst champions working girls, and her themes never changed, although she did expand her range of character types. Reviewers often responded to Hurst's work with a mixture of censure for her verbless prose and praise for her animated characterization, and this type of criticism did not alter appreciably until the publication of her last story collection, *We Are Ten*, in 1937. New York, particularly the lower East Side, dominates her settings though a few stories take place in the Midwest. Hurst's characters, in addition to working girls, include Jewish immigrants suffering or succeeding in the garment industry, traveling salesmen, boardinghouse inhabitants, circus freaks, and nightclub entertainers. The situations are always structured to manipulate the reader's emotions, the love interest is always romantic (although sometimes morbid), and the resolutions are usually sentimental.

Hurst's first award-winning story, "T.B." (*Saturday Evening Post,* 1915), was included in

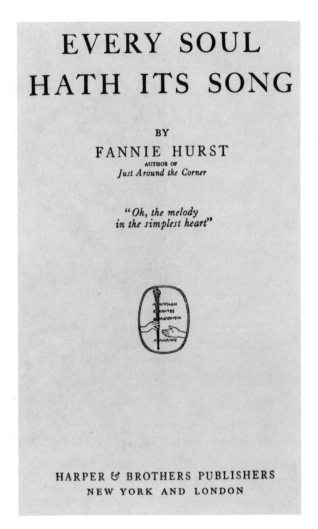

Frontispiece and title page for Hurst's second short-story collection, published in 1916

Edward J. O'Brien's *Best Short Stories of 1915* and republished in her second collected volume, *Every Soul Hath Its Song*, in 1916. Its heroine, a frail young shop girl named Sara Jukes, is doomed to daily labor in a bargain basement where "lint from white goods clogs the lungs" and the air is "putrefied as from a noxious swamp." An older and less attractive roommate, who has lost a sister to tuberculosis, admonishes Sara to guard her health, but Sara must snatch at youthful pleasures, and so she sacrifices food for fancy clothes and quiet evenings for dance hall tours. Charley, her boyfriend, urges her into ever tighter crowds, faster dances, and later hours. Sara grows thin and feverish until one evening she swoons in the middle of a dance. When she revives, she and Charley walk about the streets for air. She window-shops while he complains about

his lost evening. Suddenly a tuberculosis exhibit catches her eye, and she enters to learn about the disease, unaware that within twenty-four hours she will be informed that she has contracted it. The next night Charley abandons her amid accusations: "You got it and you been letting me eat it off your lips!" But Eddie, a former "double-lunger" who manages the tuberculosis exhibit, spirits Sara to the country to begin a cure and quickly replaces Charley.

The dialogue of "T.B." is bathetic, and the narrator's addresses to the reader are propagandistic, particularly in the story's introduction: "This is the literal under world of the great city, and its sunless streets run literal blood–the blood of the babes who cried in vain; the blood from the lungs of the sweatshop workers whose faces are the color of dead Chinese; the blood from

153

Hurst in her study (photograph by Underwood & Underwood, Albert Davis Collection/Hoblitzelle Theatre Arts, Harry Ransom Humanities Research Center, University of Texas at Austin)

the cheeks of the six-dollar-a-week salesgirls in the arclighted subcellars. But these are your problems and my problems and the problems of the men who have found the strength or the fear not to die rich." However, Hurst's descriptions—of parties in the dance halls, of evenings at home, and of the insomnia produced by fear as Sara prepares to confront her illness—are compelling and her characters alive.

Every Soul Hath Its Song earned from the critics high marks for character drawing. The reviewer for the *Boston Transcript* (6 January 1917) stated: "Here at last is a story writer who is bent on listening to the voices of America and interpreting them." More important, perhaps, was the *New York Times* (12 November 1916) reviewer's assessment: "In *Every Soul Hath Its Song* the author has placed herself among the great American writers of modern short stories."

Hurst's third story collection, *Gaslight Sonatas* (1918), includes two exceptional stories, "Ice-

Water, Pl--!" (*Collier's*, 21 October 1916) and "Get Ready the Wreaths," both of which were selected for *Best Short Stories*. All the stories in *Gaslight Sonatas* depict women who are trapped—in duncolored spinsterhoods, in soul-numbing marriages, in economic and emotional obligations to their children and their parents. On the plight of such women Hurst is always eloquent. Gertie Slayback's self-deprecatory play for an unworthy husband in "Bitter Sweet" is set against a poignant description of her fate without him: "When she unlocked the front door to her rooming-house of evenings, there was no one to expect her. . . . And when she left of mornings with her breakfast crumblessly cleared up and the box of biscuit and condensed-milk can tucked unsuspectingly behind her camisole in the top drawer there was no one to regret her." And Hannah Burkhardt's ruinous divorce from "Silent" Burkhardt in "Nightshade" is not without compellingly detailed grounds: "Across the table, a Paisley cover between them, Mr. John Burkhardt, his short spade of beard already down over his shirt-front, arm hanging lax over his chair-side and newspaper fallen, sat forward in a hunched attitude of sleep, whistling noises coming occasionally through his breathing. A china clock, the centerpiece of the mantel, ticked spang into the silence, enhancing it."

Both "Ice-Water, Pl--!" and "Get Ready the Wreaths" demonstrate that in Hurst's best fiction the situations are original as well as poignant. The stories have in common the maturity of their heroines, a focus on mother-daughter relations, and weddings between middle-aged partners as resolutions. Like so many Hurst stories, "Ice-Water, Pl--!" takes place in New York and begins with an appeal on behalf of women. In this case, much-maligned landladies are likened to Henry VIII, Shylock, Xantippe, and other scapegoats of history and literature whose arguments may have received short shrift. As a group, these ladies make a pitiful spectacle: "Tired bombazine procession, wrapped in the greasy odors of carpet-sweeping and emptying slops, airing the gassy slit of room after the coroner; and padding from floor to floor on a mission of towels and towels and towels!" But Mrs. Kaufman is a specific case, and so she wears her bombazine unspotted and with crisp net frills at the throat. She is a widow, a mother, a slave to her tenants' demands for more towels and "Ice-Water, Pl--!," as well as a beauty curiously unravaged by time. It is Mrs. Kaufman's fondest wish to see her daughter, Ruby, marry Meyer Vetsburg, president of Rosenthal Vetsburg Hosiery Company and star boarder in her rooming house. Unfortunately, Ruby's intention, unknown to her mother, is to marry Leo Markovitch, Vetsburg's nephew and a clerk in his father's Atlantic City hotel. During an all-night scene between mother and daughter, first Ruby begs to escape the middle-aged and accented Vetsburg; then, in consideration of her mother, Ruby confesses she is only infatuated with Leo and of course she means to marry "Vetsy"; and, finally, Mrs. Kaufman insists that Ruby must, of course, marry Leo, and what would she do without a boardinghouse anyway? After each has agreed to sacrifice all for the other, preparation for a romantic ending is complete. Vetsburg arrives to escort both to Atlantic City for a holiday, and, in a series of revelations, he proposes to marry Mrs. Kaufman and to invite Leo into his firm, thus securing Mrs. Kaufman's release and also the young couple's future.

Hurst, 1932 (photograph by Carl Van Vechten, by permission of Joseph Solomon, Trustee for the Estate of Carl Van Vechten, courtesy of Beinecke Rare Book and Manuscript Library, Yale University)

Much of the appeal of this story derives from Hurst's ability to invest so unromantic a situation as the daily routine of a boardinghouse and its middle-class inhabitants with vitality and sentiment. Hurst does not focus here on the poor living in the lower East Side or the privileged on Riverside Drive. The Kaufmans, neither desperate nor free, are simply confined to lives with narrow margins. And so Hurst's character sketching is all the more remarkable.

"Get Ready the Wreaths" complicates the theme of mother-daughter relations by extending it into a third generation. Its three principal characters are Selene Coblenz; her mother, Mrs. Shila Coblenz; and Mrs. Coblenz's mother, Mrs. Horowitz. Selene's grandmother immigrated to America with her daughter only after she had sacrificed a husband and son to pogroms and herself barely escaped the Pale. In America her struggle continued, for her son-in-law disappeared shortly after Selene's birth, leaving the family nothing but debts. They settled in unfashionable outskirts of St. Louis, where Mrs. Coblenz eventually established a neighborhood business known as the Convenience Merchandise Corner.

Upstairs from the store Mrs. Horowitz weeps bitterly while she weaves raffia wreaths for the graves she left in Russia. The violent deaths of her husband and son replay over and over in her mind. Downstairs, Mrs. Coblenz bargains with salesmen and customers, hoarding meager profits to finance her mother's return to Russia and to the graves there which obsess her. Mrs. Coblenz is a devoted daughter, but she is also a committed mother. And her daughter, who intends to marry Lester Goldmark, of a prominent St. Louis family, wishes to do so in style. Mrs. Horowitz's presence is bad enough: "How do you think a girl feels to have gramaw keep hanging onto that old black wig of hers and not letting me take the crayons or wreaths down off the wall?" But to spend the family's funds on the dead in Russia rather than the living in St. Louis is intolerable. Mrs. Coblenz capitulates, and the grandmother's return-to-Russia savings are withdrawn to purchase a wedding reception at the Walsingham Hotel.

On the day of the reception Czar Nicholas II abdicates, and the Romanov autocracy is overthrown. Mrs. Horowitz, who reads the news in a small room adjoining the party, needs never to know that the money for her return trip to Russia is gone now that the political opportunity has arrived, for after one grandiloquent moment in which she rises to honor the martyrdom of her husband and son in the cause now achieved, she swoons back into her rocker, softly dying with a smile on her face. Mark Haas, uncle to Lester, officer in the Mound City Silk Company, and silent admirer of Mrs. Coblenz, consoles her as she is engulfed by guilt and grief. The wreaths must still go to their respective graves, but it is not grandmother who will carry them, nor Shila Coblenz alone: "We'll take them back for her–Shila," Haas proposes. Shila responds, "We'll take them back for you mama. We'll take them back for you, darling!" Mrs. Horowitz's death and Haas's affection are, for Hurst, predictably sentimental contrivances. The story's strengths emerge elsewhere–in the cruel dynamics between Mrs. Horowitz's suffering and Selene's impatience and in the warmth and stature of Shila as she attempts to contain and resolve their conflict. Both "Get

Ready the Wreaths" and "Ice-Water, Pl--!" reveal a new depth and maturity of vision not found in Hurst's earlier stories no matter how lively their characterization.

In 1919 Hurst published her most accomplished short-story collection, *Humoresque*. Compiled from previous publications in the *Saturday Evening Post* and *Cosmopolitan*, this volume contains eight stories, all set in New York, and all featuring Jewish immigrants or working girls or both. The title story was awarded a 1919 O. Henry prize, in addition to being selected by Ray Long for *My Favorite Story* and by B. C. Williams for *Best American Stories, 1919-1924*. "Humoresque" and "Heads," from the same volume, both concern Jewish immigrant families who move, within the short span of a single generation, from lower East Side tenements to upper West Side "apartments de luxe." Both stories also end with the outbreak of World War I. In "Humoresque" America's foremost young musician departs for a tour of duty in the battlefields of Europe; in "Heads" a handsome young actor books passage to Paris on the *Lusitania*.

"Humoresque" details the development of a young prodigy, Leon Kantor, who on his fifth birthday howls for a violin until, when finally indulged with a broken-backed, single-stringed toy, he intuitively positions instrument and bow and begins to withdraw notes, "strangely round and given up almost sobbingly from the single string." At seventeen Leon tours Europe, playing for its royalty. At eighteen he purchases a Stradivarius. At nineteen he insures his fingers at ten thousand dollars a digit. At twenty-one he attracts queues that stand for hours to gain admission to his concerts.

Leon is extremely delicate (his nervous agony on concert nights mirrors Hurst's husband's own sensitivities about public performance) and devoted to his mother, who prayed to be given a musician and who first recognized his genius. But Leon is not unmanly. By the end of his long story he has engaged himself to a beautiful young opera star, and he has volunteered to defend the freedom which his immigrant parents struggled so hard to obtain. On the occasion of his departure, he plays two pieces for his family and fiancée. One is Antonín Dvořák's "Humoresque," the second a dead soldier's poem which Leon has set to music:

But I've a rendezvous with Death
On some scarred slope of battered hill,

When spring comes round again this year
And the first meadow flowers appear.

As Leon leaves, the poet's lyrics wind and wreathe about his mother, but it is "Humoresque" which lingers with the reader. According to Sarah Kantor's description of its melody, "It's like life, son, that piece. Crying to hide its laughing and laughing to hide its crying."

Some of the succeeding stories in the same volume seem at first to pale beside "Humoresque." But that is not so much because they are inferior as because they are so similar. Several critics noted this difficulty with the individual stories as they praised the quality of the volume. The *New York Times* (6 April 1919) reviewer stated: "Miss Hurst can write–she has the magic gift of bringing swift tears on the heels of laughter, but we sometimes wish she would be not quite so characteristic. However, she knows people, her figures live and breathe, her plots are well drawn, so we will not quibble over a mere sameness in style. Her fault, if it is a fault, is shared with many masters, O. Henry, for instance."

Perhaps in an effort to be less "characteristic," Hurst modified the story pattern in her next volume, *The Vertical City* (1922). The six sketches collected under that title all illustrate New York City life once again. Hurst retains her lush style and sentimental tone, but her themes have taken a morbid twist. "She Walks in Beauty," included in *Best Short Stories of 1921*, details a daughter's suffering and sacrifice for a drug-addicted mother who finally sets her free by running into an oncoming car. "Back Pay" tells the story of a woman who throws over the right man for the wrong, lives in luxury as the mistress of a war profiteer, and finally repents only to find her original lover blind and dying in a hospital. "Guilty," which was collected by Ray Long in *Twenty Best Stories in Twenty Years* (1932), presents a devoted husband and father who loses both wife and daughter to a genetic psychosis, manifested repeatedly in revulsion against him. Facing murder charges for the suicide of his mad daughter and recalling her horror of him, he acquiesces to a plea of guilty instead of arguing his innocence. The stories in this volume are both rich and sensationalistic. They are, in their own vein, more "characteristic" than Hurst's earlier works and finally not as successful as "Humoresque," "Get Ready the Wreaths," or "Ice-Water, P1--!"

Hurst published her last volume of stories, *We Are Ten*, in 1937. Many of its sketches continue the tendency of *The Vertical City* toward morbidity, but with an additional prurience and explicitness. In "Hattie Turner Versus Hattie Turner" a young woman trapped for years in a sado-masochistic marriage is freed by her husband's murder. But she sits through the long weeks of the murderer's trial neurotically confusing her obsessive desire for her husband's death with literal guilt for his murder. At the trial's conclusion the family butler confesses to voyeuristic activities which ironically provide the alibi she requires to confirm her own innocence. In "Carrousel" (*Hearst's International-Cosmopolitan*, 1930) a love triangle among two sisters and the manager of an amusement park which adjoins the sisters' home ends in a sewing-shears stabbing witnessed by Ferris wheel riders "marooned in mid-air outside the turret window." In "Soiled Dove" the principal of an all-girl high school falls passionately in love with one of his problem pupils, who cannot tame her desultorily lascivious nature until she becomes the pregnant ward of the principal, whom she later marries.

In "God Made Little Apples" (*Hearst's International-Cosmopolitan*, 1928), an exceptional story, Hurst recovers the tone of her earlier work as well as her best form in a moving, insightful tale of a husband and wife secretly in love with new partners but simultaneously unable to betray and abandon one another. This story demonstrates the same rich complexity as "Get Ready the Wreaths," but the writing is cleaner and faster paced. Hurst seems briefly to have adopted the same text as her heroine: "Modernity, whatever that harassed noun meant when shaken in the glib mouths of its disciples, like a bone in a terrier's bright teeth, dictated a clean, young, fearless, and square-shooting course of action." This story makes keen distinctions between love and infatuation, between young adulthood and middle age, and between prewar and postwar mores. Hurst's interest throughout this volume is with what she called "the turgid and dangerous currents beneath the daily surface of life." But it is only in "God Made Little Apples," the collection's least sensationalistic story, that those currents become convincing.

Reviews of *We Are Ten* were not as favorable as was customary with Hurst's story collections. The *Saturday Review* (9 October 1937) critic, Isabel Wilder, noted the crude journalistic quality of its sketches: "What Miss Hurst has done is to give with her story teller's skill and insight a three dimensional quality to merely reported front page news." The *New York Times* (26 September 1937) reviewer rated this "perfunctory and mechanical" volume as "no credit" to its author. Nonetheless, if *We Are Ten* suffered in comparison with her earlier collections, Hurst had remained a foremost writer of the American short story for well over twenty years.

Hurst's writing career extended well beyond the publication of *We Are Ten*, and she must finally be remembered for her novels as well as her short stories. Her own favorite among her novels was *Lummox* (1923), an eloquent tale of an inarticulate heroine from the slums. In it and *Appassionata* (1926), Hurst equaled or surpassed her finest short stories. Her later novels, which continued to appear throughout the 1940s and 1950s and into the 1960s, seemed curiously old-fashioned. Her florid style and sentimental tone did not endear her to contemporary tastes. Her narrative structure sometimes regressed to "amateurish" levels. Critics cited her for a deficiency of humor and lack of subtlety. But they continued to applaud her "divine energy." Criticism leveled against her work typically resolved into back-handed compliments and grudging praise such as J. W. Krutch's comments in *Literary Review* (20 October 1923): "One can account for so much bad in the midst of so much good only by imagining in Miss Hurst more talent and force than taste. . . . But it would be a great mistake to let too much fastidiousness prevent one from getting the benefits of her talent and one must merely resign himself to take the gold and accept the heavy alloy as best he may."

Since Hurst's death in 1968, fewer and fewer people recognize her name let alone read her books or argue their merit. But she contributed to American fiction a keen observation of the American scene, a compassionate perspective on America's neglected and underprivileged, and an ebullient vitality which more recent writers might well envy.

References:
A. Harrison, "Sign-Posts of Fiction," *Contemporary Review*, 128 (July 1925): 82-89;

Zora Neale Hurston, "Fannie Hurst: By Her Ex-Amanuensis," *Saturday Review of Literature*, 16 (9 October 1937): 15-16;

A. B. Maurice, "The History of their Books," *Bookman*, 69 (May 1929): 258-260;

L. Sabine, "That Elusive Something," *Independent Woman*, 13 (March 1934): 70;

H. Salpeter, "Fannie Hurst: Sob-Sister of American Fiction," *Bookman*, 73 (August 1931): 612-615;

Mary Rose Shaughnessy, *Myths About Love and Woman: The Fiction of Fannie Hurst* (New York: Gordon, 1979);

Gay Wilentz, "White Patron and Black Artist: The Correspondence of Fannie Hurst and Zora Neale Hurston," *Library Chronicle of the University of Texas*, 35 (1986): 20-43.

Papers:
The major collection of Hurst's papers is held at the Humanities Research Center, University of Texas at Austin. Smaller collections are at the Olin Library of Washington University, St. Louis, and the Goldfarb Library at Brandeis University.

Zora Neale Hurston

(7 January 1901?-28 January 1960)

Laura M. Zaidman
University of South Carolina, Sumter

See also the Hurston entry in *DLB 51: Afro-American Writers from the Harlem Renaissance to 1940.*

BOOKS: *Jonah's Gourd Vine* (Philadelphia & London: Lippincott, 1934; London: Duckworth, 1934);

Mules and Men (Philadelphia & London: Lippincott, 1935; London: Kegan Paul, 1936);

Their Eyes Were Watching God (Philadelphia & London: Lippincott, 1937; London: Dent, 1938);

Tell My Horse (Philadelphia, New York, London & Toronto: Lippincott, 1938); republished as *Voodoo Gods; an Inquiry into Native Myths and Magic in Jamaica and Haiti* (London: Dent, 1939);

Moses, Man of the Mountain (Philadelphia, New York, London & Toronto: Lippincott, 1939); republished as *The Man of the Mountain* (London: Dent, 1941);

Dust Tracks on a Road (Philadelphia & London: Lippincott, 1942; London & New York: Hutchinson, 1944);

Seraph on the Suwanee (New York: Scribners, 1948);

I Love Myself When I Am Laughing . . . And Then Again When I Am Looking Mean and Impressive: A Zora Neale Hurston Reader, edited by Alice Walker (Old Westbury, N.Y.: Feminist Press, 1979);

The Sanctified Church (Berkeley: Turtle Island Foundation, 1981);

Spunk: The Selected Stories of Zora Neale Hurston (Berkeley: Turtle Island Foundation, 1985).

OTHER: *The First One: A Play*, in *Ebony and Topaz*, edited by Charles S. Johnson (New York: National Urban League, 1927), pp. 53-57.

PERIODICAL PUBLICATIONS:

FICTION

"John Redding Goes to Sea," *Stylus*, 1 (May

Zora Neale Hurston (photograph by Carl Van Vechten, by permission of Joseph Solomon, Trustee for the Estate of Carl Van Vechten, courtesy of the Beinecke Rare Book and Manuscript Library, Yale University)

1921): 11-12; revised and republished in *Opportunity*, 4 (January 1926): 16-21;

"Magnolia Flower," *Spokesman* (July 1925): 26-29;

"The Fire and the Cloud," *Challenge*, 1 (September 1934): 10-12;

"The Conscience of the Court," *Saturday Evening Post*, 222 (18 March 1950): 22-23, 112, 114, 116, 118, 120, 122.

POETRY

"O Night," *Stylus*, 1 (May 1921): 42;

"Poem," *Howard University Record*, 16 (February 1922): 236.

DRAMA

Color Struck!: A Play, Fire!!, 1 (November 1926): 7-15;

Mule Bone: A Comedy of Negro Life, by Hurston and Langston Hughes, *Drama Critique* (Spring 1964): 103-107.

NONFICTION

"The Hue and Cry about Howard University," *Messenger*, 7 (September 1925): 315-319, 338;

"Possum or Pig," *Forum*, 76 (September 1926): 465;

"Cudjo's Own Story of the Last African Slaver," *Journal of Negro History*, 12 (October 1927): 648-663;

"Communication," *Journal of Negro History*, 12 (October 1927): 664-667;

"Dance Songs and Tales From the Bahamas," *Journal of American Folklore*, 43 (July-September 1930): 294-312;

"Hoodoo in America," *Journal of American Folklore*, 44 (October-December 1931): 317-418;

"Race Cannot Become Great Until It Recognizes Its Talent," *Washington Tribune*, 29 December 1934;

"Full of Mud, Sweat and Blood," review of *God Shakes Creation* by David M. Cohn, *New York Herald Tribune Books*, 3 November 1935, p. 8;

"Stories of Conflict," review of *Uncle Tom's Children* by Richard Wright, *Saturday Review* (2 April 1938): 32;

"Negroes Without Self-Pity," *American Mercury*, 57 (November 1943): 601-603;

"The Last Slave Ship," *American Mercury*, 58 (March 1944): 351-358;

"Bible, Played by Ear in Africa," review of *How God Fix Jonah* by Lorenz Graham, *New York Herald Tribune Weekly Book Review*, 24, November 1946, p. 5;

Review of *Voodoo in New Orleans* by Robert Tallant, *Journal of American Folklore*, 60 (October-December 1947): 436-438;

"I Saw Negro Votes Peddled," *American Legion Magazine*, 49 (November 1950): 12-13, 54-57, 59-60;

"Mourner's Bench, Communist Line: Why the Negro Won't Buy Communism," *American Legion Magazine*, 50 (June 1951): 14-15, 55-60;

"A Negro Voter Sizes Up Taft," *Saturday Evening Post*, 223 (8 December 1951): 29, 50;

"Zora's Revealing Story of Ruby's First Day in Court," *Pittsburgh Courier* (11 October 1952);

"Hoodoo and Black Magic" [weekly column], *Fort Pierce Chronicle* (11 July 1958-7 August 1959);

"The Farm Laborer at Home," *Fort Pierce Chronicle* (27 February 1959).

Zora Neale Hurston achieved moderate success during the Harlem Renaissance as a short-story writer and a collector of black-American folklore. Her stories deserve attention beyond the concerns of black or feminist literature because of their local color and strong characterization. Hurston was the most prolific black-American woman writer of her time, but the significance of her contribution to American literature and folklore has only recently been acknowledged. She has been described by her biographer, Robert E. Hemenway, as "flamboyant and yet vulnerable, self-centered and yet kind, a Republican conservative and yet an early black nationalist." Her stories reflect this complexity.

No record of Hurston's birth exists, but, as she wrote in her autobiography, *Dust Tracks on a Road* (1942), she "heard tell" she was born on 7 January 1903 in Eatonville, Florida, one of eight children. However, one brother gave 1891 as the year; another brother, Everette, was convinced by Hurston to set his age back seven years to cover the obvious discrepancies between what he said and what she wrote; and her brother John cited the 1903 date in a 1936 affidavit. Hurston used 1903 most often–but variously gave the year as 1900, 1901, and 1902. Hurston scholars Hemenway and Alice Walker use 1901. Her parents, Lucy Ann Potts, a country schoolteacher, and John Hurston, a carpenter and Baptist preacher, met and married in Alabama, then moved to Eatonville, Florida (north of Orlando), three years before Hurston's birth. Her father, as a three-term mayor, helped codify the laws of this all-black community, the first to be incorporated in the United States.

Hurston's mother died in 1904, and her father quickly remarried. In order to appease his new wife, he sent Zora with a sister and brother to a Jacksonville school. Although she fondly recalled the happiness of Eatonville where she "grew like a gourd vine and yelled bass like a gator," she bitterly remembered the racial preju-

Hurston, circa 1921, while a student at Howard University
(courtesy of Herbert Sheen)

van repertory company, she traveled around the South for eighteen months, always reading in hopes of completing her education. Later she enrolled in a Baltimore high school, Morgan Academy (now Morgan State University), while working as a live-in maid. In 1918 she entered Howard University, paying for her expenses by working as a barbershop manicurist and as a maid for prominent blacks. At Howard she met Herbert Sheen, also a student, and married him on 19 May 1927 in St. Augustine, Florida. They lived together only eight months. Sheen claims that "the demands of her career doomed the marriage to an early, amicable divorce" on 7 July 1931. In a 1953 letter to Sheen, Hurston recalls the idealistic dreams they shared in their youth, regretting nothing because she lived her life to the fullest.

A second brief marriage to Albert Price III, some fifteen years younger than Hurston, on 27 June 1939 in Fernandina, Florida, ended less amicably on 9 November 1943. Price, a Works Progress Administration playground worker, contended in a divorce countersuit that he was "put in fear of his life" due to Hurston's practice of "Black Magic" or "Voodooism," which he claimed she learned in Haiti; furthermore, Price said she possessed the power to "fix him" if he "would not perform her wishes."

Hurston's literary career began at Howard. She joined the literary society (sponsored by Alain Locke), which published her first story, "John Redding Goes to Sea," in the club's literary magazine, *Stylus*, in May 1921; in January 1926 it was republished in *Opportunity: A Journal of Negro Life*, a new magazine for beginning black writers. The story portrays a young man's inability to achieve his ambitions because his mother and wife prevent him from following his wanderlust instincts. This frustration is foreshadowed by an early childhood scene in which John plays with twigs he imagines are ships; but instead of sailing gallantly away in the stream, his ships lay stranded in the weeds. His father Alfred tells him that some people's lives end like that too. His mother Matty hinders his ambitions to explore the world, encouraging him instead to marry and settle down. Yet "his thoughts would in spite of himself, stray down river to Jacksonville, the sea, the wide world—and poor home-tied John Redding wanted to follow them." He cannot "stifle that longing for the open road, the rolling seas, for peoples and countries" unknown, but to please his mother and wife he

dice of Jacksonville, where she became just "a little colored girl," different and unwanted. When her father stopped paying her room and board (and even suggested that the school adopt her), she returned home to a miserable life of "ragged, dirty clothes and hit-and-miss meals." The four older children had left home and the four younger ones (including Zora) were passed around to their mother's friends "like a bad penny."

At fourteen Zora left Eatonville, working as a maid for whites, but refusing to act humble or to accept sexual advances from male employers; consequently, she never stayed at one job long. Hired as a wardrobe girl with a Gilbert and Sulli-

stays home until death releases him from his stifling existence. Killed in a flood, he floats at long last out to sea, a crucified figure on a timber.

While immature in comparison to later works, this story contains typical themes Hurston was to develop. Like several of her male characters, Redding the dreamer strives to improve his life, to be a man; and like many others, he never realizes his dreams. Unfortunately, he could never act upon the fantasies conjured up by his vivid imagination, transporting him to other realms—as a prince in an elegant carriage, a knight on a fiery charger, or a steamboat captain on the St. John River—always "riding away to the horizon." Another characteristic mark of Hurston's fiction is the black folklore about the supernatural that pervades the story. Matty Redding believes John's wanderlust is caused by a spell placed by a witch who sprinkled the yard with "travel dust" the day he was born to revenge Alfred Redding's not marrying her daughter. Consequently, Matty does everything in her power to keep John home. While she succeeds in this, she cannot prevent his death, portended by a screech owl's alighting on the roof and shivering forth "his doleful cry" the night John drowns. She tries charms such as burning salt in the lamp and turning her bathrobe inside out; even her husband turns his socks inside out to ward off this evil omen of death. Discussions of these folk superstitions would later be included in Hurston's anthropological study *Mules and Men* (1935).

"John Redding Goes to Sea" came to the attention of *Opportunity* founder and editor Charles Spurgeon Johnson, who subsequently wrote Hurston to solicit material; she sent him "Drenched in Light," published in *Opportunity* in December 1924. The story (republished as "Isis" in *Spunk: The Selected Stories of Zora Neale Hurston*, 1985) concerns eleven-year-old Isis (nicknamed Isie) Watts, a lively, imaginative black girl whose energies are stifled by her strict Grandmother Potts. Isie, a dreamer like John Redding, imagines herself wearing "trailing robes, golden slippers with blue bottoms," riding "white horses with flaring pink nostrils to the horizon," and "gazing over the edge of the world into the abyss." The grandmother punishes her for brazenly sitting with her knees separated, crossing her legs, whistling, and playing with boys, but Isie cannot be stopped from her lively mischief. She romps with the dogs, turns somersaults, dances, perches upon the gatepost in front of her house, races up and down the road to Orlando hailing gleefully all the travel-

FIRE!!

A Quarterly Devoted to the Younger Negro Artists

Premier Issue Edited by
WALLACE THURMAN

In Association With

Langston Hughes	Zora Neale Hurston
Gwendolyn Bennett	Aaron Douglas
Richard Bruce	John Davis

Table of Contents

Volume One   Number One

EDITORIAL OFFICES
314 West 138th Street, New York City

Price $1.00 per copy   Issued Quarterly

Table of contents for the only issue (November 1926) of the avant-garde magazine coedited by Hurston

ers, begging rides in cars and winning her way into everyone's heart. However, Grandma Potts is not pleased with Isie's antics, especially her attempt to shave the old lady's facial hair while she is sleeping. As Isie innocently explains, "No ladies don't weah no whiskers if they kin help it. But Gran'ma gittin ole an' she doan know how to shave like me." Ironically, although the grandmother sternly disciplines Isie and restricts the child's activities, she allows Helen, a white stranger, to take Isie to a hotel to dance. Having seen the youngster perform a gypsy dance at a local barbecue, Helen envisions Isie's vitality as a source for her own renewal. She confesses, "I want a little of her sunshine to soak into my soul. I need it." She needs Isie in order to be "drenched in light" herself.

Johnson praised the story for expressing "New Negro" thoughts and celebrating the beauty of being black. To be sure, Isie's energy and joyful exuberance are contrasted with the ennui and emptiness of Helen's life. Temporarily taking Isie from her home, Helen acts as if she were the white benefactor transferring a poor black child to a more privileged society; however, Helen has no intention of being a surrogate mother, for she appears interested only in what Isie can transfer to her. One is reminded of the whites who flocked to popular Harlem nightspots to be entertained by the "primitive" black dancers, singers, and musicians. To some extent the story involves racial themes, although subtle; not only does the grandmother hastily grant the white woman's request that she be allowed to take Isie to entertain her, she also tries to break Isie's high-spirited nature, perhaps to better survive in a white-dominated world. Nonetheless, "Drenched in Light" celebrates the youthful energy and independence Hurston herself describes in her autobiographical article, "How It Feels to Be Colored Me" (*The World Tomorrow*, May 1928; collected in *I Love Myself When I Am Laughing . . . And Then Again When I Am Looking Mean and Impressive*, 1979). She describes her favorite place as a child as being "atop the gate post," waving at white travelers to Orlando, even accepting rides from them, singing and dancing for them just as Isie does. Other autobiographical parallels exist as well, most notably that Hurston's mother's maiden name was Potts.

After the publication of "Drenched in Light" in *Opportunity*, the leading periodical of the Harlem Renaissance, Hurston decided in early January 1925 to move to New York, arriving with "$1.50, no job, no friends, and a lot of hope." With Johnson's friendship and encouragement she quickly became known amid Harlem Renaissance circles. Langston Hughes remembers her as the most entertaining of the group.

In May 1925 Hurston won second prize in an *Opportunity*-sponsored contest for her short story "Spunk" (*Opportunity*, June 1925; collected in *Spunk*), and at the awards banquet she met several influential people who furthered her career. Fannie Hurst, one of the judges, hired Hurston as a live-in secretary because she was impressed with Hurston's charm, her rich Southern dialect, and her laughter. Hurst recalls how Hurston ("a big-boned . . . young woman, handsome and light yellow") would get bored quickly with taking dictation and suggest that they go to "the Harlem badlands" or the wharves. Hurst soon fired her as secretary, for her shorthand was nearly illegible,

Hurston with Jessie Fauset (left) and Langston Hughes at the statue of Booker T. Washington, Tuskegee Institute, 1927 (courtesy of the Beinecke Rare Book and Manuscript Library, Yale University)

"her typing hit or miss, mostly the latter, her filing, a game of find-the-thimble"; however, she retained her as a companion and chauffeur. Hurst later wrote the introduction to Hurston's first novel, *Jonah's Gourd Vine* (1934). Another important person who befriended Hurston at the *Opportunity* banquet was Annie Nathan Meyer, a novelist and a founder of Barnard College, who arranged for Hurston to attend Barnard on scholarship. She entered in the fall of 1925 as its first black student.

"Spunk" is a story about Spunk Banks, a "giant of a brown skinned man" who goes too far in manipulating and intimidating people. Set in a black village much like Eatonville, the story follows Banks, who "ain't skeered of nothin' on God's green footstool–nothin'. " His overweening pride brings his downfall when he "struts 'round wid another man's wife" (Lena Kanty) and triggers revenge from the husband. Joe Kanty, however, is killed when he sneaks up behind Banks, for his pocket razor is no match for Spunk's army .45. Free after a brief murder trial, Spunk ironically finds he has lost his courage, for he believes he is being haunted by a big, black bobcat,

Joe's ghost "done sneaked back from Hell!" The townspeople even see Joe Kanty differently; no longer thought of as the town coward, he is considered courageous for seeking revenge with just a razor. Mysteriously caught in the saw blade at the mill, Spunk suffers a grisly death; both Spunk and the townspeople credit Joe's spirit for pushing him into the saw. Hubris is punished as the once heroic "giant" is quickly forgotten. His corpse, covered by a dingy sheet, lies on three boards on sawhorses at his wake, as the women "ate heartily ... and wondered who would be Lena's next," and the men "whispered coarse conjectures between guzzles of whiskey."

"Spunk" illustrates Hurston's growth in the way she shows rather than tells about characters. Her dialogue, using the rural black dialect of central Florida, reflects this increased narrative strength. In addition, Hurston seems more sure of her special expertise–the richness of Eatonville's folk beliefs. For example, the black bobcat (Joe's ghost), the three "cooling boards," and the turning of Spunk to the east as he dies all reflect this folklore.

"Black Death," a companion piece to "Spunk," never was published in its original short story form, even though it won an honorable mention in the prestigious 1925 *Opportunity* contest and was considered for inclusion in Locke's groundbreaking anthology *The New Negro* (1925). The story portrays an Eatonville "hoodoo" man named Old Man Morgan, who is consulted by Mrs. Boger, seeking revenge on Beau Diddeley for impregnating her daughter Docia and refusing to marry her. The traditional scoundrel stereotype, Beau is not only already married but also callous and insulting. The conjure man works his deadly magic, and, while Beau woos another girl, he dies of a heart attack–and a mysterious powder burn is found directly over his heart.

The story was rewritten as an article about Eatonville hoodoo men entitled "Hoodoo in America," and published in the October-December 1931 issue of *Journal of American Folklore*, the nation's most respected folklore journal. Undoubtedly Hurston mixed folklore reports and fiction in both versions, having become skillful at blending the folklore of many generations with her imaginative storytelling.

In 1926 Hurston again entered the *Opportunity* contest. "Muttsy" (collected in *Spunk*) was awarded a second prize and was published in the magazine's August issue. "Muttsy" contrasts the perspectives of Pinkie, an innocent young black girl who has escaped the "ill treatment and squalor" of her home in the South, and Muttsy Owens, a worldly black gambler who decides he must have her. They meet in Ma Turner's place (presumably a Harlem brothel and speakeasy) where Pinkie, in search of lodging, has been directed. Run by "Forty-dollars-Kate," the establishment caters to "women who talked of nothing but men and the numbers and drink, and men who talked of nothing but the numbers and drink and women." Pinkie immediately attracts Muttsy's attention. Smitten with her beauty and her aloofness, Muttsy slips into Pinkie's room and places his expensive diamond ring on her finger as a token of his sincere intentions. She avoids him until he gives up gambling and gets a job on the docks overseeing stevedores. However, a month after marriage, Muttsy resumes gambling, rationalizing, "What man can't keep one li'l wife an' two li'l bones?" Whether the marriage survives his backsliding is uncertain as the story concludes.

Muttsy obviously does not respect Pinkie's old-fashioned moral values. In fact, Pinkie is described throughout as a tender little piece of chicken, waiting to be eaten. Muttsy is incensed by Pinkie's leaving Ma Turner's after he has paid for her room and board for a week and has received no payment in return. Although he succeeds in convincing her of his intentions to marry her, nothing is said of their courtship or subsequent marriage. Hurston attempts in the story to contrast the woman's innocence ("Pinkie" suggesting a little, inexperienced girl) with the man's experience ("Muttsy" suggesting a worldly, though common, individual).

Whereas Pinkie and Muttsy's marriage is beginning, albeit on an ominous note, "Sweat," published in the single issue of Wallace Thurman's avant-garde magazine *Fire!!* (November 1926; collected in *Spunk*), depicts the death of a marriage. *Fire!!*, founded by Hurston, Hughes, and Thurman, advocated writing for art's sake–contrary to writers such as Locke and W. E. B. Du Bois who urged blacks to reflect a racial perspective, especially in portraying relationships with whites. In the foreword is this statement of purpose: "FIRE ... weaving vivid, hot design upon an ebon bordered loom and satisfying pagan thirst for beauty unadorned...." Hurston succeeds in blending the vivid and intense fire of passions in this portrait of the marriage of a black couple, Delia and Sykes Jones. Set in Eatonville, the story shows how the hard work ("sweat") of Delia is counter-

Hurston in the late 1930s

acted by the hatred of her adulterous husband, who beats her brutally after two months of marriage, openly flaunts his extramarital affairs from the beginning, and chooses as his mistress a woman named Bertha, a big, fat "greasy Mogul ... who couldn't kiss a sardine can ... throwed out de back do' 'way las' yeah." Delia has slaved over whites' laundry to earn a living for fifteen years; she alone has paid for the house, and now Sykes promises to give the house to Bertha. To scare off his wife, who is terrified of snakes, he first tries taunting her with his snakelike bullwhip. When the "long, round, limp and black" whip falls across her shoulders and slithers along the floor beside her, she is so frightened that "it softened her knees and dried her mouth so that it was a full minute before she could cry out or move." When that does not work, he pens up a rattlesnake near the back door. As a final resort, Sykes tries to kill his stubborn wife by placing the deadly snake in the clothes hamper just before she is to sort the clothes. Delia escapes the poisonous fangs, but Sykes is bitten and dies. Delia refuses to warn or even help him, having understood finally how deadly his hatred of her had become; she watches him with "his horribly swollen neck and his one open eye shining with hope."

As in several of Hurston's stories, the woman is strong, proud, independent; the man does not appreciate these strengths because he feels emasculated and dependent. Sykes attempts to prove his masculinity by cruelly abusing his wife. The townspeople comment on how despicably Sykes treats Delia, saying he had "beat huh 'nough tuh kill three women let 'lone change they looks." This mistreatment is described by general store owner Joe Clarke: "There's plenty men dat takes a wif lak dey do a joint uh sugarcane. It's round, juicy, an' sweet when dey gets it. But dey squeeze an grind, squeeze an' grind an' wring tell dey wring every drop uh pleasure dat's in 'em out. When dey's satisfied dat dey is wrung dry, dey treats 'em jes lak dey do a cane-chew. Dey throws 'em away. Dey knows whut dey is doin' while dey is at it, an' hates theirselves fuh it but they keeps on hanging after huh tell she's empty. Den dey hates huh fuh bein' a cane-chew an' in de way." Hurston reinforces this narrative action of Sykes's horrible abuse of Delia with the traditional symbolism of the snake to represent evil in the world. Referred to as "Ol Satan" and

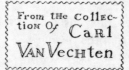

7

The more they snow, the more we see
The skirts run up, the socks run down
Jingling bells run round and round
Oh week by week, and day by day
Let's hope that things keep on this way
Let's kneel right down and pray.

49. And the women all sought him, the damsels and the matrons and the grandmothers and all those who wear the skirt, and with them his name was continually Panic.

50. And the men sought him because his raiment was such that all knew from them the styles which would come to pass.

51. And he roomed no more with Toothsome, but had unto himself swell lodgings. But one day Toothsome sought him and asked,

52. "How now dost thou come to Harlem and become Panic unto the virgin, and the matron, and the grandmatron, and unto the sheik and the Niggerati (which being interpreted means Negro literati) and unto all those above 125th street? In all my years in Babylon none has called me thus."

53. And Mandolin who is called Panic, answered him, "In my early days in Babylon was I taught to subscribe to Vanity Fair, and to read it diligently, for no man may know his way about Babylon without it."

54. Then did a great light dawn upon him called Toothsome, and he rushed forth to subscribe to the perfect magazine.

55. And of his doings and success after that, is it not written in the Book of Harlem?

From the Collection Of Carl Van Vechten

Page from the typescript for Hurston's story "The Book of Harlem," written in biblical form. The story was first published in the 1985 collection Spunk *(the Collection of Carl Van Vechten, courtesy of the Beinecke Rare Book and Manuscript Library, Yale University).*

"Ol Scratch," the snake Sykes brings home to terrify Delia is identified with Sykes's evil (the two *s*'s in his name hint at the comparison), although Freudian critics may see the snakelike whip in phallic terms as well.

"Eatonville Anthology" was published in three installments in the *Messenger* (September-November 1926; collected in *I Love Myself When I Am Laughing* . . .). This series of fourteen brief sketches, some only two paragraphs long, illustrates her artistic use of cultural experiences, fusing folklore studies with fiction. These self-contained tales include glimpses of a woman beggar, an incorrigible dog, a backwoods farmer, the village's greatest liar, and a cheating husband. They become an appropriate transition to mark the end of her short stories of the 1920s and the beginning of her work as folklorist. An English major at Howard, she took anthropology courses at Barnard and, on the merit of an excellent paper, came to the attention of anthropologist Franz Boas. She worked as his apprentice after graduating with a B.A. degree in 1928, accepting a fourteen-hundred-dollar fellowship he arranged for her so she could record "the songs, customs, tales, superstitions, lies, jokes, dances, and games of Afro-American folklore" in the South. Hurston took her work seriously; for instance, she would stop strangers in Harlem and measure their heads with calipers to study blacks' physical characteristics. However, when she went South to collect folklore, her academic approach (and her "Barnardese" dialect) alienated her subjects, and she managed to collect very few items—"not enough to make a flea a waltzing jacket," she recalled. She once admitted, "I needed my Barnard education to help me see my people as they really are. But I found that it did not do to be too detached as I stepped aside to study them." Another result of the often frustrating work as a folklorist was her article "Cudjo's Own Story of the Last African Slaver" (*Journal of Negro History*, October 1927), based on an interview with Cudjo Lewis, the sole survivor of the last slave ship to America in 1859, and blacks in Plateau, Alabama, who were descendants of the last shipped slaves. Unfortunately, Hurston had not been totally honest about her sources; in 1972 linguist William Stewart proved the bulk of the article was "culled" from Emma Langdon Roche's *Historic Sketches of the Old South* (1914) with no credit given for this obvious source of almost duplicate passages.

Nevertheless, Hurston had done considerable work collecting folklore and historical material in the four years after she graduated from college. She made a successful folklore-collecting trip in the South, subsidized with two hundred dollars a month by the wealthy Mrs. Rufus Osgood Mason, who also supported work by Alain Locke and Langston Hughes. It appears as though Hurston was at the crossroads with dual careers as a writer and folklorist / anthropologist. She was unsuccessful in her attempt to enter Columbia University to study for a Ph.D. in 1934, at which point she published her first novel (*Jonah's Gourd Vine*) and, a year later, first collection of folklore (*Mules and Men*). Hemenway speculates that she never became a serious academic anthropologist because "immediate experience takes precedence over analysis, emotion over reason and self over society, the personal over the theoretical." Hence, her fiction allowed her to affirm more forcefully the rich humanistic values of black life as opposed to the scientific objectivity of her anthropological studies. Collecting folklore gave her a new perspective as a storyteller of black culture; thus, studying anthropology both analytically and emotionally enriched her literary career.

Seven years after the "Eatonville Anthology" sketches, Hurston returned to her Eatonville remembrances in "The Gilded Six-Bits," published in *Story Magazine* (August 1933; collected in *I Love Myself When I Am Laughing . . .*). Her most frequently anthologized story, it has the most depth, the most fully developed characters, and the most skillful dialect of all her short fiction. Like several other tales, the story paints the portrait of a marriage. Missie May and Joe Banks begin happily—she keeps an immaculate home and cooks his favorite food, and he works hard

Hurston on a folklore-collecting trip, late 1930s (courtesy of the Jane Belo Estate)

and lovingly throws his week's pay into the doorway to announce his homecoming. The "gilded six-bits" are the coins of the serpent who intrudes in their garden. Otis D. Slemmons, a sly woman-chaser from Chicago, sporting showy gold teeth, a five-dollar-gold-piece stickpin, and a ten-dollar-gold-piece watch charm, causes Missie May's fall from grace in Joe's eyes. Joe's unexpected arrival early one night catches Slemmons with Missie May; she pleads for forgiveness because she just wanted to give the gold to Joe. After three months of abstaining from any contact with his unfaithful wife, Joe relents, but he leaves Slemmons's gilded half-dollar under her pillow to show his disgust of her prostituting herself. However, with the birth of a son, who definitely resembles Joe, the proud father uses the gilded half-dollar to buy molasses candy kisses for Missie May. He then throws his week's pay of fifteen silver dollars in the doorway, and she pretends to reproach him in the exact manner as she does at the beginning of the story, assuring the reader that the marriage has survived this test of their love.

That the temptations of Slemmons nearly destroy their happiness recalls the way big cities, with their gilded promises of easy money, lured blacks into situations that forced them to prostitute themselves and their values. Another theme is marital discord, showing how infidelity almost ruins the Banks's marriage, but renewed love, suggested by the birth of their child, saves it.

A departure from the Eatonville setting toward the folklore of the Bible is found in "The Fire and the Cloud," published in *Challenge* (September 1934). Edited by Dorothy West, this Harlem Renaissance magazine also published works by writers such as Langston Hughes, James Weldon Johnson, Arna Bontemps, and Frank Yerby. The first issue's lead editorial presented a challenge to young black writers to better the achievement of earlier writers who "did not altogether live up to our fine promise." "The Fire and the Cloud" fails to surpass the quality of Hurston's previous stories, yet it does briefly explore the richness of the Moses mythology, especially Moses's stature as a black folklore hero, a subject expanded in her 1939 novel, *Moses, Man of the Mountain*. In this germinal story, Moses sits on his grave on Mount Nebo and explains to a lizard how he delivered the Hebrew people from bondage in Egypt. He is not so much the great Jewish leader who gave his people the Ten Commandments; he is the great African hero who performed the greatest voodoo magic ever with his rod of power that struck terror in the Pharaoh to set the slaves free. In *Tell My Horse* (1938), a study of Caribbean voodoo practices, Hurston writes, "This worship of Moses recalls the hard-to-explain fact that wherever the Negro is found, there are traditional tales of Moses and his supernatural powers that are not in the Bible. . . ."

Hurston's devotion to anthropology disappointed those friends who wanted her to concentrate more on fiction writing. An interesting perspective is found in Wallace Thurman's satiric treatment of Sweetie May Carr, a thinly disguised portrait of Hurston, in his novel *Infants of the Spring* (1932). A short-story writer from an all-black Mississippi town, she is "too indifferent to literary creation to transfer to paper that which she told so well." Sweetie May says, "I have to eat. I also wish to finish my education. Being a Negro writer these days is a racket and I'm going to make the most of it while it lasts . . . I don't know a tinker's damn about art. . . . My ultimate ambition, as you know, is to become a gynecologist. And the only way I can live easily until I have the requisite training is to pose as a writer of potential ability." Thurman questions Hurston's commitment to writing–and in a larger context, the fate of the entire Harlem Renaissance spirit. Yet in the 1930s Hurston would produce the best fiction being written by a black woman, including the novel *Their Eyes Were Watching God* (1937), written in Haiti in seven weeks, and considered to be her best work. Despite Thurman's cynicism about Hurston's priorities, he does offer some truths about Hurston through Sweetie May Carr's character. For example, she was "more noted for her ribald wit and personal effervescence than for any actual literary work. She was a great favorite among those whites who went in for Negro prodigies. Mainly because she lived up to their conception of what a typical Negro should be. . . . Her repertoire of tales was earthy, vulgar and funny. Her darkies always smiled through their tears, sang spirituals on the slightest provocation, and performed buck dances. . . . Sweetie May was a master of Southern dialect, and an able raconteur . . . [who] knew her white folks." Thurman's fictional portrait is confirmed by Langston Hughes's comment in his autobiography *The Big Sea* (1940) that Hurston entertained wealthy whites with her "side-splitting anecdotes, humorous tales, and tragi-comic stories of the South." Hughes concludes, "no doubt she was a perfect 'darkie' in the nice meaning whites give the term– that is a naive, childlike, sweet, humorous, and highly colored Negro. But Miss Hurston was clever too. . . ."

The sixteen years between "The Fire and the Cloud" and Hurston's last published story, "The Conscience of the Court" (*Saturday Evening Post*, 18 March 1950), created an embittered writer, frustrated by the lack of popular acclaim from both blacks and whites for her four novels and two books of folklore. In the early 1940s Hurston worked for four months as a story consultant at Paramount Studios but failed to have her novels made into movies; then she lectured on the black-college circuit while she continued writing. Her autobiography, *Dust Tracks on a Road*, her most successful publication, gave a partially accurate, partially fictionalized account of her life. In the following years she made many attempts to receive funding for folklore research trips to Central America; finally, an advance on a new novel allowed her to travel in 1947 to British Honduras, where she completed *Seraph on the Suwanee* (1948), her first work that excluded blacks–and her last book. In September 1948 Hurston was arrested in New York City on a morals charge that devastated her personally and professionally. Although the accusation of sodomy with a ten-year-old proved to be false and she was cleared of this morals charge in March 1949, Hurston's world collapsed. A national black newspaper, the *Baltimore Afro-American*, gave the story sensationalized, inaccurate front-page coverage. Writing to Carl Van Vechten, Hurston explained how she was unjustly betrayed by her own race which "has seen fit to destroy [her] without reason" in the "so-called liberal North." She concludes, "All that I have ever tried to do has proved useless. All that I have believed in has failed me. I have resolved to die . . . no acquittal will persuade some people that I am innocent. I feel hurled down a filthy privy hole." However, after a brief period of depression, she attempted to restore her reputation. She taught drama at North Carolina College for Negroes in Durham for a short while and published several nonfiction articles in national magazines.

When "The Conscience of the Court" was published Hurston was working as a maid on affluent Rivo Island, one of Miami's fashionable neighborhoods. As she dusted bookshelves in the library, her employer sat in the living room reading a story written by her "girl." Hurston's unusual situation was inaccurately depicted in a *Miami Herald* feature article (and picked up by the wire services). "Miss Hurston," the interviewing reporter wrote, "believes that she is temporarily written out." (Hurston's agent was at this time holding her eighth book and three short stories–about a Florida religious colony, a turpentine worker at a political meeting, and myths explaining Swiss cheese's holes–none of which was ever published.) Hurston covered up her need for money by stating, "You can only use your mind so long. Then you have to use your hands. It's just the natural thing. I was born with a skillet in my hands. I like to cook and keep house. Why shouldn't I do it for someone else a while? A writer has to stop writing every now and then and live a little." Continuing to weave her stories, she assured the reporter that she only wanted to learn about a maid's life so she could begin a magazine "for and by domestics"–as if she did not know already from her earlier experiences. She told her employer that she had bank accounts

overseas where her books had been published, but she refused to be unpatriotic and spend the money abroad. The publicity about her being a maid and being arrested lends an irony to "Conscience of the Court," which is about a black maid arrested for attacking a white man.

The story focuses on Laura Lee Kimble, who is being tried for assaulting Clement Beasley. Refusing a defense lawyer, Laura justifies her actions by explaining that Beasley attempted to remove valuable property from the home of her white employer, Mrs. J. Stuart Clairborne, on the grounds that he was collecting on an unpaid debt incurred when the white woman borrowed six hundred dollars to pay for Laura's husband's funeral. As the lifelong maid of the Clairborne family, Laura is intensely devoted, despite the fact that she thinks her employer has now abandoned her. She protected the home as if it were her own, and when the man verbally and physically abused her, she stopped him. She tells the judge, "All I did was grab him by his heels and flail the pillar of the porch with him a few times." When the truth comes out that the money was not yet due, and that the man was trying to steal property in excess of six hundred dollars, the judge praises Laura's courage and loyalty and instructs the jury to free her. Laura then finds out that Mrs. Clairborne never knew she had been arrested. Having doubted the woman's friendship for not coming to her aid, Laura expiates her sin when she arrives home by performing a "ritual of atonement" in solemnly polishing the silver before she eats her meal.

Laura's extreme humility, dependence, and loyalty toward whites illustrate the formula writing Hurston knew would sell. The rejection of her last completed novel, about wealthy blacks, led her to believe that whites could not conceive of blacks beyond lower class stereotypes. However, in this story she helped perpetuate the stereotyped images of her race, allowing the *Post* staff to heavily edit the piece because she badly needed the nine hundred dollars she was paid for it.

A year after this last published story appeared, Hurston wrote her agent that she was "cold in hand" (penniless); she confessed, "God! What I have been through. . . . Just inching along like a stepped on worm." This once-famous writer, who had received honorary doctorates and had been on the cover of *Saturday Review*, spent the final decade of her life in relative obscu-

Hurston's gravestone in the Garden of the Heavenly Rest, a segregated cemetery in Fort Pierce, Florida. Alice Walker had the marker erected in 1973 (courtesy of Georgia Curry).

rity. From Rivo Island, she moved around Florida—Belle Glade, Eau Gallie (for five peaceful years), Merritt Island (during which time she worked briefly as a technical librarian for the space program at Patrick Air Force Base), and Fort Pierce, where she wrote a column, "Hoodoo and Black Magic," for a black weekly, the *Fort Pierce Chronicle*, from 11 July 1958 to 7 August 1959. She also taught in a black public school. In 1959 she suffered a stroke, leaving her unable to care for herself adequately. Wracked with pain, she continued to labor at a three-hundred-page manuscript about Herod the Great. Against her will she entered the St. Lucie County Welfare Home in October 1959 and died of hypertensive heart disease on 28 January 1960. No one noticed that her middle name was misspelled (Neil) on her death certificate; moreover, her funeral was delayed a week while friends and family raised the four hundred dollars for expenses. Hoping to make some money to pay Hurston's debt, a deputy sheriff used a garden hose to save the Herod manuscript from being burned, for the welfare-home janitor had been instructed to destroy Hurston's

personal effects. Hurston was buried in an unmarked grave in Fort Pierce's segregated cemetery, Garden of the Heavenly Rest.

Hurston's short stories signal the beginning of an important literary career that also produced four novels, two folklore books, an autobiography, and several nonfiction journal articles. However, "The Conscience of the Court" seems to support Darwin T. Turner's criticism of her work's "superficial and shallow" judgments because she became too "desperate for recognition" and "a blind follower of that social code which approves arrogance toward one's assumed peers and inferiors but requires total psychological commitment to a subservient position before one's supposed superiors." Yet Turner praises her early work, particularly "Sweat," for its skill in presenting the picturesque idiom of Southern blacks, its credible characterization, and its emphasis on love and hate in family relationships. Turner sums up the intensity by which Hurston herself seems to have lived: "In her fiction, men and women love each other totally, or they hate vengefully." Perhaps because she wrote against the prevailing black attitudes of protest in the 1950s, black critics often dismissed her work. Yet in 1972 Arna Bontemps (her literary executor) prophetically wrote that Hurston "still awaits the thoroughgoing critical analysis that will properly place her in the pattern of American fiction."

That comprehensive appraisal came in 1977 with Robert E. Hemenway's *Zora Neale Hurston: A Literary Biography*. Acknowledging his "white man's reconstruction of the intellectual process in a black woman's mind," he offers a favorable assessment of her literary career and tries to explain her enigmatic personality. Praising her work as a celebration of black culture, he concludes that her failure to achieve recognition in her life reflects America's poor treatment of its black artists. The critical acclaim awarded Hurston's writings in the past ten years has allowed readers to discover what Alice Walker (writing in the foreword to Hemenway's biography) finds: a "sense of black people as complete, complex, *undiminished* human beings." She honors Hurston's genius as a black woman writer and delights in her dynamic personality: "Zora was funny, irreverent (she was the first to call the Harlem Renaissance literati the 'niggerati'), good-looking and sexy."

Hurston, who produced a substantial body of literature of intense human emotions, died poor but left a rich legacy. In 1973, as a tribute to that inspiration, Walker placed a gravestone inscribed: "ZORA NEALE HURSTON / 'A GENIUS OF THE SOUTH' / 1901——1960 / NOVELIST, FOLKLORIST / ANTHROPOLOGIST."

Biography:

Robert E. Hemenway, *Zora Neale Hurston: A Literary Biography* (Urbana: University of Illinois Press, 1977).

References:

Richard Barksdale and Keneth Kinnamon, *Black Writers of America: A Comprehensive Anthology* (New York: Macmillan, 1972);

Robert Bone, *Down Home: A History of Afro-American Short Fiction From Its Beginnings to the End of the Harlem Renaissance* (New York: Putnam's, 1975);

Arthur P. Davis, *From the Dark Tower: Afro-American Writers, 1900-1960* (Washington, D.C.: Howard University Press, 1974);

Robert E. Hemenway, "Zora Neale Hurston and the Eatonville Anthropology," in *The Harlem Renaissance Remembered*, edited by Arna Bontemps (New York: Dodd, Mead, 1972);

Lillie P. Howard, *Zora Neale Hurston* (Boston: Twayne, 1980);

Langston Hughes, *The Big Sea* (New York: Hill & Wang, 1963);

Bernice Johnson Reagon, *Dictionary of American Negro Biography*, edited by Rayford W. Logan and Michael R. Winston (New York: Norton, 1982), pp. 340-341;

Darwin T. Turner, *In a Minor Chord, Three Afro-American Writers and Their Search for Identity* (Carbondale: Southern Illinois University Press, 1971);

Alice Walker, "In Search of Zora Neale Hurston," *Ms.*, 3 (March 1975): 74-90.

Papers:

Major depositories of Hurston's manuscripts, letters, and other materials are located at various libraries: the Hurston Collection of the University of Florida Library; the James Weldon Johnson Memorial Collection at Yale University's Beinecke Rare Book and Manuscript Library; the Schomburg Collection of the New York Public Library; Fisk University; Howard University; and the University of South Florida.

Ring Lardner

(6 March 1885-25 September 1933)

Michael Oriard
Oregon State University

See also the Lardner entries in *DLB 11: American Humorists, 1800-1950* and *DLB 25: American Newspaper Journalists, 1901-1925.*

BOOKS: *Bib Ballads* (Chicago, New York & Toronto: Volland, 1915);

You Know Me Al (New York: Doran, 1916);

Gullible's Travels, Etc. (Indianapolis: Bobbs-Merrill, 1917; London: Chatto & Windus, 1926);

My Four Weeks in France (Indianapolis: Bobbs-Merrill, 1918);

Treat 'Em Rough (Indianapolis: Bobbs-Merrill, 1918);

The Real Dope (Indianapolis: Bobbs-Merrill, 1919);

Own Your Own Home (Indianapolis: Bobbs-Merrill, 1919);

The Young Immigrunts (Indianapolis: Bobbs-Merrill, 1920);

Symptoms of Being 35 (Indianapolis: Bobbs-Merrill, 1921);

The Big Town (Indianapolis: Bobbs-Merrill, 1921);

Say It with Oil, published with *Say It with Bricks*, by Nina Wilcox Putnam (New York: Doran, 1923);

How to Write Short Stories (New York & London: Scribners, 1924; London: Chatto & Windus, 1926);

What of It? (New York & London: Scribners, 1925);

The Love Nest and Other Stories (New York: Scribners, 1926; London: Allan, 1928);

The Story of a Wonder Man (New York: Scribners, 1927);

Round Up: The Stories of Ring Lardner (New York: Scribners, 1929; London: Williams & Norgate, 1935);

June Moon, by Lardner and George S. Kaufman (New York: Scribners, 1930);

Lose with a Smile (New York: Scribners, 1933);

First and Last, edited by Gilbert Seldes (New York & London: Scribners, 1934);

Ring Lardner in Chicago, circa 1915

Shut Up, He Explained, edited by Babette Rosmond and Henry Morgan (New York: Scribners, 1962);

Some Champions: Sketches and Fiction by Ring Lardner, edited by Matthew J. Bruccoli and Richard Layman (New York: Scribners, 1976);

Ring Lardner's You Know Me Al: The Comic Strip Adventures of Jack Keefe (New York: Harcourt Brace Jovanovich / Bruccoli Clark, 1979).

PLAY PRODUCTION: *June Moon*, by Lardner and George S. Kaufman, New York, Broadhurst Theater, 9 October 1929.

Ring Lardner was one of the most admired American writers of the 1920s–praised by Virginia Woolf in 1925 as the author of "the best prose that has come our way" from America; compared favorably to Mark Twain, Jonathan Swift, Anton Chekhov, Bernard Shaw, James Joyce, and William Shakespeare; saluted by Edmund Wilson, H. L. Mencken, Carl Van Doren, Stuart Sherman, Gilbert Seldes, and other major critics of the day as an original and vital voice in American letters. He was proclaimed a master of the modern short story, a writer of the finest vernacular American English since Twain, a satirist unmatched in an age preoccupied with social satire. His death at the age of forty-eight in 1933 brought moving tributes from F. Scott Fitzgerald, Heywood Broun, and other eminent contemporaries. Writers as diverse as Sherwood Anderson, Ernest Hemingway, James T. Farrell, S. J. Perelman, J. D. Salinger, Mark Harris, and Philip Roth have attested not just to Lardner's excellence as a writer but to his influence on their own work (Perelman once admitted, "I was such a shameless Lardner thief I should have been arrested"). Summarizing Lardner's impact, his first biographer, Donald Elder, wrote that "Ring's influence on American prose has been so pervasive that it is easily taken for granted." In addition to other writers' testimonials, one sees much of Lardner's "Haircut" in Eudora Welty's "Petrified Man," Lardner's "Hurry Kane" in Bernard Malamud's *The Natural* (1952), Lardner's many stories of suburban pastimes in the later writings on the subject by John P. Marquand, John Cheever, and John Updike. Yet Lardner's reputation today is uncertain, his contribution to American literature a question, not a commonplace.

It is in these uncertainties themselves that one finds the key to Lardner's place in American letters. In the responses to Lardner's fiction since early in the 1920s one faces questions of vocation, audience, ambition, and form–the relationship of writer and reader in a democratic mass culture. Throughout his professional lifetime Lardner remained the working journalist, writing first for newspapers and then for the most popular magazines in order to support a large family in relative luxury. There is a partial truth in his own claim that he wrote short stories not for art's sake but "because I have four chil-

dren and a wife who has extravagant ideas about a garden." Unlike such writers as Fitzgerald and William Faulkner, Lardner did not write short stories for slick magazines in order to support his family while he worked on his more ambitious fiction. Lardner's ambition never went beyond the popular magazines. He became a "literary artist" more by accident than by design: Fitzgerald engineered his 1924 collection, *How to Write Short Stories*, with the assistance of Fitzgerald's own editor at Scribners, Maxwell Perkins, and Lardner was subsequently discovered by the literati, whose praise encouraged him to write more short stories but not to alter his practice of publishing them in the highest-paying magazines. His chief object in writing was always to make money. And he remained deaf to entreaties from both critics such as Edmund Wilson and friends such as Fitzgerald and Perkins to write the novel that would make him the true heir to Twain as humorist-turned-serious-novelist. In a characteristic remark he told one of his sons that after writing only one chapter he "would be even more bored than the reader." Lardner made his initial reputation as a popular humorist of newspaper columns and magazines pieces, and despite the acclaim that made him also a major voice in 1920s fiction, he remained, for the large majority of his audience, a popular humorist to his death. While Lardner's refusal to adopt the role of self-conscious artist helped assure his appeal to his contemporary admirers, it has worked to undermine his achievements for later generations of academic critics. Like any other author, Lardner must be judged finally for his writing, not his ambition.

That Lardner became any kind of writer at all was due more to accident than to design. Born in Niles, Michigan, on 6 March 1885–fittingly, the year in which *Huckleberry Finn* appeared in America–Lardner experienced a childhood in many ways characteristic of other American writers. Like Herman Melville and Twain before him, as well as Fitzgerald and Hemingway after, Lardner grew up in a family dominated by an artistic mother who gave him his first appreciation of literature (and music). Also like the Melvilles, Clemenses, and Fitzgeralds, the Lardners were an aristocratic family that fell on hard times–in Lardner's case, however, too late for the financial collapse to have had a crucial impact on the future writer. "I have known what it was like to be hungry," Lardner said in an interview when he was forty, "but I always went right to a restaurant." Lardner grew up as the youngest of six children in one of the first families of Niles. The several-acre Lardner estate included a tennis court and a baseball diamond, where the Lardner children played with chosen friends. Ring and the brother and sister closest to him in age each had a nurse and were not allowed out of the yard unattended until the age of eight. From their talented mother, a published poet of the sentimental school, the Lardner children learned to sing and play the piano (like his mother, Ring had perfect pitch and flawless ear), discovered the joys of parlor theatricals, and learned to play witty language games and to make jokes at the inelegancies of the illiterate. The three youngest Lardner children–Rex, Anne, and Ring–received their early education at home, first from their mother, then from a hired tutor, before enrolling in Niles High School where Ring played football, helped form a singing quartet, and graduated with honors as class poet. This last event coincided with his father's financial reversal (large losses from investments and a bank failure), but the collapse was not severe enough, apparently, to force Ring into undesired employment. Declining a scholarship to Olivet College, Ring went to Chicago where he held a handful of jobs for two weeks at a time until his father enrolled him in the Armour Institute of Technology to study mechanical engineering. Lasting less than a semester, Lardner later wrote of that experience that "I can think of no walk in life for which I had more of a natural bent unless it would be hostess at a roller rink." Returning to Niles, Lardner "rested" for a year, becoming a postal clerk, then a bookkeeper and meter reader for the gas company, until the fall of 1905 when he was employed as a reporter for the *South Bend Times* by an editor looking to hire his brother Rex. From this inauspicious entry into professional journalism Lardner became a valued member of the *Times* staff, then moved on to Chicago in 1908 for five years of daily baseball reporting, first with the *Inter-Ocean* then the *Examiner* and the *Tribune*–eventually, beginning in June 1913, writing a daily *Tribune* column, "In the Wake of the News," for six years. (In 1910-1911 he worked briefly on the *Sporting News* in St. Louis and the *Boston American*.) While reporting on Chicago baseball Lardner also waged a finally successful four-year campaign, conducted in large part by mail, to marry Ellis Abbott of Goshen, Indiana, his acceptance long uncertain in part because her father was reluctant to surrender Ellis to that "damned sporting crowd" with whom Lardner hung out. His drinking was already a topic for much conversation via letters, an occupational temptation to which few sporting journalists of the day were immune. The wedding finally took place on 28 June 1911–an event Lardner expected to increase his financial responsibilities and to keep him permanently on the "water wagon." He was right about the first, not the second.

"In the Wake of the News" served as Lardner's chief literary apprenticeship. He followed the example of his predecessor, Hugh E. Keogh, in exploring a wide range of literary forms–poems, epigrams, portraits of sports figures, letters, and verses from contributors, plus his own more original ideas for serials, parodies, and contests–that became the foundation for his mature writing. Lardner did not invent forms but perfected them, as Elder has written. Although he would later wear the mask of literary illiterate, Lardner in fact read widely, if spottily, particularly admiring Katherine Mansfield's stories, Gertrude Stein's *Three Lives* (1909), and, above all other books, Fyodor Dostoyevski's *The Brothers Karamazov* (1879-1880). The influences on his own writing, however, were not Mansfield and Dostoyevski or even Twain, but Finley Peter Dunne and George Ade, humorists who preceded him in Chicago, and Keogh, Hugh Fullerton, Charles Dryden, Charles Seymour, and Charles Van Loan–his somewhat older fellow sportswriters in a city and at a time remarkable for daily journalism. From 1908 until 1913 Lardner covered either of the two Chicago baseball teams, traveling with the Cubs and White Sox, making friends with the players and managers but more importantly listening to their talk. In transferring that talk to his newspaper reports and later his columns, Lardner was not first but best.

A turning point in Lardner's career came in March 1914, when his first series of letters from a "busher" pitcher with the White Sox, Jack Keefe, to his friend Al appeared in the *Saturday Evening Post*. Lardner modeled Keefe on an actual White Sox player with whom he had traveled in 1908, transforming fact into fiction as he had often done in his newspaper writing. This time Van Loan encouraged him to try the magazine market, a welcome suggestion to a man with a growing family. This first appearance of the busher in the pages of the *Post* has a double significance. To Lardner, it meant a new and lucrative

Lardner (right) with his brother Rex and sister Anna

outlet for his writing, his $250 fee from the *Post* eventually rising to $1,250 (and as much as $3,500 from *Cosmopolitan*). To American literature, it meant the appearance of an American original who quickly became embedded in both literary and popular culture.

What was original was not the form. Epistolary fiction had been periodically popular since Samuel Richardson developed it in *Pamela* and *Clarissa* in the eighteenth century. George Horace Lorimer himself, the editor of the *Saturday Evening Post*, had exploited the comic possibilities in his own *Letters from a Self-Made Merchant to His Son*, serialized in the *Post* in 1901 before becoming a best-selling book a year later. What was original in Lardner's version was the voice: a recognizably American voice of the small-town variety, full of the braggadocio of expansive optimism yet masking a bewilderment over the accelerated pace of modern life so complete that the character gained the readers' sympathy even as he invited their derisive laughter–a voice that revealed the speaker to readers in ways the character could never understand. Lardner's earliest admirers seized on the voice of Jack Keefe as his creator's major achievement. To Virginia Woolf, the

busher's seemingly artless vernacular conjured up a more complete and compelling portrait of small-town America than Sherwood Anderson or Sinclair Lewis had managed in any of their fiction. Gilbert Seldes declared the baseball hero dead once Lardner got hold of him. H. L. Mencken praised Lardner's flawless ear in capturing both the rhythms and the diction of the "common American."

Lardner followed the success of "A Busher's Letters Home" with twenty-five more installments. The first six of these he collected in his first substantial book, *You Know Me Al*, in 1916 (following a much slighter volume the previous year titled *Bib Ballads*). Three other busher stories became *Treat 'Em Rough* (1918) and six more *The Real Dope* (1919)–accounts of Jack Keefe's experiences in World War I, less successful in large part because they were not rooted in that world of professional baseball Lardner knew best. During this same period a brief experience as a war correspondent led to *My Four Weeks in France* (1918), another negligible early book, and four of seven stories comprised of letters from a semiliterate, wholly barbarous Chicago policeman, Fred Gross, to his brother Charley became *Own Your*

Own Home (1919). Like the busher stories in *Treat 'Em Rough* and *The Real Dope*, these sketches failed to achieve the richness of character, situation, and language of *You Know Me Al*, but they allowed Lardner to develop further the fictional techniques that would produce his best fiction. Finally, during these fruitful years in Chicago, Lardner began publishing such baseball stories as "My Roomy" (*Saturday Evening Post*, 9 May 1914), "Alibi Ike" (*Saturday Evening Post*, 31 July 1915), "Horseshoes" (*Saturday Evening Post*, 15 August 1914), and "Harmony" (*McClure's*, August 1915), all collected in *How to Write Short Stories*, as well as the loosely connected stories that became *Gullible's Travels, Etc.* (1917). Through the magazines in which all of this fiction first appeared, the Chicago newspaperman was becoming a national literary celebrity.

An offer from John N. Wheeler to write a "Weekly Letter" for the Bell Syndicate, payment to be determined by the number of subscribing papers, enabled Lardner to give up his seven-day-a-week column in 1919. As always, Lardner responded to circumstance rather than following a declared ambition. New York meant both more money and closer proximity to the theatrical and musical world that remained his first love all his life. With a family now grown to four sons (John, seven; Jim, five; Ring, Jr., almost four; and David, an infant), the Lardners moved to Great Neck, Long Island, in the summer of 1919. When he left the Midwest, Lardner was the best-known sportswriter in Chicago and the popular author of numerous stories in the *Saturday Evening Post*, *Red Book*, *McClure's*, *Metropolitan*, and the *American Magazine*. He was as yet undiscovered by the literary establishment or by the immense reading public that would eventually see his "Weekly Letter" in 156 newspapers throughout the country (paying him up to thirty thousand dollars per year). He was a funny man with a growing audience that did not yet include figures such as Mencken and Wilson. But the change in address marked a change in career as well.

The first fruit of his new circumstances was *The Young Immigrunts* (1920), an account of the cross-country auto trip from Chicago to New York purportedly written by four-year-old Ring, Jr. It was actually John who accompanied his parents, while the three younger children traveled by train with their nurse; the switch allowed Ring to put his name on the book's cover. In *The Young Immigrunts* Lardner parodied *The Young*

Illustration by Martin Justice for "A Busher's Letters Home," published in the 7 March 1914 issue of the Saturday Evening Post

Visiters, a recently popular travel book supposedly written by twelve-year-old Daisy Ashford but the work of a mature writer, Lardner was convinced. Lardner stamped the book with his distinctive voice, however, with young Ring, Jr., speaking as yet another semiliterate innocent, unconscious of the hilarity his narrative provokes. In a passage that became famous after Lardner's "discovery" in the 1920s, the child describes getting lost in the city:

> The lease said about my and my fathers trip from the Bureau of Manhattan to our new home the soonest mended. In some way ether I or he got balled up on the grand concorpse and next thing you know we was thretning to swoop down on Pittsfield.
>
> Are you lost daddy I arsked tenderly.
> Shut up he explained.

The move to New York also led directly to the series of stories that make up *The Big Town* (1921), an account of another "wise boob" such as Lardner created with Gullible, this time a husband, newly rich due to the death of his wealthy father-in-law, moving temporarily from South Bend to New York to find his wife's sister a husband. From his columns for the Bell Syndicate, Lardner also put together *Symptoms of Being 35* (1921) and *Say It with Oil* (1923). For three years in the early 1920s he also wrote a comic-strip version of *You Know Me Al*, a task he came to hate but for which he earned twenty thousand dollars a year.

During this period Lardner's writing began to attract serious attention. Mencken praised his rendering of common American speech in the second edition of *The American Language* in 1921 (in subsequent editions Mencken devoted increasing space to Lardner's philological skill). Sherwood Anderson wrote an appreciation in the *New Republic* in October 1922. Van Doren saluted him in the *Century* in July 1923 as a "Philologist among the Low-Brows." What thrust Lardner to the forefront of contemporary writers, however, was the publication in 1924 of *How to Write Short Stories*. This event has become one of those oft-repeated stories that make up the legendry as well as the history of American literature. Fitzgerald, Lardner's close friend and neighbor for a year and a half in 1922-1923, was the catalyst in transforming Lardner into a literary figure. Their friendship was rich, if brief, and it marked Lardner's life permanently. Fitzgerald made the popular journalist think of himself, however reluctantly, as a serious writer. As Great Neck neighbors, in one of the many sessions in which Fitzgerald and Lardner talked long and drank much, Fitzgerald suggested a collection of Lardner's stories. Lardner agreed, as did Maxwell Perkins. But when Lardner confessed that he had no copies of the stories, they had to be tracked down and copied from the magazines in which they had first appeared. Fitzgerald suggested the title and a mock introduction—tips from a successful writer to would-be players of the "literary game." Lardner wrote it in the familiar voice of his magazine nonfiction, that of the wise boob: "But a little group of our deeper drinkers has suggested that maybe boys and gals who wants to take up writing as their life work would be benefited if some person like I was to give them a few hints in regards to the technic of the short story, how to go about planning it and writing it, when and where to plant the love interest and climax, and finally how to market the finished product without leaving no bad taste in the mouth." Lardner also pref-

aced each of the ten stories in the volume with nonsensical explanatory headnotes, introducing the brutal boxing tale "Champion" (*Metropolitan*, October 1916), for example, as "an example of the mystery story. The mystery is how it came to get printed." This comic presentation of the best stories Lardner had written between 1914 and 1922 backfired for some readers. Edmund Wilson took him to task for misleading the reader to expect buffoonery, when the stories that follow these "half-hearted" jokes were in fact "some of the most serious and interesting work which he has yet produced." Several later critics found in the self-deprecating humor early evidence of Lardner's self-loathing and a denial of all literary ambition. The overwhelming majority of readers in 1924, however, undoubtedly saw in the title, introduction, and headnotes a well-known humorist's usual highjinks. Wilson was right in claiming the stories were something very different. Other reviewers also found in "Some Like Them Cold" (*Saturday Evening Post*, 1 October 1921), "The Golden Honeymoon" (*Cosmopolitan*, July 1922), "My Roomy," and several others not the too-frequent banality of magazine fiction but finely crafted, expertly detailed, incisive portraits of familiar American types, in the best vernacular since Twain. In a widely echoed opinion, Wilson judged Lardner superior to Sherwood Anderson and Sinclair Lewis in both his grasp of the vernacular and his rendering of reality, lacking only in sufficient artistic seriousness.

With the publication of *How to Write Short Stories*, a popular humorist had become a major voice in American fiction. The following year saw the appearance of *What of It?*—another humorously titled collection, this time of nonfiction, parodied fairy tales, nonsense plays, and other pieces from Lardner's work in magazines and for the Bell Syndicate. More important for Lardner's growing reputation, Scribners also issued a five-volume uniform edition, including *You Know Me Al*, *Gullible's Travels, Etc.*, *The Big Town*, *What of It?*, and *How to Write Short Stories*. Critics now had an opportunity to assess Lardner's career to that point, and praise was nearly unanimous.

Lardner was both startled and pleased by the reviews. Although he repeatedly declined the mantle of highbrow artist, his actions belie the denials. His son John later wrote that "it may come to the same thing as conscious artistry that he struggled constantly to make his stuff as good and as true as it could be." His youngest son, Ring, Jr., remembered that Lardner was very seri-

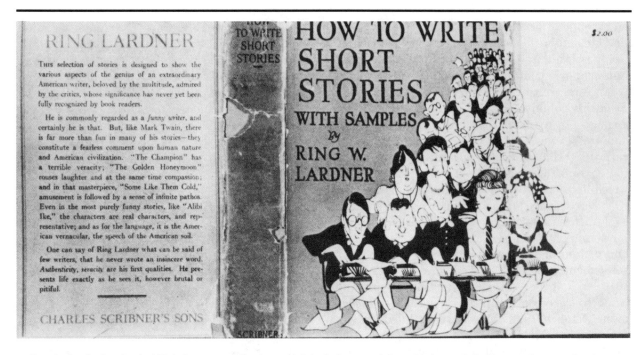

Dust jacket for Lardner's 1924 short-story collection, which includes a mock introduction and facetious explanatory headnotes

ous about his writing, but that "what he avoided at all cost was taking himself seriously in public." Most tellingly, having written no short stories for nearly three years following "The Golden Honeymoon" in 1922, Lardner became primarily a writer of short stories after 1924 and the success of his books with the critics. Between March 1925 and March 1926 he published nine new short stories, which he collected as *The Love Nest and Other Stories* (1926) to renewed enthusiasm among reviewers. In addition to the title story, the new volume included "Haircut" (*Liberty*, 28 March 1925) and "Zone of Quiet" (*Hearst's International-Cosmopolitan*, June 1925), among his acknowledged masterpieces. In the next three years he wrote twenty-one more stories, sixteen of which were included with those from *How to Write Short Stories* and *The Love Nest* to produce *Round Up* (1929), the definitive collection of Lardner's short fiction. Among the new additions, "I Can't Breathe" (*Hearst's International-Cosmopolitan*, September 1926) was the major triumph. During this same period Lardner also published his mock autobiography, *The Story of a Wonder Man* (1927), reprinted from his Bell Syndicate material. *How to Write Short Stories*, *The Love Nest*, and *Round Up* were all commercially successful. The first collection sold more than twenty thousand copies; *Round Up* was selected by the Literary Guild–in those days an honor as well as a boost to sales. When *Round Up* appeared, T. S.

Matthews's review in the *New Republic* exceeded all previous assessments, linking Lardner to Shakespeare and Chekhov as three writers who achieved both artistry and wide popularity. But Allen Nevins's emphasis on Lardner's limitations and lack of seriousness announced a new note in reviewers' responses. Just a few years before, the major critics had seemed to delight in proclaiming this supposed lightweight a serious writer. Now they began to question the earlier extravagance. Lardner's peak in both creativity and critical acclaim had occurred around 1926.

The years from 1929 to his death in 1933 were for Lardner an often painful anticlimax to a distinguished career. Admired as an author, Lardner was also revered as a man, not just his close friends but his countless acquaintances among New York celebrities regarding the tall, solemn, dignified figure with a kind of awe. His puritanical aversion to vulgar stories, his deep reserve broken suddenly by devastating wit, his epic drinking bouts that were destroying the physical man without harming the warmth and kindness he showed his friends, all made Lardner a memorable person as well as writer. "Proud, shy, solemn, shrewd, polite, brave, kind, merciful, honorable"–so Fitzgerald remembered him. Dorothy Parker's strongest impression was of "his strange bitter pity." The sad-faced clown has a perennial appeal. As Twain before him, Lardner made millions laugh but found little pleasure for himself in his last years.

Ironically, this finally sorrowful period began with the triumph of *June Moon* in 1929, a play adapted with George S. Kaufman from Lardner's story "Some Like Them Cold" and Lardner's sole success in the field where he most desired to succeed. Lardner's career as a songwriter and playwright produced but a handful of published songs, a few sketches bought by Florenz Ziegfeld for his Follies, and numerous efforts that failed either deservedly or due to others' mishandling. Lardner's writing for magazines, never easy for him, became increasingly a torture in these last years. Having been diagnosed as tubercular in 1926, a condition exacerbated by a heart ailment, recurring problems with alcoholism, and chronic insomnia, Lardner spent his last years in and out of hospitals, a seminomadic existence that took him as far away as Arizona to attempt a cure, during all of which he continued to write with increasing difficulty for a Depression-shrunk market. The *Saturday Evening Post* rejected one of his stories for the first time. *Collier's* and *Cosmopolitan* declined it as well–refusal from the three magazines that had made him wealthy by publishing most of his major fiction. The story "Poodle" was finally accepted by the *Delineator* (January 1934). Lardner wrote many more stories but none of his best, lapsing more and more into the formulas of magazine fiction unredeemed by his linguistic genius and tightly controlled sardonic tone. "Insomnia" (*Hearst's International-Cosmopolitan*, May 1931), perhaps the best of these late writings, movingly portrays Lardner's own physical and artistic frustrations, but such stories as "Mamma" (*Good Housekeeping*, August 1930), "Widow" (*Red Book*, October 1935), and "Bob's Birthday" (*Red Book*, November 1933) reveal a strain of self-pity that had not appeared before in Lardner's fiction. In 1932 he wrote a new series of busher letters for the *Post*, later published as *Lose with a Smile* (1933), but Jack Keefe's brashness had yielded to both sentimentality and defeatism, and Lardner's verbal ingenuity was reduced to proven formulas. Elder reports that at home in his last months, Lardner "sometimes . . . was observed alone, with his face in his hands, sobbing." Having dropped his weekly letter for the Bell Syndicate in 1925, writing mostly for magazines with brief returns to newspaper journalism in the late 1920s, Lardner gave his most sustained effort in these last years to "Over the Waves," a weekly column of

radio criticism for the *New Yorker*, part of which involved an "odd little crusade," as Fitzgerald later put it, against pornographic song lyrics. Flashes of Lardnerian humor appear throughout this late writing, but he was clearly a man artistically, as well as physically, exhausted when he suffered a heart attack the morning of 25 September 1933 and died within hours.

Notable writing careers and early deaths were the common lot of the Lardner men in this remarkable family. Son Jim was one of the last casualties of the Spanish civil war, David died in a freak accident while covering World War II in Europe, and John died at forty-seven following a complex of illnesses even more overwhelming than his father's. Only Ring, Jr., has lived a long life; an award-winning screenwriter, he survived the blacklists of the McCarthy era and nine and a half months in prison for contempt of Congress. Although Jim's and David's early promise as writers had no opportunity for fulfillment, John as well as Ring, Jr., were notably successful. But none of the sons surpassed their father in literary acclaim. On Ring Lardner's death, one eulogist saluted him as "the greatest American writer since Mark Twain." Most assessments were more restrained but admiring. Fitzgerald struck the note that would prevail when he saluted his friend as a brilliant writer who held too much back, a doomed genius who wrote some of the finest American short stories but fell short of his greater promise.

Lardner's place in the tradition of American short fiction rests on the ten stories in *How to Write Short Stories*, the nine in *The Love Nest and Other Stories*, and the sixteen that were added to these in *Round Up*. The sequences of stories that make up the three busher volumes, plus *Own Your Own Home*, *Gullible's Travels*, and *Lose with a Smile*, have generally remained outside consideration of Lardner as a writer of short fiction. The additional fifty or so uncollected stories have also been largely ignored, deservedly so in almost all cases. The early fiction, however, remains important to considerations of Lardner's short stories for a number of reasons: his development of a vernacular style, his refinement of his two most distinctive narrative personae (the busher and the wise boob), and his experiments with the two primary forms–letters and monologues–through which these first-person narrators expressed themselves. All of these techniques reappear in the collected stories.

Lardner in 1923 with his children, Ring, Jr., James, David (seated with his father), and John

The ten tales in *How to Write Short Stories* were published in magazines between 1914 ("My Roomy" and "Horseshoes") and 1922 ("A Caddy's Diary" [*Saturday Evening Post*, 11 March 1922] and "The Golden Honeymoon"). Seven of them deal with sports: four on baseball ("My Roomy," "Horseshoes," "Alibi Ike," and "Harmony"), two on boxing ("Champion" and "A Frame-Up" [*Saturday Evening Post*, 18 June 1921]), and one on golf ("A Caddy's Diary"). The other three ("The Facts" [*Metropolitan*, January 1917], "Some Like Them Cold," and "The Golden Honeymoon") can be loosely considered "love stories," dealing with sexual relations in courtship and marriage. Only "Champion" is written in the third person. "Some Like Them Cold" is an exchange of letters; "A Caddy's Diary" is, as the title declares, a diary; the other seven are narrated by characters in the stories: by the chief performer in "The Golden Honeymoon," by participant-observers in the rest. Dialect is virtually absent from "The Facts"; the speakers in the other six first-person stories are literate but colloquial. "A Caddy's Diary" alone among these ten stories is told in busherese.

The obvious point here is that Lardner was more versatile than is sometimes claimed. Three of the baseball stories offer amusing portraits of eccentric players: a comically compulsive excuse artist ("Alibi Ike"), a less genial lucky / unlucky mediocre ballplayer furious at the success of his talented but also more fortunate rival ("Horseshoes"), and an outfielder who sacrifices his own baseball career while inadvertently bringing his team a championship when he engineers the acquisition of a tenor for the team quartet ("Harmony"). Against these three clever but relatively slight tales, "My Roomy" is a brilliant portrait of a psychopath: a slugger whose erratic play is more than matched by his erratic off-field behavior—barely checked violence that finally explodes in serious head bashing. Lardner's black humor anticipates Nathanael West and the writers of the 1960s, as when "Buster" Elliott writes his roomy at the end of the story to describe how he attacked his ex-girlfriend and her husband with a baseball bat: "OLD ROOMY: I was at bat twice and made two hits; but I guess I did not meet 'em square. They tell me they are both alive yet, which I did not mean 'em to be. I hope they got good curveball pitchers where I am goin' [to prison]. I sure can bust them curves—can't I sport?" Of the two boxing stories, "A Frame-Up" is an O. Henry-type tale of a terrific boxer with a mild disposition who will let himself go against an opponent only when tricked into thinking a beautiful girl admires him, while "Champion" is a furious exposé of a brutal prize-fight champ promoted in the press as a Frank Merriwell of the ring. "A Caddy's Diary," finally, dissects the sporting ethics of businessmen and their wives on the golf course, where they lie about their scores and improve the lie of their balls for trivial stakes—often with the complicity of the caddy diarist who assists them for even smaller rewards: a slightly larger tip or a mere smile from the prettiest female on the course. By consensus, only "My Roomy" and "A Caddy's Diary" among these seven rank with Lardner's best stories. Some critics have praised "Champion," but others find its satire heavy-handed, its characterizations too thin. "Alibi Ike" and "Harmony" are skillfully done, if less substantial than the two best, "Horseshoes" and "A Frame-Up" slighter yet.

Of the three love stories, "The Facts" is one that "seem[s] a little magazine-made," as Edmund Wilson put it in his *Dial* review, but "Some Like Them Cold" and "The Golden Honeymoon" are masterpieces. The first is an exchange of letters between Chas. F. Lewis and Mabelle Gillespie, following their single meeting in a train station as Lewis departs Chicago for fame and fortune in New York's Tin Pan Alley. The two characters are perfectly realized—their very different voices in their letters revealing a similar capacity for self-delusion, fraudulent self-promotion, and blindness to the actual intentions of the other. Interspersed with accounts of his talentless assault on the songwriting world, Lewis blithely reports to his "friend" in Chicago about the various girls who interest him. For her part, Mabelle attempts to market herself for marriage as a combination good sport and homebody, in a manner so bald that only Lewis remains oblivious to her designs. In his final letter Lewis announces his engage-

ment to an obvious gold digger; in hers, Mabelle "congratulates" him in barely controlled fury.

In "The Golden Honeymoon" Lardner created something rare in American fiction: a pair of believable old people. Father narrates a vacation in Florida, where a chance encounter with Mother's old flame leads to rivalry at checkers, bridge, and horseshoes, even over whose beard and cafeteria are superior. Neither bitterly satiric nor sentimental as some critics have claimed, "The Golden Honeymoon" humanizes the old couple, whose pettiness reveals a typical Lardnerian bond: their partnership against outside threats. The humor is wonderful: "Mother set facing the front of the train, as it makes her giddy to ride backwards. I set facing her, which does not affect me." But the undercutting humor is perfectly balanced by a sense that the pair understand each other and are satisfied. "I guess we got kind of spoony," Father says at the end, as they remake their temporarily disrupted peace.

Inspired by the success of this first volume, Lardner published the stories in *The Love Nest* over a two-year period (1925-1926), while he was living in Great Neck, writing his "Weekly Letter" for the Bell Syndicate, and immersing himself deeper in the theatrical and musical worlds. For an author who wrote always out of personal observation, these circumstances meant a necessary shift in subject matter. Only one of the nine stories in the new collection, a particularly minor one entitled "Women" (*Liberty*, 20 June 1925), deals with sport (baseball, to be specific). In part, Lardner was simply removed now from the sports world in which he had lived in his Chicago days, but to this practical obstacle was added a disenchantment with baseball, particularly following the Black Sox scandal of 1919 and the introduction of the lively ball that, according to many fans, minimized the importance of strategy and traditional skills. Lardner's best baseball writing in the 1920s was his coverage of the 1922 World Series: brief mention of the games and copious, often hilarious detail about his wife's campaign for a fur coat. Lardner remained a football fan, particularly of Notre Dame, as well as a golfer, but perhaps the literary world's bias against sport's supposed unseriousness—comparable to its prejudice against humor—helped dictate his subject matter. In any case, three stories in the new volume focus on theatrical or musical people ("The Love Nest" [*Hearst's International-Cosmopolitan*, August 1925], and "A Day with Conrad Green" [*Liberty*, 3 October 1925], and "Rhythm"

[*Hearst's International-Cosmopolitan*, March 1926]), and three others concern the irritations of suburban life and marriage ("Mr. and Mrs. Fix-It" [*Liberty*, 9 May 1925], "Reunion" [*Liberty*, 31 October 1925], and "Who Dealt?" [*Hearst's International-Cosmopolitan*, January 1926]). "Haircut" is the sole small-town tale in the collection, "Zone of Quiet" a splendidly anomalous sketch about a hospital patient, prisoner to the babbling of his day nurse. The major shift from Lardner's previous collection, however, is the prevalence of third-person narrators. Only "Haircut" and "Who Dealt?" retain the first-person narrator that dominated the earlier volume—the latter story a somewhat contrived portrait of a painful marriage, "Haircut" the best entry in the book and Lardner's most famous and most anthologized story. Lardner had declared as early as 1917 his weariness with writing dialect stories in the first person. One suspects that the critical acclaim accorded *How to Write Short Stories* and the literary bias against humor may have encouraged Lardner's desire to write straight English in the third person. The decision is regrettable; a majority of Lardner's best stories are the dialectal ones in the first person. "Haircut" is brilliantly rendered through the monologue of a small-town barber, affectionately recalling the village prankster whose practical jokes, the occasion for masculine hilarity among the barbershop hangers-on, are only vicious and cruel. The deadpan last two lines, following the barber's account of the jokester's "accidental" shooting by the village idiot who avenges a local spinster, are simply perfect:

> He certainly was a card!
> Comb it wet or dry?

The other masterpiece in this second collection, "Zone of Quiet" is for all practical purposes another monologue by a sort of female busher, her prattle interrupted for only brief moments to allow the narrator to reorient the setting. The nurse tells her patient in exhausting detail how she attempts to steal her best friend's fiancé, oblivious to the fact that she is revealing anything unflattering about herself.

"A Day with Conrad Green," "Rhythm," and "The Love Nest" are satiric pieces in the third person. "Conrad Green," the evisceration of a venal and shameless Broadway producer, is sometimes ranked with Lardner's best but is actually as heavy-handed as "Champion." "Rhythm," on the other hand, has been as underrated as "Champion" and "Conrad Green" have been overrated. It exposes the music business as a bastion of legal plagiarism, but it simultaneously portrays the disastrous consequences of a popular artist's being discovered by highbrow critics and taking himself seriously. Much of Lardner himself is obviously in the story. "The Love Nest" is a less-subtle but better-known piece about the appalling marriage of a self-deluded movie executive and his bitter, alcoholic wife. In comparing the stories of these first two collections it seems clear that Lardner's most fruitful literary voice lay in first-person dialect. Interestingly, he continued to write most of his nonfiction in the first person behind the mask of the wise boob, a pose that served him well to his death. But he seems to have felt that a celebrated author of short stories should write in the, to him, less natural but more conventionally literary third person.

Courtship and marriage have a more prominent place in this second collection than in the first. Contrary to the claim sometimes heard that Lardner's portrait of marriage was excessively grim (provoking inevitable speculation about his own supposedly happy marriage), the truth is actually more mixed. The loveless marriages of "The Love Nest" and "A Day with Conrad Green" are offset by those in the slighter stories, "Mr. and Mrs. Fix-It" and "Reunion," in which the couples maintain a partnership against meddlers and other frustrations in the manner of "The Golden Honeymoon." The painful marriage of "Who Dealt?"—exposed gradually as the wife unconsciously reveals that her husband still loves, and feels betrayed by, the very woman sitting beside him at the bridge table opposite her own husband—is balanced by the couple who marry in "Zone of Quiet."

The sixteen stories combined with these two earlier collections to make up *Round Up*, though competent, do not show an advancement of Lardner's skill with the short story. The majority of the new stories are best described as magazine fiction; only "I Can't Breathe" ranks with Lardner's best, while several are forgettable. The only baseball story, "Hurry Kane" (*Hearst's International-Cosmopolitan*, January 1927), is a less-inventive "Alibi Ike." "Mr. Frisbie" (*Hearst's International-Cosmopolitan*, June 1928) is a less-incisive "Caddy's Diary" (these are the only sports stories). "The Maysville Minstrel" (*Hearst's International-Cosmopolitan*, September 1928) presents the type of practical joker portrayed in "Haircut" in a merely pathetic context. Several of the stories, following on

Examples of the "You Know Me Al" comic strip. Lardner provided continuity for the syndicated strip from 1922 to 1925.

the earlier "Mr. and Mrs. Fix-It," seem to have been generated simply by Lardner's gripes: the meddling neighbors of the earlier story become the compulsively hospitable hosts of "Liberty Hall" (*Hearst's International-Cosmopolitan*, March 1928), the lecturing bridge players of "Contract" (*Harper's Bazar*, March 1929), the babbling companions of "Dinner" (*Harper's Bazar*, September 1928), and "Travelogue" (*Hearst's International-Cosmopolitan*, May 1926). Lardner's own frustration in seeing his songs and sketches rejected or bowdlerized by philistine producers yields the unsubtle "Nora" (*Hearst's International-Cosmopolitan*, February 1928). A new marriage group portrays stable partnerships in "Liberty Hall" and "Old Folks Xmas" (*Hearst's International-Cosmopolitan*, January 1929), but also the grim truces or break-ups of "Now and Then" (previously unpublished), "Anniversary" (*Hearst's International-Cosmopolitan*, January 1928), and "Ex Parte" (*Hearst's International-Cosmopolitan*, November 1928). There is a weary, defeated feel to many of these stories, a greater tendency toward pathos, more emphasis on victims. Lardner viewed the world now through the eyes of a sickly, alcoholic, insomniac sufferer.

Technically, the new stories in *Round Up* present a compendium of Lardner's earlier strategies: a story in letters ("Now and Then"), ten stories in the third person, five in the first, three of these in a distinctive vernacular ("I Can't Breathe," "Hurry Kane," and "Mr. Frisbie"). The one first-rate story thus is written in the manner Lardner perfected early in his career. "I Can't Breathe" is the giddy monologue of an eighteen-year-old girl on vacation with her "ancient" aunt and uncle (they are thirty-five), sorting through the four young men she has agreed to marry. In the best Lardnerian manner she unconsciously reveals how she has created this mess: "Gordon called up this morning from Chicago and it was wonderful to hear his voice again though the connection was terrible. He asked me if I still loved him and I tried to tell him no, but I knew that would mean an explanation and the connection was so bad that I never could make him understand so I said yes." The story ends in anticipation of a convention of all the swains come to meet their fiancée at the train station. Throughout, Lardner maintains the even tone of his best stories. The girl is not vicious, only empty-headed and unintentionally cruel (the character was modeled on Floncy Rice, the daughter of Lardner's best friends and a young woman for

whom he felt particular affection). The reader both laughs and groans as the massacre of wounded hearts approaches nearer and nearer.

As a writer of short stories, then, Lardner did his best work early, in forms that came naturally to him (at least one critic claims the opposite: that Lardner's fiction became increasingly artistic through the 1920s). His growing reputation was accompanied by an increasing difficulty in writing (presumably with one eye to the critics while before both eyes had been on his popular audience). Although he wrote in bursts and revised very little, short stories were a struggle for him. Myths about his method of writing abound, such as the anecdote told by Groucho Marx that Lardner would hole up in a hotel room with a bottle or two of whiskey, get roaring drunk, and knock out a story. (Similar tales have been told of Faulkner.) But Lardner wrote sober, and with difficulty. At the work he most enjoyed–writing songs and theatrical sketches–he was distinctly unsuccessful.

Since the extravagant praise of the mid 1920s, Lardner has proven a problem for critics–not an urgent problem, to be sure, or one that has concerned a large number of the ablest minds, but a problem for that handful perennially attempting to place his work in perspective, to acknowledge both his achievements and his limitations without exaggerating either. In recent years Lardner's reputation has been most secure among a relatively small group of scholars interested in the literature of sport. For them, Lardner is a father figure: *You Know Me Al* the *ur*-text for the realistic tradition in sports fiction that has descended from Lardner through Mark Harris to such journalist-novelists in recent years as Roger Kahn and Frank Deford; a handful of the stories ("Alibi Ike," "Champion," "My Roomy," and "A Caddy's Diary" in particular) recognized as "classics" in the field. The poles of critical thought on Lardner's sports stories were established by Virginia Woolf in 1925 and F. Scott Fitzgerald in 1934, in two passages repeatedly quoted by those interested in sports fiction. In her essay "American Fiction" Woolf placed Lardner above Sherwood Anderson and Sinclair Lewis in part because to her mind Lardner had found the perfect milieu for his fiction. "It is no coincidence that the best of Mr. Lardner's stories are about games," Woolf wrote, "for one may guess that Mr. Lardner's interest in games has solved one of the most difficult problems of the American writer; it has given him a clue, a cen-

Dust jacket for the 1926 collection that includes "Haircut," Lardner's most anthologized short story

tre, a meeting place for the divers activities of people who a vast continent isolates, whom no tradition controls. Games give him what society gives his English brother." Nine years later, in his eulogy in the *New Republic*, Fitzgerald offered a radically different perspective on Lardner's interest in games. Discussing the influence of Lardner's early experience as a baseball writer on his later fiction, Fitzgerald wrote: "During those years, when most men of promise achieve an adult education, if only in the school of war, Ring moved in the company of a few dozen illiterates playing a boy's game. A boy's game with no more possibilities in it than a boy could master, a game bounded by walls which kept out novelty or danger, change or adventure.... However deeply Ring might cut into it, his cake had the diameter of Frank Chance's diamond."

Clue, center, meeting place, or Frank Chance's diamond? For obvious reasons, students of sports literature have sided with the queen of Bloomsbury. Woolf, the outsider, recognized something to which Fitzgerald, himself an idolater of athletes in his youth and follower of Princeton football to his death, was perhaps too close to see: that sport lay near the center of American culture in the 1920s and that the writer about

sport had a "serious" subject. Woolf's recognition that sport could substitute for "society" in American writing was particularly apt. The absence of a traditional, fully stratified society had driven Henry James to Europe in the nineteenth century, and American realism into its own distinctive channels. In the 1910s and 1920s, in his busher letters and stories of sport, Lardner became a Jamesian chronicler of "manners"–the manners not of the upper classes but of the wide middle class that was creating a distinctive American mass culture. Without conscious intention, no doubt, Lardner's best sports fiction presents the ball park and golf course as places where gesture, inflection, nuances of behavior in relation to rigid codes–"the half-uttered or unuttered or unutterable expressions of value" that Lionel Trilling wrote about in his well-known essay "Manners, Morals, and the Novel"–ruled with unyielding authority. In a new country without history or tradition–as both American and European commentators continually reiterated–sport even as early as the 1910s and 1920s had both a history and a rich tradition which made some of Lardner's best fiction possible. His audience was as familiar with and committed to this tradition as any English lord to the prerogatives of class.

When the busher pitcher of *You Know Me Al* blames his teammates for his own ineptitude, readers understood that beneath the speaker's comic rambling lay a serious violation of both a code of personal honor and a social contract demanded by sporting tradition. Keefe explains to Al: "They batted all round in the fourth inning and scored four or five more. Crawford got the luckiest three-base hit I ever see. He popped one way up in the air and the wind blowed it against the fence. The wind is something fierce here Al. At that Collins ought to of got under it." Similarly, when Buster Elliott, the psychotic slugger of "My Roomy," refuses to chase fly balls in the outfield and attempts to steal home in defiance of his manager's orders, these lapses in a trivial "boy's game," as Fitzgerald put it, readily represent sociopathic disruptions in any social unit, large or small. And the petty cheating of country-club golfers in "A Caddy's Diary" reveals the character of men whose ethical standards in the business world are equally low. Just as the novel of manners naturally tends toward satire, Lardner's stories of "sports manners" reveal the foibles and often the vices of an entire society. In relation to sport itself, his object was to expose the far different reality underlying a sporting myth rooted in gentlemanly standards that had never actually prevailed. In relation to middle-class America he revealed a society of atomized individuals blinded by their own egotism and desire for success.

Sport was part of Lardner's larger canvas— the leisure pursuits of the American middle class from 1914 to 1933. With the exception of a few businessmen whose occupations are never explored, the only workers in Lardner's fiction are professional athletes and theatrical people. He shows individuals at play, even his workers engaged in creating the spectacles at which others seek pleasure. Lardner described the "manners" of the ball park and the barbershop, the pullman car and the bridge table, the golf course and the resort. He wrote about what he observed, with no conscious intention of recording a dramatic shift in American culture, but the result was just that. The half-century of Lardner's lifetime saw the beginning of that large transformation from the labor-centered nineteenth century to the leisure-centered twentieth. The brilliance of many of Lardner's portraits of bewildered rubes in the big city, frustrated social climbers in suburbia, successful but miserable or misery-making celebrities, seems to have derived from Lardner's own uneasiness in the new America. Lardner gained little pleasure from his success and never fell in step with the times. In a period marked by the revolt against the village, he seemed to Mencken and others a coconspirator with Sherwood Anderson, Sinclair Lewis, and Edgar Lee Masters. But Lardner never revolted from the small town. He did not flee Niles but left because opportunity lay elsewhere, and he carried the values of Niles with him to his death. In the stories making up *The Big Town*, neither New York nor South Bend is superior to the other, and the family's return to South Bend at the end is no shameful retreat. Lardner retained the deep conservatism of his Niles upbringing–his "odd little crusade" against pornographic lyrics in the 1930s offering an appropriate culmination to a body of writing from which sexuality is virtually absent. The separate bedrooms of the Lardner household were metaphorically re-created over and over in the fiction. The sexual revolution of the Jazz Age passed Lardner by. The chasteness required for publication in popular magazines was congenial with Lardner's own reticence.

Lardner wrote consistently in reaction to his cultural context. With the rise of mass advertising, the 1920s ushered in the age of conspicuous (self-)promotion, of linguistic inflation, of the manufactured image. Lardner's specialty lay in *de*flation–in exposing the reality behind the image. In an age when intellectuals were preoccupied with Freudian psychoanalysis and the plumbing of the inner self, Lardner wrote only as a detached observer, even in his first-person narratives. Lardner was no modernist in technique, temperament, or subject matter. This objectivity in a subjective age served his own distinctive artistry well. The psychopath of "My Roomy" is brilliantly rendered, despite the author's unconcern for diagnosis or for what it feels like to be deranged. Lardner was interested in the social world in which such persons live, in the impact on others of private obsessions. The good stories never reveal only one character, but many. The satire on cheating socialite golfers in "A Caddy's Diary" turns at the end on the caddy; both letter writers in "Some Like Them Cold," the barber as well as the jokester in "Haircut," wives as well as husbands in "The Love Nest," and other stories of marriage expose an inner life at odds with outer behavior. But the revelation comes entirely by speech and act, not by reflection or stream of consciousness.

All of these Lardnerian characters seek fulfillment outside the workplace of Protestant tradi-

RING LARDNER
GREAT NECK, NEW YORK

October 7, 1926.

Dear Burton:-

It isn't often I care what the boys
and girls say about me in print,

(Author's note:That's a dirty lie!)

but honestly,Burton,
that stuff you wrote under date of October 2,well,
you must have got the information from Willie Stevens.
The first "busher" story was never sent back by the
Post;it was accepted promptly by Mr. Lorimer himself.
I didn't show it to Hugh Fullerton or Charlie Van Loan
first; I sent it to Mr. Lorimer at the Post's office,
not to his residence;I didn't write "Personal" on the
envelope in even one place; I didn't write any preliminary,special delivery,warning letter to Mr. Lorimer;no sub-editor ever asked me to correct the spelling and grammar,and I never sent any sub-editor or anyone else a bundle of letters I had received from ball
players. Otherwise—

Ellis' mother died in July and we have
had a quiet summer. But we do want you and Hazel to
come out some time. Love to her.

R.W.L.

Letter from Lardner to Burton Rascoe, editor of the Bookman *(University of Pennsylvania Library)*

tion. Many of them are hopelessly out of place in their worlds, and Lardner's point was that the new middle class was caught uncomfortably in desiring what could not make it happy. Lardner has been characterized most aptly as a disillusioned idealist. He carried a nineteenth-century family-centered, small-town, Protestant temperament into an age of frantic seeking and the triumph of the city in American life, recording the impressions of man who never accommodated himself to this changing world.

The content of Lardner's stories thus offers an insightful panorama of his age's leisure culture. But in assessing Lardner's achievement in American short fiction, one must finally emphasize his contribution to the form and technique of the short story rather than his subject matter. And one must first put to rest the debate as to whether Lardner was primarily a humorist or a satirist–a nonissue made into an issue by the liter-

ary bias against "mere" humor as an inferior art form (Lardner was most noticeably the heir to Twain in suffering from this critical prejudice). Lardner was both a humorist *and* a satirist. The shape of his career was marked by an increasing tendency toward satire, in part, one suspects, due to the encouragement of the highbrow critics who valued satire over humor. The manner of the busher letters, of the stories that comprise *Gullible's Travels* and *The Big Town*, and of early individual stories such as "Alibi Ike" (1915), "Some Like Them Cold" (1921), and "The Golden Honeymoon" (1922) is primarily humorous; while such later stories as "The Love Nest," "A Day with Conrad Green," and "Haircut" (all 1925) are more obviously satirical. On the other hand, one of his earlier stories was the fiercely satiric "Champion" (1916), one of his later ones the wonderfully humorous "I Can't Breathe" (1926). No simple, straightforward development took place, but a shift from humor toward satire marks a general tendency in his fiction. The basic distinction between the two modes is tone: relatively genial amusement in Lardner's humor, various degrees of outrage in his satire. The humorous stories are often mildly satirical as well, many of the satires humorous—no absolute distinction is possible. But an essential difference in dominant intention between the two types is easily recognizable.

Early Lardner criticism was plagued by the critics' frequent desire to identify a single Lardnerian mode. For admirers of his satire any lapse into mere humor marked a falling off. In addition, such misrepresentations as Clifton Fadiman's well-known essay, "Ring Lardner and the Triangle of Hate" (1933), also reveal this compulsion to find a consistent vision. Fadiman's thesis, reiterated by such later critics as John Berryman and Maxwell Geismar, claimed that Lardner was a thorough misanthrope, the contempt and rage of stories like "A Day with Conrad Green" serving as primary evidence. But in order to make his claim, Fadiman had to insist also that "The Golden Honeymoon" is "one of the most smashing indictments of a 'happy marriage' ever written, composed with a fury so gelid as to hide completely the bitter passion seething beneath every line." The story itself belies this claim. In several of the most celebrated statements about his art, Lardner seems to have been reduced to a mirror for the critic. Thus, like Melville, who saw his own "blackness" in Nathaniel Hawthorne, Mencken found his own contempt for the American "boobocracy" reflected in Lardner's stories, Fitzgerald saw in his older friend an image of his own failed promise, and Fadiman, when he wrote of "subhuman associations" with "the bridge-players of Great Neck," supposedly to account for Lardner's inevitable revulsion against humankind, revealed perhaps more about his own prejudices than about Lardner's. Lardner was cynical surely, and he *tended* toward self-loathing as he failed repeatedly to control his alcoholism, but he never fell to simply hating mankind.

Lardner was both humorist and satirist, then, often at the same time but in varying degrees. In some ways his artistry is most apparent in the supposedly inferior literary form. What strikes one most forcibly in reading Lardner's humorous writing today is how funny it remains, long after the topical matter that prompted it has passed. The mock introduction to *The Love Nest and Other Stories*, for example, taken by those who

insist on Lardner's failure of artistic commitment as evidence of frivolousness, and by the misanthropy school in Lardner criticism as an early sign of his self-loathing, is more accurately described as hilarious nonsense. Sarah E. Spooldripper, the supposed author of the introduction (an insider privy to "the Master's" character, as the caretaker of his wolf), reports an incident that occurred while the Master was writing "The Love Nest":

> It was in the middle of this work that the rivalry between Lardner, Scott Fitzgerald, and Opie Reade for the love of Lily Langtry reached its height. During a dinner party at which the then raging beauty and her raging suitors were all present, the toastmaster, Gerald Chapman, asked Miss Langtry to rise and drink to "her favorite." The muscles of Fitzgerald and Reade were taut; Lardner's were flabby.
>
> After a pause that seemed to endure all night but really lasted only half that long, Miss Langtry got up, raised her glass and said: "I drink to Red Grange. Heston may have been his superior on defense and Coy, Thorpe, Eckersall, and Mahan more versatile, but as a common carrier I take off my hat to the Wheaton icemonger."

Here is Lardner on marriage: "Remember always that you swore at each other at the altar that each was taking the other from bad to worse and may the best man win." Here is Lardner's parody of the ever-fashionable literary diaries: "When I got home Sousa was there and we played some Brahms and Grieg with me at the piano and him at one end of a cornet. 'How well you play, Lardy,' was Sousa's remark. Brahms called up in the evening and him and his wife come over and played rummy." And here is a Lardnerian version of Broadway gossip: "What writer on what paper is taking whose golf clubs to what Bahamas?" Inspired looniness, with an emphasis on the first word, appears throughout Lardner's nonfiction and nonsense writing and often spilled over into his short stories. Humor is notoriously difficult to discuss, short of psychoanalytic treatises on its origins—one reason for the relative neglect of this side of Lardner's short fiction. One can only read, laugh, and admire; reluctance to spoil the humor by attempting to explain it produces critical silence. But Lardner's best satire appears in his humorous stories (in first-person dialect), in which it is indirect and understated, with none of the fury that undermined many of his more overt satiric works.

*Lardner, 1927 (The Bettmann Archive, Inc.,
New York)*

If the humor itself has remained resistant to analysis, Lardner's use of the vernacular in his humorous fiction has generated some of the best criticism on his work. The seeming artlessness of Lardner's use of dialect–he himself insisted that he just "listened hard"–is clearly an illusion, the particular magic at which Lardner was most gifted. The simple *readability* of his dialect humor is not achieved simply at all. Just as Twain transformed southwestern humor into the first great vernacular style in American literature partly by rendering the sometimes unreadable language of George Washington Harris and his kind into simpler prose without sacrificing authenticity, so Lardner transformed the dialect humor of his Chicago contemporaries into a versatile and limpid vernacular that sounded like common speech without making the reader cross-eyed. Compare the language of Finley Peter Dunne's Mr. Dooley and George Ade's "fables in slang" to Lardner's Jack Keefe. First, Mr. Dooley describing an incident in the Spanish-American War:

> 'Twas this way. Th' Spanish fleet was bottled up in Sandago Harbor, an' they dhrew th' cork. That's a joke. I see it in the pa-apers. Th' gallant boys iv th' navy was settin' out on th' deck, defindin' their counthry an' dhrawin' three cards apiece, whin th' Spanish admiral con-cluded 'twud be better f 'r him to be desthroyed on th' ragin' sea, him bein' a sailor, thin to have to have his fleet captured be cav'lry. . . .

Next, the conclusion from Ade's "Fable of the Copper and the Jovial Undergrads," describing a policeman who nearly arrests three young hooligans only to discover that they are college boys whose parents rank high on the social register:

The Copper, perceiving that he had come very near getting Gay with our First Families, Apologized for Cutting In. The Well-Bred Young Men forgave him and then took his Club away from him, just to Demonstrate that there were no Hard Feelings. On the way back to the Seat of Learning they captured a Night Watchman, and put him down a Man-Hole.

MORAL: *Always select the Right Sort of Parents before you start in to be Rough.*

And now, Jack Keefe, describing how he was discovered in the minor leagues, in his first letter to his friend Al ("A Busher's Letters Home"):

I didn't know anybody was looking me over, but one of the boys told me that Jack Doyle the White Sox scout was down here looking at me when Grand Rapids was here. I beat them twice in that serious. You know Grand Rapids never had a chance with me when I was right. I shut them out in the first game and they got one run in the second on account of Flynn misjudging that fly ball. Anyway Doyle liked my work and he wired Comiskey to buy me. Comiskey come back with an offer and they excepted it. I don't know how much they got but anyway I am sold to the big league and believe me Al I will make good.

Mr. Dooley sounds like an authentic Chicago Irishman, but reading his dialect is a struggle; one can enjoy a newspaper column of such writing easily enough, but it is hard to imagine reading an entire book or even a long story written in this manner. Ade's fable, on the other hand, depends too much on the gimmicky playing with capital letters, too little on a distinctive vernacular voice. With Jack Keefe, Lardner combined the authenticity and humor of Dunne's language with the readability of Ade's, creating a voice that easily holds the reader's interest through chapter after chapter while always ringing with the truth of common speech. When Jack writes "excepted" instead of "accepted," the reader immediately recognizes the self-revealing mistake without having to work phonetically through something like "dhrawin'" or "desthroyed." Lardner's prose seems the least contrived of all three examples, yet it is a carefully crafted literary creation.

One of Lardner's most careful critics, Howard W. Webb, Jr., has traced the development of what he calls the "Lardner idiom" in the columns from "In the Wake of the News." Barely a week after assuming the column in June 1913, Lardner began a serialized novel, "The Pennant Pur-

suit," written "By the Copy Boy": "Chapter I. As Verne Dalton strod passed the jymnaseium one day in April, bound for the college ofice, where he was going to make arrangemunts for entring the college next fall, the ball nine composed of 20 (twenty) or more members came out on its way to the atheletic feild. O said Verne I wonder if Ill have a posichion on that team and fight for the glory of my ama mather, but he did not have much hope because his parents had said he must devoat all his time to study." Three months later, in a piece entitled "The First Game," Lardner offered a fictional player's account of losing the opening contest of the World Series: "We ought to of trimmed 'em. When Egan, the big shot, said I was out at second he musta been full o' hops, the big boob. I like t' known where he was at las' night, the big bum. Some o' them umps oughta be on the chain gang, the big boobs." Finally, sometime in the next six months, Lardner wrote "A Busher's Letters Home," quoted above. "The Pennant Pursuit" shows all the marks of the funny-spelling school of American humor, words like "jymnaseium" and "posichion" offering nothing to the ear, only to the eye. In addition, the reader is forced mentally to add the final *e* to "strod," a momentary pause that interrupts the flow of the language. There is no distinctive diction or syntax but essentially a bland piece of prose enlivened only by frequent misspellings. In "The First Game" the diction rings truer, a distinctive rhythm has appeared, a voice emerges through the language. But the language is insufficiently artful. The repetition of "big shot" and "big boob" probably captures the actual speech of semiliterate ball players, but it is irritating to the reader. Jack Keefe's dialect, on the other hand, sacrifices transcription for an illusion of authenticity in order to create a literary vernacular—as all the great creators of spoken English, from Twain to Hemingway to Eudora Welty, have done. For Lardner, the discipline of a daily column led to extraordinary development over a brief period.

In his short fiction Lardner's use of language is most remarkable for its versatility. The accuracy of his distinction between written and spoken vernacular has often been noted—between the language, that is, in stories comprised of letters and those that consist primarily of monologues or dialogue. Among his monologuists and letter writers, moreover, appear a wide range of character types. Jack Keefe, the busher pitcher, speaks the language of the small town, Chas F.

Lewis of "Some Like Them Cold" the masculine language of the city, and Mabelle Gillespie is his feminine counterpart. The old man of "The Golden Honeymoon" and the young girl of "I Can't Breathe" speak in the idioms of their different ages and sex, the barber of "Haircut" and the wife of "Who Dealt?" of their different classes. Race alone remains unexplored in Lardner's fiction. Lardner had a philologist's care for language itself, rooted perhaps in the aristocratic contempt in his childhood home for the mistakes made by the family's less literate and lower-class neighbors. The one time he played the role of critic, in a review of J. V. A. Weaver's *In American* in 1921, he revealed the care with which he created the vernacular in his own fiction, faulting the author for not realizing that Americans say *somethin'* and *nothin'* but not *everythin'* and *anythin'*, *thing* but not *thin'*, *fella* but not *feller*. Even his campaign against pornographic song lyrics on the radio, for which he has been patronizingly mocked, was part of a larger campaign against the inanities and bad grammar of many popular lyrics.

Lardner was thus a conservator of linguistic tradition, but his use of vernacular functioned more importantly in his short stories as a medium of unconscious self-revelation. Characters oblivious to their misspellings, malapropisms, and failed attempts to use impressive words whose meanings they do not understand reveal themselves to be ill at ease in a complex world for which they are unequipped. Lardner's first-person stories tend to be not just artistically superior but more forgiving of characters' failings as well. As the speakers reveal themselves they always seem human, however appalling their faults. Characters in the third-person stories are more liable to be stick figures, caricatures; in the third person, both Lardner's rage and his sentimentality are too easily apparent.

Lardner's chief contribution to the technique of the American short story, then, is an extremely flexible and varied first-person voice through which humor naturally merges into satire. He was a serious writer but a reluctant "artist" who wrote his best fiction before he was forced to think of himself as a short-story writer. He played no conscious role in the so-called Chicago Renaissance in the years before World War I, nor in the larger literary flowering of the 1920s. With the exception of Fitzgerald, his friends were journalists and theatrical celebrities, not the many poets and novelists whose lives could easily have intersected his. His discovery as a major writer was a mixed blessing. It brought to his work serious attention that might otherwise have missed him. But it also turned his writing in directions less productive of his superior fiction. Like so many of his best characters, he was a "natural," who, left alone to follow his own inclinations, wrote some of the best stories in the nation's literature.

Letters:

Ring Around Max: The Correspondence of Ring Lardner and Max Perkins, edited by Clifford M. Caruthers (De Kalb: Northern Illinois University Press, 1973);

Letters from Ring, edited by Caruthers (Flint, Mich.: Walden Press, 1979).

Bibliography:

Matthew J. Bruccoli and Richard Layman, *Ring Lardner: A Descriptive Bibliography* (Pittsburgh: University of Pittsburgh Press, 1976).

Biographies:

Donald Elder, *Ring Lardner: A Biography* (Garden City, N.Y.: Doubleday, 1956);

Ring Lardner, Jr., *The Lardners: My Family Remembered* (New York: Harper & Row, 1976);

Jonathan Yardley, *Ring: A Biography of Ring Lardner* (New York: Random House, 1977).

References:

John Berryman, "The Case of Ring Lardner," *Commentary*, 22 (November 1956): 416-423;

Gordon Bordewyk, "Comic Alienation: Ring Lardner's Style," *Markham Review*, 11 (Spring 1982): 51-57;

James M. Cox, "Toward Vernacular Humor," *Virginia Quarterly Review*, 46 (Spring 1970): 311-330;

James DeMuth, *Small Town Chicago: The Comic Perspective of Finley Peter Dunne, George Ade, and Ring Lardner* (Port Washington, N.Y.: Kennikat Press, 1980);

Elizabeth Evans, *Ring Lardner* (New York: Ungar, 1979);

Clifton Fadiman, "Ring Lardner and the Triangle of Hate," *Nation*, 136 (22 March 1933): 315-317;

F. Scott Fitzgerald, "Ring," *New Republic*, 71 (11 October 1933): 254-255;

Otto Friedrich, *Ring Lardner* (Minneapolis: University of Minnesota Press, 1965);

Maxwell Geismar, *Ring Lardner and the Portrait of Folly* (New York: Crowell, 1972);

Geismar, "Ring Lardner: Like Something Was Going to Happen," in his *Writers in Crisis: The American Novel, 1925-1940* (Boston: Houghton Mifflin, 1942), pp. 1-36;

Louis Hasley, "Ring Lardner: The Ashes of Idealism," *Arizona Quarterly*, 26 (Autumn 1970): 219-232;

Charles S. Holmes, "Ring Lardner: Reluctant Artist," in *A Question of Quality, Popularity and Value in Modern Creative Writing*, edited by Louis Filler (Bowling Green, Ohio: Bowling Green University Press, 1976), pp. 26-39;

Forrest L. Ingram, "Fun at the Incinerating Plant: Lardner's Wry Waste Land," in *The Twenties*, edited by Warren French (De Land, Fla.: Everett / Edwards, 1975), pp. 111-122;

Christian K. Messenger, "Lardner: The Popular Sports Hero," in his *Sport and the Spirit of Play in American Fiction: Hawthorne to Faulkner* (New York: Columbia University Press, 1981), pp. 108-128;

Michael V. Oriard, "The Sunlit Field: Country and City in American Sports Fiction," in his *Dreaming of Heroes: American Sports Fiction, 1868-1980* (Chicago: Nelson-Hall, 1982);

Walton R. Patrick, *Ring Lardner* (New York: Twayne, 1963);

Gilbert Seldes, "Mr. Dooley, Meet Mr. Lardner," in his *The Seven Lively Arts* (New York: Harper & Row, 1924);

Leverett T. Smith, Jr., " 'The Diameter of Frank Chance's Diamond': Ring Lardner and Professional Sports," *Journal of Popular Culture*, 6 (Summer 1972): 133-156;

Jonas Spatz, "Ring Lardner: Not an Escape, but a Reflection," in *The Twenties*, edited by French (De Land, Fla.: Everett / Edwards, 1975), pp. 101-110;

Allen F. Stein, "This Unsporting Life: The Baseball Fiction of Ring Lardner," *Markham Review*, 3 (February 1972): 27-33;

Carl Van Doren, "Beyond Grammar: Ring W. Lardner: Philologist among the Low-Brows," *Century*, 106 (July 1923): 471-475;

Howard W. Webb, Jr., "The Development of a Style: The Lardner Idiom," *American Quarterly*, 12 (Winter 1960): 482-492;

Webb, "The Meaning of Ring Lardner's Fiction: A Reevaluation," *American Literature*, 31 (1960): 434-445;

Edmund Wilson, "Ring Lardner's American Characters," *Dial*, 77 (July 1924): 69-72;

Virginia Woolf, "American Fiction," in her *The Moment and Other Essays* (London: Hogarth, 1947);

Norris Yates, "The Isolated Man of Ring Lardner," in his *The American Humorist: Conscience of the Twentieth Century* (Ames: Iowa State University Press, 1964).

Papers:
Most of Lardner's papers are in the Newberry Library, Chicago.

William March
(William Edward Campbell)

(18 September 1893-15 May 1954)

Michael Routh

See also the March entry in *DLB 9: American Novelists, 1910-1945*.

BOOKS: *Company K* (New York: Smith & Haas, 1933; London: Gollancz, 1933);
Come in at the Door (New York: Smith & Haas, 1934; London: Rich & Cowan, 1934);
The Little Wife and Other Stories (New York: Smith & Haas, 1935; London: Rich & Cowan, 1935);
The Tallons (New York: Random House, 1936); republished as *A Song for Harps* (London: Rich & Cowan, 1936);
Some Like Them Short (Boston: Little, Brown, 1939);
The Looking-Glass (Boston: Little, Brown, 1943; London: Gollancz, 1944);
Trial Balance: The Collected Short Stories of William March (New York: Harcourt, Brace, 1945);
October Island (Boston: Little, Brown, 1952; London: Gollancz, 1952);
The Bad Seed (New York: Rinehart, 1954; London: Hamish Hamilton, 1954);
A William March Omnibus (New York: Rinehart, 1956);
99 Fables, edited by William T. Going (University: University of Alabama Press, 1960).

OTHER: *The Last Letters of Blessed Thomas More*, edited by March (London: Manresa, 1924).

PERIODICAL PUBLICATIONS: "The Unploughed Patch," *Pagany*, 3 (October-December 1932, January-March 1933): 1-55;
"The Marriage of the Bishops," *Accent*, 1 (Autumn 1940): 15-19;
"October Island," *Good Housekeeping*, 123 (October 1946): 30, 296-312.

William March (courtesy of the William S. Hoole Special Collections Library of the Amelia Gayle Gorgas Library, University of Alabama)

When William March is remembered at all today, it is usually as the author of the sensationalistic best-seller *The Bad Seed* (1954), his last novel. Yet his narrative gifts—his wry irony, skillfully cadenced dialogue, and understated style—are realized most successfully in his short stories.

Born William Edward Campbell in Mobile, Alabama, on 18 September 1893, March lived his early years in the numerous southern sawmill towns in which his father, John Leonard Campbell, found employment. At fourteen March quit school to go to work, but he later spent a year finishing high school (1913-1914) at Valparaiso University (Indiana) and a year (1914-1915) at the law school of the University of Alabama.

When America entered World War I, March was working with a New York City law office to earn money to renew his formal education; however, he abandoned these plans and enlisted in the Marine Corps. March served heroically in some of the ghastliest fighting of the war (he first saw action at Belleau Wood) and was wounded and gassed. He emerged from the war with three medals for bravery under fire and with a shell-shocked spirit. Years later March would be unable to sleep, imagining that a German soldier he had bayoneted in battle was sitting on the edge of his bed. The war permanently altered March, forging his imagination on the anvil of its horrors into an energy that, in his fiction, often seems to be obsessed with pain.

After the war March began a successful business career with the Waterman Steamship Company. His work took him around the Midwest and the East, and eventually to Hamburg and London. He retired in New York City in 1937 to write full-time. Mentally beleaguered since his war experiences, March had a severe breakdown in 1947. Returning to Mobile, he gradually recovered. He later moved to the French Quarter in New Orleans and died there of a heart attack on 15 May 1954.

As an adolescent March made the usual efforts at poetry and fiction and even won five dollars in a National Oats jingle contest, but he did not set out to become a writer. He began his serious writing of fiction, which he found therapeutic, toward the end of the 1920s, in the middle of his career with Waterman. He submitted stories for publication under various pseudonyms, permanently adopting the family name of his mother, Suzy March, when a story under that name was accepted.

Most of March's best stories concern an average person gripped by some form of psychological aberration—for example, the protagonist of "Mrs. Joe Cotton" (*Esquire*, July 1934; collected as "Woolen Drawers" in *The Little Wife and Other Stories*, 1935) sublimates her libido into puritanical social crusades—or broken spiritually by a devastating situation beyond their control, such as the innocent radical in "George and Charlie" (*Pagany*, April-June 1932; collected in *The Little Wife and Other Stories*), who has his youthful idealism beaten out of him by police nightsticks and a ten-year jail sentence for a crime he did not commit. March's characters are not the outrageous grotesques of William Faulkner, but more the quiet ones of Sherwood Anderson. For March's charac-

Illustration by Lowell Balcom for March's story "He Sits There All Day Long," published in the November 1931 issue of Forum

ters share a bewitching surface normality, a commonness that, as Alistair Cooke (in "Introduction to William March") perceives, beguiles the reader into identifying closely with them; thus, the turbulence these characters experience once their tenuous equilibrium is unbalanced is particularly disturbing for the reader.

By the time March had collected his early tales in *The Little Wife and Other Stories* in 1935, he had already published two novels, *Company K* (1933) and *Come in at the Door* (1934), both of which strongly reflect his interest in brief forms of fiction by incorporating vignettes and fables into longer narrative structures. This first collection was well received by reviewers. All but four of its fourteen stories are set in the South, and many are situated in Pearl County, Alabama, and its seat, Reedyville. This is March's fictional empire, his own Yoknapatawpha, and he shuffles its inhabitants about from story to story with considerable, but not complete, consistency.

The volume's title story, "The Little Wife" (*Midland*, January-February 1930), is possibly March's finest and best-known short work. It was republished in *The Best Short Stories of 1930*, *O. Henry Memorial Award Prize Stories of 1930*, *50 Best American Short Stories 1915-1939*, and *50 Best*

American Short Stories 1915-1965 and was performed as a television play in 1954. Joe Hinckley,
a traveling salesman, is suddenly called home to
Mobile by a telegram informing him that his
wife, having just delivered their first baby a
month prematurely, is near death. As the train
pulls out of the station, he is handed a second telegram, which without opening he rips up and
throws away, for he realizes it contains the fateful
news of his wife's death. Unable to accept the inevitable, Joe strains desperately to keep his wife
alive by talking about her, rambling on cease-
lessly to all in his coach who will listen, until the
other passengers think him slightly demented.
But when disembarking at Mobile he sees his
mother-in-law dressed in black, Joe can no longer
sustain his illusion, and he collapses. "The Little
Wife" well illustrates March's best qualities—compression, irony, tension tempered by wry wit,
unsentimentalized compassion—all rendered in
unsettlingly plain, matter-of-fact prose.

Other notable stories in this collection include "Mist on the Meadow" (*Midland*, October
1931), which was included in *Best Short Stories of
1932*. The story focuses on Brother Hightower, a
fanatical itinerant country preacher who, obsessed with his own divine powers, crushes the
spirit of a harmless, mentally retarded boy by vio-
lently exorcising from him what the preacher
takes to be a devil. In "Miss Daisy" (*Pagany*, April-
June 1931) a saintly spinster is driven by blind-
ing, unrelenting pain to curse all she has previously held to be good and sacred. Yet another
victim of March's dark irony is Mattie Tatum in
"A Shop in St. Louis, Missouri," a story whose
theme of guilt and expiation is a March favorite.
Having denied herself for years of all pleasure
and luxury in order to save money to open her
own dress shop, Mattie suddenly is forced to decide, just when she has almost accumulated
enough money, whether to spend her earnings
on an operation that might prolong, but only for
a brief period, the life of her dying mother.
Mattie decides to be hard, which, she feels, the
world requires of one, and she keeps her money;
but when her mother dies, Mattie's guilt for her
own selfishness compels her to spend all her savings to erect an extravagant marble memorial in
honor of her mother. "Happy Jack" (*Story*, December 1932) traces the degeneration of a man unable to reconcile the fact of southern racial big-
otry with his own logical arguments against the
castration of a black farmhand found to be cohab-
iting with a white woman.

Following publication of the novel *The Tallons* in 1936, March brought out his second collection of stories, aptly titled *Some Like Them Short*
(1939). These twenty-two stories carry over the
themes and techniques of the earlier collection, although there are fewer southern stories. Three
are social protest works motivated by the Depression; but March's strength is in analyzing human
motivation, not in righting society. There are also
a few experimental stories—"This Little World" (*Alabama Rammer Jammer*, April 1938; collected as
"A Short History of England") is modeled on newspaper advertisements, and "The Shoe Drummer"
uses stream-of-consciousness—but, again, March is
no modernist, and these are not his most effective efforts.

The best-known story in *Some Like Them
Short* is "Nine Prisoners," which generated several
letters of protest when it appeared in *Forum* (December 1931). Like *Company K*, into which it was
incorporated, the story consists of brief vignettes,
each presented by an American soldier, relating
the gruesome machine-gunning of twenty-two captured Germans. Again, like *Company K*, "Nine Prisoners" employs a double structure, one that simultaneously moves forward chronologically even
while it moves inward psychologically. The focus
of each vignette is on its narrator's inner response to the mass killing, and with characteristic
conciseness March in a brief space covers a wide
emotional range. (It is not clear why, having omitted this story from the earlier collection, March included it in *Some Like Them Short*.)

The collection contains several other memorable stories. "Geraldette" (*Harper's Bazaar*, August 1937) is a tale of marital infidelity told by a
young boy: adult guilt filtered through the medium of childhood innocence is one of March's
most effective narrative methods. A subtle study
of social inhibition, "A Haircut in Toulouse"
(*Prairie Schooner*, Winter 1938) features a self-
conscious man too timid ever to fulfill his wish of
escaping conventionality. "The Funeral" (*Kansas
Magazine*, January 1939) tells of a black child
who eagerly hangs herself because she believes
that by doing so she can have a grand funeral of
the sort she has just witnessed. In a rare burst of
humor, March uses "A Memorial to the Slain" to
satirize the puritanism and the hostility to art of
southern society. A typically doomed March protagonist struggles against his own mortality in
"Time and Leigh Brothers" (*Tanager*, December
1938), futilely trying to defeat time by rigidly ar-

Illustration by Lowell Balcom for March's story "Nine Prisoners," published in the December 1931 issue of Forum

ranging each minute of his existence on index cards.

After producing his best novel, *The Looking-Glass*, in 1943, March published his collected stories, *Trial Balance*, in 1945. Here are included all of the two earlier collections (except "Nine Prisoners") plus thirteen previously uncollected stories written before *Some Like Them Short* appeared and nine stories written after. One of the best of the newly collected early works is a war story, "The Holly Wreath" (*Forum*, October 1929), which was March's first story accepted for publication. A young soldier is reminded of a holly wreath by the sight of a body lying on a battle field (red blood staining green fatigues, the head of the body meeting its toes). Recalling a sentimental childhood Christmas scene, the entranced soldier suddenly stands up from behind a protective rock to call out to his mother and is at once riddled by machine-gun bullets. Also memorable is "Not Worthy of a Wentworth," which touches on the decline-of-the-South theme March occasionally explores. The story exposes the insensitive cruelty of an aristocratic family that, in projecting its own values onto a daughter for whom those values are inconsequent, destroys the girl's sanity. "The Female of the Fruit Fly" (*Mademoiselle*, May 1943) challenges the conventional notion that intellectual understanding yields happiness. A university scientist who is plagued by the habitual infidelities of his wife realizes he will always suffer and take her back, forgiving her precisely because he understands she is not able to help herself. Sexual perversion lies beneath the outspoken public stand against vice taken by the protagonist of "Cinderella's Slipper" (*Kansas Magazine*, 1940). Verne Hollings, a fast-rising young lawyer, is sought as a candidate by a conservative political group that admires his staunch moral principles; in fact, the emotional center of Hollings's private life is a harem of stolen women's shoes, to which he makes tender love, stroking them gently as he coos sweet words of endearment.

Of the nine later stories, "The Borax Bottle" is the light tale of a boy who, to relieve the pain of a bee sting to his penis, sticks his "wounded member" into a bottle of borax–only to find that the swelling caused by the sting prevents removal of his penis from the bottle. "Dirty Emma" (*University of Kansas City Review*, Autumn 1945) depicts the murder by a filthy, pitiable woman of her brutish lover when he needlessly destroys the white hyacinth–the single clean and pure thing in her life–she had lovingly cultivated. The two spinsters of "The Static Sisters" identify so closely with their family and its aristocratic antecedents that they lack all sense of individual identity; they subsist on an unending diet of early memories and family history.

In addition to the novels *October Island* (1952) and *The Bad Seed*, March published six stories between 1945 and his death in 1954, all six of which were written in 1945 and 1946. None of these stories approaches his best earlier work; the later stories are slick fiction representative of the popular magazines (such as *Collier's* and *Good Housekeeping*) in which they appeared. (March's early stories were most often published in little magazines and academic journals.) Even had March lived to fulfill his wish of writing the forty-five stories that would "balance" at an even one hundred the fifty-five "trial" tales collected in 1945, it is by no means certain that the new stories would have matched the quality of the earlier ones.

March also wrote two novellas, each of which he expanded into a novel: "The Unploughed Patch" (*Pagany*, October-December 1932, January-March 1933), which became *The*

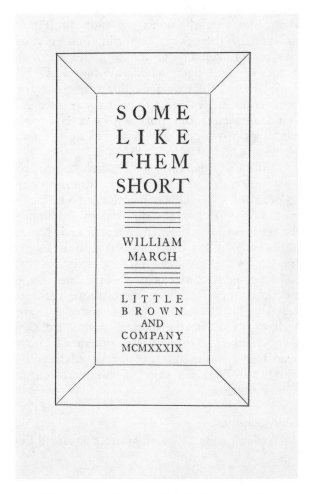

Title page for March's second short-story collection

Tallons, and "October Island" (*Good Housekeeping*, October 1946), which was separately published in 1952. "The Unploughed Patch," by means of flashbacks, compresses into a single afternoon the same action that in *The Tallons* is spread out over several years; it also eschews much of the novel's intrusive and artificial use of scenery to suggest emotional states. "October Island," a mild satire on Calvinist missionaries who find themselves attracted to the pagan spirit they have been assigned to abolish, likewise retains more force in the briefer form.

By the late 1930s March had written some 125 fables, about 50 of which he published in periodicals and newspapers. *99 Fables* appeared posthumously (1960), reprinting all but four of the previously published fables. On the whole, although more overtly moralistic, March's fables share with his stories a biting irony and a shrewd understanding of human limitations. Most are beast fables, but several treat the irrational misunderstandings between the Wittins (an anagram for "nitwits") and the Bretts (a pun on "brats"). Almost all of them are delightful; and, because they recapitulate in capsule form the dominant themes of the longer fiction (the moral of "The Pious Mantis" for example–"there is no creature more cruel in her heart than a pious woman"– well summarizes the story "Woolen Drawers"), the fables provide an excellent starting point for the new reader of March.

Alistair Cooke has called March "one of the most underrated of contemporary American writers of fiction." The little critical attention he has attracted generally has been directed toward his novels, yet it is in the short story that March is most consistently at his best. His strength is the vignette of sharp psychological insight, rather than the extended narrative of panoramic overview, so the short-story form is a mode more naturally suited to his imaginative temperament. It is for perhaps twenty stories, then, as well as for *Company K* and *The Looking-Glass*–both of which depend heavily on methods of the short story–that March will find his place in twentieth-century American fiction.

Bibliographies:

Roy S. Simmonds, "William March's 'Personal Let-

ter': Fact into Fiction," *Mississippi Quarterly*, 30 (Fall 1977): 625-637;

Simmonds, *William March: An Annotated Checklist* (Tuscaloosa & London: University of Alabama Press, 1988).

References:

Arno L. Bader, "The Structure of the Modern Short Story," *College English*, 7 (November 1945): 86-92;

Alistair Cooke, "Introduction to William March," in *A William March Omnibus* (New York: Rinehart, 1956), pp. v-xi;

William T. Going, Introduction to *99 Fables* (University: University of Alabama Press, 1960);

Going, "Some in Addition: The Uncollected Stories of William March," in *Essays on Alabama Literature* (University: University of Alabama Press, 1975), pp. 80-96;

Going, "William March: Regional Perspective and Beyond," *Papers on Language and Literature*, 13 (Fall 1977): 430-443;

Roy S. Simmonds, *The Two Worlds of William March: An Introduction to His Life and Work* (University: University of Alabama Press, 1984).

John O'Hara

(31 January 1905-11 April 1970)

Charles W. Bassett
Colby College

See also the O'Hara entries in *DLB 9: American Novelists, 1910-1945* and *DLB Documentary Series: 2.*

BOOKS: *Appointment in Samarra* (New York: Harcourt, Brace, 1934; London: Faber & Faber, 1935);

The Doctor's Son and Other Stories (New York: Harcourt, Brace, 1935);

Butterfield 8 (New York: Harcourt, Brace, 1935; London: Cresset, 1951);

Hope of Heaven (New York: Harcourt, Brace, 1938; London: Faber & Faber, 1939);

Files on Parade (New York: Harcourt, Brace, 1939);

Pal Joey (New York: Duell, Sloan & Pearce, 1940; London: Cresset, 1952);

Pipe Night (New York: Duell, Sloan & Pearce, 1945; London: Faber & Faber, 1946);

Hellbox (New York: Random House, 1947; London: Faber & Faber, 1952);

A Rage to Live (New York: Random House, 1949; London: Cresset, 1950);

The Farmers Hotel (New York: Random House, 1951; London: Cresset, 1953);

Pal Joey: The Libretto and Lyrics, libretto by O'Hara and lyrics by Lorenz Hart (New York: Random House, 1952);

Sweet and Sour (New York: Random House, 1954; London: Cresset, 1955);

Ten North Frederick (New York: Random House, 1955; London: Cresset, 1956);

A Family Party (New York: Random House, 1956; London: Cresset, 1957);

From the Terrace (New York: Random House, 1958; London: Cresset, 1959);

Ourselves to Know (New York: Random House, 1960; London: Cresset, 1960);

Sermons and Soda-Water, 3 volumes—*The Girl on the Baggage Truck, Imagine Kissing Pete*, and *We're Friends Again* (New York: Random House, 1960; London: Cresset, 1961);

Five Plays (New York: Random House, 1961; London: Cresset, 1962);

John O'Hara

Assembly (New York: Random House, 1961; London: Cresset, 1962);

The Big Laugh (New York: Random House, 1962; London: Cresset, 1962);

The Cape Cod Lighter (New York: Random House, 1962; London: Cresset, 1963);

Elizabeth Appleton (New York: Random House, 1963; London: Cresset, 1963);

The Hat on the Bed (New York: Random House, 1963; London: Cresset, 1964);

The Horse Knows the Way (New York: Random House, 1964; London: Cresset, 1965);

The Lockwood Concern (New York: Random House, 1965; London: Hodder & Stoughton, 1966);

My Turn (New York: Random House, 1966);

Waiting for Winter (New York: Random House, 1966; London: Hodder & Stoughton, 1967);

The Instrument (New York: Random House, 1967; London: Hodder & Stoughton, 1968);

And Other Stories (New York: Random House, 1968; London: Hodder & Stoughton, 1968);

Lovey Childs: A Philadelphian's Story (New York: Random House, 1969; London: Hodder & Stoughton, 1970);

The Ewings (New York: Random House, 1972; London, Sydney, Auckland & Toronto: Hodder & Stoughton, 1972);

The Time Element and Other Stories (New York: Random House, 1972; London, Sydney, Auckland & Toronto: Hodder & Stoughton, 1973);

A Cub Tells His Story (Iowa City: Windhover Press / Bruccoli Clark, 1974);

Good Samaritan and Other Stories (New York: Random House, 1974; London, Sydney, Auckland & Toronto: Hodder & Stoughton, 1976);

"An Artist Is His Own Fault," edited by Matthew J. Bruccoli (Carbondale & Edwardsville: Southern Illinois University Press, 1977);

The Second Ewings (Bloomfield Hills, Mich. & Columbia, S.C.: Bruccoli Clark, 1977);

Two by O'Hara (New York & London: Harcourt Brace Jovanovich / Bruccoli Clark, 1979).

Collections: *Here's O'Hara* (New York: Duell, Sloan & Pearce, 1946);

All the Girls He Wanted & Other Stories (New York: Avon, 1949);

Selected Short Stories of John O'Hara (New York: Modern Library, 1956);

The Great Short Stories of John O'Hara (New York: Bantam, 1956);

49 Stories (New York: Modern Library, 1963);

The O'Hara Generation (New York: Random House, 1969);

Collected Stories of John O'Hara, edited by Frank MacShane (New York: Random House, 1984).

PLAY PRODUCTION: *Pal Joey*, New York, Ethel Barrymore Theatre, 25 December 1940.

MOTION PICTURES: *Moontide*, screenplay by O'Hara, 20th Century-Fox, 1942;

The Best Things in Life Are Free, story by O'Hara, 20th Century-Fox, 1956.

OTHER: *Remarks on the Novel*, tape recording of O'Hara's 1957 Gertrude Clark Whittal Lecture at the Library of Congress (Bloomfield Hills, Mich. & Columbia, S.C.: Bruccoli Clark, 1977).

PERIODICAL PUBLICATIONS: "Entertainment Week" [weekly column], *Newsweek* (15 July 1940-16 February 1942);

"Sweet and Sour" [weekly column], *Trenton Sunday Times-Advertiser* (27 December 1953-27 June 1954);

"Appointment with O'Hara" [weekly column], *Collier's* (5 February 1954–28 September 1956);

"My Turn" [weekly column], *Newsday* (3 October 1964-2 October 1965);

"The Whistle Stop" [monthly column], *Holiday* (September 1966-May 1967).

The years since his death in 1970 have not been kind to the literary reputation of John O'Hara. Increasingly fewer readers, but especially younger ones, are aware of O'Hara's enormously productive career as the creator of fifteen novels, six published plays, and over four hundred short stories. Almost all of O'Hara's work sold well, making him probably the most popular serious writer of his era (1930-1970). Few American writers of the 1950s and 1960s could count on such widespread public appeal as O'Hara, despite the opposition of a majority of critics who characterized his work as prolix, reactionary, or shallow. None of these detractors, however, dismissed O'Hara as a hack during his lifetime, and—notwithstanding O'Hara's current eclipse—future historians of American literature will probably assess his achievements, particularly in short fiction, as noteworthy.

In fact, even before his death, O'Hara and his audience were well aware of the critical consensus which extolled his skill with the short story while denigrating his novels. A 1963 review in *Time* was typical: "John O'Hara has for so long been the acknowledged master craftsman of U.S. short story writers that whatever new peaks of performance he hits are unlikely to stir much surprise. This is a pity because in recent years, as his novels get worse and worse, his stories have been getting better and better." Academic critics, collectively more hostile to O'Hara than journalists, agreed with that estimate: "O'Hara is an extraordinarily good and important writer of short stories," wrote Prof. Charles Walcutt, "and an inferior novelist."

Given the kind of admiration for O'Hara's stories by otherwise unfriendly critics, one can

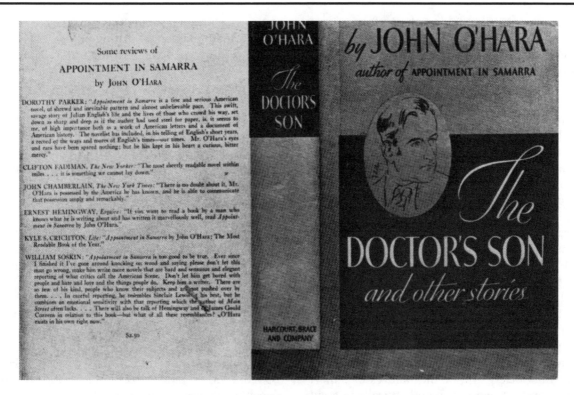

Dust jacket for O'Hara's first short-story collection, published in 1935. The book includes four stories set in the town of Gibbsville, which is based on O'Hara's hometown, Pottsville, Pennsylvania.

only wonder why O'Hara is excluded so regularly from the pantheon of modern short-story masters. Certainly O'Hara's stories were ubiquitous: twelve collections were published during his lifetime, the first in 1935, and two posthumous collections appeared in the early 1970s. O'Hara's short stories showed up regularly in the *New Yorker*, beginning in 1928, and the influence of this magazine on Americans' taste in fiction has been notable. Yet O'Hara is rarely ranked with giants such as Ernest Hemingway or William Faulkner; nor is he as highly praised as John Cheever or John Updike, whose stories are putatively akin to O'Hara's in their focus on "society." Matthew J. Bruccoli attributes O'Hara's damaged critical reputation to his refusal to allow his stories to be anthologized in school or college textbooks. O'Hara felt that his work was somehow devalued by such indiscriminate selection, but because literary reputation in America is transmitted largely through the academy, O'Hara's prestige has been diminished.

The likelihood of an O'Hara revival remains slim despite the publication of three biographies since his death. Perhaps *New York Times* reviewer Webster Schott best characterized resistance to O'Hara with this assessment of *The*

Lockwood Concern (28 November 1965): "John O'Hara is America's most distinguished out-of-date novelist." Stubbornly dedicated to plain style, accurate dialogue, verisimilitude, and specificity, O'Hara spurned those who would turn modern fiction into myth or archetype or fable. O'Hara was an old-fashioned realist, and his fiction embodied the strengths and weaknesses of this mimetic genre and of the actuality imitated.

Most contemporary literary critics are not excited by realism-naturalism, nor by the mission that O'Hara announced as his in a foreword to *Sermons and Soda-Water* (1960): "I want to get it all down on paper while I can.... The United States in this Century is what I know, and it is my business to write about it to the best of my ability, with the sometimes special knowledge that I have. The Twenties, the Thirties, and the Forties are already history, but I cannot be content to leave their story in the hands of the historians and the editors of picture books. I want to record the way people talked and thought and felt, and do it with complete honesty and variety." For every critic like Malcolm Bradbury, who honored O'Hara as "the best modern case of writer as social historian," dozens more agreed with Irving Howe, who characterized O'Hara as "stolid" for "diagramming all the hidden channels of our social arrangements."

O'Hara's calling as recorder is, of course, less obvious in his short fiction than in his novels. Nevertheless, the enormous range of O'Hara's stories, the variety of their settings and characters, the density of their revelatory detail, their ultimately interlocking themes and conclusions, all attest to his commitment to tell the truth about his time comprehensively and completely in all of his work. The economy of the short-story form, particularly in O'Hara's early stories, seemed to vitiate his historian's impulse to buttress all his characterizations with masses of detailed social information, but as he matured, O'Hara repeatedly called attention to the pattern of American life that he embodied in his fiction, short and long.

This pattern is O'Hara's exacerbated awareness of the waste and pathos that attend anyone's search for self-realization in a materialistic, status-conscious America. O'Hara writes most poignantly of the illusions that snobbery generates in this society and of the failures of American men and women to live authentically in a culture where values are more ambivalent than the characters suspect. O'Hara's America, however, even in the shortest stories, is palpable and recognizable, though sometimes more bizarre than quotidian. O'Hara's considerable audience never tired of the paradoxes of his "capitalist realism" because they shared his fascination with the seeming solidity of social forms, the symbolic value of things and rituals, and the potentially awesome power of the rich.

Concern with the power of society to define human lives leads O'Hara dangerously close to the determinism that characterizes literary naturalism, but he was never really doctrinaire about the forces that operate within his world. Relentlessly anti-intellectual in fact, O'Hara abjured abstractions as a writer: "I'm not some hairy philosopher," he insisted. "I'm just an ordinary guy who happens to write well." On the other hand, he consistently involved his characters in situations seemingly beyond their control. O'Hara's fictional world is rife with violence, fear, paranoia, despair, arrogance, frustrated desire, and hypersensitivity; no one–rich or poor, powerful or helpless, attractive or disgusting–escapes the nemesis that is social control and human weakness.

Critics have objected to O'Hara's world as too bleak, to his characters as too universally without moral resource. Frank MacShane has pointed out that given O'Hara's predilection for the real-

ist's concentration upon the norm he was faced with the dilemma of writing interesting fiction about average people. Yet somehow O'Hara managed to invest his fictional situations with a sociopsychological resonance that kept his huge audience coming back for more for decades. O'Hara's stories consistently generated shocks of recognition with their accurate dialogue and precise observation, but, more significantly, O'Hara's readers accepted his pessimism about the fate of the individuals trapped in the contradictions of American life.

Certainly O'Hara's own life had all the contradictions which he personified in his fictions. It is now a cliché to point to the feelings of inadequacy and frustration generated in O'Hara by his rank as an Irish-Catholic outsider in WASP-dominated Pottsville, Pennsylvania, his native city. But, as O'Hara himself never tired of pointing out, the O'Haras of Schuylkill County were hardly shanty Irish; his grandparents were solidly bourgeois, and John's father, Patrick Henry O'Hara, M.D., was a prominent and relatively wealthy Pottsville surgeon. Katharine O'Hara, John's mother, was a linguist, a musician, and a resourceful woman. The eight O'Hara children, John the oldest, grew up on the best street in Pottsville, drove five automobiles, and rode their own show horses on the family farm.

At the same time, Patrick O'Hara's very success in Pottsville made John all the more aware of his failure to measure up to his father's achievements. He revered his father, but John was aware that Patrick O'Hara was "the Irish doctor." And neither dexterity with the scalpel nor dancing schools for the children could break down Pottsville's elaborate caste system based on wealth, class, ethnicity, and religion. Consequently, O'Hara's well-developed doubts about himself stemmed from both paternal and public sources. Often in rebellion during his youth, O'Hara got himself thrown out of three preparatory schools, irreparably alienated his father, and acquired a local reputation as a malcontent and wastrel. He exacerbated his insecurity by falling hopelessly in love with an attractive Pottsville girl, somewhat older than he and the belle of the local Establishment; every Pottsville convention militated against their happiness.

O'Hara's world crashed completely when his father's death plunged the family into poverty in 1925. Gone was his cherished chance to enroll at Yale, gone his dream of escape from a dreary reporting job on the *Pottsville Journal*, gone his

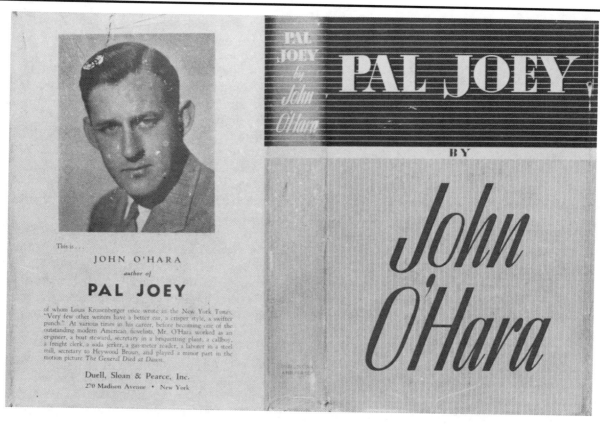

Dust jacket for O'Hara's 1940 collection, which includes fourteen epistolary stories about an exploitive nightclub entertainer named Joey Evans

family's fragile place in local society. In spite of these difficulties, Katharine O'Hara kept order in her house and among her children, save only for the eldest. Twenty-year-old John was increasingly restless, dissatisfied, guilty, and self-doubting. Alternately surly and sensitive, cynical and ambitious, bitter and hopeful, O'Hara knew that he had to leave Pottsville in order to write. He had contributed quips to Franklin P. Adams's column in the *New York World*, and Adams helped the young man get a job on the *Herald Tribune* within days after O'Hara arrived in New York City. But the fecklessness that had characterized his journalism in Pottsville continued in New York, and although O'Hara was successful in obtaining reporting jobs with various magazines and newspapers, he often showed himself to be irresponsible and was summarily fired.

A lone distinction marked these early hand-to-mouth years in New York: O'Hara placed his first piece with the *New Yorker* in May 1928, only two months after he arrived, beginning an association that was to continue stormily for four decades. In fact, O'Hara sold *all* of his fiction to the *New Yorker* in his first year in New York: 12 sto-

ries in 1928, 24 in 1929, 20 in 1930, 17 in 1931. Not until July of 1932 did an O'Hara story appear elsewhere, in *Scribner's Magazine*, and from 1928 until 1949 (when O'Hara stopped writing short stories for a decade) only 15 of O'Hara's 232 published stories were printed in other magazines.

The *New Yorker* of the late 1920s was more consciously a humor magazine than the serious journal of opinion that it later became. Accordingly, O'Hara's early fiction was satiric–often broadly ironic monologues by the confused ladies of the "Orange County Afternoon Delphian Society" or the Babbitt-like manager of Hagedorn & Brownmiller, a local paint company. Sinclair Lewis had used the absurd monologue to pillory American hypocrites for years, but O'Hara's speakers are less consciously exaggerated than Lewis's. Slight and sarcastic, these monologues– and another, later series emanating from the Idlewood Country Club–demonstrate O'Hara's enormous effectiveness as a recorder of speech. Probably no American writer more tellingly reproduces authentic conversation than O'Hara. His mimetic gifts make these apprentice monologues more than satiric ephemera; O'Hara was a practiced listener, and he never forgot what he heard.

More ephemeral was the money that O'Hara earned from these *New Yorker* contributions: generally ten cents a word. Since the monologues were inevitably short, O'Hara could not live on the few hundred dollars a year he realized from Harold Ross's magazine. O'Hara's financial stability declined more steeply after his ill-starred marriage to Helen Petit in 1931, and his seemingly constitutional inability to hold a regular job forced the couple to depend upon "Pet's" mother for support. Mrs. Petit's interference hastened their divorce in 1933.

In May 1933 O'Hara moved to Pittsburgh to edit the *Bulletin-Index* magazine, only to be driven back to New York in a few months by loneliness and boredom. Heavy drinking, violent confrontations of several sorts, even thoughts of suicide characterized O'Hara's life, yet somehow he was able to complete his first novel, *Appointment in Samarra* (1934), which required four printings by Harcourt, Brace in its first year. Critical notices were mixed, but O'Hara began living somewhat more conventionally on his royalties.

Skillful dialogue in *Appointment in Samarra* and in his *New Yorker* stories made O'Hara attractive to Paramount Studios, and he went to work in Hollywood in 1934, beginning a sequence of screen-writing jobs that would extend into the 1950s. Never an especially successful screenwriter, O'Hara nevertheless lived well on the Hollywood money and became an expert on life in the film colony. Earlier a press agent for Warner Bros. in New York, O'Hara found the competitiveness, venality, and hypocrisy of movie people an inexhaustible source of inspiration. Dreadful Hollywood characters begin appearing as early as 1932 in O'Hara's stories, often outdoing his Broadway types in their vanity and exploitiveness.

At the same time his Hollywood experience did little to control O'Hara's own drinking, womanizing, and generally dissolute life in the mid 1930s. Even though he was able to publish an average of ten stories annually and to finish two novels (*Butterfield 8* in 1935, *Hope of Heaven* in 1938), O'Hara's public behavior was often bizarre, surly, or violent, and his private moods swung from depression to self-hatred. Marriage to Belle Wylie of New York was to begin a change in O'Hara's life in 1938; he never lost his extreme touchiness, but he began to set down some roots at Quogue, Long Island, in the summers, and he worked harder than before on his writing.

During the 1930s O'Hara brought out two story collections–*The Doctor's Son and Other Stories* (1935) and *Files on Parade* (1939)–solidifying his early reputation as a master of the "*New Yorker*" short story. In fact, the coincidence of that magazine's emphases with his own themes elicited this estimate from Delmore Schwartz: "An author like O'Hara is perfect in *The New Yorker* because *The New Yorker* is in the most thoroughgoing way devoted to a sense of the social milieu, the hopes, resentments, frustrations, and fears which the American scene creates or compels."

Perhaps O'Hara's most popular character began appearing in his *New Yorker* stories in 1938: the nightclub entertainer Joey Evans. This dishonest, exploitive (yet strangely likable) charlatan reveals himself in the letters he writes to a friend. Fourteen of these epistolary stories, collected as *Pal Joey*, appeared in October 1940, at a time when O'Hara's libretto for Richard Rodgers and Lorenz Hart's musical adaptation of *Pal Joey* was in final rehearsals. The show proved a solid popular success, running on Broadway for nearly a year after its opening in December 1940.

By now, O'Hara could ask and get $1,250 a week in Hollywood, where his screenplay helped *Moontide* (1942) win an Academy Award nomination. And his growing stature led *Newsweek* to pay him $1,000 for each weekly column of show business chitchat called "Entertainment Week." He wrote eighty-four of these weekly columns in the early 1940s, but World War II engendered a fallowness in O'Hara unprecedented in his career. Rejected for military service for ulcers and bad teeth, he did publish a collection of thirty-one stories called *Pipe Night* in 1945, but nearly a third of them had been written before the Japanese attack on Pearl Harbor. A brief stint as a war correspondent in the Pacific generated only one magazine article; O'Hara felt that the important events of his time were bypassing him. The birth of his only child, Wylie, provided the sole revival of his spirits in these difficult years.

A new publisher, Random House, brought out O'Hara's next book, a collection of twenty-six stories entitled *Hellbox*, in 1947. Reviewers noted a certain extra bitterness in these stories, speculating that O'Hara may have been tiring of the form. In retrospect, the theory has some truth to it; O'Hara had been researching backgrounds for a major novel for some time. *A Rage to Live* (1949), a thorough study of the rich in a small Pennsylvania city, was a great popular success

Dust jacket for O'Hara's 1945 collection. Most of the stories in the book were first published in the New Yorker.

and O'Hara's first bona fide best-seller. Its publication signaled a change in artistic direction for O'Hara: not until 1959 was he to publish another short story.

Sharing the cause for O'Hara's desertion of the story form was his strained relationship with the *New Yorker*, which reviewed *A Rage to Live* negatively and thereby violated O'Hara's strict canons of loyalty. Because he did not feel at home with any other magazine's standards for short fiction, O'Hara simply stopped writing stories. But he became a tremendously productive writer of novels, novellas, and plays during his period of abstinence from the short story.

Underlying his increase in output was a move from the distractions of New York to the quiet of Princeton. Perhaps more important was O'Hara's decision to stop drinking after a brush with death from bleeding ulcers in 1953. Even though he was shattered by Belle's death in 1954, O'Hara made a stable third marriage with Katharine "Sister" Barnes Bryan a year later. His novel *Ten North Frederick* (1955) won the National Book Award in 1956, but he was most pleased with the huge *From the Terrace* (1958), a best-seller in the paperback edition and proof of his staying power as a novelist.

A revival of *Pal Joey* to great public and critical acclaim on Broadway made O'Hara particularly proud in the early 1950s. As the play's librettist, O'Hara won awards from the Donaldson Committee and the New York Drama Critics' Circle. Bennett Cerf, his publisher at Random House, pleased O'Hara even more by bringing out the libretto in book form in 1952 as a favor to his best-selling author. Although O'Hara continued to write plays, he was not successful in getting his subsequent efforts produced.

O'Hara was frustrated by his inability to win major literary prizes such as the Pulitzer in recognition of his achievements. Always an intensely competitive man who loved badges and plaques, O'Hara was capable of carrying on some embarrassing lobbying for prizes in the two columns of comment that he wrote in the 1950s. O'Hara's easily bruised ego dominated "Sweet and Sour" (collected as a book in 1954) for the *Trenton Sunday Times-Advertiser* and "Appointment with O'Hara" for *Collier's*, but, perhaps because he wanted them so much, he got few awards.

On the other hand, the popularity of O'Hara's fiction began to make him a wealthy man in the 1950s. He and Sister built a French provincial house on Pretty Brook Road outside Princeton and filled its garage with expensive automobiles. His economic, political, and cultural opinions grew increasingly conservative, even reactionary, and he made no attempt to hide his preference for the values of the past. "The total rejection of the standards and principles that we know were good," he wrote in "My Turn," a syndicated weekly column for *Newsday*, "will make it extremely unlikely that honesty and decency will be revived." In tweeds, flannels, and cap, he presided over his establishment in the style and spirit of the Republican elite.

Wealth did not, nevertheless, mean that O'Hara's commitment to his art abated even slightly. Indeed, his rage to write seemed to increase as he grew older. Biographers have suggested that the increased dedication that O'Hara brought to his work in the 1950s and 1960s was a more or less conscious emulation of his father's devotion to surgery during John's youth. Whatever the case, lovers of the O'Hara short story could again be satisfied when the *New Yorker* patched its differences with its erstwhile contributor and printed "Imagine Kissing Pete," a long story with a Pennsylvania setting, in its 17 September 1960 issue. The *New Yorker* published ten of his stories in 1961, and O'Hara also sold twenty-eight stories to the *Saturday Evening Post* in the 1960s, attracting a new readership and demonstrating his mastery of the short-story form.

Assembly (1961), O'Hara's first short-story collection in almost fifteen years, brought together these *New Yorker* stories with several previously unpublished works. The book was a critical and popular success. In the foreword O'Hara claimed that he "had an apparently inexhaustible urge to express an unlimited supply of short story ideas," and he gloried in "the fun of hard work" that allowed him to write these stories so readily. Accordingly, O'Hara published a collection of stories in seven of the ten years of the 1960s, regularly interspersing them with his novels, plays, and essays. As early as 1964 O'Hara declared an end to these collections, but *Waiting for Winter* (1966) and *And Other Stories* (1968) gave the lie to that announcement.

In fact, O'Hara loved writing short stories, and his trepidation about producing so many stemmed from his very facility. Somehow stories seemed not as "serious" as novels, yet O'Hara thought of his short fictions as worthy of his talent: "The way I feel about writing, which is practically a religious feeling, would not permit me to 'dash off' a story." At any rate, O'Hara pub-

lished 137 stories in hardcover collections in the 1960s, giving rise to this characterization in the *Time* review of *Waiting for Winter*: "O'Hara is a rarity in contemporary U.S. letters, a writer who never runs dry."

Even fervent O'Hara fans acknowledged, however, that O'Hara published too much during the last years of his life. His failings were less evident in the stories than in the novels, where O'Hara's ability to control plot and character seemed increasingly unstable. Consequently, *The Instrument* (1967) and *Lovey Childs: A Philadelphian's Story* (1969) lack what distinguish O'Hara's earlier novels—pace, credibility, style, bite. Ironically, the American Academy of Arts and Letters chose this time to present O'Hara with its Award of Merit for the Novel, bolstering his often-repeated claim that his longer fiction *was* best. (O'Hara frequently cited this estimate from a review of *Pipe Night* for the *New York Times* in 1945 by Lionel Trilling: "For O'Hara's talents, the novel is the proper form.")

In view of the variety of ills—back trouble, throat and stomach disorders, hypertension, and vascular disease—that beset O'Hara in the late 1960s, his friends could only admire the dogged sense of duty that sent him nightly to his typewriter. He rarely wrote until dawn as before, but he maintained his daily schedule except during his occasional visits to England and Ireland. O'Hara had completed a novel, *The Ewings*, in 1970 (it was published in 1972) and was well into its sequel when he went off to bed on 10 April complaining of chest pains. Death came in his sleep early the next morning; O'Hara was sixty-five.

Obituaries and literary retrospectives accentuated O'Hara's popularity and productivity; when themes were mentioned, O'Hara was lauded for his fictional anatomies of the rich and damned for the supposed lubricity of sexual encounters in his novels. Those critics who had never liked him (Alfred Kazin called O'Hara "a melodramatist of American social ambition and lust") were not softened by O'Hara's death, but the superiority of the short stories to his other work had become a feature of the critical litany.

Left uncollected at O'Hara's death were 15 *New Yorker* stories printed in the late 1940s, plus another 14 dating from the same period but victims of O'Hara's feud with the magazine. O'Hara's Random House editor, Albert Erskine, put together this series as *The Time Element and Other Stories* in 1972; it was roughly reviewed and sold poorly. O'Hara's final collection was *Good Samaritan and*

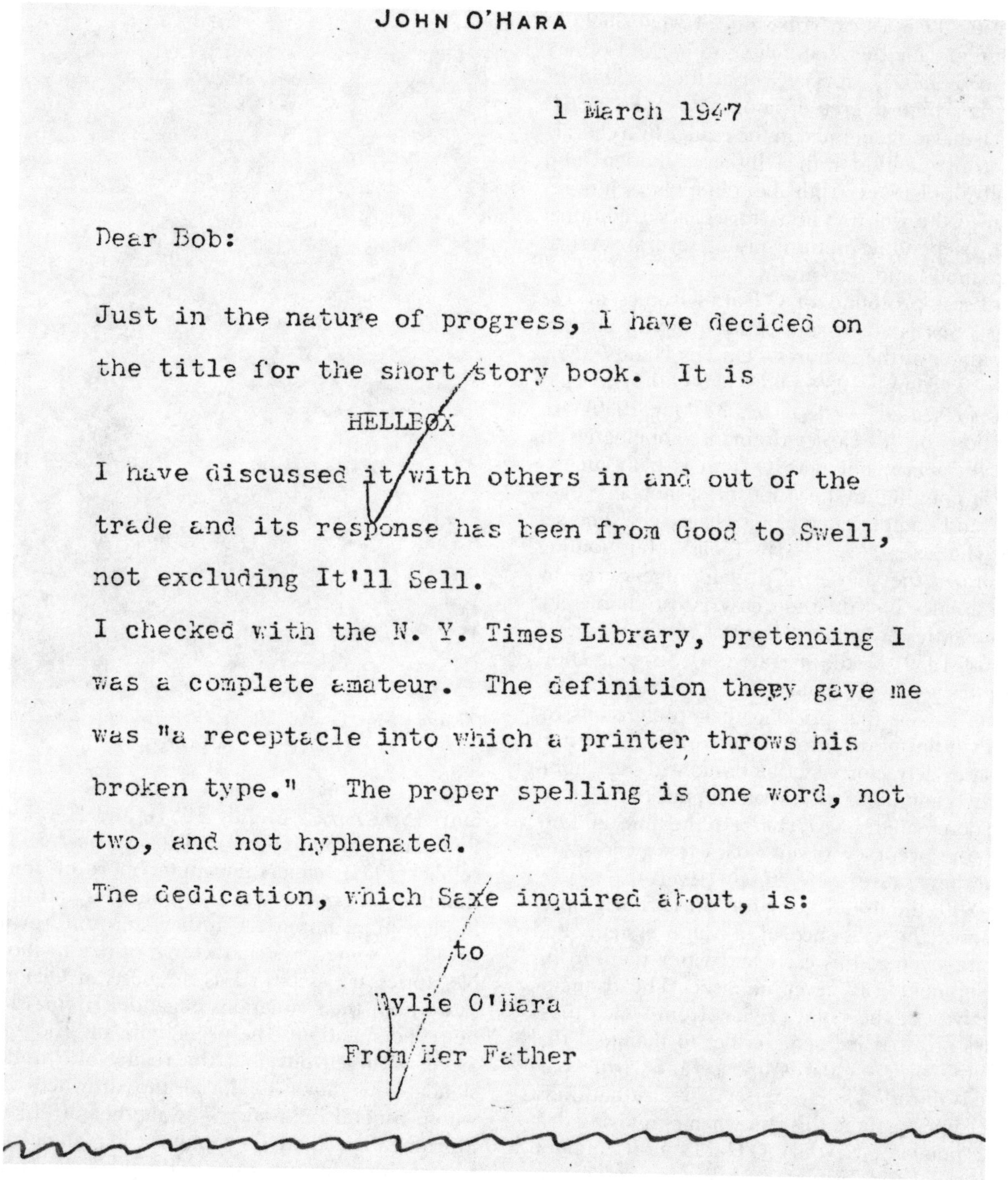

JOHN O'HARA

1 March 1947

Dear Bob:

Just in the nature of progress, I have decided on
the title for the short story book. It is

HELLBOX

I have discussed it with others in and out of the
trade and its response has been from Good to Swell,
not excluding It'll Sell.

I checked with the N. Y. Times Library, pretending I
was a complete amateur. The definition they gave me
was "a receptacle into which a printer throws his
broken type." The proper spelling is one word, not
two, and not hyphenated.

The dedication, which Saxe inquired about, is:

to

Wylie O'Hara

From Her Father

Portion of a letter from O'Hara to Random House editor Robert Linscott

Other Stories (1974), 14 pieces which Erskine dated from the 1960s. With the posthumous publication of these two volumes, O'Hara's final story count reached 402. The prodigality of this achievement caused Prof. James E. Miller, Jr., to set the agenda in the *John O'Hara Journal* in 1980: "What we need now is a good critical shifting of all those short stories. We are in the embarrassing po-

sition of not knowing just how good O'Hara is."

Early in his career O'Hara shaped most of his stories according to the space-available requirements of the *New Yorker* and other magazines; accordingly, the thirty-seven stories in O'Hara's first collection, *The Doctor's Son and Other Stories*, are usually succinct, averaging only sixteen hundred words. Nevertheless, these brief stories demonstrate O'Hara's early mastery of what Sheldon Grebstein calls the "sensibility" story (and others the *"New Yorker"* story). Crucial to this kind of story is a high degree of awareness and sensitivity to behavior generated in the reader by a character's confrontation with a hitherto hidden (and usually unpleasant) truth about him / herself in relation to the world. These stories lack traditional "plot," depending upon irony of several sorts to evoke mood and response.

Least profound of O'Hara's ironies in *The Doctor's Son* is an obvious satiric irony of characters. Many of these satires–"On His Hands" (*New Yorker*, 22 March 1930) and "The Girl Who Had Been Presented" (*New Yorker*, 31 May 1930)–are variations on his earlier dramatic monologues in the *New Yorker*, but here O'Hara is truly an expert at pointing up the viciousness, snobbery, egotism, and complacency of his characters. The satiric characters are clearly foolish, but joining O'Hara in the snicker of disdain engendered by their foibles is rather too easy. Most characters, such as Mrs. Brown of "New Day" (*New Yorker*, 23 August 1930) or the narrator of "Straight Pool" (*New Yorker*, 16 December 1933), are such minor-league villains that pricking their pretensions requires little moral effort from reader or writer. O'Hara's detractors associated him with the "lightweight champions of urban superiority" whose style dominated the *New Yorker* at the time, and despite the accuracy of his characters' voices, too often these satires were merely clever.

Still, the use of irony for satiric ridicule presupposes the existence of a value system, and O'Hara–even at this early and bitter point in his development–was never nihilistic. The dramatic objectivity of the point of view from which these stories are told led some critics to maintain that O'Hara's own standards of vice and virtue paralleled those of characters. A realist-naturalist writer must assume this risk when employing dramatic points of view like O'Hara's most common ones: speaker as witness, speaker as protagonist, interior monologue, pure dialogue. O'Hara's refusal to moralize should not be confused with immorality, particularly in the slighter satiric anecdotes.

Another half-dozen stories in *The Doctor's Son*, however, are as resonant and absorbing as any O'Hara would ever write. Irony is still O'Hara's mode, but in stories such as "Alone" (*Scribner's Magazine*, December 1931), "Hotel Kid" (*Vanity Fair*, September 1933), "Sportsmanship" (*New Yorker*, 12 May 1934), "In the Morning

O'Hara on the Queen Mary, *1959 (Cunard Line Photograph by George V. Bigelow)*

Sun" (*New Yorker*, 14 July 1934), and "Over the River and Through the Wood" (*New Yorker*, 15 December 1934) readers encounter more profound situations, a greater sense of loneliness and helplessness in an imperfect, unfair, and unforgiving world. In some ways characters in these memorable stories are as flawed as the butts of O'Hara's satires, but their situations engender compassion, not condemnation. The protagonist of "Alone" is awash with self-pity, but the reader also understands how much he loved the drowned wife whose funeral he awaits. The mother of "In the Morning Sun" can only mourn her zombielike son, and the obnoxiousness of the hotel child is excused by parental neglect. Revenge permeates "Sportsmanship," where money has spoiled any sportsman's code.

"Over the River and Through the Wood" is a classic O'Hara sensibility story: an aging ex-roué, once magnetically attractive and powerful, rides with his granddaughter and two pretty schoolmates to visit his daughter, who now presides over a house formerly the scene of the older man's successes. The girls ignore Winfield, though they hint that they have been warned of his ladies'-man reputation. Finally at the house, cold and lonely, Winfield opens a door to take some cocoa to one of his granddaughter's friends, only to find her nude. Her response– "Get out of here, you dirty old man"–is lethal. O'Hara ends this pathetic episode with two perfect sentences: "He knew it would be hours before he would begin to hate himself. For a while he would sit there and plan his terror."

Another success in *The Doctor's Son* is the title story, a novella-length growing-up narrative featuring the maturing point of view of an autobiographical protagonist, James Malloy, and set in Gibbsville, a mirror image of O'Hara's native Pottsville. Even Dr. Malloy's heroic ministrations in the influenza epidemic of 1918 closely recall O'Hara's memories of his own father's service. Whatever its personal roots, the story is memorable primarily for its juxtaposition of love with death: Jimmy's love for an older girl, the girl's mother's affair with a visiting doctor, and the death of the girl's father in the epidemic. Malloy must mature fast in this grim world where the good die, the adulterers flourish, and nothing– not training, not hard work, not love, not life itself–finally prevails. Such bleakness can only engender in Malloy a kind of qualified stoicism, O'Hara's last defense against the harsher ironies of fate.

Gibbsville and the surrounding anthracite area ("Lantenengo County") are the setting for three other stories in *The Doctor's Son:* "Mary" (*New Yorker*, 2 May 1931), "Dr. Wyeth's Son" (*New Yorker*, 28 July 1934), and "It Must have Been Spring" (*New Yorker*, 12 April 1934), a sentimental encounter between Malloy and his doctor father. O'Hara used the anthracite region (known as "The Region") in sixty stories in future collections, and Malloy turns up as protagonist / observer in fifteen stories. Moreover, O'Hara frequently features Malloy and / or The Region in such novels as *Appointment in Samarra* and *Ten North Frederick*. Nearby areas of Pennsylvania are prominent in *A Rage to Live, From the Terrace, Ourselves to Know*, and *The Lockwood Concern*. Not as imaginatively gaudy nor as symbolically rich as William Faulkner's mythical Mississippi county, Yoknapatawpha, the Lantenengo region is still a genuine literary phenomenon–its inhabitants, their values, and their conflicts unmistakably the creation of John O'Hara.

Despite the success of *The Doctor's Son* in 1935, O'Hara spent the next few years enhancing his reputation as a novelist, screenwriter, and man-about-town. Between 1935 and 1939 O'Hara published the novels *Butterfield 8* and *Hope of Heaven*; wrote treatments and scripts for Samuel Goldwyn, M-G-M, RKO, and 20th Century-Fox; married Belle Wylie; honeymooned abroad for five months; and made frequent trips between New York and Hollywood. With metronomic regularity, however, an O'Hara short story appeared in print on an average of once every forty-two days (usually in the *New Yorker*) for over four years. In the six weeks from late October to early December 1938 O'Hara published five stories, sometimes bragging that he could do one in a couple of concentrated hours of work. Harcourt, Brace's new collection of thirty-five of these stories (two of which had already appeared in *The Doctor's Son*) took the title *Files on Parade* from Rudyard Kipling to signify amplitude, variety, and a sense of doom.

Files on Parade certainly has amplitude– theater stories, Hollywood stories, city and suburban stories, country club stories–but even some friendly critics have emphasized O'Hara's increasingly pessimistic mood in these slightly longer (nineteen-hundred-word average) fictions. Frank MacShane's claim is typical: "O'Hara's picture of America is not a pretty one. Most of his characters are aggressive and selfish or defeated and lost. To O'Hara America is a jungle in which people use one another and cruelty is casual." A similar claim might be made against most of O'Hara's work, but here the morbidity has become claustrophobic.

A graphic example in *Files on Parade* is "Olive" (*New Yorker*, 17 August 1935), the story of a casually petty revenge taken by a hotel telephone operator against two guests: Miss Bishop, spinster, and Colonel Browder, recent widower. Olive, the operator, cannot believe that the daily tea shared by these two aging waifs can be innocent, and because Olive believes that the guests snub her, she destroys their genteel meetings with insinuations of impropriety. Miss Bishop leaves the hotel, and the Colonel declines into solitary despair.

O'Hara's envious and defensive characters usually manage to triumph, though not always. The forces of democracy seem to carry the day in "Price's Always Open" (*New Yorker*, 14 August 1937), a story featuring a violent confrontation between a sweet but drunken young townie and a menacing bully from the summer crowd of Ivy Leaguers. At Price's Diner, where class distinctions and sexual politics are always potentially vol-

RANDOM HOUSE INC.

457 MADISON AVENUE, NEW YORK 22, N.Y. TELEPHONE PLaza 1·2600

RANDOM HOUSE BOOKS · THE MODERN LIBRARY · LANDMARK BOOKS
LEGACY BOOKS · ALLABOUT BOOKS · THE AMERICAN COLLEGE DICTIONARY

Albert Erskine, MANAGING EDITOR

August 29, 1960

Mr. John O'Hara
Quogue, Long Island
New York

Dear John:

I have now been over the queries that I mentioned in
my letter of last week and I find that only one of
them need be referred to you:

Line 14 of galley 48, "that another generation called /
Cloud 90"

This didn't sound right to me or to others who have
read the manuscript, or to still others whom I have
asked. Some people remember Cloud 7 and some Cloud 9,
but I have discovered that the recently published
DICTIONARY OF AMERICAN SLANG gives Cloud 7 and doesn't
mention any variance. Cloud 7 seems to be the way I
remember it and I'm wondering if you were, perhaps,
thinking about Playhouse 90 when you typed this.

That's all there is unless something else turns up in
the proofreading now in progress.

Best regards,

AE:sb

Cloud 90. And don't cite dictionaries to
me, on dialog or the vernacular. Dictionary
people consult me, not I them.

Editor's query concerning the novella collection Sermons and Soda-Water *and O'Hara's reply*

canic, Mr. Price floors the elitist ruffian with his blackjack, then orders the rest of the summer crowd out. His gesture might win him admiration for its proletarian élan, but Price too well knows its ironic economic consequences: "Thinking it over, Mr. Price agreed with himself that those would be the last sounds he ever expected to hear from the summer crowd."

Even more poignant is the fate of the preparatory school "newboy," Roberts, who is baited and bullied by the pompous and sadistic master, Van Ness, in "Do You Like It Here?" (*New Yorker*, 18 February 1939). At few points in his long career of chronicling the terrors of social exclusion does O'Hara better dramatize the absolute hopelessness of the outsider. Roberts can never prove himself innocent of theft, and Van Ness will rise through self-righteousness to a more important post at the school.

Files on Parade, overwhelmingly accounted a gloomy collection, did, however, mark the first appearance of four "Pal Joey" stories, and O'Hara was able somewhat to vitiate his reputation as a pessimist with these tales of a raffish and egotistical nightclub sharpie. Joey Evans's adventures are told in epistolary form to his pal Ted, O'Hara using Ring Lardner's baseball-playing correspondent as a model. Nevertheless, O'Hara has created in Joey a vernacular wiseguy who is more than a comic stereotype; Joey is both repellent and attractive, both cynical and innocent, both user and used. O'Hara's show-business characters are notoriously rotten, but Joey breaks out of the mold in his sentimentality, his occasional good-heartedness.

The Joey stories began to appear in the *New Yorker* in 1938, and they turned out to be by far the most popular fiction that O'Hara had yet written. No one thought Joey profound or his adventures meaningful, but both O'Hara and the magazine were encouraged by public response. The *New Yorker* was eventually to carry twelve Joey stories, to which O'Hara added "A Bit of a Shock" and "Reminiss?" to make up the collection called *Pal Joey*, published in October 1940.

In a way, Joey is as upwardly mobile as O'Hara's more serious characters: in "Pal Joey" he is courting the local banker's daughter, drinking at the country club, and already planning four kids and golf clubs. A revengeful girlfriend from the past blows the lid off Joey's pretense of respectability, and his dreams evaporate. As a bush league roué, Joey can succeed with the inexperienced and the dull-witted (in "Bow Wow"), but normally intelligent and perceptive women lay him low ("Joey and Mavis" or "A Bit of a Shock"). The same skill level applies to his success with flimflam schemes: he occasionally cons the unsophisticated out of a few dollars, but he can only quail before real power ("Joey on Herta") or mature trickery ("The Erloff").

Joey still turns out to be an almost likable rogue. He will deceive, manipulate, exploit, but he is never really evil. And he hangs on, takes his lumps, bounces back, and begins again. No one would deny his social parasitism, and feminists would scorn his sexism. For all that, brash Joey Evans remains one of O'Hara's most memorable creations. Nevertheless, O'Hara could not resist ending the Joey series on a realistic note of hopeless desire. Joey too yearns for love, and "Reminiss?" is laced with envy and bitterness as Joey looks to the future and sees only emptiness.

O'Hara's creative intermission during World War II did not include a complete drought in the short story. A piece of short fiction by O'Hara appeared every other month or so throughout the first half of the 1940s, usually in the *New Yorker* but also in *Collier's* and *Good Housekeeping*. The stories in the Joey series had been slightly longer than O'Hara's usual product, but when Duell, Sloan and Pearce published *Pipe Night* in 1945, the thirty-one stories showed a return to the briefer form.

The title of *Pipe Night* derived from a custom at O'Hara's New York club, The Players, which designated as "pipe night" evenings on which members were entertained by other members: pros working for pros. And in a laudatory preface, *New Yorker* editor Wolcott Gibbs (after whom O'Hara named his fictional Gibbsville) favorably compared O'Hara's stories to Fitzgerald's and Hemingway's, but especially to Sinclair Lewis's. According to Gibbs, O'Hara had become "one of the very few considerable writers," and *Pipe Night* showed O'Hara working at the top of his form. Readers obviously agreed, buying the collection avidly enough to generate six additional printings of *Pipe Night* in 1945 alone.

The popularity of *Pipe Night* owed little to O'Hara's clearly peripheral involvement with the war; stories such as "Patriotism" and "The Lieutenant" (*New Yorker*, 13 November 1943) are O'Hara's usual revelations of infidelity among characters, some of whom happen to wear uniforms. A more likely explanation of the demand for *Pipe Night* is the sense that one gets from O'Hara's stories that American society has been al-

14——
ASSEMBLY 11|13|24½ Times Roman (RH) 3439

"No thanks. I came to fetch you to Mrs. Stratton's," said Blawen. He pointed to an old jeep with a winter top.

"How did that happen?"

"How did that happen? Why, she just called me up and said I was to go fetch you at five o'clock in my jeep. Wasn't any more to it than that. But I *imagine* she figured'd take a jeep to get you there, and she's pretty near right. You'd never get up the hill in your car, 'specially without chains. No Charley Cooper, I see."

"No, he must be counting on all this to melt away."

"Charley's all right once he gets working, but I never saw such a man for putting things off. Deliberating, he always calls it. But there's other names for it, too. Good afternoon, Mizz Reese."

"Mr. Blawen. You going to be our transportation?"

"Looks that way. She's all cleaned out inside," said Blawen. "I even got a heater in there for you."

"Not just for us, I hope," said Georgia Reese.

"Oh, no. If you mean did I put it in special," he smiled. "Oh, no. Those days are gone forever. But mind you, I seen the day when the Stratton family *would* do a thing like that. Why, they tell me she used to have a man come all the way from Philadelphia just to play a few tunes on the organ." He lowered his voice. "Paid him five——hundred——dollars." They got in the jeep. "Five hundred dollars, just to play a few tunes on the pipe organ. One time they had Woodrow Wilson here for Sunday dinner. The President of the United States. And Old Stratton wasn't even a Democrat. But him and Wilson were acquainted with one another outside of politics. Oh, yes, there was always 'something going on around here in those days. Twenty-eight people on the payroll, sometimes more."

"You don't work for Mrs. Stratton, do you?" said Evan Reese.

"Only when she has something special and I can spare the time. Like today, she knows I have my jeep, so she phoned and said would I call for you and Mizz Reese. I always try to accommodate her if I can. Never been here before, have you?"

"No, but how did you know that?" said Evan Reese.

"How did I know that? Just took a good guess. She don't have many visitors. She only got twenty acres left out of what used to be eight hundred, and I guess she feels hemmed in. Here we are."

"Thank you very much," said Evan Reese.

"Oh, I'll be here when you come out," said Blawen.

"How long will *we* be here?" said Evan Reese.

"Well, maybe that's not for me to say, but not more'n a half an hour."

Frank Stratton came out to greet them. "I heard the jeep," he said. "I'm so glad you could come."

A maid took their things and Frank Stratton showed the way to the library. Mrs. Stratton turned from gazing into the fireplace, but she did not rise. Her left hand clutched the silver mounting of a highly polished walnut walking stick. She was obviously very feeble.

"Mother, this is Mr. and Mrs. Reese."

"Good afternoon. I'm glad you could come," said Mrs. Stratton. "Did you have a nice ride in Elwood Blawen's hideous conveyance? But it does do the trick, doesn't it?"

"My first ride in a jeep," said Georgia Reese.

"And you, Mr. Reese? Your first ride in a jeep too?" said the old lady.

"Oh, no. I did some painting for the Navy during the war, and I rode in a lot of jeeps."

"What kind of painting? Camouflage?" said Mrs. Stratton.

"No. I did some pictures of the landings at Iwo Jima, in 1945."

"Photography?"

Galley proof for O'Hara's 1961 short-story collection with his annotations for "Mrs. Stratton of Oak Knoll" (John O'Hara Collection, Pennsylvania State University Libraries)

tered not at all by World War II. "The Next-to-Last Dance of the Season" (*New Yorker*, 18 September 1943) takes place in 1942, but–save for references to gasoline coupons and sons in service–the time could be 1922 or 1962. Nazis and Pacific atolls are offstage in O'Hara's world, and readers of *Pipe Night* derived commonplace and secure satisfaction from reading O'Hara's usual mordant anatomies of Hollywood stupidity ("The Magical Numbers," *New Yorker*, 18 January 1941) and violence ("The King of the Desert," *New Yorker*, 30 November 1940). Life–such as it is–goes on.

Although several of the stories in *Pipe Night* are built on revelations of hidden evil–pride in "On Time" (*Collier's*, 8 April 1944), cuckoldry in "Radio" (*New Yorker*, 22 May 1943), social exclusion in "Where's the Game?"–O'Hara can be genuinely compassionate in a story such as "Now We Know" (*New Yorker*, 5 June 1943): a Jewish bus driver and an Irish secretary can never consummate their hopeless love and thus separate. "Bread Alone" (*New Yorker*, 23 September 1939) involves the shy love shown by a black son who presents his father with a baseball after a Yankees game. Some critics have argued that O'Hara verges on the sentimental when he really *likes* his characters, but these stories work effectively.

Nevertheless, O'Hara is undoubtedly at his best in the sensibility story that reveals the weaknesses just below the social surface of the recognizable American. "Graven Image" (*New Yorker*, 13 March 1943) is prototypical: a powerful Washington bureaucrat is interviewing a Harvard acquaintance for a wartime job. The job looks to be all set until the applicant expresses relief that his formerly obscure classmate bears no grudges at not having been elected to an elite undergraduate club years ago. But of course the now-powerful under secretary has never forgiven the snub, and the applicant will not get the job. Both men come off badly–one still a snob, the other a hypersensitive parvenu. The husband in "Civilized" (*New Yorker*, 4 December 1943) similarly reveals his cynicism, manipulativeness, and egocentricity; his wife can now divorce him with a clearer understanding of the reasons that their marriage failed.

One of the few academic critics to take these characters and their concerns seriously was Lionel Trilling, who–in a review of *Pipe Night* in the *New York Times* (18 March 1945)–claimed that O'Hara was "at present the only American writer to whom America presents itself as a social scene as it once presented itself to Howells or Edith

Wharton." The Modern Library would use a modified version of this review as an introduction to *Selected Short Stories of John O'Hara* in 1956. Relations were always cordial between Trilling and O'Hara, who allowed one story from *Pipe Night*, "Summer's Day" (*New Yorker*, 29 August 1942), to be one of his rare anthologized stories in a textbook edited by Trilling.

Trilling's choice of "Summer's Day" was apt because this story is at once typical and yet outstanding O'Hara. Set at a Long Island beach club, the story's center of consciousness is A. T. Atwell, an old-money aristocrat whose social eminence is inherited but whose poise is nevertheless fragile. In dramatic contrast to Atwell is the Irish arriviste, Mr. O'Donnell, father of seven sons but still full of frustrated social aspiration dating back to his years at Yale. O'Hara's dialogue reveals that the Atwells' only daughter hanged herself, that Mr. and Mrs. Atwell are too old to conceive other children, and that Mr. Atwell's pride in his family name is badly wounded. He will die without hope, just as Mr. O'Donnell's life is darkened by thwarted hopes of superiority. Each is the measure of the other's failure.

By now O'Hara's short stories were recognizable hallmarks of his characteristically tough and unsparing vision of American life. Reviewing O'Hara's next story collection, *Hellbox*, in the *New York Times Book Review* (17 August 1947), Richard Sullivan contended that O'Hara wrote with "not only accuracy and brilliance, but with a kind of terrible, unmerciful disgust" and with a "grim, almost moralistic attitude toward his subjects." The twenty-six stories in *Hellbox* (a box into which printers throw pieces of lead type before melting them down for reuse) come together more gloomily than ever before.

The moral disgust supposedly so evident in *Hellbox* has been attributed by some critics to O'Hara's own low self-esteem at this point in his career. In any event, something close to pure alienation reigns in such stories as "Someone to Trust" (*New Yorker*, 22 March 1947), where no one can be trusted. The protagonist of "Ellie" (*New Yorker*, 19 October 1946) turns out to be a narcissistic racist, and Mr. Osgood in "Wise Guy" (*New Yorker*, 26 May 1945) plots an assignation during a meeting with his disillusioned son. The aristocratic rich exercise feudal control over the lives of their dispirited retainers in "Other Women's Households" (*New Yorker*, 24 May 1947). The total effect of O'Hara's arctic vision in *Hellbox* goes beyond sensibility to near misanthropy, the compassion of *Pipe Night* having given way to emptiness, sadness, loneliness, and failure.

Perhaps the chief cause of this unhappiness in O'Hara's fictional world is the disorderly sexuality of his characters. Sexual attraction, sexual competition, and sexual assertion move O'Hara's characters helplessly, and regularly the conflict in an O'Hara story will occur between society's demand for moral order and the anarchy of sexual desire. O'Hara consistently argued that as a realist, he had to depict life as it was and that sex was at the core of all human activity. Love was sexual but so was hate. The anomalies inherent in sexually motivated conduct had always been inspiring to O'Hara, particularly in his novels, but the stories in *Hellbox* increasingly feature overt sexual conflict.

Of course O'Hara's focus on the dangers of human sexual activity did not originate in *Hellbox;* critics were attacking O'Hara's explicitness about sex as early as *Appointment in Samarra*. Nevertheless, overt sexual themes were for a long time excluded from his short stories because of the rather more prudish standards set by the popular magazines in which O'Hara's short fiction first appeared. The *New Yorker* would bend more than *Collier's* or *Good Housekeeping*, but even there Harold Ross kept a lid on O'Hara's treatment of sex. That sexual themes are more common in *Hellbox* says less about O'Hara's views than about increasingly liberal attitudes toward sex in popular magazines and perhaps in American society generally.

Even the *New Yorker*, however, could not print one story appearing for the first time in *Hellbox:* "A Phase of Life" is set in a bordello and features the dazed consciousness of an alcoholic pimp at its center. The perversions of the local aristocracy are contemptible, but no one comes off well in the story. Less sordid is a story with a strong undercurrent of potential sexual license, "The Moccasins" (*New Yorker*, 25 January 1947). Doc Fothergill is a society parasite with the cool amorality of a procurer; yet he is still "romantic" enough to send away a girl who will get hurt in his reptilian world.

Disruptive sexual desire and its ramifications among the aristocratic landed gentry constituted a theme which O'Hara incorporated in *A Rage to Live*, and the novel form was to preoccupy him for an entire decade. In fact, O'Hara sporadically insisted that his longer works were more significant. In 1955 he wrote: "I don't think I'll write any more short stories. In very re-

cent years I have been made sharply aware of the passage of time and the preciousness of it, and there are so many big things I want to do. But during the Thirties and Forties stories were part of me as I was part of these nights and days, when time was cheap and everlasting and one could say it all in two thousand words." At the same time O'Hara was fully aware of his own achievements in short fiction, and the 1950s saw the beginning of O'Hara's experimentation with a hybrid fictional form–the novella.

Literary historians have for years struggled unsuccessfully with the distinctions which set off the novella from the short novel, or the novelette, or the *nouvelle*. Bruccoli contends that an O'Hara novella is an augmented short story, an O'Hara novelette a truncated novel. O'Hara himself distinguished his novellas as works "written from memory with a minimum of research" dependent upon "the limits of my own observation." Certainly a novella is shorter than a novel but longer than a story; in O'Hara's case, a novella ranges from eighty-five hundred to forty-seven thousand words.

Nancy Walker has characterized an O'Hara novella as "a detailed portrait of a single character, relationship or conflict over a considerable period of time." Often the narrative voice is more personal, ruminative, descriptive, and the novella has a sense of resolution absent from the story. In any event, O'Hara himself became increasingly comfortable with the form, and he was to use it repeatedly in the 1950s and 1960s.

O'Hara's first experiment with the novella form was "The Doctor's Son" in his first collection of short stories in 1935. The relatively short time scheme of "The Doctor's Son" may put Walker's definition to the test, but the work does feature the perspective that O'Hara uses again in the three novellas collected in *Sermons and Soda-Water*, the novellas serving as a transition to his full return to the short-story form a year later.

Malloy's function in these three novellas–*Imagine Kissing Pete, The Girl on the Baggage Truck*, and *We're Friends Again*–is to unify the events of the characters' lives by imposing on them the logic of his own perceptions. However, Malloy remains detached from the action, much more an observer than the participant that he is in "The Doctor's Son." Likewise Malloy has aged commensurately with his creator, and he is content to tell these stories with more compassion and tolerance than would have been possible for the angry young man of the earlier fiction.

Reviewers were quite enthusiastic about *Sermons and Soda-Water*, celebrating O'Hara's mastery of the novella form and unanimously praising the economy with which he used the experiences of his characters and their narrator to present social and political reality. It was the novellas in *Sermons and Soda-Water*, in fact, that began the eventually routine critical judgment that O'Hara's short fiction is better than his novels.

O'Hara does use the novella form very skillfully to portray the forces of time and history which change character. The vividness of his images of the excesses of the rich on Long Island is ultimately more interesting than the central figure, Charlotte Sears, in *The Girl on the Baggage Truck*. And the politics and atmosphere of the wartime years enliven *We're Friends Again*. Probably best in terms of character development is *Imagine Kissing Pete*, a Gibbsville story recounting the drunken and infidelity-filled marriage of aristocratic Bobbie McCrea and her ineffectual husband, Pete. O'Hara accentuates her snobbery and disappointment, his resentment and envy. Illness and poverty reduce Pete and Bobbie to despair, but their marriage endures, at least partly because of their love for and pride in a brilliant son. Malloy joins in their tears sentimentally at the son's graduation exercises, knowing that some order has returned to their lives because they have developed tolerance (or at least resignation).

Malloy's increased forbearance in *Sermons and Soda-Water* does not vitiate a theme that haunts all three novellas: loneliness. Ubiquitous on all social levels and in all regions of the country, loneliness is Malloy's fate. "What, really, can any of us know about any of us," Malloy muses, "and why must we make such a thing of loneliness when it is the final condition of us all? And where would love be without it?" This quasi-Emersonian theory of compensations adds a glimmer of optimism to the novellas, making even James Malloy (called "the lonesomest son of a bitch I know" by a friend) more serene.

If either O'Hara's critics or his audience had taken the more sentimental nostalgia of *Sermons and Soda-Water* to have become habitual, they were returned to reality in 1961 by O'Hara's first collection of short stories in almost fifteen years, *Assembly*. The twenty-six stories in this book are not as monotonously frigid in their themes as were the stories dating from the 1940s, but O'Hara's fictional world has hardly become Edenic by the 1960s. The traditional O'Hara situations and conflicts reappear in *Assembly*: failed love, obsessive infidelity, potential and real danger in sexual competition. O'Hara belied imputations of softening with stories such as "In a Grove"; this gruesome tale features a murderous ex-Hollywood producer, exiled to the desert after repeated failures in his films, who lures an old acquaintance into bed with his own wife, then kills them both. Or a story such as "The Sharks" with its own "love" murder and the impending invasion of a formerly staid summer colony by homosexuals. O'Hara began his moral animadversions against homosexuality in *Assembly*, although he was later to concentrate his disgust on lesbianism as the more perverse and dangerous of sexual preferences.

On the other hand, the majority of stories in *Assembly* are less egregiously violent and perverse than "The Sharks." Like O'Hara and his alter ego Malloy, the other protagonists are aging, showing less impetuosity in their affairs, limiting their desires (in "The Lighter When Needed" and "You Can Always Tell Newark") so as to preserve the decency of order in their marriages. Promiscuity may be the opiate of the masses ("Mary and Norma," *New Yorker*, 5 August 1961), but "Mrs. Stratton of Oak Knoll" dramatizes the perseverance of mother love in the face of disastrous weakness in children and society. Accordingly, O'Hara—speaking through Malloy—settles for a qualified stoicism in *Assembly*: "After you've lived a good many years I don't see how you can be anything but cynical, since all any of us have a right to expect is an even break, and not many get that."

Assembly, then, marks a new beginning for O'Hara as a writer of short stories. By 1961 his stories had grown longer (an average of fifty-seven hundred words in *Assembly*, over twice the length of the 1940s stories in *Hellbox* and almost three times the length of O'Hara's stories from the 1930s). The increasingly relaxed pace of O'Hara's narration allows for more overt commentary on events by Malloy and other (editorially omniscient) narrators and for the inclusion of more specific historical and cultural detail in the longer stories. "A Case History," a novella-length story in *Assembly*, involves a typical O'Hara theme—the ironic difference between the public and private selves of an ordinary Gibbsville physician—but the story demands length because of the narrative strategy that O'Hara adopts. The protagonist, Buz Drummond, is revealed to the reader by an omniscient author, by Buz himself, by his wife,

O'Hara in his study at Linebrook, Princeton, New Jersey

by his mistress, and by a local politician. Multiple points of view are more common in a novel than in a story, but O'Hara's fondness for an intermediate form like the novella became increasingly evident in the last decade of his life.

Moreover, O'Hara could assert his creative independence more easily in the 1960s. No longer was he dependent for his living on the publication of his stories in magazines; as a best-selling novelist, O'Hara could write the kind of story *he* wanted and yet be certain that Random House would include it in the next collection. Before 1961 only ten percent of O'Hara's stories were original to his collections, that is, not previously published in magazines. After 1961 fifty percent of the stories first appeared in O'Hara's own collections. Consequently, an O'Hara story of the 1960s was more likely to have been shaped entirely by its creator, exclusive of the requirements or limitations of magazine editors.

For the next several years O'Hara published dozens of short stories from the "unlimited supply" that he bragged of in *Assembly*. The first collection to appear was *The Cape Cod Lighter* (1962), its title deriving from a device used to kindle fires in fireplaces and signifying human fires ignited by some outside agency. Audiences may have been mystified by the obscurity of the title, but *The Cape Cod Lighter* proved to be O'Hara's most

popular collection of short stories: seven Random House printings and three Bantam softcover printings. Eventually the book sold over half a million copies in the paperback edition.

Such large sales are surprising since O'Hara did nothing in *The Cape Cod Lighter* that he had not done in earlier collections. Furthermore, although the general level of the stories is high, it is no higher than usual. What impressed audiences in all of O'Hara's last collections of short stories was the enormous range of his interests and curiosity. The twenty-three stories in *The Cape Cod Lighter* depict Gibbsville's working-class bars, the adulteries of the country club set on Long Island, the lonely despair of bourgeois spinsters. O'Hara seems not to be quite as obsessed with aging and death as he was in *Assembly*, where more than half the stories are so centered, but the best stories in *The Cape Cod Lighter* focus on loss.

"The First Day," for example, concerns the return of a once-famous journalist to a job on his small hometown newspaper; alcoholism and who knows what else have diminished this proud man who cannot even keep the interest of his editor at lunch. In "Sunday Morning" (*New Yorker*, 13 January 1962) a housewife suddenly realizes that she can no longer content herself with husband-children-house, that her life is mostly futile.

Loss is the theme of "Pat Collins," generally conceded to be the best story in *The Cape Cod Lighter*. Another novella-length examination of the ironic consequences of sexual license and relations among the social classes of Gibbsville, the story is about a man whose wife destroys his relationship with a close friend by sleeping with him. Both Pat Collins and his wife Madge are attracted to Whit Hofman for his aristocratic grace, but adultery destroys their association. Pat will have another friend, but Madge will never know his name; her sexuality will not disrupt Pat's new world. Still, "Pat Collins" ends not with hope but with an echo of the lost friendship between Pat and Whit.

It is a tribute to O'Hara's versatility to contrast the mature despair of the cuckolded Pat Collins with the deftly rendered adolescent infatuation of Ted for an older girl in "Winter Dance" (*New Yorker*, 22 September 1962). Replicating O'Hara's own experiences, this story's dialogue strikes the perfect combination of love, embarrassment, and hope. Leavening O'Hara's nostalgia is the story's awareness of the real pain of the boy's plight.

Indeed, a greater compassion betokens O'Hara's attitude in more stories than ever before in *The Hat on the Bed* (1963). The more cynical reviewers maintained that O'Hara had begun watering down some of his more severe ironies once he found a new market for his short stories in the rigorously optimistic *Saturday Evening Post*. Yet perhaps this collection's most sentimental story, "The Man on the Tractor," first appeared in the *New Yorker* (22 June 1963), site of the traditionally savage O'Hara story. At any rate, "The Man on the Tractor" features the Denisons, once Gibbsville's Scott and Zelda Fitzgerald, who have returned to their hometown after thirty years of the fashionable life in New York and Connecticut. Gibbsville, their childhood friends, the past itself is decaying, dying. George Denison's response is tempered romance: "Life has been awful to them, Pam, the town and the people, and it hasn't been nearly as bad to you and me. Not yet, anyway. But our luck will start running out. We're getting there. And I always wanted to bring you here and tell you that I've always loved you. Here, where I told you the first time." Such sentiment, now unabashedly admirable in O'Hara's eyes, has become characteristic of the middle-aged heroes and beyond. These men (and sometimes their women) embrace James Malloy's candor, honesty, and willingness to share.

The Hat on the Bed recalls the old superstition that a hat on a bed will bring bad luck. With this motif in mind, O'Hara consistently contrasts the enduring love of the Denisons or the realization of two friends of forty years in "The Flatted Saxophone" (*New Yorker*, 1 June 1963) that remaining friends is better than becoming lovers with situations as bleak as any in the early pathetic stories. The good fortune and good sense of *some* O'Hara characters is hardly universal, and "Exterior: with Figure" (*Saturday Evening Post*, 1 June 1963) brings back a sense of jeopardy dating from his very first writings, and the major theme in *Appointment in Samarra*. "There are, most definitely, such things as hard-luck people, hard-luck families," James Malloy insists in "Exterior: with Figure"; "we hesitate to bring up the family name for fear of hearing one more bit of evidence that bad luck begets bad luck, may have to endure not a single disaster but a life-time of it." Malloy is recounting the fall of the Armour family from upper-middle-class rectitude to poverty, madness, and despair in Gibbsville. Their descent is an example of hereditary misfortune, but

Malloy, more stoic with age, can only puzzle over the calamities of the Armours: "I do not know. I wish I knew."

Malloy's puzzlement did not prevent his creator from continuing to pour out stories. Exactly a year after *The Hat on the Bed* came an even longer collection of twenty-eight stories, *The Horse Knows the Way* (1964). In his foreword to this collection O'Hara once again announced his decision to forgo the writing of more short stories, in part because his critics acknowledged how good he was with this form. O'Hara had for years used the forewords to his collections of stories to repay the hostility of "what I contemptuously refer to as the academics" with his own ill will and assertiveness. "I have work to do," he proudly informed readers of *The Horse Knows the Way*, "and I am afraid not to do it."

O'Hara included some excellent work in *The Horse Knows the Way*, further proof that he was continuing to experiment with the short-story form. In a note prefaced to "The Lawbreaker" (*Saturday Evening Post*, 16 November 1963), O'Hara claimed that "the so-called 'popular' plot stories did bear little relation to truth and life. But having been one of the leading practitioners of the oblique and plotless, I have recently been putting action back into my stories." O'Hara is right about "The Lawbreaker," which does involve some suspense and complicated action, but O'Hara's stories remain quintessentially his, still more concerned with the psychological and ethical effects of events than with the action itself. The expanded length of the typical O'Hara story in the 1960s (including the several novellas included in the collections of this decade) does allow room for more action, but complications of plot are never really characteristic of O'Hara's work.

What became more characteristic of O'Hara's stories in the 1960s is his increasing use of The Region, his Gibbsville-Lantenengo anthracite territory, as the setting for his stories. Even the title of *The Horse Knows the Way* evokes the past in its quotation from Lydia Maria Child's poem "Thanksgiving Day": "Over the river and through the wood, / To grandmother's house we go; / The horse knows the way / To carry the sleigh / Through the white and drifted snow." O'Hara set twelve of the stories in *The Horse Knows the Way* in The Region, and yet–in reflection of his personal ambivalence toward the area of his youth–O'Hara is rarely nostalgic about the coal country. "Zero" (*New Yorker*, 28 December

1963) is representative: Dick Pfeister is a melancholy bank clerk caught in a joyless adultery. He has paid off his mistress, temporarily, with an abortion and cash. But his wife knows, and when he slaps her, she threatens to kill him: " 'Go ahead, you'd be doing me a favor,' he said. The strange simple words shocked her. Whatever else he said to her, those words she recognized as the truth; at this moment he wished to be dead and free. More than free of her, he wished to be free of the other woman. . . . She was looking at destruction and she had had no part of it."

Another first-rate story, demonstrably concerned with sensibility and not action, is "The Bonfire" (*Saturday Evening Post*, 10 October 1964). Its author was particularly proud of this story, which dramatizes the distinctive O'Hara theme of loneliness. A young widow, finally determined to emerge after her mourning, approaches a neighbor's bonfire on the beach: "She walked on and the voices grew more distinct, the voices of young women and young men, a harsh and frightening chorus of people who did not want her. . . . Though they were ignorant of her existence they were commanding her to stay away." Kitty ends the story in despair, running all the way home.

Few of the stories in *The Hat on the Bed* and *The Horse Knows the Way* are full-scale novellas of the kind O'Hara perfected in *Sermons and Soda-Water*. Several of the stories in *The Hat on the Bed* are quite long, including "Ninety Minutes Away" and "Yucca Knolls" (*Show Magazine*, April 1963). Walker has shown that sheer length is not determinative of an O'Hara novella; both of these long narratives above remain stories because their characters are static and their actions unresolved. Nevertheless, O'Hara returned to the fully developed novella form frequently in his next collection, *Waiting for Winter* (1966).

Four novellas dominate the twenty-one stories in *Waiting for Winter*: two are set in The Region ("The Skeletons" and "Andrea") and two in Hollywood ("James Francis and the Star" and "Natica Jackson"). Edgar Shawen has found in this collection an increased emphasis upon individual initiative in creating a situation in which love and security can flourish. Courage and discipline can free O'Hara's characters from the deterministic forces formerly circumscribing them. At the same time, other critics have stressed a pure futility in the lives of the wife killers in "Fatimas and Kisses" (*New Yorker*, 21 May 1966) and "The Neighborhood" (*New Yorker*, 15 May 1965), or O'Hara's

emphasis upon alcoholic weakness of will in "The Assistant" (*New Yorker*, 3 July 1965). Finally, "Natica Jackson," with its vengeful Medea echoes, can be interpreted as an amoral collapse as well as a discovery of surrogate parents. Both the Pennsylvania novellas are gloomy accounts of loveless, self-satisfied people.

Still, decency and responsibility triumph in "The Weakling," in which a rich Chicagoan agrees to help care for an institutionalized old girlfriend as long as his associates realize that he does so altruistically, not guiltily. James Francis's long friendship with Rod Fulton does survive in "James Francis and the Star," and Dixon and Sophie Hightower have an interesting marriage in "The General" because of (not in spite of) Dixon's transvestism. Finally, a January-June "romance"–based on trust and solidity, not sexual whim–looks as if it might succeed in "Yostie" (*Saturday Evening Post*, 4 June 1966).

In his foreword to *Waiting for Winter* O'Hara explains that he wrote these short stories during the summer, reserving the more solemn and portentous winters for his novels; yet the title "has other implications as well." Even as rigorously nonsymbolic as O'Hara tried to be, he wanted his readers to catch the undercurrent of mortality in *Waiting for Winter*, embodied especially well in "Flight," the best story in the collection. This is a tight and perceptive tale of an aging playwright who falls on winter ice, goes over his life with his wife in a clearheaded, rational way, then drifts into a dream of his past. Frightened, Charles Kingsmith tries to be optimistic: "I'm convinced that most people really know just about how long they're going to last, and they guide their lives and expend their resources accordingly. If you ask a man when he's going to die, he won't be able to tell you, but he knows. I know when I'm going to die, but it isn't to be from this fall." Notwithstanding, Kingsmith dies. This summary does not touch the chief effect of the story, which is the love of Charles and Emily Kingsmith, a love that has endured for forty years.

The Kingsmiths' marriage, like the Denisons' in "The Man on the Tractor," stands in direct contrast to the loveless and barren unions that typify marriage in O'Hara's novels. Of course, emotionally stunted characters exist in O'Hara's later stories, but their aridity is no match for that shown by the protagonists of *The Instrument* or *The Lockwood Concern* (1965). Symptomatic of the desiccation of relationships in the unhealthiest corners of O'Hara's fictional world is the lesbianism that became an almost obsessive component of the later fiction. Heterosexual relationships in O'Hara had always been freighted with peril, or, as John Cheever put it, "O'Hara's vision of things is the premise of irony generated by a ceremonial society and an improvisational erotic life." However, lesbianism became the most grievous sin in the canon of morality for O'Hara's characters.

And Other Stories (1968), the last collection to be published during O'Hara's lifetime, includes twelve stories that bear witness to the "moral disgust" stirred by lesbianism in O'Hara's world. Nowhere is the danger of such perversion more obvious than in "The Broken Giraffe." Here a characteristically brutal and vulgar lesbian villain, Margo, seduces the aristocratic Mary Brewer, and O'Hara obviously believes that only disaster can follow. Less clear is Isabel Barley's bisexuality in "A Few Trips and Some Poetry," a novella. Once again the setting is Lantenengo County and the narrator James Malloy, who carries on a long, sporadic, but sensuously satisfying love affair with Isabel. Malloy is at his most philosophical about art and religion and life in "A Few Trips and Some Poetry," yet all the men in this story fear and hate lesbians: "But when Bobbie [a lesbian] gets through with a woman she's corrupted her, psychologically. . . . I consider her the most evil woman in New York." Isabel takes a lesbian lover and lives contentedly with her for twenty years, a relationship that even the hypermasculine Malloy must honor when he sees the two together. Malloy's tolerance may be helped along when Isabel reveals that she is dying of cancer, but she is certainly not the most evil woman in Lantenengo County. "A Few Trips and Some Poetry" ends with more pity than anger.

Furthermore, if corruption reigns, courageous compassion can banish it. A very subtle demonstration of this thesis occurs in "We'll Have Fun," the story of an Irish stableman made redundant by the automobile and a lonely, pretty young woman whose lesbianism is only suggested. These two superfluous outsiders can forge a tentative (because noncarnal) bond in the face of a world that excludes them, and even the homophobic O'Hara can only wish this odd alliance well.

Isabel Barley's uncontrolled sexual appetite could easily have moved her into the gallery of evil harpies who dominate O'Hara's novels. Yet none of the females in the stories can compare

O'Hara's tombstone, Princeton Cemetery (Willard Starks)

with the truly memorable wantons of the longer fiction–Gloria Wandrous of *Butterfield 8*, Grace Tate of *A Rage to Live*, Hedda Millhouser of *Ourselves to Know* (1960), Mary Eaton of *From the Terrace*. Perhaps O'Hara needed the scope of the novel in order to do misogynic justice to this heedless and brazen matronage, but whatever the case, women in the stories, though often wicked, lack the unregeneracy of the novels' sirens.

By no means, however, has rectitude and peace come to Gibbsville in *And Other Stories*. "Barred" (*Saturday Evening Post*, 7 October 1967) concerns a callow young Irishman who is causing trouble for the local madam; "The Gangster" (*Saturday Evening Post*, 18 November 1967) is about another ambitious Irishman who fails to cut in on the monopoly of the boss bootlegger of Lantenengo County. "How Old, How Young" (*New Yorker*, 1 July 1967) involves embezzlement and adultery in the country-club set. Personal relationships and relationships among the classes have improved little from the surly, sensitive, competitive conflicts of earlier collections.

All of O'Hara's short-story collections of the 1960s sold well; *Waiting for Winter*, for example, required eight printings in Bantam paperback edition. Even *And Other Stories*, a collection which raised the total number of O'Hara stories published in the 1960s to 137, sold out its first Random House hardcover printing of fifty thousand copies and required a large second printing as well. Therefore, when Albert Erskine, O'Hara's Random House editor, proposed issuing a posthumous book of uncollected stories, most of which O'Hara had written in the 1940s, few doubted its sales potential. For once, however, the doubters had their day when *The Time Element and Other Stories* (1972) could sell only about half of its single hardcover printing and was not printed in a paperback edition at all. Perhaps the public had had enough of O'Hara; perhaps the especially dismal critical reception of *The Time Element* ("phonier than life," grumped the *New York Times* reviewer Anatole Broyard) discouraged buyers; perhaps these stories from the 1940s paled beside O'Hara's more mature work in the 1960s. At any rate, *The Time Element* failed to achieve the popularity that O'Hara's other recent short-story collections had unfailingly won.

Probably *The Time Element* failed because its audience never understood what such a collection demonstrated about O'Hara. Erskine argued that an acknowledged master of the short story such as O'Hara deserved to have even fugitive pieces collected: "his reputation does not need enhancing," Erskine wrote in a foreword, "nor can it suffer from the exposure of work below the level of his best. . . ." The thirty-four stories selected by Erskine are not as good as the majority of stories in *Pipe Night* and *Hellbox*, but their configuration is similar–terse (twenty-two-hundred-word average), urban, heavily ironic, seemingly more anecdotal and contrived than his best. One especially hostile critic called these stories "finger sandwiches," cunningly made but ultimately unsatisfying.

The critics were too harsh on *The Time Element*. If its stories are not O'Hara's best, they do flesh out the concerns that dominated O'Hara's middle period. No experienced reader could fail to recognize a story such as "Not Always" (*New Yorker*, 11 January 1947) as O'Hara's. The despair that Melvin Langley feels after his wife's cool snub reminds him that *her* wealth and social position are responsible for his success is intrinsic to O'Hara's understanding of the operations of the ego. Moreover, O'Hara's tone in "Not Always" is

at its most scrupulously dispassionate; it is apparent that Langley has brought this emptiness on himself with his anger and envy.

Most of the stories dating from the 1940s in *The Time Element* share the bleakness and irony of "Not Always." As sensibility stories, they engender either disgust or aversion in the reader for the manipulators and cheaters who dominate their weaker contemporaries in such works as "The Time Element" and "Memorial Fund." Occasionally O'Hara allows the sentimental to slip through: a murderously unhappy man is redeemed by the kiss of a little boy in "The Dry Murders" (*New Yorker*, 18 October 1947), and the last story of the collection, "That First Husband" (*Saturday Evening Post*, 21 November 1959), looks forward to the successful, if necessarily compromised, marriages of older folk.

Erskine had promised that *The Time Element* would be the first of several projected volumes of uncollected O'Hara stories; it was followed by *Good Samaritan and Other Stories*. The fourteen stories in this collection, the last to be published, were written during the 1960s, and only two had previously been published in magazines. "The Good Samaritan" (*Saturday Evening Post*, 30 November 1968) is a particularly nasty little tale, told almost exclusively through dialogue, of adultery among the rich. The aging, bitter, pathetic creatures who bicker and fence in this story had been appearing in O'Hara's stories for decades, but their petty vengefulness never entirely stales. A reader would remember Willoughby Wood clearly had not O'Hara created other, more interesting villains in "Andrea" or "Zero." The stories in *Good Samaritan* are better than most of those in *The Time Element*, and O'Hara's last short-story collection showed a modest success critically and at the bookstores.

Erskine arranged *Good Samaritan* so that the last story in the last collection would be "Christmas Poem" (*New Yorker*, 19 December 1964). This story is personal, sentimental, nostalgic. Echoing O'Hara's own Christmases in Pottsville in the 1920s, "Christmas Poem" bears upon Billy Warden's desire to escape home for a gala house party being thrown by the wealthy Coopers upstate. Billy considers his family outrageously middle class and dull until he discovers that his father secretly writes a poem each Christmas for his mother, and has for a quarter of a century. "He wondered if Henrietta Cooper's father had ever written a poem to her mother. But he knew the answer to that." The triteness of this "home is best" sentimentality is vitiated by Billy's social ambitiousness and his parents' bourgeois shortcomings. But they love him, and he discovers that he loves them.

Certainly scholar-critics who attempt Miller's "good critical sifting" of fourteen volumes of O'Hara's short stories have set themselves a monumental task. Furthermore, the thorough researcher must plow through back files of the *New Yorker* and other magazines in order to read 82 additional O'Hara stories still uncollected. Most of the uncollected fiction is early ephemera, but occasionally one is struck by some solid fugitive story (such as "Little 'Chita," *Esquire*, August 1936) that should have displaced a marginal story in the collections. Faced with these 402 stories, however, an overworked scholar might well find it easy to join the chorus of O'Hara's traditional detractors: O'Hara wrote too much; he focused his fictional attentions too obsessively on adultery or snobbery (or both); his technical virtuosity faded in the later stories, and his sentimentality increased.

Yet any reader, a scholar, or the layman who constituted O'Hara's normal audience, will recognize a solid core of truly major short stories in the O'Hara canon. Those willing to seek out the best of O'Hara's stories will come to admire the careful and precise economy with which he dramatizes so many crises in the lives of his stories' protagonists. And despite critical animadversions that his range was narrow, the comprehensive O'Hara reader will discover that O'Hara's short fiction deals expertly with elemental concerns: inferiority, shame, pride, viciousness, guilt, resentment, parental neglect, violence, passionate sexual impulse, love, and death.

In the stories of the 1930s and 1940s O'Hara most often embodied his significant themes in monologues and dialogues, always ironic and often satiric, establishing the "perceptual distance" that is one of the trademarks of an early O'Hara story. Author and reader share a cool remoteness from the reality that the character understands, and the effect can be comic but is most often savage. As O'Hara's life and career progressed, his narrative technique became less dramatic, his intrusions more ruminative (especially in the voice of James Malloy, the author's surrogate), and his attitudes more compassionate. For all the softening of mood and tone in many of the stories of the late 1960s, O'Hara never wrote with philosophical serenity; to the end, a typical O'Hara story is most often a chronicle of the inability of twentieth-century Americans to cope with contradictory values.

What disturbed so many of O'Hara's critics was his unblinking attention to the social locus of his characters, to the paraphernalia of their bourgeois existence. An O'Hara story grounded all of its thematic abstractions and psychological acuity in a solidly explicit milieu. The short-story form forced O'Hara to suggest rather than enumerate the components of social status–begetting a concision that made particularly his early stories such spare little tales–but all of O'Hara's memorable characters are certifiably of this time, of that place.

Such attention to accuracy and material credibility, combined with a spare, nonmetaphoric style and a refusal to comment overtly on his characters, places O'Hara squarely within the realist-naturalist community. O'Hara was wholly comfortable within that tradition, proud of his precise observation and his correct rendering of the symbols of value in America. His dialect is flawlessly characteristic; his narration and description careful and exact. The people in his stories seem more often to be venal, greedy, and weak than imaginative, compassionate, and steadfast. No O'Hara character reaches for ideas or ideology, though most are incurably curious about their own caste and their betters.

The most serious criticism leveled at O'Hara is that he fails to create characters whose souls or minds soar, that they (and by inference their creator) are prisoners of sexual instinct and class envy. And in his more pedestrian stories, O'Hara does fail to reveal the motivations of his characters adequately. O'Hara confessed that he did not always know how his characters thought ("I wish I knew"), and the character-as-fate moving his men and women is sometimes left unexplained. They just act, and O'Hara records. For an author so committed to realistic, even positivistic explanations, O'Hara's failure thus to "see" constitutes a genuine flaw.

Nevertheless, at his best, O'Hara is truly excellent. His contemporaries have called him "a great professional" who lent "a ruthless perfection to some of the stories." Frank MacShane said it as well as anyone has: "O'Hara dramatizes the human condition in stories that are set in social conflict, but their point is usually not social at all." In fact, O'Hara's world is Manichean; his lubricious matrons and manipulative poseurs have ironic counterparts–the Denisons, the Kingsmiths, Mrs. Stratton of Oak Knoll, Dr. Malloy–

who personify love and loyalty and dedication and forgiveness and compassion. Even when O'Hara is unmasking hypocrisy, envy, or self-pity, he is always fair to his miscreants, careful to reveal the social and psychological pressures which generate their often deadly mischief. Above all O'Hara dealt honestly with his art and with his audience, and he created a truly significant body of short fiction during his four decades of work.

The clearest demonstration of the quality of O'Hara's accomplishment in short fiction is the unmistakably personal stamp that he put on his stories. He was indeed a great professional, accomplishing his thematic missions with pellucid prose, tight and inevitable structures, and rhythmic alterations of narrative technique that make any O'Hara story readable. Perhaps O'Hara's devotees cannot hope for the popular revival of an old-fashioned realist in the age of deconstructionism, but American literature will be diminished if readers forget John O'Hara. He was a short-story writer of tremendous virtuosity, variety, and significance.

Letters:

Selected Letters of John O'Hara, edited by Matthew J. Bruccoli (New York: Random House, 1978).

Bibliography:

Matthew J. Bruccoli, *John O'Hara: A Descriptive Bibliography* (Pittsburgh: University of Pittsburgh Press, 1978).

Biographies:

Finis Farr, *O'Hara: A Biography* (Boston: Little, Brown, 1972);

Matthew J. Bruccoli, *The O'Hara Concern: A Biography of John O'Hara* (New York: Random House, 1975);

Frank MacShane, *The Life of John O'Hara* (New York: Dutton, 1980).

References:

Charles Bassett, "John O'Hara: Irishman and American," *John O'Hara Journal*, 1 (Summer 1979): 1-81;

E. Russell Carson, *The Fiction of John O'Hara* (Pittsburgh: University of Pittsburgh Press, 1961);

Beverly Gary, "A Post Portrait: John O'Hara," *New York Post*, 24 May 1959, pp. 18-22;

Sheldon Grebstein, *John O'Hara* (New York: Twayne, 1966);

John O'Hara Journal, special issue, 3 (Fall / Winter 1980);

Robert Emmet Long, *John O'Hara* (New York: Ungar, 1983);

John Portz, "John O'Hara Up to Now," *College English*, 16 (May 1955): 493-499, 516;

Don Schanche, "John O'Hara Is Alive and Well in the First Half of the Twentieth Century," *Esquire*, 72 (August 1969): 84-86, 142-149;

Edgar Shawen, "The Unity of John O'Hara's *Waiting for Winter*," *John O'Hara Journal*, 5 (Winter 1982-83): 25-32;

Charles Walcutt, *John O'Hara* (Minneapolis: University of Minnesota Press, 1969);

Nancy Walker, " 'All That You Need to Know': John O'Hara's Achievement in the Novella," *John O'Hara Journal*, 4 (Spring / Summer 1981): 61-80.

Papers:

The largest collection of O'Hara's correspondence and manuscript material is in the John O'Hara Study of Pattee Library, Pennsylvania State University, University Park.

Dorothy Parker

(22 August 1893-7 June 1967)

Lucy M. Freibert
University of Louisville

See also the Parker entries in *DLB 11: American Humorists, 1800-1950* and *DLB 45: American Poets, 1880-1945*.

BOOKS: *Men I'm Not Married To*, published with *Women I'm Not Married To*, by Franklin P. Adams (Garden City, N.Y.: Doubleday, Page, 1922);

Enough Rope (New York: Boni & Liveright, 1926);

Sunset Gun (New York: Boni & Liveright, 1928);

Close Harmony, or The Lady Next Door: A Play in Three Acts, by Parker and Elmer Rice (New York & London: French, 1929);

Laments for the Living (New York: Viking, 1930; London: Longmans, Green, 1930);

Death and Taxes (New York: Viking, 1931);

After Such Pleasures (New York: Viking, 1933; London: Longmans, Green, 1934);

Not So Deep as a Well (New York: Viking, 1936; London: Hamilton, 1937); republished as *The Collected Poetry of Dorothy Parker* (New York: Modern Library, 1944);

Soldiers of the Republic (New York: Alexander Woollcott, 1938);

Here Lies: Collected Stories (New York: Viking, 1939; London: Longmans, Green, 1939); republished as *The Collected Stories of Dorothy Parker* (New York: Modern Library, 1942);

The Viking Portable Library Dorothy Parker (New York: Viking, 1944); republished as *The Indispensable Dorothy Parker* (New York: Book Society, 1944); republished as *Selected Short Stories* (New York: Editions for the Armed Services, 1944); revised and enlarged as *The Portable Dorothy Parker* (New York: Viking, 1973); republished as *The Collected Dorothy Parker* (London: Duckworth, 1973);

The Best of Dorothy Parker (London: Methuen, 1952);

The Ladies of the Corridor: A Play, by Parker and Arnaud d'Usseau (New York: Viking, 1954);

Constant Reader (New York: Viking, 1970); republished as *A Month of Saturdays* (London & Basingstoke: Macmillan, 1971).

Dorothy Parker

PLAY PRODUCTIONS: *Chauve-Souris* (revue), by Parker and others, New York, 49th Street Theatre, 1 February 1922;

Nero, by Parker and Robert Benchley, New York, Punch and Judy Theatre, 7 November 1922;

Round the Town (revue), New York, Century Root Theatre, 21 May 1924;

Close Harmony, or The Lady Next Door, by Parker and Elmer Rice, New York, Gaiety Theatre, 1 December 1924;

Shoot the Works (revue), New York, George M. Cohan Theatre, 21 July 1931;

The Coast of Illyria, by Parker and Ross Evans, Dallas, Margo Jones Theatre, April 1949;

The Ladies of the Corridor, by Parker and Arnaud d'Usseau, New York, Longacre Theatre, 21 October 1953.

MOTION PICTURES: *Business Is Business*, by Parker and George S. Kaufman, Paramount, 1925;

Here Is My Heart, Paramount, 1934;

One Hour Late, Paramount, 1935;

Mary Burns, Fugitive, Paramount, 1935;

Hands Across the Table, Paramount, 1935;

Paris in Spring, Paramount, 1935;

Big Broadcast of 1936, Paramount, 1935;

Three Married Men, screenplay by Parker and Alan Campbell, Paramount, 1936;

Lady, Be Careful, screenplay by Parker, Campbell, and Harry Ruskin, Paramount, 1936;

The Moon's Our Home, additional dialogue by Parker and Campbell, Paramount, 1936;

Suzy, screenplay by Parker, Campbell, Horace Jackson, and Lenore Coffee, M-G-M, 1936;

A Star Is Born, screenplay by Parker, Campbell, and Robert Carson, Selznick-United Artists, 1937;

Woman Chases Man, by Parker and Joe Bigelow, United Artists, 1937;

Sweethearts, screenplay by Parker and Campbell, M-G-M, 1938;

Trade Winds, screenplay by Parker, Campbell, and Frank R. Adams, United Artists, 1938;

Weekend for Three, screenplay by Parker and Campbell, RKO, 1941;

Saboteur, screenplay by Parker, Peter Viertel, and Joan Harrison, Universal, 1942;

Smash Up: The Story of a Woman, screen story by Parker and Frank Cavett, Universal, 1947;

The Fan, screenplay by Parker, Walter Reisch, and Ross Evans, 20th Century-Fox, 1949;

Queen for a Day, United Artists, 1950.

TELEVISION SCRIPTS: *The Lovely Leave, A Telephone Call*, and *Dusk Before Fireworks*, adapted for the Festival of Performing Arts, WNEW-TV, 8 May 1962.

OTHER: *The Portable F. Scott Fitzgerald*, edited by Parker (New York: Viking, 1945);

Short Story: A Thematic Anthology, edited by Parker and Frederick B. Shroyer (New York: Scribners, 1965).

PERIODICAL PUBLICATIONS: "Such a Pretty Little Picture," *Smart Set* (December 1922): 73 + ;

Bobbed Hair, collaborative novel, chapter 7, *Collier's* (17 January 1925);

"A Certain Lady," *New Yorker*, 1 (28 February 1925): 15-16;

"Travelogue," *New Yorker*, 2 (30 October 1926): 20-21;

"A Terrible Day Tomorrow," *New Yorker*, 4 (11 February 1928): 14-16;

"The Garter," *New Yorker*, 4 (8 September 1928): 17-18;

"But the One on the Right," *New Yorker*, 5 (19 October 1929): 25-27;

"Mrs. Carrington and Mrs. Crane," *New Yorker*, 9 (15 July 1933): 11-12;

"The Road Home," *New Yorker*, 9 (16 September 1933): 19-20;

"The Game," by Parker and Ross Evans, *Cosmopolitan* (December 1948): 58, 90 + ;

"Advice to the Little Peyton Girl," *Harper's Bazaar* (February 1953): 46-47, 84, 86;

"The Banquet of Crow," *New Yorker*, 33 (14 December 1957): 39-41.

In the 1920s and 1930s Dorothy Parker, the pampered, yet feared, darling of the New York smart set, was the most quotable, quoted, and misquoted person in America. She earned this reputation by creating humorous and satiric verse, writing trenchant and biting reviews for the *New Yorker* and *Vanity Fair*, and making clever and stinging comments often repeated in the conversations and columns of her Algonquin Hotel Round Table associates–Robert Benchley, Franklin Pierce Adams (F.P.A.), and Alexander Woollcott. Her verses and remarks, such as "Men seldom make passes / At girls who wear glasses," "a girl's best friend is her mutter," and "Verlaine was always chasing Rimbauds," became sophisticated parlance. Parker's permanent place among American writers, however, depends on the critical reputation afforded her short stories.

Parker was born Dorothy Rothschild in West End, New Jersey, of a Jewish father and a Scottish mother, J. Henry and Eliza A. Marston Rothschild. Her mother died when Parker was an infant, and Parker's relationships with her father and stepmother were marked by fear and hatred. Dismissed from Blessed Sacrament Convent school in New York for identifying the Immaculate Conception as spontaneous combustion, Parker entered Miss Dana's, an exclusive New Jersey girls' school, where she received an excellent classical education, read La Rochefoucauld, wrote poet-

Painting by Will Cotton of the Algonquin group's poker club. Parker is standing, far left; at table (counterclockwise from Parker): Franklin P. Adams, Henry Wise Miller, Gerald Brooks, Raoul Fleishmann, George S. Kaufman, Paul Hyde Bonner, Harpo Marx (with George Backer looking over his shoulder), Alexander Woollcott (with Alice Duer Miller looking over his shoulder), Heywood Broun; standing: Robert Benchley, Irving Berlin, Harold Ross, Beatrice Kaufman, Herbert Bayard Swope, Joyce Barbour, Crosby Gaige.

ry, and became interested in social issues. She graduated in 1911.

When her father died in 1912, leaving the family without money, Parker found work writing captions at *Vogue* for ten dollars a week. Two years later she moved to *Vanity Fair*, where, under Frank Crowninshield's tutelage, she developed the wit and critical taste that allowed her to move into New York's literary circles. In 1917 she married a young Wall Street broker, Edwin Bond Parker II. She divorced Parker in 1928 but retained his name even after marrying Alan Campbell in the early 1930s. Parker continued her work at *Vanity Fair*, becoming drama critic in 1918.

The 1920s proved a time of achievement and tension. Fired from *Vanity Fair* in 1920–chiefly for panning Billie Burke (wife of Florenz Ziegfeld) in the play *Caesar's Wife*–Parker turned to free-lancing and writing a drama column for *Ainslee's*. Her poems and short prose appeared in *Life*, the *Saturday Evening Post*, *Everybody's*, and the *Ladies' Home Journal*. *Smart Set* published her first short story, "Such a Pretty Little Picture," in its December 1922 issue.

Parker collaborated on plays with Benchley and Elmer Rice, on a book with F.P.A., and on a film script with George S. Kaufman. In 1926 she collected her best poems in *Enough Rope*, which quickly achieved best-seller status. From October 1927 to May 1928 and intermittently thereafter until 1933 she reviewed books for the *New Yorker* under the byline "Constant Reader." She praised Ernest Hemingway and Ring Lardner but demolished others, as demonstrated by her response to A. A. Milne's *The House at Pooh Corner* (1928): "Tonstant weader fwowed up." In 1928 Parker published a second volume of poems, *Sunset Gun*, and wrote a column for *McCall's*. In 1929 "Big Blonde" (*Bookman*, February 1929; collected in *Laments for the Living*, 1930) won the annual O. Henry short-story prize.

During this period Parker's personal life altered dramatically. In the early 1920s she frequented speakeasies and parties in uptown apartments. Her friends and acquaintances now included Irving Berlin, Deems Taylor, Paul Robeson, Neysa McMein, Hemingway, Lardner, and Zelda and Scott Fitzgerald. Twice she traveled to Europe as the guest of Sara and Gerald

Title page for Parker's first short-story collection. "Big Blonde," for which Parker received the 1929 O. Henry Memorial Award, is included in this volume.

Murphy. Always, she drank more. By the end of the decade, she had had several affairs, an abortion, a divorce from Eddie Parker, and three times had attempted suicide. In spite of everything, Parker continued to write, though suffering from writer's block. She told journalist Marion Capron a story took six months: "I think it out and then write it sentence by sentence—no first draft. I can't write five words, but that I change seven." Her perfectionism, inability to fit into the traditional woman's role, and increasing alcoholism kept her always at odds with herself and others.

The 1930s brought another spurt of productivity. Parker continued reviewing plays for the *New Yorker* and published her first two collections of short stories—*Laments for the Living* and *After Such Pleasures* (1933)—and two more volumes of poems—*Death and Taxes* (1931) and *Not So Deep as a Well* (1936). In 1933 or 1934 she married Campbell and moved to Hollywood. Parker contributed dialogue to screenplays and wrote screenplays herself, and with Campbell and others.

Though affluent, she spent the money as fast as she made it. She hated Hollywood and frequently returned to New York. In 1938 she and Campbell bought a farm retreat in Bucks County, Pennsylvania. In the same year Parker became pregnant but miscarried.

In the 1940s and 1950s Parker's literary output diminished. *Here Lies: Collected Stories* (1939) was followed by a second edition (1942) and *The Viking Portable Library Dorothy Parker* (1944). In 1947 Parker divorced Campbell, complaining of his homosexual affairs, but they remarried in 1950. Despite their differences, he moderated her drinking and took care of her.

Like other literary and film personalities of the 1930s and 1940s Parker supported many radical causes. She demonstrated for Sacco and Vanzetti, backed the Spanish Loyalists (Parker went to Spain in 1937 as a reporter for *New Masses*), and helped found the Screen Writers Guild and the Anti-Nazi League. Consequently, Hollywood studios blacklisted her in the McCarthy era, HUAC subpoenaed her, and the New York Joint Legislative Committee questioned her. Asked whether she were a Communist, Parker pleaded the Fifth Amendment.

Parker spent her final days mainly in New York, where she wrote a play, *The Ladies of the Corridor* (1953; published in book form, 1954), with Arnaud d'Usseau. In 1958 she received the Marjorie Peabody Waite Award from the American Academy of Arts and Letters, and the following year the academy made her a member. In 1963-1964 Parker was distinguished visiting professor of English at California State College, Los Angeles. Parker's later years were marked by financial instability. Lillian Hellman, her staunchest friend, and possibly the only person about whom she never made an unkind remark, came to her aid at this time. Most of her other friends were dead—Campbell had died in 1963—and she was losing her sight. She lived alone at the Hotel Volney, where she was found dead on 7 June 1967. As a final social statement, Parker left her estate (about twenty thousand dollars), plus copyrights and royalties, to Martin Luther King, Jr., to be passed at his death to the NAACP.

The classical traditions of satire and wit inform Parker's work. Her stories, generally set in New York, comment on human behavior, both satirically and compassionately. She perceives human beings as frustrated yet inactive, cruel yet obtuse, and insensitive yet victimized. Her targets, chiefly upper class, include the envious, jealous, egotistical, self-pitying, shallow, and boring. She embraces the oppressed, frustrated, lonely, immobilized, and unmotivated. Her themes include jealousy, disintegrating relationships, failure of communication, dead marriages, women's dependency on men, emptiness of women's lives, and selfishness of the wealthy. The autobiographical nature of her work adds to its ironic density.

Parker combines starkly honed and understated prose with banal language and uses paradox, exaggeration, zeugma, synecdoche, symbolic names, and epithets that sum up characters with concision and succinctness, often implying that they are little more than the "green lace" or "chocolate-brown suits" which they wear. Her stories, always focused on a single scene, take the forms of monologue, dialogue, or narrative and sometimes combine all three.

Parker's first published story, "Such a Pretty Little Picture," ranks among her best. The Wheelocks have a comfortable suburban home, which Mrs. Wheelock runs "economically and efficiently," and a daughter called Sister, whom she overprotects. Mrs. Wheelock's one-sided conversations are satiric thrusts at her husband's earnings, which prevent their giving Sister a brother, and her jokes expose his ineptness. Locked into the role of husband and father, Wheelock would like to challenge his wife's jokes with a "what of it?" or say, "Oh, hell!" and walk off forever. As he clips the hedge, speculating how long it will take to muster courage to leave, and Mrs. Wheelock sits on the porch holding the delicate Sister, passing neighbors admire the trio bathed in golden afternoon sun. Few writers have achieved such ironic density. Unfortunately, the story was excluded from Parker's collections and is not widely known.

Other uncollected early stories bridge Parker's sketches and later collected works. "A Certain Lady" (*New Yorker*, 28 February 1925) characterizes Mrs. Legion, who cannot afford to live on Park Avenue but follows the activities of those who can. "Travelogue" (*New Yorker*, 30 October 1926) portrays the society matron whose nonstop chatter reduces a young male traveler to speechlessness. "A Terrible Day Tomorrow" (*New Yorker*, 11 February 1928), a dialogue between "the woman in the leopard-skin coat" and "the man with the gentian-blue muffler," occurs in a speakeasy, where drink turns Bohemian small talk into senseless wrangling. Typical monologues reveal women hurt or bitter or both, magnifying awkward situations. In "The Garter" (*New Yorker*, 8

Parker (right) with Lillian Hellman at a benefit for the Spanish Refugee Appeal Campaign, 27 March 1945 (Culver Pictures)

September 1928) the protagonist, whose garter has snapped at a dance, spikes her ramblings with literary allusions and a classic zeugma—"never trust a round garter or a Wall Street Man." The protagonist of "But the One on the Right" (*New Yorker*, 19 October 1929) struggles through dinner, trying to draw conversation from the man on her left while anguishing that the "Greek god" on her right ignores her. The speaker in both monologues is ironically named Dorothy Parker.

Parker's first collection, *Laments for the Living*, comprising thirteen stories and sketches previously published in magazines, received mixed reviews. Critics found the stories "admirable" but limited, perfect "of their kind," "biting, satiric and witty," but "too few and too slight." Fanny Butcher spoke of "brilliant prose, . . . more impressive in a book" than in the magazines (*Chicago Daily Tribune*, 21 June 1930). Of the author, T. S. Matthews remarked: "No one could write with such unhappy wit, no one could manage such a savage humor, who did not feel herself a blood sister to her victims. . . . Dorothy Parker is very much of our day. . . . her most sympathetic gesture always has some horror in it" (*New Republic*, 17 September 1930).

Many of the stories of this collection "make themselves," in Parker's words, "by telling themselves through what people say." In "The Mantle of Whistler" (*New Yorker*, 18 August 1928) the inane patter of Alice French and Jack Bartlett epitomizes the flapper era. "A Telephone Call" (*Bookman*, January 1928) records with extraordinary sensitivity the anguish of a woman awaiting a man's call. Suspecting that their relationship is over now that they have had sex, she rationalizes, prays, and counts to "five hundred by fives." The protagonist of "New York to Detroit" (first published as "Long Distance," *Vanity Fair*, October 1925) breaks the social code by calling the man who has neither called nor written. Her words make abundantly clear her awful loneliness as she pleads for love and hints at pregnancy; his are an exercise in evasion. In "The Last Tea" (*New Yorker*, 11 September 1926) "the girl with the artificial camelia" and "the young man in the chocolate-brown suit" preface their breakup by boasting of other liaisons. The protagonist of "Just a Little One" (*New Yorker*, 12 May 1928), instead of pretending another interest, indulges in jealousy and sarcasm until drinking turns sarcasm into self-pity. Her drunken counterpart, "the woman in the petunia-colored hat," turns "Dialogue at Three in the Morning" (*New Yorker*, 13 February 1926) into a monologue, allowing "the man with the ice-blue hair" no rebuttal. In each instance Parker's focus is on conversation, not action.

Several other pieces work in the same manner. In "The Sexes" (*New Republic*, 13 July 1927) the jealous "girl in the fringed dress" confuses the "young man with the scenic cravat," tricking him into blunders and double entendres. She maneuvers for compliments, he for sexual advantage. "You Were Perfectly Fine" (*New Yorker*, 23 February 1929), one of Parker's lightest and funniest pieces, follows "the clear-eyed girl" as she helps "the pale young man" recall the previous evening. Her repetition of the title phrase magnifies the vulgarity of his conduct. "Arrangement in Black and White" (*New Yorker*, 8 October 1927) exposes a self-styled liberal socialite who blunders repeatedly while trying to demonstrate tolerance in a conversation with black singer Walter Williams.

The more substantial stories in the collection employ primarily third-person narrative.

Three such pieces deal with extremes of egotism and selfishness. "Mr. Durant" (*American Mercury*, September 1924), one of Parker's most frequently anthologized stories, indicts male chauvinism. When Durant, a minor administrator, learns that Rose, the secretary with whom he has been having a casual affair, is pregnant, he "gallantly" insists on giving her twenty-five dollars for the abortion, even though he could use the money for "Junior's teeth, and all!" Urging her to consider the recuperation period a "vacation," he promises to "put in a good word for her" whenever she wants her job back. When she leaves, he chuckles "Well, that's that!"

Durant's treatment of Rose is his worst but by no means his only sexist action. He is, in fact, the quintessential womanizer. His ego assures him that every woman in his range desires his attention. As he waits for the streetcar that will carry him home to his dinner, his children, and his wife (in that order), his eye lights on a young woman waiting nearby. When she steps up into the car, his eye follows the run in her stocking, and his thumbnail itches to extend the flaw down to her shoe. When she accidently bumps against him, he perceives her action as deliberate and instinctively starts to follow but then changes his mind. He hurries along his street in order to watch two young neighbors "run up the steps, their narrow skirts sliding up over their legs," his mind meanwhile dwelling on the run in the stocking.

Entering his home, Durant reenacts his treatment of Rose by refusing to allow his children to keep a stray female dog that might become pregnant and look "disgusting." The interview with his wife in which he makes known his plans to dispose of the dog takes place in his "truly masculine" study decorated with "a drawing of a young woman with wings like a vampire bat," a watercolored photograph of "September Morn," "a tanned and fringed hide with the profile of an unknown Indian maiden painted on it," and a leather pillow "bearing the picture, done by pyrography of a girl in a fencing costume." Having rid himself of Rose and the dog, Durant complacently lays his arm on his wife's shoulders and goes to dinner.

Selfishness within the family emerges in "The Wonderful Old Gentleman" (*Pictorial Review*, February 1927). While an old man lies dying in his daughter's shabby home, conversation among his heirs, intended to praise his strong will and alertness, unwittingly reveals that he has

Parker with her second husband, Alan Campbell, circa 1945 (Culver Pictures)

driven away his son and grandson, enslaved the daughter he lives with, and willed his fortune to a wealthy daughter who has room for his possessions but not for him. In "Little Curtis" (first published as "Lucky Little Curtis," *Pictorial Review*, February 1927) the wealthy Matsons adopt a boy from "the best place in New York," hoping to make him fit to inherit their fortune and prevent their relatives' going through it "like Sherman to the sea." They do their best to make Curtis self-ish and snobbish, but his natural generosity and exuberance persist. Their rigidity suggests the ironic appropriateness of Parker's original title.

The O. Henry prizewinning story "Big Blonde" (*Bookman*, February 1929), Parker's most fully developed work, crowns the collection. About the piece, Parker said, "I knew a lady–a friend of mine who went through holy hell. Just say I knew a woman once." Though the title ill describes tiny, dark-haired Parker, the story of Hazel Morse, a New York model, whom the men call a "good sport," hints at Parker's agonies. A "large, fair woman of the type that incites men when they use the word 'blonde' to click their

tongues and wag their heads roguishly," Hazel strives to fulfill society's expectations. She prides herself on her small feet pushed into high-heeled slippers of "the shortest bearable size" and on her social skills.

At twenty Hazel laughs at men's jokes, praises their neckties, and enjoys the meals they buy. At thirty her desires shift, and she enters wearily into marriage–"a new game, a holiday," a promise of security and peace. Losing his "good sport" does not amuse husband Herbie, who begins to party alone. Finding herself insecure, ineffectual, and "completely bewildered" in the role of the "little woman," Hazel joins Herbie in his evenings out. She turns to drinking with him, with her neighbor Mrs. Martin, and alone. When drinking and fighting drive Herbie away, other men provide varying degrees of economic and emotional security. Hazel drinks "industriously" until drinking no longer gives her a high, and she attempts suicide. Hazel, like Parker, cannot find fulfillment in relationships. Many of Parker's stories featuring the "little woman" ridicule characteristics of the socially conditioned woman Parker

Parker in Hollywood, 1963 (Wide World Photos)

despised—emotional and economic dependency, tearfulness, intellectual and cultural paucity, emptiness, bewilderment, and emphasis on physical beauty. In "Big Blonde," however, Parker gives her most powerful feminist statement: Hazel as victim achieves true tragic stature. As Nancy Walker writes, Parker "pushes the 'little woman' beyond humor into pathos."

Parker epitomizes Hazel's plight in a single image. Blown out of her whiskey drowsiness as she crosses Sixth Avenue one evening, "consciously dragging one foot past the other," Hazel sees a scared horse "crashed to his knees before her." Lashed by the driver, the horse struggles to rise on the icy pavement. Unable to shake the vision, Hazel attempts suicide, but she fails even in this and seems doomed to an existence of continued agony, alone and terrified.

Writing "Big Blonde" did not exorcise Parker's demon; instead, it sharpened her focus. Consequently, each story of her next collection, *After Such Pleasures*, treats, both satirically and sympathetically, some dilemma arising from woman's traditional conditioning. "The Waltz," a previously unpublished story, is frequently antholo-

gized and has been dramatized and often performed. It centers on a woman's plight when she chooses to dance with a clumsy partner rather than be a wallflower. Her acquired social graces thinly and humorously disguise her resentment of the social code. "The Little Hours" (*New Yorker*, 19 August 1933) and "Sentiment" (*Harper's Bazaar*, May 1933) reveal the anguish of the woman alone. The former, which takes place at 4:20 A.M., is a brilliant example of Parker's ability to handle stream of consciousness narration; the latter records a woman's sentimental drive through a neighborhood where she once lived with a lover. "The Young Woman in Green Lace" (*New Yorker*, 24 September 1932) exposes a pseudosophisticated woman just back from three weeks in Paris. Dressed in green lace and pearls as fake as her French, she plays the demure maiden in order to catch a naive young man. "Dusk Before Fireworks" (*Harper's Bazaar*, September 1932) presents three social types: the new woman who initiates dates with men, the traditional woman devoured by jealousy, and the facile man who sheds women, one after the other. All three perspectives emphasize the male's advantage and the woman's dependency. "Lady with the Lamp" (*Harper's Bazaar*, April 1932) exposes both the woman who rejoices over a rival brought low and her victim. As Mona Morrison suffers from what she calls "nerves," her self-styled best friend visits Mona's hospital room, dismays her with gossip about Mona's recent lover, and links Mona's "illness" to an abortion. "From the Diary of a New York Lady" (*New Yorker*, 25 March 1933) reveals the emptiness of a socialite's life and charts the actions by which she is alienating her husband Joe. The "Lady" spends her evenings partying with a last-ditch companion, Ollie Martin, and her days recovering, and gossiping with her manicurist Miss Rose. Repetition and banal language illustrate the futility of such a life.

The four strongest stories of the collection range from frivolous to grim. Arthur F. Kinney places "Here We Are" (*Cosmopolitan*, March 1931) at the top of the list. He compares it to Hemingway's "Hills Like White Elephants," though he finds it "gayer in tone." "Here We Are," a dialogue between newlyweds, contrasts the groom's jocular anticipation and the bride's fearful hesitancy. The sexual aspect of marriage, never mentioned, informs every word. "Too Bad" (*Smart Set*, July 1923), Kinney's second choice, examines a "perfect marriage" that disintegrates after seven years. The couple's problems, never articulated, stem from sexual incompatibility and the wife's lack of a meaningful occupation. "Glory in the Daytime" (*Harper's Bazaar*, September 1933), which wins Edmund Wilson's highest praise, explores the pain of three women. Stage-struck Mrs. Murdock goes to tea to meet the actress Lily Wynton. After watching the great lady swill brandy, despite Hallie Noyes's attempt to keep her sober for the evening performance, Mrs. Murdock, ambivalent but euphoric, goes home to face her realistic but insensitive husband who understands Hallie's (he calls her Hank) relationship to the actress. Another grim story is "Horsie" (*Harper's Bazarr*, December 1932), an episode in the life of Miss Wilmarth, a trained nurse hired to tend Camilla Cruger and her infant daughter. Its irony stems from the value traditionally placed on beauty in a woman. Because of Miss Wilmarth's facial structure, she is an easy target for humor. The Crugers call her "Horsie" and constantly joke at her expense, while pretending kindness in her presence. The hypocrisy culminates in Gerald Cruger's bringing "Horsie" gardenias as a parting gift. Here, as in all her works, Parker's biting tongue and sympathetic heart collide.

Though some critics decried the paucity of Parker's output, *After Such Pleasures* fared well. The *New York Times* (24 October 1933) reviewer praised Parker's "inestimable gift of jeering at sentimentality without utterly destroying it," and Ogden Nash, no mean wit himself, called Parker "truly great" in his critique for the *Saturday Review of Literature* (4 November 1933).

Here Lies, a combination of the two previous collections, replaces "Dialogue at Three in the Morning" and "A Young Woman in Green Lace" with "Clothe the Naked" (*Scribner's*, January 1938), "Soldiers of the Republic" (*New Yorker*, 5 February 1938), and a previously unpublished story, "The Custard Heart." The first two new stories reflect Parker's radical interests of the 1930s. "Clothe the Naked" reveals the helplessness of poor blacks, the short-sightedness of wealthy do-gooders, and the baseness of uneducated whites. When Raymond, Big Lannie's blind grandson, wears the cast-off clothing given him by Big Lannie's employer, Mrs. Ewing, white construction workers nearly kill him. Contrasting the generosity of the impoverished blacks and the selfishness and cruelty of the whites points the social comment. "Soldiers of the Republic," a factual report of one of Parker's experiences in Spain,

shows the generosity of the poor, through the response of some Spanish soldiers to the gift of a pack of cigarettes. "The Custard Heart" returns to the themes of *After Such Pleasures*. Wealthy and wistful Mrs. Lanier is so sensitive that everything pains her. Her one thought is that she needs a little baby, but whenever a young man offers to give her one, she drops him. When Gwennie, the perfect maid, becomes pregnant by Kane, the perfect chauffeur, who immediately disappears, Gwennie's physical condition and Mrs. Lanier's emotional predicament contrast in what Parker might call a "killing" irony.

Here Lies, like the preceding volumes, received mixed, though predominantly favorable, reviews. Clifton Fadiman, writing in the *New Yorker* (29 April 1939), thought the stories "as good as they ever were, and they were always good." William Plomer, writing in the *Spectator* (17 November 1939), characterized the collection as "technically skillful and full of clever observation and telling touches."

Stories written in 1933 but not collected include "Advice to the Little Peyton Girl" (*Harper's Bazaar*, February 1933) and two minor pieces—"Mrs. Carrington and Mrs. Crane" (*New Yorker*, 15 July 1933) and "The Road Home" (*New Yorker*, 16 September 1933). "Advice to the Little Peyton Girl" depicts Miss Marion, a teacher, giving excellent advice to a young woman whose possessiveness is alienating her boyfriend. The student, amazed at how well Miss Marion understands the difficulty, never suspects that the teacher is so perceptive precisely because their experiences are parallel.

The Viking Portable Library Dorothy Parker compiles Parker's previously collected stories as well as five additional pieces from the 1930s and 1940s. In "Song of the Shirt, 1941" (*New Yorker*, 28 June 1941) Parker continues to expose the insensitivity of the wealthy. Mrs. Martindale, a patriotic matron who wears a flag especially designed from her "spare" diamonds, rubies, and sapphires, works diligently through the summer, sewing shirts for military hospitals. Although she hates the task and does it poorly, she is at a loss when asked who might give work to poor Mrs. Christie. Like Mrs. Ewing of "Clothe the Naked," Mrs. Martindale is socially obtuse, comfortably ensconced in the accoutrements of wealth and privilege. "The Standard of Living" (*New Yorker*, 20 September 1941) is a wryly humorous story that depicts the rude awakening of two secretaries when they learn the cost of real pearls and reveals their pristine ignorance that their own dress, speech, and manner betray their "standard of living" to the jewelry-store employees whom they regard as inferiors. "Cousin Larry" (*New Yorker*, 30 June 1934) ridicules the foolish wealthy woman who supports her philandering husband and allows herself to be destroyed; it exposes the husband's insensitivity and makes the "other woman" the butt of her own words. "Mrs. Hofstadter on Josephine Street" (*New Yorker*, 4 August 1934) exposes the inexperience of a couple who allow themselves to be duped by the employment agent and dominated by Horace Wrenn, a black servant supposedly recommended by Mrs. Hofstadter.

The most complex story of the previously uncollected group is "The Lovely Leave" (*Woman's Home Companion*, December 1943). Like many women, Mimi McVicker finds life dull while her husband, Steve, is in service. Envious of the energy and concern he puts into his work, she had ruined his previous leave but wants to make the next one happy. An unexpected change of plans upsets her, and again she explodes. Parker also focuses on the husband's insensitivity, thereby subtly demonstrating the different ways in which women and men handle affection.

The 1973 edition of the collection, retitled *The Portable Dorothy Parker*, adds three important stories of the 1950s. All treat by now familiar themes–dependency, jealousy, failed marriages, and selfishness–but with obvious touches evocative of the 1950s. "I Live on Your Visits" (*New Yorker*, 15 January 1955) carries many of the undertones of "The Lovely Leave." It pictures an idle, alcoholic divorcée who wastes her son's brief visit by railing against his father and stepmother. Instead of living within the present, the protagonist seeks her future in the cards of a fortune-telling parasite. "Lolita" (*New Yorker*, 27 August 1955) shows Parker's deep understanding of mother-daughter jealousy. Mrs. Ewing, a widow, always thought that she would remarry but doubted that Lolita, her rather plain daughter, would find a man. When Lolita marries handsome and successful John Marble, Mrs. Ewing feels bewildered and cheated; yet she never gives up hope that Lolita will be abandoned.

"The Bolt Behind the Blue" (*Esquire*, December 1948), another story contrasting wealth and poverty, surprises with an unusual feminist twist. Mrs. Hazelton, a wealthy widow, occasionally invites Mary Nicholl, a poor working girl, to her home for cocktails, but never for meals. While Miss Nicholl envies Mrs. Hazelton's closets of unworn clothes, the lonely Mrs. Hazelton envies Miss Nicholl the friendship of Miss Christie, who shares her evenings and, more important, her confidence. Although each recognizes her envy of the other, each tells herself that she would not exchange places. The narrator wonders that a bolt from behind the blue does not strike both.

In a significant uncollected story, "The Banquet of Crow" (*New Yorker*, 14 December 1957), Parker's treatment of the failed marriage comes full circle. Like Wheelock of "Such a Pretty Little Picture," Guy Allen lives for years in a "perfect" marriage. Unlike Wheelock, after years of fruitless explanation, Allen walks out. Bewildered, Maida Allen seeks out Dr. Marjorie Langley, a psychiatrist, who assures her that Guy is merely "going through the change." When Guy attempts a final explanation, Maida still does not hear. Instead, she creates a fantasy of his return "gnawing on a leg of cold crow." But fantasy also fails, and Maida calls the psychiatrist. Parker seems to be saying that people like Maida will never learn, but Emily Toth, perceiving Parker's subversive intent, sees Maida's fantasy as a beneficial product of anger.

In over thirty years as a fiction writer Parker produced fewer than fifty stories; yet her reputation is secure. Structurally, her works show the influence of the classical traditions of wit and satire coupled with modernist techniques. Like Hemingway and Lardner, she believed that "a good short story is much 'larger' than its wordage," and her own works illustrate that point. Their spare ironic surface contains, in equal measure humor and pain. Her innovation lies in her recognition of the unequal status of women and her ability to catch the plight of women in carefully constructed stories and in poignant dialogue. She had no time for women who wrote what she called fantasies. She told Capron, "I'm a feminist, and God knows I'm loyal to my sex, but you must remember that from my very early days when this city was scarcely safe from buffaloes I was in the struggle for equal rights for women. But when we paraded through the catcalls of men and when we chained ourselves to lamp posts to try to get our equality–dear child, we didn't foresee *those* female writers." Parker's stories are certainly not fantasies. As Suzanne L. Bunkers, Toth, and others have made clear, Parker deals with complex feminist issues that psychologists and sociologists have probed only since the 1970s. Consequently, although much of her poetry now seems dated, her stories remain contemporary and invite further study.

The publication in 1988 of Marion Meade's *Dorothy Parker: What Fresh Hell Is This?* has rekindled interest in Parker. The absence of a substantial bibliography and a complete edition of Parker's fiction continues to impede critical study. Still, since readers today are finding deeper meanings in Parker's work than previous generations could perceive–particularly concerning women's issues–the future should bring the recognition her work deserves.

Interview:

Marion Capron, "Dorothy Parker," *Paris Review*, 13, no. 4 (1956): 73-87; republished in *Writers at Work*, edited by Malcolm Cowley (New York: Viking, 1957), pp. 69-82.

Biographies:

John Keats, *You Might as Well Live* (New York: Simon & Schuster, 1970);

Marion Meade, *Dorothy Parker: What Fresh Hell Is This?* (New York: Villard, 1988).

References:

Suzanne L. Bunkers, " 'I Am Outraged Womanhood': Dorothy Parker as Feminist and Social Critic," *Regionalism and the Female Imagination*, 4 (Fall 1978): 25-34;

Wyatt Cooper, "Whatever you think Dorothy Parker was, she wasn't," *Esquire* (July 1968): 56-57, 61, 110-114;

Frank Crowninshield, "Crowninshield in the cub's den," *Vogue* (15 September 1944): 162-163, 177-201;

Lillian Hellman, *An Unfinished Woman* (Boston: Little, Brown, 1969);

Arthur F. Kinney, *Dorothy Parker* (Boston: G. K. Hall, 1978);

Emily Toth, "Dorothy Parker, Erica Jong, and New Feminist Humor," *Regionalism and the Female Imagination*, 3 (Fall 1977 / Winter 1977-1978): 70-85;

Nancy Walker, " 'Fragile and Dumb': The 'Little Woman' in Women's Humor, 1900-1940," *Thalia*, 5 (Fall / Winter 1982-1983): 24-29;

Alexander Woollcott, *While Rome Burns* (New York: Grosset & Dunlap, 1934).

Papers:

There is no central collection of Parker's papers. Letters, in very small numbers, are scattered in over twenty libraries. The largest group of letters (twenty-two) is at the Houghton Library, Harvard University.

Damon Runyon

(3 October 1880-10 December 1946)

Guy Szuberla
University of Toledo

See also the Runyon entry in *DLB 11: American Humorists, 1800-1950*.

BOOKS: *The Tents of Trouble. Ballads of the Wanderbund and other Verse* (New York: Fitzgerald, 1911);

Rhymes of the Firing Line (New York: Fitzgerald, 1912);

Guys and Dolls (New York: Stokes, 1931; London: Jarrolds, 1932);

Blue Plate Special (New York: Stokes, 1934);

Money From Home (New York: Stokes, 1935);

More Than Somewhat, selected by E. C. Bentley (London: Constable, 1937);

Take It Easy (New York: Stokes, 1938; London: Constable, 1938);

Furthermore: A Companion Book of Stories to "More than Somewhat," selected by Bentley (London: Constable, 1938);

The Best of Damon Runyon, edited by Bentley (New York: Stokes, 1938);

My Old Man (New York: Stackpole Sons, 1939; London: Constable, 1940);

My Wife Ethel (London: Constable, 1939); with different material (Philadelphia: McKay, 1940); London edition republished as *The Turps* (London: Constable, 1951);

A Slight Case of Murder (New York: Dramatists Play Service, 1940);

Runyon à la Carte (Philadelphia: Lippincott, 1944; London: Constable, 1946);

The Three Wise Guys and Other Stories (New York: Avon, 1946);

In Our Town (New York: Creative Age Press, 1946);

Short Takes, Reader's Choice of the Best Columns of America's Favorite Newspaperman (New York & London: Whittlesey House / McGraw-Hill, 1946; London: Constable, 1948);

Poems for Men (New York: Duell, Sloan & Pearce, 1947);

Trials and Other Tribulations (Philadelphia: Lippincott, 1948);

Damon Runyon

Runyon First and Last (Philadelphia: Lippincott, 1949); republished as *All This and That* (London: Constable, 1950);

Runyon From First to Last (London: Constable, 1954).

Collections: *The Damon Runyon Omnibus* (New York: Blue Ribbon Books, 1939);

More Guys and Dolls (Garden City, N.Y.: Garden City Books, 1951).

PLAY PRODUCTION: *A Slight Case of Murder*, by Runyon and Howard Lindsay, New York, 48th Street Theatre, 11 September 1935.

When Alfred Damon Runyon moved to New York City, sometime in late 1910, he was thirty years old, a seasoned journalist, and a stranger to the city. Though he had published a handful of short stories in *McClure's, Lippincott's,* and *Metropolitan,* and his poetry had appeared in *Collier's,* he had made his living for almost fifteen years as a writer for newspapers, including the *Pueblo Evening Press,* the *San Francisco Post,* and the *Denver News.* In moving to New York he ended his years of rough-and-tumble journalism and the drinking binges that threatened to doom him to lifelong alcoholism. He began a rise to fame and fortune that, even now, seems phenomenal. Throughout the 1930s he was ranked as America's most popular short-story writer and called the century's greatest journalist. *Saturday Evening Post* and *Collier's* paid him their highest fees; Hollywood producers besieged him with rich offers for film rights and story lines. He remains the nonpareil chronicler of Broadway, the maker of a lingo and syntax dubbed Runyonese, and the proprietor of a reputation notched just below that of Ring Lardner, his onetime pressbox rival.

During his first six months in New York, Runyon wrestled with uncertain prospects and mixed ambitions. He looked for newspaper work while he sold articles and stories to slick, large-circulation magazines. In these months Runyon lived in Brooklyn with his friends Mr. and Mrs. Charles Van Loan. In exchange for the use of the Van Loans' spare room, he spun out plot lines for stories that Charles Van Loan embroidered and published. Van Loan, once the star sportswriter for William Randolph Hearst's *New York American,* had found it more profitable to turn out short stories for the *Saturday Evening Post* and other magazines. He had invited Runyon to New York so that he might replenish his supply of short-story plots. But Van Loan wearied of their arrangement, and Runyon himself grew restless when Ellen Egan, his fiancée back in Denver, demanded he secure a steady income before they marry. Egan, a society reporter for the *Rocky Mountain News,* had earlier insisted that he give up drinking. Just as spring baseball practice was about to start, Van Loan set Runyon up with a job as a sportswriter on the *American.* Once he won his place on the paper, Runyon, in May 1911, married Ellen Egan in Brooklyn.

Runyon worked for the rest of his life as an *American* reporter and columnist. If, in these thirty-five odd years, he conceived of a conflict between writing a daily column and writing fiction–the kind of trap Gertrude Stein magisterially

warned Hemingway against–he never complained of it openly. Perhaps he was fated or willing to so divide his energy and talents; he never attempted a novel and framed most of his fiction within a *Saturday Evening Post* type format and word limit. For all these constraints, Runyon was prodigiously productive: no bibliographer has hazarded a tally of his hundreds of stories, articles, and sketches. Jean Wagner, in *Runyonese: The Mind and Craft of Damon Runyon* (1965), has listed sixty-six "Broadway sketches"; Patricia Ward D'Itri, in *Damon Runyon* (1982), counts approximately eighty stories and one play under a similar heading. They list, of course, stories such as "The Idyll of Miss Sarah Brown" (*Collier's,* 28 January 1933) and "The Bloodhounds of Broadway" (*Collier's,* 16 May 1931), Broadway tales that will forever bind Runyon's name to the musical *Guys and Dolls* (1950). However, the western stories collected in *In Our Town* (1946), some early hobo stories, parodistic detective stories, the domestic comedy of the "My Wife Ethel" series, and the hundreds of stories and sketches written for his daily or weekly columns in now defunct magazines and papers remain unlocated.

Runyon was born in Manhattan, Kansas, and raised in the mining town of Pueblo, Colorado. His grandfather William Renoyan had been a printer and an original settler of Kansas in the 1850s. His father, Alfred Lee Runyan, a journalist in Kansas and Colorado, had served under George Armstrong Custer in 1868. It was his father, a saloon orator and flamboyant dresser, who sought, single-handedly, to bring up young "Al," his only son. Runyon's mother, Libbie J. Damon, died in Colorado in 1887, when Runyon was only seven years old, and his three sisters were taken to live with relatives in Abilene, Kansas. Under his father's rule he was free to attend Hinsdale school or to play hooky. When he was expelled for "horseplay" in the sixth grade, the print shop and Pueblo saloons became his schoolroom and college. His father became his first editor, publishing his son's premiere stories in the *Pueblo Evening Press;* Alfred Damon Runyan (the name was not yet altered) was then thirteen years old. At age fifteen he was a full-fledged reporter for the *Evening Press;* his first assignment, so he later told it, was to report a lynching.

Such experiences, braced by a steady reading of dime-novel Westerns, were to indelibly stamp Runyon's imagination. The West, its ethos and mythos, shaped a matrix for the narrative

Runyon (seated third from left) and unidentified colleagues at the Denver Press Club, circa 1909 (courtesy of the Denver Press Club)

forms of his fiction. He undoubtedly borrowed sentimental colors and character types from Bret Harte; his "Little Miss Marker" (*Collier's*, 26 March 1932; collected in *Blue Plate Special,* 1934), Calvin S. Brown has shown, recasts plot devices taken from "The Luck of Roaring Camp" and "The Outcasts of Poker Flat." The Old Cattleman, narrator of Alfred S. Lewis's "Wolfville Yarns," proved to have an undying influence on Runyon's present-tense narration. Lewis, as John O. Rees and Jean Wagner have shown, anticipated Runyon's systematic avoidance of past verb tenses. Lewis's *The Apaches of New York* (1912), a series of muckraking tales about Manhattan's underworld, influenced the language and design of Runyon's Broadway stories. If Rees is right, many of Runyon's Broadway "guys and dolls" are named after Lewis's "Apaches." Runyon himself transplanted characters he had encountered in Colorado and California. Nicely-Nicely Jones, Sky Masterson, and Nathan Detroit are among the Broadway characters whose roots are in Runyon's Western past.

However deeply Runyon ventured into the wilds of Broadway, he oriented himself by values and a sense of character mapped out in the literary traditions of western humor and a loosely framed western code of honor. D'Itri, in her chapter on the Broadway stories, emphasizes the western bearing in cataloging Runyon's prevalent themes: (1) the western code of instant justice or revenge; (2) defense of the underdog; (3) a code

of loyalty based on individual trust and defiance of a dominant culture; (4) a sense of integrity defined by a defiant subgroup; (5) the force of circumstance in shaping character.

These values and themes, not surprisingly, emerged in rough outline in Runyon's earliest fiction. His first works of fiction in major magazines–"The Defense of Strikerville" (*McClure's*, February 1907), "Two Men Named Collins" (*Reader*, September 1907), and "Fat Fallon" (*Lippincott's*, October 1907)–upheld the underdog and spoke a rebellious defiance of legal authority. In them, ragtag irregular soldiers, in opposition to handsome officers and cleanly uniformed regulars, defy army rules and regulations. Like the honor-bound gangsters and gamblers of the later Broadway tales, Private Hanks and his companions recognize no higher law or duty than loyalty to friends.

These stories, collected in *Runyon First and Last* (1949), are told by dialect narrators who hold forth in the "squad room" or "barrack hall." Their tales and the heroics in them thus owe an obvious debt to Rudyard Kipling's *Barrack Room Ballads* (1892). But their language, especially the incongruous blends of learned diction and lively slang, recalls the speech of Mark Twain's naive narrators and con men. The stock pranks and overblown rhetoric suggest, as well, that Runyon knew the rebellious ways and rough tricks of the southwestern humorists. J. Wallace Hanks, the dialect narrator in "The Defense of Strikerville,"

Runyon, circa 1910, as a sportswriter for the New York
American *(United Press International)*

tells his story with mock bravado: "Lemme relate
the sad circumstances of J. Wallace Hanks' enlist-
ment in the Colorado State milish, and if you all
don't weep, you haven't got no hearts." His adventure, and the story's action, turns on a comic battle between some well-dressed regular troops and
Hanks's veteran militia unit. Though hired "to
suppress" strikers, they decide that they "were
already pretty much suppressed." Together, the
strikers, their women and children, and Hanks's
militiamen ambush the H troops with rock-
plugged snowballs. Their alliance, despite
Hanks's flashes of radical rhetoric, finally bears
no particular political meaning. The rough militiamen, Hanks assures his listeners, had forsaken
their soldierly duties and joined the strikers to protect "a girl baby" from the snow and the cold.

Runyon's stories of tough-skinned soldiers
with soft hearts grew out of his experiences in
the army. He enlisted during the Spanish-
American War and saw action in 1899 during the
Philippine Insurrection. For his "hobo" stories–
"As Between Friends" (*Adventure*, May 1911),
"The Informal Execution of Soupbone Pew"
(*American Weekly*), and "The Breeze Kid's Big Tear-

Off " (*Hampton's*, January 1912)–he reached back
to the times after his discharge when he rode the
rails between San Francisco and Colorado. Frisco
Shine, Manchester Slim, the Honey Grove Kid,
Chicago Red, Squirt McCue, and his other hobo
characters are bound together by an ardent sentimentality and a peculiarly unforgiving code of
vengeance. They are gentlemen of the road and
men of leisure, but they also know how to crack
a safe and can sleep peacefully in a jailhouse
after having killed a railroad dick.

Runyon's command of criminal argots and
his knowledge of the technical details of crime
were probably as complete here as they would be
in the Broadway stories. But these tales were published in 1911 and 1912, and his early handling
of slang is neither as controlled nor as artfully understated as it would be in the 1920s and 1930s fiction. As D'Itri has pointed out, Runyon's slang-
making in his early fiction seems circumspect and
often hesitant. Some lines of hobo talk, in apparent deference to middle-class readers, are
translated parenthetically: "We had jungled up–
camped." Other slang expressions are set off
from the text by self-conscious quotation marks.
The first-person narrator of "The Informal Execution of Soupbone Pew," for example, recalls
that he and Chicago Red "had been 'vagged' for
ten days each."

"The Informal Execution of Soupbone
Pew," the best of Runyon's early fiction, must
stand, then, as an apprentice piece. While Runyon carries off an O. Henry-style twist ending,
cleverly embedding one story of an execution
within another, he has not quite found the inside
narrator or narrative voice that gave his later
work distinctive power. Red, who has "been a
gun and a crook for many years," tells the story
of Soupbone Pew's cruelty in words that too
often make him sound more like a nineteenth-
century omniscient author than a dialect character. Red and a band of hoboes "execute" Soupbone to avenge the death of Manchester Slim.
Red's speech, a blend of conventional literary diction and slang, is not invariably intended to be
comic. When he says, "on a bitter cold night, in a
certain town that I won't name, there was five of
us in the sneezer . . . ," he speaks with unmodu-
lated earnestness. Such fusions of polite and pro-
fane diction, in later Runyonese, are carefully
bent toward comic periphrasis.

By 1913 Runyon had become the official humorist of the *American*. He had also become
Damon Runyon: his editor clipped back Alfred

Runyon with Jack Dempsey, Joe Bannon, and Joe Benjamin, Atlantic City, 1921 (United Press International)

Damon Runyon, telling him that the three-name bylines that had served Richard Harding Davis's generation had passed out of fashion. Runyon had earned the title of humorist not only because slang and irreverence peppered his sports stories, but because few of his reports followed a traditional or chronological lineup of facts. He might focus a whole story on a single player or fan, seldom following the game's action in any direct way. Runyon was as likely to picture a baseball game from the vantage point of an earthworm–as he once did–as he was to see it with the eyes of an ordinary reporter, looking down from the press box. The promotion department of the *American*, with good reason, billed him as a humorist: "Mr. Runyon has entertained for several seasons narrating the game in his inimitable humorous style and at the same time furnishing enough detailed description to satisfy the most rabid fan." In 1914 he had earned the right to his own column, "Th' Mornin's Mornin' "; there he served up abbreviated short stories, doggerel poems about the West, and, occasionally, straight news reports.

From the moment Runyon joined the *American* staff he aggressively pursued his career as a newspaperman. He was a sportswriter, a crime and court reporter, and, when the occasion de-

manded, he took on the national political conventions and the border raids of Pancho Villa. He worked, in his first two years, seven days a week, writing with the cold ferocity that led the veteran reporter Bugs Baer to say, "he could write you out of the paper." Though in 1911 he had married, and had a daughter, Mary Elaine, in 1914, he frequently absented himself from his Manhattan home for long junkets during spring training and for the weeks leading up to a big prizefight. With the outbreak of World War I he ached to go overseas, and in 1918 he managed to wrest an assignment covering the American front. According to Edwin P. Hoyt, he felt no qualms "about leaving wife and family, although a baby boy [Damon Runyon, Jr.] had been born in June 1918."

Working as an all-around reporter and regular columnist left Runyon with little time to perfect his short-story technique or, for that matter, to write anything other than newspaper copy. Between 1912 and 1929 he appears to have written almost no short stories and published few other works outside the pages of the *American*. Though he did manage to publish a second book of Kiplingesque poetry, *Rhymes of the Firing Line* (1912), like the antecedent *Tents of Trouble*, it was largely a gathering of verse he had written in Colorado.

Hoyt, in omitting newspaper work from his checklist, suggests that for almost seventeen years Runyon gave up his rough-hewn literary efforts, but this is a bit misleading. Throughout these years Runyon wrote character sketches, encapsulated short stories, fictive sports reports, and columns that casually appropriated the narrative forms and language of fiction and poetry. It may not be possible to trace a unified pattern of development across the oscillating lines of his reportage, but it seems clear that he was trying out different writing styles, different voices, and a variety of personas. In several of his 1916 "Th' Mornin's Mornin'" columns, for example, Runyon wrote extended monologues using the voices of obviously fictive dialect characters. Under the heading "Confessions of Successful Men: How I Made a Great Fighter," a Famous Manager told–in an ironic play of sports clichés–how he made "such a remarkable fighter out of Young Yegg." Kid Botts, in another column, gave readers advice on "How to Have Muskels like Mine." The subheading intimated Runyon's burlesque intentions: he was reporting "Extracts from an Address Delivered at a Smoker of the Boys' Gowanus Athletic Union by Brooklyn's Rugged Lightweight, World's Challenger at 140 Pounds." The "Kid" solemnly stated that his listeners should "beware of liquor": "I do not think Mr. Willard is as strong as me if he was my size. I done it by not drinking wines, liquors, and cigars. I have my lager in the mornings and sometimes in the afternoons and evenings, but champagne is bad for a boy who wants good muskels. So is dago red and other things which are drank in Brooklyn." Such acts of ventriloquy, and the truncated narratives accompanying them, seem in retrospect a necessary prologue to Runyon's creation of fully worked-out short stories where he draws this carnival of voices together.

The creation of A. Mugg (first, A. Baseball; later Amos Mugg) in 1919 was the most important of Runyon's early experiments with an inside narrator. Hoyt and D'Itri trace a straight line of development from Mugg to the "I" narrator of the Broadway stories. Mugg, like Kid Botts, had first appeared in a daily column, "Th' Mornin's Mornin'"; in the newspaper's Sunday magazine, however, he assumed a larger role and a different voice. Mugg maintains a distanced perspective on another Broadway mug, Chelsea McBride. He uses language and circumlocutions that are not far from the more practiced idiom of the later Broadway narrators. One of the first of these stories, published 10 August 1919, introduces McBride as a returning war veteran: "In the old days before the Kaiser gets to be such a stinker, this Chelsea McBride is one of the lads around Broadway, and is well known to one and all, though what Chelsea's racket is nobody knows, except that he does thus and so, and one thing and another. He is just a good man, which is a way of saying he does the best he can, and he does all right at that." Runyon's later Mugg stories for the Sunday *American* enlarged the narratives and indirectly defined the elusive outlines of this wisely innocent narrator. In one installment of the "Reveries of a Retired Rounder, by A. Mugg (retired), per Damon Runyon" series, Mugg recalled some advice his father gave him when he was a "young squirt":

> "Son," he says, "no matter where you go or how smart you get, I want you always to remember one thing. Some day," my old man says, "a guy is going to come up and show you a nice brand new deck of cards, still in the original package, and with the seal unbroken, and he is going to offer to bet you that the jack of spades will jump out of this deck of cards and hit you a crack in the ear.
> "But son," my old man says, "do not bet him that the jack of spades will not do as he claims, because," he says, "as sure as you bet you are going to get a cauliflower ear."

This advice, almost word for word, was repeated in two later Runyon stories. When Nathan Detroit, the hero in "The Idyll of Miss Sarah Brown," repeats his father's warning, he does not seem to be another version of A. Mugg. But the similar memories and their near-identical paternity suggest that Runyon, as early as 1919, was beginning to conceive of Mugg as more than a punching bag for jokes. He had a family, a past, and a memory of both.

Between 1922 and 1924 Runyon used the "Grandpap Mugg" and then the "My Old Home Town" stories as a bridge back to his own memories of the past. Starting in late 1922 Runyon wrote a series of encapsulated stories about a small town "out West," tales of slickers and settlers, Indians, Indian fighters, and cardsharps. At the center were Grandpap and Grandmaw, who represented the loving family Runyon never had. The tales construct a nostalgic if comic version of Runyon's boyhood Pueblo, Colorado. Run-

Runyon at the 1924 World Series (United Press International)

yon wrote most of these stories for the Sunday editorial section of the *American* and saw them published under the heading "Greatest American Humorists." Bugs Baer, Gene Fowler, and Ring Lardner also contributed stories to this weekly column. Runyon's "My Old Home Town" stories were humorous and generously suffused with sentimentality, even when they sounded a bitter or a sardonic note in closing.

In many of the tales Grandpap and Grandmaw tell their grandson–a mask for Runyon, the narrator–about adventures and moments that are slipping out of memory and into myth. Grandpap, for example, recalls a night "At Dead Mule Crossing" as a "historic battle" between "fifteen of us men with the women and children . . . and four thousand Injuns pressing in from all sides." Grandmaw then corrects him, saying there were but four Indians, and these were chased off by Ella May Wintergreen, wielding a kettle of scalding hot water. She knows this because old "Chief Tomato who sells hot tamales . . . tells me many times there are only four in the bunch, and they are just looking to steal a horse or a mule. . . ." Rather than remembering

this as a story of fifteen men fighting against four thousand, she recalls it as a prelude to Ella May's wretched marriage to Dods Campbell. "She will be a lot better off," she says, "if the Injuns get her this night at Dead Mule Crossing." Grandmaw then ends the story looking at Grandpap: "maybe some of the rest of us poor women will be better off if the same thing happens to us."

The "My Old Home Town" stories were, Hoyt believes, a way of reckoning with the impending breakup of his own marriage. Runyon and his wife separated in 1924. The stories of the town may represent a dream wish for primordial innocence and a vision of a happy family and a secure childhood. But Runyon also used them to fashion an Edenic image of men without women. One of the best of these tales, "The Old Men of the Mountain," happily crosses the "Rip Van Winkle" legend with the narrative motifs of Tom Sawyer's Jackson Island adventures. Over several weeks the old men of the town, in groups of six and seven, form rescue parties to bring back Old Zeb Griscom who "hauls off and drops out of sight leaving his wife . . . mourning for him more

Dust jacket and title page for Runyon's first short-story collection

than somwhat." Rescue parties are formed to rescue other rescue parties. The men, in fact, are fleeing their wives. Grandmaw discovers them in a cave in the Greenhorn Mountains: "she busts right into as jolly a party as anybody will wish to find with Mr. Hathaway, the banker, doing some cooking over a big fire, and my Grandpap dealing out drinks, and everybody laying around looking very happy indeed, until they see my Grandmaw." The "good time" ends, as the men are forced to follow Grandmaw back to town. Though they must leave the Greenhorn Mountains and go home to their wives, they are returning to a town where the Greenlight saloon still offers a nightly sanctuary for men and their games.

What meager home life Runyon clung to in the last four years of his marriage was submerged under the set routines of his leisure and work. He had become a prominent figure on Broadway by 1920 and seldom returned home before dawn. He spent his nights listening to the stories told by gangsters, chorus girls, bookies, cops, and boxers. For many years he was, according to Tom Clark, a constant companion of Arnold

Rothstein, a bookie and loan shark known as The Brain. Runyon sat at Rothstein's table–at Churchill's, Jack's, Reuben's, and, later in the 1920s, Lindy's. He watched and listened as The Brain held court; gamblers and other petitioners lined up for their chance to hear Rothstein say, "tell me the story." Runyon kept no notes and rarely said anything at these sessions, but from such nights he collected the stories and the talk that he later distilled into the stylized lingo and narratives he poured into his daily columns and, later, into his Broadway tales.

He naturally slept late, waking at two or three in the afternoon. He was moody when he awoke, though as he shaved he might talk to his daughter and son. At breakfast he read newspapers and would drink the first of the forty or fifty cups of coffee he consumed daily. After an hour in the bathroom, and another spent choosing the tie, jacket, and the pocket handkerchief he always sported, he was ready for another night on the town. Runyon favored bold checks and lively patterns, the kind gamblers and sporting men wore. These he bought at Nat Lewis's on Broadway; legend has it that he owned twelve hundred suits. The few waking hours he spent at home were mostly given over to dressing for the next night on Broadway or writing. When he wrote at home, he sequestered himself in a room away from his wife and children.

According to Gene Fowler, a newspaper friend from Denver, Runyon wrote his daily column at home during the 1920s. He also wrote some of his short stories there. When he lived with his wife and children, the family was obliged to keep "a sort of quarantine of silence." His son, Damon Runyon, Jr., remembered his father as "an agony writer": "Writing was a heavy labor for him and each word hit the paper bathed in sweat. . . . For his short stories he resorted to long hand to write the first draft, sometimes doing this chore in bed. . . . The final draft was the result of several rewriting sessions at the typewriter. It was heavy going not only for him but for the rest of us around the house since he became more moody than ever and was difficult if not impossible to deal with during these periods." Oddly enough, many newspapermen remember Runyon, whom they nicknamed "the Demon," as someone who "detested being alone." Clark reports that he told friends he was happier working at a typewriter in a noisy newsroom or at a crowded ringside table than writing in the solitary quiet of his apartment.

If the "My Old Home Town" stories encoded the unhappy secrets of Runyon's childhood and the painful solitude he found in his first marriage, they also, in Wagner's view, opened the way to the Broadway stories. That Runyon should conceive of New York–its moral and social structure–through the metaphor of a small town may be less paradoxical than it first seems. Wagner points up a series of parallels between the Broadway and "My Old Home Town" stories, arguing, for example, that the "three slickers from Omaha" who fleece Grandpap in poker resemble Nathan Detroit and Ikey the Pig, equally slick Broadway gamblers. The Greenlight saloon "looks very much like a prefiguration of such later New York hangouts as Good Time Charley's speakeasy and Miss Missouri Martins's Three Hundred Club. . . ." He concludes that "Broadway looks so strikingly like My Old Home Town because its characters are swayed by the same tremendous forces that govern the actions of human beings everywhere. Love, revenge, and especially the lust for money and power are all-important themes in any of Runyon's stories, what-

ever their settings, East or West, they are shown at work . . . shaping the fundamental patterns of a social order to which many submit for simple self-defence, but against which just as many other characters in the Runyonese universe rise in secret or open rebellion."

Runyon abruptly abandoned the Sunday "My Old Home Town" series in 1926, when he, Bugs Baer, and Gene Fowler discovered that someone in the Hearst organization was selling their Sunday features to papers outside the syndicate. The swindle so angered Runyon and the other contributors to the "Greatest American Humorists" column that they stopped writing Sunday features. For roughly the next three years Runyon worked as Hearst's chief reporter and turned out a daily column. From 1926 to the summer of 1929 he published no fiction. He covered the big fights, handled other sports stories, and became the Hearst syndicate's ace reporter on three of the most sensational trial stories of the 1920s. He reported the Halls-Mills case (the famed "Pig Woman" case), the Snyder Grey case that he nicknamed "A Dumbell Murder" ("Dumbell because," he said, "it was so dumb"), and the execution of Sacco and Vanzetti. In the summer of 1928, about the time he tackled the Republican National Convention, he changed the title of his column from "Th' Mornin's Mornin' " to "I Think So." And in 1929 he renamed it again, calling it "Between You and Me." Although Runyon was obviously attempting to create an intimate stance toward his readers, he was also laying the final groundwork for his Broadway stories, hinting that he was to speak only in the first person singular.

Runyon wrote the first of his Broadway stories, "Romance in the Roaring Forties," for the July 1929 issue of *Cosmopolitan*. For it he received one thousand dollars; Ray Long, the magazine's editor, quickly called for more stories like it and raised Runyon's already astounding fee. Before the year's end he had written and published three more Broadway tales for *Cosmopolitan*. At least one of his biographers believes that he wrote the first story to pay for his appendicitis operation. Since he had formally separated from his wife in 1928, he might have felt equally compelled to find extra income for the maintenance payments he owed her and his children. At the rather ripe age of forty-six, Runyon had launched a series of stories that were, more than anything else he wrote, to insure him a lasting fame. *Guys and Dolls* (1931), his first collection of

Runyon (right) with fellow sportswriter Arthur Bugs Baer (United Press International)

short stories, includes "Madame La Gimp," "Dark Delores," "Butch Minds the Baby," "Blood Pressure," "The Brain Goes Home," and "Social Error." Throughout the Depression years the popularity of such Broadway stories brought him a rich harvest of publication fees, royalties, and film work.

"Romance in the Roaring Forties" set the pattern. The story traces the crisscrossed loves of Waldo Winchester (a thinly disguised Walter Winchell) and Dave the Dude, a "kind-hearted" rumrunner and much-feared gangster. They both love the same "doll," Miss Billy Perry, a tap dancer at the 1600 Club. Like many a Runyon doll after her, she is grasping and greedy, fickle and fluff-headed. And yet she is fatally attractive. When Dave discovers Waldo and Billy holding hands at the 1600 Club, he "knocks Waldo Winchester bow-legged." From there he goes to the Chicken Club, where he spends three days drinking bootleg hooch. Then, in a quick change of heart, he decides that because Billy truly loves Waldo he must give her up. As in another *Guys and Dolls* tale, "Madame La Gimp" (*Cosmopolitan*, October 1929), Dave nobly assumes the role of a hard-punching and oversized Cupid. He kidnaps Waldo, who naturally believes that he is about to be "scragged." Dave, in fact, is setting up an elaborate and expensive wedding for Billy and Waldo

at the Woodcock Inn. The mob is invited to the roadhouse wedding, and Runyon takes delight in cataloging them and their "monikers": "Miss Missouri Martin with all her diamonds hanging from her in different places, and Good Time Charley Bernstein, and Feet Samuels, and Tony Bertazzola, and Skeets Bolivar, and Nick the Greek, and Rochester Red, and a lot of other guys and dolls from around and about." They drink noisily as they await the ceremonies and the marriage feast.

What neither Dave, Billy, the invited guests, nor the reader knows is that Waldo Winchester is already married to Lola Sapola "of the Rolling Sapolas." The strong-armed Lola, having somehow learned of the marriage, breaks into the Woodcock Inn, body punches Dave the Dude twice, and carries off Waldo over one shoulder. Lola and Waldo are blissfully reunited. Billy, now recognizing that Dave is a gentleman, and seeing that he is a most generous and free-spending one, agrees to marry him. All ends happily or seems to. But the narrator gives the plot yet one more quick twist in the epiloguelike close: "I see Mr. and Mrs. Dave the Dude the other day, and they seem very happy. But you never can tell about married people, so of course I am never going to let on to Dave the Dude that I am the one who telephones Lola Sapola at the Marx

*Runyon and his second wife, Patrice Amati del Grande
(United Press International)*

guy" who says yes to "propositions" of which he silently disapproves or questions.

But while he tells his stories in what Runyon calls a "half-boob" air, he shows himself to be observant and even shrewd. In "Dark Dolores" (*Cosmopolitan*, November 1929), for example, he notices, though the mob bosses he is with do not, that the sinuous Dolores "may know more than she lets on." When he later observes that she "is from Detroit with me" and "from Cleveland" with Benny the Blond Jew, his suspicions of this dark and doughnut-eyed temptress are rightly aroused. But to the end–long after Dolores has led Benny, Black Mike, and Scoodles Shea to their deaths–he is wisely innocent, insisting with his silence that he knows nothing. Reluctant to express anything that might sound like a moral judgment, he can string out long and circuitous explanations to show that "you never can tell." Wagner has pointed out that the Runyon narrator typically allows his "own first-person report to be confronted on an equal footing with those of other characters." In his carnival of first-person narration Runyon makes the reader "conscious of his keen sense of relativity."

His narrator, then, seldom judges, and seems never to act willingly. In "Blood Pressure," the first of Runyon's *Saturday Evening Post* (3 April 1930) Broadway stories, Rusty Charley, who has just "guzzled" Gloomy Gus Smallwood, makes him his unwilling companion. As their adventures veer toward the violent, the narrator's blood pressure rises higher and higher. Near the story's end, he is safe but "dizzy" and "wobbling." In "The Brain Goes Home" (*Cosmopolitan*, May 1931) the narrator voices no objection aloud as others bend his feeble will to theirs. He is comically but sympathetically passive. Before he knows it, he and Big Nig Skolsky are wandering through New York carrying the fatally wounded body of the gambler Armand Rosenthal. The four women he has kept–each in turn–send the wounded Brain away from the "homes" he rented for them. And, though Daffy Jack stabbed The Brain, Runyon's narrator nervously fears that *he* may be charged with the murder: "cops just naturally love to refuse to believe guys like Big Nig and me, no matter what we say." In "Butch Minds the Baby" (*Collier's*, 13 September 1930) the narrator is first forced to take Harry the Horse, Little Isadore, and Spanish John to Big Butch's brownstone. Before he can muster the courage to leave them, he finds himself, much against his will, drawn into a safecracking

Hotel, because maybe I do not do Dave any too much of a favor, at that." As many readers have noted, the narrator's delayed revelation of a suppressed or omitted plot piece re-creates Harte's and O. Henry's "snapper" finishes. Here, the narrator's confessional aside–to an undefined and undramatized audience–openly discloses the Rube Goldberg engine that turns the wheels of most Runyon plots.

The narrator's closing revelations have yet another effect. They graft the action of the story to an ambiguous time present and, in turn, call the reader's attention back to the unnamed narrator himself, to the process of narration and the character of the "I" who tells the story. Wagner refers to this as the "egocentristic organization" of Runyon's short stories. Other critics regard the "I-narrator" as Runyon's persona, his comic mask. His narrator is obviously a knowledgeable "citizen" of Broadway, a nervously cautious soul, frightened of cops, gangsters, and con men, and oddly unwilling to drink freely or get mixed up with dolls. By his own admission, he is a "nod-

job. His characteristic understatement does not hide his fear of the "three parties from Brooklyn" who have muscled him around. He knew, even before they "put the arm" on him in Mindy's, what no-goods they were. Though Runyon's use of the passive voice mutes any direct judgment, the narrator rather flatly categorized the three as thugs who were "always doing something that is considered a knock to the community, such as robbing people, or maybe shooting or stabbing them . . . and carrying on generally."

Between 1929 and 1931 Runyon produced Broadway stories at a regular and rapid pace, enough of them, thirteen in all, to make *Guys and Dolls* (1931) a sizable short-story collection. Heywood Broun wrote the introduction, asserting that "the mantle of O. Henry" had fallen to Runyon. The book quickly became a best-seller. Reviewers for the literary journals and magazines, for the most part, sniffed cautiously at the collection. The anonymous reviewer for the *New York Times Book Review* (6 September 1931) declared that "Mr. Runyon knows what interests most people, arouses their curiosity and makes them laugh." Though he argued that the "characters are too thin for any long life," he rounded out his review by praising Runyon's fidelity to the "language of Broadway." The reviewer for the *Saturday Review of Literature* (12 September 1931) posed a balanced critique: "nearly all of Mr. Runyon's stories are ingenious. Most of them are ingenious and cheap; a few are ingenious and good." Like the *Times* reviewer, he valued Runyon's handling of "slang," "the rich and varied phraseology of a class with whom language, like crime, is a debased but well-cultivated art." Following Broun's lead, he linked Runyon's name with O. Henry and with Lardner, a double pairing that soon became commonplace. He singled out for praise "Butch Minds the Baby" and "The Brain Goes Home," stories he found notable for "humor, kindliness, and surprise."

Hollywood's opinion, in many ways, proved far more important to Runyon's career as a short-story writer. His stories, during the 1930s and after, moved, as if on an endless conveyor belt, from magazines to books to the screen. Film rights and screen writing became a major source of income, though the first returns promised only a modest profit. Shortly after the publication of *Guys and Dolls*, Fox studios took an option on the book for one thousand dollars. According to Hoyt, John Francis Dillon and other Fox read-

ers decided the book had "no picture value." Their decision proved to be fortunate. Had they exercised their option Runyon could have realized no more than fifteen thousand dollars for the sale of his film rights. Instead, the subsequent sale of individual stories earned him many more times that figure. On his first sale, of the story of "Madame La Gimp," he was able to earn thirty-five hundred dollars. When the film–titled *Lady for a Day* (1933)–was nominated for several academy awards, the price for other Runyon stories rose.

"Madame La Gimp" seems to have been written for the screen. When Dave the Dude discloses his plans for marrying Madame La Gimp's daughter to a Spanish grandee, the ordinarily cautious narrator responds tartly: "It is commencing to sound to me like a movie such as a guy is apt to see at a midnight show. . . ." Dave the Dude's plans sound like the plot of a 1930s screwball comedy. Runyon's story pivots on a series of impersonations, all designed–by Dave the Dude–to convince a visiting Spanish family that Madame La Gimp and her daughter are rich and respectable. Madame La Gimp, in fact, is "a busted-down old Spanish doll" who scratches out a living selling day-old newspapers and wilted flowers. At a party for the Spanish aristocrats Guinea Mike successfully poses as Vice President Curtis; Wild William Wilkins, "who is a very hot man at this time," impersonates "The Honorable Police Commissioner, Mister Grover A. Whalen." Wagner and D'Itri see, in these deceptions and social inversions, a strong vein of social satire. Wagner, citing "Social Error" (*Collier's*, 22 March 1930; collected in *Guys and Dolls*), "The Old Doll's House" (*Collier's*, 13 May 1933; collected in *Blue Plate Special*), and several other Runyon tales, argues persuasively that through such parodies of high society Runyon suggests "that nothing much would be changed if Gangland and respectability were made to take each other's places." The thesis of Wagner's study is that Runyon was a "respectable rebel." Despite his "over-all optimism," he nourished a skepticism and irony that he leveled at "the actual depreciated values by which success was measured in the America of his age." "Madame La Gimp," and the humor and irony of other Broadway stories Wagner scrutinizes, illustrates Runyon's covert rebellion.

Runyon's scattered statements of his artistic credo are ambivalent on this point. Near the end of his life he wrote a mock review of his own work that, in part, said:

Runyon with one of his racehorses, All Scarlet, in 1935 (United Press International)

Damon Runyon, in a simulation of humor, often manages to say things which, if said in a serious tone, might be erased because he is not supposed to say things like that. By saying something with a half-boob air . . . he gets ideas out of his system on the wrongs of this world which indicate that he must have been a great rebel at heart but lacking in moral courage. . . .

I tell you Runyon has subtlety but it is the considered opinion of the reviewer that it is a great pity the guy did not remain a rebel out-and-out, even at the cost of a good position at the feed trough.

His ambivalence about art and money would seem to have been resolved in two newspaper columns, "Magnificent Mammon" and "Get the Money" (collected in *Short Takes*, 1946). In "Get the Money," with lines much quoted by Runyon critics and biographers, he said, "I would like to have an artistic success that made money, of course, but if I had to make a choice between the two I would take the dough." Such statements, no doubt, were intended to suggest to newspaper readers that he was, as he liked to put it, a "mercenary-minded old skeezicks." To Wagner, his comic overstatements carry an underlying irony and point to Runyon's alienation from American plutocracy and to his running satire of its social order. His subversive impulses are, in other words, encoded in short-story formulas and the slang that subtly inverted social values. Runyon often disclaimed a high-minded artistic intent and ridiculed prissy critics who were shocked over his saying that for him money outweighed "artistic merit." At the same time he sweated out as many as a dozen drafts of a story. In his vaunting cynicism about "art" he may well have been staking a claim to his own true artistic merit.

Boosted by the popular demand for the Broadway stories, Runyon's income rose mightily during the Depression years. He published nine short-story collections between 1929 and 1939; in the same years at least fifteen films were made from his stories, and Runyon himself collected as much as two thousand dollars a week for screen writing. He did all this while working as Hearst's highest-paid columnist. The money was spent on horses, hunting dogs, and prizefighters. In addition, Runyon bought property on Hibiscus Island in Miami harbor and began to spend winters in Florida. On 7 July 1932, with his friend Mayor Jimmy Walker presiding, he married Patrice Amati del Grande, a dancer from the Silver Slipper. (His first wife had died 9 November 1931; they had not divorced.) The marriage may have made him feel less bound to Broadway. Following it, he built a large white house on his island property (near Al Capone's winter retreat) for seventy-five thousand dollars. He and Patrice had chosen the Miami location so that he might, according to Hoyt, "find material for his column and amusement for himself and Patrice."

Ed Weiner, a friend of Runyon's in the 1930s and the first of his biographers, said in 1948 that "the majority and the best of his stories were written . . . from 1931 to 1936." The Runyon stories that anthologists and critics have canonized were written then: among them, "Bloodhounds of Broadway" (1931), "Little Miss Marker" (1932), and "The Idyll of Miss Sarah Brown" (1933). The three collections of his work published during the Depression–*Guys and Dolls* (1931), *Blue Plate Special* (1934), and *Money From Home* (1935)–constitute the recognized core of the Broadway tales. In 1939 and again in 1944 the three books were published in one volume entitled *The Damon Runyon Omnibus*. Perhaps it is mere coincidence that his most productive years were also the happy years of his marriage to Patrice. The 1930s were clearly money-filled and rewarding times. When magazine editors discovered the extent to which a Runyon tale increased sales, they bid up his price for a single short story to five thousand dollars. The Depression hardly seemed to touch him.

Though Runyon's second collection of Broadway tales was entitled *Blue Plate Special*, its somber title did not reflect any particular emphasis on Depression blues or simple and plain living. Runyon, perhaps to play off the success of his first collection of Broadway tales, had wanted to name the book *More Guys and Dolls*, but his editors at Stokes objected. They no doubt wanted to distinguish it from the earlier collection of Broadway fables. Few of these stories make direct reference to hard times; the characters seem more conscious of the waning of prohibition than the coming of the NRA. "The Snatching of Bookie Bob" (*Collier's*, 26 September 1931) stands as something of an exception, since the narrator states in the opening that "times are very tough indeed, with the stock market going all to pieces, and

banks busting right and left. . . ." The "many citizens of this town," he adds, "are compelled to do the best they can." But even this grim reminder is washed away in humor. In the following paragraph the narrator solemnly states that they are "wearing last year's clothes and have practically nothing to bet on the races or anything else, and it is a condition that will touch anybody's heart."

"Little Miss Marker" (*Collier's*, 26 March 1932) seems the most important–certainly the most emotionally charged–of the *Blue Plate Special* stories. Wagner calls it one of Runyon's "most representative stories," noting its fusion of Dickensian sentimentality and its biting social satire. Marky, a three- or four-year-old girl, has been left with a bookie named Sorrowful by her father as a marker for his bet. When, after a long day, her father does not return to claim her, the miserly old bookmaker reluctantly takes her home to his flophouse apartment. He slowly comes to love her and, with uncharacteristic generosity, makes a home for her. Marky and Sorrowful, along with an odd assortment of Broadway characters, become an idealized family. Calvin S. Brown has read in this a parallel to Bret Harte's "The Luck of Roaring Camp." Like "Luck," the foundling infant of Harte's story, Marky becomes a redemptive figure. Gamblers and touts, and most significantly Sorrowful, are softened by her innocence and goodness. When, after a long absence, her father does return to reclaim his "darling child," his motives–he can now inherit a fortune through Marky and her deceased mother–are questioned, and his pretensions to respectability are bitterly satirized. Long ago he had abandoned his wife in Paris either because he succumbed to amnesia or because his family snobbishly disapproved of his "marriage to a person of the stage."

The general outlines of this story suggest that Runyon drew, as he did in the "Grandpap Mugg" stories, on the bitter memories of his own lonely childhood. The father's rejections of Marky, and her mother's early death, seem to frame the tale within the shadows of Runyon's past. In Sorrowful and Marky's love he projects the bright image of the loving and happy family he never had. Marky dies, in part, because she became "lonesome." Awaking one night to find her sitter, Mrs. Clancy, asleep, she runs barefoot through the snow to the nightclub where she will find Sorrowful. When she embraces him there, she inadvertently shields him from the deadly aim of Milk Ear Willie and saves his life. Within

Illustrations by Garth Williams for Runyon's 1946 short-story collection In Our Town *(copyright © by Garth Williams)*

a few days she dies of pneumonia: "her hands fall across her breast as soft and white and light as snowflakes, and Marky never again dances in this world." The film version of the story, starring Adolph Menjou and Shirley Temple, proved to be a great commercial success. Not surprisingly, Marky, as portrayed by Shirley Temple, has her stirring sickbed scene and lives to have her bows, hugs, and kisses in the final reel.

"Dream Street Rose" (*Collier's*, 11 June 1932) is a story of revenge, a much darker vision of youth betrayed and despoiled. Dream Street Rose, an "old tomato," compels the narrator to listen to the story of her youth and, in telling her tale, tacitly announces that she has just killed the man who wronged her thirty-five years ago. Though she tells it as a story "about my friend," it is evident from her emotion, and the intimate details of her story, that she is chronicling her own life. The device of the story within a story–Rose's autobiography within the frame of a murder mystery–serves Runyon well. The narrator does not immediately realize what Rose is saying. She implicitly confesses that she has just killed a prominent society figure, Frank Billingsworth McGuigan, a man who wronged her when she was young. In abandoning her, he destroyed her dreams of "love . . ., a nice little home, children. . . ." Rose has waited thirty-five years to take her revenge. She has waited until Frank has a family and reputation to live for, and then, she says, she forced him to kill himself to save his family and good name.

Rose's story, like the much earlier tale "The Informal Execution of Soupbone Pew," may be said to originate in Runyon's western code of honor. Frank had falsely promised to marry her when she was a beautiful young woman in Pueblo, Colorado. Whatever else Rose's Pueblo birthplace may suggest, it stands as a reminder that a western code of revenge frequently governs the moral structure of Runyon's Broadway tales. That she suffers degradation at the hands of a social better also links her story to Runyon's many tales of chorus girls manhandled and mistreated by society swells: principal among them, "Bloodhounds of Broadway" and "What, No Butler?" (*Collier's*, 5 August 1933; collected in *Blue Plate Special*). But the mode of narration distinguishes it from these tales. Here, as in other Runyon stories, the narrator listens, piecing together the buried story from fragments he slowly collects from different sources. The narrator and Charley, reading the morning papers that report

McGuigan's "suicide," can puzzle out the meaning of the tale Rose has told. As they try to reconcile the newspaper's version of events with Rose's tale, Charley futilely tries to mop away the tarred tracks that Rose left on his tavern floor the night before. They lead back to McGuigan's apartment.

Few reviewers commented on Runyon's narrative techniques in *Blue Plate Special;* most simply repeated what had been said about *Guys and Dolls*. The characters seemed "thin" and the Broadway lingo authentic. D'Itri has pointed out that reviewers were slow to discover the narrator's central importance. An anonymous reviewer in the *New York Times*, for example, noted his "knowing and dumb, brutal and tender" character but largely ignored his mediating function as a narrator. Fred T. Marsh, in a *New York Times* (13 March 1938) review of *The Best of Damon Runyon*, finally focused on his double role as narrator and character; he commented on his " 'pawky' way of telling a story by understatement" and went on to describe him as "an unforgettable mug in the rogue's gallery of American fiction."

In 1935 Runyon published *Money From Home*, and, for the third time running, he had a best-selling short-story collection. For some, however, Runyon's plot formulas and stock characters were turning stale. A book critic for the *Saturday Review of Literature* (18 August 1934) flippantly categorized Runyon's tales as "midget yarns." *Money From Home* again collected tales of Broadway; characters such as Harry the Horse, Mindy, and Johnny Brannigan, as principals or supernumeraries, reappeared in a kind of New York Yoknapatawpha County saga. But Runyon's Broadway citizens also wandered far from the roaring forties: to Florida ("A Story Goes with It," *Cosmopolitan*, November 1931; "Pick the Winner," *Collier's*, 11 February 1933), to Managua, Nicaragua ("Earthquake," *Cosmopolitan*, January 1933), to Connecticut for the Harvard-Yale boat race ("A Nice Price," *Collier's*, 8 September 1934). All the tales were imprinted with Runyon's now-familiar manner. Adverbial markers, a stylized present or present-progressive tense, and other devices free him from any standard usage of the past tense ("It is along toward four o'clock one morning, and I am sitting in Mindy's restaurant . . ."). Flurries of coincidence fall upon the plots of most stories (Brannigan, a New York cop, meets and arrests a fugitive named Earthquake during an earthquake in Nicaragua). Narratives are punctuated, even structured, by gnomic sayings (Sam the Gonoph, in "A Nice Price," says, "I long ago come to the conclusion that all life is 6 to 5 against"). Once more, murderous gangsters make grand sentimental gestures (Harry the Horse, like Dave the Dude before him, acts as a matchmaker). Under improbable circumstances, in encounters sometimes made plausible by the dislocations of the Depression or the crossroads of the city, gamblers and gangsters come together with Harvard swells or "old family" dolls ("Money from Home," *Cosmopolitan*, October 1935; "A Nice Price"; and "Breach of Promise," *Cosmopolitan*, January 1935). Wagner has asserted that Runyon uses such meetings of high society and the underworld "to set off the blemishes of respectability"; he cites, by way of illustration, satiric contrasts in two *Money From Home* stories, "Undertaker's Song" (*Collier's*, 24 November 1934) and "Broadway Complex" (*Collier's*, 28 October 1933).

Runyon wrote and published Broadway tales almost until the end of his life. In 1938 he published *Take It Easy*, which included the finely comic "A Piece of Pie" (*Collier's*, 21 August 1937) and "Tight Shoes" (*Collier's*, 18 April 1936). The latter story was a burlesque of politics akin to Charlie Chaplin's *Modern Times* (1936). "A Piece of Pie" is a tall tale, an account of an eating contest that piles one absurd eating feat on top of another. Nicely-Nicely Jones–"maybe five feet nine inches tall, and about five feet nine inches wide"–squares off against Violette Shumberger. They fall in love and elope after the contest.

In *Take It Easy* Joe and Ethel Turp, a blue-collar couple from Brooklyn, make their first book appearance. Runyon had begun publishing fictive letters from Joe in his column and in *Pictorial Review* in the 1930s. D'Itri compares Joe's letters and the stories about the daffy doings of his wife to Lardner's *You Know Me Al* missives. The Turps' banter and manipulative play can be linked as well to the comedy and repartee of George Burns and Gracie Allen. In *My Wife Ethel* Runyon published differing sets of Turp tales, one for sale in Great Britain (1939) and the other in the United States (1940). A generous sampling of the Turp letters was published in *Short Takes* (1946). Domestic comedy and a play of manners, sometimes read as a sign of class conflict, lift and lighten most of these short, short stories. Clark Kinnaird, in his foreword to the Modern Library *A Treasury of Damon Runyon* (1958), recalled that the Turps were, next to "My Old Man," Runyon's favorite characters. He notes that the Turp story "Home-Cooking" was among the last he wrote.

Not surprisingly, the Brooklyn couple and their all-American virtues proved popular enough for a film, *Joe and Ethel Call on the President* (1939), based on the *Saturday Evening Post* (13 August 1937) story "A Call on the President."

Hoyt believes that, after 1940, the genial image of home life and American society presented in the Turp columns concealed Runyon's almost complete "alienation." Other stories and columns reveal a "sourness" about marriage and declining American values. After the war began he and Patrice spent little time in each other's company, and by 1944 they were no longer living together. Between 1943 and spring 1944 Runyon belatedly discovered that a persistent pain in his throat was a sign of a malignant cancer. In the beginning of 1944 his health was such that his column began to appear irregularly.

Though Runyon's production of short fiction also waned during the war years, he continued to write, collecting enough material to fill one notable collection, *Runyon à la Carte* (1944). Few of the stories that Runyon wrote for the *Runyon à la Carte* collection during the 1940s matched the conventional happy endings of his earlier works. "Little Pinks" (*Collier's*, 27 January 1940), a tale of unrequited love and violent revenge, might stand as a representation of Runyon's sentiments and fiction of this period. Little Pinks, once a busboy at the Canary Club, gives up his own life to wait upon the invalid "Your Highness." Once a chorus girl, this redheaded "Judy" was injured by Case Ables so that she can never walk again. Not until her life's end, after Little Pinks has avenged her, does she thank him, saying, "Little Pinks, I love you." To earn her gratitude he battered Ables's spine until it was permanently injured. In 1942 Runyon produced *The Big Street*, a film based on this story starring Lucille Ball and Henry Fonda.

"Blonde Mink" (*Collier's*, 29 September 1945) and "Big Boy Blues" (*Collier's*, 4 August 1945) were the last Broadway stories published in Runyon's lifetime. "Big Boy Blues," a sentimentalized tale of World War II, traces an improbable reconciliation of a tough gangster father and a gentle son. Though larded with black bile, "Blonde Mink" is at one level a comically constructed ghost story. When Slats Slavin dies and is buried, he rests uneasily in his grave because Beatrice Gee, his unfaithful fiancée, has failed to buy a promised gravestone. She has spent his bequest on an expensive blonde mink. As a ghostly apparition he instructs his loyal friend Julie the

Starker to remind her of the promise. Hoyt suggests that, while the story cannot be taken to be autobiographical, it nevertheless projects Runyon's final fears and preoccupations. Like the dying Slats, he was a "long shot," not worth a doctor's time. He was haunted in his last days by his illness and the impending divorce from his second wife. Critical opinion holds that this is a lesser Runyon tale: the multi-layered narration seems confusing; the irony of the situation, bitter and heavy-handed. The character of Beatrice Gee bulks too wantonly cold and cruel. The relativity of perspective Wagner prizes in the Broadway tales is absent. At this late date in his life Runyon could not, probably did not try to, distance himself from his characters.

Runyon died after a prolonged illness on 10 December 1946. For the last two years of his life he had no power of speech; he carried a pad of paper with him at all times and communicated by writing on it. During his illness he and his son, who had been estranged for many years, were reconciled. Runyon willed that his body be cremated: eight days after his death, a large transport plane carrying an urn with his ashes flew first over Woodlawn Cemetery, where his first wife was buried, over the Statue of Liberty, and then over Times Square. There, three thousand feet above the busy thoroughfare, Runyon's friend of many years, Capt. Eddie Rickenbacker, scattered Damon Runyon's ashes over Broadway.

In the forty odd years since his death, Runyon's name has endured and most of his Broadway stories have stayed in print. *Guys and Dolls, The Damon Runyon Omnibus,* and other standards were reprinted in facsimile form in the late 1970s; since 1958 Modern Library has kept in print, under two different titles, a well-stocked anthology of his poems, sketches, columns, and stories. And recently Tom Clark edited two new anthologies of his Broadway stories. Sports commentators, aided and abetted by the staying power of the musical *Guys and Dolls,* have made his name synonymous with broken syntax and pleonastic locutions that seem either colorful or comic. He remains popular, but none of this means that a Runyon revival in academia is here or is coming. In 1982 Patricia Ward D'Itri compared his narrative technique to Sherwood Anderson's and Ernest Hemingway's, mustered the evidence for the power and authenticity of his underworld lingo, and, like Runyon defenders before her, complained of serious critical neglect. Whether her study, any more than Wagner's reading of the Broadway tales in 1965, heralds a critical revaluation of his fiction remains to be seen. Since the 1930s Runyon has been categorized as a lesser O. Henry or Lardner, and critical opinion has coalesced around those views.

Though a minor writer, Runyon cannot be reduced to an example of antique popular culture. To say, as many have, that he was the master of the magazine short story is to damn him with the faintest of praise. In his tales of the underworld and America's underclass he wrestled with the dreams of success and fears of failure that have possessed the greatest of American writers. His densely detailed plots, his persistent present-tense narration, and the slang language of his characters, at their best, illuminate an angry ambivalence. In his sentimentality and his melodramatic flourishes he was the last of our Victorian authors; his cool, understated reckoning with the violence, confusion, and corruption of urban life places him among the first of our twentieth-century writers.

References:

Calvin S. Brown, "The Luck of Miss Marker," *Western Humanities Review,* 11 (1957): 341-345;

Tom Clark, *The World of Damon Runyon* (New York: Harper & Row, 1978);

Patricia Ward D'Itri, *Damon Runyon* (Boston: Twayne, 1982);

LaRocque DuBose, "Damon Runyon's Underworld Lingo," *University of Texas Studies in English,* 32 (1953): 123-132;

Gene Fowler, *Skyline: A Reporter's Reminiscence of the 1920s* (New York: Viking, 1961);

Edwin P. Hoyt, *A Gentleman of Broadway: The Story of Damon Runyon* (Boston: Little, Brown, 1964);

Clark Kinnaird, Foreword to *A Treasury of Damon Runyon* (New York: Modern Library, 1958);

John O. Rees, "The Last Local Colorist: Damon Runyon," *Kansas Magazine,* 7 (1968): 73-81;

Damon Runyon, Jr., *Father's Footsteps* (New York: Random House, 1954);

Jean Wagner, *Runyonese: The Mind and Craft of Damon Runyon* (Paris: Steckert-Hafner, 1965);

Edward H. Weiner, *The Damon Runyon Story* (New York: Longmans, Green, 1948).

Papers:

The University of California, Berkeley, and Temple University hold a significant number of Runyon letters.

William Saroyan

(31 August 1908-18 May 1981)

Greg Keeler
Montana State University, Bozeman

See also the Saroyan entries in *DLB 7: Twentieth-Century American Dramatists; DLB 9: American Novelists, 1910-1915;* and *DLB Yearbook: 1981.*

SELECTED BOOKS: *The Daring Young Man on the Flying Trapeze and Other Stories* (New York: Random House, 1934; London: Faber & Faber, 1935);

Inhale & Exhale (New York: Random House, 1936; London: Faber & Faber, 1936);

Three Times Three (Los Angeles: Conference Press, 1936);

Little Children (New York: Harcourt, Brace, 1937; London: Faber & Faber, 1937);

Love, Here Is My Hat (New York: Modern Age, 1938; London: Faber & Faber, 1938);

The Trouble with Tigers (New York: Harcourt, Brace, 1938; London: Faber & Faber, 1939);

Peace, It's Wonderful (New York: Modern Age, 1939; London: Faber & Faber, 1940);

My Heart's in the Highlands (New York: Harcourt, Brace, 1939);

The Time of Your Life (New York: Harcourt, Brace, 1939);

Three Plays: My Heart's in the Highlands, The Time of Your Life, Love's Old Sweet Song (New York: Harcourt, Brace, 1940);

My Name Is Aram (New York: Harcourt, Brace, 1940; London: Faber & Faber, 1941);

Jim Dandy (Cincinnati: Little Man Press, 1941); republished as *Jim Dandy: Fat Man in a Famine* (New York: Harcourt, Brace, 1947; London: Faber & Faber, 1948);

Three Plays: The Beautiful People, Sweeney in the Trees, Across the Board on Tomorrow Morning (New York: Harcourt, Brace, 1941); republished as *The Beautiful People and Other Plays* (London: Faber & Faber, 1943);

Saroyan's Fables (New York: Harcourt, Brace, 1941);

The Time of Your Life and Two Other Plays (London: Faber & Faber, 1942);

William Saroyan

Razzle-Dazzle (New York: Harcourt, Brace, 1942; revised edition, London: Faber & Faber, 1945);

The Human Comedy (New York: Harcourt, Brace, 1943; London: Faber & Faber, 1943; revised edition, New York: Harcourt, Brace & World, 1971);

Get Away Old Man (New York: Harcourt, Brace, 1944; London: Faber & Faber, 1946);

Dear Baby (New York: Harcourt, Brace, 1944; London: Faber & Faber, 1945);

Why Abstract?, by Saroyan, Hilaire Hiler, and Henry Miller (Norfolk, Conn.: New Directions, 1945);

The Adventures of Wesley Jackson (New York: Harcourt, Brace, 1946; London: Faber & Faber, 1947);

The Saroyan Special (New York: Harcourt, Brace, 1948);

Don't Go Away Mad and Two Other Plays (New York: Harcourt, Brace, 1949; London: Faber & Faber, 1951);

The Assyrian and Other Stories (New York: Harcourt, Brace, 1950; London: Faber & Faber, 1955);

The Twin Adventures (New York: Harcourt, Brace, 1950);

Rock Wagram (Garden City, N.Y.: Doubleday, 1951; London: Faber & Faber, 1952);

Tracy's Tiger (Garden City, N.Y.: Doubleday, 1951; London: Faber & Faber, 1952);

The Bicycle Rider in Beverly Hills (New York: Scribners, 1952; London: Faber & Faber, 1953);

The Laughing Matter (Garden City, N.Y.: Doubleday, 1953; London: Faber & Faber, 1954);

Mama I Love You (Boston & Toronto: Little, Brown / Atlantic Monthly, 1956; London: Faber & Faber, 1957);

The Whole Voyald and Other Stories (Boston & Toronto: Little, Brown / Atlantic Monthly, 1956; London: Faber & Faber, 1957);

Papa You're Crazy (Boston & Toronto: Little, Brown / Atlantic Monthly, 1957; London: Faber & Faber, 1958);

The Cave Dwellers (New York: Putnam's, 1958; London: Faber & Faber, 1958);

The William Saroyan Reader (New York: Braziller, 1958);

Sam, The Highest Jumper of Them All, or The London Comedy (London: Faber & Faber, 1961);

Here Comes, There Goes, You Know Who (New York: Simon & Schuster / Trident, 1961; London: Davies, 1962);

Boys and Girls Together (New York: Harcourt, Brace & World, 1963; London: Davies, 1963);

Me (New York: Crowell-Collier / London: Collier-Macmillan, 1963);

Not Dying (New York: Harcourt, Brace & World, 1963; London: Cassell, 1966);

One Day in the Afternoon of the World (New York: Harcourt, Brace & World, 1964; London: Cassell, 1965);

After Thirty Years: The Daring Young Man on the Flying Trapeze (New York: Harcourt, Brace & World, 1964);

Horsey Gorsey and the Frog (Chippewa Falls, Wis.: Hale, 1965);

My Kind of Crazy and Wonderful People (New York: Harcourt, Brace & World, 1966);

Short Drive, Sweet Chariot (New York: Phaedra, 1966);

Look at Us: Us? US?, by Saroyan and Arthur Rothstein (New York: Cowles, 1967);

Letters from 74 Rue Taitbout, or Don't Go, But If You Must, Say Hello to Everybody (New York & Cleveland: World, 1969); republished as *Don't Go, But If You Must, Say Hello to Everybody* (London: Cassell, 1970);

Three New Dramatic Works and 19 Other Short Plays (New York: Phaedra, 1969);

Days of Life and Death and Escape to the Moon (New York: Dial, 1970; London: Joseph, 1971);

Words and Photographs (Chicago: Follett, 1970);

Places Where I've Done Time (New York: Praeger, 1972; London: Davis-Poynter, 1973);

The Tooth and My Father (Garden City, N.Y.: Doubleday, 1974);

An Act or Two of Foolish Kindness (Lincoln, Mass.: Penmaen Press & Design, 1976);

Morris Hirshfield (New York: Rizzoli International, 1976);

Obituaries (Berkeley, Cal.: Creative Arts Books, 1979).

SELECTED PLAY PRODUCTIONS: *My Heart's in the Highlands*, New York, Guild Theatre, 13 April 1939;

The Time of Your Life, New York, Booth Theatre, 25 October 1939;

A Theme in the Life of the Great American Goof, New York, Center Theatre, 11 January 1940;

Love's Old Sweet Song, New York, Plymouth Theatre, 2 May 1940;

Across the Board on Tomorrow Morning, Pasadena, Pasadena Community Playhouse, February 1941; New York, Theatre Showcase, March 1942; New York, Belasco Theatre, 17 August 1942;

The Beautiful People, New York, Lyceum Theatre, 21 April 1941;

Hello Out There, Santa Barbara, Locerbo Theatre, 10 September 1941; New York, Belasco Theatre, 29 September 1942;

Jim Dandy, Pasadena, Pasadena Community Playhouse, 1941;

Saroyan (seated at center) with his siblings: Zabel, Henry, and Cosette (courtesy of Aram Saroyan)

Talking to You, New York, Belasco Theatre, 17 August 1942;

Get Away Old Man, New York, Cort Theatre, 24 November 1943;

The Hungerers, The Ping Pong Game, and *Hello Out There*, New York, Provincetown Playhouse, 23 August 1945;

Sam Ego's House, Hollywood, Circle Theatre, 30 October 1947;

Don't Go Away Mad, New York, Master Institute Theatre, 9 May 1949;

The Son, Hollywood, Circle Theatre, 31 March 1950;

Once Around the Block, New York, Master Institute Theatre, 24 May 1950;

A Lost Child's Fireflies, Dallas, Round-up Theatre, 15 July 1954;

Opera, Opera, New York, Amato Theatre, 21 December 1955;

Ever Been in Love with a Midget, Berlin, Congress Hall, 20 September 1957;

The Cave Dwellers, New York, Bijou Theatre, 19 October 1957;

Sam, The Highest Jumper of Them All: or, the London Comedy, London, Stratford East Theatre Royal, 6 April 1960;

Settled Out of Court, by Saroyan and Henry Cecil, London, Strand Theatre, 19 October 1960;

High Time Along the Wabash, Lafayette, Purdue University Playhouse, 1 December 1961;

Ah Man, music by Peter Fricker, Suffolk, England, Aldeburgh Festival, 21 June 1962;

Bad Men in the West, Stanford, Stanford University, 19 May 1971;

People's Lives, by Saroyan and others, New York, Manhattan Theatre Club, August 1974;

The Rebirth Celebration of the Human Race at Artie Zabala's Off-Broadway Theatre, New York, Shirtsleeve Theatre, 10 July 1975.

MOTION PICTURES: *The Good Job*, Loew, 1942; *The Human Comedy*, M-G-M, 1943.

TELEVISION: *The Oyster and the Pearl*, 1953; "Ah Sweet Mystery of Mrs. Murphy," *Omnibus*, NBC, 1 March 1959; "The Unstoppable Gray Fox," *GE Theatre*, CBS, 1962; *Making Money and Thirteen Other Very Short Plays*, ETV, 12 November 1970.

RADIO: "Radio Play," *Columbia Workshops*, CBS, 1940; "The People with Light Coming Out of Them," *Free Company*, CBS, 1941.

OTHER: *Dentist and Patient* and *Husband and Wife*, in *The Best Short Plays, 1968*, edited by Stanley Richards (Radnor, Pa.: Chilton Press, 1968); *The New Play*, in *The Best Short Plays, 1970*, edited by Richards (Radnor, Pa.: Chilton Press, 1970).

William Saroyan's life, so crucial to an understanding of his controversially autobiographical short fiction, was fraught with instability and change. When Saroyan was three his father, Armenak Saroyan, died, and William and his brother and two sisters had to leave their hometown of Fresno, California, to live in an orphanage in Oakland. In 1915 they returned to Fresno, where they joined their mother, Takooki Saroyan, then working as a domestic servant. Saroyan attended public schools and eventually got a job as a messenger boy for a telegraph company, a job which later became one of the major sources for his fiction and drama. After dropping out of high school he moved to San Francisco, where he worked at various jobs and eventually became a clerk, then a telegraph operator, for Postal Telegraph Company. In 1928 he published his first story in *Overland Monthly and Outwest Magazine* and took a trip to New York, hav-

ing decided to make writing his career. In 1939 he began a prolific career as a playwright. In 1943 he married Carol Marcus, a wealthy New York socialite. They had two children, Aram and Lucy, divorced in 1949, remarried in 1951, and divorced again in 1952.

Through much of Saroyan's life his personal experiences were as diverse and, at times, unhinged as the disparate genres through which his work ranges. His early success with the short story led to his interest in drama and the novel and to a fascination with film and television and even into the realm of popular music. His 1951 song "Come On-a My House," cowritten with his cousin Ross Bagdasarian, was a hit in America and abroad. But while his fame spread, his personal life seemed to suffer, for as his later memoirs repeatedly illustrate, he was obsessed with gambling and alcohol, even to the extent that he would complete works specifically to pay off gambling debts. Perhaps if it were not for his Armenian heritage (his father had come to America from the Armenian-Kurdish town of Bitlis in eastern Turkey in 1905), Saroyan would never have found the coherence and stability for which he spent the major portion of his years searching, both in his life and in his fiction, for the Armenians and their plight became his personal metaphor. Their expatriation and loss of identity were deeply felt in the Armenian community in which Saroyan was raised, and, during the Depression years especially, many Americans who brought Saroyan his success respected the pain and hardship that the Armenian people had endured for centuries.

When Saroyan died in Fresno on 18 May 1981 of cancer, America was far from the Depression years, and the values which the country had found important in his short stories seemed distant. Many of his stories were first published in magazines, and a complete bibliography of his periodical publications has not been compiled. Yet the vitality of his early short fiction, with its passion and seemingly unfulfilled promise, continues to ensure his importance as an American writer.

Despite a prolific career, Saroyan's reputation as short-story writer still rests largely on his first collection, *The Daring Young Man on the Flying Trapeze and Other Stories* (1934). As in so many of his later collections, Saroyan dashed these stories off at an amazing speed, yet the manner of composition seemed to add to the urgency of his tone. When the title piece was published in *Story*

Saroyan in 1939

magazine in February 1934, the public response was so favorable that in less than a year Random House had compiled the collection. Saroyan sets the tone of the volume in a preface, in which he advocates the abandonment of traditional short-story forms and asserts that the will of the author is the crucial element of unity. Thus, *The Daring Young Man on the Flying Trapeze* fit the literary vogue of the day both in its rebellious stance and in its advocacy of the individual.

As in many of his stories, Saroyan's narrator in "The Daring Young Man on the Flying Trapeze" is a young writer, a thinly veiled representation of the author himself. The young man, unable to rationalize his position in a materialistic society, finds fulfillment only in death. He metaphorically carries the problems of a civilization on his back as he tries to find work, gets disgusted with the bureaucracy, gives up on physical sustenance, falls back on the literary fare which has sustained him psychically, and gives himself up to death: "Then swiftly, neatly, with the grace of the young man on the trapeze, he was gone from his body." In this story Saroyan establishes one of the main themes that permeates al-

most all of his subsequent writings—the brilliance and importance of life in the face of death—usually emphasized by Saroyan's direct, autobiographical narrative but often finding a more distinct objective presentation.

In "Seventy Thousand Assyrians" (1934) Saroyan speaks directly to the reader, using a barber shop as his public forum. Here is the collection's first strong assertion of Saroyan's Armenian heritage, for when the narrator finds that the barber, Badal, is an Assyrian, whose people, like the Armenians, have lost their physical locality and are being driven to extinction, he realizes the value of Badal's identity as well as his own. He then lets this stark contrast of the endurance of their two small lives against the hugeness of the deaths of the two nations carry his theme. And in the defiant pose typical of this collection, he asks, "Why don't I make up plots and write beautiful love stories that can be made into motion pictures?" and answers his own question: "Well I am an Armenian."

Like "Seventy Thousand Assyrians," "A Cold Day" (1934) emerges through Saroyan's own voice; in fact, it is the most direct story of the collection in that it takes the form of a letter from Saroyan to Martha Foley, the editor of *Story* magazine. In "A Cold Day" Saroyan tells his editor of the hardships of writing in a cold apartment. Though the idea of this story may seem overly simple, it, perhaps more than any other story in the collection, links Saroyan personally to the concept of the daring young man. The metaphorical significance of the cold is obvious: it is Saroyan writing in the face of death.

Some other stories in this collection narrated in the author's undisguised, direct voice are "And Man" (1934), where the young narrator skips school to spend a day coming to grips with his increasing maturity; "A Curved Line" (1934), where the narrator asserts the value of common people's creative capacities in a night school art course; and "Myself Upon the Earth" (1934), where Saroyan lets a description of the process involved in writing the story become the work itself. In these pieces the author constantly alerts the reader to the immediate intentions of his craft, where plot, setting, and other trappings of traditional short fiction are subordinated to the basic struggle of a clear mind posing life against death.

In addition to these strong personal narratives, Saroyan includes several objective third-person stories in *The Daring Young Man on the Fly-*

ing Trapeze. In "Laughter" (1934) the young protagonist, Ben, laughs in class at his teacher, Miss Wissig, who forces him to stay after class and, as punishment, laugh. The protagonist of "Laughter" may be a thinly veiled young Saroyan, similar to the narrator of "And Man," but Ben is Italian instead of Armenian, putting some distance between author and narrator. Felix Otria, the narrator of "Dear Greta Garbo" (1934), is also Italian, and the extremity of his epistolary story about appearing in a newsreel where he is clubbed in a riot reveals even more distance. These objective characterizations provide early evidence of Saroyan's ability to utilize the traditional precepts of short-story writing which the preface disclaims.

Saroyan's next collection, *Inhale & Exhale* (1936), is the longest and perhaps the most divergent in style and quality of all of his works. Saroyan divided the stories into nine titled subdivisions which can be grouped into three unstated categories: stories of childhood, stories of young men, and stories of travel. Perhaps it is the stories of childhood that reveal most clearly both the worst and best in this stage of Saroyan's development.

The basic flaw in stories such as "The World and the Theater" (1935) stems from Saroyan's desire to load his narrative with emotional import rather than to let it develop within the text. The narrator, a young newsboy, through his perceptions of headlines on the papers he sells, conveys a picture of a national mind, yet his words and thoughts are obviously more mature, more Saroyan's; thus, the character and his situation are less believable.

In "The War" (1935) the young narrator witnesses an incident where, because of strong anti-German feelings, several boys beat up an innocent German boy. Here the perspective is more believable as the language remains in the range of the narrator's natural capabilities. The language is less abstract and more typical of a confused young mind: "Those boys out there. What they did today. That was nothing fine. I hate that. That is the thing I hate."

"Five Ripe Pears" (1935), because of its adult perspective on a childhood experience, also averts the confusion of adult speaking through child. The adult narrator has valuable hindsight on his childhood. He realizes the importance of nonownership as he recounts an incident where, as a child, he was punished for "stealing" pears which he thought should have been free by the mere strength of their beauty and his desire to have them. In retrospect, the punishment still seems unfair, and the child's attitude is given an intensified validity through the mature narrator.

Whether in these stories of childhood or in those of young adulthood and travel, the strongest thematic development between *The Daring Young Man on the Flying Trapeze* and *Inhale & Exhale* concerns Saroyan's Armenian background. For it is in *Inhale & Exhale* that his future optimistic themes of national identity and strong personal independence, first developed in the earlier collection, begin to solidify. To some critics this solidification of style, which led to the more objective, more tightly structured narratives of his later collections, was positive in that it was in keeping with the developing tenants of the new criticism, stressing an objectification of the narrative voice. To others, the solidification of his Armenian themes and the resulting traditional and highly crafted stories represented a diminishing of the original direct first-person voice used in *The Daring Young Man on the Flying Trapeze*. Instead of an improvement in craftsmanship, the stories of *Inhale & Exhale* revealed, to some critics, a departure from cynicism and independence toward triteness and sentimentality.

In stories such as "A Broken Wheel" (1935) Saroyan writes of his experiences in the Armenian community in Fresno with a narrative distance reinforced by the story's remote temporal setting. Saroyan's theme is implied, not forced, and the story's strength emerges in a single image: the narrator and his brother, Krikor, find a correlative for their Uncle Vahan's death in a broken bicycle wheel. Thus, the story's impact comes from the imagery more than from any direct statement of theme. Yet, "A Broken Wheel" depends heavily on a sense of nostalgia which, when combined with the emotional resolution, brings the story to the brink of sentimentality.

However, in the last story of *Inhale & Exhale*, "The Armenian and the Armenian" (1935), Saroyan reasserts his direct personal narrative style and thus eschews any sentimentality. Here, in a manner perhaps more powerful than in "Seventy Thousand Assyrians," without subtlety and with the arrogance for which his young voice was so well known, Saroyan portrays the strength of the individual in the face of oblivion, of two Armenians in the face of extinction: "Go ahead, see if you can do anything about it. See if you can stop them from mocking the big ideas of the world. . . , go ahead and try to destroy them."

Saroyan and drama critic George Jean Nathan (courtesy of Aram Saroyan)

After Saroyan's brilliant and promising beginning with *The Daring Young Man on the Flying Trapeze*, most critics were disappointed in *Inhale & Exhale*: some thought it a boring continuation of the personal diatribes of the first collection; others wondered how long he could show promise without fulfilling it. The volume includes some of the strongest stories Saroyan wrote and also some of the weakest. This polarization is perhaps due to Saroyan's attempt to answer the charges of critics concerned with the looseness of his narrative style yet preserve the integrity of his own voice.

Saroyan's next book, *Three Times Three* (1936), arose from a suggestion made by three university students who visited him while he was working on scenarios for B. P. Schulberg in Hollywood. Saroyan and the students, in an attempt to create an "uncommercial and easy-going" market for a book, created their own publishing company, Conference Press. *Three Times Three* contains nine stories and, to some degree, further marks Saroyan's progress toward more formal, belletristic narratives. "Public Speech" (1936), an ironic parody of an orator, paraphrases Chaucer's "Pardoner's Tale" and satirizes Andrew Mellon, John D. Rockefeller, and J. P. Morgan. Though the parody remains consistent through most of this story, Saroyan is unable to do away with his ever-present sympathy for his characters, thus softening the satire and reducing its effects.

By becoming his own editor in this collection, Saroyan forced himself into a new role where he was responsible for the ultimate product. Because of this, he began to soften his hard, rebellious literary posture: "Critics are happiest with my stuff I think, when I try for almost nothing, when I sit down and very quietly tell a little story. In a way I don't blame them. I myself enjoy writing and reading a very simple story, that is whole and with form." Thus, "The Man With the Heart in the Highlands" (1936), a fantasy about Fresno and Saroyan's Armenian background, finds its theme through the concrete language of its six-year-old narrator.

With *Little Children* (1937) Saroyan continued his movement toward more traditional, more stylized narratives. T. S. Matthews claimed in the *New Republic* that these stories "are told by a Saroyan who is less a show-off and more of a writer than he was a year ago." This collection is a continuation of the Fresno stories found in his earlier collections, but here these accounts of childhood and ethnic experiences are not exceptions, but the rule, just as is the newer, more formal style. The stories are not just about little children, as the title might suggest; they concern the fresh, unbroken spirit associated with youth, a spirit constantly threatened by the harsh lessons of human experience.

In "Sunday Zeppelin" (1936) two boys are fooled by an ad in their Sunday-school paper into withholding their money from the collection plate to send off for a cardboard zeppelin. What they get however, falls far short of what the ad had pictured. The simplicity of the details in this story carries a more complex theme of disenchantment with basic American values.

Jef Logan of "The Crusader" (1936) is a young man who returns to his home in the San Joaquin Valley to relocate his past. He winds up at a hotel cigar counter playing a pinball machine appropriately named "crusader." The machine becomes symbolic of his quest and his split from his past. Saroyan's selective omniscient perspective on Logan and his reliance on symbols for thematic development is further evidence of the author's compromise between his urgency of expression and his desire to conform more strictly to traditional literary forms.

With *Love, Here Is My Hat* (1938) Saroyan attempted to produce an entire book of stories connected by a single unifying theme and a tightly knit network of plots. Perhaps due to the ambitious scope of the project, the volume was greeted with enthusiasm by many reviewers; yet because of this optimistic theme–that only through love and compassion can people realize their human potential–these stories seem to be the first clear evidence of the softness and sentimentality which was to increase in Saroyan's later work. In these stories Saroyan seems to have become what he had warned against in his preface to *The Daring Young Man on the Flying Trapeze* when he insisted: "If you write as if you believe that ultimately you and everyone else alive will be dead, there is a chance that you will write in a pretty earnest style. Otherwise you are apt to be either too pompous or too soft." Yet at the beginning of the title story, "Love, Here Is My Hat" (1937), he writes, "Love is absurd, always has been, always will be. It's the only thing, but it's absurd." In the story that follows, two lovers meet briefly and have a pleasant affair. Then they decide to break it off and make no commitments to each other. The story ends as follows: " 'Isn't it wonderful?' she said. 'It certainly is,' I said."

Saroyan's earlier concern with the cutting edge between life and death softened just as his stories began to harden into more commonly structured forms. Only occasionally does the old first-person Saroyan intervene in these stories. In "For My Part I'll Smoke A Good Ten Cent Cigar" (1937) Saroyan doles out advice on life in general, just as in his earlier works, yet here smugness seems to have replaced the earlier uncompromising idealism: "The best I can do is get comfortable and smoke a fine panatela cigar."

At its best, *Love, Here Is My Hat* contains several entertaining, objectified stories that use suspense, foreshadowing, and other traditional devices. "Three, Four, Shut the Door" (1937) is the story of a mulatto youth unjustly accused of murder and rescued by his white friend Glenn Lyle. By using Lyle as the first-person narrator Saroyan manages to understate a clichéd situation and provide mystery and suspense to the plot. In "The Filipino and the Drunkard" (1937) Saroyan sustains a similar intensity by deftly manipulating plot and action. Here a young Filipino, cornered by a bigoted drunk on a ferryboat, stabs his assailant after receiving no help from the other people on the boat. The lack of love and sympathy in this story perhaps emphasizes Saroyan's central

Saroyan and Carol Marcus between marriages in 1950. They divorced twice (courtesy of Aram Saroyan).

theme better than their presence in the other stories of *Love, Here Is My Hat*.

Two subsequent collections follow a similar thematic arrangement: *The Trouble with Tigers* (1938) and *Peace, It's Wonderful* (1939). Both of these books continue Saroyan's movement toward tightly structured narratives and away from the more abrasive stance of his earlier works.

The stories of *The Trouble with Tigers* are bound together by a theme stressing the value of common existence, the importance of everyday life and the basic fears which give it intensity. The title story (1937) resembles Saroyan's earlier, more amorphous monologues except that the author relies more heavily on imagery and symbolism. Tigers in the story symbolize not only death but those negative parts of the human psyche over which we have little or no control; thus, the first-person narrator and the autobiographical tone of *The Daring Young Man on the Flying Tra-*

peze are still present, but vignettes and symbols hold what used to be a wandering voice to a steady thematic course. Most of the other stories in this collection, however, have more conventional plots, characters, and settings. "Summertime" (1938) reflects the concern for minute changes in everyday life, the structured plot and the common settings so typical of *The Trouble with Tigers*. In this story John Cobb goes to his office on a summer morning and, because of a few small changes, watches joy turn to depression. He clowns around in his office and, on a whim, jokingly tells his secretary that he would like to be swimming naked out in the country. The secretary is not amused, the weather outside becomes stormy, and John Cobb's mood changes accordingly. Because of the understatement in stories such as this, *The Trouble with Tigers* is less sentimental than *Love, Here Is My Hat*, yet its stories still lack the more forthright oppositions of *The Dar-*

ing Young Man on the Flying Trapeze.

Peace, It's Wonderful forms a thematic balance for the "tigers" or basic fears of daily life in *The Trouble with Tigers.* Saroyan here stresses the brief elusive encounters between people seeking peace; once more, the encounters are in common settings, yet the subtle, positive effects of peace are just as pronounced as the negative ones in the preceding collection. However, too often in these traditionally structured stories Saroyan allows his resolutions to come from clichéd situations and stereotyped characters. In "Noonday Dark" (1938) the narrator finds a southwestern dust storm to be a fitting vehicle for his feelings about the shortsightedness of man and the dehumanizing effect of cities. Yet contrary to the main thrust of the story, the narrator finds a peace, a positive answer through God which, compared to Saroyan's stronger resolutions, seems contrived for the sake of thematic consistency.

Some of the interrelated stories in Saroyan's next collection, *My Name Is Aram* (1940), feature the now familiar optimism bordering on sentimentality and nostalgia, while others retain the hard irreconcilability between the characters' illusions of life and the flat truth of the events that they confront. Of the former type are stories such as "The Summer of the Beautiful White Horses" (1939). Here Aram and his cousin Mourad secretly borrow their neighbor's horse and take it on early morning rides. The neighbor, for a while, thinks that his horse is stolen but soon finds that the boys have it. He does not get mad and is happy when the boys return it, for, due to the exercise, it is in better shape than ever. The clear, concise descriptions and understated emotions help to give this story and others like it a quiet intensity, yet the nostalgic tone softens the ultimate effect.

"The Three Swimmers and the Grocer from Yale" (1939) is representative of the stories of disillusionment in *My Name Is Aram.* These pieces, though sometimes not as vivid in their imagery, find a surer balance between the darker side of life and the glow of nostalgia. In "The Three Swimmers" Aram and his friends try to swim in a local ditch but end up waist deep in mud with rain pelting them. This slight, childish letdown finds a more serious parallel in the mind of a grocer who runs a store where the boys go for refuge. The grocer's fantasies interfere with the practicality required for being a successful businessman, so when the boys return to the store later, they find he has transformed himself into a dull clerk. The mud and rain find a more serious embodiment in a life of tedious necessity.

My Name Is Aram was well received. Some critics saw it as Saroyan's most accomplished collection of short fiction because of the sure themes and apparent ease yet conciseness with which the stories were crafted. However, this work can also be seen as a further compromise of the cold, hard insights promised behind the posturing and braggadocio of *The Daring Young Man on the Flying Trapeze. My Name Is Aram* comes close to realizing in more concrete, less personal terms the unflinching stance between being and nonbeing that the first collection proposes, yet the warm nostalgia that makes it more generally palatable also causes it to retreat from the thematic standards of its predecessor.

Saroyan's next collection, *Dear Baby* (1944), though not as widely praised as *My Name Is Aram,* is perhaps as close as Saroyan's work ever comes to the thematic standards proposed in *The Daring Young Man on the Flying Trapeze.* In these stories Saroyan combines the craftsmanship he learned over the years with the bright, original insights that emerged with such fervor in his first collection. Much of the nostalgia has been stripped away from works more totally fabricated, yet perhaps more true to themselves, than the semiautobiographical pieces which precede and follow *Dear Baby.* Yet even as Saroyan's last important collection of short fiction, *Dear Baby* does not completely measure up to the promise of his first, for as bluntly as it deals with life and death it still relies on a level of sentimentality that the voice in *The Daring Young Man on the Flying Trapeze* might find inexcusable.

In "Dear Baby" (1939) a boxer, Joe, and his wife decide to have a baby despite the wife's poor health. Using time shifts, Saroyan weaves the tragic events of the woman's death during childbirth into the boxer's struggles in the ring. The tragedy of death, the craftsmanship behind the time shifts, and the understatement of events all combine to give the title a sharp irony, yet at the end of "Dear Baby" Saroyan falls into the overstatement and sentimentality typical of much of his work: "The Phonograph was playing, and the fighter was sitting on the bed with his head in his hands and he was crying.... 'Dear Baby,' the fighter kept saying over and over again."

After *Dear Baby* Saroyan worked mainly on plays, novels, and memoirs. The short fiction that he did publish frequently repeated the patterns he set during his prolific period between *The Dar-*

Saroyan and his son, Aram, 1957 (Richard Tolbert)

ing *Young Man on the Flying Trapeze* and *Dear Baby*. In the late 1940s he was having so much trouble in his personal life that he wrote little and summed up his life as follows: "Suicide was suicide, divorce was divorce. I flipped a coin." The latter part of his life Saroyan devoted mainly to memoirs, and although his best work remained in the past, he had definitely made his mark in American letters. Saroyan's best work was written in the voice of a Depression-burdened Armenian, bereft of his heritage and seeking a personal and national identity. His personal dilemma was a national dilemma; thus, he gained an immediate importance in a confused country searching for stability.

Saroyan's scorn of wealth and power led him to gamble away what money he could acquire, to reject the Pulitzer Prize for his play *The Time of Your Life* (1939) on the grounds that businessmen were not qualified to judge art, and to carry on a running battle with literary critics and

Hollywood producers. Yet even when his life seemed to be falling apart and his work seemed to be slipping into obscurity, he retained his optimism and his sense of humor, evident in his later memoirs. Not long before his death Saroyan phoned in his official last words to the Associated Press: "Everybody has got to die, but I have always believed an exception would be made in my case. Now what?" At seventy-one and in failing health Saroyan was still joking in the face of death, the voice not all that different from the one in *Inhale & Exhale* that said, "See if you can stop them from mocking the big ideas of the world, you sons of bitches, a couple of Armenians talking in the world, go ahead and try to destroy them."

Interviews:

Annie Brierre, "William Saroyan à Paris," *Nouvelles Littéraires*, 1665 (30 July 1959): 5;

Budd Schulberg, "Saroyan: Ease and Unease on the Flying Trapeze," *Esquire*, 54 (October 1960): 85-91;

Zori Balayan, "Arguments for Soviet Power . . . ," *Soviet Literature*, no. 12 (1977): 159-166;

Herbert Gold, "A 20-Year Talk with Saroyan," *New York Times Book Review*, 20 May 1979, pp. 7, 49-51.

Bibliography:

David Kherdian, *A Bibliography of William Saroyan 1934-1964* (San Francisco: Beacham, 1965).

References:

Frederic I. Carpenter, "The Time of William Saroyan's Life," *Pacific Spectator*, 1 (Winter 1947): 88-96;

William J. Fisher, "What Ever Happened to Saroyan?," *College English*, 16 (March 1955): 336-340, 385;

Howard R. Floan, *William Saroyan* (New York: Twayne, 1966);

Edmund Wilson, *Classics and Commercials* (New York: Farrar, Straus, 1950): pp. 26-31, 327-330.

Papers:

The most substantial collection of Saroyan's manuscripts is at the John M. Olin Library, Cornell University; the University of California Research Library, Los Angeles, has an extensive collection of letters.

Wilbur Daniel Steele

(17 March 1886-26 May 1970)

Mel Seesholtz
Pennsylvania State University

BOOKS: *Storm* (New York & London: Harper, 1914);
Land's End and Other Stories (New York & London: Harper, 1918);
The Shame Dance and Other Stories (New York & London: Harper, 1923);
The Giant's Stair (New York & London: Appleton, 1924);
Isles of the Blest (New York & London: Harper, 1924);
Taboo (New York: Harcourt, Brace, 1925);
The Terrible Woman and Other One Act Plays (New York: Appleton, 1925);
Urkey Island (New York: Harcourt, Brace, 1926);
The Man Who Saw Through Heaven and Other Stories (New York & London: Harper, 1927);
Meat (New York & London: Harper, 1928);
Tower of Sand and Other Stories (New York & London: Harper, 1929);
Undertow (New York: Jacobsen, 1930);
Post Road, by Steele and Norma Mitchell (New York, Los Angeles & London: Samuel French, 1935);
Sound of Rowlocks (New York & London: Harper, 1938);
That Girl from Memphis (Garden City, N.Y.: Doubleday, Doran, 1945);
The Best Stories of Wilbur Daniel Steele (Garden City, N.Y.: Doubleday, 1946);
Diamond Wedding (Garden City, N.Y.: Doubleday, 1950);
Full Cargo: More Stories by Wilbur Daniel Steele (Garden City, N.Y.: Doubleday, 1951);
Their Town (Garden City, N.Y.: Doubleday, 1952);
The Way to the Gold (Garden City, N.Y.: Doubleday, 1955).

PLAY PRODUCTIONS: *Post Road*, by Steele and Norma Mitchell, New York, Masque Theatre, 4 December 1934;
How Beautiful with Shoes, by Steele and Anthony Brown, New York, Booth Theatre, 28 November 1935.

Wilbur Daniel Steele (photograph by Doris Ulmann)

PERIODICAL PUBLICATIONS:
FICTION
"On the Ebb Tide," *Success Magazine*, 13 (June 1910): 339-401;
"Gloomy on the Gridiron," *Success Magazine*, 13 (November 1910): 739-763;
"The Insurrecto," *National Magazine* (May 1911): 29-40;
"The Admirable Admirals," *Success Magazine*, 14 (October 1911): 27-46;
"Thumbs Down," *Harper's Weekly*, 56 (3 August 1912): 16-17;
"An Officer Born," *American Magazine*, 75 (May 1913): 24-28;

"The Islanders," *Harper's Magazine*, 127 (July 1913): 268-273;

"The Handkerchief Lady's Girl," *Harper's Magazine*, 128 (February 1914): 463-471;

"Captain Ulysses G. Dadd, Retired," *Scribner's Magazine*, 56 (July 1914): 117-128;

"The Wickedness of Father Veiera," *Atlantic Monthly*, 114 (July 1914): 59-69;

"The Younger Twin," *Harper's Magazine*, 129 (August 1914): 464-472;

"Pa-Jim," *Scribner's Magazine*, 56 (November 1914): 627-637;

"The Miracle," *Masses*, 6 (January 1915): 5-6;

"On Moon Hill," *Century Magazine*, 15 (April 1915): 2-13;

"A Matter of Education," *Harper's Magazine*, 141 (May 1915): 894-900;

"The Real Thing," *Century Magazine*, 90 (May 1915): 2-13;

"Free Agent," *Collier's Weekly*, 55 (17 July 1915): 5-6;

"Heritage," *Harper's Magazine*, 131 (July 1915): 298-309;

"Before the Mast," *Harper's Magazine*, 132 (March 1916): 625-633;

"The Last Fletcher," *Good Housekeeping*, 63 (September 1916): 35-37;

"An Escape from Freedom," *Harper's Magazine*, 133 (October 1916): 739-748;

"The Killers of Provincetown," *Harper's Magazine*, 134 (March 1917): 457-466;

"Mr. Timmons Tackles Life," *Harper's Magazine*, 134 (April 1917): 620-635; 134 (May 1917): 849-862; 135 (June 1917): 126-137;

"Free," *Century Magazine*, 94 (August 1917): 518-526;

"The Half Ghost," *Harper's Magazine*, 135 (August 1917): 518-526;

"A Point of Honor," *Harper's Magazine*, 135 (November 1917): 848-855;

"You're Right, at That," *Collier's Weekly*, 60 (23 February 1918): 16-34;

"Eternal Youth," *Scribner's Magazine*, 63 (April 1918): 473-483;

"Mr. Scattergood and the Other World," *Harper's Magazine*, 137 (July 1918): 258-269;

"The Perfect Face," *Harper's Magazine*, 137 (August 1918): 362-368;

"A Taste of the Old Boy," *Collier's Weekly*, 62 (28 September 1918): 11-25;

"The Heart of a Woman," *Harper's Magazine*, 138 (February 1919): 384-391;

"Goodfellow," *Harper's Magazine*, 138 (April 1919): 655-656;

Steele, circa 1914

"Accomplice After the Fact," *Good Housekeeping*, 69 (August 1919): 22-25;

"Clay and Cloven Hoof," *Harper's Magazine*, 139 (October 1919): 683-699; (November 1919): 889-906;

"God's Mercy," *Pictorial Review*, 30 (July-August 1920): 17-88;

"Fouled Anchor," *Harper's Magazine*, 142 (April 1921): 591-602;

" 'Toinette of Maisonnoir," *Pictorial Review*, 20 (July 1921): 13-44;

"The First Born," *Pictorial Review*, 24 (December 1922): 14-42;

"Ginger Beer," *Pictorial Review*, 25 (November 1923): 10-132;

"Marriage," *Pictorial Review*, 25 (August 1924): 12-13;

"Sauce for the Goose," *Pictorial Review*, 26 (January 1925): 12-13;

"Beauty," *Good Housekeeping*, 82 (January 1926): 14-17;

"Now I Lay Me," *Pictorial Review*, 27 (April 1926): 10-11;

"New Deal," *Scribner's Magazine*, 82 (August 1927): 138-147;

"Speed," *Pictorial Review*, 28 (August 1927): 14-15;

"Lightning," *Pictorial Review*, 29 (June 1928): 23-24;

"Satan Am a Snake," *Harper's Magazine*, 157 (August 1928): 304-313;

"Winter Wheat," *Pictorial Review*, 29 (September 1928): 19;

"From One Generation to Another," *Pictorial Review*, 30 (October 1928): 20-21;

"The Silver Sword," *Pictorial Review*, 30 (March 1929): 18-19;

"Pioneers," *Harper's Magazine*, 159 (July 1929): 199-210;

"Quicksilver," *Harper's Magazine*, 159 (August 1929): 316-330;

"Surprize," *Pictorial Review*, 30 (September 1929): 16-17;

" 'Ki,' " *Pictorial Review*, 31 (February 1930): 16-17;

"Wife of a Viking," *Pictorial Review*, 31 (April 1930): 13-14;

"Diamond Wedding," *Woman's Home Companion*, 57 (September 1930): 17-19;

"Green Vigil," *Ladies' Home Journal*, 47 (September 1930): 18-19;

"Light," *Ladies' Home Journal*, 47 (November 1930): 18-19;

"The Hills of Heaven," *Good Housekeeping*, 92 (January 1931): 20-23;

"Daughter of the Soil," *Pictorial Review*, 32 (March 1931): 18-19;

"Twenty-seven Minutes," *Ladies' Home Journal*, 49 (April 1932): 10-11;

"Where There's Smoke," *Ladies' Home Journal*, 49 (October 1932): 14-15;

"Will and Bill," *Ladies' Home Journal*, 50 (January 1933): 14-15;

"Somebody," *Harper's Bazaar* (November 1933): 56-104;

"Landfall," *Liberty*, 12 (12 January 1935): 20-27;

"Son of His Father," *Saturday Evening Post*, 208 (12 October 1935): 12-13;

"The Second Mrs. Brown," *Collier's Weekly*, 99 (6 February 1937): 14-15;

"Baptism," *Good Housekeeping*, 109 (August 1939): 20-21;

"Through Road," *Collier's Weekly*, 105 (16 March 1940): 25;

"A Life Is So Little," *Good Housekeeping*, 111 (October 1940): 22-23;

"Prescription for Success," *Woman's Home Companion*, 69 (May 1942): 18-19;

"Her Hand in Marriage," *Cosmopolitan* (July 1943): 21-22;

"The Crystal-Gazer's Daughter," *Good Housekeeping*, 118 (January 1944): 38-39;

"The Bogeyman," *Magazine of Fantasy and Science Fiction*, 15 (October 1958): 99-113.

NONFICTION

"Moving-Picture Machine in the Jungle," *McClure's Magazine*, 40 (January 1913): 329-337;

"At the Ocean Crossroads," *Harper's Magazine*, 135 (October 1917): 681-693;

"Beleaguered Island," *Harper's Magazine*, 136 (May 1918): 817-829;

"Contact," *Harper's Magazine*, 138 (March 1919): 485-493;

"Commuters in Barbary," *Harper's Magazine*, 143 (July 1921): 137-150;

"Fourth Pillar," *Harper's Magazine*, 143 (August 1921): 367-379;

"The Mendenine Road," *Harper's Magazine*, 143 (October 1921): 587-601;

"In the Mountains of the Desert," *Harper's Magazine*, 143 (November 1921): 784-797;

"In the Mzab," *Harper's Magazine*, 144 (April 1922): 636-646.

In a career spanning five decades, Wilbur Daniel Steele produced nearly two hundred short stories, seven short-story collections, ten novels, and several plays, including two one-acts written for the Provincetown Players. He received four O. Henry Awards (three first places, one second), a Harper's Prize (first place), and a Special O. Henry Award for "maintaining the highest level of merit." With his second wife, actress Norma Mitchell, he coauthored the successful Broadway play *Post Road* in 1934, and in 1935, with Anthony Brown, he dramatized his story "How Beautiful with Shoes" (*Harper's*, August 1932) for a Broadway run. Nonetheless, he is today virtually unknown and unread. Although a few of his best stories infrequently appear in anthologies and prose readers, none of his works is currently in print. Yet for a quarter century Steele was popularly and critically acclaimed as one of America's great short-story writers. His impressionistic, romantic yarns, which combine exotic escape with reaffirmation of traditional American values, were favorites among educated, middle-class readers

Illustrations for Steele's story "Land's End," published in the 25 March 1916 issue of Collier's

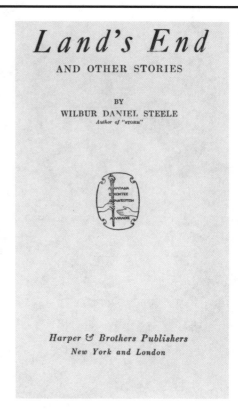

Frontispiece and title page for Steele's first short-story collection, published in 1918

of popular magazines such as *Harper's, Collier's,* and *Good Housekeeping.* And although championed by Edward J. O'Brien, who dedicated the 1917 edition of his influential *Best Short Stories* anthology to Steele, by 1938 his reputation was in decline. On 4 March of that year F. Scott Fitzgerald wrote to question Dayton Kohler about one of the selections Kohler had made for a planned survey of contemporary literature: "Why Wilbur Daniel Steele, who left no mark whatever, invented nothing, created nothing except a habit of being an innocuous part of the O'Brien anthology?" Although his reign was short, Steele remains a key figure in a period which did much to shape the modern short story.

The third child of the Reverend Wilbur Fletcher and Rose Wood Steele, Wilbur Daniel Steele was born in 1886 on St. Patrick's Day in Greensboro, North Carolina, also the birthplace of William Sydney Porter, better known as O. Henry. Steele may have been born in the South, but as his father pointed out in a letter dated 1 July 1920, he was descended from "like worthy New England stock and New York Dutch." The Steeles were only in Greensboro from 1881 to 1888, living at Bennett Seminary while the reverend served as principal. At age four Steele left

with his family for Germany, where his father continued his graduate studies and he practiced his German in Fräulein Froebel's kindergarten.

In 1893 Wilbur Fletcher Steele received his Ph.D. from Syracuse University and accepted a position as professor of Bible at the University of Denver, from which he retired in 1923. Wilbur Daniel Steele called Denver home until 1907, when, after receiving his B.A. in history and economics (a minor in mathematics) from the University of Denver, he left Colorado to begin formal training in his desired profession at the Boston Museum School of Fine Art. His art education would be as important in shaping his literature as his family and home life. The Bible, religion, and moral struggle as the ontology of life unify many of his stories; the American West serves the same function in his novels.

The two years in Boston were followed by study at the Académie Julien in Paris. Steele's aesthetics led him away from the study of painting in Paris and to the study of etching in Italy in 1909. The internal intricacies and delicate complexities of etching inspired him. In 1910 Steele returned to the United States to Provincetown, Massachusetts, with a desire to paint and etch not with the tools of an artist but with the words of a writer.

Although he began publishing stories in 1910, Steele's short-story career began in earnest with the publication of "White Horse Winter" in the April 1912 issue of *Atlantic Monthly*. The birth of his literature was, for him, a painful one, "every word coming out of me with a scream." In the spring of 1912 Steele was lured to the bohemian life-styles and literary trends of Greenwich Village. He married Margaret Orinda Thurston, whom he had met at the Boston Museum school, on 17 February 1913. Totally inept at melancholy bohemianism, Steele returned to Provincetown the following summer. By the end of 1914 Steele had published his first novel and five short stories, and he had been proclaimed–much to his embarrassment–a short-story writer second only to Rudyard Kipling. As Steele was given to excesses in his fiction, so too were many of his reviewers.

Steele's first collection, *Land's End and Other Stories* (1918), includes ten previously published stories: "Land's End" (*Collier's*, 25 March 1916), "The Woman at Seven Brothers" (*Harper's*, December 1917), "White Horse Winter," "Down on Their Knees" (*Harper's*, July 1916), "The Killer's Son" (*Harper's*, January 1916), "A Devil of a Fellow" (*Seven Arts*, November 1916), "The Yellow Cat" (*Harper's*, March 1915), "A Man's a Fool" (*Metropolitan*, June 1918), "Ked's Hand" (*Harper's*, September 1917), and "'Romance'" (*Atlantic Monthly*, June 1915). In his introduction to the volume, O'Brien pronounced Steele's literary "permanence" and praised his technical skills. And like one of Steele's narrators, closed with exaggeration and intrigue: "Almost without exception they [the stories] represent the best that is being accomplished in America to-day by a literary artist. But Mr. Steele will never be elected to an Academy. Such is the fate of all pioneers."

As the titles suggest, the stories of *Land's End* are heavy with atmosphere, local color, and folklore. Half the stories deal with a Portuguese-American fishing village, much like those on Cape Cod that Steele knew intimately. Looking through romantic prisms, Steele's narrators examine the spectrum of these immigrants' trials and tribulations, and the triumph of their ultimate victories.

The stories of *Land's End* all bear Steele's signature: romantic, melodramatic plots laced with ad hoc mystification; story lines involving the supernatural and / or mental illness, derangement,

insanity, either acquired or inherited; black comedies of coincidental errors; impressionistic dramas confirming America's pre-World War I values; and, of course, O. Henry-like surprises and climaxes. Although his best, most enduring stories were still years into the future, the Steele formula was already well refined.

An impressionistic painter and master etcher in words, Steele lavishly captures the ambience of New England coastal landscapes and the folk who inhabited them. His narratives create a tapestry of past and future woven into a story of the present. Emphasis is on the unity of the narrative experience. Steele's narrators strive to "reduce to writing" this wholeness. More often than not, they are successful.

Nevertheless, the operative term in the *New York Times* appraisal of *Land's End* was "weird." The *Dial* was less amused. The "Notes on New Books" editor pointed out how Steele's odd themes served to highlight the stories' pervasive mediocrity. Most reviewers recommended the collection primarily to antiquarians and lovers of lore. The popular magazine audience, however, now becoming increasingly female, was already his; many critics were soon to be.

In his second collection Steele assembled twelve stories which offered readers an extended excursion into the exotic twilight zones of the South Seas and the Caribbean, North Africa, and the Middle East. The excesses that characterize his fiction are well represented in the individual pieces that make up *The Shame Dance and Other Stories* (1923): "The Shame Dance" (*Harper's*, December 1920), "The White Man" (*Harper's*, February 1918), "La Guiablesse" (*Harper's*, September 1919), "Both Judge and Jury" (*Harper's*, January 1910), "Always Summer" (*Harper's*, April 1918), "At Two-in-the Bush" (*Harper's*, October 1920), "The Anglo-Saxon" (*Harper's*, August 1922), "The Marriage in Kairwan" (*Harper's*, December 1921), "'He That Hideth His Secret'" (*Harper's*, February 1922), "From the Other Side of the South" (*Pictorial Review*, August 1922), "'Arab Stuff'" (*Harper's*, January 1923), and "The Man Who Sat" (*Pictorial Review*, September 1922). Wild, exotic settings, improbable plots, strange characters, ingenious narratives, and topical issues underwritten by traditional Christian morality fill the pages of *The Shame Dance*. "La Guiablesse" (the title is taken from a voodoo term which translates as "devil woman") is overflowing with exaggerated dialogue, caricatured characters, and dense melodramatic plots replete with deus ex machina climaxes. In "The Anglo-Saxon," an O. Henry Award story set in Middle Eastern splendor straight from *The Arabian Nights' Entertainments*, the narrator passes judgment via outlandish plots and characters on the nature / nurture question. Nature seems to take the day, but after a double denouement, nurture seems the victor.

The exotic, lavishly depicted settings and otherworldly nature of *The Shame Dance* stories earned the volume critical praise and considerably enlarged Steele's audience. The author was hailed in the *Literary Review* as "a master narrator," whose stories, according to the *Detroit News* reviewer, were "unexcelled by those of any other living writer." By the time his third collection, *Urkey Island* (1926), was published Steele's popular magazine audience and literary backers had become a familiar community–old friends gathering for some tall tales, such as "White Hands" (*Pictorial Review*, January 1917), "Ching, Ching, Chinaman" (*Pictorial Review*, June 1917), "The Wages of Sin" (*Pictorial Review*, March 1918), "Out of Exile" (*Pictorial Review*, November 1919), "Crocuses" (*Pictorial Review*, May 1923), " 'Lost at Sea' " (*Pictorial Review*, May 1924), "Six Dollars" (*Pictorial Review*, March 1925), and "Out of the Wind" (*Pictorial Review*, October 1925). In the author's note that prefaces *Urkey Island*, Steele etches an impressionistic panorama of his short-story canon: "These recollections of a town at sea, some at first hand, some got by hearsay, and some gathered out of a common body of knowledge which is as near as anything we yet have in America to a local legendry, I have thought better to offer here in the somewhat random order in which they have been reduced to writing, rather than in the more precise chronology of their years. And this despite the shock it may prove to the nodding reader to find a fellow he has considered safely dead and buried this long while, of a sudden not yet even born." His comments to Winnifred King Rugg in an unpublished 1932 interview give a sense of the man: "I seem to be pretty much the common or garden variety of person, anxious about the well-being of my family, always losing everything, and having difficulty with my income tax returns. My main desire is to have the moon."

Some reviewers reveled in the human melodramas and picturesque New England settings of the *Urkey Island* stories. Others, such as the "New Books in Brief " editor of the *Independent*, found the stories "dismally aloof." In general, the volume stood in the shadow of a story Steele published in 1925, profiting by association, paling by comparison. Not coincidentally, that 1925 story would be the title piece for Steele's fourth collection.

"The Man Who Saw Through Heaven" (*Harper's*, September 1925) won the 1925 O. Henry Award and is generally regarded as one of Steele's best works. *The Man Who Saw Through Heaven and Other Stories* (1927) also includes "Sooth" (*Harper's*, August 1927), "Sailor! Sailor!" (*Pictorial Review*, July 1927), "Bubbles" (*Harper's*, August 1926), "Luck" (*Harper's*, August 1919), "Blue Murder" (*Harper's*, October 1925), "When Hell Froze" (*Harper's*, May 1925), "Autumn Bloom" (*Pictorial Review*, November 1926), "A Drink of Water" (*Harper's*, January 1927), "The Thinker" (*Pictorial Review*, December 1924), "Fe-Fi-Fo-Fum" (*Pictorial Review*, August 1926), and "What Do You Mean–Americans?" (*Pictorial Review*, April 1924). "The Man Who Saw Through Heaven" is the tale of fundamentalist missionary Rev. Hubert Diana's "enlightenment" in a Boston observatory while gazing at Messier 79 the night before leaving for darkest Africa. Some fifty months later the narrator tells of his African adventures with Mrs. Diana and their discoveries as they track down the "insane" minister, now known locally as "Our Father Witch," who had been compelled by that night in the observatory "to measure the Infinite with the foot rule of his mind." Steele's characterization of Hubert Diana and the creation of his post-relativity God captivated the imagination of loyal readers as well as those who discovered Steele through this story. The concepts and ideas were popularizations but offered profound insights into Man and his spiritual evolution at a time when America was grappling with enormous change. For new readers "The Man Who Saw Through Heaven" was a most enticing introduction to Steele. With the publication of a critically acclaimed short story overflowing with potential, an audience swollen with anticipation, and a critically applauded fourth collection, the "permanence" of Steele's fiction seemed certain.

The December 1929 issue of the *Bookman* included a photo gallery of America's favorite writers: Robert Frost, Sherwood Anderson, Thornton Wilder, Thomas Wolfe, and Wilbur Daniel Steele. However, *Bookman* literary critic Paul Allen lamented what he called the "machine-made" quality of *Tower of Sand and Other Stories* (1929), Steele's fifth collection, which includes "Tower of Sand" (*Pictorial Review*, June 1923), "A

Life" (*Pictorial Review*, August 1921), "Mary Drake and Will Todd" (*Pictorial Review*, March-April 1928), "For They Know Not What They Do" (*Pictorial Review*, July 1919), "For Where Is Your Fortune Now?" (*Pictorial Review*, November 1918), "The Mad" (*Pictorial Review*, July 1922), "Footfalls" (*Pictorial Review*, October 1920), and "Never Anything That Fades" (*Harper's*, June 1928). Steele's formulaic stories were still favorites among popular magazine audiences, but the American short story and modern literature were going in other directions.

By the end of World War II the stories of Wilbur Daniel Steele were already part of the genre's history but not its future. As if in acknowledgment, Doubleday published *The Best Stories of Wilbur Daniel Steele* in 1946. Henry O'Neil, who selected the stories and to whom the volume was dedicated, did preserve the best of Steele in a single collection. The volume drew overwhelming popular and deferential critical praise and would have been a fitting conclusion to a remarkable career in short fiction. The final collection, however, was *Full Cargo: More Stories by Wilbur Daniel Steele* (1951), a dismal assemblage of previously published stories, many of which had already been collected, dating from 1915 to 1939.

The world and literary tastes had changed. The reviewer for *Time* characterized Steele as "a reactionary and flavorful old fogy" whose formulas were of a different time and place: "At his best, Author Steele can stir a jigger of irony, a dash of adventure, a sprig of the exotic and a pinch of mystery into a tippling good yarn. At his worst, he makes the tricks of Fate look like the hoked-up tricks of the trade."

During the first third of the twentieth century Steele was popularly and critically regarded as one of America's premier short-story writers. Exaggerated caricatures as characters, melodramatic plots in lavish settings of intrigue, narratives which tried to "reduce to writing" the unity of oral tradition, the values and beliefs of pre-World War I America: Steele's formulas for fiction, which had led to such popular success, never evolved and led inevitably to his short stories' literary extinction. However, it is that rapid rise to the top and equally rapid plunge into virtual extinction that signals Steele's key role as a transitional figure in the history of the modern American short story.

In his review of "The Man Who Saw Through Heaven" *New York Times* critic Clifton

Fadiman acknowledged Steele as "master [of] a complex bag of tricks," but he also wrote that "he is incapable" of writing "literature." As skillful and ingenious as he was in varying the "tricks," the number of combinations was finite. In perfecting the formulas he exhausted their possibilities. Steele's "machine-made" fiction was not able to evolve. For some time his stories remained popular culture's pleasant diversions, but they could offer little more and have slowly faded into obscurity. Ironically, if there is a lost or forgotten treasure in Steele's short fiction, it is "The Man Who Saw Through Heaven," the story of one who, like the author, faced a need to evolve and failed.

Interviews:

Frank B. Elser, "Oh, Yes . . . Wilbur Daniel Steele," *Bookman*, 62 (February 1926): 691-694;

Harvey Breit, "Talk with Mr. Steele," *New York Times*, 6 August 1950, p. 12.

References:

Martic Bucco, *Wilbur Daniel Steele* (New York: Twayne, 1972);

Edith R. Mirrielees, "The Best of Steele," *New York Times*, 14 July 1946, pp. 5, 20;

Hassell A. Simpson, "Wilbur Daniel Steele's Influence on William Faulkner's Revision of 'Beyond,'" *Mississippi Quarterly*, 34 (Summer 1981): 335-339;

Ernest W. Sullivan, "Flowers, Verse, and Gems: Names in Wilbur Daniel Steele's 'How Beautiful with Shoes,'" *Publications of the Arkansas Philologic Association*, 4 (1978): 63-65;

Mary Heaton Vorse, *Time and the Town* (New York: Dial, 1942);

Warren S. Walker, "'Never Anything That Fades': Steele's Eleusian Mysteries," *Studies in Short Fiction*, 17 (1980): 127-132;

Blanche Colton Williams, *Our Short Story Writers* (New York: Dodd, Mead, 1926), pp. 372-384.

Papers:

The largest collection of Steele's papers, letters, and manuscripts is at Stanford University Library. The archives at the University of Denver house the papers of Prof. Wilbur Fletcher Steele and other Steele memorabilia.

Gertrude Stein

(3 February 1874-27 July 1946)

Bobby Ellen Kimbel
Pennsylvania State University–Ogontz Campus

See also the Stein entries in *DLB 4: American Writers in Paris, 1920-1939* and *DLB 54: American Poets, 1880-1945, Third Series.*

BOOKS: *Three Lives: Stories of The Good Anna, Melanctha and The Gentle Lena* (New York: Grafton Press, 1909; London: John Lane, Bodley Head / New York: John Lane, 1915);

Portrait of Mabel Dodge at the Villa Curonia (Florence, Italy: Privately printed, 1912);

Tender Buttons: Objects, Food, Rooms (New York: Claire Marie, 1914);

Have They Attacked Mary, He Giggled. (West Chester, Pa.: Printed by Horace F. Temple, 1917);

Geography and Plays (Boston: Four Seas, 1922);

The Making of Americans, Being A History of A Family's Progress (Paris: Contact Editions, 1925; New York: A. & C. Boni, 1926; London: Owen, 1968); abridged as *The Making of Americans, The Hersland Family* (New York: Harcourt, Brace, 1934);

Descriptions of Literature (Englewood, N.J.: George Platt Lynes & Adlai Harbeck, 1926);

Composition as Explanation (London: Leonard & Virginia Woolf at the Hogarth Press, 1926);

A Book Concluding with As a Wife Has a Cow, A Love Story (Paris: Editions de la Galerie Simon, 1926; Barton, Millerton & Berlin: Something Else Press, 1973);

An Elucidation (Paris: transition, 1927);

A Village Are You Ready Yet Not Yet A Play in Four Acts (Paris: Editions de la Galerie Simon, 1928);

Useful Knowledge (New York: Payson & Clarke, 1928; London: John Lane, Bodley Head, 1929);

An Acquaintance with Description (London: Seizin Press, 1929);

Lucy Church Amiably (Paris: Plain Edition, 1930; New York: Something Else Press, 1969);

Dix Portraits, English text with French translations by Georges Hugnet and Virgil Thomson (Paris: Librarie Gallimard, 1930);

Gertrude Stein, 1913 (photograph by Alvin Langdon Coburn, courtesy of the Beinecke Rare Book and Manuscript Library, Yale University)

Before the Flowers of Friendship Faded Friendship Faded, Written on a Poem by Georges Hugnet (Paris: Plain Edition, 1931);

How to Write (Paris: Plain Edition, 1931; Barton: Something Else Press, 1973);

Operas and Plays (Paris: Plain Edition, 1932);

Matisse Picasso and Gertrude Stein with Two Shorter Stories (Paris: Plain Edition, 1933; Barton, Berlin & Millerton: Something Else Press, 1972);

The Autobiography of Alice B. Toklas (New York: Harcourt, Brace, 1933; London: John Lane, Bodley Head, 1933);

Four Saints in Three Acts, An Opera To Be Sung (New York: Random House, 1934);

Portraits and Prayers (New York: Random House, 1934);

Lectures in America (New York: Random House, 1935);

Narration: Four Lectures (Chicago: University of Chicago Press, 1935);

The Geographical History of America or The Relation of Human Nature to the Human Mind (New York: Random House, 1936);

Is Dead (N.p.: Joyous Guard Press, 1937);

Everybody's Autobiography (New York: Random House, 1937; London & Toronto: Heinemann, 1938);

A Wedding Bouquet, Ballet Music by Lord Berners, Words By Gertrude Stein (London: J. & W. Chester, 1938);

Picasso [in French] (Paris: Libraire Floury, 1938); translated into English by Alice B. Toklas (London: Batsford, 1938; New York: Scribners / London: Batsford, 1939);

The World is Round (New York: William R. Scott, 1939; London: Batsford, 1939);

Paris France (London: Batsford, 1940; New York: Scribners / London: Batsford, 1940);

What Are Masterpieces (California: Conference Press, 1940; expanded edition, New York, Toronto, London & Tel Aviv: Pitman, 1970);

ida A Novel (New York: Random House, 1941);

Petits Poèmes Pour un Livre de Lecture, French translation by Madame la Baronne d'Aiguy (Charlot, France: Collection Fontaine, 1944); republished in English as *The First Reader & Three Plays* (Dublin & London: Maurice Fridberg, 1946; Boston: Houghton Mifflin, 1948);

Wars I Have Seen (New York: Random House, 1945; enlarged edition, London: Batsford, 1945);

Brewsie and Willie (New York: Random House, 1946);

Selected Writings, edited by Carl Van Vechten (New York: Random House, 1946);

In Savoy, or Yes Is for a Very Young Man (A Play of the Resistance in France) (London: Pushkin, 1946);

Four in America (New Haven: Yale University Press, 1947);

The Mother of Us All, by Stein and Thomson (New York: Music Press, 1947);

Blood on the Dining Room Floor (Pawlet, Vt.: Banyan Press, 1948);

Two (Hitherto Unpublished) Poems (New York: Gotham Book Mart, 1948);

Last Operas and Plays, edited by Van Vechten (New York & Toronto: Rinehart, 1949);

Things As They Are, A Novel in Three Parts by Gertrude Stein, Written in 1903 but Now Published for the First Time (Pawlet, Vt.: Banyan Press, 1950);

Two: Gertrude Stein and Her Brother and Other Early Portraits [1908-12], volume 1 of *Unpublished Works of Gertrude Stein* (New Haven: Yale University Press / London: Cumberlege, Oxford University Press, 1951);

In a Garden, An Opera in One Act, libretto by Stein, music by Meyer Kupferman (New York: Mercury Music, 1951);

Mrs. Reynolds and Five Earlier Novelettes, volume 2 of *Unpublished Works of Gertrude Stein* (New Haven: Yale University Press / London: Cumberlege, Oxford University Press, 1952);

Bee Time Vine and Other Pieces 1913-1927, volume 3 of *Unpublished Works of Gertrude Stein* (New Haven: Yale University Press / London: Cumberlege, Oxford University Press, 1953);

As Fine As Melanctha (1914-1930), volume 4 of *Unpublished Works of Gertrude Stein* (New Haven: Yale University Press / London: Cumberlege, Oxford University Press, 1954);

Absolutely Bob Brown, or Bobbed Brown (Pawlet, Vt.: Addison M. Metcalf Collection, 1955);

Painted Lace and Other Pieces 1914-1937, volume 5 of *Unpublished Works of Gertrude Stein* (New Haven: Yale University Press / London: Cumberlege, Oxford University Press, 1955);

Stanzas in Meditation and Other Poems [1929-1933], volume 6 of *Unpublished Works of Gertrude Stein* (New Haven: Yale University Press / London: Cumberlege, Oxford University Press, 1956);

Alphabets & Birthdays, volume 7 of *Unpublished Works of Gertrude Stein* (New Haven: Yale University Press / London: Oxford University Press, 1957);

A Novel of Thank You, volume 8 of *Unpublished Works of Gertrude Stein* (New Haven: Yale University Press, 1958; London: Oxford University Press, 1959);

Gertrude Stein's America, edited by Gilbert A. Harrison (Washington, D.C.: Robert B. Luce, 1965);

Writings and Lectures 1911-1945, edited by Patricia Meyerowitz (London: Owen, 1967); republished as *Look at Me Now and Here I Am: Writing and Lectures, 1909-1945* (Harmondsworth & Baltimore: Penguin, 1971);

Lucretia Borgia, A Play (New York: Albondocani Press, 1968);

Stein, age four, in Passy, France (courtesy of the Beinecke Rare Book and Manuscript Library, Yale University)

Motor Automatism, by Stein and Leon M. Solomons (New York: Phoenix Book Shop, 1969);

Selected Operas and Plays, edited by John Malcolm Brinnin (Pittsburgh: University of Pittsburgh Press, 1970);

Gertrude Stein on Picasso, edited by Edward Burns (New York: Liveright, 1970);

I Am Rose (New York: Mini-Books, 1971);

Fernhurst, Q.E.D., and Other Early Writings (New York: Liveright, 1971; London: Owen, 1971);

A Primer for the Gradual Understanding of Gertrude Stein, edited by Robert Bartlett Haas (Los Angeles: Black Sparrow Press, 1971);

Reflections on the Atomic Bomb, volume 1 of *The Previously Uncollected Writings of Gertrude Stein,* edited by Haas (Los Angeles: Black Sparrow Press, 1973);

Money (Los Angeles: Black Sparrow Press, 1973);

How Writing is Written, volume 2 of *The Previously Uncollected Writings of Gertrude Stein,* edited

by Haas (Los Angeles: Black Sparrow Press, 1974);

The Yale Gertrude Stein: Selections (New Haven & London: Yale University Press, 1980).

PERIODICAL PUBLICATIONS: "Normal Motor Automatism," by Stein and Leon M. Solomons, *Psychological Review,* 3 (September 1896): 492-512;

"Cultivated Motor Automatism," *Psychological Review,* 5 (May 1898): 295-306;

"Henri Matisse" and "Pablo Picasso," *Camera Work,* special number (August 1912): 23-25, 29-30;

"From a Play by Gertrude Stein," *New York Sun,* 18 January 1914, VI: 2;

"Aux Galeries Lafayette," *Rogue,* 1 (March 1915): 13-14;

"A League," *Life,* 74 (18 September 1919): 496;

"Two Cubist Poems. The Peace Conference, I and II," *Oxford Magazine,* 38 (7 May 1920): 309;

Review of *Three Stories & Ten Poems* by Ernest Hemingway, *Chicago Tribune,* European edition, 27 November 1923, p. 2;

The Making of Americans, transatlantic review, 1 (April 1924): 127-142; 1 (May 1924): 297-309; 1 (June 1924): 392-405; 2 (July 1924): 27-38; 2 (August 1924): 188-202; 2 (September 1924): 284-294; 2 (October 1924): 405-414; 2 (November 1924): 527-536; 2 (December 1924): 662-670;

"The Life of Juan Gris The Life and Death of Juan Gris," *transition,* no. 4 (July 1927): 160-162;

"Bibliography," *transition,* no. 14 (February 1929): 47-55;

"Genuine Creative Ability," *Creative Art,* 6 (February 1930), supplement: 41;

"Scenery and George Washington," *Hound & Horn,* 5 (July / September 1932): 606-611;

"Basket," *Lion and Crown,* 1 (January 1933): 23-25;

Review of *Roosevelt and His America* by Bernard Fäy, *Kansas City Star,* 20 January 1934;

"Why Willows," *Literary America,* 1 (July 1934): 19-20;

"Plays and Landscapes," *Saturday Review of Literature,* 11 (10 November 1934): 269-270;

"Completely Gertrude Stein: A Painting Is Painted as a Painting," *Design,* 36 (January 1935): 25, 28;

Review of *Puzzled America* by Sherwood Anderson, *Chicago Daily Tribune*, 4 May 1935, p. 14;

"English and American Language in Literature," *Life and Letters Today*, 13 (September 1935): 19-27;

"A Portrait of the Abdys," *Janus* (May 1936): 15;

Dialogue with Nunez Martinez, *Ken*, 1 (2 June 1938): 103-104;

"The Situation in American Writing" [symposium], *Partisan Review*, 6 (Summer 1939): 40-41;

"Ballade," *Confluences*, 11 / 12 (July 1942): 11-12;

"Liberation, Glory Be!," *Collier's*, 114 (16 December 1944): 14-15, 61-63; 114 (23 December 1944): 51, 74-76;

"Now We Are Back in Paris," *Compass* (December 1945): 56-60;

"Capital, Capitals," by Stein, with music by Virgil Thomson, *New Music*, 20 (April 1947): 3-34;

"I Like American and American," *'47*, 1 (October 1947): 16-21;

"Jean Atlan: Abstract Painting," *Yale French Studies*, no. 31 (May 1964): 118.

Gertrude Stein, who lived and wrote as though she knew she would be legendary, is more than that now: she is an icon. The image of Stein, sitting under the Picasso portrait of her in the living room at 27, rue de Fleurus, in Paris, has permanently entered the consciousness of literate people everywhere. The image carries with it a myriad of associations: the brilliant hostess around whom gathered a dazzling array of avant-garde writers and artists–among them Ernest Hemingway, F. Scott Fitzgerald, Pablo Picasso, Henri Matisse, Sherwood Anderson, Alfred Steiglitz, Carl Van Vechten, Guillaume Apollinaire, Georges Braque, Marie Laurencin, Robert Delaunay; the powerful personality, alternately brusque or charming as the situation or her mood dictated; the dominant half of a famous and apparently harmonious lesbian relationship with Alice B. Toklas, with whom she lived for thirty-seven years; the originator of the phrase, "A rose is a rose is a rose," words familiar even to those who know little or nothing of the woman who wrote them. Indeed, so unique are the facts of her life that they have continually overshadowed her contribution to the whole range of American literature: fiction, poetry, drama, theory, and criticism.

Although she is regarded as an experimentalist, the works for which she is best known are her most conventionally written: *Three Lives* (1909) and her series of memoirs–*The Autobiography of Alice B. Toklas* (1933), *Everybody's Autobiography* (1937), and *Wars I Have Seen* (1945). Her critical works–*Composition as Explanation* (1926), *Lectures in America* (1935), and *What Are Masterpieces* (1940), which explain, analyze, or justify her method–have historically been useful only to Stein scholars or to those writers, like her, who wish to pursue answers to philosophical or epistemological questions. The remaining works–portraits, still lifes, geographies, plays, novels, operas, and philosophical disquisitions–shatter conventional notions of genre and function as explorations into the nature and function of mind, human nature, perception, language, and art. "Language is a real thing," she said, it is not "an imitation of sounds or colors or emotions it is an intellectual recreation." In an attempt to catch this "real thing" she invented new rhetorical strategies, bringing to language a purity, simplicity, and joy, but in the doing she effectively alienated a whole generation of readers and writers who saw her as an eccentric ("The Mother Goose of Montparnasse"), cloaking herself in a deliberate verbal obscurity.

Gertrude Stein was born in Allegheny, Pennsylvania, on 3 February 1874, the fifth and last child of Amelia Keyser and Daniel Stein, neither of whom, it seems, was able to engender filial devotion in their daughter. About her mother, frequently sickly and always passive, she would later write in *The Making of Americans* (1925), "She was very loving in her feeling to all her children, but they had been always ... after they stopped being very little children, too big for her ever to control them. She could not lead them nor could she know what they needed inside them." Amelia Stein died of cancer in 1888, but, wrote Gertrude Stein in *Everybody's Autobiography*, "we had already had the habit of doing without her." Daniel Stein died three years later: his moodiness and tyranny over his children led Stein to generalize: "fathers are depressing." This emotional estrangement from her parents was shared by her brother Leo Stein, and it resulted in an intricate bond between them, characterized by alliance (they called themselves the "happy exiles" during their early years at home) and later by long periods of bitterness and antagonism as Gertrude Stein's celebrity and productivity grew far beyond that of her brother, who saw her as possessing an intellect inferior to and wholly dependent upon his own.

The Stein children (Gertrude, Leo, Bertha, Simon, and Michael) with their governess and tutor in Vienna, circa 1876 (courtesy of the Beinecke Rare Book and Manuscript Library, Yale University)

Nonetheless, her early years in the Stein household provided, both by way of Leo's influence and the family's years in Europe, the crucible in which was forged her extraordinary adult life and work. In 1875, when Gertrude Stein was one year old, Daniel Stein moved his family to Vienna, where he had developed business interests, and then three years later to Passy, France. Her exposure to German and French–in both of which she early became fluent–undoubtedly helped to shape her later daring experiments in language. In 1879 the Stein family went to stay with Amelia Stein's family in Baltimore, and the next year they moved to Oakland, California, where they lived for a year in Tubb's Hotel, and then rented a ten-acre farm just outside the city. The fresh beauty of this environment was one of her earliest aesthetic experiences. As she recalls it in her massive *The Making of Americans*: "There was, just around the house, a pleasant garden, in front were green lawns not very carefully attended and with large trees in the center whose roots always sucked up for themselves almost all the moisture, water in this dry western country could not be used just to keep things green and pretty and so, often, the grass was very dry in the summer, but it was very pleasant then lying there watching the birds, black in the bright sunlight and sailing, and the firm white summer clouds breaking away from the horizon and slowly moving . . . and

then when the quail came it was fun to go shooting, and then when the wind and the rain and the ground were ready to help seeds in their growing, it was good fun to help plant them, and the wind would be so strong it would blow the leaves and branches of the trees down around them and you could shout and work and get wet and be all soaking and run out full into the strong wind and let it dry you, in between the gusts of rain that left you soaking. It was fun all the things that happened all the year then."

These early years were relatively unstructured, and, although Gertrude's formal schooling was limited and erratic, she and Leo shared in the discovery of George Eliot, Mark Twain, Jules Verne, and William Shakespeare, and they read widely in history and science books and in encyclopedias. Their hunger for all aspects of culture was already in evidence: they made frequent excursions to art galleries and attended, with regularity, opera and theater productions.

Following Daniel Stein's death in 1891, Michael, the eldest of the Stein children, became guardian of the family. In 1892 he arranged for Gertrude and her sister, Bertha, to move to Baltimore to live with an aunt, and Leo, who had been attending the University of California at Berkeley, transferred to Harvard. His matriculation there was crucial to Gertrude Stein's development, for she followed him in 1893 and began study at Radcliffe College.

It was here that she came under the tutelage of the father of American pragmatism, philosopher William James, who was later to remember Gertrude Stein as one of his most brilliant students. Her assessment of him, if somewhat presumptuous (she was twenty at the time she recorded it), shows the emergence of her powerful intellect and fearless judgment. He was, she wrote in an essay for an English composition course, "truly a man among men, . . . a scientist of force and originality embodying all that is strongest and worthiest in scientific spirit, . . . a metaphysician skilled in abstract thought, clear and vigorous and yet too great to worship logic as his God, and narrow himself to a belief merely in the reason of man." From James she learned the absolute necessity of retaining an open mind in the inquiry into the nature of all things, spiritual as well as material. (He told her, "Never reject anything. Nothing has been proved. If you reject anything, that is the beginning of the end as an intellectual.") Under James's supervision she experimented with automatic writing, attempting to discover the nature and function of the subconscious mind, an enterprise which may well have stimulated her interest in capturing the rhythms of speech, but which led as well to her observations on character (the fiction writer emergent) and to a tendency to group people according to type. Thus, in the paper published as a result of her work in the Harvard psychology laboratory, "Normal Motor Automatism," she described two kinds of personality: the first is "nervous, high strung, very imaginative, has the capacity to be easily roused and intensely interested"; the second is "distinctly phlegmatic. If emotional, decidedly of a weakish, sentimental order."

In general, Stein's life at Radcliffe, where she earned an A.B. degree in 1898, was marked by social as well as academic success. According to the accounts of classmates, she enjoyed a measure of popularity although she tended to display airs of superiority. She earned only a C in her English composition course with the poet William Vaughn Moody, and her writing for the course is more significant for its autobiographical content than for its suggestiveness about her later method. A theme titled "In the Library" describes the experience of a young woman who, while sitting in the college library, feels suddenly suffocated and rushes out to find an ocean view that brings her fresh air and a sense of freedom:

"Now the time had come when her old and well-beloved companions had begun to pall. One could not live on books, she felt that she must have some human sympathy. Her passionate yearnings made her fear for the endurance of her own reason. Vague fears began to crowd on her. Her longings and desires had become morbid. She felt that she must have an outlet. Some change must come into her life, or she would no longer be able to struggle with the wild moods that now so often possessed her." Moody found the theme lacking in organization and in literary method but displaying considerable psychological insight and emotional intensity.

This extraordinary candor about the turmoil of her emotional life may well indicate that at about this time Stein had begun to recognize the conflicting sexual impulses eventuating in her love affair with May Bookstaver in 1900. Following the advice of William James, who advised her that a career as a professional psychologist required a medical degree, she had enrolled in the Johns Hopkins Medical School in 1897, did reasonably well for the first two years, and then began to fail miserably. Commentators on Stein's life have suggested that Leo Stein's decision in 1900 to live in Europe may have left her despondent and unable to perform academically, but, in fact, her grades show a marked decline before he left Baltimore, where he had been engaged in independent biological research. She had met a group of young feminists, several of them graduates of Bryn Mawr College. Among them was May Bookstaver, for whom she had developed a strong sexual attachment but who, after a brief liaison, chose another woman in the group as her lover. Letters between Stein and Bookstaver documenting the relationship were destroyed by Alice Toklas years later, but we know Stein referred to them as she was composing *Q.E.D.*, her work of lesbian fiction. Published posthumously as *Things As They Are* (1950) and later in *Fernhurst, Q.E.D., and Other Early Writings* (1971), *Q.E.D.* is the story of a female love triangle in which the character representing Gertrude Stein suffers a painful rejection and is cast as the lonely outsider. Her next love relationship–with Alice B. Toklas–was to be a deep and satisfying one and was to last the rest of her life.

Between 1900 and autumn 1903 when she decided to live in Paris, Stein made three trips to Europe, either visiting or accompanying Leo, who had decided to devote his life to the study of painting and aesthetics. During her intermit-

Gertrude and Leo Stein, Cambridge, Massachusetts, circa 1897 (courtesy of the Beinecke Rare Book and Manuscript Library, Yale University)

tent sojourns in America, she tried, repeatedly, to reconcile with May Bookstaver; finally, accepting the futility of her efforts, she moved in with her brother at 27, rue de Fleurus, in Paris. After a visit to the United States in early 1904, she did not return to her native land for thirty years. When Stein moved in with her brother, she was twenty-nine years old, at a point, she was to write in *Fernhurst,* when "the straight and narrow gateway of maturity and life which was all uproar and confusion narrows down to form and purpose and we exchange a great dim possibility for a small hard reality." This "small hard reality" was, for Stein, the commitment to a life of writing.

Her written work up to this time included *Q. E. D., Fernhurst,* and the early draft of *The Making of Americans,* a combining of novel, biography, and history. Over the next two years she met Paul Cézanne and Pablo Picasso and was enormously impressed and then very much influenced by their paintings. In spring 1905 Stein began to write what has become her best-known

fiction work, *Three Lives.* The importance of this collection of three stories is in the subtle power of each portrait and in the narrative technique, which reflects her growing disenchantment with traditional fictional forms. The avant-garde painters who became her friends were in the process of rejecting conventional (that is, "realistic") ways of seeing and had begun to break up the spatial planes depicted on the canvas so that completed paintings appeared no longer to mirror the objects in the material world which they represented. Similarly, over the next decade she made herself the writer of the nonrepresentational. Her aim was to capture the "movement of thoughts and words," and at the same time to give the sense of character as existing in a continuous present, divorced from history or description. Being is not remembering, she said, "at any moment when you are you you are you without the memory of yourself." The result was a simple, unadorned prose, emptied of associations and largely composed of nouns and verbs subtly modulated to reveal what she called "entity." In her word portrait, "Miss Furr and Miss Skeene" (first published in *Geography and Plays,* 1922), it looked like this:

> The voice Helen Furr was cultivating was quite a pleasant one. The voice Georgine Skeene was cultivating was, some said, a better one. The voice Helen Furr was cultivating she cultivated and it was quite completely a pleasant enough one then, a cultivated enough one then. The voice Georgine Skeene was cultivating she did not cultivate too much. She cultivated it quite some. She cultivated and she would some time go on cultivating it and it was not then an unpleasant one, it would not be then an unpleasant one, it would be quite richly enough to be a pleasant enough one.

The stripping down of language, removing its complex connotations, creating the word as a thing in itself (as in the words *cultivate* and *pleasant* and their variations), and defining character by way of a fixed moment of consciousness were extraordinary innovations forcing readers to perceive language, mind, and world in new ways. Nonetheless, Stein's contemporaries were not ready for such distortions of conventional prose, deriding most of her work as nonsensical, fraudulent, or worse. More recently, there has been a resurgence of interest in her experimental work–in part from feminists who applaud her break with a patriarchal literary tradition, but from a wide range of scholars in other disciplines as well. These include film and theater theorists, poets, literary deconstructionists, philosophers, and composers–all of whom turn to her work for examples of the sophisticated use of language pressed to its limits of purity and innocence.

The bridge to the later abstract prose forms is *Three Lives,* a work of enormous influence on a small number of writers of her time, notably Sherwood Anderson and Ernest Hemingway, who found in Stein's insistent focus on the present moment an alternative to looking to a past that seemed to have failed them and the generation for whom they became spokesmen. Critic Donald Sutherland has summed it up this way: "*Three Lives,* more radically than any other work of the time in English, brought the language back to life. . . . Gertrude Stein in this work tried to coordinate the composition of the language with the process of consciousness" by using simple words "to express the most complicated thing" and then by employing "repetition and dislocation to make the word bear all the meaning it has." Thus, he

concludes, "One has to give her work word by word the deliberate attention one gives to something written in italics." *Three Lives,* although not widely read at the time of its publication (Stein had to subsidize its printing), and understood by only a small coterie among those who did read it, created new possibilities for the short-story form.

Several convergent forces led to the writing of *Three Lives.* The lessons she learned under the tutelage of William James at Harvard and her concomitant fascination with language and its relationship to the workings of the mind remained with Stein long after her apprenticeship with him. Her ideas on this subject and her application of them to her writing left her brother Leo either indifferent or unabashedly hostile. (He later characterized her experimental work as "an abomination.") Her sensitivity to his rejection led to her writing during the quiet hours after midnight when she could avoid his scrutiny. The need of a creative sensibility akin to her own was met in Pablo Picasso, who by late 1905 was a frequent visitor at 27, rue de Fleurus. For several months in 1905 and 1906 Stein sat for him as he painted her portrait, and during this period they engaged in an ongoing, mutually supportive dialogue. Stein's biographer, James R. Mellow, describes their artistic relationship this way: "Picasso had . . . a way of summing up, in razorsharp and emphatic statements, his ideas about art and the creative life that complemented and influenced her own way of thinking. When he told her, for example, that the artist who first creates a thing is 'forced to make it ugly,' that 'those who follow can make of this thing a beautiful thing because they know what they are doing, the thing having already been invented, but the inventor because he does not know what he is going to invent inevitably the thing he makes must have its ugliness,' she set it down as one of the larger truths to be gained from listening to a genius." In return "she might offer her own breathtaking generalizations, such as her belief that the reason that she and Picasso were so responsive to each other was that they represented the most advanced and most backward of modern nations, America and Spain. They had, therefore, the affinity of opposites."

The effect of this enduring friendship, while characterized by the occasional turbulence that would naturally exist between two such powerful personalities, was to release Gertrude, gradually, from a dependence on Leo and to instill in her the confidence she desperately needed to go

Stein at Johns Hopkins University, circa 1897 (courtesy of the Beinecke Rare Book and Manuscript Library, Yale University)

on with her innovative work. During this period she came increasingly under the influence of paintings by Henri Matisse, as well as Picasso and Cézanne–all of whose works the Stein family (Leo, Gertrude, and Michael and his wife, Sarah) were purchasing and promoting with regularity. Indeed, the salon at 27, rue de Fleurus, had become a small but important museum in which many of the finest avant-garde canvasses could be seen. One of the earliest important paintings on her walls was by Cézanne, a portrait of his wife seated in a red chair and wearing a blue dress. The artist had departed from the established techniques of photographic or representational portraiture by structuring color planes so that areas of color gave a solidity and monumentality to the work and captured the essential nature of his subject. At the same time the model did not dominate the painting as in traditional portraiture but was related to everything else in the painting equally, achieving a kind of democratization of composition. Stein sat in front of the painting calculatedly and began to write the stories that were to become *Three Lives*. She later had this to say about the impact of Cézanne's painting on

the writing that took place in front of it: "I came to Cézanne and there you were, at least, there I was, not all at once, but as soon as I got used to it. The landscape looked like a landscape that is to say what is yellow in the landscape looked yellow in the oil painting, and what was blue in the landscape looked blue in the oil painting and if it did not there was still the oil painting, the oil painting by Cézanne. The same thing was true of the people there was no reason why it should be but it was, the same thing was true of the chairs, the same thing was true of the apples. The apples looked like apples the chairs looked like chairs and it all had nothing to do with anything because if they did not look like apples or chairs or landscapes or people they were apples and landscapes and chairs and people. They were so entirely these things that they were not an oil painting and yet that is just what the Cézannes were they were an oil painting. They were so entirely an oil painting that it was all there whether they were finished, the paintings, or whether they were not finished. Finished or unfinished it always was what it looked like the very essence of an oil painting because everything was there, really there. . . . This then was a great relief to me and I began my writing."

At about this time Gertrude Stein, at her brother's suggestion, had begun reading Gustave Flaubert, and as part of her immersion in the technique and vision of the French novelist, had begun to translate his *Trois Contes* (1877). The consequence of this experience was the decision to begin three tales of her own, tales at whose center were servant women modeled on real women from her childhood. The mood is set in the epigraph which Stein took from a work of Jules Laforgue: "Donc je suis un malheureux et ce n'est ni ma faute ni celle de la vie" (So I am unhappy and neither I nor life is responsible for it). The first and last stories, "The Good Anna" and "The Gentle Lena," are closely related to the rhetorical and thematic tradition of the naturalists writing in this period; that is to say, the prose style, while rhythmic and poetic, is relatively conventional, and the characters are depicted as passive victims who, almost from the beginning, are seen as doomed by fate to a tragic end. But in the middle tale, "Melanctha," one can see the transition to an entirely new perception of the role of fiction. The central character struggles with the conflicting forces that seem, all unbidden, to dominate her existence, and the narrative now dispenses with conventional means of structuring plot and time.

"The Good Anna" is closely patterned after Flaubert's "Un Coeur Simple" in *Trois Contes*. Anna, like Flaubert's young woman, is a servant girl, who, like Flaubert's Félicité, depends on the events in other people's lives for the meaning of her own. Since she moves from position to position and since her energies are so heavily invested in those for whom she works, her history is one of a series of losses, the greatest of which is that of Miss Mathilda, the large, phlegmatic woman with whom she spends her last years and who eventually moves to Europe to live. The pride she cannot feel about her own achievements, possessions, and appearance is displaced onto her mistress: "With Miss Mathilda Anna did it all. The clothes, the house, the hats, what she should wear and when and what was always best for her to do. There was nothing Miss Mathilda would not let Anna manage, and only be too glad if she would do. . . . Anna was proud almost to bursting of her cherished Miss Mathilda with all her knowledge and her great possessions, and the good Anna was always telling of it all to everybody that she knew." When Mathilda, going out

one evening, puts on an old dress, Anna stops her, insisting, "You can't go out to dinner in that dress, Miss Mathilda. You got to go and put on your new dress you always look so nice in." The most original aspect of this work is the way in which much of the narrative perpetuates the style of the character's voice. As a consequence, one has the sense that everything within the narrative is perceived by Anna, is given her conceptual limitations, her values, her mind-set. Here is the narrator describing a brief period in Anna's life: "All this time Anna was leading her happy life with Dr. Shonjen. She had every day her busy time. She cooked and saved and sewed and scrubbed and scolded. And every night she had her happy time, in seeing her doctor like the fine things she bought so cheap and cooked so good for him to eat. And then he would listen and laugh so loud, as she told him stories of what had happened on that day." The effect of this device—the inversions, the rhythmic repetitions, the colloquialisms—is to place the narrator on the same social and epistemological plane as the character and, thus, to yoke together character, narrative persona, and vision. Stein's great contribution here is her demonstration that working-class characters can be as interesting psychologically as those from the middle class, who are traditionally the subjects of fiction. In her treatment of Anna, she avoids even the faintest patronizing tone which could easily have resulted had the tale been told from the point of view and in the voice of a socially superior narrator.

Anna's eccentricities, in part rooted in her German-immigrant background, make her complex: although well motivated and relentlessly moral, she is not simply a "good Anna" but a tough-minded, at times irritable, and occasionally badgering woman. That which Stein has also caught in Anna's occasional rebelliousness is the repressed anger predictably experienced by members of the servant class, for whom there is a preordained and changeless requirement that they perform smilingly, an exacting of courteous and cheerful behavior no matter what their spirits may in actuality dictate. The story ends with the departure of Miss Mathilda and then, very quickly, the death of Anna. Given the dependency which alone characterizes her existence, there is literally nothing further she can live for. Anna has known that Miss Mathilda never lives in one place for long, but she has "made herself forget it. This last year when she knew that it was coming she had tried hard not to think it

Leo, Gertrude, and Michael Stein, outside 27, rue de Fleurus, circa 1907 (courtesy of Edward M. Burns)

would happen.... The dreary day dragged out and then all was ready and Miss Mathilda left to take her train. Anna stood strained and pale and dry eyed on the white stone steps of the little red brick house that they had lived in. The last thing Miss Mathilda heard was the good Anna bidding foolish Peter say good bye and be sure to remember Miss Mathilda." The report of Anna's death is given by way of a letter to Miss Mathilda, and its contents make clear that the good Anna died in precisely the same way she lived–her thoughts rooted in concern for those outside herself:

> "Dear Miss Mathilda," wrote Mrs. Drehten, "Miss Annie died in the hospital yesterday after a hard operation. She was talking about you and Doctor and Miss Mary Wadsmith all the time. She said that she hoped you would take Peter and the little Rags to keep when you come back to America to live. I will keep them for you here Miss Mathilda. Miss Annie died easy, Miss Mathilda, and sent you her love."

In "The Gentle Lena" Stein reveals with

even greater force the relationship between language and power. Like Anna, Lena is a German immigrant, but she has a less assertive personality and an even greater linguistic inadequacy in her adopted country; so she is overwhelmed by others of her group who, in their need to compensate for their own feelings of powerlessness, succeed in manipulating the events of her life.

Early in the story we learn of the influence on Lena of her aunt, Mrs. Haydon, whose own daughters are unmanageable and who consequently chooses the young, gentle Lena for the exercising of her maternal prerogatives. "Mrs. Haydon thought it would be a fine thing to take [Lena] back with her to Bridgepoint and get her well started.... Lena's age just suited Mrs. Haydon's purpose. Lena could first go out to service, and learn how to do things, and then, when she was a little older Mrs. Haydon could get her a good husband. And then Lena was so still and docile, she would never want to do things her own way. And then, too, Mrs. Haydon, with all her hardness had wisdom, and she could feel the rarer strain there was in Lena."

The search for a husband begins: for four years Mrs. Haydon is "busy looking around among all the german people that she knew for the right man to be Lena's husband, and now at last she was quite decided. The man Mrs. Haydon wanted for Lena was a young german-american tailor, who worked with his father. He was good and all the family were very saving, and Mrs. Haydon was sure that this would be just right for Lena, and then too, this young tailor always did whatever his father and his mother wanted." But neither Lena nor Herman Kreder wish to marry: she remains silent, impassive; he runs away. When Lena stands before her aunt, mute, intimidated, she is berated: "You just stand there so stupid and don't answer just like you ain't heard a word what I been saying to you. I never see anybody like you, Lena. If you going to burst out at all, why don't you burst out sudden instead of standing there so silly and don't answer." Of course, "bursting out" is totally inconsistent with Lena's character, and so, when her aunt asks if she likes Herman, she responds: "Why I do anything you say, Aunt Mathilda. Yes, I like him. He don't say much to me, but I guess he is a good man, and I do anything you say for me to do."

Even though Lena has been jilted by Herman Kreder, when the reluctant bridegroom finally reappears, the two young people find they have no power to fight the communal forces urging their union. They capitulate, and Lena, now living with Herman and his parents, retreats even further into silence and isolation. So few are her articulated needs and so infrequent are her demands that it is as though she has no existence at all. When she dies in childbirth, the event is given only a passing reference, the narrative structure emulating her inconsequentiality, the lack of impact her introverted nature has had on the lives of others: "When the baby was come out at last, it was like its mother lifeless. While it was coming, Lena had grown very pale and sicker. When it was all over Lena had died, too, and nobody knew just how it had happened to her."

With "Melanctha," the second story in the collection but the last to be written, Stein's break with traditional fictional forms was complete. In this story of a young black woman's struggle to understand her troubled and passionate nature, Stein not only stretched the linguistic parameters of narrative strategy, but she found a way to enter the black experience with a rare authenticity. There have been, admittedly, those critics whose views of "Melanctha" have been less than sanguine. Black-American poet and novelist Claude McKay wrote, "In the telling of the story I found nothing striking and informative about Negro life.... Melanctha seemed more like a brief American paraphrase of Esther Waters than a story of Negro life. The original Esther Waters is more important to me." The most openly hostile response to the story came from British writer and artist (and frequent nay-sayer) Wyndham Lewis, who called it "the most wearisome dirge it is possible to imagine.... What is the matter with it is, probably, that it is *dead*." He went on to charge that "The monstrous, desperate *soggy lengths* of primitive mass-life.... are undoubtedly intended as an epic contribution to the present mass-democracy. The texture of the language has to be jumbled, cheap, slangy, and thick to suit."

Both these critics either inadvertantly or willfully misrepresented Stein's intention and achievement. A careful reading of "Melanctha," even from the vantage point of today's heightened consciousness in matters of race and ethnicity, reveals an authorial attitude of compassion, wisdom, and sensitivity. It is precisely this astuteness that Richard Wright caught in the story at the time of his first reading. He claimed it was "the first long serious literary treatment of Negro life in the United States" and, in a 1945 review of Stein's *Wars I Have Seen*, described discovering the story while browsing in a public library in Chicago and taking *Three Lives* home so that he could read "Melanctha": "As I read it my ears were opened for the first time to the magic of the spoken word. I began to hear the speech of my grandmother, who spoke a deep, pure Negro dialect and with whom I had lived for many years. All of my life I had been only half hearing, but Miss Stein's struggling words made the speech of the people around me vivid. From that moment on, in my attempts at writing, I was able to tap at will the vast pool of living words that whirled around me." After reading a left-wing literary critic's charge that Stein was a decadent writer who opposed social revolution, Wright "contrived a method to gauge the degree to which Miss Stein's prose was tainted with the spirit of counter-revolution." He read "Melanctha" to a group of semiliterate black stockyard workers: "They understood every word. En-

Alice B. Toklas and Stein in Vienna, circa 1908 (courtesy of the Beinecke Rare Book and Manuscript Library, Yale University)

thralled, they slapped their thighs, howled, laughed, stomped, and interrupted me constantly to comment upon the characters. My fondness for Steinian prose never distressed me after that." The anecdote emphasizes the authenticity of dialect and character, the truthfulness of events and behaviors, the accuracy of language patterns in this rendering of the stormy life of a young black working-class woman by an upper-middle-class white one.

The story of "Melanctha" is loosely patterned after Stein's earlier *Q.E.D.* and, like that work, is rooted in the experience of an oppressed social group. Yet here she has replaced the lesbian love relationship and its difficulties

with the struggle of a beautiful young light-skinned black woman to discover her place in a world whose limits and values she cannot really fathom any more than she can understand the conflicting and constantly changing emotional forces that seem to drive her. That Stein should have an interest in and sensitivity to oppressed groups–lesbians, German immigrant women, black working-class women–is not surprising. As an intellectual Jewish lesbian she could not have been more outside the mainstream of contemporary culture. What is surprising, however, is the degree to which she was able to shape language into a tool for the subtle communication of thought processes and lived experience as no one ever had before her.

Stein said that "Melanctha" is a pattern of "beginning again and again." Thus, in Melanctha's relationship with each person who enters her life, she moves toward, then away from, then nearer to, then back again from the intimacy that she seems so urgently to need–a dizzying dance of tentative acceptance and rejection that ends, repeatedly, in Melanctha's isolation. The pattern first emerges in her friendship with Jane Harden, a young black woman who, the narrator says, introduces Melanctha into the ways of "wisdom." The sexuality at the heart of this story has been for many decades unacknowledged, or at best glossed over. That Melanctha is defined mainly, although not only, by a powerful eroticism is clear from the beginning in her flirtations with the men at the railroad station and shipyard. This appetite is expressed in her lesbian relationship with Jane Harden as well as in the heterosexual liaisons both women openly seek: "It was not from men that Melanctha learned her wisdom. It was always Jane Harden herself who was making Melanctha begin to understand. . . . Jane had many ways in which to do this teaching. She told Melanctha many things. She loved Melanctha hard and made Melanctha feel it very deeply. She would be with other people and with men and with Melanctha, and she would make Melanctha understand what everybody wanted, and what one did with power when one had it . . . . In every way she got it from Jane Harden. There was nothing good or bad in doing, feeling, thinking or in talking, that Jane spared her. Sometimes the lesson came almost too strong for Melanctha, but somehow she always managed to endure it and so slowly, but always with increasing strength and feeling, Melanctha began to really understand."

Melanctha's nature is complex: although she possesses great vitality and an enormous appetite for experience and "knowing," she desires, too, "peace and gentleness and goodness." But like so many other young fictional heroines whose characters are tested as they move outward into the world, Melanctha lacks a moral guide; she is, in a very real sense, parentless. Although her mother and father are married, they do not live together. Her mother has been responsible for raising her, but, as the narrator explains, "Melanctha had not liked her mother very well." Her mother "had always been a little wandering and mysterious and uncertain in her ways," and these "things she had in her of her mother never made her feel respect." Though she has "almost always

hated" him, she more closely identifies with her father. She resents and fears his coarseness and brutality, but she loves "the power in herself that came through him."

After a few years of "seeking wisdom" with and through Jane Harden, Melanctha meets Jefferson Campbell, an attractive, but quiet, serious, young black physician, who until Melanctha "has never yet in his life had real trouble." They meet when Jeff is called in to treat her mother in the last days of a terminal illness. The long, agonizing wait draws them together, but Jeff is a "thinking" man, Melanctha a "feeling" woman; the relationship is doomed despite their early strong attachment to one another. The long, complex, continually shifting texture of this romance is revealed in subtly modulated language, expressive of both the inner thoughts and spoken words of each character. Key words appear and reappear, defining the distinctive and sharply contrasting emotional structures of Melanctha and Jeff as they grope futilely toward an understanding. This extended dialogue reveals the rhetorical strategy Stein uses to establish the psychological nature of her two characters:

"You see it's this way with me always Miss Melanctha, I really certainly don't ever like to get excited, and that kind of loving hard does seem always to mean just getting all the time excited. That certainly is what I always think from what I see from them that have it bad Miss Melanctha, and that certainly would never suit a man like me. You see Miss Melanctha I am a very quiet kind of fellow, and I believe in a quiet life for all the colored people. No Miss Melanctha I certainly never have mixed myself up in that kind of trouble."

"Yes I certainly do see that very clearly Dr. Campbell," said Melanctha, "I see that's certainly what it is always made me not know right about you and that's certainly what it is that makes you really mean what you was always saying. You certainly are just too scared Dr. Campbell to really feel things way down in you. All you are always wanting Dr. Campbell is just to talk about being good, and to play with people just to have a good time, and yet always to certainly keep yourself out of trouble. It don't seem to me Dr. Campbell that I admire that way to do things very much. It certainly ain't really to me being very good. It certainly ain't any more to me Dr. Campbell, but that you certainly are awful scared about really feeling things way down in you, and that's certainly the only way Dr. Campbell I can see that you can mean, by what it is that you are always saying to me."

"I don't know about that Miss Melanctha, I certainly don't think I can feel things very deep in me, though I do say I certainly do like to have things nice and quiet, but I don't see harm in keeping out of danger Miss Melanctha, when a man certainly knows he don't want to get killed in it, and I don't know anything that's more awful dangerous Miss Melanctha than being strong in love with somebody. I don't mind sickness or real trouble Miss Melanctha, and I don't want to be talking about what I can do in real trouble, but you know something about that Miss Melanctha, but I certainly don't see much in mixing up just to get excited, in that awful kind of danger. No Miss Melanctha I certainly do only know just two kinds of ways of loving. One kind of loving seems to me, is like one has a good quiet feeling in a family when one does his work, and is always living good and being regular, and then the other way of loving is just like having it like any animal that's low in the streets together, and that don't seem to me very good Miss Melanctha, though I don't ever say that its not all right when anybody likes it, and that's all the kinds of love I know Miss Melanctha, and I certainly don't care very much to get mixed up in that kind of a way just to be in trouble."

Jefferson stopped and Melanctha thought a little.

"That certainty does explain to me Dr. Campbell what I been thinking about you this long time. I certainly did wonder how you could be so live, and knowing everything, and everybody, and talking so big always about everything, and everybody always liking you so much, and you always looking as if you was thinking, and yet you really was never knowing about anybody and certainly not being really very understanding."

On a later occasion Jeff protests, "I certainly do think I feel as much for you Miss Melanctha, as you ever feel about me, sure I do"; and she responds, "I certainly do care for you Jeff Campbell less than you are always thinking and much more than you are ever knowing."

Throughout the story, Melanctha is described as always "wandering," "looking for excitement," having "too much feeling," and always finding "trouble." Given what we know of her history with Jane Harden and her early flirtations with the railroad and dockyard workers, the terms could be construed as having specifically sexual connotations, but Stein's shaping of her character transcends the merely primitive or titillating. While Melanctha's nature is frankly sensual, and while it is clear that she has experienced intimacy with several men (as well as with Jane Harden),

this eroticism is a metaphor for her openness and responsiveness to life, a childlike delight in the myriad of experiences presented to her sensibility. This distinguishes her from Jeff Campbell, who lives "so that he could understand what troubled people, and not just to have 'excitements.' " He is a practical man, a rationalist; she is a sybarite, and it is her very need and ability to enjoy a diversity of sensuous experiences that charms others while it troubles her. She lives completely in the here and now, a creature of the immediate (exemplifying both through the prose that describes her and the experiences she lives through, Stein's concept of the continuous present: "being is not remembering"; "at any moment when you are you you are you without the memory of yourself"). Consequently, she has great difficulty in "remembering right"; her own history is elusive to her. Jeff's accusation that she never is "remembering anything only what you just then are feeling in you," is precisely her predicament. Much of the dialogue between the young lovers is centered around the issues of trust and fidelity: "no man can ever really hold you," Jeff tells her, "because you mean right Melanctha, but you never can remember. . . ."

Although their efforts to establish a strong and lasting union are thwarted by their differences, Jeff, through his closeness to Melanctha, is able to move beyond the narrow emotional limits he has placed upon his life. From her he learns to think less and feel more; first, he begins to "feel a little"; then he becomes less "sure of what he wants"; he stops "thinking in words"; he begins to "wander" and finds he is "losing himself in strong feeling." Finally, one afternoon, Jeff finds he can, like Melanctha, respond fully to the glories of the physical world: "He loved all the colors in the trees and on the ground, and the little, new, bright colored bugs he found in the moist ground and in the grass he loved to lie on and in which he was busy searching. Jeff loved everything that moved and that was still, and that had color, and beauty, and real being. Jeff loved very much this day while they were wandering. He almost forgot that he had any trouble with him still inside him. Jeff loved to be there with Melanctha Herbert. She was always so sympathetic to him for the way she listened to everything he found and told her, the way she felt his joy in all this being, the way she never said she wanted anything different from the way they had it. It was certainly a busy and a happy day, this their first long day of really wandering." For the

Gertrude Stein in 1919, seated beneath Pablo Picasso's 1906 portrait of her (courtesy of Edward M. Burns). When Stein's friends had complained that she did not resemble the recently completed portrait, Picasso had replied, "She will."

first time Jeff finds "real being." He achieves the freshness and innocence that so defines Melanctha and tells her: "You see Melanctha, it's like this way with me. I got a new feeling now, you been teaching to me . . . and I see perhaps what really loving is like, like really having everything together, new things, little pieces all different, like I always before been thinking was bad to be having, all go together like, to make one good big feeling." Jeff, through loving her, has achieved spiritual and psychological integration, a wholeness not available to Melanctha. Her function is to provide for others what they do not have without her, but hers is a restless spirit. She

seems destined to move on from relationship to relationship like a principle of energy, giving much, taking little.

Following her affair with Jeff Campbell, she enters one with the irresponsible gambler Jem Richards, to whom cards and travel mean more than any woman, and from this to a complex, strangely satisfying friendship with the rigid, scolding, authority figure Rose Johnson, a woman Melanctha feels has "worked in to be the deepest of all her emotions." But Rose, fearing the effect the unwittingly seductive Melanctha might have on her husband, Sam, rejects her, forbidding her ever to come to her house again.

This act is a fatal blow; Rose has been a source of strength to Melanctha; she has been able to give her a feeling of safety she has not experienced before: "And now Rose had cast her from her. Melanctha was lost, and all the world went whirling in a mad weary dance around her." She feels that "nothing any more could ever help." It is as though she is all used up, as though the intensity of the emotional investment she has made in each of her doomed encounters has left her drained, empty. The short time that remains to her is marked by loneliness and despair, and then by weakness and a fatal illness. As in the stories of "The Good Anna" and "The Gentle Lena," her life ends in a phrase: "They sent her where she would be taken care of, a home for poor consumptives, and there Melanctha stayed until she died."

While Stein's story of this troubled, spirited young woman has interest in and of itself (and may have significant autobiographical resonance in the heroine's unsuccessful search for a parent figure), it is her technique, a deliberate departure from past fictional prose forms, that warrants most attention. The careful limitation of vocabulary, the emphatic repetition, the distortion of diction and syntax suggest a rudimentary level of consciousness, a mirroring of the mind as it experiences feelings and perceives events. The texture of this prose style is halting, hypnotic, incantatory. Each character is depicted, not by way of narrative description or conventionally deployed dialogue, but rather by the unique linguistic patterns that establish his or her personality. The rootedness of each individual within limited, repeated word patterns emphasizes both the struggle to achieve understanding and the inability of language to act as a medium of communication. Absent from "Melanctha" is fiction's socially elevated tone, its occasional over-reliance on description, plot, and dialogue, its gratuitous building to denouements, and its ever-present authorial voice. Absent, too, is the aggrandizement of one character, one event with the resultant diminution of all others. Stein had achieved in writing *Three Lives* the democratization of composition that had so struck her as she sat and gazed at Cézanne's portrait of his wife.

In 1907, not long after she completed the writing of *Three Lives,* Michael and Sarah Stein introduced Gertrude Stein to Alice B. Toklas, who had traveled to Paris from her home in California with a companion, Harriet Levy. Toklas's recollection of this meeting in *What Is Remembered*

(1963) makes wonderfully vivid the impact Stein immediately had upon her: "In the room were Mr. and Mrs. Stein and Gertrude Stein. It was Gertrude Stein who held my complete attention.... She was a golden brown presence, burned by the Tuscan sun and with a golden glint in her warm brown hair. She was dressed in a warm brown corduroy suit. She wore a large round coral brooch and when she talked, very little, or laughed, a good deal, I thought her voice came from this brooch. It was unlike anyone else's voice–deep, full velvety like a great conralto's, like two voices. She was large and heavy with delicate small hands and a beautifully modeled and unique head." Later she was to remark after meeting the philosopher Alfred North Whitehead, "He was my third genius for whom the bell rang. The first two had been Gertrude Stein and Picasso."

There are several ways in which the two women must have been drawn to each other. Each was well educated, well informed about, and vitally interested in the arts; each had a Jewish background which, from the standpoint of orthodox rituals, each had renounced; each had lost parents while still young; each had spent time in the vast openness of the American West; each had traveled to and fallen in love with Paris, which was to become home for them in their shared life; and each was sexually woman-oriented, a fact about Toklas that Stein possessed even before their meeting.

But the ways in which they differed are of equal importance; Toklas, in her greater passivity and in her taking over most of the domestic responsibilities (she developed a reputation as cook; the *Alice B. Toklas Cookbook* still enjoys great popularity), made it possible for Stein to expend her energies on her increasingly difficult, ever more innovative writing. Toklas became integral to the composing process itself. Her fine literary instincts and her openness to the unconventional nature of Stein's work led her at first to encourage Stein, then to begin editing and typing the manuscripts. Since Gertrude's relationship with Leo had been rapidly disintegrating, the entrance of Toklas into Stein's life could not have been more felicitous. Here at last was someone who was vitally interested in every aspect of her existence and whose pleasure came, not in competing with her as her brother did, but in creating an environment in which Stein's creativity could flourish. Not long after their meeting, Harriet Levy returned to California, and Toklas moved

Toklas and Stein, late 1920s, in the Model T Ford "Godiva," so named by Stein because it lacked all accessories (courtesy of the Beinecke Rare Book and Manuscript Library, Yale University)

into 27, rue de Fleurus. In 1914 Leo moved out, announcing later that Toklas was not responsible for his departure; the growing rift between sister and brother had made their continuing to live together impossible.

In *European Experiences* (1935), volume two of her *Intimate Memories*, Mabel Dodge Luhan describes Alice Toklas this way: "slight and dark, with beautiful gray eyes hung with black lashes—and she had a drooping Jewish nose, and her eyelids drooped, and the corners of her red mouth and the lobes of her ears drooped under the

black folded Hebraic hair, weighted down, as they were with heavy Oriental earrings." To Luhan, "She looked like Leah, out of the Old Testament, in her half-Oriental get-up–her blues and browns and oyster whites–her black hair–her barbaric chains and jewels–and her melancholy nose. Artistic." Clearly not beautiful, Toklas nonetheless seems to have possessed an exoticism, a charm, and an air of elegance that attracted people to her. She had been born to an upper-middle-class San Francisco family that later suffered severe financial setbacks. Her mother died when she was nineteen, and she was sent to her grand-parents to keep house for them and the adult sons who lived with them; this arrangement placed severe restrictions both on her social life and on her ability to develop her emerging talent for music into anything like a career. While she took what she could of the culture then beginning to develop in the San Francisco area, by the time she was twenty-eight she yearned for more, and, having come into a small inheritance from her grandfather, arranged with her friend, Harriet Levy, to spend the winter in Paris. The celebrated meeting with Gertrude Stein gave her her vocation. Not only did she act as listener, critic, and appreciative audience for Stein, but she frequently entertained her with wry and lively anecdotes. Her role as raconteur is caught in Stein's word portrait "Ada" (*Geography and Plays*): "Someone who was living was almost always listening. Someone who was loving was almost always listening. . . . That one who was loving was telling about being one then listening. That one being loving was then telling stories having a beginning and a middle and an ending."

The two women took up their lives together very much as husband and wife, with Toklas guarding Stein from unwanted visitors and interruptions and entertaining the wives of guests at their Saturday night salons: "The geniuses came and talked to Gertrude Stein and the wives sat with me," Stein has Toklas report in *The Autobiography of Alice B. Toklas*. They fell into comfortable, unvarying patterns: Toklas cooked and Stein ate; Toklas tended the garden and Stein chopped wood; Toklas prepared the shopping lists and Stein drove the car; Toklas proofread the manuscripts and found publishers for them; Stein continued to write. While Toklas's role seems to have been defined by a general subservience to Stein, she gained immediate exposure to a lively world of art and artists that would never have been hers without the entrance of Stein into her life. She found herself suddenly, astonishingly, at such events as the famous Banquet Rousseau in 1908 at Picasso's studio, where some of the most famous artists of the day became increasingly drunk waiting for a dinner that never arrived, Guillaume Apollinaire sang songs to the accompaniment of Henri Rousseau on the violin, and a donkey ate the feathers off Toklas's hat.

It is interesting to note that after Alice Toklas moved to 27, rue de Fleurus, Gertrude Stein's writing became more joyous, more rooted in the domestic scene which she experienced daily, and more openly erotic, as in "Lifting Belly" (first published in *Bee Time Vine and Other Pieces 1913-1927*, 1953):

> Kiss my lips. She did
> Kiss my lips again she did
> Kiss my lips over and over and over again she did.

Clearly, although her work found no responsive audience in the larger literary world, her new living arrangement and the total fulfillment it brought led to confidence in her work and abandonment to a myriad of creative impulses. Before the beginning of World War I, she had completed a series of portraits (her impressionistic and often acute responses to specific people or to character types), among the most interesting of which are "Matisse," "Cezanne," "Picasso," and "Portrait of Mabel Dodge at the Villa Curonia," all written between 1909 and 1912. Dodge had her portrait published privately in an edition of three hundred copies and bound in opulent Florentine wallpaper, and she distributed it to friends whom she thought would be open to this unconventional writing. "Portrait of Mabel Dodge" later appeared in the June 1913 special number of Alfred Steiglitz's avant-garde and widely distributed *Camera Work*, which earlier had published "Matisse" and "Picasso" (special number, August 1912), and Stein's reputation as a modernist writer was launched. A number of avant-garde artists and art patrons flocked to 27, rue de Fleurus–Roger Fry, Augustus John, Francis Picabia, Jacob Epstein, Lady Ottoline Morrell, Marcel Duchamp–to be amused or enlightened by the woman who had dared to transpose the cubist impulse to the written word.

From 1906 to 1911 Stein was at work on her thousand-page book *The Making of Americans*. Although it was not published until 1925, it achieved notoriety while she was writing it since all who knew her were aware of the notebooks she diligently kept, notebooks in which were entered her observations on the people with whom she came in contact. No one escaped her notice; all were grist for her literary mill; all were scrutinized for their potential function as character types in this "history of every one who ever can or is or will be living." Although Stein came to regard this work as her magnum opus, her challenge to Proust's *Remembrance of Things Past* (1913-1927) and to Joyce's *Ulysses* (1922), she was alone in this assessment. James Mellow describes the work as "a sprawling, jerry-built structure,"

Toklas and Stein in New York before their first airplane flight, 7 November 1934 (photograph by Carl Van Vechten, by permission of Joseph Solomon, Trustee for the Estate of Carl Van Vechten, courtesy of the Beinecke Rare Book and Manuscript Library, Yale University)

whose "writing style . . . was slow and ponderous; the simplest ideas and observations are introduced and worried over endlessly. The pace of the novel is elephantine; the plot, such as it is, lumbers forward, foraging about in strange jungles of psychological observation. Gertrude was to make no concession to the patience and endurance of her readers." Yet, Mellow concludes, the book served "as the laboratory of her later style, of her antic philosophy of human nature, and

even of her habits as a creative writer." *The Making of Americans* is purported to be a history of the Dehning and Hersland families, but its content is more nearly a series of vignettes—descriptive bits and pieces, character analyses, personal confessions ("I am all unhappy in this writing")—often seemingly unrelated, unfocused. Her interest was in using the history of her family as a parable of the history of America—its vast openness, its spirit of adventure, its incredible energy. Early in the book she articulates her purpose: "There are many that I know and they know it. They are all of them repeating and I hear it. I love it and I tell it. I love it and now I will write it. This is now a history of my love of it. I hear it and I love it and I write it. They repeat it. They live it and I see it and I hear it. They live it and I hear it and I see it and I love it and now and always I will write it." These lines demonstrate Stein's enormous enthusiasm for life, her great interest in all kinds of people, and her attempt, through rhythmic repetition and greatly reduced vocabulary to catch, not individual identities, but what she called the "bottom nature in people." Yet they demonstrate as well the enormous egotism of assuming that nearly one thousand pages of seemingly unmediated impressions would be of interest to anyone but herself, and, presumably, to Alice Toklas. In fact, when the book was finally published in 1925, only 103 of the 500 copies in the first edition were sold. In his hugely influential critical work *Axel's Castle* (1931) Edmund Wilson expressed enthusiasm for Stein's early work but said that he had been unable to finish *The Making of Americans*, and he doubted that anyone could.

Other creative work during this period culminated in a long prose poem, *Tender Buttons: Objects, Food, Rooms* (1914), more dense, more abstracted a word patterning than anything she had attempted before. In *Lectures in America* she had this to say about the work: "And so in *Tender Buttons* and then on I struggled with the ridding of myself of nouns. I knew that nouns must go in poetry as they had gone in prose if anything that is everything was to go on meaning something. . . . Poetry is . . . a vocabulary entirely based on the noun . . . concerned with using with abusing, with losing with wanting, with denying with avoiding with adoring with replacing the noun." She invites the reader into her mind as it searches for new strategies: "Was there not a way of naming things that would not invent names, but mean names without naming them." The result was the series of linguistic still lifes that suggest, not the image of the subject depicted, but the energy of the thing seen, or, as Marjorie Perloff has observed, "a way of happening rather than an account of what has happened, a way of looking rather than a description of how things look." There is a resultant playfulness and freshness embodied in the individual pieces in *Tender Buttons*, whose subjects could easily have led to facile clichés: "Elephant beaten with candy and little

pops and chews all bolts and reckless reckless rats, this is this" ("A Sound"); "It is a winning Cake" ("Salad"); "Celery tastes tastes where in cured lashes and little bits and mostly in remains. A Green acre is so selfish and so pure and so enlivened" ("Celery"); "In the middle of a tiny spot and nearly bare there is a nice thing to say that wrist is leading. Wrist is leading" ("A Leave"). The work, predictably, was widely quoted and ridiculed by friends and enemies alike when it appeared in 1914. "Stirred by the publication of Tender Buttons," Stein wrote in *The Autobiography of Alice B. Toklas*, "many newspapers had taken up the amusement of imitating Gertrude Stein's work and making fun of it. Life [the weekly magazine] began a series that were called after Gertrude Stein." To review *Tender Buttons* now is to be struck by its antipatriarchal stance. The subjects are insistently those of feminine domesticity: sensual and sexual pleasures, parts of the female body, nursery rhymes, characters from life or from fiction, food, rooms, the autonomy of women. The traditional subjects of male fiction writers—battles, jobs, travels, families or nations in crisis—are conspicuous by their absence.

When World War I broke out in August 1914, Stein and Toklas found themselves stranded in England, where they had been visiting Alfred North Whitehead and his wife (Bertrand Russell, George Moore, and Lytton Strachey were there as well). They were forced to remain there for several weeks before they could safely return to Paris. Frightened by the zeppelin raids and concerned about the potential lack of food and fuel, they fled to Spain, returning to Paris in 1916 following the Battle of Verdun. Feeling called upon to devote some energies to the war effort, they bought a Model T Ford, had it converted to a truck (which they christened "Auntie"), and transported medical supplies to depots throughout France for the American Fund for French Wounded for the remainder of the war. Their activities were acknowledged by the French: at war's end they each received a Medaille de la Reconnaissance Française.

"If you write not long but practically every day you do get a great deal written," Stein once asserted. Indeed, her productivity during and after the war was considerable. Attentive to every facet of her experience, she reworked her impressions into poems, plays, and portraits, most of which, finding no publisher courageous enough to print them, did not reach the public until late in her life or after her death. In spite of the indiffer-

Stein and Toklas with Carl Van Vechten during Stein's 1934 American lecture tour (courtesy of the Beinecke Rare Book and Manuscript Library, Yale University)

ence (or worse, the derision) that greeted her work, she remained resolute in her attempts to revitalize language. As Richard Kostelanetz observes in his introduction to *The Yale Gertrude Stein* (1980), she wanted to treat words "as autonomous objects, rather than symbols of something else, rather than windows onto other terrain. They cohere in terms of stressed sounds, rhythms, alliterations, rhymes, textures, and consistencies in diction–linguistic qualities other than subject and syntax; and even when entirely divorced from semantics, these dimensions of prose have their own powers of effect." Stein's lonely project was to reveal that "meaning" lies not in symbolic references, that is, with reference to another, separate reality, but in the relationship that words have among themselves.

In insisting on the divorce of word from referent and in keeping character and narrative remote from traditional structures, Stein was implicitly challenging the authority of myth in literary modernism. In this fictional mode, practiced by the acknowledged literary giants of the period–

James Joyce, Virginia Woolf, D. H. Lawrence, and William Faulkner–power lies in rich, symbolic suggestiveness, in a multi-referential structuring of both plot and character, clearly the very antithesis of Stein's spare, antihistorical approach to the creative use of language. Although she might have befriended Joyce, who for a time lived in Paris and expressed an interest in meeting her, she assiduously avoided any contact with him other than a brief introduction at a party. She may well have felt that their talents and their interests were too disparate for any mutually satisfying relationship to ensue; or, more than likely, she was jealous of the success that had come to the Irish writer and that had so far eluded her. Hemingway was later to remark about visits to 27, rue de Fleurus: "If you mention Joyce's name twice, you'll never be invited back."

There were many literary figures who did become her friends, including Ernest Hemingway, F. Scott Fitzgerald, and Sherwood Anderson. The friendship between Stein and Hemingway was the most notorious. Hemingway and his wife,

Hadley, came to dinner one evening in 1922, having been introduced by way of a letter from Anderson to Stein and Toklas. Stein was charmed by him. (Toklas was less so; she was easily threatened by those who might make any claim on Gertrude's affections.) There was an immediate feeling of kinship between them, Stein being particularly impressed by the younger writer's ability to listen, his hunger for advice on fiction writing, his emerging talent. They met frequently after that evening, taking leisurely walks along the Left Bank, discussing Hemingway's writing as well as his personal difficulties. ("Gertrude Stein and me are just like brothers, and we see alot of her," Hemingway wrote in a letter to Anderson.) He courted her energetically, pleased to be a clear favorite among the growing number of Stein partisans. And he convinced Ford Madox Ford to serialize *The Making of Americans* in the *transatlantic review* (April-December 1924). And, as the Hemingway style emerged, it was clear how indebted he was to his mentor for his spare, simple, declarative sentences, for his repetitions, and for his restricted vocabulary. There emerged, ultimately, some resentment on Hemingway's part as he witnessed Stein's growing admiration for Anderson's prose fictions; he was much less sanguine about the older writer's work and, in fact, parodied Anderson cruelly in his novel, *The Torrents of Spring* (1926). Biographers point to no single event that caused the rift; there may have been simply a slow dissolution of the affection they had once felt for one another intensified by Stein's growing (and very astute) suspicion that Hemingway's obsession with violence and death masked a painful vulnerability, and his predictable discomfort at her discovery.

The estrangement of the two writers eventually became public, finding its way into their works. Stein referred to Hemingway as "yellow" in *The Autobiography of Alice B. Toklas;* he responded by way of parody in *For Whom The Bell Tolls* (1940): " 'An onion is an onion is an onion,' Robert Jordan said cheerily and, he thought, 'a stone is a stein is a rock is a boulder is a pebble.' "

Throughout the 1920s and into the 1930s Stein was wholly dependent upon little magazines for the publication of her poetry, fiction, portraits, plays, and literary and psychological theories. She remained, to general readers at least, unknown, unread, unheralded. But when *The Autobiography of Alice B. Toklas* appeared in 1933 she achieved instant celebrity. The book is not, of

course, an autobiography. It is a fascinating and important social record of Stein's and Toklas's life among the artists and writers in Paris in the early decades of the century, and while it masquerades as Toklas's memoir, it is, in actuality, written by Stein as though she were Toklas reporting on Stein. This device allowed Stein to create a Gertrude Stein of her own making, one somewhat idealized. Indeed, several of those represented in the book protested at the distortions, publishing their counterclaims in a *transition* article titled "Testimony Against Gertrude Stein" (February 1935). The genesis and method of *The Autobiography of Alice B. Toklas* are clarified in its closing sentences: "About six weeks ago Gertrude Stein said it does not look to me as if you were ever going to write that autobiography. You know what I am going to do. I am going to write it for you. I am going to write it as simply as Defoe did the autobiography of Robinson Crusoe. And she has and this is it." That the book was and still is the most widely read of all Stein's publications is ironic; for she regarded it as an inferior work, one sullied by her awareness of the audience for whom she was writing. "When you are writing before there is an audience," she said, "anything written is as important as any other thing and you cherish anything and everything that you have written. After audience begins, naturally they create something that is they create you, and so . . . something is more important than another thing, which was not true when you were you that is when you were not you as your little dog knows you." Despite her reservations about the aesthetic purity of *The Autobiography of Alice B. Toklas*, it is important because it demolishes the complaint by Leo Stein and others that she was incapable of writing coherent, conventional prose; because it is filled with lively, significant anecdotal material about her life and work; and because it is a witty, charming social chronicle, offering brief, penetrating characterizations of the famous, or the soon to be famous, in Paris's Left Bank community during the early years of the twentieth century.

The book enjoyed immediate success on both sides of the Atlantic; in 1933 it was a Literary Guild selection, and the conservative *Atlantic Monthly* serialized it in four installments (May-August 1933). Stein had wished, probably rather desperately, for the recognition she saw others receiving through the years; now both recognition and celebrity were hers. Although nervous at the prospect of returning to the United States after a

Stein singing her favorite song, "On the Trail of the Lonesome Pine," at Bilignin, summer 1937 (photograph by W. G. Rogers, courtesy of the Beinecke Rare Book and Manuscript Library, Yale University)

thirty-year absence, she acceded to her agent's proposal that she undertake a six-month American lecture tour. She need not have worried; she was greeted everywhere as though she were a diva–hounded for interviews, photographed relentlessly, applauded, and cheered. Reporters were waiting when her ship arrived in New York Harbor, and she saw her name in lights moving around the *Times* building. Her lectures, while occasionally on rather lofty subjects ("What is English Literature?," "Portraits and Repetition," "Poetry and Grammar"), were always well attended and dutifully reported in the nation's newspapers. Even her appearance did not escape notice: her closely clipped hair, her odd deerstalker hat, mannish oxford shoes and shirt, coarse tweed suit and vivid vest were commented upon everywhere, and as John Malcolm Brinnin reports, "every story about her bore the inevitable Steinese caption. Typical among them was:

GERTY GERTY STEIN STEIN IS BACK HOME HOME BACK."

Among the people she visited or met during her October 1934-May 1935 tour were Eleanor Roosevelt (in the White House), Thornton Wilder, George Gershwin, F. Scott and Zelda Fitzgerald, Charlie Chaplin, Ellen Glasgow, William Saroyan, Dashiell Hammett, and Sherwood Anderson. While the attention she received was beyond anything she might have imagined, the paradox of being praised by the public and ridiculed or ignored by most in the literary community could not have escaped her notice. Still, as she observed: "It is very nice being a celebrity a real celebrity who can decide who they want to meet and say so and they come or do not come as you want them."

Stein had been convinced, even during those increasingly troubling times in the late 1930s, that there would be no war. When it came, in September 1939, she and Toklas left their Paris apartment at 5, rue Christine, where they had moved shortly after their return from the United States to live year-round at their country house in Bilignin. Then in 1943 they went to live at Le Columbier, in Culoz, where during one brief period German officers and then Italian troops were billeted with them. As Jews, Americans, and lesbians, the danger for them was very real; the combined protection given them by the town officials, their neighbors, and their friend, Bernard Fäy, a member of the Vichy government and director of the Bibliotheque Nationale, made possible their survival.

Gertrude Stein had always seen herself as essentially American. Although separation from home for most of her creative life was, as with so many expatriates (Wharton and James among them), absolutely necessary for her work, her lifelong identification with the country of her birth was a powerful force, frequently expressed in her writing. The experience of the war and her distance from home for its duration reinforced even more her nationalistic fervor. When peace was declared, she broadcast an emotionally charged speech to America: "What a day is today that is what a day it was day before yesterday, what a day! I can tell everybody that none of you know what this native land business is until you have been cut off from that same native land completely for years. This native land business gets you all right. Day before yesterday was a wonderful day. First we saw three Americans in a military car and we said are you Americans and they said yes and we choked and we talked, and they took us driving in their car, those long-awaited Americans. . . . And now thanks to the land of my birth and the land of my adoption we are free. . . . I am so happy to be talking to America today so happy."

Just as they had during World War I, Stein and Toklas developed close relationships with American soldiers. "It was pretty wonderful and pretty awful to have been intimate and friendly and proud of two American armies in France apart by only twenty-seven years," Stein said. These relationships led her to write a book of soldier dialogues, *Brewsie and Willie* (1946). The two characters who give the book its title are temperamentally opposed: Willie is aggressive, cynical, practical; Brewsie is quiet, meditative, emotional. Their conversations allow Stein to explore several subjects: sex, money, jobs, food, the atom bomb. Her attitude about contemporary American politics and culture as engendering immaturity and conformity, particularly in men, is everywhere in evidence as are her convictions about the shortcomings of industrial capitalism. "We are ruled by tired middle-aged people," she says in one of the dialogues, "tired business men, the kind who need pin-ups, you know the kind, only they can afford the originals. . . ."

In March 1946 Stein completed the libretto for an opera, *The Mother of Us All* (1947), written in collaboration with the composer Virgil Thomson. He was later to describe the work as "an evocation of nineteenth century America, with its gospel hymns and cocky marches, its sentimental ballads, waltzes, darn fool ditties and intoned sermons." But its thematic impulse was less innocuous than this description suggests: the feminist stance implicit in *Brewsie and Willie* is now overt. Through the opera's central character, Susan B. Anthony, the nineteenth-century woman whose life was defined by her struggle to achieve equal rights for women, the idea that women are in every way superior to men is repeatedly articulated: "[Men] do not know that two and two make four if women do not tell them so."

Gertrude Stein did not live to see *The Mother of Us All* performed. She collapsed on 19 July 1946, during a brief vacation in the country; friends rushed her to the American Hospital at Neuilly, where she died of inoperable cancer on the evening of 27 July. Alice B. Toklas reported the event this way: "I sat next to her and she said to me early in the afternoon, What is the answer? I was silent. In that case, she said, What is the question?

Then the whole afternoon was troubled, confused and very uncertain, and later in the afternoon they took her away on a wheeled stretcher to the operating room and I never saw her again."

The anecdote reveals about Stein not only her philosophical turn of mind, and, given the circumstances, her courage, but her sense of humor—a facet of her personality not generally remarked upon by critics. It is this same humor, at times expressed as wit, at other times as a sense of play, which dominates so much of her "inaccessible" writing. While the serious questions of contemporary philosophy—those that deal with fragmented twentieth-century reality and its emphasis on the nonrational, of art no longer seen as primarily representative or mimetic—find in her work answers no less brilliant than they are astonishingly original, her value lies equally in her ability to revitalize our language, to bring to it a childlike freshness, a sense of words made new. It is no small contribution. To examine her prose—her more abstract, impersonal, spare, and "difficult" prose—is to discover, in a phrase she delighted in, that "it shows shine."

Interview:

Robert Bartlett Haas, "Gertrude Stein Talking: A Transatlantic Interview," *Uclan Review*, 8 (Summer 1962): 3-11; 9 (Spring 1963): 40-48; 9 (Winter 1964): 44-48.

Letters:

Sherwood Anderson / Gertrude Stein Correspondence and Personal Essays, edited by Ray Lewis White (Chapel Hill: University of North Carolina Press, 1972);

Dear Sammy Letters from Gertrude Stein & Alice B. Toklas, edited by Samuel M. Steward (Boston: Houghton Mifflin, 1977);

The Letters of Gertrude Stein and Carl Van Vechten, 2 volumes, edited by Edward Burns (New York: Columbia University Press, 1986).

Bibliographies:

Robert Bartlett Haas and Donald Clifford Gallup, *A Catalogue of the Published and Unpublished Writings of Gertrude Stein* (New Haven: Yale University Library, 1941);

Robert A. Wilson, *Gertrude Stein: A Bibliography* (New York: Phoenix Bookshop, 1974);

Ray Lewis White, *Gertrude Stein and Alice B. Toklas: A Reference Guide* (Boston: G. K. Hall, 1984).

Biographies:

W. G. Rogers, *When this you see remember me: Gertrude Stein in person* (New York & Toronto: Rinehart, 1948);

Elizabeth Sprigge, *Gertrude Stein: Her Life and Work* (New York: Harper, 1957);

John Malcolm Brinnin, *The Third Rose: Gertrude Stein and Her World* (Boston: Little, Brown, 1959);

Alice B. Toklas, *What Is Remembered* (New York, Chicago & San Francisco: Holt, Rinehart & Winston, 1963);

Four Americans in Paris: The Collections of Gertrude Stein and Her Family (New York: Museum of Modern Art, 1970);

James R. Mellow, *Charmed Circle: Gertrude Stein & Company* (New York & Washington: Praeger, 1974);

Janet Hobhouse, *Everybody Who Was Anybody: A Biography of Gertrude Stein* (New York: Putnam's, 1975).

References:

Shari Benstock, "Gertrude Stein and Alice B. Toklas: Rue de Fleurus," in her *Women of the Left Bank: Paris, 1900-1940* (Austin: University of Texas Press, 1986), pp. 143-193;

Richard Bridgman, *Gertrude Stein in Pieces* (New York: Oxford University Press, 1970);

Marianne DeKoven, *A Different Language: Gertrude Stein's Experimental Writing* (Madison: University of Wisconsin Press, 1983);

Robert Bartlett Haas, ed., *A Primer for the Gradual Understanding of Gertrude Stein* (Los Angeles: Black Sparrow Press, 1971);

Frederick J. Hoffman, *Gertrude Stein* (Minneapolis: University of Minnesota Press, 1961);

Cynthia Secor, "The Question of Gertrude Stein," in *Essays in Feminist Criticism*, edited by Fritz Fleischmann (Boston: G. K. Hall, 1982);

Donald Sutherland, *Gertrude Stein: A Biography of Her Work* (New Haven: Yale University Press, 1951);

Jayne L. Walker, *The Making of a Modernist: Gertrude Stein from "Three Lives" to "Tender Buttons"* (Amherst: University of Massachusetts Press, 1984);

Edmund Wilson, *Axel's Castle: A Study in the Imaginative Literature of 1890-1930* (New York & London: Scribners, 1931).

Papers:

The major repository for Stein materials is the Beinecke Rare Book and Manuscript Library at Yale University, which has most of Stein's manuscripts, correspondence, and unpublished notebooks. There are also significant collections at the Bancroft Library, University of California at Berkeley, and the University of Texas at Austin.

Arthur Train
(6 September 1875-22 December 1945)

Philip Stevick
Temple University

BOOKS: *McAllister and His Double* (New York: Scribners, 1905);

The Prisoner at the Bar (New York: Scribners, 1906; revised and expanded, 1908);

Mortmain (New York: Appleton, 1907);

True Stories of Crime (New York: Scribners, 1908);

The Butler's Story (New York: Scribners, 1909);

Confessions of Artemas Quibble (New York: Scribners, 1911);

Courts, Criminals and the Camorra (New York: Scribners, 1912);

"CQ"; or, In the Wireless House (New York: Century, 1912);

The Goldfish (New York: Century, 1914);

The Man Who Rocked the Earth, with Robert Williams Wood (Garden City, N.Y.: Doubleday, Page, 1915);

The World and Thomas Kelley (New York: Scribners, 1917);

The Earthquake (New York: Scribners, 1918);

Tutt and Mr. Tutt (New York: Scribners, 1920);

As It Was in the Beginning (New York: Macmillan, 1921);

By Advice of Counsel (New York: Scribners, 1921);

The Hermit of Turkey Hollow (New York: Scribners, 1921);

His Children's Children (New York: Scribners, 1923);

Tut, tut! Mr. Tutt (New York: Scribners, 1923);

The Needle's Eye (New York: Scribners, 1924);

The Lost Gospel (New York: Scribners, 1925);

On the Trail of the Bad Men (New York: Scribners, 1925);

The Blind Goddess (New York: Scribners, 1926);

Page Mr. Tutt (New York: Scribners, 1926);

High Winds (New York: Scribners, 1927);

When Tutt Meets Tutt (New York: Scribners, 1927);

Ambition (New York: Scribners, 1928);

The Horns of Ramadan (New York: Scribners, 1928);

Illusion (New York: Scribners, 1929);

The Adventures of Ephriam Tutt (New York: Scribners, 1930);

Arthur Train

Paper Profits (New York: Liveright, 1930);

Puritan's Progress (New York: Scribners, 1931);

The Strange Attacks on Mr. Hoover (New York: John Day, 1932);

Princess Pro Tem (New York: Scribners, 1932);

No Matter Where (New York: Scribners, 1933);

Tutt for Tutt (New York: Scribners, 1934);

Jacob's Ladder (New York: Scribners, 1935);

Manhattan Murder (New York & London: Scribners, 1936);

Mr. Tutt Takes the Stand (New York: Scribners, 1936);

Mr. Tutt's Case Book (New York: Scribners, 1936);

Old Man Tutt (New York: Scribners, 1938);

From the District Attorney's Office (New York & London: Scribners, 1939);

My Day in Court (New York & London: Scribners, 1939);

Tassels on Her Boots (New York: Scribners, 1940);

Mr. Tutt Comes Home (New York: Scribners, 1941);

Yankee Lawyer: The Autobiography of Ephriam Tutt (New York: Scribners, 1943);

Mr. Tutt Finds a Way (New York: Scribners, 1945);

The Moon Maker, by Train and Wood (Hamburg, N.Y.: Krueger, 1958);

Mr. Tutt at His Best, edited by Harold R. Medina (New York: Scribners, 1961).

PERIODICAL PUBLICATIONS:

FICTION

"McAllister's Christmas," *Scribner's,* 36 (December 1904): 655-668;

"Extradition," *Scribner's,* 37 (March 1905): 354-366;

"The Governor-General's Trunk," *Scribner's,* 37 (April 1905): 486-496;

"The Golden Touch," *Saturday Evening Post,* 178 (1 July 1905): 3-5, 16;

"In the Court of Justice," *McClure's,* 25 (September 1905): 516-525;

"The Pursuit of a Teapot," *American,* 61 (October 1905): 37-46;

"More Tricks of the Trade," *Saturday Evening Post,* 178 (6 January 1906): 7-8, 24;

"The Hand of Holofernes," *Saturday Evening Post,* 178 (17 February 1906): 5-7, 18;

"The Sentence," *Saturday Evening Post,* 178 (3 March 1906): 8-9, 17-18;

"The Verdict," *Saturday Evening Post,* 178 (28 April 1906): 8-9;

"Confessions of a Juror," by Train as Percival Saltus, *Saturday Evening Post,* 179 (30 March 1907): 3, 26;

"A Finder of Lost Persons," *Saturday Evening Post,* 180 (4 April 1908): 18-20;

"The Dare Devil," *Saturday Evening Post,* 180 (13 June 1908): 18-21;

"Up Against It," *Saturday Evening Post,* 182 (5 February 1910): 5-7, 35-37;

"Shall He Go Back?," *Saturday Evening Post,* 182 (5 March 1910): 15-17, 47;

"The Other Man," *Scribner's,* 47 (April 1910): 408-420;

"The Inheritance," *Saturday Evening Post,* 182 (11 June 1910): 9-11, 46;

Train, circa 1912

"The Never Winks," *Collier's,* 47 (1 July 1911): 21-29;

"Monsieur X," *Everybody's,* 26 (February 1912): 161-172;

"A Friend of the Family," *Collier's,* 49 (11 May 1912): 22-23;

"The Madonna of the Blackbird," *Everybody's,* 28 (January 1913): 3-13;

"House of the Open Heart," *Everybody's,* 28 (April 1913): 502-511;

"Men Who Live on Nothing," *Saturday Evening Post,* 186 (30 May 1914): 19-21, 57-59;

"The Purple Monkey," *Saturday Evening Post,* 188 (26 February 1916): 18-20, 48-50, 53-54;

"Helenka," *Saturday Evening Post,* 189 (27 January 1917): 6-8, 61-62, 65-66;

"New York City on Guard," *Saturday Evening Post,* 189 (26 May 1917): 16, 37-38, 41-42;

"Tutt vs. the 'Spring Fret,'" *Saturday Evening Post,* 192 (2 August 1919): 22-23, 66, 69-70;

"Matter of McFee," *Saturday Evening Post,* 192 (30 August 1919): 20-21, 148, 150, 153-154, 157;

"Ways That Are Dark," *Saturday Evening Post*, 192 (29 November 1919): 8-9, 69-70, 73-74;

"Hocus Pocus," *Saturday Evening Post*, 192 (3 January 1920): 24-25, 173-174, 177-178;

"The Passing of Caput Magnus," *Saturday Evening Post*, 192 (17 April 1920): 20-21, 145, 149, 152;

"Honor Among Thieves," *Saturday Evening Post*, 192 (24 April 1920): 20-21, 94, 99;

"Twelve Good Men and True," *Saturday Evening Post*, 193 (22 January 1921): 10;

"Blindfold Chess," *Saturday Evening Post*, 193 (29 January 1921): 12-13, 59-60, 62-63, 66;

"The Presumption of Ignorance," *Saturday Evening Post*, 193 (9 April 1921): 18-19, 54, 59, 60;

"Old Duke," *Delineator*, 101 (September 1922): 5-7;

"Status Quo, or Nine Points of the Law," *Saturday Evening Post*, 197 (26 July 1924): 16-17;

"Mr. Tutt Lays a Ghost," *Saturday Evening Post*, 198 (29 May 1926): 14-15;

"The Acid Test," *Saturday Evening Post*, 198 (12 June 1926): 12-13;

"Findings-Keepings," *Saturday Evening Post*, 199 (24 July 1926): 14-15;

"The Man Who Fell Over Backwards," *Saturday Evening Post*, 199 (25 September 1926): 40-43;

"Mr. Tutt's Revenge," *Saturday Evening Post*, 201 (1 September 1928): 8-9;

"The Perfect Goldfish," *Saturday Evening Post*, 202 (28 September 1929): 25;

"The Law and Minerva McCann," *Ladies' Home Journal*, 51 (March 1934): 14-15;

"A Dark Man in Her Life," *Ladies' Home Journal*, 51 (June 1934): 16-17;

"Tit, Tat, Tutt," *Saturday Evening Post*, 209 (13 March 1937): 16-17;

"No Parking," *Saturday Evening Post*, 209 (29 May 1937): 28;

"Mr. Tutt and Mr. Jefferson," *Saturday Evening Post*, 210 (25 September 1937): 16-17;

"Her Father's House," *Saturday Evening Post*, 210 (1 January 1938): 14-15;

"Clean Hands," *Saturday Evening Post*, 210 (11 June 1938): 16-17;

"Private Enemy No. 1," *Saturday Evening Post*, 211 (8 April 1939): 18-19;

"Salmon for the White House," *Saturday Evening Post*, 212 (19 August 1939): 20-21;

"King's Whiskers," *Saturday Evening Post*, 212 (30 December 1939): 16-17;

"Sun in His Eyes," *Saturday Evening Post*, 213 (16 November 1940): 38;

"His Honor, The Judge," *Saturday Evening Post*, 213 (29 March 1941): 24-25;

"Camels Are Coming," *Saturday Evening Post*, 213 (28 June 1941): 22-23;

"With His Boots On," *Saturday Evening Post*, 215 (12 September 1942): 22-23;

"King Wagamoc's Revenge," *Saturday Evening Post*, 215 (20 March 1943): 23;

"Exit Mr. Machiavelli," *Saturday Evening Post*, 216 (12 February 1944): 21;

"Mr. Tutt Corners a Fox," *Saturday Evening Post*, 217 (2 September 1944): 21;

"Gold of Ophir," *Saturday Evening Post*, 217 (10 February 1945): 23.

NONFICTION

"William Travers Jerome," *Saturday Evening Post*, 178 (9 December 1905): 3-5, 28;

"The Patrick Case," *American*, 64 (June 1907): 97-107;

"Detectives and Detective Work," *Collier's*, 47 (5 August 1911): 22-23;

"Did Leo Frank Get Justice?," *Everybody's*, 32 (March 1915): 314-317;

"Unhooking the Hyphen," *Saturday Evening Post*, 191 (10 August 1918): 21-22, 24, 26, 28;

"Following the Front," *Saturday Evening Post*, 192 (15 May 1920): 18-19;

"In Defense of Authors," *Forum*, 76 (August 1926): 206-215;

"The Portrait That Sargeant Forgot," *Atlantic*, 143 (May 1929): 663-664;

"I Cannot Refrain," *Saturday Evening Post*, 203 (17 January 1931): 8-9;

"Are You Psychic?," *Scribner's*, 99 (March 1936): 153-160;

"Should I Apologize?," *Saturday Evening Post*, 216 (26 February 1944): 9-11, 52, 54-55;

"Mr. Tutt Pleads Not Guilty," *Saturday Review of Literature*, 27 (2 December 1944): 16-18, 27, 71.

Arthur Train, a colorful and accomplished lawyer, for two periods an assistant district attorney for the county of New York, a skilled prosecutor, and a learned and ingenious student of the law, was also one of the most popular and gifted writers of his time, with a body of work extending from true tales of crime and courtroom to social history, from autobiography to novels of manners, and embracing a large body of short fiction of uncommon narrative grace. Several times Train argued that the law was destructive of the

Illustrations for Train's story "The Meanest Man," published in the 4 June 1927 issue of the
Saturday Evening Post *(reprinted from the* Saturday Evening Post © *1927 The Curtis Publishing Co.)*

MR. TUTT'S CASE BOOK

BEING A COLLECTION OF
HIS MOST CELEBRATED TRIALS AS
REPORTED AND COMPILED

BY

ARTHUR TRAIN, A.B., LL.B.

*Formerly Assistant District Attorney of New York County and Special Deputy
Attorney-General, State of New York*

Annotated by
FERDINAND J. WOLF, Litt.B., LL.B.
of the New York Bar

With an introduction by
JOHN HENRY WIGMORE
*Formerly Dean of the Law School of Northwestern University
Author of "Wigmore on Evidence"*

NEW YORK
CHARLES SCRIBNER'S SONS
1948

*Title page for a later edition of Train's 1936 collection of
stories about trial lawyer Ephriam Tutt*

talents of a writer, corrupting the style and encouraging all of the wrong habits of mind. If such arguments seem at first playful self-derogation, as one reads on they seem authentic and sincere; Train's reasons are persuasive and devoid of irony. Yet, if he was right, he was his own conspicuous exception. The subject matter of his most popular, and best, fiction is drawn from the experience of the law, and his style echoes the possibilities of the legal voice at its best—ingratiating, unobtrusively knowing, urbane, and with a flawless sense of timing.

Arthur Cheney Train was born on 6 September 1875, the son of Charles Russell Train, then attorney general of Massachusetts, and the former Sarah Maria Cheney. He attended public schools in Boston, St. Paul's School in Concord, New Hampshire, and entered Harvard in 1892, gradu-

ating cum laude in 1896. He married Ethel Kissam, with whom he had four children, on 20 April 1897. Kissam died on 15 May 1923. Train married Helen C. Gerard on 6 January 1926; they had one son.

Not given to reminiscing about his rather proper childhood, Train would later recall his Harvard years with great fondness, especially his literature classes. From boyhood he had wished to be a writer; but his family encouraged him to enter the law, and he received his LL.B. degree from Harvard Law School in 1899. After practicing briefly in Boston he moved to New York where, after persistent application, he was appointed assistant district attorney of New York County in the reform administration of William Travers Jerome, serving in that position until 1908, then again from 1913 to 1915. It was during the later period that he successfully prosecuted Henry Siegel, a banker involved in a variety of interlocking illegal ventures.

It was less the cases themselves than the atmosphere of the court and that notorious prison "The Tombs" that fascinated Train, with its endless panorama of con men, ne'er-do-wells, and psychopaths, with an occasional innocent victim. It was an interest that, together with his natural talents as a raconteur, led him to begin writing down, as stories, the human drama of the New York court. As early as 1904 he had written a fictionalized account of a remarkable and complicated case involving the theft of the Mexican crown jewels that was published as "The Maximilian Diamond" in the July issue of *Leslie's Monthly*. Within a year he had published seven more stories and began what was to be a long association with *Scribner's* and the *Saturday Evening Post*.

From the start Train's idea of the nature of narrative was uncomplicated. Aware of the claims of the densely interior fiction of writers like Henry James, he remained committed to the traditional plotted story. (For Train the resolution of the plot tended to be the *verdict*.) Not only were most of the models from which he might have learned his craft realistic and plot oriented, but his legal subject matter contained, as he put it, "a ready-made plot of its own."

Not all of Train's writing in the early years of his career was short fiction with a subject matter drawn from the courtroom. In fact, he became widely known as a result of his nonfictional descriptions of the working of the legal system. But in 1919 he conceived of a character, Ephriam Tutt, who was to dominate his reputa-

Dust-jacket illustration for Train's 1938 short-story collection, Old Man Tutt

tion. Although he continued to work in other forms and subjects, it was as the creator of Ephriam Tutt that he was always best known. And even now, insofar as he is read and remembered, Train is inevitably associated with Tutt.

Long after Ephriam Tutt had established himself firmly at the center of Train's fiction, the author reminisced about his genesis. Physically, Tutt derived from a painted image, in a clamshell ashtray in Train's childhood home, of a pair of figures, one with frock coat, stovepipe hat, and cigar. Although he had come to know lawyers like Tutt in some respects, the character was not modeled on a real person. Train summarizes: "Spiritually, I suppose that Mr. Tutt is a combination of most of the qualities which I would like to have, coupled with a few that are common to all of us. One critic has disposed of him by saying that his popularity is due to the fact that he is a hodgepodge of Puck, Robin Hood, Abraham Lincoln and Uncle Sam. I am willing to let it go at that." The unnamed critic, if flip, was nonetheless right in seeing Tutt in relation to certain mythic figures. For Tutt is less a character–he thinks and feels rather perfunctorily, behaves, as Train admitted, quite inconsistently–than he is a

myth. The myth has elements of style, uniting Tutt's anachronistic dress and courtly manners to a total ease with the modern world. It has elements in common with that long tradition in American popular culture of the single figure– the cowboy, the private eye–opposing his quiet convictions to the world of power and privilege. It has elements of class: like many mythic figures, Tutt is aristocratic in his bearing, populist in his compassion. But the true mythic power of Ephriam Tutt resides in the manner in which he demonstrates that higher principles of justice and decency can be made to prevail within a system of law which ostensibly serves those principles but often fails.

It is not only the presence of Tutt as character and myth, however, that gives the stories their distinction. For one thing, the stories always rest upon a basis of fact which is both interesting in itself and integral to the story. Sometimes it is the facts of place, often New York, the buildings and street names, the lesser-known businesses, the odd pockets of unusual people, handled with a light touch but, in the best O. Henry manner, unmistakably verifiable. Sometimes it is the facts of technology–the railroad signal system, methods

*Dust jacket for a selection of Train's "Mr. Tutt" stories
published in 1961*

of prospecting for oil—suggestive of the omnivorous curiosity projected by Sir Arthur Conan Doyle. As Train himself put it, "If I wanted to write about coal mines I went down in the bucket and, if I wanted to describe the life of a young vaudeville 'magician,' I joined the Society of American Magicians." For another thing, the stories turn upon a union of the mysteries of the law and the persuasiveness of common sense, the law being so credibly presented that one of the collections of stories, *Mr. Tutt's Case Book* (1936), contains legal annotations by Ferdinand J. Wolf, a member of the New York Bar, heavy with precedents, citations, and interpretation, and a foreword by John Henry Wigmore, former dean of the Northwestern University law school. Finally, the stories are executed in a style at once elegant, knowing, often arch, ingratiating, charming—in a word, comfortable.

Train eventually published some one hundred Tutt stories and fourteen collections of them in book form, and it was Tutt who provided the occasion for the most publicized event

in Train's career. In 1943 Train published *Yankee Lawyer: The Autobiography of Ephriam Tutt.* Train's name does not appear either on the spine or the title page, and the copyright notice reads "Copyright, 1943, by Ephriam Tutt." The book includes an introduction credited to Train in which he claims for himself only the role of admiring recorder of Tutt's career in pages other than these. The "autobiography" begins with Tutt's birth in Vermont of a stern, Calvinist father and a saintly mother, both of whom are pictured in early photographs, as is Tutt himself at the age of five. The account proceeds through Tutt's education at Harvard, his early law practice, his pleasures, recreations, and domestic crises, ultimately his most famous cases. Along the way Tutt describes his friendship with a gallery of public figures, from Calvin Coolidge to Edith Wharton. At one point Tutt describes a conversation with his friend Arthur Train, who discourses on how being a lawyer corrupts a man's prose style. "No lawyer can spend ten years drawing papers and retain his freedom of expression. . . . It's not only the saids, aforesaids, whereases, hereinafters and befores, it's because the factual attitude becomes part of his make-up. His style ceases to be free. He becomes literal, pedantic, over-precise." The book ends with Tutt's "Indian Summer," a graceful gathering of his opinions on manners and morals, the state of the republic, and the eternal disparity between law and justice. The illusion is never broken: the book seems, start to finish, a book by Tutt, not Train. It is a remarkable tour de force.

Since nothing but a prior knowledge of the real Train and the fictive Tutt could have prepared the public to accept the work as fiction, Train might have anticipated that a few readers would take it as autobiography. Nothing, however, could have prepared him for the nature or the extent of the response he received. Indignant readers refused to be persuaded that Tutt was a mere invention. Letters arrived from lost relatives and would-be clients of Tutt. *Who's Who* invited Tutt to submit his résumé. And a Philadelphia lawyer brought suit, seeking to recover a portion of the price of the book on the grounds that a fraud had been perpetrated. Train responded with disclaimers in the *Saturday Evening Post*, later writing in the *Saturday Review* an urbane and thoughtful defense of the long tradition of the fictional "autobiography." An episode by turns hilarious and embarrassing, it established Ephriam Tutt as one of those fictional creations, like Frankenstein's monster or Sherlock Holmes, more famous, seemingly more alive, than its creator.

Train's own autobiography, *My Day in Court* (1939), displays not only the anecdotal art one would expect, given his flair for shaping an episode and his eye for the colorful. It shows also a mind immensely engaged by experience–by travel, the natural world, and the company of good friends. It demonstrates furthermore a capacity to reflect, again and again, on the nature of authorship, a subject upon which Train was sensitive and astute. It was his concern with the legal situation of the author that led him, in 1912, to cofound the Author's League of America, an organization devoted to the reform of copyright law and contract procedure. Such activity added much to the affection and esteem with which he was regarded by his fellow writers. Many years later he was elected president of the National Institute of Arts and Letters, then reelected only a week before his death.

Train died of cancer on 22 December 1945 in New York. He was seventy. None of his fiction, including the Tutt stories, is likely to endure. But a reader who happens upon his fiction now will be struck with its ease and grace and the wisdom with which he takes the measure of his fellow man and woman. And the historian of our culture's myths will be obliged to acknowledge the extraordinary power, for two decades and more, of the image of Ephriam Tutt.

References:

D. L. Mann, *Arthur Train, Man of Letters and Man of Laws* (New York: Scribners, n.d.);

Grant Overton, "The Documents in the Case of Arthur Train," in *American Night's Entertainment* (New York: Appleton, 1923).

Papers:

Substantial collections of Train's correspondence are located at Princeton University and at the Beinecke Rare Book and Manuscript Library, Yale University. The American Academy of Arts and Letters, New York, also maintains a Train collection, including letters and several manuscripts.

William Carlos Williams

(17 September 1883-4 March 1963)

Kim Flachmann
California State University, Bakersfield

See also the Williams entries in *DLB 4: American Writers in Paris, 1920-1939; DLB 16: The Beats: Literary Bohemians in Postwar America;* and *DLB 54: American Poets, 1880-1945.*

BOOKS: *Poems* (Rutherford, N.J.: Privately printed, 1909);

The Tempers (London: Elkin Mathews, 1913);

Al Que Quiere! (Boston: Four Seas, 1917);

Kora in Hell: Improvisations (Boston: Four Seas, 1920);

Sour Grapes (Boston: Four Seas, 1921);

The Great American Novel (Paris: Three Mountains Press, 1923);

Spring and All (Paris: Contact Editions, 1923);

GO GO (New York: Monroe Wheeler, 1923);

In the American Grain (New York: A. & C. Boni, 1925; London: MacGibbon & Kee, 1967);

A Voyage to Pagany (New York: Macaulay, 1928);

A Novelette and Other Prose (1921-1931) (Toulon, France: TO Publishers, 1932);

The Knife of the Times and Other Stories (Ithaca, N.Y.: Dragon Press, 1932);

The Cod Head (San Francisco: Harvest Press, 1932);

Collected Poems 1921-1931 (New York: Objectivist Press, 1934);

An Early Martyr and Other Poems (New York: Alcestis Press, 1935);

Adam & Eve & The City (Peru, Vt.: Alcestis Press, 1936);

White Mule (Norfolk, Conn.: New Directions, 1937; London: MacGibbon & Kee, 1965);

Life Along the Passaic River (Norfolk, Conn.: New Directions, 1938);

The Complete Collected Poems of William Carlos Williams 1906-1938 (Norfolk, Conn.: New Directions, 1938);

In the Money: White Mule—Part II (Norfolk, Conn.: New Directions, 1940; London: MacGibbon & Kee, 1965);

The Broken Span (Norfolk, Conn.: New Directions, 1941);

William Carlos Williams (photograph by Charles Sheeler)

The Wedge (Cummington, Mass.: Cummington Press, 1944);

Paterson (Book One) (Norfolk, Conn.: New Directions, 1946);

Paterson (Book Two) (Norfolk, Conn.: New Directions, 1948);

The Clouds, Aigeltinger, Russia, & (Aurora, N.Y.: Wells College Press / Cummington, Mass.: Cummington Press, 1948);

A Dream of Love: A Play in Three Acts and Eight Scenes (Norfolk, Conn.: New Directions, 1948);

Selected Poems (Norfolk, Conn.: New Directions, 1949; enlarged, 1968);

The Pink Church (Columbus, Ohio: Golden Goose Press, 1949);

Paterson (Book Three) (Norfolk, Conn.: New Directions, 1949);

The Collected Later Poems (Norfolk, Conn.: New Directions, 1950; revised, 1963; London: MacGibbon & Kee, 1965);

Make Light of It: Collected Stories (New York: Random House, 1950);

A Beginning on the Short Story [Notes] (Yonkers, N.Y.: Alicat Bookshop Press, 1950);

Paterson (Book Four) (Norfolk, Conn.: New Directions, 1951);

The Autobiography (New York: Random House, 1951; London: MacGibbon & Kee, 1968);

The Collected Earlier Poems (Norfolk, Conn.: New Directions, 1951; London: MacGibbon & Kee, 1967);

The Build-Up: A Novel (New York: Random House, 1952; London: MacGibbon & Kee, 1969);

The Desert Music and Other Poems (New York: Random House, 1954);

Selected Essays (New York: Random House, 1954);

Journey to Love (New York: Random House, 1955);

I Wanted to Write a Poem, reported and edited by Edith Heal (Boston: Beacon Press, 1958; London: Cape, 1967);

Paterson (Book Five) (Norfolk, Conn.: New Directions, 1958);

Yes, Mrs. Williams: A Personal Record of My Mother (New York: McDowell, Obolensky, 1959);

The Farmers' Daughters: The Collected Stories (Norfolk, Conn.: New Directions, 1961);

Many Loves and Other Plays: The Collected Plays (Norfolk, Conn.: New Directions, 1961);

Pictures from Brueghel and other poems (Norfolk, Conn.: New Directions, 1962; London: MacGibbon & Kee, 1963);

Paterson, books 1-5 and notes for book 6 (New York: New Directions, 1963; London: MacGibbon & Kee, 1964);

The William Carlos Williams Reader, edited by M. L. Rosenthal (New York: New Directions, 1966; London: MacGibbon & Kee, 1967);

Imaginations, edited by Webster Schott (New York: New Directions, 1970; London: MacGibbon & Kee, 1970);

The Embodiment of Knowledge, edited by Ron Loewinsohn (New York: New Directions, 1974);

A Recognizable Image: William Carlos Williams on Art and Artists, edited by Bram Dijkstra (New York: New Directions, 1978);

The Collected Poems of William Carlos Williams, 2 volumes (New York: New Directions, 1986-1988).

TRANSLATIONS: Philippe Soupault, *Last Nights in Paris* (New York: Macaulay, 1929);

Yvan Goll, *Jean sans Terre: Landless John*, translated by Williams, Lionel Abel, Clark Mills, and John Gould Fletcher (San Francisco: Grabhorn Press, 1944);

Pedro Espinosa (Don Francisco de Quevedo), *The Dog & the Fever*, translated by Williams and Raquel Hélène Williams (Hamden, Conn.: Shoestring Press, 1954);

Sappho: A Translation of One of the Two Existing Complete Poems by Sappho (San Francisco: Poems in Folio, 1957).

Best known as a poet, William Carlos Williams was an accomplished writer in many genres. He produced twenty-three volumes of poetry, five collections of short fiction, six novels, seven books of nonfiction, five plays, and four translations. His work, in all genres, is characterized by a direct treatment of reality, creating an artistry of immediacy and native freshness.

Williams was born and lived his entire life in Rutherford, New Jersey. His father, William George Williams, was English by birth and remained a British citizen his entire life, even though he left England at age five. Williams's mother, Raquel Hélène Rose Hoheb (called Elena by her family), was partly French, Dutch, Spanish, and Jewish. An exotic and romantic personality, she exerted a strong influence on her son, as did his paternal grandmother, Emily Dickinson Wellcome. As a youth Williams was passionately devoted to sports, especially track, until, at age sixteen, he began to suffer from an ailment diagnosed as adolescent heart strain. His abundant energy was then rechanneled into the study of literature. From 1902 to 1906 Williams attended medical school at the University of Pennsylvania, where he formed lasting friendships with Ezra Pound, H.D., and Charles Demuth. After his internship in New York hospitals, he pursued two professions—medicine and writing—with equal vigor. Much to his satisfaction, he found that these two careers complemented rather than contradicted one another: in his *Autobiography* (1951) Williams insists, "As a writer, I have been a physician, and as a physician a writer."

In 1909 Williams had his first book, entitled *Poems*, privately published (this less than success-

Williams (seated in front) with his father, William George, his mother, Elena, and his brother, Edgar, circa 1899 (courtesy of Dr. William Eric Williams)

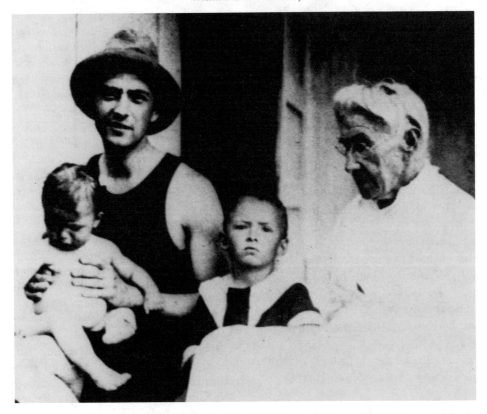

Williams with his sons, Paul and Bill, and his grandmother Emily Dickinson Wellcome, 1917 (photograph by Irving B. Wellcome, courtesy of Dr. William Eric Williams)

Self-portrait by Williams, 1914 (by permission of the University of Pennsylvania, gift of Mrs. William Carlos Williams, 1965)

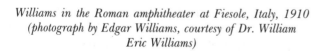

Williams in the Roman amphitheater at Fiesole, Italy, 1910 (photograph by Edgar Williams, courtesy of Dr. William Eric Williams)

ful work shows the overriding influence of John Keats and Walt Whitman). In 1910, after an additional year of study in Leipzig, Williams set up his own medical practice. In 1912 he married Florence ("Flossie") Herman. His second book of poems, published in 1913, was followed by the birth of two children, William Eric in 1914 and Paul in 1916, and a third book of poems in 1917.

During the 1920s Williams established himself as a prose writer as well as a poet with the publication of *Kora in Hell* (1920), a collection of prose "improvisations"; *The Great American Novel* (1923), a short novel; *In the American Grain* (1925), a collection of historical essays; and his first full-length novel, *A Voyage to Pagany* (1928). In 1924 he was honored with the Guarantor's Award by *Poetry* magazine, and in 1926 he received a two-thousand-dollar Dial Award for general excellence in writing.

Williams's short-story collections began to appear in the 1930s with *The Knife of the Times and Other Stories* (1932), which includes eleven stories, and *Life Along the Passaic River* (1938), which includes nineteen stories. Williams seems to have turned to fiction at this point because of the consistent discouragement he met with in his attempts to be recognized as a poet. In his frustration, he found the short story "a good medium for nailing down a single conviction. Emotionally." Williams's short stories are not traditional in form but are sketches or fragments of his experience and imagination that begin and end on impulse. Episodic in nature, they rely on juxtaposed observations to relay their message, much like an imagist poem, with few figurative or symbolic distractions. In isolated, brief moments, these stories capture the realism of Sherwood Anderson, early Ernest Hemingway, and Gertrude Stein in a blend of vitality, wit, and humanity.

Many of Williams's stories are autobiographical, having to do with a doctor-narrator and his patients: "The actual calling on people at all times and under all conditions . . . when they were being born, when they were dying, watching them die . . . has always absorbed me. I lost myself in the very properties of their minds." His characters are revealed objectively by their responses to their immediate environment and are raised to the level of individuals in the midst of depraved insensitivity. Often designed as casual, spontaneous conversations in which Williams is a participant, his stories evolve from nascent speech patterns, or what he calls "the American id-

Williams and his mother in Rutherford, New Jersey, circa 1918 (courtesy of Dr. William Eric Williams)

iom," a narrative technique that heightens the intensity and immediacy of his short fiction.

Williams's short fiction deals in particular with poverty and suffering. His sketches are about the insignificant people in America (often immigrants), who live along the banks of the Passaic River. The stories themselves are a product of his belief that all art must begin in the "local": a person's immediate environment, claims Williams, is the only legitimate source of imaginative work, the only means of discovering the universal. Most of these sketches derive meaning from the juxtaposition of opposing forces that creates a tension which is slowly resolved during the course of the story through a subtle revelation of new self-knowledge on the narrator's part. Some of Williams's main themes are oppression, poverty, pessimism, sickness, gloom, boredom, hopelessness, and their opposites. In a composite, these works are a testimony to Williams's faith in human dignity and strength in a time of depression and destruction.

The stories that comprise *The Knife of the Times and Other Stories* dramatize the fortitude and perseverance of Williams's characters in spite of the oppression ("the knife") of the times. Most of these stories (only one of which was first published in a periodical) illustrate the power of love and identity as forms of survival. One of the first reviews of this publication praises these stories for their "clinical calm" and "even-colored tone."

The best-known story in this collection is "Old Doc Rivers," a character sketch of a small-town, suburban doctor. In spite of his use of drugs and his tendency toward inexplicable eccentricities, Doc Rivers's undeniable medical abilities earn the trust of his patients. The story is told in a series of anecdotes about the doctor as seen from a variety of perspectives, depicting him as an archetypal study in contrasts; he is abrupt and kind, aloof as well as dedicated, constant yet inconstant.

The courage to distinguish himself from others causes him to attract numerous foes, but he is a good doctor. Though sensitive and able, he is a victim of America's shift from a rural to an urban temperament. As his conflicts with contemporary America increase, drug use causes Rivers to make professional errors. Nonetheless, his character has reached mythic proportions; the townspeople believe in him for the sake of ritual. His failure at the end of the story characterizes a tragic waste of talent.

Williams claimed that *Life Along the Passaic River* was a continuation of the stories in *The Knife of the Times.* He admitted, however, that he was a more mature writer at this stage, seldom needing to revise his work. Among these stories, called by one early reviewer "stabs, brilliant and inspired, at truth," are some of Williams's most incisive social commentary. His autobiographical narrator becomes even more deeply involved in the lives of the people he knows along the banks of the Passaic. With passionate authenticity, Williams writes about their hopes, their fears, their weaknesses, their strengths, shifting the point of view from tough to tender and from indifferent to sympathetic.

The title story (first published in the *Magazine,* January 1934) moves by free association from scene to scene, giving the impression that activity throughout the story is continuous and often simultaneous. At the beginning of the story the image of a solitary figure in "a spot of a canoe" in the midst of an industrial environment establishes a focal point that centers on a tension between nature and industry. From this image the story moves forward with a series of juxtaposed scenes depicting this perpetual conflict between industry and nature, the conflict between the factory and the river. Williams implies that the salvation of the country is in the hands of the youth; only they can stop the relentless movement toward destruction. The story ends as it began—in the heat of a July day in the industrial city of Passaic with industry the victor, but with new hope for salvation.

The most frequently anthologized of Williams's stories is "The Use of Force" (*Blast,* November-December 1933), which dramatizes a struggle between life and death, or more specifically, between control and loss of control. In this story the doctor-narrator is called upon to diagnose the problem of a child with a fever; but the child, Mathilda, refuses to let the doctor look at her throat. A strong sense of distrust between doctor and child at the beginning of the story sets the scene for the different levels of conflict that take place: between life and death; cure and disease; self-control and anger; attraction and repulsion. The battle itself consists of two conflicts. Initially, Mathilda is trying to hide the sickness within her. If it is not discovered, it does not exist; but if it is discovered, she knows she will lose control. The doctor, on the other hand, becomes angry with himself when he has to resort to force to accomplish his mission. In three progressively intense stages the struggle becomes one in which basic instinct takes full possession of the senses of each character. The sexual overtones of the conflict are obvious. Mathilda loses the battle to the possibility of cure and survival, but the most profound element she loses is control of her own life. Her secret has been forcefully taken from her by a stranger.

Williams's own favorite among his stories was "Jean Beicke" (*Blast,* September-October 1933), about an eleven-month-old girl who dies of undiagnosed acute purulent mastoiditis. Williams asks the question of whether society should attempt to save a "scrawny, misshapen, worthless piece of humanity." For the months that the child clung to life, she became a fascinating paradox for the narrator: objectively, she was a drain on society, with no quality of life; but for those in the hospital who grew to know her, she became the child with the alert eyes who ate her food with zest and vitality every three hours. When she

Sept 29, 1951

Dear Upton Sinclair:

One of my patients during my office hour today called my attention to your letter in last weeks issue of New Republic. In ~~which~~ you asked some questions, very pleasantly I must say, about the modern poem. Since you quoted from two of my poems it might be appropriate for me to try to answer you. ~~I'll try~~

If you will try rhythmically to analyse even those bits of poems, a person of your abilities and experience as a writer will quickly get to the heart of the matter: it is the <u>hearing</u> of the poem in modern practice rather than its physical appearance on the page which is the important thing. And you know also, where the artist's choice is concerned, that for him it is important to be free to elect ~~what~~ to ~~him is important~~ vary from accepted standards. When one line runs over into another, where no pause in the sequence of words is wanted, he will terminate his line whereever he pleases. It's a matter of the sound - which must be allowed to vary as he may desire it.

You see, the measure, the actual measuring, of the line has been brought into question ever since "free verse" (which does not exist) came to be seriously practiced. But I don't want to go inot a long progression on the stages of modern ~~progression in the~~ measurement of the line. It wouldn't help me to get you clear on this one elemental point.

Dropping that, I ought to speak of the materials, the sort of image that has come into the modern poem : the factory, the dump heap, anything "ugly" you choose to name. Don't you see that <u>anything</u> can be used in a poem? It isn't the quality of the object that makes a picture, for instance, it is the light we are painting. It doesn't matter what the object is that we write about, it's what you do with it that counts. The poem is a device for saying something above or beyond or in# addition to the mere images used. And that something is carried by the structural amplifications the modern world has discovered (or wants to discover) as opposed to a world lived in the past.

Well, that's a beginning at any rate, if you're interested we might go further with the argument# - if we consider it worth while. In any case the face of the modern poem has been altered, for better or worse.

Sincerely

9 Ridge Rd, Rutherford, N.J.   William Carlos Williams

*Letter from Williams to Upton Sinclair (*William Carlos Williams: Selected Letters. *Copyright 1957 by William Carlos Williams. Reprinted by permission of New Directions Publishing Corporation; courtesy of the Lilly Library, Indiana University)*

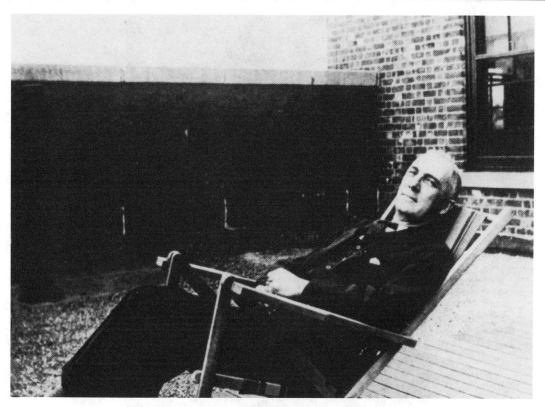

Williams in 1936 on the roof of the Passaic General Hospital

died those who knew her felt compassion and sorrow. In the final scene the narrator comes to understand that Jean Beicke's death is a loss to science, but her life had been a salvation to humanity.

During the 1930s Williams also published *A Novelette and Other Prose (1921-1931)* (1932) and the first installment (*White Mule*, 1937) of what is known as the "Stecher trilogy." This particular novel represented Williams's first real public success. During this period he also published four new books of poetry, two collections of his poems, and his first play.

The 1940s were especially productive for Williams: he continued the Stecher trilogy with *In the Money: White Mule–Part II* (1940); he wrote three plays; and in 1946 he began to produce, over a period of eight years, the epic poem he had prepared his whole life to write–*Paterson*. In addition, he wrote five new books of poems. In 1948 Williams suffered the first in a series of heart attacks, which were accompanied by serious depression.

In 1950 Williams was elected to the National Institute of Arts and Letters; he won the National Book Award for *Selected Poems* (1949) and *Paterson* (*Book Three*) (1949); and New Directions

published *The Collected Later Poems*. At this time Williams was simultaneously working on a libretto for an opera, book four of *Paterson*, his autobiography, a novel, and an edition of his collected short stories.

Make Light of It (1950) includes the stories collected in Williams's first two volumes of short fiction and a third group of twenty-one stories entitled "Beer and Cold Cuts." All but two of these pieces ("The Insane" and "Lena") had been previously published. Regarding this collection, a 1950 review claims that "its chief quality is the gusto that is Williams' signature."

To create "The Zoo" (*Decision*, February 1941), one of the best known of the previously uncollected stories, Williams extracted characters and scenes from the Stecher trilogy. The plot concerns a trip to the zoo and back home again, emblematic of Williams's focus in the narrative on the tension between freedom and confinement. The story begins as Elsa, the maid, prepares to take her two charges, Lottie and Flossie, on a trip to the zoo; there they first encounter the caged ape, wolves, foxes, deer, elk, and bears. These animals are wild, yet confined–a paradox which holds Elsa's attention throughout the story.

Williams with his granddaughters Erica and Emily (courtesy of Dr. William Eric Williams)

The next four scenes take the trio in and out of varying degrees of confinement as the girls and the maid wend their way from caged birds to caged pachyderms, from the fury of a lion to the frustration of a confined monkey. Elsa is fascinated by this world of contradictions–naturalness juxtaposed with unnaturalness, wildness with civilization, freedom with confinement. Although Elsa and the children leave the world of enforced confinement behind, they return to a world which stifles their natural growth and behavior as much as the zoo stifles that of the animals. The only difference between the two worlds is that confinement among humans is self-imposed.

After 1950 Williams entered a period of physical decline, though this did not restrict his productivity. In 1951 he published *Paterson* (*Book Four*), *Autobiography*, and *The Collected Earlier Poems*. In 1952, though Williams completed the Stecher trilogy with *The Build-Up*, he suffered a serious depression and another heart attack, accompanied by a loss of speech. This was followed in March 1953 by yet another heart attack and depression that sent him to a mental hospital until June.

At this point he retired from medicine and devoted the rest of his life to writing. In 1952 Williams was also invited to serve as consultant in poetry at the Library of Congress; this appointment was delayed by Williams's health and then abandoned by the Library of Congress after a traumatic investigation into Williams's political association with Ezra Pound.

In 1961 Williams published final collections of his stories (*The Farmers' Daughters: The Collected Stories*) and his plays (*Many Loves and Other Plays: The Collected Plays*). *The Farmers' Daughters* includes all the author's previously collected stories and one uncollected work entitled "The Farmers' Daughters. A Long Short Story," originally published in the Autumn 1957 issue of the *Hudson Review*. Much like "Life Along the Passaic River" in form, it is comprised of a series of related scenes and images about two southern farmers' daughters named Margaret and Helen and their doctor, who often serves as the liaison between the girls themselves and between the girls and reality. Williams forces his readers to derive meaning from the various juxtaposed incidences that separate the characters and bring them back together again. Though not one of his best stories, it adds new dimensions to Williams's accumulation of truths derived from immediate experience.

His last effort before his death was *Pictures from Brueghel and other poems* (1962). Following his death on 4 March 1963 he was awarded the Pulitzer Prize in Poetry and the Gold Medal for Poetry of the National Institute of Arts and Letters.

In his brief tapestries of fiction and fact Williams is searching for those characteristics that enable the human being to survive, the threads of human fortitude that make the difference between health and disease, life and death. Throughout his career he became intensely involved in his patients' conditions, then worked, through his short fiction, to give those experiences meaning and significance. Williams reveals the psychological complexities of his characters with the detachment of a scientist, developing, in the process, a deep respect and concern for them that is aesthetically convincing. A work of art, says Williams, has the potential to save the world because it filters thoughts, observations, and perceptions through the imagination, thus creating an imaginative view of life that improves upon reality. In his attempt to come to terms with his surroundings, Williams creates a corpus of tightly structured short stories that are poignant and vital to an understanding of human nature's basic drive for survival.

Letters:
William Carlos Williams: Selected Letters, edited by John C. Thirwall (New York: McDowell, Obolensky, 1957).

Interviews:
Interviews with William Carlos Williams: "Speaking Straight Ahead," edited by Linda Welshimer Wagner (New York: New Directions, 1976).

Bibliographies:
Emily Wallace, *A Bibliography of William Carlos Williams* (Middletown, Conn.: Wesleyan University Press, 1968); with addenda included in various issues of the *William Carlos Williams Newsletter* and the *William Carlos Williams Review;*

Neil Baldwin and Steven L. Myers, *The Manuscripts and Letters of William Carlos Williams in the Poetry Collection of Lockwood Memorial Library, State University of New York at Buffalo: A Descriptive Catalogue* (Boston: G. K. Hall, 1978).

Biographies:
Mike Weaver, *William Carlos Williams: The American Background* (Cambridge: Cambridge University Press, 1971);

Reed Whittemore, *William Carlos Williams: Poet from Jersey* (Boston: Houghton Mifflin, 1975);

Paul Mariani, *William Carlos Williams: A New World Naked* (New York: McGraw-Hill, 1981).

References:
Charles Boyer, ed., *William Carlos Williams: The Critical Heritage* (London: Routledge & Kegan Paul, 1980);

James E. Breslin, *William Carlos Williams: An American Artist* (New York: Oxford University Press, 1970);

John Engels, *Checklist of William Carlos Williams* (Columbus, Ohio: Merrill, 1969);

James Guimond, *The Art of William Carlos Williams: A Discovery and Possession of America* (Urbana: University of Illinois Press, 1968);

Vivienne Koch, *William Carlos Williams* (New York: New Directions, 1950; revised edition, New York: Kraus, 1973);

Linda Wagner, *The Prose of William Carlos Williams* (Middletown, Conn.: Wesleyan University Press, 1970).

Papers:
The bulk of Williams's manuscripts and letters is housed in three libraries: the Lockwood Memorial Library, State University of New York at Buffalo; the Beinecke Rare Book and Manuscript Library, Yale University; and the Humanities Research Center, University of Texas at Austin. There are also smaller but important collections of papers at the Alderman Library, University of Virginia; the University of Delaware Library; and the Lilly Library, Indiana University.

Books for Further Reading

Aldridge, John W. *After the Lost Generation: A Critical Study of the Writers of Two Wars*. New York: McGraw-Hill, 1951.

Allen, Frederick Lewis. *The Big Change: America Transforms Itself, 1900-1950*. New York: Harper, 1952.

Allen, Walter. *The Short Story in English*. New York: Oxford University Press, 1981; Oxford: Clarendon Press, 1981.

Bates, H. E. *The Modern Short Story: A Critical Survey*. Boston: Writer, 1949; London: T. Nelson & Sons, 1948.

Bridgman, Richard. *The Colloquial Style in America*. New York: Oxford University Press, 1966.

Bryer, Jackson R., ed. *Sixteen Modern American Authors: A Survey of Research and Criticism*. New York: Norton, 1973.

Canby, Henry S. *The Short Story in English*. New York: Holt, 1909.

Cowley, Malcolm. *Exile's Return: A Literary Odyssey of the 1920's*. New York: Viking, 1951.

Cowley, ed. *After The Genteel Tradition: American Writers 1910-1930*, revised edition. Carbondale: Southern Illinois University Press, 1964.

Friedman, Melvin. *Stream of Consciousness: A Study in Literary Method*. New Haven, Conn.: Yale University Press, 1955.

Grabo, Carl H. *The Art of the Short Story*. New York: Scribners, 1913.

Hicks, Granville. *The Great Tradition: An Interpretation of American Literature Since the Civil War*, revised edition. New York: Macmillan, 1968.

Hoffman, Frederick J. *Freudianism and the Literary Mind*. Baton Rouge: Louisiana State University Press, 1945.

Hoffman. *The Twenties: American Writing in the Postwar Decade*, third edition. New York: Free Press, 1965.

Hoffman, Charles Allen, and Carolyn Ulrich. *The Little Magazine: A History and a Bibliography*. Princeton: Princeton University Press, 1947.

Kazin, Alfred. *On Native Grounds*. New York: Reynal & Hitchcock, 1942.

Kenner, Hugh. *A Homemade World: The American Modernist Writers*. New York: Knopf, 1974.

Madden, David. *Tough Guy Writers of the Thirties*. Carbondale & Edwardsville: Southern Illinois University Press, 1968.

Malin, Irvin, ed. *Psychoanalysis and American Fiction.* New York: Dutton, 1965.

May, Charles E., ed. *Short Story Theories.* Athens: Ohio University Press, 1976.

Mott, Frank Luther. *A History of American Magazines,* 5 volumes. Cambridge, Mass.: Harvard University Press, 1957.

O'Connor, Frank. *The Lonely Voice: A Study of the Short Story.* Cleveland: World Publishing, 1963.

O'Faolain, Sean. *The Short Story.* New York: Devin Adair, 1951.

Peden, William. *The American Short Story: Front Line in the National Defense of Literature.* Boston: Houghton Mifflin, 1964.

Peterson, Theodore. *Magazines in the Twentieth Century.* Urbana: University of Illinois Press, 1964.

Reid, Ian. *The Short Story.* London: Methuen, 1977.

Ross, Danforth. *The American Short Story.* Minneapolis: University of Minnesota Press, 1961.

Spiller, Robert E. *The Cycle of American Literature.* New York: Macmillan, 1955.

Stevick, Philip, ed. *The American Short Story, 1900-1945.* Boston: Twayne, 1984.

Swados, Harvey. *American Writers and the Great Depression.* Indianapolis: Bobbs-Merrill, 1966.

Thorp, Willard. *American Writing in the Twentieth Century.* Cambridge, Mass.: Harvard University Press, 1960.

Trilling, Lionel. *The Liberal Imagination: Essays on Literature and Society.* New York: Viking, 1950.

Voss, Arthur. *The American Short Story: A Critical Survey.* Norman: University of Oklahoma Press, 1973.

West, Ray B., Jr. *The Short Story in America: 1900-1950.* Chicago: Regnery, 1952.

Contributors

David D. Anderson ....*Michigan State University*
Charles W. Bassett...*Colby College*
Elizabeth S. Bell...*University of South Carolina, Aiken*
Winifred Farrant Bevilacqua ....*Universita Degli Studi di Torino*
Laurie Buchanan...*Bowling Green State University*
Susan Currier ....*California State Polytechnic University*
Kim Flachmann ....*California State University, Bakersfield*
Lucy M. Freibert ....*University of Louisville*
Wade Hall...*Bellarmine College*
Greg Keeler ....*Montana State University, Bozeman*
Bobby Ellen Kimbel.......................*Pennsylvania State University–Ogontz Campus*
Michael Oriard...*Oregon State University*
Ruth Prigozy ....*Hofstra University*
Michael Routh...*Utrecht, The Netherlands*
Paul Schlueter ....*Eastern, Pennsylvania*
Robert Schmuhl ....*University of Notre Dame*
Mel Seesholtz ....*Pennsylvania State University*
Rodney Simard......................................*California State University, San Bernardino*
Philip Stevick ....*Temple University*
Guy Szuberla ....*University of Toledo*
William P. Toth, Jr..*Bowling Green State University*
Ellen Serlen Uffen ....*Michigan State University*
Laura M. Zaidman...*University of South Carolina, Sumter*